GOLD SEEKER

Adventures of a
Belgian Argonaut
during the
Gold Rush Years

JEAN-NICOLAS PERLOT

Translated by
Helen Harding Bretnor
Edited and
with an introduction
by Howard R. Lamar

Yale University Press
New Haven and London

Designed by Nancy Ovedovitz and set in Cheltenham type by The Composing Room of Michigan, Inc. Printed in the United States of America by Murray Printing Company, Westford, Mass.

Library of Congress Cataloging in Publication Data

Perlot, Jean-Nicolas, 1823–1900.
  Gold seeker.
  (Yale Western Americana series ; 31)
  Translation of: Vie et aventures d'un enfant de l'Ardenne.
  Includes index.
  1. California—Description and travel—1848–1869. 2. Oregon—Description and travel.
3. California—Gold discoveries. 4. Perlot, Jean-Nicolas, 1823–1900. 5. Belgians—California—Biography. 6. Belgians—Oregon—Biography. I. Lamar, Howard Roberts. II. Title. III. Series.
F865.P45513 1985   979.4′04   84-17378
ISBN 0-300-01996-3 (alk. paper)

The paper in this book meets the guidelines for permanence and durability of the Committee on Production Guidelines for Book Longevity of the Council on Library Resources.

10 9 8 7 6 5 4 3 2 1

To the memory of
Helen Harding Bretnor
and her parents
Sidney T. Harding and
Evelyn Rosso Harding

Helen Harding Bretnor
(1912–1967)

Although Helen Harding Bretnor lived almost all her life in Berkeley, California, her intellectual interests were far-ranging. Bretnor, the daughter of Sidney Twitchell Harding, a professor of irrigation engineering, attended Pomona College for two years, after which she received her A.B. with a major in French from the University of California. Some years later, in 1943, she received a certificate for graduate work at the School of Librarianship on the Berkeley campus and became a Junior Librarian at the Bancroft Library. There she remained, a dedicated member of the library's Public Services Division, her ability and knowledge of her field increasing steadily during almost a quarter-century, until illness forced her to retire just a few months before her death in 1967 at the age of fifty-five.

At the Bancroft, Helen Bretnor assisted scholars and general readers, through comprehensive reports in immaculate handwriting or through oral replies delivered in her charming voice, which barely rose above a whisper. She was noted for the attractive, ingenious small exhibits that she mounted in the glass cases of the Reading Room and for the more elaborate ones prepared for the great gathering of the year: the annual meeting of the Friends of the Bancroft Library.

Mrs. Bretnor's meticulous research and her impressive store of information are noted in countless acknowledgments and commendations in works published by the users of Bancroft, but she also made valuable bibliographical contributions as a member of library committees. Her major publication, prior to this translation, was a substantially augmented edition of the nineteenth-century classic *A History of California Newspapers, 1846–1858*, by the pioneer printer, publisher, and editor Edward C. Kemble.

Her familiarity with esoteric material in Bancroft's stacks enabled Mrs. Bretnor to turn up *Vie et aventures d'un enfant de l'Ardenne*, the autobiography of the adventurous young Belgian Jean-Nicolas Perlot, which was published in his native country in 1897. Bretnor was intrigued by this work, which vividly described the twenty-six-year-old emigrant's experiences during the gold rush that brought him to California and led him to make his fortune as Portland's first landscape gardener. Through careful research she discovered that although Perlot finally retired in Belgium, where some of his family still lived, he had a granddaughter in Oregon who bore the delightful name of Ghislaine LeJeune. Correspondence with Miss LeJeune resulted in her gift to the Bancroft Library of a number of Perlot's graphic letters describing his long voyage around Cape Horn and his experiences on the west coast of America, as well as other memorabilia, including some philosophic manuscripts and nine photographs of the pioneer.

Helen Bretnor worked on the translation of Perlot's memoir for a long time, polishing and repolishing it right down to the last year of her life. Now at last we have this work in print to serve both as a vivid historical document and as a tribute to the literary and scholarly accomplishments of its translator.

James D. Hart
Director
The Bancroft Library

Contents

Author's Preface

Some friends, who occasionally took pleasure in making me tell my adventures, persuaded me to write them. I wrote them without being begged. They then exhorted me to publish them. This time I resisted. Compose a book! I exclaimed, what are you thinking of? It's not my profession. To write a book, one must first, it seems to me, know how to write.

They assured me that this was not necessary. Moreover, they said, the book is done: all that remains is to print what you have just written. As for not being by a professional writer, it won't be worth any the less for that. On the contrary.

—But will that be worth the trouble of printing it? My story is quite simply that of a man at grips with the difficulties of life who finally manages to surmount them; it can interest some friends, not the public. At the very least it would be necessary, in order to present it to the public, that the insignificance of the content be somewhat relieved by the merit of the form.

—Too much modesty! First, the spectacle of a man struggling obstinately against adverse fortune is instructive and inspiring; it always interests. And, for another thing, a personal account has something to please with, even if deprived of the attractions of style.

—Possibly, but this has other faults. I have chronicled my memories as they come to my pen, without order or method; it abounds in repetitions, extensions, excursions. I would have to cut out three-quarters of it to make it readable. I didn't have time, you understand, to make it any shorter.

—Publish it as it is; there will be, at least, one category of readers who will not be repelled by the tedious portions: your friends, your children and—later—your grandchildren.

I was not convinced, and yet I let myself be persuaded. Why? I don't quite know; perhaps to put an end to the discussion, perhaps too because, at heart, I felt a secret satisfaction in seeing myself in print while yet alive, and bound in calf or otherwise. Man has many weaknesses!

After all, this book, here it is. If it bores you, benevolent reader, close it.

Translator's Preface

A copy of *Vie et aventures d'un enfant de l'Ardenne*, by Jean-Nicolas Perlot, was given to the Bancroft Library in 1953 by Harry N. M. Winton, librarian to the United Nations, who had picked it up in Seattle some twenty years before. The title, at first glance, appeared far afield for a library devoted to Western America. An examination of the contents, however, showed that the adventures included the gold rush and that the most important years of the life were spent in California and Oregon. An initial reading of the text revealed the unusually interesting and detailed experiences of a Belgian, first in the Southern Mines and as a friend and interpreter of the Yosemite Indians, and finally as Portland's first landscape gardener. He was observant and intelligent, with the ability to turn his hand to whatever needed doing; he also had stability, honesty, and a sense of humor. In addition, he was a gifted storyteller—a rare and precious quality among writers of pioneer narratives.

Despite all this, Perlot's account was unknown to scholars in the field. The book was printed in a very small edition for distribution to the author's family and friends by F. Brück in 1897–98 at Arlon, capital of Belgian Luxembourg, with a population of 5,700. A check of major library catalogues has so far failed to reveal another copy. None of the appropriate bibliographies consulted mentions it. Two years' searching and advertising have failed to turn up a copy for sale. Possibly the small edition, the deceptive title, and the book's unavailability to the English-speaking reader, who would be most likely to be interested in it, account for its obscurity.

At any rate, it was immediately obvious that this situation should be remedied. The value of the account as sheer entertainment was more than matched by its historical importance in matters of local interest in California and Oregon, and its apparent rarity argued for translation and publication.

Helen Harding Bretnor

Editor's Preface and Acknowledgments

Jean-Nicolas Perlot's penchant for storytelling was not confined to his experiences in California and Oregon. In the original edition of *Vie et aventures d'un enfant de l'Ardenne* he traced his family's origins back to the Middle Ages in chapters that relied more on family legends, perhaps, than on facts. Because that history, however delightful and intriguing, is not part of the gold rush narrative or the story of his sojourn in Oregon, it has been omitted from this edition. In this volume Perlot's account begins after he has been living in Paris for three years while holding a job as a *calicot*, or linen-draper's assistant. Sometime in the fall of 1848, either in October or November, he learned of the discovery of gold in California.

In the California portion of the narrative, Perlot sometimes told the story of his explorations for gold or his lonely travels in regions of the central Sierra in a way that defies precise dating or geographic identification. Where these obscure passages add little to the narrative, or to the historical record, they have been omitted.

Perlot also mentioned in passing the names of many persons whom it has been impossible to identify. Many were foreign nationals whom Perlot met briefly but with whom he established a bond because they spoke French or were from Belgium. Although their origins and careers remain obscure, they are vitally important historically as examples of "invisible Europeans" in the gold rush, and where it seems useful I have called attention to the pattern of their relationships or activities, either in a brief preface to a chapter or in a footnote. Similarly, when Perlot's life intersected with important events in California and Oregon history, some explanation of the larger context has been provided.

Besides acknowledging the splendid accomplishment of Helen Harding Bretnor as the translator of Perlot's memoirs, I wish to thank Reginald Bretnor of Medford, Oregon, who has been of invaluable assistance to me in the editing of the translation. Further, I am indebted to Dr. James D. Hart, director of the Bancroft Library, not only for his tribute to Helen Bretnor, but for making available various manuscript materials written by Perlot that are now deposited in the Bancroft Library. Julia Macleod, Estelle Rebec, and Marie Byrne of the Bancroft have also been helpful.

A very special thanks must go to Christiane Fischer Dichamp, formerly of the University of Nancy, who collected materials from the Bibliothèque Nationale about the French response to the California gold rush and who assisted me in translating the more difficult texts. Largely through her researches the tremendous impact of the gold rush on France has become apparent to me. I am grateful as well to Jay Gitlin, historian, musician, and devoted Francophile, who identified records in the Portland Historical Society relating to Perlot's years in Portland.

Not only did Abraham P. Nasatir provide me with much information in many personal interviews in 1978, when we were both fellows at the Henry E. Huntington Library, but his many books and articles on the French in the California gold rush were indispensable in editing Perlot's memoirs. Indeed, no one could begin to understand the European response to the gold rush and the French experience in California without consulting his remarkable *French Activities in California* (1945).

Mary Lee Spence, editor of the Papers of John C. Frémont, provided material on Les Mineurs Belges, a company of workers from Liège who came to Frémont's Mariposa Estate. Both Charles Capen McLaughlin, editor of the Papers of Frederick Law Olmsted, and Victoria Post Ranney, who is editing the volume on Olmsted's years in California as the manager of the Mariposa Estate, shared their still unpublished findings with me. I am grateful as well to John McCullough of North Bennington, Vermont, and to Muriel Palmer and the staff of the Park-McCullough House for calling to my attention their remarkable collection of Carleton E. Watkins photographs of the Southern Mines of California.

Three Yale colleagues, John Merriman, associate professor of French history, Irving Rouse, professor of anthropology, and Archibald Hanna, former curator of the Western Americana Collection in the Beinecke Rare Book and Manuscript Library, have furnished me with much crucial information. In the final weeks of editing, George A. Miles, curator of the Western Americana Collection, and the staff of the Beinecke Library, Yale University, were unstinting in their kindnesses. Richard Leder, of the class of 1979, and Andrew Campbell, of the class of 1984, Yale College, have been assiduous in their efforts to find materials in the Yale University Library relating to Perlot. Rose Stone of the Yale College Dean's Office and Florence Thomas and Mary Whitney of the Yale History Department have assisted in the preparation of the final manuscript. And finally, I am indebted to Edward Tripp, Editor-in-Chief of Yale University Press, whose patience while awaiting this manuscript has been monumental.

Howard R. Lamar

Introduction

On April 7, 1851, Jules Lombard, the French vice-consul at Monterey, California, noted that a sailing vessel, *Le Courrier de Cherbourg*, had anchored in the
harbor. Six months out of Le Havre, it had on board seventy-two passengers, of
whom forty-five were members of a Parisian gold-seeking society or company
called La Fortune, so named because they had banded together under the slogan
Audaces fortuna juvat—Fortune to the bold.[1]

Consul Lombard also reported that bitter disappointment awaited the members
of La Fortune, for he and a company representative, who had arrived some time
before, had to inform them that the firm was bankrupt. Company supplies were
seized to pay outstanding debts, and even the ship itself was detained for a time
when its captain was unable to pay American customs fees.[2] The argonauts
became even more dispirited when they sought the advice of Consul Lombard.
Unlike his predecessor at the consulate, Jacques Antoine Moerenhout, who had
urged his government to send French citizens to participate in the gold rush,
Lombard was still convinced that the placers on the Sacramento and American
rivers were but a temporary phenomenon. For him the future of California lay in
agriculture, not mining, so he strongly advised the workers of La Fortune company
to turn to farming and give up their dreams of gold.[3]

1. "Lombard to Minister, Division Commerciale, Bureau d'Amérique, Number 8, Agence Consulaire
de France à Monterey, Monterey, April 25, 1851," correspondence summarized in Abraham P. Nasatir,
French Activities in California: An Archival Calendar-Guide (Stanford: Stanford University Press, 1945),
pp. 290–91.

2. "Lombard to Minister, . . . April 25, 1851," and "Lombard to Minister, . . . June 14, 1851,"
Nasatir, *French Activities in California*, pp. 290–91.

3. Moerenhout was an able and observant civil servant who had been consul for the Netherlands in
Valparaiso and for the United States in Tahiti. He was also trained as a civil engineer and thus could comment
with some authority about the California gold discoveries. Moerenhout visited the placer operations on the
American, Sacramento, and San Joaquin rivers as early as May 15, 1848, and dispatched an intelligent and
favorable report to his superiors on August 17, 1848. See *Inside Story of the Gold Rush*, trans. and ed.
Abraham P. Nasatir, with George Ezra Dane (San Francisco: California Historical Society, Spec. Pub. no.
8, 1935), pp. iv, 4ff., 52ff., 75–76. See also Nasatir, *The French in the California Gold Rush*, Franco-
American Pamphlet Series, no. 3 (New York: American Society of the French Legion of Honor, 1934), pp.
7–8, and *French Activities in California*, pp. 28–31.

For a summary of Lombard's views see Nasatir, "A French Pessimist in California," *California Historical
Society Quarterly*, 31 (1952), 139–48, and *French Activities in California*, pp. 34–36.

The steward of the company, a spirited young Belgian named Jean-Nicolas Perlot, felt otherwise. Ignoring Lombard's advice, he and nine companions formed a new Company of Ten. Having secured a few maps from Lombard that promised to guide them from Monterey to the San Joaquin River, they struck out for the Southern Mines in the foothills of the central Sierra.

Many years later, Jean-Nicolas Perlot used the notes he kept during his long sojourn on the west coast of North America to fashion a witty, informative, and intriguing account of his life in the California gold regions from 1851 to 1857 and his later career as a landscape gardener in Portland, Oregon, as well. That account, virtually unknown to historians of the gold rush until a decade ago, has been translated into English by the late Helen Harding Bretnor and published in this volume.

Perlot's memoir, entitled *Vie et aventures d'un enfant de L'Ardenne* and published privately at Arlon, Belgium, in 1897, is not only a rare, perhaps unique, story of a Belgian argonaut, it is exceptionally valuable in that it covers so long a period and records the experiences of scores of other French and Belgian nationals who participated in the California and later western gold rushes. It is, in fact, a new gold rush journal in that it traces for the first time the daily life of one of the several thousand French-speaking placer miners who came to the Southern Mines of California between 1849 and 1855.

One might well ask at this point: Who was Perlot and why has he escaped our notice for so long? Jean-Nicolas Perlot was born on December 6, 1823, in the village of Herbeumont, the arrondissement of Neufchâteau, in the province of Luxembourg, Belgium. Enormously proud of his Belgian heritage, Perlot traced his ancestors back to the Middle Ages. Although he made no claims to their being noble or wealthy, he stressed their sense of independence, their bravery on occasion, and their firm belief in the work ethic. In the three opening chapters of his memoirs, which have not been included in this edition, Perlot made much of the fact that in his younger years his parents were hardworking but poor. Whatever the facts may have been, his father, Joseph Perlot, worked at, and appears to have been part owner of, a slate quarry that employed between fourteen and eighteen persons. When he was able to sell his share of the quarry for a good price, he used his new wealth to send his four surviving children, three sons and a daughter, to good schools.[4]

Jean-Nicolas was the youngest and—if we may judge by his own confession—the most restless and rebellious of the sons. Later, he remembered that he had learned little from his stay at the Collège de Boillon or during a term at the normal

---

4. The details of Perlot's ancestry are available in the original edition: Jean-Nicolas Perlot, *Vie et aventures d'un enfant de l'Ardenne* (Arlon, Belgium, 1897), chaps. 1–4. Perlot's parents, Joseph and Jeanne (Boulanger) Perlot, had five children, four of whom survived: Nicolas-Joseph, Jean-Baptiste, Jean-Nicolas, and Marie-Joséphe (ibid., p. 12). Helen Bretnor provided a typescript translation of Perlot's first four chapters, and this information is also available there (pp. 11–12).

school in Bastogne. Even a private-school master in Neufchâteau, whom Perlot liked and respected, had only limited success with his spirited charge. Perlot's last stint, at the Athenaeum in Arlon, was also not very productive: "At Boillon I had learned to skate, at Bastogne to make watch chains, at Neufchâteau I was in the midst of acquiring an incontestable skill at catching loaches in the river. That was just about the whole of my studies."[5]

Perlot's formal education was cut short by his father's early death. Called home to assist the family, Jean-Nicolas—or Jean Ka, as his family called him—came into increasing conflict with his older brother, Jean-Baptiste, who had become head of the household. It was also true that Jean-Nicolas felt the heavy hand of the Catholic church, for his family were pious communicants in a devoutly religious village. To make matters worse, the local curé was convinced that Jean-Nicolas was a freethinker and therefore a disturbing force. After reviewing his prospects, young Perlot decided that he must leave; so in 1845 he boarded a diligence at Sedan to seek his fortune in Paris.

He chose Paris partly because that was where many young Belgians went to find work and partly because he had an uncle there who was employed in the townhouse of the Duchess de la Force.[6] Perlot's uncle soon found him a job as a *calicot,* or linen-draper's assistant, in the shop of the kindly Monsieur Dupont. To Perlot, the shop was but the doorstep to Paris. In his free time he explored the whole of the city on foot and haunted the bookstalls, where, he tells us, he purchased some sixty volumes. Almost obsessed with the idea of educating himself, he became proficient in mathematics and engineering, skills he acquired by attending an arts and trades school at night. These skills and the ability to use a compass undoubtedly saved his life later, when he was lost in the Sierra Nevada.[7]

As Perlot explored the cultural riches of Paris, he also followed with fascination and dismay the last days of the troubled regime of Louis Philippe. Perlot was in the city when the Revolution of 1848 occurred after the king had refused to reform the election laws. After Louis Philippe had fled to England and the efforts of Louis Blanc to form a socialist government had failed, the French Assembly established the Second Republic, and by December 1848 Louis Napoleon had been named its new president.[8]

The revolution also triggered a severe economic depression. The number of unemployed laborers grew, and during June 1848 street riots occurred in Paris, Limoges, Lyons, and elsewhere in France. Food was so short that Paris almost experienced a famine. There were so many shortages that the unemployed began to

5. Ibid., pp. 13–15.

6. Ibid., pp. 15–18, 20–21, 30–31.

7. Ibid., pp. 32–37 passim. See chap. 16.

8. A convenient summary of the Revolution of 1848 and the establishment of the Second Republic can be found in Philippe Vigier, *La Seconde République* (Paris: Presses Universitaires de France, 1975), which has a useful bibliography (p. 127).

cut down trees in the Bois de Boulogne to use as fuel.[9] Perlot recalls that beginning in May 1848 his employer did "one sou's worth of business where usually we did one franc's worth."[10] As the depression continued, Perlot became restless. Like Mr. Micawber, he was waiting for "something to turn up" when news of the discovery of gold in Captain John Sutter's millrace at Coloma, California, reached Paris late in the fall of 1848.[11]

For many Frenchmen—and eventually for the French government as well— California gold offered a way out of the bitter economic, political, and psychological sense of despair the nation was experiencing. As Perlot put it, Paris exchanged "the revolutionary fever" for "the gold fever." The story of France's reaction to the California gold rush is by itself a touching melodrama of great expectations, naive self-deception, and deliberate fraud.[12] At the same time, its importance for France and western Europe can scarcely be exaggerated, for while it was a major event in American history, to Europeans it was the most exciting news to come out of the United States since the Revolution of 1776.

Accounts of the California gold discoveries reached France through several avenues. Jacques Antoine Moerenhout, the capable and articulate French consul at Monterey, first reported the news to his government in a dispatch dated May 15, 1848. After visiting the diggings himself in July of that year, he sent an intelligent and highly favorable report to his superiors on August 17—the very day, as Abraham P. Nasatir has noted, that Acting Governor Mason of California sent his report of the discovery to President Polk.[13] Moerenhout also forwarded the news and a box of nuggets to the admiral in command of the French fleet in the Pacific, who was stationed in Valparaiso at the time. He in turn forwarded the information and the gold samples to the French government.[14] Meanwhile the French had learned of the discovery in late October or early November via vessels returning from New York. By the end of the year official

9. The long depression lasted until 1854 (Vigier, *La Seconde République*, pp. 17–18, 89–108). See also John M. Merriman, *The Agony of the Republic: The Repression of the Left in Revolutionary France, 1848–1851* (New Haven: Yale University Press, 1978).

10. Perlot, *Vie et aventures*, p. 36.

11. Accounts of the discovery and the subsequent gold rush are legion. For a detailed account of the discovery see James P. Zollinger, *Sutter: the Man and his Empire* (New York, 1939); see also Rodman W. Paul, *California Gold: The Beginning of Mining in the Far West* (Lincoln: University of Nebraska Press, 1964). An excellent older account can be found in Theodore H. Hittell, *History of California* (San Francisco: N. J. Stone, 1897), vol. 2, pp. 682–700, and vol. 3 (1898), pp. 43–160.

12. The French response to the gold rush has been the subject of many historical studies. The standard account, Daniel Levy, *Les Français en Californie* (San Francisco, 1884), pp. 67–71, is also one of the earliest. Nasatir, *French Activities in California*, and *The French in the California Gold Rush*, have been cited in nn. 1 and 2. His accounts are complemented by Léon Lemonnier, *La Rueé vers l'or en Californie* (Paris: Gallimard, 1944), and Gilbert Chinard, "When the French Came to California: An Introductory Essay," *California Historical Society Quarterly*, 22, no. 4 (1943), 289–314.

13. Nasatir, *Inside Story of the Gold Rush*, p. iv.

14. Nasatir, *French Activities in California*, p. 281.

American reports confirming the discovery had also reached western Europe. Chief among them were Governor Mason's account and President Polk's annual message to Congress, which, having been delivered on December 5, reached Paris on December 23, 1848.[15]

At first Paris greeted the news with skepticism, but Moerenhout's exuberant words, "Never, I think, . . . has there been such excitement in any country of the world," were echoed in the reports of mining engineers sent out by the French government to investigate.[16] It was then that depression-ridden Paris went wild. Brochures and books on California appeared almost overnight. Auguste La-Coste's *Californie* (1849) went through three editions. Hipolyte Ferry, a common sailor who had visited California, published a good account of the state that became a best seller.[17] The Paris newspapers, writes Nasatir, "published every scrap of information about California."[18] Etienne Derbec, a prominent French journalist, went to California in 1849 to report on events firsthand. His letters, full of details about his visits to the mining regions, soon appeared in the influential Paris newspaper, *Journal des debats*.[19] Even a bimonthly publication, *La Californie*, appeared, which, as its name suggests, retailed news of the gold rush.[20]

Parisians were all the more favorable in their response since they were already familiar with John C. Frémont's famous reports on the overland routes to California, which had been published in 1845, and his prominent if controversial role in the American conquest of California in 1846–47.[21] Now not only was Frémont a senator from the new state of California, his name was also associated with rich placers found on his Mariposa Estate, in the foothills of the central Sierra Nevada,

15. Chinard, "When the French Came to California," p. 292.

16. A. P. Nasatir, "The French Consulate in California, 1843–1856," *California Historical Society Quarterly*, 13 (1934), 57.

17. Auguste Lacoste, *Californie. Fragments inédits d'un voyage autour du monde* (Paris, 1849); Hipolyte Ferry, *Description de la Nouvell-Californie: geographique, politique et morale* (Paris, 1850), which was published previously in a newspaper series in 1849.

18. Nasatir, *The French in the California Gold Rush*, p. 4.

19. *A French Journalist in the California Gold Rush—The Letters of Etienne Derbec*, ed. A. P. Nasatir (Georgetown, Calif.: Talisman Press, 1964). Eventually Derbec settled in San Francisco, where he wrote a column in French for the *Evening Picayune*, "the first evening newspaper on the Pacific Coast." In June 1852 he founded his own *L'Echo du Pacifique*, "the first permanent French paper in San Francisco." Edward A. Kemble, *A History of California Newspapers, 1846–1858*, ed. and with a foreword by Helen Harding Bretnor (Georgetown, Calif.: Talisman Press, 1968), pp. 107, 111, 124.

20. Nasatir, *French Activities in California*, p. 37.

21. Frémont's *Report of the Exploring Expedition to the Rocky Mountains in the year 1842, and to Oregon and North California in the year 1843–44* (1845), and his *Geographical Memoir upon Upper California in Illustration of His Map of Oregon and California* (1848), were available to the French by the time of the gold rush. For a superb summary of Frémont's explorations and achievements, see William H. Goetzmann, *Army Exploration in the American West, 1803–1863* (New Haven: Yale University Press, 1959), pp. 65–108. Frémont's role in the conquest of California is covered in Allen Nevins, *Fremont, Pathmarker of the West* (New York, 1939).

in 1848–49.[22] Giving way to flights of imagination, a variety theater in Paris produced a panorama entitled "Journey to California," based on Frémont's exploits in the West. The production was actually a series of tableaux painted on a giant canvas mounted on a vertical cylinder. The canvas was slowly rolled past the audience to give the illusion of traveling with Frémont across the plains and mountains to California. The final section of the painting depicted life in the gold fields.[23] Frémont himself appears to have promoted French interest in California mines, for as Henry Blumenthal has noted, Le Nouveau Monde society of Paris purchased California lands from him while another company, Les Mineurs Belges, bought a quartz mine from him soon after the gold rush began.[24]

By far the most accurate indicator of the gold fever in France, however, was the fact that eighty-three societies and companies were organized there to carry passengers to California, exploit the mines, or send supplies for sale at a good price.[25] One company announced that it intended to send prefabricated portable iron and wooden houses to California for sale. Another promised to build hotels on the west coast. The prospect of easy gold led other groups to form charitable organizations with such names as L'Espérance and La Société de Jésus et Marie. Sometimes these were endorsed by prominent churchmen or public figures. Their stated purpose was to collect gold to alleviate the miseries of the poor.[26]

Such endeavors capitalized on an already popular faith in clubs and associations in France. "During the 1840's," writes John M. Merriman, "faith in association was the central theme of the social programs of most republicans." There were 348 mutual-aid societies in Paris alone in 1848. Some took the form of agricultural improvement societies; others focused on labor organization or political reform.[27] Unfortunately, enthusiasm was paralleled by public gullibility, since a firm founded by one Christophe Colomb and named "America" appears not to have excited suspicion.[28]

By far the most interesting and ambitious French enterprise associated with the

22. The Southern Mines are described in Hittell, *History of California*, 3, 161–76; *A History of Tuolumne County, California* (San Francisco: B. F. Alley, 1882); and Raymond F. Wood, *California's Agua Fria: The Early History of Mariposa County* (Fresno, Calif.: Academy Library Guild, 1954). While there are scores of memoirs and reminiscences by miners in the Southern Mines, one of the most succinct accounts of the region, and of the role Stockton played in its development, is Catherine Coffin Phillips, *Coulterville Chronicle: The Annals of a Mother Lode Mining Town* (San Francisco: Grabhorn Press, 1942), pp. 51–80.

23. "The Trip to California: An Explanatory Note of the Panorama. Presented for the first time to the public, at the Theatre des Variétés, Paris, August 8, 1850," *Frontier and Midland*, 14 (Jan. 1934), 160–61, 168–69.

24. Henry Blumenthal, "The California Societies in France, 1849–1855," *Pacific Historical Review*, 21 (1956), 258, n. 25.

25. Ibid., pp. 251–60.

26. Chinard, "When the French Came to California," p. 296; Blumenthal, "California Societies in France," p. 252.

27. Merriman, *Agony of the Republic*, p. 52; Chinard, "When the French Came to California," pp. 293–94.

28. Lemonnier, *La Rueé vers l'or en Californie*, p. 128.

California gold rush was the Société des Lingot d'Or, which was organized by the prefect of police in Paris as a lottery offering 224 prizes, the largest of which was a solid gold ingot. Ostensibly the lottery was designed to assist those interested in going to California by paying for part of their passage; but it also had a political purpose because the police hoped to use the funds raised to ship 5,000 suspected radicals or undesirables—many of them participants in the Revolution of 1848— to California.[29] To publicize the effort, Alexandre Dumas *fils* was hired to write a history of lotteries and to praise the activities of the society.[30] The first prize, a gold ingot valued at 4,000 francs, was displayed in a Paris storefront window as a further effort to entice the public to buy lottery tickets. Meanwhile, the walls of Paris were being covered with posters advertising other companies and societies and offering stock for sale.[31]

The naive qualities of the response to California eventually led French humorists and illustrators to lampoon the gold craze. One cartoonist depicted a man sitting on a pile of gold surrounded by three cannon and attempting to sleep while holding a lighted match in each hand in order to fire the cannon in case of robberies. The laconic caption read: "Slight precaution which it is advisable to take in California if one wants to spend a peaceful night and still possess one's gold upon reawakening." Another pictured men struggling to lift nuggets so large that they soon fell exhausted from the effort; a third showed a clever merchant filling a large shipping crate with pretty women, for he had heard they were "in great demand" in California.[32] The skepticism of the lampooners apparently had limited effect, for more French citizens emigrated to the United States between 1846 and 1851 than at any other time in the nineteenth century. Before the gold rush was over, some thirty thousand French-speaking immigrants could be found in California alone.[33]

When Perlot himself succumbed to the gold excitement, he decided to cast his lot, as he explains in his memoirs, with the La Fortune company, headed by one

29. Ibid., chap. 5, esp. pp. 133–45.

30. Ibid., pp. 140–43; "Alexandre Dumas fils and the Lottery of the Golden Ingots," translated, with introduction and notes by A. P. Nasatir, *California Historical Society Quarterly*, 33 (1954), 125–42.

31. Blumenthal, "California Societies in France," p. 252. See chap. 1.

32. *Charivari*, Jan. 21, 1849, Apr. 11, 1849. I am grateful to Christiane Fischer Dichamp for locating these cartoons in the Bibliothèque Nationale and making them available to me.

33. Blumenthal, "California Societies in France," p. 258; also Henri Bunle, *Mouvements migratoires entre la France et l'étranger* (Paris, 1943), and Louis Chevalier, "L'émigration français au XIX siècle," *Etudes d'histoire moderne et contemporaine*, 1 (1947), 126–71. Emigration from France to the United States was 847 between 1821 and 1830, 4,552 between 1831 and 1840, and 7,722 between 1841 and 1850. The three peak periods of French migration to the United States were 1846–60; immediately after the Franco-Prussian War and the Commune of Paris, 1870–71; and 1886–90.

The number 30,000 probably needs some qualification. There were many French-Canadians and persons of French descent from Louisiana in the gold mines. Gold seekers of French origin had also come from Mexico, Chile, Peru, the Sandwich Islands, Tahiti, and the United States. All of them were usually identified as "Frenchmen." See Levy, *Les Français en Californie*, p. 66. Nasatir, *French Journalist*, p. 15, estimates that the number was between 22,000 and 30,000 by December 1851.

Thibeau (Lemonnier, *La Rueé vers l'or en Californie*, p. 128, spells it "Thibaut") and his two sons. Although the Californienne was the largest society with the greatest amount of stock for sale and attracted the most publicity, La Fortune published a handsome brochure in which the directors claimed to have purchased a machine that could easily separate gold from earth and gravel and therefore pay great dividends.[34] Perlot had received part of his inheritance from his father's estate shortly before the gold rush began, but even with that sum he lacked the necessary funds to buy a full share of La Fortune stock. Since he knew one of the Thibeaus personally he resolved the difficulty by combining the deposit of his savings with an agreement to serve as the company steward. Thus in the fall of 1850 he was able to march off to Le Havre under the company flag with its optimistic motto, *Audaces fortuna juvat*.[35] There, after some delay, he boarded the *Courrier de Cherbourg*, which sailed around the tip of South America and landed at Monterey on April 7, 1851.

One must not anticipate Jean-Nicolas Perlot's own fascinating narrative by attempting to summarize it here. Nevertheless, some of his experiences in California and Oregon deserve comment for they illustrate larger themes in both European and American history that are quite important. Even though Perlot wrote retrospectively and sought to verify his own first impressions by reading or by consulting others, he was not really aware of the significance his narrative would have one day as a historical document.

The first of these themes, the profound effect of the California gold rush on France and, indeed, on all of western Europe, has already been suggested.[36] Even the origins of Perlot's shipboard companions suggest just how wide a swath the gold rush cut. Among the passengers on the *Courrier de Cherbourg* was an Alsatian named Margraff who claimed to be the nephew of the duke of Baden. The other company members Perlot identified included a Swiss doctor and a Swiss farmer, a daguerreotypist, a hatter, a schoolmaster's son, a plumber, a trumpeter who had seen army service, a stationer, a lumber salesman, a baker, a silverer of forks and spoons, a drunkard, a French waiter from Madrid, and withal, a garrulous liberal named Badinier who was fond of quoting the speeches of Mirabeau.[37] Among the remaining passengers were an abbé and five women, one of whom appears to have been either an English schoolmistress or a teacher of English. Perlot's shipmates were also representative of the French and European gold seekers who came to

---

34. Chinard, "When the French Came to California," pp. 300–01, contains a drawing of the "Machine for Washing and Amalgamating Gold."

35. See chap. 1.

36. Levy, *Les Français en Californie*, pp. 67–68, observed that it was seen as a wonderful act of Providence. "It gave courage to the heart and produced a spirit of adventure."

37. See pp. 19–20.

California by virtue of the fact that the migration represented all classes rather than a largely worker-peasant class.[38]

The French presence in California has been ably documented by French journalists and visitors as well as government officials and French scholars. Further, these resources have been supplemented by the admirable scholarly publications of Abraham P. Nasatir, who has spent much of his distinguished career documenting, editing, and chronicling the story of the French in California.[39] On the other hand, the everyday experiences of European miners in California remain somewhat obscure.

Moreover, the Belgian presence has seldom been either recorded or acknowledged, although something is known about the group of artisans from Liège, Les Mineurs Belges, who came to do deep-shaft mining at Frémont's Mariposa Estate.[40] A Belgian painter, Théodore T'Scharner (1826–1900), made some of the first sketches of the gold fields, but unfortunately most of them have been lost or destroyed. In 1862 Hendrik Conscience, a prolific Flemish writer, published a novel about three Belgian youths in the gold rush which he entitled Het Goudland! The book enjoyed immense popularity in both Belgium and France.[41] A Belgian emigré to California, J. J. F. Haine, later presented an account of gold rush San Francisco to the Royal Geographic Society in Antwerp that has now been translated into English and published.[42] Even so, relatively little is known about the experiences of the individual gold seekers from Europe who actually worked in the placers for a sustained period of time. Thus, Perlot's narrative about a group of almost invisible and almost inarticulate French and Belgian argonauts is of crucial evidence of their response to the gold rush frontier.

Perhaps equally important is the fact that although Perlot eventually prospered in America, whereas most of his shipmates did not, on the whole his experiences reflected those of other Francophone immigrants to the West Coast. Even when Perlot and his companions landed at Monterey and discovered that La Fortune was bankrupt, their experience was representative, for virtually all of the eighty-three societies and companies turned out to be impractical ventures or fraudulent enterprises.[43]

38. One of the main themes of Levy, Les Français en Californie, is the incredible variety of French nationals who came to California. In A Frenchman in the Gold Rush. The Journal of Ernest de Massey, Argonaut of 1849. Publication no. 2 of the California Historical Society (San Francisco, 1927), p. 8, Margaret Eyer Wilbur, the translator, argues that the majority of the French who came were "mainly younger sons of the nobility, lawyers, doctors, bankers, scholars, and political free-thinkers rather than men of brawn and muscle." Perlot's shipmates fell somewhere in between: they were neither aristocrats nor noblemen, nor were they peasants.

39. The range of Nasatir's contributions may be seen in footnotes 1–4 and 12–20.

40. Blumenthal, "California Societies in France," p. 258n.

41. "A Belgian in the Gold Rush: A Memoir by Dr. J. J. F. Haine," translated, with an introduction by Jan Albert Goris, California Historical Society Quarterly, 37 (Dec. 1958), 312.

42. Ibid., pp. 311–46.

43. Blumenthal, "California Societies in France," pp. 251–60.

When Perlot and his friends set out on foot to the Southern Mines, some two hundred miles distant, they were ignorant of the terrain and the nature of the people and wildlife they might encounter on the way. Hampered by a poor understanding of either English or Spanish, they were sometimes reduced to a comical situation when seeking directions from Americans. Perlot's friend Messent, who was one of the Company of Ten, could understand English but could not speak it; Perlot could not understand Americans but could speak passable English.[44] In short, they underwent a variation of the classic American experience of pioneering as they struggled across the San Joaquin Valley and up the Merced River before reaching Mariposa. At times Perlot's company dwindled from ten to himself and one other companion. They became lost, ran out of food, and often were so terrified of Indians and bears that much of the trek was made in an atmosphere of crisis and fear.

Nevertheless, it seems significant that the young linen-draper's assistant not only survived his American "pioneer" experience, he and his companions became good miners and soon reveled in the crude life of the camps in the foothills of the Sierra. Perlot became such a fine marksman that he supplemented his income from gold digging by supplying local butchers with game. He was, in fact, engaged in market hunting, a business that Daniel Boone, David Crockett, Kit Carson, and even Annie Oakley had pursued at some point in their careers.

Armed with compass, gun, and his ever-present pipe, and accompanied by his dog, Miraud, Perlot also explored, Daniel Boone style, the rugged terrain of the Hetch Hetchy and Yosemite valleys only a few years after the discovery of the latter by James Savage and the Mariposa Battalion in 1851.[45] Perlot's life in California suggests that pioneering was not an experience that only Americans understood and appreciated. Indeed, it was universal in the sense that man's will to survive and his insatiable curiosity are universal.

As a member of a foreign minority on the frontier, he had, of course, a different experience. His economic and political status was often in doubt. Shortly before Perlot arrived in California, for example, American miners persuaded the California legislature to impose a prohibitive tax or license fee of twenty dollars a month on all foreign miners. After heated protests from Mexican and French miners it was repealed, but a license costing four dollars a month was substituted.[46] Because of

44. See chap. 4.
45. The exact date that the first Europeans or Americans saw the Yosemite Valley will always remain in doubt, but Major James Savage, a friend and follower of John C. Frémont and a pioneer Indian trader along the Tuolumne, Merced, and Fresno rivers in 1848, is generally given credit for the discovery. Savage and a group of volunteers from Mariposa marched into that awesome valley in the spring of 1851 while in search of marauding bands of Yosemite Indians. See Hittell, *History of California*, 3: 129, 189, 837, 846–48; Wood, *California's Agua Fria, County*, pp. 37–57; and Carl P. Russell, *One Hundred Years in Yosemite: The Story of a Great Park and Its Friends* (Berkeley: University of California Press, 1947), pp. 8, 40–50.
46. When the more reasonable fee of four dollars per month was imposed in March 1851, sheriffs were made collectors but they seldom enforced the law except, as Hittell notes, "for the purpose of harassing Chinamen" (*History of California*, 3: 706–09).

the language barrier, Americans sometimes mistook the French for Mexican miners and threatened and bullied them. In several instances only Perlot's toughness and personal leadership saved his friends from the assaults of American miners.[47]

Perlot's angle of vision was so different from that of American miners that when one reads the diary of Robert Eccleston, an American who was mining in the same area at the same time that Perlot was there, the discrepancies in perception are vast.[48] Eccleston's account is concerned with military action against local Indians or focused on legal actions to secure property or enact justice. Whereas Eccleston was full of talk about newspapers, political crises, and local government, Perlot referred to these only in passing. Another American miner of sorts whose sojourn in the Southern Mines overlapped that of Perlot and who kept a journal was Samuel Ward, brother of Julia Ward Howe and cousin to Ward McAllister. Although Ward ran a store at Belt's Ferry and mined only incidentally, he was, like Perlot, a keen observer and a witty, articulate writer. But Ward's world was one of business rivalry, speculation, and class distinctions, while that of another miner, Benjamin Butler Harris, was full of election news, jury trials, and confrontations with foreigners.[49]

Perlot also had a different perspective when it came to dealing with the small bands of Miwok Indians in the central Sierra.[50] Although he and his friends arrived in the Southern Mines at the time of the Mariposa War and other Indian–white conflicts, Perlot's initial fear and hate of the red man began to dissipate when he realized that groups of Indians were bringing gold to the town of Coulterville to buy sugar, flour, and coffee. He realized that they were miners like himself, and he began to befriend them in order to learn where they panned for gold. In the process of parleying he came to know and respect individual Indians; in turn, they eventually allowed him to mine for gold in their territory.[51]

Once he made successful contact by presenting himself to one of the Yosemite chiefs—he troubled to learn their language, took intelligent notes on their religious beliefs, and even participated in a skirmish between the Yosemites and the Tuolumnes.[52] It may well be that Perlot is the only known recorder of the names of certain native leaders and the acts and customs of certain bands in the Mariposa–

47. See chap. 18.

48. C. Gregory Crampton, ed., *The Mariposa Indian War, 1850–51: Diaries of Robert Eccleston: The California Gold Rush, Yosemite and the High Sierra* (Salt Lake City: University of Utah Press, 1957).

49. *Sam Ward in the Gold Rush*, ed. Carvel Collins (Stanford, Calif.: Stanford University Press, 1949); Benjamin Butler Harris, *The Gila Trail: The Texas Argonauts and the California Gold Rush*, ed. and annot. Richard H. Dillon (Norman: University of Oklahoma Press, 1960), pp. 109–62.

50. A standard if older account is S. A. Barrett, *The Geography and Dialects of the Miwok Indians*, University of California Publications in American Archaeology and Ethnology, vol. 6, no. 2 (Berkeley: the University Press [*sic*], 1908), pp. 333–80. See also Alfred L. Kroeber, *Handbook of the Indians of California* (Washington, 1925), and Robert F. Heizer and M. A. Whipple, *The California Indians: A Source Book* (Berkeley: University of California Press, 1971), esp. pp. 332–40, 375–84, 520–32.

51. See chaps. 15–18.

52. See chap. 18.

Yosemite region.[53] And although Perlot appears to have admired Major James Savage, frontiersman, Indian trader, and member of the Mariposa Battalion that captured marauding Indians who were then placed on a reservation, he appears to have set down his impressions without having been affected by the American attitude of hostility toward Indians that the Mariposa conflict had exacerbated.[54]

By 1853 Perlot had succeeded at mining well enough to employ other miners to work for him. He began to spend more time hunting for new placers or simply exploring. That year he came within a few miles of penetrating the main portion of the Yosemite Valley, which Savage and the Mariposa Battalion had discovered in 1851.[55] By 1857 he was so familiar with the approaches to the valley that he was hired by George W. Coulter and a group of San Francisco businessmen to open a trail from Coultersville to Yosemite for use by tourists. Two years before, J. M. Hutchings, an architect and journalist from San Francisco, and Thomas Ayres, an artist-illustrator, had visited Yosemite and had returned full of plans to publicize and exploit the wonders of Yosemite.[56]

Accounts of the opening of the trail from Coultersville in 1857 suggest that it was done by Americans, some of whom were surveyors or engineers, and by some Indian workers. Perlot, on the other hand, states that Huguet, a shipmate from *Le Courrier de Cherbourg* who had become a butcher in Coultersville, told Coulter of Perlot's knowledge of the trails and, in turn, urged Perlot to assist the party. Perlot claims that it was he who directed the ten Indians as they hacked a way through the undergrowth or cleared boulders so that the pack mules could pass into the valley and, eventually, a wagon road could be constructed for tourists.[57]

Perlot spends as much time describing the activities of the Indian guides in the party and the native bands they found camped in the valley as he does the actions of the Americans. He also recalls that once they were in the valley and moved forward to see Yosemite Falls, a party of musicians preceded them. Their instruments and tunes so intrigued the local Indians that they forced the performers to play throughout the day. Perlot's pied-piper scene is a charming complement to the more sober account by Dr. Lafayette H. Bunnell, a veteran miner and promoter of the valley. While surveyors measured the heights of the massive walls and domes, an artist, possibly Ayres, sketched scenes, Perlot made his own survey with homemade instruments.[58] Once again Perlot played the role of the invisible man whose observations place standard accounts in a new perspective.

53. Jean-Nicolas Perlot, index, "mots indiens" (ca. 1850–55), MS notebook in Bancroft Library, Berkeley, California. See also chap. 14.

54. See n. 48; Hittell, *History of California*, 3: 839–51.

55. See chap. 15.

56. Lafayette Houghton Bunnell, *The Discovery of the Yosemite and the Indian War of 1851* (Chicago: Fleming H. Revell, 1880), pp. 303–16. Hutchings' own account may be found in the *Mariposa Gazette*, July 12, 1855.

57. Russell, *One Hundred Years in Yosemite*, pp. 48–50.

58. See chap. 21.

By 1857 Perlot had made enough money to invest in a mortgage loan firm in California.[59] While his investments appear to have been successful, he was still young and restless. The California placers had almost been exhausted and his fellow miners were pessimistic.

> They had told me that everywhere, on the placers they knew, people were shoving and elbowing each other; everywhere there was a great number of people who did not find enough to pay for their labor, who did not earn enough, often, to pay for the supplies they consumed. They saw some, they said, who were working for a dollar a day. This gave me something to think about.[60]

As Perlot tried to figure out what his next course of action would be, reports reached San Francisco that gold had been discovered at Fort Colville, an old Hudson's Bay Company post on the upper Columbia River. After having persuaded themselves that the strike was legitimate, Perlot and his friend, Margraff, set off in the summer of 1857 for Oregon with the intention of ascending the Columbia. This, and the Fraser River finds in the spring of 1858, were the first of a series of siren calls that lured many thousands of miners from California to other parts of the West, so much so that some observers predicted that the California camps would soon be depopulated.[61]

Perlot arrived in the Pacific Northwest so late in the season that he was forced to spend the winter in Portland, Oregon, rather than push on to Fort Colville. There, without ever intending to do so he began a new American career—less exciting than mining, but in many ways more profoundly challenging; for Perlot, alone in a predominantly Yankee city without any French or Belgian compatriots to sustain him, had to learn to deal with Americans, on American terms, in an urban setting.

It was perhaps symbolic of the new order of things that every occupation at which he had succeeded so well in California seemed to go badly in Oregon. While waiting for the weather to break so that he could go up the Columbia, he expected to support himself by market hunting, but a scarcity of game around Portland and the sufficiency of domestic cattle and pigs left him with disinterested customers and low prices. He then became a woodcutter for a local protestant minister, but that proved to be a grueling job that paid little cash. Moreover, the minister's condescension toward Perlot, whom he regarded as a benighted foreigner, rekindled in him his long-smoldering dislike of men of the cloth.

All the while Perlot had been baffled, even horrified, by the paradox that was

59. See chap. 22.

60. See ibid.

61. Gold was discovered at Fort Colville in 1855, but hostilities between Indians and whites that year erupted into the Yakima Indian War. It was unsafe for miners to go there or to the western slope of the Rockies until treaties were signed and reservations established in 1856. See Rodman W. Paul, *Mining Frontiers of the Far West, 1848–1880* (New York: Holt, Rinehart & Winston, 1963), pp. 37–38, and Levy, *Les Français en Californie*, p. 42.

Portland. Here was a burgeoning town, about to become a city, in which there were many elegant homes being built by newly rich merchants who had made money shipping grain and timber to San Francisco or by those who were busy furnishing the interior gold mines and settlements with supplies.[62] Portland's mercantile elite were full of civic pride, but if we can believe Perlot, none of the elegant houses boasted either flower or vegetable gardens. Forthwith, the rational and ever-practical Perlot befriended a number of Portland's business and professional men, among them Alexander P. Ankeny, a former sea captain who had become a successful butcher and merchant. Perlot volunteered to spade and plant a garden for Ankeny if the two could share the profits from the sale of the vegetables produced there.[63]

From the start Perlot's gardening enterprise was a sensation, for vegetables were so scarce in Portland that he and Ankeny sold all that they could raise. Ankeny then asked Perlot to landscape his property. The effort was such a success that other wealthy homeowners soon wanted the "French gardener" to landscape their city lots, always with the request, as Perlot noted with amusement, that he use the same design as their neighbors had chosen. Almost overnight he became a nurseryman and was soon traveling to San Francisco to buy seeds and shrubs.[64]

Once established in the nursery and landscaping business, Perlot began to enlist the help of French and Belgian miners who had been disappointed in the Fraser River diggings and had drifted back to Portland. Later in 1861 and 1862 fellow nationals who had joined the Salmon River and Boise Basin rushes also came to see him. By the mid-1860s Perlot's Portland house had become a center for French and Belgian immigrants in the Pacific Northwest. With an understandable lack of modesty he remarked that it was he, a Belgian, who kept the French consul in San Francisco informed of affairs in Portland. His narrative of these everyday events constitutes another firsthand record of the Franco-Belgian presence in yet another region of the American West.[65]

Certainly Perlot felt that he had achieved his greatest success, however, when he persuaded one of his brothers, Nicolas-Joseph, and his family to emigrate to America and to join him in the nursery business. In October 1867, having been in America for seventeen years and away from Belgium for twenty-three—except for a hurried visit from Paris in 1849—Perlot finally returned to his homeland to see the rest of his family. As he made the journey to Nicaragua and from there to New

---

62. Gordon B. Dodds, *Oregon, A History* (New York: Norton, 1977), pp. 71–75; Earl Pomeroy, *The Pacific Slope: A History of California, Oregon, Washington, Idaho, Utah and Nevada* (Seattle: University of Washington Press, 1965), pp. 50, 135–39. See also Sidney Warren, *Farthest Frontier: The Pacific Northwest* (New York: MacMillan, 1949), pp. 131–37, 140–43, and Terence O'Donnell and Thomas Vaughan, *Portland, A History and a Guide* (Portland: Oregon Historical Society, Western Imprints, 1976).

63. Eugene E. Snyder, *Skidmore's Portland: His Fountain and its Sculptor: From Buckboards to Bustles* (Portland: Binfords & Mort, 1973), pp. 139–40. Also see chaps. 23 and 24.

64. See chaps. 25 and 26.

65. Ironically for Perlot, who held anticlerical views, several of the Catholic missionaries and churchmen in Oregon were from Belgium, among them Reverend John F. Fierens of Portland, whom Perlot befriended.

York, he moved along a lifeline of French and Belgian compatriots to whom he could turn for advice, housing, or companionship. A friend kept a Franco-Belgian hotel in Portland; another Belgian emigré ran a small hotel in San Francisco. Once in New York he called on the Belgian consul there, and later he chose to stay at a Belgian hotel in London. From there he traveled to Paris and finally to his native Herbeumont.

The attention Perlot's return attracted must have pleased him immensely. He had left Herbeumont mourning his father's death, angry at not having finished his schooling, and hurt and puzzled by the hostility of the local Catholic priest, Curé Mangin, who had been assiduous in describing Perlot as a person of bad character. Over the years, however, rumors of Perlot's adventures and financial success in America had grown so that friends and relatives called upon him day and night and strangers came seeking advice about emigrating. Fifteen young men of the village announced their intention of returning to America with him, a piece of news that led the local curé to denounce him for creating a generation of old maids in the village. By the time of his departure Perlot had won the hand of Victorine Gaupin, whose family he had known since childhood and to whom he was distantly related.

Perlot's visit to Herbeumont, however triumphal it may have seemed at the outset, brought him face to face with many problems. He was dismayed at the persistence of family feuds and appalled at the number of rules and regulations imposed by both church and state on the daily lives of Belgian citizens. At the same time, he was infuriated by the prejudices of his countrymen against America, which they referred to as *le pays inconnu*. Having felt like a sojourner in the United States for nearly seventeen years, Perlot now realized that even he had become an American. Thus it was with a special pleasure—if indeed not a little malice—that, when he left Herbeumont to return to America, he took with him his new bride and fifteen young men from the village.

After his return to Portland Perlot continued to prosper. By 1870 the properties on which he had raised vegetables and shrubs were in demand as house lots and brought excellent prices. Perlot felt at home with the Americans of Portland and he liked doing business with them, but his wife and his brother's wife and children were separated from the American community by language and other subtler barriers. When Ivon Voet, a close friend and compatriot who was a local carpenter, became despondent and committed suicide, Perlot began to doubt the wisdom of remaining in Portland, a doubt his wife, who was homesick for her family, undoubtedly cultivated. Perlot's candid recital of the self-doubts of the immigrant family is not only a revealing piece of social history, it is a very moving one.

In 1872 the Perlots finally decided to return to Belgium. They journeyed first to San Francisco, where they boarded the Union Pacific Railroad for New York. Always the acute observer, Perlot appears to have seen as much of the West from his train window as some overland immigrants had witnessed in the first days of the gold rush. Once back in Belgium, he and his wife and children settled at Arlon, where, as he tells us in the final chapter of his memoirs, he gardened and hunted until old age confined him to his own acreage. There he smoked his pipe, told his

children and grandchildren stories about America, and, in the last days of 1897
and the beginning of 1898, completed the writing of *Vie et aventures d'un enfant de
l'Ardenne*. Three years later he died at Arlon, at the age of seventy-seven.

Unlike many of his companions in La Fortune company, fifteen of whom died
within a few years after reaching California, Perlot achieved financial success.[66]
There is a cruel irony in the fact that all eighty-three of the societies and companies
created to allow France to take its share of California gold became bankrupt or
failed to live up to their promises. And yet the Lingot d'Or, which was organized
to ship political undesirables to America, managed to sell 6 million lottery tickets
and to persuade 3,740 French nationals to leave France. The society's very
success clouded the reputation of other French immigrants in California. When
Pierre Saint Amant arrived in California to take up his post as French consul at
Sacramento, he complained that every Frenchman he met asked him: "What crime
have you committed to be here?"[67]

The irony becomes more profound when one realizes that while the gold rush
dashed so many hopes and caused so much hardship to individual Frenchmen,
France itself benefited enormously from California gold, for by 1851 French
miners had sent 400 million francs back to their homeland. Meanwhile, Paris
became the headquarters for the encouragement of European investments in California.[68]

There is, of course, a more positive side to the story. Many of the 30,000
French nationals who came to California in the 1850s remained there. Some
6,000 of them could be found in San Francisco alone. Those who panned for
gold are commemorated in more than seventy places in the state with "names
which include the word French."[69] Others developed vineyards, ran hotels and
restaurants, and launched merchandising firms. Some opened branches of Parisian banking houses.[70] The sheer variety of enterprises they engaged in and the
many ways in which they enriched the cultural life of California are so manifest
that one should be cautious in making generalizations about the role of the French
in gold rush California. As was the case with Perlot, however, there do appear
to be common themes: a determination to succeed under new and trying circumstances, a desire for adventure, and a capacity to adapt. These qualities have not

66. Perlot discusses the fate of his shipmates in chap. 25.

67. Blumenthal, "California Societies in France," p. 258; P. C. F. de Saint Amant, *Voyage en
Californie, et dans L'Oregon* (Paris, 1854), p.451.

68. Blumenthal, "California Societies in France," p. 251.

69. Erwin G. Gudde, *California Place Names* (Berkeley and Los Angeles: University of California
Press, 1969), p. 115.

70. Levy, *Les Français en Californie*, traces the roles of the French all over the state in the latter part of his
book. His comments are confirmed for the area of the Southern Mines in John Heckendorf and W. A. Wilson,
Miners' and Business Men's Directory (Columbia, Calif., 1856), see esp. pp. 93–95.

been understood, because the rank and file of the Francophone immigrants have not been fully studied. Daniel Levy, who did understand and appreciate the accomplishments of the French in California, perhaps captured these characteristics best when he wrote that, as one traced the activities of Frenchmen in that vast region west of the Rocky Mountains from the southern placers to the Bering Straits, "il est permis de dire que le go-aheadism n'est pas une qualité exclusivement américaine."[71]

Perlot's career also illustrates another important but unappreciated theme in the experiences of the French and other west European gold seekers. He did not like rules and regulations, and free spirit that he was, he was not only jealous of his independence, he also appears to have been truly egalitarian in his dealings with everyone from the Yosemite tribes to Portland's elite merchants. Although his periodic reunions with the surviving members of La Fortune company suggest that they continued to find happiness with Francophone companions rather than in American society, their sense of not belonging seems to have been compensated by a sense of freedom and an opportunity to move around that they did not want to give up. Perlot's friend Huguet, who had himself gone from the trade of a hatter to that of the butcher at Coulterville, California, expressed this sense eloquently after he had returned from a visit to Paris in the 1860s.

> He, accustomed for nine years to the free and easy life one leads in America, judged that it was not safe for him to live in a country where everyone spoke of liberty without daring to speak freely; where they lived tranquilly, moreover under the paternal surveillance of the police; tranquil, in the phrase of P. L. Courier, as one is on the eve of going to prison.[72]

Perlot, who was fully as proud of his Belgian origins as he was of his independence, would object to being classified as an example of the French response to California and the American West. He was, in fact, a minority within a minority, and as such deserves the distinction by nationality that his compatriots Dr. J. J. F. Haine and Theodore T'Scharner have received.[73] But in a larger sense he remains one of the best Francophone reporters of the gold rush and its aftermath in terms of detailed, on-the-spot description, range of coverage, and a sensitivity to the character and personality of everyone he met. Indeed, both he and his memoir are something of a paradox, for although Perlot himself was logical, objective, and witty and detested the mysterious and obscure, his account is so intensely personal that it might almost be called a confession. Here human emotions and personal relations are discussed with a mature candor and analytical bent that one seldom finds in either American or European gold rush journals.

71. Levy, *Les Français en Californie*, p. 88.
72. See chap. 27.
73. Levy, *Les Français en Californie*, pp. 67–68, interestingly suggests that the French consuls in California treated Belgian nationals as their compatriots.

Perhaps it is fortunate that he did not write for a public audience as did Hipolyte Ferry and the talented journalist Etienne Derbec, or for government superiors as did consuls Moerenhout, Lombard, and Dillon. Because this was a personal account written for friends, and because it is from his unique perspective, Jean-Nicolas Perlot deserves recognition as a perceptive and articulate commentator on the California gold rush and the profound and unexpected consequences it had for all European argonauts.[74]

74. Kevin Starr, *Americans and the California Dream* (New York: Oxford University Press, 1973), pp. 52–58, describes the profoundly disorienting effects of the gold rush on American argonauts. They experienced, he writes, both "Iliad and Odyssey."

Gold Seeker

I

THE VOYAGE TO CALIFORNIA: LE HAVRE TO MONTEREY 1850–1851

Never, I think, . . . has there been such excitement in any country of the world.
Jacques Antoine Moerenhout
Monterey, 1848

This is the law of compensation: The Orient is depopulated for the benefit of the Occident; the birth of San Francisco compensates for the death of Constantinople.
Alexandre Dumas fils
Un Gil Blas en Californie
(Paris, 1852)

Chapter One

"Fortune to the Bold"

The first of November [1848] I returned to Paris, gay, lighthearted, weighed down by neither money nor cares. Our family affairs were settled, my uncles had shown me that they were satisfied with me, the clouds raised for a moment between them and me were dissipated. Not a black speck remained on the horizon. I was going to live happily and peacefully—provided however that business picked up a little, for my salary was always too short for the length of the month; but I knew that for the moment M. Dupont could not raise it.

The winter passed after a fashion, rather bad than good. Spring followed it without bringing the upswing of business; the felicity which I had promised myself no longer appeared to me, thenceforth, except as a distant prospect; I had a long time to wait, before returning to my magnificent situation of the first of January, 1848.

Now, I was impatient, for I was reaching the age of twenty-six years. In the state of spirits in which I found myself, an opportunity was all that was needed to determine me to abandon the trade of a *calicot* [linen draper] and to tempt fortune in another career. The opportunity presented itself.

Some months before, in a distant and almost unknown country of North America, called California, a certain Captain Sutter, while digging a canal to bring water to his mill (for this captain was a miller), had found gold in abundance. [1] He had immediately informed the government of the United States, which had recently annexed this territory following a war with Mexico, and the news had spread with astonishing rapidity. Therefore, in the course of the season, the banks of the

1. In 1839 John Augustus Sutter (1803–80), a Swiss adventurer who had traveled all over the world, arrived in Mexican California, where he secured a land grant of nearly 50,000 acres in the Sacramento Valley. He named his estate New Helvetia, in honor of his native land, and made Fort Sutter, constructed of adobe, its headquarters. By combining cattle ranching, fur trapping, and farming with profits made from selling supplies to overland immigrants from the states, Sutter was soon on the road to financial success.

On January 24, 1848, James W. Marshall, a carpenter and wheelwright, found gold in the race being dug for Sutter's mill at Coloma. Ironically the discovery of gold spelled Sutter's ruin, for his lands were overrun by gold seekers, who also seized his cattle for food. Although he was engaged in litigation for the remainder of his life, he never recovered his holdings or his fortune. See James P. Zollinger, *Sutter: The Man and his Empire* (New York: Oxford University Press, 1939), and Richard H. Dillon, *Fool's Gold: The Decline and Fall of Captain John Sutter of California* (New York: Howard-McCann, 1967).

Sacramento River had been overrun by an innumerably large crowd of miners rushing from Mexico, the United States, Peru, and Chile.[2]

When the first deposits were exhausted, the workers, forced to scatter, found others. In brief, the reports of the agents sent by the government stated that California was a gold-bearing land par excellence and possessed the richest deposits in the world.

The news had soon crossed the seas; it arrived in time to provide a diversion from the preoccupations born of the political and economic situation of the moment. The gold fever succeeded the revolutionary or reactionary fever, or, at least, gave it rough competition.

Companies were formed for the exploitation of the gold mines of California.[3]

All the walls, in Paris, were covered with their announcements, and these were filled with alluring promises. They aimed at finding both shareholders and workers; each of them presented to the former as to the latter the prospect of a swift fortune: the latter, after two years—three years at the most—should all return rich.

The least lucky would have 100,000 francs, rather more than less; but—for there was a but—it was a prerequisite 1,000 francs to pay for the crossing.

That done, one embarked on some sort of a sailing vessel, one doubled Cape Horn and at the end of a six months' voyage, one arrived in California—if one arrived, for not everyone arrived.

The chance to tempt fortune thus presented itself; I seized it and decided to leave for California.

There was only one obstacle: that was the 1,000 francs which had to be paid first, and I vainly scratched my head to find the means of surmounting it.

Chance served me. It happened that the manager of one of these Californian companies was a M. Thibeau, bookkeeper for M. Dupont, my employer. This latter, to whom I often talked about my project, spoke of it one day to M. Thibeau, who came only twice a week to the store.

We had an interview; his enterprise seemed well on its way to success; I insisted that he take me away, whether as working member or as employee, or under any title whatever; I insisted on only one thing—leaving.

Once there, I felt in myself enough courage and strength to carry it off, whatever the country might be, whatever might be the work to do and the fatigues to endure.

But the difficulty was always that I had no money; the problem was to turn it up in one way or another.

    2. There are hundreds of histories of the California gold rush, but especially valuable are Rodman W. Paul, *California Gold: The Beginnings of Mining in the Far West, 1848–1880* (Cambridge: Harvard University Press, 1947; reprint Lincoln, Neb., 1964), and his edited work, *The California Gold Discovery: Sources, Documents, Accounts and Memoirs Relating to the Discovery of Gold at Sutter's Mill* (Georgetown, Calif.: Talisman Press, 1966).

    3. Henry Blumenthal, "The California Societies in France, 1849–1855," *Pacific Historical Review*, 25 (1956), 251–60.

We separated without concluding, but also without breaking off, negotiations.

Finally, in the course of the month of May 1850, M. Thibeau, manager of the company of La Fortune, having set the departure for California for the 20th of August, proposed that I leave as a worker on condition of contracting a five-years' engagement and of signing a note to him for the sum of ten thousand francs which he would have the right to raise on my earnings during the five years. In return, he would take me in the capacity of *Steward* of the company and, as such, I was fed, lodged, clothed, armed, and, in case of illness, nursed, at his expense. I had, moreover, my share in the 40% previously deducted for the use of the workers from the benefits which the company would realize during the extent of my engagement, on the expiration of which the company would return me at its expense to Paris, if I still wanted to return.

I accepted with pleasure; I was saved, I was leaving!

As I still had three months before leaving, I proposed to my employer that I stay with him until then, without salary, provided that he permit me to absent myself three times a week to take lessons in English, the language spoken in California since 1846, that is, since that country belonged to the United States. The excellent M. Dupont consented to all, except to the decrease of my salary.

I wrote to my brothers to let them know of my resolution. I told them meanwhile that, although supplied with everything by the company, I would be happy to have a hundred or two francs in my pocket, for fear of annoying accident. As for the question of knowing how they would be repaid these funds, they had only to have an understanding with our uncles and to use my property during the years of my absence; in case I didn't return, they would have better than the use of my property: they would inherit it.

In the month of August, I received from my uncles, in agreement with my brothers, the authorization to retain two hundred francs from a sum of six hundred and fifty francs which I had to send them and, at the same time, the order to place their papers (railroad shares, bank shares and others, the whole adding up to eighteen thousand francs) in the hands of M. Champion, who was willing to take care of their affairs as I had done, that is, to collect their income from their notary and the coupons of shares at their falling due; then, by the intermediary of the public treasury, to make this money available to them, without expense, at Sedan, where they went to get it.

The day fixed on for leaving Paris arrived. All the workers of the company of La Fortune, numbering forty-three, were gathered at No. 62, Faubourg Poissonnière; they were all from the départements, except a Belgian from the environs of Wavre, named Latuy, and me.

On the sixth of September we left Paris and arrived at Le Havre, where we were supposed to embark immediately; but our ship was not yet ready.

The manager put us in a boarding house run by a man named Thiry, No. 16 Rue St.-Julien, our departure being delayed by a month.

During our stay at Le Havre, M. Thibeau installed me as steward of the company. I had the duty of supervising the loading of our provisions and especially the packing, in order to check what the contractors delivered to us.

At last, on the third of October, at six o'clock in the morning, we climbed aboard.

Whoever has seen, in any seaport whatsoever, the sailing of a ship, has seen them all: there are always the same incidents, the same scenes, the same tumult. There was a crowd to witness our departure; indeed, our ship carried, besides the forty-three workers of La Fortune, fifteen independent passengers, of whom twelve were for California and three for Chile, where we would put into port and stop several days.

Now, during our stay of a month at Le Havre, each of us had a visit from a relative: father, mother, brother or sister, or from a friend who had wanted to see him one last time, perhaps, and say goodbye to him.

All these people, increased by the curious, covered the quays until the falling tide forced us to cast off, and our ship slowly started moving, drawn by the ebbing current.

At this moment, everybody is on the deck, and each one seeks to distinguish in the crowd the loved one from whom he has just parted, in order to address a last word to him, a last gesture of farewell. On one side and on the other, handkerchiefs wave, adieux are exchanged.

As for me, I had in this crowd neither relative, nor friend, nor even an acquaintance, and none of these words of affection was addressed to me. I was leaving—would I ever return? nobody asked himself this question, which interested nobody. As at my arrival in Paris, I had the bitter feeling of my isolation. Ought I, after all, to rejoice or regret not seeing anyone weep for my departure? I did not know. And nevertheless, witnessing these scenes of farewell, I began to be sorry that I too did not have someone to embrace, to shake by the hand. I was there on the deck, walking haphazardly, looking without seeing. I met Latuy, who also was looking without seeing anything, for it was only a few days since he had left Wavre, and no one had accompanied him.

You will understand the sentiment which, as soon as we saw each other, made us approach each other and join our steps.

After some seconds of silence, I told him what I was feeling; without saying a word, he looked at me fixedly then, covering his face with his handkerchief, he fled; I remained alone, mournful, my eyes turned toward Le Havre, which was slowly receding.

The voice of the captain, giving the order to raise the standing jib (first sail which a ship unfurls in leaving), drew me from my reverie; I understood that we were on the open sea, that, in consequence, the farewells were ended and that our voyage was beginning.

Chapter Two

In Passage

The ship on which we were embarked was called *Le Courrier de Cherbourg*, Captain Hairon, Mate Coquet, a captain too, but who, for lack of a ship to command, had accepted this employment on board the *Courrier*. The second mate or boatswain was named Bourgouin; then we had three sailors, an apprentice, a cabin-boy, and a cook; altogether, we were seventy-three persons aboard, counting the forty-three workers of La Fortune and fifteen independent passengers, ten men and five women.

I think I should, beginning now, present to the reader those of my companions on board who have the right to a special mention, whether because they have, for whatever reason, more particularly attracted my attention, or because their names will reappear in the course of this narrative.

First there were the two sons of M. Thibeau, manager of the company of La Fortune, of whom the elder, an ex-noncommissioned officer, was supposed to replace his father on board and to command the expedition. As for the latter, he was going to take the Panama route and be at Monterey, the place of debarkation, to receive us on our arrival. Then there was the doctor and engineer of the company who, I might mention in passing, did not seem to me to be gifted with great genius.[1]

I pass to the working members of the company. Here is Clavel de Vérance, ex-Zouave, an imaginary nobleman, whom we nicknamed Portos, to humor him, for he was proud of his bodily strength, although it appeared as debatable as his coat of arms; Poinsignon, café waiter, returned from Madrid; then the Messieurs Conqui, Briet and Waslin; these three hadn't yet, I think, made anything of their lives, but they were, like the two preceding, children of Gascony or of Saintonge—that was something.

Messent, himself, was Norman; son of a schoolmaster, he had been a clerk in England, had grown bored there, and at the end of four months had returned to his

---

1. Dr. Pierre Garnier was both the company doctor and the ship's doctor. He kept a journal and, after a brief stay in California, he returned to Paris, where, in 1854, he published his recollections of the voyage in installments in *L'Union médical: Journal des interets scientifiques et pratiques moraux et professionnels du corps médical* (Paris, 1847–58), 1st ser., vol. 8. Happily an English version is available. See *A Medical Journey in California*, introd. and annot. Doyce B. Nunis, Jr., and trans. L. Jay Oliva (Los Angeles: Zeitlin and Ver Brugge, 1967), p. 2. Hereafter cited as Garnier, *Medical Journey*.

village, situated in the neighborhood of Cherbourg. He had married there, but not finding anything that he, a former shop-clerk in England, could do to earn his living in a village of Lower Normandy, he was going away with us to seek his fortune in California.

Marcan, his compatriot, had been a seller of lumber for shipbuilding. Although he was not a drunkard, he seemed to have less taste for work than for the divine bottle, especially if the divine bottle contained brandy, and that explained, doubtless, why he was on board the *Courrier de Cherbourg*, en route for the new world; he was a small man, lively, and frank to the point of telling people, without hesitation, the most disagreeable things, under pretext of expressing his way of thinking.

The young Lemériel, a Breton, an only son, was leaving the school of the friars-minor, who had not succeeded in inculcating the virtue of obedience in him, for he was leaving without his mother's consent.

Béranger and Bigot were, the one a baker, the other a silverer of spoons and forks. This latter squinted horribly—I have not known him to have any other fault.

Psalmon, although a Norman, was a boy completely lacking in shrewdness, but a good worker and a good lad. When we had passed the Canary Islands, they nicknamed him Tenerife because of his nose; when Psalmon slept, flat on his back, his olfactory organ reminded us, in fact (in smaller proportions, it is true), of the famous peak of that name.

Mercier senior had done almost nothing until then but beget Mercier junior, a young boy of fifteen who accompanied him aboard; his specialty was composing and delivering speeches, but he rarely brought them to a successful conclusion.

The Alsatian Margraff, son of a doctor who flourished during the First Empire, called himself a nephew of the Duke of Baden and perhaps he really was. Whether he was or not, he certainly was not raised at his uncle's court; he had served in the French army, at first as a militiaman, then as a volunteer, had fought in Africa and had reached the grade of noncommissioned officer. Far from having obtained, in the old world, a position suitable to his illustrious origin, he hoped to be happier in the new world, and that was why he was aboard the *Courrier*. He had been entrusted with the Company's flag, on which was written: *Audaces fortuna juvat*.

Ragache was a tanner; he was going to America partly to make a fortune, but principally, he said, to put the ocean between him and his wife with whom he did not agree—his ruby nose indicated sufficiently the true cause of this misunderstanding.

Braconnier, son of a harness-maker, had been a curé's servant; something of it stuck with him.

Salard had served as trumpeter in a regiment of cavalry; returned to civil life, he had become a carpenter, but, a mediocre workman, had not made a fortune.

Duléry, a plumber, and Viot, a stationer, were two children of Paris; the first, married and father of two children, was a sensible man, peaceable and with pleasant manners; the second, more lively, gayer by reason of his age or perhaps in his role as bachelor; as I was able to prove in the end, an intrepid worker.

Salomon, confectioner, was a frank and open Burgundian, to whom I quickly became attached; a nature fundamentally honest, a character that was benevolent and at the same time strong and true, he was esteemed and respected.

Gaillot, his compatriot, was a young man of distinguished features and jovial humor; he seemed to have received a good education.

Zacarie was a clamorous, garrulous, fidgety little man, a good lad at bottom although a little pretentious; his sharp and piercing voice, which was heard too often, caused him to be called *Cricri*.

For foreigners, there were two Swiss: Schmutz, who had been a farmer, a calm, peaceable man, but a little mistrustful; and Schérrer, a doctor, a respectable person according to all reports, who could be reproached with nothing but that he spoke and understood French with difficulty.

Finally, two Belgians, Latuy and I. Latuy, son of a cotton-manufacturer, had traveled for his father; he was an easy-going young man, naturally drawn to the good and, like so many others, too easily letting himself be led to the bad.

Among the independent passengers, that is, those not forming a part of the Company, I will mention the following:

M. Vénard, a merchant of I-forget-what, returned from Constantinople, a very talkative little old man, knowing all about life, well-informed on everything and, I think, the most intelligent man aboard.

Badinier, a lumber dealer of Orléans, whom the revolution of 1848 had ruined and who, unlike so many others, held no bitterness against it—quite the contrary. He was nicknamed "Mirabeau" and "the Father of the people," because on any occasion and even without any occasion, he talked to us about his love for the people and delivered harangues which were doubtless very beautiful, but which were Greek to us and perhaps to him too, so elevated was the point of view—and so incoherent the form.

Kaine, man of a grave exterior, with a harsh voice; he had been a photographer in Paris, and tried on board to become a doctor by magnetizing.

Huguet, son of a notary in Clermont (Auvergne). He was a simple journeyman hatter in Paris. This was a young man of good manners, who lacked neither wit nor judgment, although he became enthusiastic too easily. He gave me the impression of a son of good family whose education had been neglected. We joined forces on board and I taught him fractions, of which he was completely ignorant. I found in him a sure and sincere friend.[2]

To finish up with the men, I will name the Abbé Laubert, who performed on board the functions of almoner. He was going to evangelize the savages of California and in the meantime he evangelized us. In his character as missionary, he wore a

2. Although Perlot claimed to be a friend of Huguet's, Dr. Garnier perhaps understood him better, for he noted that Huguet, age twenty-two, was a consumptive whose father and brother also suffered from tuberculosis. Since the *Courrier de Cherbourg* had a goat on board, Garnier placed both Huguet and another consumptive, Lartigue, on a regimen of goat's milk diluted with seawater. Later Garnier reported with satisfaction that Huguet was cured of his disease. See Garnier, *Medical Journey*, p. 84.

long red beard. He was an educated and liberal priest, perhaps a little heretical. Was that why he was going far from the oldest daughter of the Church? It might be. The explanation which he gave us of the birth of Jesus Christ, son of a ghost, although he swore he did not believe in incubi, completely passed my understanding.

The ladies were: Mlle. Pauline, thirty years old; Mlle. Delètre, eighteen; Mme. Thomas, thirty-six; Miss Tournach, uncertain age, who made herself a teacher of English while on board; and a lady, flanked by her husband, whose name I have forgotten.

At the end of some hours, Le Havre disappeared on the horizon. Each of us, drying his eyes, busied himself with his unpacking, tried to put things in a little order and succeeded only with difficulty, for the weather was stormy, the wind contrary; consequently the sea was rough, and we hadn't our sea-legs yet. Toward midday they rang the *Ratatouille* [name of a vegetable stew; that is, dinner bell], but already the sea had taken our appetite and few tried to eat. As responsible agent in charge of supplies, it was I who distributed the rations; in the evening, I was excused from this drudgery, considering that everybody was sick. The cook, who had experience with the sea, had foreseen the situation; for supper he had brought only hot water, which would serve to make tea.

Next day, few people were able to come up on deck. The sea was very choppy, the wind still contrary. We were in sight of Cape La Hague, a little to the west of Cherbourg, and we made tack after tack in order to hold ourselves against the wind, which was blowing directly from the west. As for me, I was not yet sick, but neither did I still feel as usual; the fresh air which I breathed on the deck did me good and I held my own—held is the word, for it was impossible for me to stay upright without hanging onto a rope or without supporting myself against some sort of object. I profited from the circumstance to admire the sea at my ease, the sea which I saw for the first time in all its beauty.

This contrary wind held us for six days in the Channel, when three days, in ordinary weather, suffice for the passage; but on the seventh, the wind calmed a little, and at the same time we observed that the waves were becoming longer, higher, more majestic, which indicated that we were entering the waters of the Atlantic.

The day after, we changed direction, that is, instead of continuing to make for the west we bore south-southwest. A west wind, fairly gentle, permitted us to sail slowly and pleasantly. We began then to recover from the tossing which we had just experienced in the Channel, a tossing which naturally had made us sick, novice navigators that we were; but already a goodly number were feeling better, and those nursed the others who were suffering more.

This good weather lasted until we had reached the Bay of Biscay, which extends between Brest and Spain, then it changed all at once from white to black. Then it was that we could judge what the Ocean is. This time we had a real tempest, for we had had, in the Channel, only a shadow of one. A fair number of us who, at that time, had only frowned, were weeping now when they looked toward the absent shore, convinced that their last day was come. Certainly, when seeing in the port of Le Havre great ships which gauged two or three thousand tons, I never would have imagined that the sea had enough power to make these colossi pirouette like nutshells.

The motions of two ships in distress which we had in sight made us aware of the movements which ours was performing. One of them seemed hardly out of gunshot; we could perceive it only when it found itself, like us, on the top of a wave; sometimes launched toward the sky, we saw it almost upright on its prow or on its poop, sometimes it appeared to us completely upset and let us see only its keel. It was just the same with ours. Sometimes it stayed so thoroughly upright on its bow or stern that the deck fled from under my feet and I remained suspended from the rope which I had twisted around my arm; at other times, the roll put the deck on a vertical line and half the yards in the water; then all at once, it dove between two waves and the surge passed over the deck and I was astonished at not being engulfed.

As long as the tempest lasted, I remained on the deck, unable to stop admiring the terrible and grandiose spectacle of the sea in fury. Perhaps I might have preferred to admire it from the shore; but no longer having the choice of a point of view, I forced myself to keep a good countenance in the face of danger.

The interest inspired in me by the struggle I witnessed between our frail skiff and the tempestuous ocean, hardly left room, besides, for personal preoccupations. This struggle seemed incomprehensible at first sight. Why is the ship, so rudely shaken, not broken by the first shock, or engulfed? How is it possible for so much weakness to resist so much power and most often end by triumphing? It is this: though the forces of nature are grand, the genius of man is superior to them. Applying, even before having recognized and formulated them, the laws of gravity, he has found the secret of constructing a ship and of steering it on the waves against wind and tide; he has invented, in a word, the art of navigation. This art defies the tempest.

That is why, novice though I was, I could contemplate it at that moment without shuddering too much. I did not disdain the danger, I appreciated it; I had faith in the science of the one who had built this much-buffeted vessel, faith in the cleverness of the one who directed it. Suspended between the enflamed sky and the half-open abysses of the ocean, I did not curse, as did the poet, him who first adventured on the open sea in a fragile bark; rather I congratulated myself on belonging to the audacious race of Japhet.

It was only at the end of three days that we saw the sun again and, with it, more bearable weather, which accompanied us as far as Madeira.

Chance had it that on the eve of the day we arrived in sight of this island, our distillation machine suffered some damage which obliged us to land at Funchal.[3] It is one of the most primitive of ports. One arrives at the roadstead, one approaches within five hundred meters of the shore, one anchors at fifteen fathoms, one lowers the shoreboat to the water, one gets in it, then one rows as far as the beach, one jumps to earth, and that's that!

Funchal is built in the form of an amphitheater on the southeast coast of the island, of which it is the capital. The houses are built of bricks; the streets are paved with pebbles, which makes walking painful and not too steady. No vehicles, moreover, roll on this pavement. To transport merchandise, they attach to the head of an ox, by means of two leather straps, a dry hide, untanned, on which they put the load which is thus drawn on the pavement to its destination. Only the people of the lower class go on foot; the young people of both sexes ride horseback; for four sous, they have a footman who follows them all day. This servant holds the horse and brushes away the flies, and, when the cavalier mounts the saddle, he seizes the horse's tail and follows it in all its gaits: at a walk, at a trot, at a gallop. Some others have themselves carried in a litter or palanquin; this is a curtained bed, with a very low roof to which are fastened shafts which two men place on their shoulders. They will carry you this way all day for eight sous.

The leisure class speaks French and English; the people know only a sort of Portuguese dialect. These people seem miserable, they are poorly clothed, stockings are for them an unknown luxury; in place of shoes they wear a simple sole of untanned leather; this sole, which is long and wide, is held on the foot by means of a cord laced through eyelets placed at intervals and, when turned up, envelops the foot almost entirely.

Victuals are cheap; one dines at the hotel for eighteen sous: soup, vegetables, three kinds of meat, fish and wine—authentic Madeira wine, which costs three sous a bottle; it is good, in spite of its low price, and equals, I think, the wine which is sold for three francs in France, but it is little suited for a table wine because it provokes thirst rather than appeases it. At Funchal, they do not drink it pure, they add half orange-blossom tea; thus mixed, it is refreshing, but it intoxicates those who are not used to it.

Madeira is a charming little island, a true earthly paradise. A goodly number of English men and women go there to repair their shattered health, especially tuberculars; we encountered many of them in the streets, on horseback, or being carried while nonchalantly reclining in a palanquin.

Of the three days which we spent in Funchal, I had to employ half in putting our cargo back in order and in making a summary inventory of what we had aboard, for, in my position as steward, I had to handle the distribution of supplies for each meal.

3. Garnier also mentioned the stop at Funchal and added that the date was October 21, 1850. Once at sea again, twenty-six passengers and crew became very ill from eating tainted tunny fish which had been taken on board at Funchal. See *Medical Journey*, pp. 30, 80ff.

At our departure from Le Havre, everything was in such disorder that during the eighteen days which had passed before our arrival at Funchal, I had been really overwhelmed with work, to the point that I had to have the help of an assistant; this way, I had a little leisure during the rest of the crossing, and I profited from it by studying English, which I was going to need when I arrived in California.

I was just speaking of the management of supplies and of the culinary service on board; here are a few details on this subject.

At our departure from Le Havre, I repeat, this double service was not organized and it did not seem at first necessary that it be, so much had our appetite failed. But at the end of several days, seasickness ceasing to make its effects felt, each one took separately and at his own time the road to the office; as the delivery of supplies and the distribution of rations was made without order and without control, the head cook used it practically according to his fancy and, in fact, was almost sole master.[4]

It was necessary to put an end to this confusion of powers and to emerge from this state of anarchy. We considered the problem. It was decided first that meals would be taken regularly and at sea times, which would permit the steward himself to make, each time, a regular distribution of supplies. Then the passengers were divided in ten squads. The workers of La Fortune formed eight of them, and the independent passengers, two; each squad had its kettle or mess from which all its members ate together; each named its mess cook, who, at the appointed hour, brought his empty kettle to the head cook, received seven or eight portions, according to the number in the squad, and took it away no matter where, on deck or elsewhere.[5] Then those having the right surrounded the mess, squatting or lying down or in any other position that seemed more convenient to them, each trying, with the help of a spoon or a fork, according to the case, to take his share; they generally succeeded in it well enough in ordinary weather; with some precautions and some skill one managed to finish his meal as well as not. But when the sea was rough or it rained, the thing was complicated; one was forced to take refuge between decks, in a vast room which, at night, was a dormitory filled with superimposed hammocks, and, by day, was a public room where everyone went to attend to his various occupations. In bad weather, therefore, this dormitory, this public room, became a dining room; each squad, after having folded its hammocks to have more room and to see more clearly, installed itself around its kettle, balanced and braced as well as possible on the floor. How many times that damned wind came to disturb the order and the religious silence which ruled in that solemn moment! How many times we had the bitter experience of that truth, that there is many a slip 'twixt the spoon and the lip!—if I may be pardoned this slight alteration of the text. In fact, at the moment when, this utensil in hand, we were

4. Garnier confirmed Perlot's sense of disorder on board when he complained that discipline was lax and there was careless handing of food (*Medical Journey*, p. 30).

5. The division of the passengers into "squads" or "messes" was precisely what occurred on the overland trail to California, particularly during the gold rush years, 1849–51, when the migrants were largely male.

preparing to eat, the rolling or pitching forced us to seize precipitately at a post, a rope, a piece of woodwork of whatever kind, or else at a comrade who was already holding one of these objects; whoever missed his aim rolled from port to starboard and from starboard to port, and this shuttle movement continued until the deck had regained the horizontal position; happy was he who, in these successive and rapid voyages from one side to the other, did not happen to overturn one or another of the kettles, or to put his foot in one; this accident would immediately start a dispute which had to be settled in front of the kettles whose contents had been respected by the rolling. It concerned knowing who should skip dinner, and it was discussed a long time before being settled, one invoking article 1382 of the civil code, the other pleading the case of main force. However, the quarrel never became very serious because, most of the time, the cook, as a wise man, furnished more rations than there were guests. Ordinarily, one ended where one had had to begin; one reported the kettle empty and he filled it again.

This affected, however, only the unfortunate workers of La Fortune, the pariahs on board; the independent passengers, themselves, were not exposed to these tribulations; they had cabins instead of hammocks and, for their meals, were seated at table, on benches; this privilege was the consequence of another: they had in their squads the more beautiful half of humankind, or, at least, that which represented it on board.

The fourth day after our debarkation, we set sail again, steering for the south; the wind was fair, the sea calm; the ship began to skim speedily toward the Canary Islands. As early as the third day we perceived the peak of Tenerife, although we were more than thirty leagues distant from it; it is one of the highest peaks I have seen: its head seems to touch the sky, clouds cling to its foot. Beside it, the other islands of the group seem hardly to rise from the ocean; I passed the day in contemplating it; it disappeared only at eight o'clock at night, for the sun, an hour after setting, still lit its summit.

From there on, we headed a little more to the west, and having a good wind, well placed, we spun along admirably, so that at the end of a few days we perceived the islands of Cape Verde, or rather we saw there some lights, still rather faint, for it was night. When day appeared, we had passed them; seeing these lights on the west, I understood that we were between these islands and Senegambia, perhaps not far from the coast; however, we did not see it when the sun rose.

The second day after, we steered southwest and six days later we reached the Equator at 25° west of Paris.

The crossing of the *line*, that is, the Equator, is a festival which is always religiously observed on board ship. Captain Hairon gave his crew a banquet, to which we naturally were invited, for the passengers are in some ways the heroes of the festivities; this day they receive baptism.

In fact, according to an ancient and still-respected custom, each person who crosses the line for the first time must be baptized by the old-timers; it naturally follows that the neophyte pays the expenses of the ceremony.

Here is how things happen:

The day before the crossing, toward evening, the mate, armed with his telescope, attentively scrutinizes the horizon, then after several false alarms, cries to the man at the helm: "Hold the wind, the line is in sight." He says these words in a way that attracts attention, then he takes a few more sights through the glass as if to be sure he is not mistaken. The news spreads, and everyone rushes to the deck, trying to perceive the line; they look, they squint their eyes, they rub them, they look again; in vain! They see nothing. Then the mate advances, glass in his hand, and obligingly offers to show you the famous line: You approach, you look; ah! this time you see very clearly a line which extends all the length of the horizon.

The complaisant officer is careful, it's understood, to direct the instrument only toward the Equator; otherwise, one would notice that, whatever part of the horizon is observed, one sees the line, and one would soon guess that this line is nothing but a hair placed between the two large glasses of his telescope; no one thinks, however, of making this experiment; everyone has proved *de visu* that he is coming to the line.

Next day, at dawn, a rattling of hail is heard on the deck. Reveille sounds, and everyone rises precipitately, because no one has to dress, that is to say that the men wear only shirt and trousers, and the ladies . . . I don't know exactly, but not much.

Then the captain leaves his cabin, comes up on deck and in an irritated voice asks what means this hail and this tapping which have somersaulted him out of bed (it is well to inform you that on the open sea, on the Equator, and in a zone 10° wide, it never hails).

A voice which seems to come from the heavens makes itself heard: "Who are you, audacious mortals, who do not fear to adventure upon my waters? Know that I am the Equator and that I permit no one to cross me."

"However," says the captain, "we have been told, in our distant lands, that previously voyagers had encountered his Lordship the Equator and had been able, under certain conditions, to cross beyond without being destroyed by the fires with which he defends his realms."

"That's true," replies the Equator from on high, "but those travelers had submitted to my conditions; submit in your turn and you will pass."

"Well," says the captain, still looking at the heavens, "what are your conditions?"

"Here they are," replies the voice from above, "I wish each person who passes here to change his name and be baptized in my waters; I wish him after the baptism to bear no name other than *shellback*."

The captain accepts the conditions and gives the order that everyone shall be baptized, with an injunction to each to call himself *shellback* thenceforward.

Shortly afterward, the most attentive among us saw descending from the top of the main mast a sailor whom a sail had hidden from the sight of all; this sailor had doubtless lent his voice to the Equator, and an empty sack which he held in his hand let one guess where the morning's formidable hail came from and why the deck was covered with peas and beans.

After these preliminaries, they proceeded to the ceremony of the baptism; they had improvised on the deck, by means of four sails, a sort of room; in the middle, an enormous tub full of water and above the tub a plank suspended by two ropes; all this represented the baptismal fonts.

The godfather and godmother came to get the neophyte, brought him to this room, made him sit down on this plank, then an assistant poured a pail of water over his head, during which the godfather spoke the sacramental words. At the moment he reached the word *Amen,* the assistant let loose the ropes by which the plank was suspended, and the baptized one fell in the tub where he found himself plunged in water almost up to his neck. That done, it was the turn of another one.

The ceremony was going along well enough, everybody was amused, especially the young people, when a passenger, an Alsatian, finding that a sailor had jostled his wife more than he had to, became angry; very bitter words were exchanged, and, finally, they led to violence. The captain had to intervene, then, himself becoming angry, he stopped the baptism; and the ceremony was left there, when hardly seven or eight persons had received the sacrament.

However, before the end of the day, peace was made, and at four o'clock in the afternoon the baptismal banquet took place.

A great table was set on the poop; we all seated ourselves there, officers, sailors, and passengers, and the dinner was splendid: food, beer, all kinds of wine were served to us with profusion, and the guests did honor to all; each one helped himself to his heart's content, knowing that he would not again find himself at such a feast during the rest of the crossing.

This had quite the air, moreover, of a family party; during the five or six weeks that we had been together on the same ship, we had ceased to be strangers to one another; people had approached each other, they had become intimately ac- quainted, they were even beginning to group themselves according to the law of affinities. In brief, the passengers' relations among themselves as well as with the crew were marked by a frank cordiality. Without a care, what's more; they had forgotten those of the day before and they did not worry about the morrow. The state of health could not have been better; not a sick person aboard.[6]

So it seemed that the feast should come to an end as peacefully as any in the world. It was not quite like that, however. The demon of discord, who had succeeded that morning in disturbing the baptismal ceremony, had promised him- self to disturb the feast too. He stirred up, to this end, the Alsatian Margraff, our flag-bearer.

Toward the end of the meal, the nephew of the Duke of Baden, who had eaten well and drunk superlatively, got up and asked to speak. Everyone was quiet, everyone listened; doubtless he was going to offer a toast. Not at all; Margraff had something else in mind; he proposed to discuss a question of domestic economy; he

---

6. Garnier catalogued their ills as seasickness, heat prostration, suffering from tainted tunny fish, overeat- ing oranges, and, after their stop in Valparaiso, some cases of venereal disease (*Medical Journey*, pp. 30, 80– 84).

intended to stop the wastage of supplies on board . . . He found that not enough care had been taken of the biscuit, salt pork, wine, etc.; what he said perhaps was true, but it was not the moment to say it.

He had forgotten the precept of Horace that one must say things in their place, or maybe he just never knew it. Besides, supposing that he was basically right, he sinned incontestably as to form. Margraff, the former trooper, spoke straight out, without circumlocution; he either did not know or disdained the art of oratorical prudence, so much so that, when he had finished speaking, Mercier senior thought himself obliged to reply to him. He undertook to demonstrate that Margraff, if he was not entirely wrong, was not absolutely right; he carried it off in one way or another, rather worse than better. When he had finished, Margraff replied, then Mercier senior got up to respond again; but Margraff, still in his character of former trooper, did not like anyone to answer him.

He became red with anger and, getting up in his turn, he walked straight—as straight as he could—toward Mercier senior. From his gestures, from his voice, it was easy to see that he proposed to prove to this latter that he could beat him in an argument. The discussion would infallibly have ended in a pugilistic scene, if the Abbé Laubert, realizing better than anyone what was going to happen, had not judged that it was time to intervene. Just before sitting down at table, our worthy almoner had made an address in which, flattering the vanity of his auditors, he had borne witness to the good conduct, the excellent deportment, of each and every one, and had attested to the spirit of concord and brotherhood which reigned among us. So he got up and requested permission to speak. Using once again the resources of his insinuating eloquence, he launched into a discourse, in which he found a way of saying things that were agreeable to everybody, and made it very long, without doubt to give tempers time to cool.

When he saw that he had succeeded in restoring calm to everyone's spirits and Margraff to his proper place, he stopped talking. The demon of discord slunk away shamefaced and left us in peace for the rest of the day.

It did not end, however, without the production of a new incident, though a gayer one this time. M. Badinier, the one who was nicknamed the father of his people, rose also, and asked also to speak.

There was a profound silence. They knew the pacific character and the humanitarian sentiments of M. Badinier, and they were very sure that if he asked to speak, it was not to excite a quarrel.

In fact, it was to pronounce one of those discourses where he put in everything, where he omitted nothing, except to connect his sentences and his ideas:

"Messieurs, at Le Havre, Messieurs, we did not know the ship and the ship did not know us; we have become as brothers and at Le Havre Thiry's boarding house meant nothing and we were strangers; long live Fraternity! Myself, I'm nothing but a simple citizen of Orléans, although I don't see why I should be any simpler than another; long live Equality!

"The Republic ruined me, I lost twenty-five thousand francs worth of wood

which I had floated on the Seine; I also lost twenty-five th———." (interruption)
"Yes, Gentlemen, it's to tell you what my principles are; long live the Republic!
in spite of all, it is the salvation of the people, I will always defend their rights.
They have the right of self-government; and I have voted against the bishop of
Orléans, he's not a citizen, that's not the man we need; read Mirabeau and you
will see . . . ; I've read him myself, I am the brother of the people and the people
are my brothers. For the moment we are on board and we have to behave as one
behaves at sea. Before long we'll be in California and there too it is a republic;
long live the United States! You will always find in me a man of good will, but
before all else a republican; long live Ledru-Rollin! as for me I like universal
suffrage, there is a man! and Barbès too."[7] (interruption) "Well, Gentlemen, I
conclude by saying that . . ." (noise). "But after all, it is necessary to
know . . ." (tumult). ". . . Therefore, I will explain myself in private . . . since . . ." but it is impossible for him to continue; a deafening noise, a
formidable clamor, covering the orator's voice, force him to reseat himself and to
be quiet. Everyone gets up from the table, but the day is not ended; suddenly
several harebrains begin to shout: "Long live Badinier, the father of the people!
long live Mirabeau!" And Gaillot and Viot, in their enthusiasm, propose on the
instant to carry in triumph the father of the people, the Demosthenes, the Mirabeau of the ship.

Suiting the action to the word, they seize a spar and despite the protestations and
the efforts of Badinier, who, in his modesty, sought to escape from this excess of
honor, they pass the enormous stick between his legs and, helped by other comrades, succeed in keeping him astraddle, then they lower him thus from the poop to
the deck; Gaillot, leading the parade as drummer, beats the drum or at least
imitates its sound: *ran plan plan, ran pataplan, plan plan.* After having made the
tour of the ship three or four times in the midst of the acclamations of the multitude,
and on the pretext of enabling him to explain himself in private—as he had
promised—they go at last to deposit the triumphant one in I don't know what secret
resort "which smelled much stronger but not better than the rose."

7. Alexandre Auguste Ledru-Rollin (1807–74), a French lawyer and politician, was famous for his
defense of the advocates of a French Republic throughout Louis Philippe's reign. During the Revolution of
1848 he was elected as a deputy to the National Assembly as a spokesman for the workers of France, but his
intemperate speeches, unwise political maneuvers, and his strong opposition to the rise of Louis Napoleon
forced him to seek exile in England. He lived there for twenty years before returning to France in 1870 after
having been granted amnesty. See Pierre et Paul, *Portraits, critiques et biographiques des Candidats à la
Présidence* . . . (Paris: Garnier Frères, Libraire, 1848), pp. 83–93, and "Ledru-Rollin, *Encyclopedia
Britannica* (Chicago, 1958), 13: 860–61.

Armand Barbès (1809–70), an idealistic revolutionary who was a friend of George Sand, Flaubert, and
Victor Hugo, also opposed Louis Philippe's government, but his conspiracies were so impractical and ill-
timed that in 1839 he was condemned to death, a verdict that Lamartine and Hugo succeeded in changing to a
prison sentence. Although liberated from prison during the Revolution of 1848, he was soon in such difficulties
that he went into exile for sixteen years. See Roger Merle, *Armand Barbès: un revolutionnaire romantique*
(Toulouse: Eduoard Privat, 1977).

This folly ended the festival; in sum total, it was a joyful day.

The next day we were able to economize on breakfast and to a great extent on dinner; nobody was hungry, but everyone was a little thirsty; each one complained of pain at the roots of the hair.

Chapter Three

Wreck of La Fortune

The northwest wind pushed us, always slowly and peacefully, toward the south, so that if we advanced little, at least the movement was agreeable; but the wind became more and more feeble, so much so that the fourth day after the banquet, we found ourselves in a flat calm at the latitude of 6° south and 25° west from Paris.

Little by little we saw the waves disappear, the swell flatten; and at last the motionless sea presented the uniform surface of a mirror; not the least breath of wind; it was in vain to spread the sails in any direction, they fell softly the length of the masts.

This calm held us back there for twenty-two days—twenty-two days which seemed to us as long as twenty-two years, and twenty-two years of purgatory. Each day, the sun passed almost vertically above our heads, and with no protection whatever against its fires, not the least breeze to refresh us; the water which we drank was hot.[1]

When on account of supplies or of drinking water I had to descend into the hold, I took off all my clothes, my drawers alone excepted, and when I came up again, perspiration covered me with water as if I had just come out of a bath.

All contact became unbearable to us because everything was burning hot. The tar ran the length of the ship's sides and the length of the masts; during half the day, the sunlight, reflected by the uniform surface of the sea, dazzled us and hurt our eyes.

To be on board a ship is to be in prison; but when this prison is motionless on the sea, it becomes less bearable than a prison cell. It reduced us to regretting the squalls we had endured in the Channel, indeed even the tempest of the Bay of Biscay, which nevertheless we had found quite disagreeable.

Our savants on board claimed, perhaps with reason, that it was because of these calms, so frequent in these parts, that the ancient navigators had believed the Equator absolutely impassable.

At last on the morning of the twenty-third day, some light clouds appeared on the horizon; they climbed slowly, approached, and shortly afterward the royals, for so long a time motionless on the masts, were agitated, then gradually were filled;

1. Garnier recorded a calm of twenty-eight days rather than twenty-two, during which he notes that they suffered "the most savage heat" (*Medical Journey*, p. 30).

at the same time, we saw the surface of the sea begin to wrinkle; it was for us a true delight to breathe the first puffs of the breeze, very weak to begin with, but which soon rose appreciably.

So the sails were filled and the ship began again at last to make headway on the reborn wave, in such a way that by three o'clock in the afternnon we were spinning along at three leagues an hour on a sea that was almost rough. The rolling, then, seemed agreeable to us, so happy were we to be moving.

To profit from the wind, which was only half favorable, we were heading south; next day we were able to put it to the southwest. A steady and pleasant wind rocked us softly and led us to our heart's desire.

We arrived thus in sight of the island of Trinidad, which we passed during the night. That night was a sleepless one for the captain and mate; they probably were anxious to see this island, for toward evening they had established a lookout near the bowsprit to signal it; it was, I suppose, in order not to run upon the rocks which border it, doubtless also to verify their logbook, to be assured that their chronometer was exact and that their observations agreed with that fixed point which is well known to navigators.

When the island was passed, the run continued to the southwest, and two days afterward we crossed the tropic of Capricorn. Then the weather changed all at once; from the north, the wind jumped to the south, then became violent and brought us rain, which in its turn brought us the west wind. Then, for eight days, it was detestable weather; never two hours of the same wind and never a good wind.

Nevertheless, by means of tacking, now to the south, now to the southwest, we succeeded in getting out of this bad spot. A quite pronounced and favorable enough breeze permitted us to steer for ten days to the southwest; it carried us to a point opposite the mouth of the Rio de la Plata; that is to say on a line with Buenos Aires, and probably at a great distance out on the open sea, for we did not see land; but various indications announced it to us: first the color of the water, which had passed from azure to green, then the masses of seaweed which were perceived floating here and there on the waves, and, later, the land birds, who came to rest on our cordage, then resumed their flight to the west.

With the same wind continuing to blow, though with some variations, we arrived in sight of Patagonia. We followed the coast for three days, always keeping our distance of six to eight leagues.

This coast seemed barely to rise from the water, and the whole countryside gave the effect of an immense forest. So far as living beings were concerned, we saw nothing but a flock of birds who came to rest on our rigging, then, with evening, regained the coast in a single flight. The distance from this coast at which we sailed did not permit us to distinguish any quadruped whatever there; very far in the interior we perceived two volcanoes in eruption.

The smoke of one of these volcanoes made a half-luminous trail in the evening, almost four leagues long; the other belched flames only at intervals.

We coasted along here peacefully for three days before a very violent west wind forced us to gain the open sea. In less than two days, this wind became a tempest and we remained hove-to another three days, during which we drifted forty leagues.

However the wind calmed a little and permitted us to head to the southwest. Three days of sailing in this direction brought us in sight of the Falkland Islands, which at first we had some trouble in recognizing. In fact, it had been a good ten days since we had seen the sun, and the captain did not know exactly where we were because he had no confidence in his dead reckoning. That is why, for two days, we had a lookout who watched what happened in front of the ship, for fear that it might strike the reefs which border these islands. The precaution was not superfluous: at ten o'clock at night, the lookout gave the alarm and the ship stayed hove-to until day; then we recognized the Falklands, and we had to sail a day to the west in order to avoid them.

These islands are covered with very high mountains on which nothing can be seen but snow: no living being the length of the coast, not even birds.[2]

The weather continuing rather bad than good, we sailed slowly and painfully toward the south and that lasted until we were in sight of Tierra del Fuego (which seemed to me to be rather the land of snow than that of fire), with its cliffs as high as mountains.

There, by good luck, the weather became better, and two days afterward we cleared the strait of Le Maire, between Tierra del Fuego and Staten Island, having a violent wind astern. The weather then was admirable, in spite of fairly sharp cold; we were approaching Cape Horn with a good west-northwest wind; joy reigned on board, we were going to have the unexpected luck of doubling, unimpeded, the terrible Cape! and still while casting a last look on Staten Island, which was fleeing far behind us, each one got ready for a passing salute to the island, or rather the rock which bears this name, the terror of navigators, whom it reminds of so many wrecks: Cape of Storms! That evening, we went to bed gay and happy, promising ourselves to get up early in order to enjoy the view of the redoubtable cape.

Hardly had we gone to sleep when we were awakened by the noise of a maneuver which the sailors were executing on deck; then as the rolling became stronger we supposed there was a change in weather. In fact, with the maneuver barely finished, a frightful west wind blew, and we were shaken as we had not yet been since we had left Le Havre. The billows rolled over the waist of the ship; almost every wave passed over the vessel. Day came, the same weather continued. Toward noon, it became impossible to hold to the cape any longer.

The topsail, fully reefed, the only sail which had been left set, was torn by the winds, as if someone had tried, with a machine made expressly, to make it into a

2. Perlot's remarks about the Falklands were inaccurate. British rule was established in 1833, and after ten years of rule by naval officers, a civil administration was created which has lasted until the present. While the flora and fauna of the Falklands are at best sparse, birds do exist there in considerable numbers.

canvas sieve. It was necessary to fly before the storm and we put the wind astern. I leave you to guess if we made good time, pursued by a wind of an unheard-of violence.

The ship literally leaped from one wave to another, so rapid was the headway and so short was the interval from the crest to the trough of the wave. Besides, what waves!

Truly, only Cape Horn can raise waves to equal them. Each one, in descending, seemed certain to precipitate us into a gulf ready to swallow us—and nevertheless we always found ourselves, more or less soaked, it's true, on the top of the following wave. Each surge passed over the ship and left us a foot or two of water on deck.

One must pardon sailors the invocations which, in such moments, they address to Sainte Barbe [the gun-room], or as they say: to the all-seeing Mother. For one who does not know the laws of hydrostatics, it is impossible to understand that one can escape, otherwise than by a miracle, from such a danger; he who knows that every accident at sea implies an error committed in the application of the principles of the science, is preoccupied solely in learning if the ship is constructed according to the rules and if the captain knows the theory and practice of his trade.

This flight lasted two days, during which we made one hundred and sixty leagues, but in a direction diametrically opposed to our route. However the wind fell a little and permitted us to try to regain the distance lost by tacking here and there. Three days afterward, the wind recommenced with a new violence and we were forced to heave-to. This situation lasted for twelve days during which we had fifteen leagues of drift a day; after which we were able to begin tacking again. We had magnificent weather, not a cloud in the sky, but always a very strong wind from the west; in spite of that, during five days, our tacks were successful enough and we regained our westing, but we were forced to go too far south.

On the sixth day, as the wind was diminishing in violence, we hoped to be able to cease deviating toward the south; then the weather became foggy and cold. Next day all the ropes were covered with a layer of grime an inch thick; it was impossible for us to put about that day and the next; it was not till the third day, toward noon, that, breaking the ice which encased the ropes, we succeeded in putting about and going back toward the northwest. The weather was clearing, but we had a fairly strong west wind.

At this moment we found ourselves at longitude 62° west and latitude 61° south. It was the 18th of December; that day we had twenty-one hours of sun followed immediately by three hours of aurora clear enough to permit us to read and play on deck as in full daylight. The sun turned almost horizontally round us, but, although nothing stopped its rays, for no cloud altered the azure of the sky, we froze on deck, where we liked to stay in order not to miss the opportunity, if it was presented, of seeing a floating iceberg. But the lookout, already posted for three days, had not yet pointed out one of these enormous blocks which navigators dread encountering, when finally the order was given to put about, and to sail toward the northwest.

Since we had passed the 56th degree of south latitude, our existence on board had become the strangest in the world. The night was suppressed, or virtually so. Daily habits were found to be completely upset. Thus, the cook would have had to stay permanently at his stove, if he had wanted to satisfy everybody. This one, who had just got up, claimed his breakfast while that one, up for a long time, demanded supper in order to go to bed; one claimed that the sun had just risen, the other affirmed that it was going to set; both were wrong, for it was noon. The fact is that at noon, the sun was no higher on the horizon than it is in our climate an hour after its rising or an hour before its setting. What contributed the most to disorient us, we people of the northern hemisphere, is that at noon it was directly north, which was absolutely contrary to all its habits as we knew them. We were not less amazed during the few hours of aurora which served us as night, when it was barely hidden behind the south pole. If one went down below deck at any time whatever, one always found some passengers sleeping, others who were going to bed, and others who were getting up; this kind of life disrupted conversation, meals, amusements, as well as repose, because never were we all together at any one place.

Our progress to the northwest continued without interference. We stayed nine days on the same tack, with weather which became more and more propitious.[3] The sun, each day, took a step toward the zenith; the nights, while lengthening, progressively extinguished the aurora borealis; and the cold became from day to day less rigorous. The tenth day, we were heading north, when the island of Chiloé came in sight. So we had been floating for several days in the waters of the Pacific Ocean, which seemed to want to justify its name, for we were sailing as peacefully as possible, though nonetheless with speed.

We followed the coast in the intention of putting into port for several days at Valparaiso (Chile). We had no more fresh supplies, and the doctor [Garnier] on board had declared that we needed them to avoid scurvy, which would not have failed to appear as we returned to a warmer latitude. It was necessary, moreover, to unload the few goods we had for Chile.

One morning, we sighted a ship which was sailing in our waters. We spoke it at noon: it was the *Anne-Louise*, a three-master which left Le Havre a month before us.

Signals were exchanged between the two ships. The *Anne-Louise*, without however asking for help, let us know that she had lacked fresh supplies for a long time, that she had several invalids on board, and that she was going to put into Valparaiso. As we were all well on board the *Courrier de Cherbourg*, we offered to share with her what we had left of supplies; she accepted, and next day launched one of her landing boats, which came over to take what we had to give her.

We had to hear the story of the unhappy passengers of the *Anne-Louise* concerning the passage of Cape Horn, which they had spent six weeks in rounding! What harsh ordeals, and how small ours were in comparison! Like us, they had

---

3. Garnier recalled that they spent a month "tacking about" off Cape Horn (*Medical Journey*, p. 30).

taken the Strait of Le Maire, like us too, they had been pushed back by a very violent west wind, but instead of turning to the south, they had headed north and had returned within sight of the Falkland Islands; two times they had tried to double the cape and two times they had seen themselves pushed back in the same manner. Returning then anew in sight of the Falklands, they had decided to attempt the passage of the Straits of Magellan, in which they had succeeded well enough, for they, no more than we, had any serious damage. The two ships separated after setting a rendezvous in Valparaiso.

We then followed, as I have said, the coasts of Araucania, peacefully and pleasantly. Each one on board, joyful and content, got himself ready to go ashore and enjoy himself, to lead the good life for a few days, in order to make use of the short time that we were going to stay in Valparaiso, which should not be very far to the north, and to which each day brought us sensibly closer. Preparing for this debarkation, each one thought of tidying up a little, a thing completely neglected since our departure from Funchal. Several of the passengers found this an occasion for using their special skills: François, called La Houlette, the former valet de chambre, brushed everyone's suits and polished their shoes, in consideration of an honest reward. Haubourg, former tailor, sewed buttons on, and gave a lick of the iron to coats and trousers, in order to get rid of the abundant wrinkles. Mme. Thomas took charge of giving a presentable appearance to shirts, undershirts, collars, cuffs, and handkerchiefs. Huguet, the ex-hatter, brushed the hats which, sure enough, needed it: victims, during the whole crossing, of the sun and rain, of rolling and pitching, our unfortunate headpieces were truly in a lamentable state.

We had reached that point when a very thick fog rose, which hid from us the view of the coast. Night having come, we perceived faint lights toward shore; the wind had, at the same time, become so weak that we hardly moved. Seeing these lights, we believed ourselves opposite Valparaiso; we let ourselves arrive, that is, we let the ship follow the movement that the rising tide imposed on it, which pushed us in the direction of the lights. Shortly afterward, the sails fell limp along the masts, for lack of wind; we were thus in the roadstead of Valparaiso.

But imagine our surprise, when the sun rose, to find ourselves in we knew not what gulf, less than a hundred feet, perhaps, from the rocks of the coast; the fog was so dense that one could not see ten feet, but we heard the swell which broke with a crash on an invisible object and we saw it return, covered with a thick spume, to beat against the sides of the ship. Suddenly there appeared, forward to port, an object which cut down our shrouds and snapped our rigging. This object was none other than the bowsprit of a ship which the thickness of the fog had prevented us from seeing and which found itself in the same danger as we.

The mate, to warn it that we were there and to beg it to withdraw its bowsprit, took his megaphone and cried out: "Look out for your bowsprit!" A voice replied in English: "What?" This response was a question; we were dealing with an Englishman who had not understood what had been said to him; then the mate, helped by Miss Tournache, our English teacher, called to him: "Look out bowsprit." We heard the voice reply "all right" and, a little later, our neighbor disencumbered us of his bowsprit. During this time, the sun in mounting had somewhat penetrated the fog, and we were beginning to realize the danger of our position. We recognized first what had led us astray. At some distance were three other ships, which probably were seeking Valparaiso like us, and which, having lost their way thanks to the fog, had lighted their lanterns in order no doubt to try to see clearly; it was these lanterns which we had taken for the lights of Valparaiso.

Toward nine o'clock, the fog dissipated. We then saw rising before us a high sheer cliff, toward which the tide was pushing us imperceptibly, but with an irresistible force; we were hardly two hundred feet away from it. Not the least breath of wind to help us escape. The sea, although comparatively peaceful, threw itself against the jagged rocks, as if pushed by an invincible force, then, tired of its vain efforts, recoiled toward us loaded with spume—it was horrible to see! No hope, moreover, if the ship touched and sank; death was inevitable; nowhere was there access to the shore; to cling to the rocks, to climb them and gain the heights, was impossible. All these black cliffs were overhanging, licked by the waves that broke there with a crash on reaching a height of fifteen or twenty feet. They offered no recesses where the unfortunate castaway could find a refuge, even momentarily.

As soon as it was possible to take account of the situation, a mournful silence reigned on board, and the most intrepid paled. The women, despairing, returned to their cabins, covering their faces with their hands; one saw some of the men run aimlessly from one side to the other, then hide themselves, as if they had lost their reason. However, the greatest number remained immobile, silent, and seemed resigned to everything.

The captain, mounted on the poop, commanded the maneuver; realizing that because of the absolute calm the sails would be no help whatsoever, he had the shore boats put in the water, then he asked that eight men armed with oars descend into each of them. I thought for a moment that I was going to be left alone with the captain on the ship; everybody wanted to jump into these longboats, understanding very well that the danger was greater on board than in a shore boat, which could always be rowed to an accessible spot on the coast. However, on the remark of the captain that only two longboats would put to sea, they calmed themselves.

These longboats were attached by a cable to the ship, then by dint of rowing, the sixteen men who manned them succeeded in towing us for a certain distance. Then—it was about eleven o'clock—a breeze came up, strong enough to fill the royals; we were saved!

The three other ships had to have recourse to the same maneuver, and I think that it succeeded for them as for us. However, one of them had approached so near the coast that it escaped shipwreck only by means of long spars attached end to end, then supported at one end against the ship and at the other against the rock.

Toward noon, the breeze filled all our sails. The order was given to the longboats to return, then we gained the open sea.

The next day, at three o'clock in the afternoon, our ship cast anchor in the roadstead of Valparaiso, where the *Anne-Louise* had been awaiting us for twenty-four hours.[4]

Since we had left Madeira, the Abbé Laubert had entered into the practice of his duties, that is to say that every Sunday, when the weather permitted, he installed himself on the forecastle, improvising a sort of altar there; then he said a low mass, interpreted for us the Gospel of the day, and recited several prayers—meteorological—in order to ward off storms. He began again the following Sunday if the weather permitted, which did not happen every time—and likewise when we approached the bad passages, the weather no longer allowed it at all.

Few people, anyway, attended mass; a few Provençaux, a few Bretons and Normans and that was all. That doubtless did not seem enough to the Abbé Laubert, who soon stopped saying it.

Valparaiso is a city of about four [*sic*; that is, forty] thousand inhabitants, pretty enough, but not to the point of justifying the name which has been given it (Valley of Paradise). This name, however, is that of a valley which lies to the east of the roadstead, and the city is situated on a plateau to the south of the bay, at a sufficient height above sea level and at the foot of a fairly high mountain with an earthy slope, that is to say, where the rock is little apparent.

The valley of which I was just speaking is to the east of the city, on the road to Santiago (Saint James), capital of Chile.

This valley, if it resembles paradise, does not give a very high idea of it; it seems beautiful to the inhabitants, doubtless, because it is the only one there is in the country, which is nothing but an immense honeycombed plateau.

The city is well enough built; the houses have only one story, rarely two, because of the earthquakes, frequent in the country. It is for this same reason that the walls of these houses are very thick, which does not prevent them from tumbling down on occasion. Three weeks before our arrival, a shock had toppled fifteen houses, among others, that of the French consul, the walls of which were still lying in the street at our arrival.

The people speak Spanish, but one can make oneself understood almost everywhere by speaking French. The price of commodities is about the same as in France and the products of the soil are about the same; however, wages are three times as high. To cite only one example, one of our passengers, named Poinsignon, hired out in this city as a café waiter; he got twelve francs a day, room, and board. I should add that he spoke the two languages.

Beer, bad enough, was sold at eight sous per bottle; water, scarce at this season of the year (the end of January), was sold at three sous; they brought it to the city on mule back and it was sold in the streets by the bottle.

Policing is done by blasts of a whistle. They take over the street at nine in the evening; after that, moving around is still permitted, I think even all night, but talking is forbidden, unless in a low voice. Nevertheless, houses stay open all night

---

4. The passengers came ashore on February 9, 1851 (ibid., p. 31).

for entertainment; only the street is silent. Three of our passengers, being inspired to sing on their way back to the ship, were arrested and put in prison; that cost each one a night in the lockup and fifty sous' fine. As for the *moeurs* [morals], they are very free there, I will say even very depraved.

All the hills and mountains around the city are absolutely arid, what little grass grows there being thoroughly burned by the sun. They told us that this year the spring, a season which begins in September and ends in December, had been extraordinarily warm there and that they hoped for an exceptional vintage in autumn, that is in April.

At the end of the five days, after amusing ourselves to the best of our abilities in Valparaiso and having restocked fresh supplies, we raised anchor and continued our voyage, heading northwest.[5] We arrived at the line (Equator) at 125° west longitude, in twenty-eight days, without once changing the sails, always having good weather and fair winds. It really was agreeable sailing; the roll was scarcely felt, so joy reigned on board.

One would not have said that we were leaving the valley of Paradise, but rather that we were in Paradise itself. This constant serenity of the sky permitted us to give ourselves up to all sorts of diversions which bad weather had prevented.

We amused ourselves, in fact, as best we could; the games of draughts, chess, and cards were going all day. In the evening, it was the promenade on deck, an agreeable moment when we relaxed from play in conversation.

We had established an exchange on board. Every day, after noon, for an hour, the values of public stocks were announced. They fell or rose according to the gain or loss which one had made in play; they represented rations of wine, brandy, bread (they baked on Sundays and Thursdays), tobacco, etc., even of coined silver; but this last article was very scarce in that spot. The one who lost his allowance of brandy (five centiliters), if he did not prefer to do without it, had to buy some at the exchange; he paid for it with a ration of wine or tobacco or bread. As in the infancy of society, exchanges were made in kind, a forced consequence of the absence or rarity of money.

Finally, the spirit of enterprise was developed with the new needs to be satisfied. A society was formed to start a theater. The director was M. Passeau, former Zouave and former *zéphyr* [military police in Algeria]; having engaged six actors and two actresses, he played for us successively "The Tower of Nesle," "The Debutante's Father," "The Sister of Jocrisse," etc.

Our orchestra was composed of a cornet (M. Salard), a flute (M. Latuy), an accordion (M. Waslin) and a flageolet. It was M. Conqui who played this last instrument, but only when he was not an actress, for he and M. Mercier junior took the roles of women. The fair sex on board had consented to lend their gowns but not their personal assistance.

5. Five passengers deserted at Valparaiso (ibid.).

These performances were given in the afternoon; now, as the days were long and as the play was over quickly, after the spectacle, M. Salomon who, in his character of confectioner, had studied literature a little, declaimed selected passages to us, such as the recitation of Waterloo, the Isle of Saint Helena, the speech of Théramène or Athalie's dream. As we would have been considerably bored if we had not been amused, we had the good sense not to be difficult and, in the final account, we passed the time agreeably enough.

That lasted from Valparaiso to the Equator, and two or three days beyond; the weather, then, became unpleasant again, and games and laughter fled distracted.

Since we had recrossed the line, our route was due north; the wind blew from the west with sufficient strength, and we were sailing the best in the world, when it turned to the northeast all at once and forced us to take another direction. For more than fifteen days, we had to sail northwestward. From time to time, we tried to regain our course, but at the end of several hours we were forced to follow anew the direction which we had quitted. However, about the 25th of March, when we found ourselves at longitude 145° west and latitude 30° north, the bad weather ceased for several days; the west wind came up again and carried us, slowly, it is true, to the east-northeast.

Already we were making our preparations for the debarkation; the most impatient, at sunrise, were trying to discover land, when the wind turned from the west to the north. It also became very violent, and we were forced to beat back and forth for five days without making headway.

However, in the end, while continuing from the north, it became gentler and permitted us at last to head for Monterey. We approached it slowly but smoothly for two days.

On the third day, at eight o'clock in the morning, the lookout cried: "Land, California!" Three hours later, the *Courrier de Cherbourg* cast anchor in the bay of Monterey. It was the sixth of April, six months and three days after our departure from Le Havre.

To understand the joy which we experienced in hearing the cry "Land," in seeing it with our own eyes, one must have been six months at sea, six months separated from the world, between the serene or stormy sky and the treacherous sea; this joy touches at times on delirium, and that was somewhat the case on board. We ran here and there on the deck without knowing where or why; when we met each other, we began to laugh without saying a word; if we spoke it was by laughing and pointing to land.

Hardly had our anchors touched bottom when all of us, men and women, young and old, intoned in chorus, with a tremendous voice, by way of a *Te Deum*, some patriotic song or other, and after that one, several others.

The population of Monterey, which, apparently, had not passed six months at sea, was flurried by it, perhaps scandalized, but the ships in the roadstead applauded deafeningly.

Only toward two o'clock was this wild joy calmed a little, and then we remembered, not without some confusion, that we had not dined. Salard, former trumpeter, who, parenthetically, had sounded mess call during the whole crossing, took his instrument and gave the signal to come to table; we obeyed eagerly, appetite having returned to us in the cold light of reason; we had a splendid and copious repast, with a triple ration of wine, that is, everyone had his bottle.

About four o'clock, a longboat left the quay and steered toward our ship; it brought the vice-consul of France and the customs officers who came to take possession of our deck. We thought that it also brought us M. Thibeau, who should have been there a long time ago to receive us. We got ready to give him an ovation, and someone in the society, I no longer know who, set himself to deliver a lengthy discourse, long prepared, when the longboat touched. As I said, it brought the vice-consul [Jules Lombard] and messieurs the customs agents, but no M. Thibeau.

General stupefaction! What had become of our manager? and what had happened? As we were asking ourselves these questions, the vice-consul, accompanied by the captain, with whom he had doubtless consulted previously, came to announce to us:

That M. Thibeau, impatient at not seeing us arrive, had left for the placers in order to prepare everything for our installation, and that he would return in a few days. The most credulous believed these words; some others doubted. Whatever it might be, this news was like a douche of cold water thrown on our enthusiasm; we stopped singing on board, though we did not yet go so far as sadness; we were perturbed and we waited, that was all.

Next day we landed and we learned the truth.

The society, less fortunate than its members, had been wrecked! shortly after our departure from Le Havre, it had been declared bankrupt. To crown the misfortune, our ship was seized by the customs, since we did not have anyone to act as surety for unloading what we possessed; but after all, they told us, they were going to take measures to pull us out of the business. The blow was terrible, and one will understand the reversal which made extreme dejection follow extreme joy in us; all were mournful, silent; many wept.[6]

There we were, thrown on the shore like castaways, without money, without resources, in an unknown land whose language we did not understand. Each one asked what would become of him and found no reply.

It took us a little time to recover from our depression, to be in a state to face the situation coolly.

We were on land, camped in our tents, which the customs had permitted us to unload. We were fed, they told us, at the expense of vice-consul; we had open credit with the butcher, the baker, and the grocer who had been pointed out to us,

6. Perlot's account of the passengers' joy upon arriving in Monterey Bay contrasts with that of Garnier, who recalled that the passengers were full of doubt and fear (ibid.).

and we got wood for ourselves in the neighboring forest. We did our cooking ourselves, in our shipboard kettles; at night we slept on the bare ground, wrapped in our blankets, which we had also brought from the ship. But that could not last very long; we had to decide what to do. The engagements contracted before our departure from Europe being broken, we had to provide for ourselves.

One of us, M. Tampié, a Provençal and a former businessman, a fox who was a bit of a clerk, as de La Fontaine said, got it into his head that the cargo of the ship belonged to us and, with the civil code under his arm, he tried to persuade us that we should go find the vice-consul and reclaim, as our property, all that the ship contained, sell it, then divide the money among us. As we were too numerous to take this step together, we contented ourselves with naming a committee of five delegates who went to find the vice-consul to make our claims known to him.

Had these claims any basis? It is possible. The committee waited on the vice-consul once, perhaps twice, then I heard nothing more of it, and didn't worry myself otherwise about the result of the affair. I had something else in mind.

ILLUSTRATIONS

1. Jean-Nicolas Perlot (1823–1900), Belgian-born author of *Gold Seeker*. Courtesy of Bancroft Library, Berkeley, California.

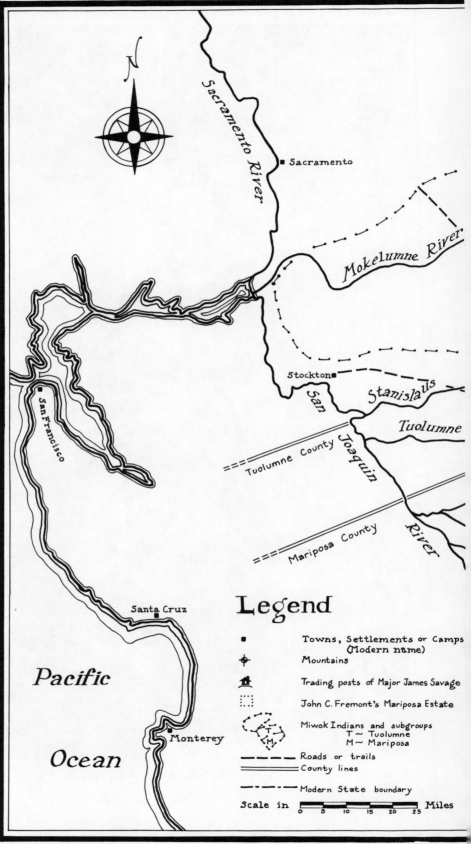

N

Sacramento River

■ Sacramento

Mokelumne River

Stockton ■

San

Stanislaus

Tuolumne

═══ Tuolumne County

Joaquin

River

═══ Mariposa County

■ San Francisco

Santa Cruz ■

Legend

■   Towns, Settlements or Camps
             (Modern name)

⊕   Mountains

🏠   Trading posts of Major James Savage

⋮⋮⋮   John C. Fremont's Mariposa Estate

      Miwok Indians and subgroups
           T ~ Tuolumne
           M ~ Mariposa

– – – –   Roads or trails

═══ County lines

— · — · —   Modern State boundary

Scale in   [0 5 10 15 20 25]   Miles

Pacific

■ Monterey

Ocean

2. Southern Mines region of California, which by common understanding extended from the
slope of the Central Sierras.

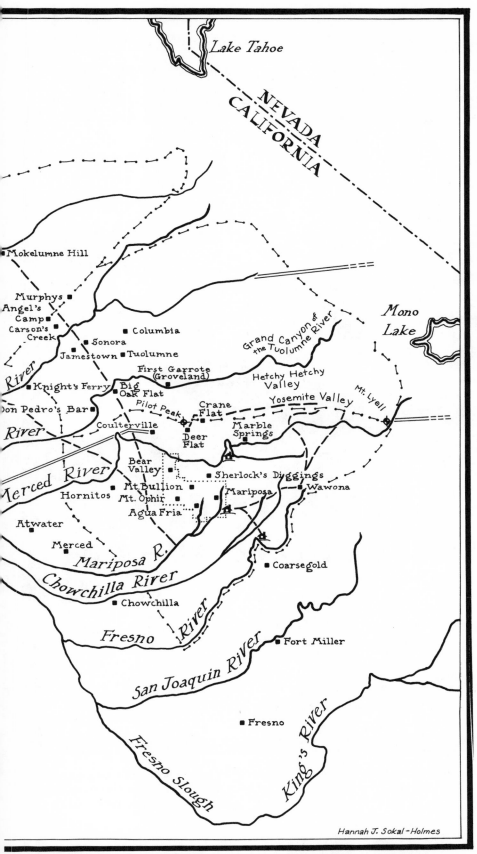

Lake Tahoe

NEVADA
CALIFORNIA

Mono
Lake

Mokelumne Hill

Murphys
Angel's
Camp
Carson's
Creek

Columbia
Sonora
Jamestown   Tuolumne

Grand Canyon of
the Tuolumne River

River

First Garrote
(Groveland)

Hetchy Hetchy
Valley

Knight's Ferry   Big
Oak Flat

Yosemite Valley   Mt. Lyell

Pilot Peak   Crane
Flat

Don Pedro's Bar

River

Coulterville   Deer
Flat   Marble
Springs

Merced River

Bear
Valley

Sherlock's Diggings

Mt. Bullion   Mariposa   Wawona
Hornitos   Mt. Ophir
Agua Fria

Atwater

Merced

Mariposa R.

Chowchilla River   River

Coarsegold

Chowchilla

Fresno   River   Fort Miller

San Joaquin River

Fresno

King's River

Fresno Slough

Hannah J. Sokal-Holmes

Mokulumne southward to the Fresno River and eastward from the San Joaquin to the western

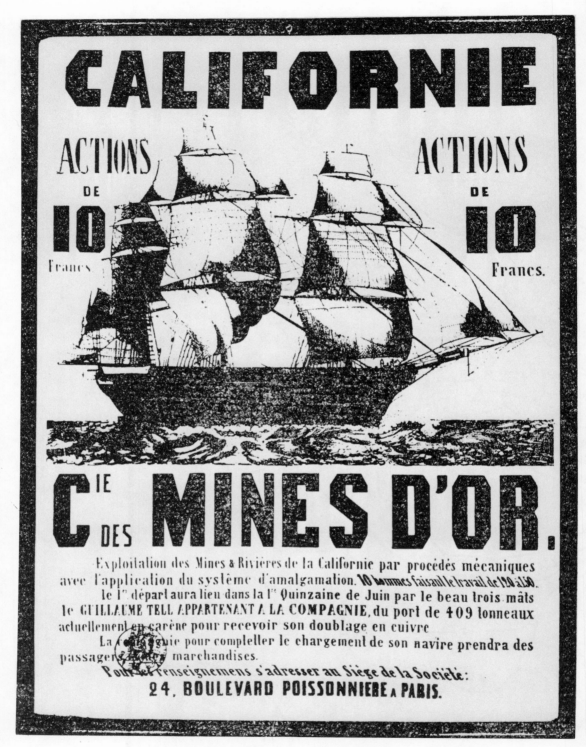

3. Broadside advertisement issued ca. 1850 by Société Cie Mines d'Or, one of the many Parisian companies or societies formed to exploit the California gold fields. From *A French Journalist in the California Gold Rush: The Letters of Etienne Derbec*, ed. A. P. Nasatir (Georgetown, Calif.: Talisman Press, 1964), p. 21.

4. Mr. Williaume exporting to California an "item" which is in very great demand. *Charivari*, no. 101 (11 April 1849) (Yale University Library).

5. The way California looks now that bigger and bigger ingots can be found there. *Charivari*, no. 101 (11 April 1849) (Yale University Library).

6. —I've had a very good day. I've dug 10,000 francs' worth of gold. I'd like to have dinner now.
—I'm sorry, Sir, I can't cook dinner for less than 15,000 francs! *Charivari*, no. 14 (14 January 1849) (Yale University Library).

7. A family arriving in California.
—Oh! My God! Our servants are already leaving to run to the mines! Perhaps we should offer to raise their wages a little! *Charivari*, no. 29 (29 January 1849) (Yale University Library).

8. Slight precautions which it is advisable to take in California if one wants to spend a peaceful night and still possess one's gold upon reawakening. *Charivari*, no. 21 (21 January 1849) (Yale University Library).

9. Machine for washing and amalgamating gold bought by La Fortune Mining Company. *Charivari*, no. 176 (25 June 1850) (Yale University Library).

10. Bear Valley, where Perlot lived in a log cabin during his second winter in California (1852–53). Carleton E. Watkins glass slide, courtesy of Beinecke Library, Yale University.

11. Mariposa Creek, scene of one of the first gold discoveries in the Southern Mines. Perlot first mined here in 1851. Carleton E. Watkins glass slide, courtesy of Beinecke Library, Yale University.

12. The town of Mariposa, shown above, was where Perlot first began mining in 1851. This glass slide impression by Carleton E. Watkins was probably taken in the early 1860s. Courtesy of Beinecke Library, Yale University.

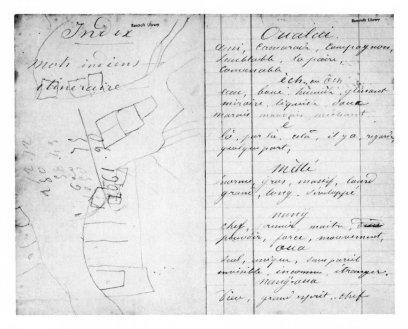

13. Perlot's "Index of Indian Words" began with "Oualai," the word for friend which he used so often that he himself came to be called "Mr. Oualai." Courtesy of Bancroft Library, Berkeley, California.

14. Yosemite Indian in dance costume. Photograph by J. T. Boysen.

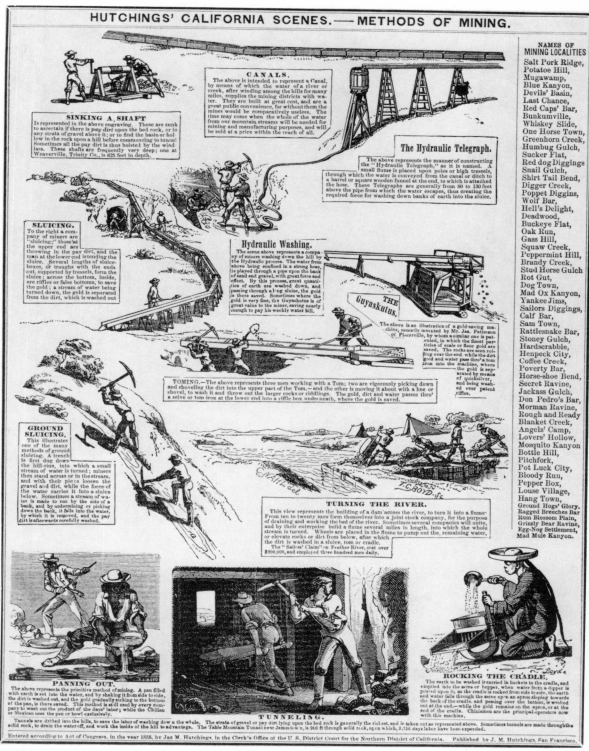

15. San Francisco publisher James M. Hutchings not only described some of the methods that Perlot used, as shown above, but was one of the first to describe the wonders of Yosemite Valley in his popular *Hutchings' Illustrated California Magazine*. Courtesy of Beinecke Library, Yale University.

16. Hutchings' "The Miner's Ten Commandments" was a popular spoof on the mining codes and rules of behavior that miners sought to enforce in the camps. Illustrated broadsides such as these were mailed to families back east. Courtesy of Beinecke Library, Yale University.

17. Yosemite Valley: Half Dome and the Merced River. Photograph by Carleton E. Watkins, courtesy of Beinecke Library, Yale University.

18. *Yosemite Valley: Bridalveil Falls from the Coulterville Trail.* Photograph by Carleton E. Watkins, courtesy of Beinecke Library, Yale University.

19. Alexander Ankeny, Perlot's mentor and employer in Portland. Courtesy of Portland Historical Society.

20. Ankeny's home. There is no date on the photograph, but this is probably the first garden Perlot leveled and designed. Courtesy of Portland Historical Society.

21. Simeon G. Reed residence in 1873 showing recent plantings; it is likely that Perlot landscaped this garden. Courtesy of Portland Historical Society.

22. *Mines D'Or de la Californie*. This rare French woodcut news-poster, published in Metz in 1849, shows California gold miners working with pickaxes, pans, and spades and then weighing up their ingots at a counter. It dramatically illustrates the way the gold fever seized the European imagination.

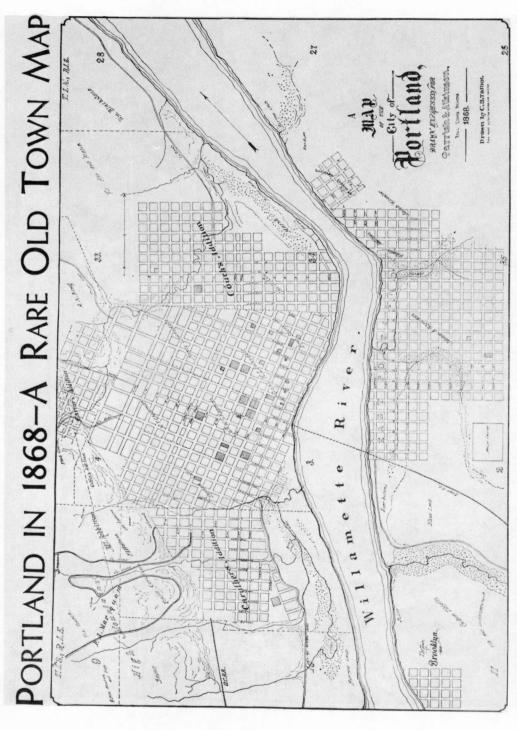

23. Map of Portland in 1868, by which time Perlot had purchased property in Couch's Addition, near Tanner's Creek, where he lived and had his nursery. Courtesy of Portland Historical Society.

II

FROM MONTEREY
TO MARIPOSA
1851

*The gold regions are difficult of access from
Monterey, for lack of roads.*
> Jacques Antoine Moerenhout
> April 25, 1849

*Before the discovery of the mines, Rancho
Pacheco was the end of the inhabited country.
We replenished our supplies there and started into
the California mountains. The roads were not yet
marked, and we walked at random for two days,
crossing a hundred times the streams that wind
through the ravines of these mountains.*
> Etienne Derbec
> Letter from Agua Frio,
> May 16, 1850

*Shall I tell you, sir, about the city of Mariposa?
Good Heavens, to call that a city! . . . a city
without houses is a curious thing!*
> Etienne Derbec
> Letter from Mariposa,
> September 1, 1850

By the time Perlot and his companions reached California in the spring of 1851, most vessels carrying gold seekers were landing at San Francisco rather than Monterey. Not only did San Francisco have one of the greatest natural harbors in the world, but one could go directly by steamer from there to the Northern Mines, which, by common but informal agreement, consisted of those districts north of "the ride on the north side of the north fork of the Mokelumne River."

Generally speaking the northern mining camps were located on the eastern slope of the Sacramento River valley. Indeed, the river port city of Sacramento was both entrepôt and major supply center for the hundreds of camps that sprang up on the Feather, Yuba, and American rivers and their tributaries. Here could be found the famous settlements of Placerville, Grass Valley, Nevada City, Marysville, Oroville, and Coloma. It was at Coloma that James W. Marshall first found gold in Colonel John Sutter's millrace.

The Southern Mines extended southward from the Mokelumne to the Fresno River. They could be called a rough mirror image of the Northern Mines in that they, too, lay on the eastern slope of a river valley—in this instance the San Joaquin—and had as their major supply center the town of Stockton, which would be reached by steamer from San Francisco. Besides the southern tributaries of the Mokelumne, the watersheds of the Calaveras, the Stanislaus, the Tuolumne, the Merced, and the Chowchilla rivers helped define the Southern Mines. Although some mining was done on the Fresno River to the south of these, and even on the San Joaquin, for all practical purposes, the town of Mariposa marked the southernmost of the major mining towns.

For reasons that are not entirely clear, the members of La Fortune company appear to have been attracted to the Southern Mines and to the town of Mariposa in particular. Placer gold had been discovered in the region at Woods Creek as early as 1848, and along the Merced River and Mariposa Creek soon thereafter. By 1849 Mexican and American miners could be found all along the banks of the two streams. In the summer of 1850 even more spectacular strikes were made— among them the discovery of rich quartz veins at the southern end of the so-called Mother Lode near Mariposa.

Nevertheless it seems likely that La Fortune company chose to go to the Southern Mines because of their knowledge of John C. Frémont, whose fame as an explorer and whose participation in the American conquest of California were well known in France. Frémont was also viewed as being sympathetic because he was of French descent. But there were other more practical reasons as well: Frémont owned the fabulous Mariposa Ranch or "Estate," on which could be found some of the richest placers and veins in California. While they were still in Paris, Perlot and his companions may also have heard about Frémont's negotiations with two emigrant companies: the Mineurs des Belge and the Nouveau Monde Company, who wished to establish mining operations on Frémont's estate. And finally, the Southern Mines had the reputation of being the region where most foreign nationals—and especially Frenchmen—had congregated.

Once they had landed at Monterey, Perlot and his friends decided to go directly overland to Mariposa rather than journey to San Francisco and take a steamer to Stockton. The fact was that they did not have the money to pay for such a trip. The route Perlot and his companions followed was actually the one the earliest Spaniards had taken to explore the San Joaquin Valley. They journeyed first from Monterey to Salinas, then to Mission San Juan Bautista, and from there eastward to Pacheco Ranch, which was seen as the eastern limit of settlement during the Mexican period. They then crossed the Coast Range via Pacheco Pass and recruited at a small station called San Luis. From there they headed for an outpost called "Round Tent" before reaching Woods Ferry on the San Joaquin. From a post or point Perlot identified as "Griffine" (which appears to correspond with the location of the present town of Stevinson, California), near the confluence of the San Joaquin and Merced rivers, they ascended the banks of the latter until they could turn south to Hornitos and from there to Mariposa.

At least part of the route followed by La Fortune company was already well known to Mexican miners who had come from Sonora to the Southern Mines in 1849, and to American argonauts who had come over the Southern Trail across Texas, New Mexico, and Arizona to the gold fields. Benjamin Butler Harris went from southern California into the Tulare or San Joaquin Valley to Agua Fria, while George W. B. Evans and his party traveled from Santa Barbara to Mariposa.[1]

While Perlot could hardly be called a pathmarker as he made his way to Mariposa, he had already begun to make original contributions to our knowledge of California Indian culture. Shortly after crossing the San Joaquin he and his friends encountered three Indians who shouted, "Walai! walai!" on seeing the whites. Assuming that it was a form of greeting, Perlot also shouted, "Walai! walai!" After the company shared some biscuits with the Indians they left peacefully. These may have been Miwok Indians, probably Tuolumne or Mariposa, although at the time Perlot was on the lower Merced, where Yokuts tribes could be found.

Instantly attracted to the language these Indians spoke, Perlot began to keep a list of Indian words and phrases which correspond with those found in the Mariposa and Tuolumne dialects.[2]

Perlot's Indian word *walai* presents an intriguing mystery. In his list of Indian words, found in his notes deposited in the Bancroft Library, he states that *oualai* or

1. Benjamin Butler Harris, *The Gila Trail: The Texas Argonauts and the California Gold Rush*, ed. and annot. Richard H. Dillon (Norman: University of Oklahoma Press, 1960); G. W. B. Evans, *Mexican Gold Trail: The Journal of a Forty-Niner*, ed. Glenn S. Dumke (San Marino, Calif.: Huntington Library, 1945), pp. 195–217.

2. See introduction to part V and chap. 17.

walai means "ami, camarade, compagnon, sembable, . . . convenable." He always greeted Indians with the term by which he meant "friend." Stephen Powers, who wrote about the California Indians and their languages in the 1870s, observed that the "extensive tribe of Wallies" lived on the Stanislaus and the Tuolumne; but he went on to say that "some assert it is a word applied by the pioneers to the Indians without any particular meaning; others, that it is an aboriginal word denoting 'friend.' The latter theory probably had its origin from the fact that these Indians on meeting each other, frequently cry out 'Wallie! Wallie!'"

Powers himself believed that "wallie" came from the word *wallim*, meaning "down below," which the Yosemite Indians "applied to the lower tribes with a slight feeling of contempt." Powers noted that the Indians on the Stanislaus and Tuolumne used the term freely in conversing among themselves, "but on the Merced it is not heard, except among Americans." Powers's conclusions, while interesting, do not seem that persuasive.[3]

A quick search through the most common words in the Mariposa and Tuolumne dialects, however, suggests only one word that resembles Perlot's "oualai," and that is *ōyea*, which means "white man" (Tuolumne: *ūyeayū*). While the Mariposan word for earth, dirt, or world is *wallī*, it seems to make no sense as a greeting. The Pomo word for the phrase "on both sides" is *wa'lī*, which could suggest "together." Whatever the original meaning of the word, Perlot used it as a greeting so often and so successfully that his friends jokingly called him "Mr. Oualai."[4]

In addition to his efforts to comprehend California Indian words and phrases, during the trek to Mariposa Perlot also emerged as a leader of men. His jaunty optimism, his great physical strength, and his complete faith that they would succeed gave his companions courage when they were lost and spurred them on when the trail was difficult.[5] Although the 206-mile journey from Monterey to Mariposa bears no comparison with the grueling overland trip of the American argonauts of 1849, it is important to remember that Perlot and his friends went by foot and were short of supplies and pack animals the entire way. They experienced hunger and thirst, were terrified by the tracks of unknown animals, encountered bears and rattlesnakes, and even had an Indian scare, so that they, too, felt they had "seen the elephant" by the time they had arrived at the Southern Mines.

3. See Stephen Powers, "The California Indians," no. 7, The Meewocs, *Overland Monthly*, 10 (1873), 322–33, reprinted in *Contributions* of the University of California Archaeological Research Faculty, 25, ed. and annot. Robert F. Heizer (Berkeley, Calif., 1975), p. 67.

4. For a vocabulary of Mariposa and Tuolumne words, see S. A. Barrett, "The Geography and Dialects of the Miwok Indians," *University of California Publications in American Archaeology and Ethnology*, VL, no. 2 (Berkeley: The University Press, 1908), 362–68. See also L. S. Freeland and Sylvia M. Broadbent, *Central Sierra Miwok Dictionary with Texts*, University of California Publications in Linguistics, 23 (Berkeley and Los Angeles: University of California Press, 1960).

5. Perlot not only used a compass to guide his party, he kept a careful table of distances. See his manuscript "Itineraire de Monteréy à Mariposa . . ." (Berkeley: Bancroft Library).

Chapter Four

The Company of Ten

I had taken some English lessons in Paris, and aboard ship I had attended the school held by Miss Tournache, so that arriving at Monterey I thought I could manage.

Imagine my astonishment when, hearing the people of Monterey speak, I realized that I did not understand them at all! It is true that I had never heard English spoken by the English.

A strange thing: rarely did they make me repeat what I said, but I could not understand the reply unless it was *yes* or *no*. No way of catching a sentence, unless it was written.

One of us, called Messent, found himself in the opposite situation. He had been a clerk four or five months in England and understood a little English, but did not speak it at all.

Here is what we dreamed up: when we went into the town in search of information, I asked the question, then Messent translated the answer for me. They laughed at us, but, at least, we understood and we were understood.

At Monterey, everybody tried to persuade us to become farmers. The work at the mines, they said, was too hard; it was difficult even to reach the placers and when one did get there, one was exposed to death from hunger, for there was no road and they could not take in provisions, to such an extent that the previous winter three-quarters of the population there had died of hunger and hardship. Instead of which agriculture was an easy and productive industry here, which led to fortune as quickly and as surely as the extraction of gold from ore.

A goodly number of the band let themselves be persuaded and took engagements with different farmers in the neighborhood.

The company of La Fortune was thus in the course of being transformed into an agricultural enterprise. But I could not make up my mind to undertake a career other than that for which I had left Paris and crossed the seas. I wanted, at the very least, to get to the placers and to try them, cost what it might, before trying something else if that didn't work—and if I returned, for the rumor ran that they were dying there like flies, and that the survivors spent their time killing each other.

So, to go to the placers was my fixed idea, in spite of difficulties, and the difficulties were not small. It was a matter of covering two hundred and six miles (sixty-eight leagues) across an uninhabited and pathless land, of avoiding Indians, bears, panthers, wildcats, coyotes, and snakes of all kinds, including rattlesnakes; but the greatest difficulty of all was that I could not go there alone. In the first place, I hadn't even the money necessary to purchase the mule I would need to carry my provisions, and a gun to defend myself with on occasion; without counting that it was more dangerous to attempt the adventure alone than with companions. A Mexican, with whom I was bargaining for an old donkey, asked four hundred francs; I had only a hundred and sixty left!

On the chance, I called on the vice-consul and asked him the way from Monterey to Mariposa, a placer discovered the previous summer and where, it was said, they were finding much gold.[1]

The consul opened his eyes wide and tried to turn me from my enterprise by repeating what others had already told me: that it was too far, too dangerous, that one would be hungry there, not for lack of gold but for lack of supplies, seeing that there was no road yet and that the miners who ventured that far had soon exhausted the few provisions which they took with them.

I thanked him for his counsels, which I believe were sincere, for M. le Consul seemed a fine man and was much concerned over us; but I made him understand that my mind was made up and that all I wanted from him was the route to follow. That way he could save me from long detours, for, knowing only the general direction, I ran a great risk of getting lost.

"Very well," he said, after some moments of reflection, "come back tomorrow; I will consult my reports and establish your itinerary as well as I can."

I bowed, thanking him, and withdrew.

On my way, I encountered one of our people, named Duléry, the former plumber, who still didn't know what to decide on. I told him about my visit to the consul and the purpose of this step; I asked him if he did not think it possible to organize an expedition, and proposed that he be in it. He listened to me and was at first quite astonished; the idea of forming another company had not even entered his mind. After having listened to my explanations, he made some objections, to which I replied, but, in the end, I could not entirely persuade him; he doubted its success.

Next day, I went to get the itinerary which the consul had ready, as well as the additional information.

1. It seems likely that Mexican miners discovered gold on Mariposa Creek in 1848, but the first solid evidence suggests that Alexander Godey and a number of Mexican miners began to extract gold there in 1849. Mexicans also reputedly discovered gold at Mount Ophir nearby in 1848. Still another strike was made at Princeton, which soon came to be called Mount Bullion in honor of John C. Frémont's father-in-law, Senator Thomas Hart Benton, whose hard-money views led him to be nicknamed "Bullion" Benton. Located about five miles northwest of Mariposa, it proved to be one of the richest gold mines in the state. News of rich discoveries made by "Quartz" Johnson near Mt. Ophir in 1850, and all along the southern end of the Mother Lode, may have persuaded Perlot to locate at Mariposa. See Erwin G. Gudde, *California Place Names: The Origin and Etymology of Current Geographical Names* (Berkeley and Los Angeles: University of California Press, 1969), p. 193; idem, *California Gold Camps* (Berkeley and Los Angeles: University of California Press, 1975), pp. 207–08, 227–28, 276–77; and C. B. Glasscock, *A Golden Highway: Scenes of History's Greatest Rush, Yesterday and Today* (Indianapolis: Bobbs-Merrill, 1934), pp. 304, 311–12.

This itinerary traced the route to follow only as far as the San Joaquin (river), that is, a scant half of the distance to be covered. Farther on, the country was unknown and information was lacking. All that they knew in Monterey was that the San Joaquin had a tributary a river named the Merced, and that the previous summer some Mexicans, after having worked on this river, had headed east and, ten or fourteen leagues beyond, had found some gold on another watercourse, which they had called Mariposa, because of the numerous butterflies (in Spanish *Mariposa*) which they had seen on its banks.[2]

In addition, the vice-consul knew, from reports he had received the previous autumn, that some miners leaving from San Francisco had followed the San Joaquin as far as a place indicated on the itinerary, then had turned toward the mountains by going up the Merced. There ended all that he could tell me for sure. I had to be content with this information, however insufficient it might be. Duléry, who had not been able to sleep all night, accosted me, and renewed his objections, with a good many others which his nocturnal meditations had suggested. I replied by showing him my itinerary and by explaining it; at last I succeeded in persuading him. So there was a first partner; to join the two of us we chose another, then the three chose a fourth, and so on until we made a dozen.

I thought for a moment that we were going to break up the camp and all leave together—everybody wanted to be in on it; after reflection, we resolved to admit no more new partners. Twelve was enough; more would perhaps have been too many. We held council; it was decided that we would buy the donkey which the Mexican was offering to sell me. We would load it with what provisions and effects it could carry, and each of us would carry a load of fifty to sixty livres in the bag with which he should be equipped.

I shouldn't omit mentioning that some other passengers of the *Courrier de Cherbourg*, numbering eleven, all natives of the beautiful land of Provence, had formed a company, following our example, and were getting ready to leave at about the same time. As for the rest of the members of the late company of La Fortune, those who were not employed by the farmers were preparing to leave for San Francisco with the intention of settling there or of traveling from there to the mines.

Two of us had double-barreled guns and three others, pistols; it seemed to us that this armament was sufficient, considering the state of our finances. Our donkey and provisions cost us six hundred and fifty francs, and when that was paid we had only seven hundred and twenty francs left. Moreover, in order to realize this capital, it had been necessary for many of us, myself included, to sell shirts, pants,

2. When Gabriel Moraga led an expedition into the San Joaquin Valley in 1806, his troops encountered hosts of yellow butterflies on Mariposa Creek, which led them to call it the place of the mariposas (butterflies). Two Mexican land grants in the area took the name of Las Mariposas, and when Frémont purchased a ranch there in 1847, it came to be called the Mariposas Estate. After gold was discovered on the estate, the miners who came there abandoned the plural name *Mariposas* for Mariposa, the name they gave the camp which sprang up there. The name was also given to the surrounding area in 1850, when it was made a county. See Gudde, *California Place Names*, p. 193.

drawers—especially drawers, as these were objects of luxury, since a pair of pants sufficed for modesty; in our situation, luxury was no longer permitted us.

On the eve of the day set for the departure, two of the members, Margraff and Huguet, came to inform me that they would not leave—for fear, they said, of being killed by the Indians or else of dying of hunger. They asked for the return of their money, to which we consented.

So there were ten of us left, to wit:

Duléry, Messent, Marcan, Ragache, Viot, Béranger, Braconnier, Schmutz, Bigot, and I.

Finally, on the 16th of April 1851, at about nine o'clock in the morning, we left Monterey, driving before us a donkey who carried three hundred livres of provisions and clothing. As I have said, each of us had on his back a load of fifty to sixty livres. We directed our steps to the east, making our way over terrain that was not too uneven, but sandy and dry, and therefore uncomfortable. It was rather a curious thing to see our exodus: the greater part among us carried the military knapsack commonly called the *ace of diamonds;* as for me, I had preferred to attach some leather straps to my carpetbag and to arrange it as best I could on my back. Our donkey walked in the lead, but he had been so badly loaded at our departure that, after having gone a little bit of the way, the load slipped to one side; we were forced to put down our packs to untie the load to replace it on the back of the animal. This time we took all possible precautions to fasten it well. That done, we set forth anew, but after a few steps, there goes the load, leaning and turning again—though, it's true, on the side opposite to that on which it had fallen the first time; again, we put down our knapsacks, and we reload the ass.

We had, this first day, to begin this exercise over again so often that each one of us had unloaded and reloaded the poor beast at least two or three times, and each one in his own fashion; for as many as we were not one of us had ever loaded a beast of burden or seen one loaded. At last the evening came; we camped near a stream in order to have something to drink and above all something with which to make our coffee.

On leaving Monterey that morning, we had the firm intention of reaching a good stage and of going at least as far as Salinas to sleep, that is, a distance of eighteen miles (six leagues); but the difficult road, the loads which more or less hindered our movements and weighted our steps, the time lost in loading and unloading our donkey, and night arriving perhaps a little too soon—all these circumstances made us find a camping place about halfway to the place we expected to reach; but we hoped to do a longer stage the next day. Someone of the troop—it was Braconnier—had offered to concoct a pack-saddle for our donkey, so that we would no longer have to lay hand to his load so often.

While we were at supper, the company of Provençaux arrived. They had left Monterey at noon; but as they had two pack animals, a mule and a donkey, they were less laden than we, put more bounce in their step, and, after leaving, covered more of the road. They came to camp beside us in order to save a sentinel. Supper was composed of a beefsteak, which we had carried since Monterey, potatoes baked in their jackets, and a cup of tea. This frugal repast ended, we each drew a number; we had to stand, in turn, two hours of sentry duty, loaded gun on one's arm. These precautions taken, each one made his bed, as he wanted to retire. The weather was fine, we had not pitched our tent, we were content to roll ourselves in our blankets, the knapsack serving as pillow. We slept little, because of uneasiness, for it was the first night that we lay thus under the stars; however, the night passed tranquilly. Next day, we were up early; while the water was heating for the coffee, we helped our saddlemaker to concoct a pack for the donkey; by means of six cloaks and a certain number of cords and strings, the object was patched up quickly enough. After breakfast, each one repacked his knapsack, then helped to reload the animal, who, parenthetically, had passed the night at pasture attached to the end of a rope twelve meters long whose other extremity was fastened to a stake planted in the ground. That done, we were on our way again.

The Provençaux, who, being better equipped than we, claimed to walk faster, proposed to leave us behind; therefore they had left the encampment well before us, after I had given them a copy of the itinerary which the consul had delivered to me.

What I had not given them, indeed, was the pocket compass by means of which I assured myself of the direction to follow; but as three or four of them flattered themselves on almost speaking Spanish, they had judged it useless to get themselves this precious instrument, because one always had a chance of encountering Mexicans on the way, of whom one could ask the necessary directions.

It was at least seven o'clock before we were on the march again. We went better than the day before, because each one, taught by experience, had adjusted his knapsack better, and our donkey, itself better loaded, gave us much less trouble; moreover, we were leaving a wooded and mountainous terrain and were entering a plain, or rather a vast prairie, where we had only to pick up one foot after the other.

Toward noon, we were able to rejoin the Provençaux, who in their turn were suffering vexations. They had had the mischance, ordinary enough anyway, of happening upon a mule who had a head typical of his species and who in addition had some fantasies of his own; thus they could not persuade him to cross the smallest stream except on a bridge. Now, bridges were rare, in 1851, on the watercourses of California. Our Provençaux, when we caught up with them, were properly stopped at the edge of a stream twelve feet wide, which the mule obstinately refused to enter; vainly they endeavored to overcome his resistance.

To begin with, at the first blows that he received, he had started to kick so wildly that in a short time he had scattered around him on the ground all the objects which constituted his load. These gentlemen had then carried this load to the other side, then had passed a rope around the neck of the animal, and two of them, crossing the stream, were pulling with all their strength while the others caressed his rump by beating him with sticks. However, it was only on our arrival that, seeing our donkey enter the water beside him, no doubt spurred to emulation, he decided to cross in his turn, but so suddenly that he barely missed passing over the bodies of the two men who were pulling him toward themselves.

With our beast of burden, less nimble but of more compliant temperament, we were walking peacefully, without hindrance, and it was our turn, in the afternoon, to take the lead.

About one o'clock we were at Salinas (salt mines, in Spanish), which was composed of two houses built of adobe (sun-dried bricks), occupied by two Spanish farmers.

The plain, properly speaking, ends at Salinas, and the whole afternoon was spent in climbing and descending hillocks, which were more or less high, but almost always steep and wooded.

We had to make our stage longer because we found no more water, and it was only at eight o'clock in the evening that we encountered a spring at the foot of a mountain behind which was San Juan. The weather, which was overcast, forced us to pitch our tent.

For supper we had to eat what we had left of the fresh meat, if fresh it could be called, for already it was acquiring a taste that was hardly appetizing, so that several delicate stomachs in the company preferred to withdraw it from their supper menu. Toward ten o'clock we were rejoined by the children of Provence, still quite red with anger and giving voice to a formidable *trounn de l'airre* which echoed in the silence of the night, intended for their mule, who had played the farce for them five or six times during the day. This night we slept better than the first, for fatigue began to make itself felt, without counting that one rests better under a tent than in the open air. The next day, as the weather was clouding over, our sentinel woke us early in order to reach, if possible, the summit of the fairly high mountain which we had ahead of us before the way was flooded by the rain; but hardly were we midway when it began to fall. We continued, nevertheless, to climb, although more slowly; but the water in making the way slippery had at the same time made heavier the load of our donkey, who suddenly staggered and fell. We attempted to raise him; it was in vain. We first had to carry our own load to a point a kilometer higher, that is to the summit of the hill, then, leaving a man on guard there, we returned to get the load of the poor animal. When this was done, we were at the end of the climb; it was noon, and we had no water with which to prepare our dinner. We decided that each one would content himself with a biscuit and a half-piece of chocolate, and that we would push on at once to San Juan, which we should find at the base of the mountain. But if the climb had been difficult, the descent was not easy. The rain had almost ceased, but the path—steep, slippery, and full of ruts— was dangerous. However, after having many times unloaded, raised, and re-loaded our donkey, who slid and fell at almost every step, we ended by finding ourselves on the plain. It was time, for shortly afterward the rain began again and when, toward evening, we entered San Juan, it was raining still.

The Provençaux arrived two hours after us, soaked to the bone, covered with mud, exhausted and out of breath. To hear them, they had had much more trouble than we. The truth is that they had had the same crosses and had not borne them as well.

San Juan was then a city composed of about sixty houses, all of them business houses. It served as center to the population, scattered in a radius of four leagues, who gathered there on Sunday to hear Mass at the Mission, which was built on a little rise not far from the plateau where the houses were grouped.[3] In the afternoon, countrymen and city dwellers together gave themselves up to amusements of all kinds.

On our arrival, we were in the midst of setting up our already damp tent in the rain, when an American, who was building a butcher-shop, offered us shelter for several days in his house, then under construction, an offer which we accepted without being begged. This house had only walls and a roof as yet; no doors or windows. But that did not prevent us from finding ourselves comparatively well off; having lit an enormous fire in the fireplace we dried our effects and our provisions, then prepared a splendid supper—that is, as sumptuous as the resources of the city and the state of our purse permitted. The carpenter's shavings served us as mattress and there we enjoyed a delicious and uninterrupted slumber, for we kept no guard, considering that we were in the city and that the doors and windows were closed by boards. In the evening, rolled in our blankets, before going to sleep we had held a council and decided, unanimously, to buy a second beast of burden; our donkey was too heavily loaded and we ourselves were beginning to find the knapsacks we carried on our backs a little heavy. So, we had to add to our means of transport.

Next day, Easter Sunday, my companions set out in search of a donkey or mule. By eight o'clock, they had one, purchased very reasonably because he had a foreleg curved in a half-moon. They had paid sixty dollars (300 francs) for him, so that we had only two hundred and twenty francs left in the company.

Our original capital was one thousand, three hundred, and seventy francs; we had disbursed six hundred and fifty francs of it for purchase of provisions and the acquisition of our donkey; we had had to repay the two deserting members their two hundred and ten francs. At San Juan, we bled it again for three hundred francs, and we had still to pay, before leaving, twenty francs for coffee, meat and brandy; for it had been decided, in a second council, that in future each one would have, every morning, his glass of brandy, on the pretext that this was necessary to put us in a state to face the fatigues and trials of the route. That reduced the cashbox to 190 francs.

While my partners were in search of a mule, I had gone to visit the "Mission," on

3. The San Juan Bautista Mission was founded June 24, 1797, by Father Fermin de Lasuén and was still being used for parish services in 1851. Located in the San Benito Valley, it was a logical stopping place for Perlot's party. See ibid., p. 287; "San Juan Bautista," in Howard R. Lamar, ed., *Reader's Encyclopedia of the American West* (New York: Thomas Y. Crowell, 1977), pp. 1077–78; and Zephyrin Engelhardt, *Mission San Juan Bautista* (Santa Barbara, Calif.: Mission Santa Barbara, 1931).

the subject of which, when in Paris, I had seen such fine reports in my uncle's journal (Journal des missionnaires, year 1845); I wanted to see these Indians whom the reverend Fathers had converted, and to learn for myself what these pretended savages were like; and then I wanted to try to obtain from them some information on the country lying beyond my map. But I saw there only three or four Indians, more or less authentic, whom nothing differentiated from the mass of the faithful. The buildings were almost in ruins; the chambers of the Fathers and the church alone were kept up. A palisade, seven or eight feet high, rather poorly maintained, served as surrounding wall for the Mission; this wall was a pentagon, more or less regular, whose sides were each about sixty meters in length.

The Mission and the church were built of adobe and seemed ancient; in the church was a mass of ornaments, neither beautiful nor rich, but very brilliant and similar to those trinkets which dazzle the villagers at the fair. For furniture, there was an altar; neither benches nor chairs. During the sermon, which took place with collect twice every Sunday, the faithful seated themselves like Turks on the uneven and dirty area which served as pavement for the church. The preacher did not mount to the pulpit, for there was no ladder leading to it; he reached it by a door cut in the wall, which probably communicated with the Mission; one would have said it was a balcony rather than a pulpit for preaching.

What especially attracted my attention was, in the lower part of the church, a great number of statues representing Indians. They told me that these were the Indians who had been outstanding for their good conduct during the hundred and twenty years [actually fifty-four years] of the mission's existence. Presently, seeing that the church was filling with the faithful who came to celebrate the festival of Easter, and that I had no chance of finding what I sought, I returned to find my partners.

Some of them wanted to delay the departure in order to attend the ten o'clock mass; first, because it was Easter and also to give the road a chance to dry a little, for it had rained during part of the night; but the majority was of the opinion that we should leave, because we were consuming our supplies and money was going to be short. About nine o'clock then, we set off again in the direction of the east, with the hope of going to bed at the foot of the California mountains, whose still snow-covered summits could be seen on the horizon.

The Provençaux decided otherwise; they wanted to attend mass, so they could not leave San Juan before one o'clock in the afternoon.

From San Juan to Pacheco, we had eighteen miles (six leagues) to cover over a terrain that was slightly rolling and very little wooded. After having crossed the little river of San Juan, which twists its way through an even plain three kilometers wide and of indefinite length, we found ourselves on a terrain composed of little hillocks completely covered with wild oats, which seemed to us to be of the black species, and which were approaching maturity. Our astonishment was great to see all this country covered, as far as the eye could reach, with a superb crop which passersby trampled without a care for property rights. It was only after having walked four or five hours in this immense harvest that we acquired the conviction that it had not been sown and that it grew spontaneously throughout the country.

What confirmed us in the conviction was seeing, in the environs of Pacheco, immense herds of cattle, horses, and sheep, pasturing, running, and rolling freely in this illimitable field of grain. In approaching one of these herds of cattle, we ran a rather serious danger. These animals see man only when mounted on a horse, the Californian's sole manner of traveling, and doubtless, like the Indians of the time of Christopher Columbus, they imagine that the two are but one; it's still the man on horseback who is the only one they know and the only one they fear, especially if he has the terrible lasso in hand. The lasso is a long rope of untanned leather, ending in a running knot, which the Mexican uses, with marvelous dexterity, for catching horses and wild cattle. So now, these cattle, seeing a species of man without the ordinary appendage, were doubtless struck with astonishment and wondered what sort of animals we could be. They stopped, contemplated us with attention, and finally some of them, pushed by an irresistible curiosity—for I do not believe that they had evil intentions—approached us, began to follow us and, thanks to the sinuosities of the way, soon surrounded us. Then we pushed back those who crowded us too closely; they fell back on their companions who were following them, and began to bellow.

Immediately we saw the whole plain agitated, moving, and heading toward us, and there we were in the midst of two or three thousand cattle who pushed, collided with each other, and came close, forming around us a cricle which grew more and more constricted. It was time to consider; we made a halt, put down our knapsacks, and after having taken our stand around the two beasts of burden, who did not have a reassured air at all, we strove bravely against our enemies with cudgels, stones, and even with gunshots. The combat lasted a good hour, or so it seemed to me, and God be thanked, the victory was ours; that is, the cattle, seeing with whom they had to deal, scattered a little and left us a free passage.

We were disengaged but did not yet dare start off again, because our enemies, who had beaten a retreat with slow steps, had stopped, turning toward us their big blue eyes and above all their horns, those cursed long, sharp horns which did not fail to cause us a certain anxiety. They ended, however, by withdrawing, but slowly and in good order; we ourselves set off again. Hardly had we gone a kilometer when we saw those who, nearby, had put on such a brave display, now abandon themselves to a disordered flight.

It was because, at that moment, a Mexican horseman arrived at full speed from the top of a hill, where he had seen what was happening and so came running to our rescue. He seemed as surprised as pleased to see us delivered; he spoke to us in Spanish but, in spite of the pocket dictionary which I had at my disposal, I could not succeed in understanding what he said; he was more intelligible when he spoke the language of signs and gestures.

He explained that it would have sufficed to twirl a rope around our heads like a slingshot, to scare away the whole herd, who would have taken this rope for a lasso, for anything resembling it makes them flee. It was very simple, but one would have to know it or guess it.

Two hours later, we were at Pacheco, which was composed of three buildings, a shed, a chicken-house, and living quarters; all this belonging to Señor Pacheco, a Spaniard who had come to establish himself in this place some twenty-five years ago.[4] He had been granted fifteen square leagues of land and lived there, occupying himself by raising livestock; as far as agriculture was concerned, he did not even have a garden.

Like the good Catholic he was, he let the Mission livestock graze at will on the immense plain which we had just crossed and which belonged to him.

In any case, this pious liberality did not remain without recompense; it enabled him to live in peace and security on his domain, seeing that the good fathers, thanks to their influence over the Indians, protected him against their depredations.

But, one will say, where did the missionaries get so many bulls, cows, horses, and sheep?

And how, occupied with the cure of souls, did they find the time to discharge the duties demanded by the administration of so many riches?

This demands some explanation.

When the missionaries establish themselves in a country occupied by Indians, they begin by learning the language or dialect spoken by the natives. That done, they try to seize control of the mind of the chief. Ordinarily they succeed by studying his tastes, perhaps his passions, and by applying themselves to satisfying them. The chief, in return, as gauge of his friendship, has his tribe baptized; he can do no less. One fine day, he brings all his people to the Mission; the Father takes the branch of a tree, dips it in a stream which he has taken care to bless, sprinkles with it all the Indians, men, women, old folk and children—and there they are, Christians.

The Christians, according to the ideas the Indians have of them, are people who live peacefully, who say their prayers to be happy during their life and after their death; who go to hear sermons to learn how they ought to behave, and who, when they have the misfortune to commit a sin, go and tell it to the Father, so that he can teach them what they must do in order that the sin may be forgotten by the Great Spirit.

The Indians, turned Christian, follow this program exactly; they learn their

4. Perlot was undoubtedly referring to Francisco Pérez Pacheco, who was awarded the Ausayamas y San Felipe grants in 1833 and 1836, located at San Felipe in San Benito and Santa Clara counties. Although Pacheco was not a native Californian—he had migrated there in 1819—he became one of the most prominent men, first in the Mexican province, and then in the new American state. He was one of the few rancheros who owned a library. The San Luis Gonzaga grant in the same vicinity, awarded to Juan P. Pacheco in 1843, stretched into Santa Clara and Merced counties. Together the Pacheco holdings embraced Pacheco Pass, Pacheco Peak, and Pacheco Canyon. See Gudde, *California Place Names*, p. 233, and Robert G. Cowan, *Ranchos of California, A List of Spanish Concessions, 1775–1822, and Mexican Grants, 1822–1846* (Fresno: Academy Library Guild, 1956), pp. 6, 17, 83–84.

prayers, go to hear sermons, and above all go to confession, if only to imitate the chief, who goes there often.

This latter is never punished or is punished only lightly. But these reverend persons are more severe with the common run of the faithful.[5] As soon as an Indian, male or female, has committed any sin whatsoever, he or she must go and tell it to the Father, who becomes more or less angry and imposes a more or less severe punishment, according to the case. It seems that the indignation of the confessor is in proportion to the number of head of cattle which the penitent possesses. He undertakes to appease the Great Spirit by means of the gift of a sheep, of a calf, and sometimes of a bull or a horse. The Indian receives the reply, that is to say the absolution, only when he has brought to the missionaries' herd the animal which serves him as ransom.

Among the converts, there are ardent neophytes who, the better to assure their salvation, consecrate their life to the service of the Mission, that is, serve as domestics to the Fathers. As recompense, after their death they are sometimes made saints, and their statues are placed in the Mission church. It was these statues which I had noticed in the lower part of the church of San Juan. But this recompense is not squandered, first because it must not be lessened in the eyes of the Indians, who consider it as the extreme beatitude, and next because it's expensive, for it is necessary to buy the statue.

When a mission attains the possession of three or four thousand horses or horned beasts, these devout Indians of whom we have just been talking undertake to drive this immense herd to Mexico or Texas, where it is sold, to the profit of the Mission, at the rate of sixty to a hundred francs a head.[6]

The sheep, on the other hand, is skinned and the fleece is sent on muleback to some port or other where it is put aboard ship for Europe. Pigs are eaten on the spot, except the parts which can be salted and smoked and which they sell to the ships which come to anchor in the coastal ports.

And now, one has the answer to the double question which we posed just now; if the Fathers have numerous herds, it is because there are many sinners among the Indians; if the care of these herds does not form an obstacle to the exercise of their sacred ministry, it is because there are also among the Indians many saints or aspirants to sanctity.

We made a halt at Pacheco to profit by the water of the fountain, for since San Juan we had not encountered the least spring or the least stream. The kettles are unpacked and the water is heated for the coffee which we carried ready ground. As we have seen not a few cows on the plain, there should be some milk at the Pacheco house, and I undertake to go look for some to whiten our coffee. There I go,

5. Spanish and Mexican mission fathers in California did exploit and mistreat Indian neophytes on occasion, but Perlot's account here is clearly biased against the padres.

6. California horses were taken east—some to New Mexico, and from there to Texas or even Missouri or Louisiana—but it seems that Perlot is in error when he states that California cattle were driven to Texas.

supplied with a pot and my pocket dictionary. The door of the house is open; on entering I throw a scare into thirty or forty hens who are strolling and pecking at their ease in the court. When their cries are somewhat appeased, not seeing anyone, I call at the top of my voice; then I hear something moving in a corner; I turn and find myself face to face with the Señora Pacheco, whom I have just awakened. She has been lying, fully dressed, in a string hammock suspended in a corner of the room. When I say fully dressed, it is a manner of speaking; she was wearing simply a shift and a calico dress which she had unfastened in order to take her siesta more comfortably. I salute her, then, showing her my pot and a twenty sous piece, I say: Leche (pronounced létché). She stretches her arms very hard to wake up better, then walks around and around me without saying a word. The examination ended, she goes out and lets loose a great shout; shortly afterward there arrives an Indian of a sort, also half-naked, to whom she says several words and who retires to return soon, mounted on a horse and with his lasso in hand; thus he gains the plain.

While I was in front of the door to await his return, my attention was drawn to a sort of pen closed on all sides by a palisade, which was full of calves in the flower of their age; I was about to ask myself why they were thus enclosed when I saw the Indian return, driving before him six or seven cows. Soon leaving them behind, he runs at a gallop, opens the barrier of the pen and makes a calf cry; the cows run up immediately. He then closes the barrier, catches them one after another with the lasso, then ties them and makes me a sign to give him my pot; all that in the wink of an eye. He goes to work at milking one cow, then another, and while he milks on the right, the calf suckles on the left; when my pot is full, he returns it to me. Re-entering the house then, I offer my piece of money, the señora makes a sign that she wants nothing and delivers a beautiful discourse to me in a gibberish which is impossible for me to understand, but where the word "leche" often appears. The harangue ended, I salute profoundly, saying *gracias* (thanks), a word which I have just found in my book, and I withdraw.

I took back in my pot at least eight liters of milk, which we drank with delight to the last drop; we had mixed it with our coffee, but the result of this mixture was rather milk with coffee than coffee with milk.

The same men of delicate stomach who, two days before, at Salinas, had not wanted any meat because it lacked a little freshness, regaled themselves now with unfiltered milk drawn by the dirty hands of an Indian; it was because fatigue and exhaustion were beginning to make themselves felt.

When the repast was ended, it was still far from being night. In order to do the next day's stage more easily, a stage entirely in the mountains and thirty miles long, we repacked our animals' loads and our own, and we set off again with the intention of walking until evening.

We climbed up the bed of a dry river; however, it must have had a great deal of water in the winter, for the bed, fairly deep, was not less than ten to twelve meters wide.

Four or five miles from Pacheco, the way was beginning to rise in a rapid slope when we arrived beside a spring. As we were not sure of finding water higher up, and as night was approaching, it was decided to camp in this place for the night, all the more so as this was the most beautiful flat we had come upon in our last hour of walking in wooded country; also, we hoped that the Provençaux would come to rejoin us there before the darkness of night.

The day had been warm and, although our packs had each been lightened by fifteen livres, which we had loaded on our second beast, we were sweating and exhausted. So every one was sleeping a deep sleep when at three o'clock in the morning, being on guard, I had to awaken the camp. In a moment, all were up. I heard, coming from the wooded hill beside us, a strange noise; soon, by the feeble light of dawn, we saw, leaving the thicket, a brown bear accompanied by three cubs, which doubtless she was bringing to drink at the spring near us.

At the sight of the monsters, our terrified mule breaks the rope which holds him, and flees; the donkey wants to do the same, but, powerless to break his tether, succeeds only in turning a somersault. As I was at the moment the widest awake of the ten, I throw myself without loss of time into the pursuit of the mule and I luckily succeed in catching the end of the rope, which he was dragging behind him; I manage to master him and to bring him back near the tent, set up a hundred feet from the spring. In the interval, someone else had untied the donkey and was bringing him, too, back near the mule; thus our two auxiliaries were provisionally in safety. However, the bear stops on hearing the noise, for she has not seen us, I think; then, arching her back like a cat confronted by a dog, she starts to cut back and forth through the grass, constantly herding her little ones who are trying to climb to the spring. We have taken arms, but these arms add up only to two double-barreled guns. Messent gives me his and promises to take care of the mule; then I advance a few steps with Ragache, possessor of the second gun, and we wait. The bear has started forward again and continues to climb, but slowly; at last her cubs reach the spring and quench their thirst, then the whole family makes its way into the woods again and disappears. At last! we breathe! I dare affirm that we all were pale. Two years later, a similar encounter would have moved us no more than one with a fox. We did not know then that the bear never attacks, and fights only in self-defense; we were convinced that we had just escaped from a great danger.

We could not get back to sleep; it was useless for me to observe that I had been up since one o'clock in the morning, that my watch was ended, and that I needed rest; nobody wanted to go back to bed or to consent that I do so. We must not, in fact, abandon ourselves to a mistaken security. Who knows? the bear had perhaps gone to seek reinforcement and was going to return well attended. . . .

It was decided that everyone should be on watch until it was broad daylight. We kept, in fact, a good guard until sunrise, but the bear did not return. At five o'clock, we breakfasted with a good appetite, then we broke camp.

The Provençaux had not rejoined us; we learned later that they had arrived toward evening at Pacheco, and that they had passed the night there.

Chapter Five

In Search of the San Joaquin

In consequence of the event which had interrupted our sleep, we set off at an earlier hour than was our habit. Two hours after our departure, we arrived at the mountain, properly speaking.

The path we were following, leaving the banks of the dry river which we had been climbing since Pacheco, wound among masses of great rocks. We set ourselves to scale the mountain. Scale is the word: the way was so steep that one had to put a hand on the ground to help in climbing. Our animals were exhausted; they climbed for two minutes, then, out of breath, they stopped.[1]

At last, at two o'clock in the afternoon, we attained, as by a miracle, the summit; I say by a miracle, for if, in climbing, one of our animals had made the least false step, he would infallibly have rolled down the ravines opening into abysses which surrounded us on all sides, where he would have landed in shreds, torn by the sharp edges of the rocks before touching bottom; and those leading him could have thought themselves fortunate not to have been dragged along in his fall.

At last, we were at the top; there was nothing more but to rest an instant, gather strength, and come down again.

We found on the plateau neither spring nor glade where we could prepare our dinner; nevertheless we put down our knapsacks and unloaded the animals, then we made a frugal repast composed of crackers and chocolate bars, sharing two bottles of water which we had taken the precaution of bringing with us that morning. A curious phenomenon—on that mountain we shivered, while on the plain we were overwhelmed by the heat. During the short time that we stopped, we had to make a huge fire and put on our cloaks; even so, we were forced to cut short our halt in order not to freeze.

We went down the other side by a path that was fairly easy but winding and long.

We saw at our feet a magnificent plain which extended before us farther than the eye could reach; but in vain did we descend and then descend some more, still we did not reach it.[2]

1. Perlot's description of this part of the route is so general that it is difficult to state exactly where they were, but it does seem certain that they went over Pacheco Pass in the Coast Range and down Pacheco Canyon.

2. Perlot and his party were seeing the western slope of the San Joaquin Valley.

54

It was the torture of Tantalus, augmented by blistered feet.

When at last we arrived at the bottom, the sun had been down for more than an hour.

Most of us were at the end of our strength; three, among others, had such bruised feet that they could walk only with great difficulty. Marcan, a Norman from the environs of Cherbourg, stained the path with the blood which ran from his shoes. Now, nothing showed that we might be in the neighborhood of San Luis, the end of our stage as indicated on the itinerary. Perhaps we were still a league from it, perhaps two, perhaps three. It was pitch dark: impossible to consult the horizon, and we had perceived nothing during our descent of the mountain. Some were of the opinion that we should seek water and, if we found it, camp on the spot. It was easy to see from the nature of the terrain that there wouldn't be any water; however, we searched the vicinity to a distance of three or four hundred meters, but all was dry; no one dared, even going in pairs, to go any farther, and we had to give up finding water. Some wanted to camp anyway, but everyone was dying of thirst, our animals had not drunk all day, and it was quite impossible to let them pass the night without drinking. So it behooved us to continue on our way. What added even more to the fatigue and anxieties of the march was our ignorance of the path still to be covered.

Those who were most exhausted lightened their knapsacks; one threw away pants, another shirts, a third boots. There were two of them who threw away everything: their packs, their effects, and their reserves; still they had trouble keeping up.

After half an hour of this forced march, in order to prevent the laggards from lying down, I had to take the tail of the column and really force them to march; if they had stopped, at the end of ten minutes it would have been impossible for them to start walking again. Our situation, certainly, was not gay, but extremes meet and the swan, they say, sings at the moment of dying. So, there was one of us striking up the Marseillaise in a loud voice. At once, as each one doubtless felt the need of reacting against his overwhelming gloom, we began to repeat in chorus the revolutionary hymn. I do not affirm that its execution was irreproachable—it naturally felt the effects of the artists' fatigue; but the song resounding in the night did us good. It was a diversion, and then the ordinary effect of the hymn of "Rouget de Lisle" is to excite or reanimate courage. It had another, on this occasion, which we were not expecting. A dog who had heard us began to bay in the distance.

We were approaching San Luis!

Noah, seeing the dove return to the Ark with the olive branch in its bill, did not experience a greater joy than we felt in hearing the voice of that dog.

We then picked up courage completely, no one thought any more of going to bed, and even those whose feet were lacerated doubled their pace. At ten o'clock, we arrived at San Luis.

Everyone was of the opinion that it was too late to make supper; we drank

copiously and we contented ourselves, by way of supper, with a plain biscuit; after
which each one, having laid down, slept a deep sleep. The sentinel was not relieved
all night, which proves that he slept as deeply as those whom he was charged to
guard, for otherwise he would not have missed awakening the one who was
supposed to replace him.

San Luis, a kind of oasis of five to six hectares, about a league from the foot of
the mountain, was composed quite simply of a one-room house, with a garden and a
roof fifty meters long, supported by posts. This roof served, in the hunting season,
as a stable for the wild horses which each year the Mexicans lassoed on the plain of
the Tulares, which begins at San Luis and extends to the lake which gives it its
name.[3] This plain, through which winds the San Joaquin, separates the California
mountains, which we had just crossed, from the Sierra Nevada, to whose base we
were going; it is a hundred and twenty miles from south to north, and forty to fifty
from west to east.

Of the five or six Mexicans who formed the population of San Luis, only two
were there on our arrival. Seated under a live oak, they were playing cards by the
light of a fire on which, I think, they had cooked their supper. They played to see
who would drink from a bottle which they had near them, and as they were winning
by turns, they had both almost lost their reason. It was impossible for us to draw
anything from them except the water of their well, and that is why we judged that
the best thing for us to do was to go to bed and deliver ourselves to a healing sleep of
which we were in great need.

It was late the next day when we got up, that is, when we unrolled our blankets
to get out of them.

As soon as I was up, I went to see for myself that our animals were still there, for
the sentinel knew nothing; then I returned to the Mexicans, in order, if possible, to
obtain some fresh meat from them for our breakfast. I found them breakfasting,
themselves; they each had a turnip which they had peeled in the manner of a radish,
then plunged it into a tin box containing a mixture of salt and pepper, and bit it
savagely between two mouthfuls of a tortilla which they had just cooked.—Tortilla
means omelette, but this omelette is nothing but water and flour made into a hard
paste which one pats between the hands, then cooks either on a cookstove or, more
simply, on the coals.—After the turnip, which was doubtless intended to whet the
appetite, they each ate an enormous beefsteak, cooked by the heat of the fire in a
process which was quite new to me, which I will describe: in front of the fire, they
had each stuck a strong switch, four feet long, in the ground, and the end of the stick
was run through a piece of meat, with the fat part on top.

From time to time they turned the switch, holding it much inclined toward the
coals, and so the meat roasted perfectly. I disclosed to them the object of my
mission, and I had some trouble in making myself understood. Finally one of them

---

3. Perlot's "San Luis" is most likely a reference to the San Luis Gonzaga (Merced County) land grant
mentioned in chap. 4, n. 4 (Gudde, *California Place Names*, p. 289).

gets up, comes to show me half a beef hanging from an oak, gives me an enormous knife, and signs to me to cut what I want. I hasten to profit from the authorization. After having cut off ten or twelve livres of meat from various parts of the beast, I ask, putting my hand in my pocket: Quanto? (how much?) He replies: Nada (nothing). I say gracias, as at Pacheco, salute, and return to the others. My companions, ravished by the sight of this appetizing meat, receive me with enthusiasm, and dream of nothing but breakfast. Coffee being ready, there is nothing more to do but cook the meat.

"Messieurs," said I, "in this country, this is how beefsteak is cooked," and I set myself to roasting a piece of meat as I had just seen it done by the Mexicans. Several imitated me and found the process good. We made an excellent repast without other seasoning than a robust appetite sharpened by several days of walking.

We had slept well and eaten well; however, no one spoke of leaving. Finally Béranger said: "Gentlemen, it is late, let's leave, I'm going to look for the animals." No one replied. Three or four of our companions were still occupied in dressing their aching feet. When Béranger returned shortly afterward with the donkey and the mule, only four made a start on the job of loading them; the others seemed to raise the question not of when we would leave but if we would leave. We tied the animals to a tree and we held council. About half were disposed to continue the course, the others wanted to retrace the path and return to Monterey, following the example, they said, of the Provençaux. These had not rejoined us because without any doubt one of their animals, perhaps both, had rolled into a ravine while climbing the California mountains, and so, deprived of beasts of burden, perhaps of victuals, they had retraced their route, at least as far as San Juan. In the middle of the discussion, suddenly Marcan leaps upon Messent's gun and tries to kill himself. We jump and one of us arrives in time to stop his arm at the moment when he is about to accomplish his fatal design. "Ah!" says the unhappy Marcan, "why prevent me from putting an end to my sufferings? I can neither go forward nor retrace my steps, for it is impossible for me to walk; either kill me or let me kill myself, that would be better than abandoning me here." And he dissolves in tears.

This scene, although impressing us vividly and sadly, seemed to renew some energy in the sick ones, who accused Marcan of pusillanimity. Each one made it a point of honor to appear healthy and active; there was no longer any question of turning back. However, as Marcan could renew his desperate attempt, as his despondency could even become contagious, we took precautions; those who had pistols carried them, and Messent and Ragache each took his gun; then, in hiding, they removed the caps. We were all looking each other in the face without daring to express any kind of an idea, when Messent, coming close to me, said in a low voice: "Well, Perlot, what shall we do?" I replied out loud: "What shall we do! Stay, of course! Ten we are, ten we must remain. Marcan does us an injury by believing us capable of abandoning a companion. That would be a low thing to do. Tomorrow, perhaps, he will be in a condition to walk, then we will leave; if not, we will wait. If anyone is not of this opinion, let him go; as for me, I stay." "Me too," said one, "me too," said another, and so with all nine; Marcan didn't say anything more. "If the supplies are giving out," I added, "instead of abandoning anyone whatsoever, let's abandon the baggage, and carry only the supplies. In case of need, we can put a sick man on the mule, another on the donkey, and so reach the San Joaquin where, according to the itinerary, we can find a place to procure supplies and clothes." That said, everyone seemed content to stay. We were going to unload the animals who, if they had understood me, would have been just as content as our invalids with the resolution taken, when I saw one of our two Mexicans, mounted on a mule and leading another by a rope; he arrives at the cabin, addresses some words to his comrade, then says to him: *A Dios* (goodbye), and leaves at a trot on the road which we should follow.

An idea comes to me at once; I stop the Mexican in passing and ask him where he is going; he does not understand me and wants to go away. I hold the mule. I open my dictionary and find, opposite the French words: *où allez-vous* (where are you going?) these Spanish words: *A donde va?* He then replies to me: San Joaquin. Without saying anything more and without letting go the bridle, I tell Messent to bring Marcan's blankets; we fold them three times, we tie them with the rope which served to make his pack, then I tell him: "Mount, the Mexican will lead you to the San Joaquin and we will rejoin you there tomorrow." He makes some difficulty at first, but Messent, his countryman (they were both from the environs of Cherbourg), forces him to mount. Once on the mule, we put somebody else's knapsack on the crupper, for he had thrown his away the day before; the sack we gave him contained supplies in case of need. This done, turning toward the Mexican, who probably had ended by understanding what we wanted, I say to him, indicating the horizon with my finger: San Joaquin. He replies: *Está bueno* (Good enough), pricks his mule with the spur, and so they leave. I say with the spur, because the Mexican horseman has but one, attached to the left foot, and its rowel is not less than three inches in diameter, with iron trinkets on each side, which weigh, I think, a half-pound.

With Marcan gone, I tear a pocket-handkerchief to rags, I help to treat the feet of the injured, then we agree to set sail (if I may be pardoned this maritime reminiscence) for the Round Tent (*Tente Ronde*).

We had fifteen miles to cover and it was eleven o'clock; no one thought of dinner, we had dined so well and so late! and then what emotions!

So there we were en route, hobbling along; but fortunately we were on a plain and had only to lift one foot after another; moreover, we had lightened our packs by augmenting the load of our mule, and the sick ones had nothing to carry, but they had the job of leading the animals on a rope. In spite of these wise arrangements, we were obliged to walk slowly so that everybody could follow.

After leaving San Luis, the road forked at every step. In these emergencies, my compass was a precious help to us, for it showed me the direction to follow and the road we had to choose, a fairly difficult thing because in the plains paths separate and rejoin at very narrow angles.

About one o'clock, we made a halt to prepare for dinner, without waiting until we were near a spring or a stream, knowing well that we had no chance of encountering one on the plain. We contented ourselves with the two essential bottles of water, to wash down our few biscuits. The meal ended, we set out on our way immediately in order to be surer of reaching the Round Tent before night, for we could not dream of spending it anywhere else, considering the lack of water. Hardly were we on the march, when what was our surprise to see before us, at some distance, a river which could only be the San Joaquin! One more hour of walking and we would reach it.

Now, from San Luis we had fifteen miles to cover to go to the Round Tent, and from the Round Tent, fifteen miles to reach the San Joaquin, total thirty miles (nearly eleven leagues). How explain, according to this, that after barely three hours at a very slow walk, the San Joaquin was in front of us? And the Round Tent, which we had not seen! The most general opinion was that we were led astray, that the itinerary was inaccurate, or else that my compass was no good. Some expressed the opinion that we must return to San Luis, in order to take the right road there, if we did not want to expose ourselves to getting lost on the plain and dying there.

Must we then retrace this road, so painfully traversed! was our effort pure loss? As, behind us, the peak of San Luis was still in sight on the horizon I again consulted my compass and, having assured myself that the way we were following was right, I insisted that we continue the march. It was so decided after a long debate. After having gone a little way, we saw before us, grazing on the plain, a herd of wild horses. They let us approach within about five hundred paces, then all together left at a gallop; there were two or three hundred. That was a curious spectacle made by these proud and beautiful animals flying before us, spurred by the love of liberty and the instinct, or perhaps experience, which denounces man to them as an enemy. After having run the distance of four hundred paces, all stopped at the same time as by a command and turned toward us, heads high, manes and tails streaming; then, after a few moments, they made a half-turn and renewed their wild race, disappearing in the depths of the plain.

The encounter with these horses convinced the least pessimistic that we were off the right road, for it indicated, it seemed, that we were caught in an unfrequented part of the plain. Consequently, it was agreed that we would go to the river to camp, then the next day we would return to San Luis, which the horizon hid behind us. Impatient to arrive beside this water where we were going to rest and quench our thirst, we marched bravely, and even the invalids had become active again; however, two hours after we had encountered the wild horses and while still walking at an accelerated pace, we noticed that this San Joaquin, which we had before us, was still at the same distance, although some of us claimed that we were approaching it. In short, night was coming, it was five o'clock and the river was still far; with fatigue and uncertainty helping, discouragement was beginning to spread among us, when suddenly, we heard a gun-shot some distance ahead of us. A cry of joy and hope escaped our breasts! We were not then alone on this immense plain, we were going to find someone who would tell us where we were and would set us on the right road, if we had strayed. A half hour later we saw before us the Round Tent.

Imagine our stupefaction!

It was beyond understanding and, in fact, we didn't understand it at all.

When we reached the Round Tent, the German who occupied it gave us the explanation of the enigma, through the medium of Schmutz, one of us, who was Swiss. This river which we had seen all afternoon and which we had vainly pursued, was simply the effect of the phenomenon known by the name of mirage; it was pure illusion, there was not the least sign of a river in this arid plain. We were left quite sheepish by this revelation. Some, not wanting to believe the word of the German, persisted in believing in the river. As for me, if I, like the others, had been the dupe of the mirage and if I had believed like them that the itinerary had misled us, I had at least had confidence in the compass. The consul, in tracing the route, might have been mistaken on the length of the road to travel before reaching the San Joaquin, but I could not admit that he was mistaken concerning the direction to follow; that is why I had persisted in believing and in saying that we were on the right road.

The Round Tent was, in fact, a round tent and nothing more. It was the home of a German who spoke Spanish, a little English, and also a few words of French. His wife was Mexican; they had no children. Our German raised a few sheep and hunted wild horses: that was his entire occupation. The water he needed was supplied by a well, dug by he didn't know whom, which was not less than two hundred feet in depth; finding it abandoned, he had deepened it by a few feet and found water in it at all times. He informed us that Marcan and the Mexican had come to drink at his well, at one o'clock in the afternoon; he supposed they had arrived at the San Joaquin. One can believe without difficulty that we supped with good appetite and slept a deep sleep.

The next day, early, we again set off on our way. The cripples walked better; the resident of the Round Tent had given them, the night before, a kind of grease with which they had rubbed their feet and they felt better for it.

We walked slowly all the same, to avoid fatigue. The weather was clear and warm, not a cloud impaired the clarity of the air, and the view stretched unbroken as far as the limit where sky and earth seemed to unite and mingle. It was the first time I found myself on a plain where the earth's curvature alone ended the view; it gave us the same effect as when we found ourselves on the open sea in a moment of calm. This limitless plain was covered only by a thin grass which the ardor of the sun had already almost dried out. No bush, no tree, not even a mole-hill where the eye could rest. Here and there, sand covered great surfaces where the print of no step was visible, perhaps because the wind, in lifting this sand, ceaselessly leveled the ground; when we reached these sandy surfaces, walking was painful and slow, and we had to maintain the closest attention to keep from losing our way, for very often we had to walk thirty or forty minutes before reaching any kind of turf where we could recover a trace of the path. If, by misfortune, we had lost our direction on this uniform surface, it would have been impossible for us to turn around and retrace our steps, whose imprint was effaced behind us.

To guard against this danger, at the first sandy places we encountered, I had established the direction by means of the compass; but since the Round Tent had disappeared over the horizon, whose uniform line offered not the slightest land-mark, we had to stop too often, for fear of having lost the direction. We had to fall back on another method, which was to take our land-mark from ourselves.

Placing ourselves, like so many stakes, at 50 paces from one another on the same line, we set off on the march; I took the lead and turned around every two or three minutes to align myself on the procession, which only had to follow me. Thus we succeeded in maintaining the original direction all day.

In short, we carried it off, and about one o'clock in the afternoon the banks of the San Joaquin, covered with alders, willows, and aspens, appeared on the horizon.

It was not the mirage, this time!

At the sight of this ribbon of verdure, our joy was great; we forgot our fatigues and the hard trials of the day, our legs seemed less feeble to us, and our packs less heavy.

As we progressed, the grass became less sparse under our feet; the path, more and more visible, was better marked, thus assuring us that we were on the right road; small birds, which had disappeared since our departure from San Luis, began to show themselves again. The eagle and the bare-necked vulture were, with the ring-dove and the swallow, the sole representatives of the winged tribe which we had met while we were crossing the plain. Now, life reappeared in all its forms and soon surrounded us on all sides.

The trees bordering the river became noticeably bigger.

Soon, above their tops, we perceived an object floating in the sky at the will of the wind. It was the red and white striped flag of the United States, raised to the top of a very tall pole. It announced to those who could see it that the pioneers of civilization had come this far.

By four o'clock, we were seated on the bank of the river, "mug" in hand, about to quench our thirst—the mug is a tin cup with a handle which we carry hung from our belt.

The San Joaquin is a beautiful river which, on our arrival, could have been a hundred meters wide by five or six deep, in which was flowing a yellow-white water, full to the banks and almost rapid. It deposited on its banks a very fine sand composed of copper mica and of emery reduced to powder. It carried mosses, grasses, animals, branches of trees and even whole trees, torn, doubtless, from its sides which, according to the ferryman, were two or three meters above low water, that is to say, in September. When the water was rising, this flotsam became the terror of this good man who, once already, had seen it carry away both his raft and his cable. So, since then, he had raised by three meters the point where the one was attached and had guarded the other more carefully. The water, taken in a bucket, appeared clear and beautiful but with time deposited a fine, impalpable mud, and I think it was this silt which gave it its color. Fish of all kinds abounded and formed the wealth of the river, as the swan, the goose, the duck and other palmipeds formed its ornament.

We were at Woods' Ferry; there we found Marcan well rested and half cured. He had arrived the day before toward evening. The Mexican, after having received his thanks, had that same evening continued on his way by following the banks of the river. Marcan, not knowing which direction to take, had stayed and was waiting for us.

At Woods' Ferry, there was only one house, that of the ferryman, who transported travelers from one bank to the other on his raft; it was made of boards.[4] There were three Germans there who had no other support than this business. A rope or cable went from one bank to the other of the river which was, as I have said, about a hundred meters wide at this place; they asked fifty sous per person and five francs per animal. Seeing greener grass on the other side, out of consideration for our animals we crossed the same evening and went to camp for the night in a little wood, not far from the bank. Our Swiss, knowing German, had an interview with the boatman, entered his house, and came back to us carrying a whole quarter of beef on his shoulder. It is true that this meat was not of the first freshness, but tired and hungry men are not difficult, and we gave him a good welcome. No sooner was our meal ended than we went to bed; half an hour later everyone was sleeping profoundly, most of us with pipe in mouth, so much had fatigue overcome us. I think that I would never have slept better in my life had it not been for a pain in the loins which, at the least movement, made me suffer cruelly. While we were crossing the sandy parts of the plain, I had had, as I have said, to march at the head, and as I was obliged to turn back at every moment to be sure that we were walking in a straight line, I had acquired this pain, which I had noticed only on our arrival.

Next morning, everyone turned over in his blanket but nobody got up, except Marcan, who had gone to look for dead wood and was making a fire to prepare breakfast while waiting for the others to get up. Seeing that nobody was budging, I started making coffee and cooking as many beefsteaks as we were men, enormous beefsteaks of which one alone would have been enough to make a meal for three people. I didn't stint the meat, seeing that we intended to leave behind what remained, for fear that it would not be edible at noon. You will understand that, harassed as we were, we were not eager to overload ourselves needlessly.

4. Woods' Ferry does not appear on any of the early maps in Carl I. Wheat, *Maps of the California Gold Region, 1848–1857* (San Francisco: Grabhorn Press, 1942). Woods' Ferry should not be confused with Woods' Creek or Woods' Crossing on the upper Tuolumne, where the Reverend James Woods first discovered gold in the Southern Mines region in 1848.

However, at the smell of the broiling meat, each one opens an eye, stretches, yawns several times, and at last gets up. Not one walked in a straight line; one leaned to the right, the other to the left; all suffered, some in the foot, some in the leg; another hunched an aching shoulder. As for me, it was in the loins that I was taken, but only slightly; the pain had partly disappeared with the restorative sleep of the night.

Most of us thought that we should stay there twenty-four hours, claiming that a day of rest would restore our strength so that next day we would make twice the distance. Nevertheless, upon the observation being made that we had only eight more miles to go before reaching the last stop indicated on our itinerary, it was decided that we would leave.

In consequence, about eleven o'clock, after having had a second breakfast, we set off on our way; but first Schmutz, the Swiss, went to the quarter of beef, took from it what still seemed good to him, and put a piece in each of our knapsacks for us.

The country which we were crossing was no longer the Tulare plain, but it was another plain, raised about forty feet higher than that which we had just left. It did not have the desolate aspect of that one; the eye rested now on a little wood or on a clump of bushes, now on a slight hillock; at other times, it presented the appearance of a prairie planted with fruit trees with tall trunks; but these fruit trees, when one approached, were enormous oaks, distant from one another by thirty to forty meters.

Game abounded there; at each step we saw fleeing or flying before us a rabbit, a partridge, or a quail; this last wears an aigrette on its head. It was there that we saw our first deer and our first elk, which we took for a stag; we had somehow surprised him in a fold of the ground; he looked at us with an astonished air, then, slowly making a half-turn and lowering to his shoulders his inordinately long and thick horns, he gained the neighboring wood in a few bounds.

As we had only eight miles to cover, we did it in one stage. At three o'clock in the afternoon we were crossing the river La Merced in a sort of ferryboat, and we were arriving at Griffine.[5]

---

5. I have been unable to locate "Griffine" on available maps, but Perlot's "Itineraire" suggests that Griffine, which he described as being at the confluence of the San Joaquin and Merced rivers, may have referred to Stevinson, which was close by,. Gudde states that James J. Stevinson acquired land on the lower Merced in August 1852, but it seems likely that he was there in 1851 when Perlot passed by. See Perlot, "Itineraire," Bancroft Library MS, and Gudde, *California Place Names*, p. 321.

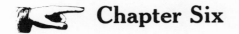 **Chapter Six**

Following the Merced

Griffine was the extreme point of the itinerary which the French vice-consul had given me. At Monterey, in fact, nothing more was known beyond that, and we were hardly half-way to the end of our journey. We had before us an unknown land, unexplored. We knew, it is true, that some miners had worked the previous autumn on the tributary streams of the Merced; we thus had a chance of meeting some, supposing that they were still there; we knew, moreover, that the road coming from San Francisco, from Sacramento and from Stockton crossed the Merced at Horse-Shoe Bend (courbe en fer-à-cheval); if we did not know how far we were from this place, I hoped, at least, that we could find someone there and could gather information. But that was all.

We knew nothing, from there on, of the route to follow, not even the general direction; the compass could no longer guide us; it could serve us no more unless we had to retrace our path.

Our guiding thread in these obscurities was the Merced, on whose banks we found ourselves, a league from its confluence with the San Joaquin.

This river, at Griffine, had the power of the Meuse at Sedan; therefore it came from far away. Its banks, similar enough to those of the San Joaquin, were covered with the same deposit. I said to myself that, in order to grind a sand as fine as that, its rapids must be far from us, which suggested a great plain to cross before arriving at the mountains where the river has its source. Then, having reached the foot of these mountains, could one cross them? And if we lost our guiding thread, that is, if we could no longer follow the Merced, what direction should we take? Game abounded; so we wouldn't be hungry, at least as long as the three livres of powder and the twenty livres of lead we were carrying lasted. But the proverb, "Where there are hares, there are dogs to chase them," returned to me in memory and worried me. In a wild country it should be translated thus: "Where game is found, there also are found the carnivores who live on it." We must therefore expect in these places to encounter bears, panthers, coyotes, and *tutti quanti;* What welcome would they give us?

I was asking myself all these questions while my companions, after having unloaded the animals and having put them out to graze, were lying on the grass, without seeming otherwise preoccupied with our situation and the means of getting out of it. They were at the end of their strength, anyway; out of the ten we numbered, there perhaps were not four who would have been in a state to go any farther if it had been necessary to leave immediately. I was about to regret having set off with such companions; I was wondering if we would all arrive at Mariposa; but I was silently promising myself that I would never leave one of them behind, as long as he was alive. After all, the die was cast, we had to follow the enterprise until the end, and it was useless to stop any longer to reflect on it.

Being, thank God, one of the most able of the band, I resolved to appear also the most assured, and to affect, on all occasions, an absolute confidence in the final success of our enterprise: it was the sole means of restoring the courage of my companions, whose morale as well as whose strength was obviously weakening.

We had decided to set up our tent in that place, and to stay there two or three days on the pretext of waiting for the Provençaux, left behind since San Juan. The true motive of our decision was the need we felt to get some rest and also to collect ourselves, before venturing into a country where the simple track of the barefooted Indian was our sole guide.

Griffine, like all the localities in these uninhabited regions, was composed of a single house of superimposed tree trunks. As yet it was not finished. While waiting till it was, the proprietor slept with wife and children under a tent made of four bedspreads sewn together; he was the man who kept the ferry. We could obtain nothing from him in the way of provisions because he was no better supplied than we.

It was impossible for us to use the meat we had brought; it was too tainted, even for us. We cooked what potatoes we had left, and ate them spread with grease. It was a treat in this desert, but it was the last of the kind, for we were at the end of our supplies although we had covered only half the distance, which did not prevent us, however, from going to bed cheerful and lighthearted.

Next day, those who were the first to be hungry, got up to prepare breakfast; at ten o'clock there were some who were still breakfasting. When one had eaten, he went back to bed; it was the same at the other meals, and, in fact, we needed the rest.

The second day, finding myself sufficiently rested, I took Messent's gun and went out to hunt. During the night it had seemed to me that I heard ducks passing and at first the idea came to me of following the banks of the river, but it was impossible for me to come near; it was boxed between two wooded bluffs which made it inaccessible. So I set off across the plain and it was a good thing I did: at every step, I started quail, partridge, rabbit, or hare, so that well before noon I returned with one hare, three rabbits, one red partridge, and six quail; these quail were in a covey near a little pond of muddy water and I had killed four of them with a single shot.

I had made myself a gamebag from the empty potato sack: I had attached the end of a rope to one of the bottom corners, the other end served to close the opening; then I had passed my head and arm between the rope and the sack. All this constituted a gamebag that was hardly elegant, no doubt, but . . . after all, it was full of game, that was the point. I amazed my companions when I returned; but I was amazed, in my turn, when I saw, spread on the floor of the tent, I don't know how many fish of all sizes and kinds.

Bigot and Viot, supplied with a box of fishhooks bought at Monterey, and with a ball of string, had gone angling, using for bait the meat which we had had to throw away. It seemed that the fish were less difficult than we, for they bit heartily at this lure and were taken in quantity. By noon, our fishermen had a good thirty livres of them; we made a copious and excellent dinner of them, reserving the game for the evening.

We were astonished not to see the Provençaux arrive. Had they retraced their steps or had they lost their way? In any case, we could not wait for them any longer, because our supplies were becoming exhausted; we had only a little biscuit and a little grease left, and we had not provided enough flour and beans. It is true that we were entering a region where game was plentiful, but nothing but meat—and especially game—to eat, was not a hygienic régime, as proved by the sort of dysentery by which most of us had been attacked for the last three days.

We resolved, nevertheless, to remain yet one more day and to leave on the next, whether the Provençaux had arrived or not.

While waiting for that next day, the fishermen returned to their fishing and the hunters to the hunt.

I left accompanied by Ragache. We covered the same territory where I had hunted the day before, keeping about five hundred meters apart; around nine o'clock, as I was skirting a hillock on one side while Ragache was skirting it on the other, I heard a shot, soon followed by a second. I headed for the side they came from to rejoin my companion, and as I was going through a wood of several hectares, I started a bird which I took at first for a hazel-hen; I succeeded in shooting that one, then a second, then a third; this last had a bare throat like a turkey—so it wasn't a hazel-hen! the hazel-hen is not made like this. Never having seen a bird of this kind, I wisely concluded that I should abstain, until more fully informed, from giving it any name whatever. Shortly afterward, I left the wood and, not seeing Ragache any more, I continued to hunt on the plain; this time I shot, besides some rabbits, an enormous hare which weighed at least fourteen livres; he was so large that I could not get him into my gamebag. I had to tie his feet with the string of my powderflask, then hang him from my neck. Thus harnessed, I returned triumphantly to the camp, where Ragache had preceded me by two hours. He had brought back two rabbits and had killed an enormous snake which, he said, had prevented him from coming to rejoin me because he had feared encountering others. He claimed also to have seen a wolf or something like it; having seen the animal enter the wood and having heard soon afterward my two shots coming fairly close together, he had announced to these gentlemen that I had killed the wolf. Now, seeing me from afar returning with an animal on my back, they believed that I was bringing back the wolf. Ragache, judging by the color of the beast, claimed that it really was that animal which he had seen. How great was everyone's surprise, especially Ragache's, to ascertain that this alleged wolf was a simple hare! As for my birds, Schmutz claimed to recognize them as grouse, and I learned later that he was right.

The fishing having been equally fruitful, we ate only fish for dinner. For the evening meal, Duléry offered to make us an excellent ragout from the enormous hare, which would form, all by itself, the menu for supper.

Although our Vatel lacked many of the things necessary to prepare a hare properly, this stew smelled good and we prepared to regale ourselves with it; about six o'clock, the usual hour of supper, Duléry begs his guests to wait, as the ragout is still a little tough. We build up the fire, we relight our pipes; the alluring prospect of this succulent dish makes us wait patiently. Thirty minutes later, we taste the stew again; it is still a little tough; we rebuild the fire, and at the end of thirty minutes, already longer than the preceding ones, we taste it yet again; the devil! but it is still tough! However, we have patience, although our appetite begins to make the time seem extremely long. We make, this time, a hellish fire, then thirty minutes afterward, everyone says: "It's late; here it is, coming time to go to bed; serve the stew." We serve it, but everyone can gnaw as he will, no one can succeed in detaching a fiber. I think it was tougher than when we put it on the fire. We had to content ourselves with drinking the sauce, which, however, was excellent; if we had been stubborn about wanting to cook that damned hare, I think we would not have supped that day. Still, it had an excuse: judging by the size of the bones, it was at least eight to ten years old, and a hare, at that age, has the right to be leathery.

Later, taught by this experience, I killed small hares in preference to the big ones; those, at least, could be cooked and eaten.

It was late when we had finished supper. Seeing nothing of the Provençaux, we decided to break up camp early the next day; that settled, there remained the question of knowing which bank we should follow.

The Merced was too strong to hope to be able to cross it elsewhere without danger. Here we had the ferry, consequently our choice of sides; once on the way, we could not count on a bridge or ford before reaching Horse-Shoe Bend, located at an unknown distance. The choice of bank on our departure was therefore important; but we lacked sufficient data to resolve this problem, and so, for the sole reason that those who had discovered Mariposa had taken the east side of the Merced, that is, the left bank, we took it too, promising ourselves, in any case, not to go too far from the river, to be sure that somewhere we would cross the road from the Merced to Mariposa, which, according to the consul, was ten or twelve leagues long. The next day, we reloaded our animals, who also were rested, and we left, following the plan of march agreed upon the night before.

To give yourself an idea of the trip we were undertaking, you need only imagine that the Meuse crosses uninhabited lands and that we follow it, beginning at Maastricht, as far as the Vosges. The comparison would be even more exact if the summits of the Vosges were covered with eternal snows.

From Griffine, the path that followed the river was faintly traced, because since the preceding year the Indians seldom passed that way.

In fact, the Mexican miners had invaded the mountains, and the Indians, who did not understand why people came to trouble them in their retreat, had not received them well.[1] Hostilities had followed, in consequence of which they had been crowded back beyond the first chain of mountains, which borders the plain we were crossing. The way was easy enough, but excessively winding; it followed exactly the meanderings of the river and left it only to return soon, so that, if we walked without difficulty, we advanced little. Besides, we dared not leave the track we were following, for fear of throwing ourselves into some impassible section which would have obliged us to retrace our steps. This track, faint as it was, was at least an indication that one could get through; so it still was better to follow all its detours than to risk the adventures of the straight line.

We encountered, this first day, a great number of wild animals: deer, elk, coyotes, gray squirrels, hares, rabbits, partridges, quail, grouse, brown pheasants; but these weak or inoffensive animals were not the only guests of the woods, thickets, and brambles through which we were traveling. In approaching a sort of ford in the river, we saw on the sand the paw-print of a bear and that of another animal who could be a lion, a tiger, or at the very least a panther. All that we could determine was that it had retractile claws like a cat and that its footprint was as big as that of an ox. We stayed a long time contemplating these tracks, but each one kept his impressions to himself; he feared that, by communicating them, he would spread the terror which seized him. We started off on our way again at last, but walking slowly and with caution, for the tracks which caused us so much apprehension were directed, on leaving the river, toward the path we were following; in pushing our pace too much, we risked overtaking the animal, and if that happened, how would we get ourselves out of that bad spot? We had, at all events, loaded our two double-barreled guns with ball, and Ragache and I, who were their bearers, were walking at the head, having, in order to be more agile, put our knapsacks on the mule's back. Our anxiety lasted until, leaving the irregular, brush-covered terrain where we were entangled, we found ourselves on a sort of little plain where only dry grass covered the earth. It was all of three o'clock when we reached the end of this plain. There, the terrain became irregular again and more or less wooded, and the two banks of the Merced rose steeply once more. However, the path which wound over the plateau being fairly easy, we traveled quickly.

Having arrived, well before evening, beside a stream which flowed into the Merced, we resolved to camp there for the night in order to have until the next day to make a decision as to the direction which we should take. We had, in fact, to choose between two paths, that which climbed the Merced and another which climbed its tributary.

At the moment we were crawling into bed, that is to say, into our blankets; the one who was on guard made the observation that he had never had a gun in his

1. There had been difficulties between the local Indian bands and Mexican miners on the Mariposa, but it is possible that Perlot was referring to the more recent troubles between the Indians and American miners in 1850–51 that took on the exaggerated title: the Mariposa War. See introduction to part IV.

hands and that he probably could not shoot if the need arose. It was agreed that I would go to bed not far from his post so that he could wake me if he saw or heard anything unusual.

The tracks which we had seen during the day did not cease to disturb us, and we expected to receive some annoying visit before morning. We took the precaution, before going to bed, of going after our animals and of tying them to a bush within reach of the place where Ragache and I were spending the night. For barely an hour had I been tasting the sweets of sleep when the sentinel came to rouse me; he saw nothing, but he had heard something; I listen, hear nothing, and go back to bed. Hardly asleep again, I am awakened anew—this time he saw an animal approaching; this time, like the first, I listen and hear nothing. Meanwhile, another's turn has come to stand guard; as that one is able to shoot a gun, I give him the weapon I had, then go back to bed, hoping at last to sleep in peace. But at the end of an hour, a detonation is heard. In a moment, the entire camp, jolted awake, is up, they all look at each other in fright, not knowing what to do. The first moment of surprise over, we notice that the most surprised of all is the watchman. He had good reason! his gun, to hear him, had gone off without being touched; what is more likely is that he had sat down with the loaded gun beside him, then had become a little drowsy, and on waking up had involuntarily pressed the trigger. After all, if he had killed neither bear nor panther, at least he had not killed any of his comrades, and that was lucky!

When day had come and after we had breakfasted, we decided to continue to follow the river, although the path was hardly visible, and off we went. After some time—it was about ten o'clock—the path disappeared; as, on the other hand, we were no longer on a plateau, but on a steep slope whose foot plunged into the water, we had to leave the river and try to climb to the summit of this declivity, in order to determine the direction of our route by means of the heights. We had chosen for this ascent a place where the hillside was less steep and the wood not so thick; only, from time to time, we had to climb for fifteen or twenty minutes over gravel or little, round, rolling stones, which made walking extremely laborious, especially for our animals, so that they had a great deal of trouble to keep from falling. However, toward noon, we attained the summit of the height, where we found again a sort of path, very probably the same which left the river at the confluence of the stream where we had passed the night and which we should have taken. We followed it the rest of the day and it brought us back, by a gentle slope, to the river.

During this afternoon, we encountered several snakes, among others a rattlesnake; it was three and a half feet long and, in its greatest thickness, measured nearly a foot around. I could then verify for the first time that it is not always possible to beat these dangerous animals to death with a stick; this one, each time that someone wanted to approach him, coiled up to put himself on the defense, then unfolded and rewound himself with such speed that in the wink of an eye he was between our legs or five paces beyond, and at each of his movements his tail made that noise, similar enough to the sound of a not very loud alarm clock, which has given him his name. As he barred our path, and as he seemed little disposed to go away, Ragache broke his head with a shot; then he rolled up like a ball, while hissing almost like a cat; then, his movements became slower, but he floundered for a long time, and we left him while he was still moving.

When we arrived on the plateau, we could assure ourselves that the path did not cross the river. It was a terrain of alluvium, forming a meadow, and grass was plentiful; to let our animals profit from it, we resolved to spend the night there.

A surprise of a new kind awaited us there. On going to get water at the river for our supper, we found some prints of a man's naked foot; the sand bordering the river was covered with them, and these tracks seemed quite fresh.

The Indians, those men of Nature so dreaded by civilized man, could therefore not be far, but nevertheless, during the day, no indication had made us suspect their presence; that threw us into a great perplexity. The encounter with the tracks of a bear, a panther, or no matter what wild beast, could doubtless cause us some disquiet, but, after all, we knew what had to be done to defend ourselves from them and our measures were taken in case of attack; but man is for man a more redoubtable enemy than the bear, than the panther, and even than the rattlesnake; at the sight of these traces which revealed to us the presence of our fellow-man we were left speechless, not knowing what to do or what to resolve.

Evening arrived while we were still contemplating these prints and asking ourseves how we could face the danger by which we were menaced. At the end, however, we recalled that we should eat supper, whatever might be the number of the Indians by whom we believed ourselves surrounded. So we made supper and we ate, then we deliberated.

We decided first that we were too near the wood and too far from the place where our animals were grazing, and that we must move our camp to the open meadow and near the banks of the river, which was done. In this way we were protected on one side by the river, while on all the other sides the Indians could attack us only in the open, for we were at least two hundred meters from the bushes where they doubtless were hiding. We placed two guards in such a way as to put the camp at the apex of the triangle of which they would be the two other angles, each of them being able to see at the same time what happened on the side of the river and on the side of the other guard.

In case the enemy should come in too great a number, the guards, after giving the alarm, were to retreat to the camp while bringing in the animals, and we would defend ourselves as best we might. If resistance became impossible, everyone should grab the baggage, throw everything in the river, including the animals, then throw himself in (helping himself to swim, if possible, with both baggage and animals), and try to rejoin the others a kilometer downstream, where they would fish out what they could. Having made these wise strategic preparations and having reconnoitred the posts assigned to the guards, who would report to them only when night had fallen to hide their approach, we went to bed; but I believe that few among us slept.

The night passed tranquilly until about three o'clock in the morning. A cry, similar to that of a lost dog and seeming to come from fairly far away, was then heard in the wood; this cry was like the signal for a frightful uproar with which the wood echoed all around us. One would have believed that we were in the midst of a hundred dogs fighting among themselves. In an instant we all were up; even our animals, lying down for some time, got on their feet. Our two guards, not knowing what was happening, had judged it prudent to retreat to the camp. Neither of them had seen anything.

The noise ceased all at once. Before we had had time to recover from our surprise, the lost dog was heard again and again the uproar began, but a little farther away, on the hill which bordered the river; from the moment that the noise departed, whatever was its cause, there was no more danger; on this conclusion, the guards returned to their posts and the others to their blankets.

We knew later that this uproar was produced by some coyotes and that their presence was a sure sign that the Indians were not prowling around us. But when one does not know, one is afraid of everything: our emotion was excusable.

Hardly had day begun to break when the guards came to make breakfast, so that we were able to leave early, congratulating ourselves on having so happily escaped from a great danger. As we still feared a surprise from the Indians, Ragache, with a gun, walked a hundred paces in advance of the body of the army and I, with the other gun, I walked a hundred paces to the rear. We made our way without difficulty across valleys that weren't very deep and mountains that weren't very high.

We were observing a profound silence and hastening our steps; fear seemed to have restored strength to our legs; the very ones who, the day before, were complaining of fatigue and proposing to set up the tent for a day or two, today were quiet and walked at the same pace as the others.

As we had made a very early start, we decided to call a halt at noon, a thing that had not happened to us since Griffine; but fatigue was beginning to make itself felt again and the day seemed long to us.

About eleven o'clock, then, finding ourselves again on the river at the confluence of a large stream, we put down our loads, then prepared dinner. The provisions were disappearing, the knapsacks were becoming light.

We would have to reach the end of the trip soon or else decrease our rations, and already we had to stop eating while we were still hungry. How were we going to manage to walk all day with an insufficient ration? We still had some biscuit, some beans, flour, chocolate, coffee, pepper and salt, but all those in small quantity; and no more grease, no more meat, no more sugar; it was time to arrive. It was decided that beginning with this evening we would camp early and that those who were in a state to hunt would try to kill some game, which was not scarce, for all day we came upon tracks of deer, hare, rabbit, pheasant, etc. As for the bear, we had not yet reached the point of considering it as game and when we saw its tracks, which happened fairly often, we felt more fear than desire. It would, however, have been quite necessary to kill one to refill our two grease-boxes, which we had been carrying empty for two days.

After dinner, Bigot took his hooks and went off to fish, putting bits of frog on them for bait. At the end of an hour he returned with eight to ten livres of fish; immediately, we cleaned them, we cooked them in water, then we divided them. Although we had just finished dinner, each one disposed of his share with an appetite which would have been pleasing to see if it had not been an indication of our distress.

We were occupied in reloading our pack animals to continue on our way, when, at the bend of the river, at a distance of a hundred meters, we saw three Indians appear.

They were completely naked, and their bodies were about the color of poorly smoked ham. On seeing us they seemed as surprised as we were ourselves, and they stopped for some time; then one of them began to cry, "Walai, walai."[2] As I found myself one of those nearest them, I repeated mechanically, "Walai, walai"; then they walked toward us, but slowly. I said to Ragache and Messent, who happened to be near me: "Beware of weapons and let's watch out that others do not try to surround us." And, putting ourselves on the defensive, we waited. At fifty meters, the same Indian repeated, "Walai, walai," and all of us replied again, "Walai, walai." These three gentlemen then approached us. Two of them were each carrying a stick fifteen feet long teminated by something resembling a peg tapered at both ends and fastened to the long stick; the other had in his hand a bow four feet long and on his back a quiver filled with arrows two feet long. This quiver consisted of a stretched-out skunk skin to which he had fastened the sinew of some kind of animal, which served as strap; this passed over his forehead, the quiver bumping on his back. They seemed just as embarrassed as we. They were speaking among themselves, but it was Hebrew to us, even for our Swiss who spoke German, and who himself, at that moment, was finishing eating his biscuit. Seeing that he was the only one eating, the Indians approach him and one says: "Pane éia," pointing to the biscuit. Then I say to Schmutz: "Give them your biscuit, so we can see if that is what they want." The Indian takes the biscuit which Schmutz presents him, breaks it in three pieces, gives two of them to his two companions and all three retire, while saluting us again with their "walai, walai," which we repeat in chorus and which signifies, as we later learned: *Friend, friend.* "Well," said one of us, putting his pistol in his pocket, "the Indians are not as bad as we thought, it's better to meet them than a bear or a panther."

This encounter with the Indians forced us to some reflections of an entirely new order. These Indians traveled in a group of three without weapons—or practically so; they knew, even better than we, how many panthers, bears, and other ferocious animals there were in this country. However, they didn't have the air of worrying about that. Why this assurance when we, more robust and better armed, were

2. The significance of Perlot's efforts to understand Indians and his subsequent use of the greeting "walli" or "oualai" is discussed at length in the introduction to part II.

afraid? It was because they knew better than we, doubtless, the habits of these wild
animals; they knew them from experience, and we knew them only from hearsay or
from reading. They were surer of their knowledge than we of ours, these savages
who, assuredly, did not know how to read. It was we who were the ignorant ones.
Be that as it may, we were reflecting; as we claimed to be at least as redoubtable as
they, we concluded that we were very wrong to be afraid of what did not frighten
them. The fear, then, diminished in us, but wariness survived. Shortly after the
disappearance of the Indians, we set off on our way again, continuing to go up the
river, which they were descending. The trail was easy at first, but, about three
o'clock, we had to leave the Merced; the hill, whose foot plunged into the water,
was precipitous and covered with thick brush; we even had to backtrack as far as a
fault in the hillside which we had noticed when coming up, in order to be sure of
being able to reach the summit with our animals, where we hoped to find a path; but
we were mistaken in that attempt. From the top of the hill, we saw the river turning
or rather coming from the left in a very long curve which we did not expect. Not
having a path, we walked the rest of the day a little haphazardly, taking care
however not to get too far away from the river, for we still hoped that farther along
we would find the trail which followed it.

On the way, Ragache and I had our guns in hand in order to profit by the
opportunity if game of any sort presented itself within range; but it did not present
itself.

The preceding days, we were encountering it at every step and we had only to
take it; but, for fear of loading ourselves down, like the heron in the fable, we
waited.

Now that hunger was coming, in fact had come, game had disappeared. We
then bitterly regretted having profited so little from the lesson of the good de La
Fontaine.

Toward evening, we had to climb a mountain covered with pines, the first we
had seen since crossing the California mountains. These trees were scattered, but
big, and as the mountain leveled off gradually as we climbed, we walked rather
easily and fast, so much so that our animals were in a sweat before reaching the top.
Although night was coming, as we saw no indication of water we were obliged to
continue our march; that is what we did until an hour after sunset; even then we had
only a verdant plateau where we could see no water on the surface; but by digging
with sticks and with our hands—for we had no kind of tool—to a depth of a few
inches, we managed to get enough to make our supper and to water the animals.

That evening there could be no question of hunting; that was put off till the next
morning. Then, having tied the animals in the midst of abundant-enough grass, and
having placed our guard, we went to sleep. During the night, two hours apart, the
sentinel awakened us two times. Two times, we were put on the defensive and two
times the noise we heard went away without our being able to see or to suspect its
cause. The second time, however, it rather resembled the trot of a horse which
might have run through the scattered bushes around us.

Toward dawn, just as the sentry was going, as had been agreed, to wake

Ragache and me, who were to go hunting early, a strange concert was heard around us, a vocal concert similar to that which might be produced by a hundred roosters shut in casks and beginning to crow, one not waiting to begin until the other had finished. We listened, quite overwhelmed, without being able to figure out what it could be. One said that the noise was far away, another affirmed that it was quite close; this one claimed that it was coming from the earth, that one believed that it came from the trees. But it was very difficult to tell whence and how our ears were reached by these deep and half-muffled sounds which deafened them. If we had not all been, as much as we were, more or less free-thinkers, we would have willingly believed that the devil had something to do with it.

Meanwhile day had come, the concert continued and we saw nothing; no movement around us. All at once, while casting my glance on all sides, I saw a sort of hen flying from one tree to another; as I was approaching the tree, I startled into flight two other winged creatures of the same species; I advanced cautiously then and at the end of ten minutes, perhaps, I saw one sitting on the ground and making the noise we had been hearing; I shot it, it was an enormous grouse. My gunshot had naturally ended the effect with the cause; we heard nothing more. I brought my grouse back to camp, saying: "Here is the bear we heard growling"; some of us, in fact, had uttered the opinion that we were surrounded by bears and that it was the growling of the little cubs that we were hearing.

Certain now that this frightful uproar was the song of the grouse and hearing this same uproar begin again, we set off on the hunt, Ragache and I, and at seven o'clock, breakfast time, we returned with seven of these birds. Everyone plucked, cleaned, roasted them, but alas! no grease for so fine a dish! What a pity! What a feast it would have been with this condiment! But after all, one must suit oneself to the times, and although they were seasoned only with pepper and salt, we ate four of them between the ten of us.

While they were repacking the baggage and reloading the animals, we still had time to shoot two more of this excellent gamebrid.

It was late when we broke up camp, taking with us six grouse, in case we didn't find any in the place where we were to camp that night. We walked with a firm step. In less than two hours of hunting, the pair of us had killed ten grouse. While reviving our health, it raised our morale: we were strong and joyful, and for very little we would have started singing upon our departure; but, thinking of bears and Indians, we judged it better to keep quiet.

Having neither path nor river to guide us, I had recourse to my pocket compass to find the direction of our route.

Since our departure from Griffine, the course of the Merced has been from the northeast to the southwest; our march, in going up the river, had therefore been toward the northeast. Now, finding ourselves at the time on the east side of the river, and in the hypothesis that the part to be followed ran in the same direction as the part already followed, we should still, in order to approach the river, have headed toward the northeast, but deviating just a little to the north.

After having walked in this direction for some time, we realized that instead of being on the crest of the mountain, as we thought, we were only half-way to the top.

Moreover, the rise to the northeast became so rapid that we had to make for the north. We had to climb that way until one in the afternoon.

After a slope there was a flat, then a slope, then a flat, and so on all the way. Fortunately, the forest was of full-grown trees; otherwise we would have been forced to break a path. At last we reached the summit; instead of having a long hill to go down, as we expected, we found a plateau unrolling before us almost as far as we could see. It was covered with great scattered oaks, which were surrounded by thickets composed of shrubs which much resembled hawthorne or crabapple.

After having descended a little in the direction of the Merced, whose course we perceived on our left, indicated by a deep and long cut in the mountain, we began to cross this great plateau, which we were in haste to leave, for the nature of the terrain announced that we would find no water there, and we hoped to find some on the opposite slope.

This plateau must have been burned during the preceding winter or autumn, for only the oaks were living, all the brush was dead, half burned and all black. After two or three hours of march among these shrubs, we were frightful to see. Not one of us had kept his coat whole, most of us had our trousers in ribbons, our legs bleeding and our faces torn. Besides that, what we had left of trousers, coat and face was blackened by the charcoal; charcoal-burners at work would have looked neat and dainty next to us. Our animals, who were suffering like us, became restive and advanced only by grace of the intervention of Martin Stick. We ended, however, by getting out of it, but night was approaching and no water! As we then found ourselves at the foot of a comparatively high and steep hill, we set off along it, at the same time coming closer to the Merced. About eight o'clock, we arrived beside a little spring where luckily there was enough grass for the donkey and the mule. The poor beasts were dying of fatigue and thirst. Since our departure from San Juan, I had not yet seen them so spiritless, they were so far gone that after having drunk, instead of starting to graze as usual, they lay down. When approaching the spring, we had noticed that the grass was trampled all around it. By what foot? That was what we could not discover, because of the thickness of the turf. However, by dint of searching, we found a sort of path which came to a turn a hundred paces from the spring, then climbed a dry stream whose bed cut the hill in two.

This made us suppose that we were on the trail of the *Walais*, as we called the Indians, and that, in consequence, we had to stay on our guard at night, all the more so because the Indians perhaps were not the only ones who had so trampled the grass around the spring.

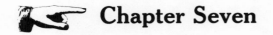 **Chapter Seven**

On the Miners' Highway

It was the fourth night since we had left Griffine; we had walked a lot during these four days and we had been poorly fed; each night, almost, we had to leap to arms, and we had hardly slept at all. Today, at last, we arrived late at the camping place, after having suffered all day from the march, from the brush, and from thirst. The result was that most of us were at the end of our strength, and to these exhausted men it still was necessary to say: "Take up the gun, do two hours of guard duty, then you may go to bed, subject to being awakened with a start, perhaps, an hour later by a cry of alarm, in order to try to save your life."

It was too much. Most of them stretched out on their blankets, too tired to bother even with their supper, refusing to take their watch, and preferring to leave to chance the trouble of saving them from the perils of the night. Several began to doubt that Mariposa existed, or that it was possible for us to reach it; the placers were a dream or, if reality, it was no longer within their reach. In no condition to go there, in no condition to return to Monterey, what did it matter to them whether they perished here or farther on? Were they even sure of waking up the next day, quite aside from the chance of being butchered by Indians?

This talk was going back and forth while Béranger built up the fire and made the dough to bake our bread in the frying-pan; another, in spite of the late hour, started to pluck the grouse, claiming that it would be quickly done and that a good supper was well worth the trouble; finally all of those who were on their feet joined in, we ended by having supper, and even those who had gone to bed did not sleep till after they had eaten copiously like the others.

Seeing that there could be no question of following the order of the lots, I asked Béranger if he wanted to stand two hours of guard before going to bed, myself undertaking to watch over the safety of the camp the rest of the night. Béranger having consented, I went to bed after going to wake up our animals so that they could start to browse, which they did.

Before going to sleep, I heard the furious voice of Marcan, the desperate fellow of San Luis, a small and lively man, who, on my word, was singing my praises, and under the pretext of taking in hand the interests of justice, wronged in my person, according to him, was inveighing against his unfortunate companions in fine style, in terms as energetic as hastily chosen: "Thunder! as for me, I don't want anyone to wake Perlot; it isn't his turn to stand guard. And then, if there is an alarm, he is always the first one on his feet and running to danger; because he shoots well, won't he be allowed to sleep? Even today, he's the one who marched in the lead all day and who parted the bushes for us, he's the one who kills what we have to eat. If that man there were to fall, what would we do? he is our guide, he alone can lead us; all of you, whatever you are, you are too stupid, saving the respect I owe you, to understand anything about a compass; if a while back he had listened to you, we would have taken a turn to the right instead of taking the left and, instead of being here, we would still be back there parching from thirst. He guessed well, he did, that there was water here. Since we need him, let us try at least not to let him kill himself and let's let him sleep for once like everybody else. He's worn out, he can't take any more, he does not complain, no, he doesn't dare, and surely he is more tired than those over there, who are already snoring and who couldn't walk any farther because there was no more brandy to drink; while there was any, they were always drunk and now, because of them, we are deprived of the little glass which we took in the morning. They are the ones, those imbeciles, who say that there aren't any placers, just when we are about to reach them. If I despaired at San Luis, myself, and wanted to kill myself, it was because my feet were lacerated and swollen and it was impossible for me to walk; I could not resolve to see you leave when I could not follow you. Now that my feet are healed, I will walk anyway and I will follow Perlot to the end, even if I have to endure hunger and thirst; but they, who are not wounded, who are only a little fatigued, there they are lamenting like women. Wet hens! cowards! who are good for nothing but to discourage everyone else. Messent, give your gun to Béranger, and you, Béranger, take your watch until about midnight, then wake me, I'll undertake to keep good watch until day. If tomorrow these . . . mugs don't wake up in time, we will plant them there and we will leave without them, by the . . . lord, since they believe that they won't get there."

Thus Marcan vociferated in his bad humor, mixing in almost equal doses the true and the false. However flattered I might find myself to hear him pronounce, with the accent of conviction, this magnificent panegyric on myself, I realized, in my inner judgment, that he was exaggerating things, or rather (which happens too often with panegyrists as with detractors) that he was seeing only one side. If I took the most robust part in the fatigues of the expedition, it was only justice, for, after all, I had the responsibility for it. It was I who had conceived the project, who had dragged my companions into this adventure full of perils. I alone, perhaps, had remained immune to discouragement and to lassitude, because I had faith in the final success of the enterprise, of which I had weighed the chances, favorable and unfavorable. I was young; besides that I was strong, and I belonged to that energetic and robust race of the children of the Ardenne, whom the harshness of the native climate prepares so well to support fatigues and privations. The services which I had been able to render and which Marcan recalled with too much emphasis, cost me little and, in all conscience, I did not deserve the praises which he sang so loudly.

Béranger did his two hours on watch, then went to awaken Viot, another volunteer sentinel, who two hours afterward awakened Marcan, who, still grumbling, kept his watch till daybreak.

During the night, the coyotes, it seemed, had returned to make their usual uproar. Viot, who was then on guard, had heard them come from afar in a large pack, pass fairly close to us, then go away. He was not otherwise disturbed by the incident, for we were beginning to recover; he had let the camp sleep, and only three or four among us had heard the noise. As for me, I woke up only when Marcan came to shake me to tell me that breakfast was ready.

During the night, he had cooked some beans in which floated the two grouse left from the night before. We breakfasted in silence, then each one set to work to make up his pack without saying anything.

When all was ready for the departure, Béranger, who usually led the mule, said: "Gentlemen, which way are we going today?" As nobody replied, he came to me and asked me if it would not be good to follow the stream-bed rather than to continue along the hillside; I approved and we left, one following the other, with mournful eye and lowered head.

The creek, whose bed was dry and was ten to fifteen meters wide, served as our road most of the time. At the end of two hours, it became steep and scattered with stones so big that our animals could hardly step over them, and advanced only with difficulty.

From time to time, however, on the alluvial flats, we came upon a sort of path which made us hope that we would reach the top of the slope without too many difficulties. In the meantime, the banks were becoming more and more precipitous and rocky, so that there was reason to fear that, if we encountered a waterfall, we would be forced to retrace our path. Nevertheless, we kept advancing, until at last the two banks, by drawing together, became no more than two completely vertical walls of rock, which made our route resemble a street bordered, on each side, by houses having a height of ten or twelve stories. Even the public squares were not lacking, for the street, of an average width, as I have said, of twelve to fifteen meters, sometimes took a double or triple width for a length of more than a hundred meters.

It was really a curious sight, if we had been of a humor to admire the beauties of the countryside. But we had other preoccupations; we were thinking rather of what we could do to preserve ourselves if by chance we should encounter a bear, a lion, or a panther promenading on this street in the opposite direction to our march. However, we got off with only the fear. Soon the street turned to the left, then the walls became less and less high and buttressed a little on the sides, which made us hope that we were at last going to leave this deep cut; but there it was that another difficulty awaited us. All at once, the way became so steep that our animals could no longer climb. The bed of the torrent was rock, without a single stone, and this rock, although dry, was fairly slippery. Perforce we had to stop and consider.

We had to try everything before resolving to retrace our steps, considering the length of the route which we had covered since morning. Two of us left to explore the terrain ahead, and we soon returned to inform our companions that this steep slope ceased after about four hundred meters, and that from there on an easy terrain extended at least as far as the twistings of the stream had permitted us to see. After having carried our packs to the top of the rise, we returned to get the loads of our animals on our own backs, then, by pulling the beasts with ropes and pushing them from behind, we ended by making them climb.

So this great obstacle was happily surmounted. A crack in the rock which served as bed of the stream furnished us some potfuls of water which could have been improved upon but which, nevertheless, for lack of something better, we used to make a light collation composed of coffee and biscuit. During this time, our animals being unsaddled, we let them too have a modest repast, for fear of soon seeing them exhausted as they had been the night before. Shortly, after we set off again on our march, continuing to climb the creek, in which the water began to flow more abundantly as we advanced. At the end of an hour we entered a sort of plain; the stream became dry again and the path there seemed a little better marked. Seeing that the water was going to disappear again, some of us, fearing that we would lack it in the evening when we made a halt, were of the opinion that we should camp in this place, a thing moreover which it was better to do by daylight in order to be able to hunt, for without game from then on there would be no meal, unless a very meager one. But as it was only three o'clock in the afternoon, this opinion did not prevail.

On leaving the plain, the path left the creek, which turned to the right; we followed the trail which seemed to lead toward the Merced. About six o'clock, it brought us at a right angle, without climbing, to the top of a hillside, at the foot of which we discovered a plain as long as the eye could reach, and at least two kilometers wide, which was traversed by a big stream. We descended this not very high and not very steep slope and we came to the stream, which we had some trouble in crossing without removing our trousers. The path crossed it and continued in a straight line through the valley, while another, as well and even better marked, went up it along the bank. Considering the advanced hour, we decided to spend the night in this place. While they were preparing the supper—a very frugal supper, for it was composed of beans cooked that morning, of biscuit, and coffee— I took the gun and started off. My aim was indeed to hunt but, at the same time, to investigate where this road up the river could lead; it seemed to me that the one we had been following for two hours wandered a little too much from our direction; it took us almost to the west.

Hardly was I out of the plain and climbing the hill by going up the river which, itself, led us too far to the east, when I came to another fairly big stream (and therefore, consequently, one coming from a distance) which joined it. The path then changed in direction; it followed the banks of this fork and seemed definitely to leave the river. After having followed it the distance of five or six hundred meters, I was convinced of the fact, and I returned to the camp through the woods in order to try to shoot some kind of game. I was not lucky; I returned with two gray squirrels and a partridge, having found nothing else. Ragache, on his part, had brought back a little hare and two rabbits, the product of eight shots. In ordinary times, we would have cried out against this useless expenditure of ammunition; what hope we had of not dying of hunger rested solely in our supply of powder, and each fruitless shot drew a sigh from us. However, nobody complained because everybody was hungry. Ragache brought something to eat, and he had gone on the plain and had seen three or four hares, which he hoped to find again the next day.

At last, we supped, then prepared the game for next day's breakfast, leaving to the last guard for the night the duty of cooking it when it should be time.

The night was tranquil and each one slept a deep sleep, including, I think, the sentinel. Alone, perhaps, I was troubled in my sleep: at I don't know what hour of the night, having thought I heard a call, I get up, look for the gun and don't find it; I listen, I hear nothing more; I walk to the fire, it was extinguished; seeing no one move, I dare not shout for fear of troubling this profound peace. I went back to bed without having seen anyone up, not even the guard. At breakfast, I told the story, but the four guards of the night competed in protesting their innocence, each claiming to have done his two hours without sleeping. I was ready to ask myself if I had been dreaming. While discussing it, we were going to sit down at table without waiting for Ragache who, his duty ended toward morning, had gone searching for the hares he had seen the evening before. All at once we heard talking on the side of the river, upstream, then the voices were silent. Our restless animals had stopped eating and were watching the hillside; shortly afterward we saw coming into view a band of Indians. There were eighteen, as many men as women and children; one would have said that they were moving from one home to another. The women were carrying a sort of hamper made in the form of a cone, which was filled with baskets of the same shape, and with furs. This hamper was held on the back by a bark strip forming a circlet which passed across the forehead.

They were doubtless warned of our presence, for, on seeing us, they continued on their way without showing any hesitation, and walked toward us with an assured step; however, while approaching, the two or three foremost saluted us with the famous walai, walai, which we returned to them as courteously as they had given it to us. The women kept themselves discreetly to one side; they were, like the men, entirely naked, except that they had a belt three inches wide to which was attached from front to back a band of the same width which passed between their legs. The men wore their hair, of a dull black, pulled together and tied in a big tuft on the top of the head, while the women let theirs hang naturally, keeping it short only over the forehead to clear the eyes. On almost all, the breasts hung lower than the waist; they had their ears pierced by some kind of bird's feather: it was their only jewelry. The children of both sexes, completely naked, seemed very timid. Most of the men had on their back a skunk-skin quiver full of arrows and a bow four to six feet long. Our Indians made the rounds of the camp, gathered the skins of the hares, rabbits, and squirrels which we had thrown away, then after having said, "Walai, walai," to us again, continued on their way.

Reassured by their peaceful mien, I had tried to obtain some information from them, but it had been impossible for me to make myself understood.

The Indians gone, we dispatched our breakfast, which was no longer too warm.

As we were preparing to depart, leaving near the fire the share of the absent Ragache, we saw him running at full speed, gun in one hand, hat in the other, leaping over the bushes with the agility of a goat; he was heading for us, with a terrified air and gesticulating wildly. Fearing that he ran some danger, I take the gun and advance toward him with accelerated step. Seeing me approach, he wants to speak, but, out of breath and all in a sweat, he cannot articulate a word; I succeed, however, in understanding that he has just seen an innumerable troop of Indians hidden in the brush, that he has managed to flee without being seen by them, and that he runs to warn us to be on our guard, because before long they will reach our camp. I inform him then that these terrible Indians have just passed, that they are of a peaceful disposition and scarcely armed, that, moreover, there are only fifteen or twenty, including women and children, and that there is no danger to fear.

"Not at all," he tells me, "they are very numerous, it cannot be the same, we must watch out."

We return to the camp and we are on our guard for an hour; after which, seeing nothing appear and persuaded that Ragache is mistaken, we break camp.

So we filed along the path which followed the river, by which the Indians had come. At the end of a little time, we came to and went up the stream I had seen the evening before. The path didn't rise too rapidly; only the bushes, thick and high, interfered with the animals' progress, and it took us nearly two hours to reach the summit of the hill which we were climbing.

We arrived at the place where the Indians had spent the night. Great was our surprise to find there an empty sardine-tin, then the leg of a knitted sock. Either some miners had passed there before us, or, if it was the Indians who had abandoned these objects, they themselves had necessarily passed by a place where there were sardine-tins and socks, a place, consequently, where there were civilized beings, evidently miners.

So we were on the right road, we were going to reach the placers! These deductions were of an irreproachable logic, and that is how the sight of these sordid remnants of civilization restored our courage with hope, and why joy shone instantaneously on all our faces; these long, sad, tired and dejected visages took on new life; the pack which overloaded our shoulders became lighter, and we gaily set off again on the march.

The path, instead of going down the hill again, which seemed not very high, followed the heights and seemed to bring us back to the Merced, which probably had left us in a great curve to the west, for we had covered more of the trail to rejoin

it than to get away from it. Whatever it was, from the place where we found
ourselves we could prejudge nothing, because the wood, although comparatively
clear, being composed of oaks and pines, hid the country from us completely.
However, as the path was approximately in the right direction, we followed it,
lengthening our steps.

Shortly after, one of us claimed to have heard a shot; in which direction he did
not know exactly. We agreed to talk no more in order to hear better; we were
walking thus in silence for more than an hour when our donkey began to bray; his
song made us start and caused a general astonishment. Since the departure from
Griffine, that had not happened to him. We discussed this unexpected event, but
we could not come to an agreement on the prognosis which should be drawn from it.

The trail, leaving the height, began to descend a hillside that was passably steep
and rocky. We had some trouble not to lose the trail, because the grass was sparse
and steps had left few imprints on the stones and rocks.

However, past two o'clock in the afternoon, we reached the bottom of the hill.
We found water there and we refreshed ourselves; then, as the path forked, we
took the direction which came nearest to ours and soon we arrived on a dry terrain,
slightly wooded although rough. We had been walking on this terrain for an hour
when we heard, very distinctly, two gunshots echoing on our left. They had been
fired at a great distance; no matter, that reanimated us: we were sure, at least, that
there was someone there, and that this someone was not an Indian since Indians shot
only arrows. Shortly afterward, our donkey began to bray again; everyone this
time was of the opinion that it was a good sign. Without doubt the sense of smell,
that sense of such great subtlety in certain animals, revealed to him the presence of
one of his kind in the neighborhood. Whatever it might be, his song, disagreeable as
it could seem in ordinary times, sounded a delicious music to us; this was even worth
some consideration for him. He had doubtless guessed what we desired, and he
was announcing it to us. Among the services which we demanded of him, we had
not thought of that one; we were grateful to him for it; we didn't go so far as to
embrace him, but we sweetened for him the rigors of command; instead of saying
gee! with a stick, we said it with a hand—it was more polite; he seemed sensible of
these attentions and witnessed it by a particular movement of his ear.

It was about five o'clock, and we were worried that we had not found water;
evening perhaps would come before the nature of the terrain had changed, and we
had no place in sight where we could have hoped to find anything with which to
quench our thirst. We were about to regret not having camped at the base of the
hill, although it was then hardly past two o'clock; there, at least, there was water
and grass. The little bit of grass that there was where we were now, was dry on the
stalk. All at once, at the turn of a hill, we fell upon a path that was perfectly worn,
not by the bare foot of the Indian, but by the feet of men shod as we were, without
counting the feet of horses, donkeys, and mules whose prints could be distinctly
recognized. Oh! for once, joy shone on all visages, and our muscles took on new

strength. We took this trail which cut ours almost at a right angle, and we began to walk as gaily as in leaving Monterey; we had forgotten that we were thirsty and that night was about to fall; but we soon came to a meadow planted with big trees, where neither water nor grass was lacking.

Around the spring, the earth was trampled as if a regiment had camped there for several days; we saw numerous places where fires had been made, one among others where the ashes were still warm. So there was no longer any doubt, we were really on the trail of the miners who were coming from San Francisco, Sacramento, and Stockton. We should have the Merced not far behind us, and ahead of us Mariposa. At what distance? We did not know, but according to the reports of the vice-consul, there was at the maximum, from the Merced to the Mariposa, only twelve leagues. What did it matter to us, from then on, to know the distance exactly? We were on the trail, that was the thing—we were saved.

Here and there, we found, scattered on the turf, trousers, shirts, hats, even an umbrella, all almost new. These objects had been abandoned, probably by foot travelers exhausted from fatigue. Shoes with crooked heels, the indication of a long march, as well as twisted and broken boots, were not lacking either. The terrain, moreover, was strewn with empty sardine-tins, old biscuit-boxes, and with papers of all dimensions, all colors, all sources, which had served to wrap comestibles of whatever kind. At first sight, and if we had not known what to make of it, we could have believed that we were arriving on the spot where the witches had held their Sabbath.

A notice nailed to an oak attracted our attention. This notice, written in pencil, said in English: "I abandon here my bag with all it contains, lucky if I reach Mariposa, even reduced to my lowest terms! still luckier is the one who will have the courage to carry there what I leave! it will be his, he will have earned it well, and will not have to thank me.—J. L. Ogan."[1]

At the bottom of this notice, somebody else had added: "let each one take what can be useful to him and leave to others what does not suit him. Remember that to destroy is a crime." This was signed: *A civilized man.*

The valise in question was new, of black leather; all around were found trousers, shirts, vests, socks, and shoes.

Seeing all these objects thus placed at our disposal, we regretted having loaded ourselves with heavy baggage; we could not profit from the windfall, for each of our packs, although containing only what was strictly necessary, was too full and too heavy. The notice said: "Lucky if I reach Mariposa." Therefore, the proprietor of the valise was going to Mariposa; therefore, we were on the road to Mariposa.

The trail led to the east. According to all our calculations, it was utterly impossible that we should be more than a dozen leagues from the Merced, which we had on the west; even the distance of three leagues did not seem probable to me. So

1. I have been unable to identify J. L. Ogan.

J. L. Ogan, proceeding to Mariposa, was going to the east and covering the twelve leagues which, according to the statement of the consul, separated this locality from the Merced.

While we were in contemplation before this placard, trying to draw from it as much light as possible, we heard a noise at some distance; then we perceived a man on horseback, followed by thirty or forty mules which other men, also on horseback, were driving before them. When they reached the plateau where we were and where they were evidently coming to camp for the night, they removed the pack-saddle from the back of each animal; one of the three attached a bell to the neck of a mare and hobbled her forefeet, then let all these animals graze at liberty. That done, they lit the fire and occupied themselves with their supper. Then we approached them; they were Mexicans and did not know a word of French; however, by means of my Spanish dictionary, we succeeded in learning from them that the Merced was four miles behind us and Mariposa twenty-five miles ahead. They had left the latter place that morning and were returning to Stockton, whence they had come; there, they would reload their mules with provisions and return again. I also asked them if there was nothing to fear from Indians or wild animals. They told me there was not, but that sometimes, however, the Indians stole the animals and ate them; that from time to time, too, they killed someone in order to take his trousers or shirt, but that that happened rarely, especially since the weather turned warm.

I should remark here that all the miner's clothing consists of a hat (which the Indian doesn't care about—on the contrary), a shirt, trousers, and then a pair of boots, which the Indian doesn't want any more than the hat.

Our Mexicans, having given this information, rolled themselves in their blankets and began to snore tranquilly. Seeing their calmness, we did as they did, and without posting a guard, we all slept a peaceful and profound slumber.

In the morning, before leaving, I returned to the Mexicans to get *el Camino*, the road *por la Mariposa;* one of them reached in his pocket, took his notebook, then dictated to me: "Paso, three miles; Arroyo, four miles, Hornitos, nine miles; Bear Valley, six miles; Mariposa, three miles."

Not hoping to make our twenty-five miles that day, because it was too much for half of us, we cut the stage in two, proposing to sleep at Hornitos (little ovens) after having done our sixteen miles (nearly twenty-six kilometers, the English mile equaling about 1609 meters).

Soon after our departure, we had arrived at the place the Mexican called Paso; it was a pass, in fact: that is, after having climbed nearly an hour and reached the summit of the mountain, one found oneself in a narrow defile which wound among enormous blocks of granite so close to one another that very often our mule's load grazed the walls on both sides. Once out of this defile, which it took us a long time to pass, we found ourselves, after an easy little descent, on a superb plateau, with a gentle slope where we only had to pick up our feet, which ended at the stream El Arroyo.

Since we began following the miners' trail, we had noticed here and there, and we still continued to notice, places where the earth had been disturbed; most often it was nothing but a very small hillock, or, if you wish, a very big mole-hill, but sometimes too this earth, freshly piled, resembled the grave of a person newly buried. When we reached the plateau, these hillocks became so numerous to the right and left that the trail almost resembled the path in a cemetery; only the tombs and the crosses were lacking. Each one was conjecturing to himself on this subject, when we saw a piece of clothing hanging out from one of these graves; we approached and saw that some animal, in digging, had exposed the leg of a corpse buried fully clothed. Instinctively, we pushed the earth back with our feet, having no other instrument, and covered this half-devoured leg.

What sad and also what salutary reflections this incident suggested to us! We were very sure now that all these humps which we had passed and which we were still passing, were as many graves, where slept the miners the vice-consul had told me about. These unfortunates, for the most part, were dead of hunger; and we, sybarites, were sorry for ourselves because we had no more grease to prepare our meat! Perhaps, even probably, there were also those who had died of illness; had we the right to lament so much, we who did not count one sick person among us? Then we lacked courage, decidedly! And forgetting our own miseries, we began to commiserate the fate of these unfortunates. There they were in the midst of the forest, scattered at random, probably as they had fallen; three hundred, four hundred perhaps, had found death in the space of three leagues which we had just traversed; how many, by this count, were left along the hundred and twenty miles which separate Stockton from Mariposa? And then, these tombs of yesterday, already abandoned, these tombs scattered without order in this distant and desert country, had something that was really heartbreaking. Those whom they enclosed had doubtless remembered, in falling, their native soil and their paternal roof, but they could never have hoped that a friend, a compatriot, or an unknown passerby might stop, if only for an instant, to accord them a regret, a memory, a thought of whatever kind. Their burial place would forever remain unknown. Would they even have a burial? Had they not died with the thought that their bodies would serve as food for the coyote, the wolf, and the hyena, and that the Indian alone, in passing, would stumble over their bones? Yes, this cruel thought must have obsessed them at their last moment and added to the sufferings of their agony.

Would the destiny of these men be ours? Hardly six months ago they were full of life; in six months, what would it be for us?

While forming these reflections, we were walking, mournful, silent, drawn together as if we had been following a funeral convoy. One of us had made the remark that there was hardly two feet of earth over these corpses; but what astonished me, myself, was that there was any. I could not explain how and by whom they could have been buried. On arriving at El Arroyo, we had the explanation of the fact.

There were six tents there, inhabited by miners, that is, by the men who washed the sand of the stream in order to extract from it the gold which it contained. It was there that the placers began. It was not yet noon, but as we had water there and as we found someone there to talk to, we made a halt.

An enormous notice, attached to an oak, drew our attention. It was written in longhand, in English, in French, and in Spanish. It begged the passersby, whether they were arriving at the placers or returning to the coast, to be so good as to bury the dead they might encounter on their way. "God has willed," it said, "that civilization should begin, in this place, with this duty which a man owes to his kind, to his brother, in order that he may never forget it. Every man believing in a God knows that to bury the dead is a duty; I entreat you to fulfill it, you who are civilized. God is great, He does not forget good works. Replace, in these distant lands, the absent relatives, and do unto others that which we wish others should do unto us."

This too was signed: A civilized man.

We were all agreed in recognizing that this notice had been written by a truly civilized man, as he called himself; but having neither pick nor shovel, it was impossible for us to do what he asked of us.

Seeing the miners who were working along the creek, I climbed toward them and addressed them. Among about fifteen who were there, only one, a former sailor, Irish of nationality, spoke a little French. Quite happy to find a man who understood me, I shook his hand.

This made my companions come running, believing that I had encountered someone of my acquaintance.

I asked my Irishman if he had been working there long. "No," he said, "only fifteen days."—"But," I said to him, "where do you find anything to eat?"— "Well, I bought a mule-load from the Mexicans when they passed, and they will return before I have finished; otherwise I would have to go to Hornitos, nine miles from here, to get supplies. There are, in fact, two or three tents there were they sell provisions to the miners of the environs."—"But, do you find any gold?"—"Oh! yes, though not too much, because I don't yet know how to mine very well, but my neighbors, farther down, are finding about an ounce a day apiece."—"Why don't you go to Mariposa or else to Hornitos?"—"Because I know my neighbors, who have let me sleep in their tent, and besides they have told me that gold is no more abundant there than here; consequently one place is as good as another."—"You have posted a big sign back there," I said. — "It was there when I arrived, but," he added, "you must have seen the same notice every ten miles along the road, since Stockton."—"Oh," I said, "we climbed the Merced, we came from Monterey and, from that direction, the path is not marked. But, on the subject, who are all these dead whose graves we have encountered along the way?"—"Those are last year's miners. In the autumn, many of them came this way, and the provision merchants were poorly supplied when winter began, so that the miners who did not want to or were not able to go down to Stockton, were hungry. It rained three months and no one could bring them supplies. There were two feet of snow; the mules could not walk because the earth was too soaked; moreover, the snow had made all the game descend to the plain, where the snow did not last, so that the miners had to leave the placers and try to return to Stockton; but the greater part fell along the way, dead of hunger. When I came up here, just fifteen days ago, I still had to bury some of them, but already they were half eaten by the wild animals.

"Didn't you notice, in coming along the way, that so many of the piles were not made like graves?"—"Yes."—"Well, that is where they buried the remains of those who were half-eaten; we made any kind of hole, then we rolled in the remains pellmell. Ah! this Protestant minister who posted the notices is a courageous man. I have seen him, myself, at Stockton, preaching on the public square. It was at the end of winter; nobody dared yet go up to the mines because all the rivers were over their banks. He preached in his church, he gathered, by means of a collection, enough money to buy three mules, loaded them with supplies, then, with one other, came as far as the Merced by swimming across all the rivers; already they had found many bodies along the way. In recrossing the Calaveras (name of a river) by swimming, his companion was drowned with another sick man they had found en route. He himself returned to Stockton with the two other mules, loaded with three sick men; he followed on foot. You should have seen him, on the public square, describing the miseries he had not been able to alleviate; he made everyone cry, me as well as the others. It was he, no one but he, who caused all these unfortunates to be buried; the eve of our departure, he preached again about it and for two hours he recited the prayers for the dead for those we were going to bury along the way."

"But," I asked him, "are there any Catholic priests in Stockton?"—"Oh, yes, there is a Mission; but they are not anxious to venture this way; when we see them, they will come to seek and not to bring. That will be when there are provisions and there is no more danger."—"I think," I said to him, "that you are not a Catholic?"—"Pardon me," he said quickly, "I am a Catholic, an Irishman who is not Catholic is not an Irishman; but that does not prevent me from recognizing that that Protestant is worth more than the priests of Stockton. They have a big church and preach for themselves, that's all, while this Protestant has nothing for a building but a little plank shack, and occupies himself with the unfortunate."

I left him because the hour was growing late, and after having shaken my hand he went back to work.

This work consisted in putting into a sort of wooden pan (what we would call a big Vachaî at home) the earth and rock he had dug from the bottom of his hole, which was four feet on a side and three in depth, then in washing the whole—about the contents of a bucket—in the creek nearby. When there was gold in this dirt, he found it, after the washing was done, at the bottom of his pan, put it in his purse of dressed deerskin, then began the operation all over again.

We set off for Hornitos. The terrain being passable, the road easy and well marked, we walked quickly and without fatigue; in each stream, in each ditch which we crossed, we saw holes worked or abandoned, and a fair number of people occupied in seeking gold. Midway, a caravan, part on horseback and part on foot, joined us. Having left Stockton six days before in a party of one hundred and twenty, they were now no more than forty; the others had been left behind, scattered the length of the road and following as well as they could. As they had nothing to carry, the animals being loaded with all their baggage, they went faster than we and soon passed us. Forced to a more modest gait, we reached Hornitos only toward evening.

III

LIFE IN THE SOUTHERN MINES 1851–1852

To me a new life opened in the mines—a life widely differing from anything before anticipated or dreamed of. People culled from every race and nation formed a cosmopolitan, composite, varicolored, and Babel-tongued group, free from social or legal restraint, free in every sense, standing on an equal plain, a nobility whose title was manhood.

Benjamin Butler Harris,
*The Gila Trail: The Texan
Argonauts and the California
Gold Rush,* p. 112.

The California gold rush has been characterized as chaotic, wasteful, marked by needless human tragedy, and blessed by pure luck. Yet the gold regions themselves were not only definable, there were obvious clues as to where and how gold could be found and how it could be extracted. The first Mexican miners to come to California after the beginning of the rush acknowledged these characteristics by calling the gold-bearing regions the *veta madre*, or mother lode, a phrase used in the mining province of Mexican Sonora. By mother lode they referred to a sequence of California hills and limestone outcroppings that ran roughly in a northwest-southeast direction in the foothills of the Sierra Nevada. These contained the gold; and where the westward flowing rivers had sliced through the hills, their waters carried loose ore downstream and deposited it in the gravel and sands of the riverbeds.[1]

Thus the placer miners of the Southern Mines gathered on streambanks to pan for gold or diverted streams from their courses to search for gravel in the dry beds. Others dug ditches or constructed flumes to channel water into riffled sluices into which they shoveled gravel for washing. Mexican miners often dug deep "dry" holes near a stream and washed the soil and gravel they found at different levels rather than build flumes or pan gold standing in an icy stream.

By the time Perlot arrived in Mariposa, mining society had evolved from the stage of individual miners working on a streambank with few rules to obey, to a point where towns had begun to develop, mining codes had been adopted, and local and county governments were being formed. Because Perlot spent his entire gold-mining career in the Southern Mines—a period of seven years—it may be well to note who had preceded him in the region and where camps and towns had appeared.

The first gold strike in the region of the Upper Stanislaus was made by the Reverend James Woods, a Philadelphia clergyman, on a stream that came to be called Woods Creek. The unusually rich finds there attracted so many people that the town of Columbia sprang up nearby. Later that season James H. Carson, a sergeant on leave from Stevinson's regiment, and his partner named Angel discovered gold at Carson Creek and Angel's Camp. Other discoveries south of the South Fork of the Stanislaus by Mexican miners led to the founding of the lively town of Sonora only a few miles from Columbia. By February 1850, Sonora had become the seat of Tuolumne County.

Meanwhile James D. Savage, a former member of Frémont's California Battalion turned Indian trader, had come into the area with the Reverend Woods, and found gold at Big Oak Flat near the Tuolumne. Then Colonel George F. James found more gold on Woods Creek four miles southwest of Sonora. That camp grew into the town of Jamestown.

1. Adolph Knopf, "The Mother Lode System of California," U.S. Geological Survey, *Professional Paper No. 157* (Washington, D.C.: Government Printing Office, 1929).

The following year seven Frenchmen found such a large amount of gold at Mokelumne Hill in the northernmost section of the Southern Mines that they were able to return to France on the profits. Mokelumne Hill subsequently became one of the richest mining areas in California.

Although the names of Reverend Woods, Major Savage, and Colonel James have been immortalized by their discoveries in the Southern Mines, the name of Colonel John C. Frémont dominates the history of the southeastern sector. After the American conquest of California in 1846–47, Frémont, as did many other Americans, began to acquire Spanish or Mexican land grants, often for ridiculously small sums. Frémont gave Oliver S. Larkin, who had been the American consular agent at Monterey at the time of the conquest, $3,000 to purchase one of these grants. For reasons that remain obscure Larkin bought the Alvarado grant, about eleven square leagues of land on the western slope of the Sierra through which ran Mariposas Creek. It soon bore the romantic name of the Mariposas Estate. Some observers felt that Frémont had been bilked, for the property was two hundred miles from the coast and not easily accessible. At the time of purchase it had no obvious economic value except as ranchland.

When gold was discovered in the Southern Mines area, Frémont immediately sent Alexander Godey, a mountain man and faithful lieutenant, to see if gold existed on his estate. Either late in 1848 or early 1849 Godey, accompanied by twenty-eight Mexican miners, found gold there. Suddenly it began to appear that Frémont was the owner of one of the richest pieces of real estate in the world, for in 1850 a miner named Johnston located a quartz vein along the line of the Mother Lode twelve miles east of Mariposas but on Frémont's property. Fantastic strikes at Princeton (Mount Bullion) and Mount Ophir, and later at Agua Fria in Bear Valley, the latter on Frémont's property but not part of the Mother Lode, led Benjamin Silliman to exclaim, when he visited the Mariposas Estate some years later, that it was more of a "principality than an estate."[2] Two other camps that were emerging as towns were Coulterville, a few miles northeast of Horseshoe Bend on the Merced River, and Hornitos on Burns Creek. Although neither was on the Mariposas Estate they were seen as part of the Mariposa mining area (see map following p. 34).

By the time Perlot arrived at the town of Mariposa (which soon replaced the older spelling *Mariposas* in all instances), the first flush of discovery had passed, and although the streambanks were lined with miners, they had not only taken up the best claims, they were beginning to experience disappointing returns. Nevertheless the town was to endure as a major mining and supply center and soon became the seat of Mariposa County.

During the months that Perlot was still in transit around the Horn, Indians in the Mariposa mining region had begun to attack isolated miners for food or livestock.

2. Benjamin Silliman, Jr., *A Report of an Examination of the Mariposa Estate in California, Made in May, 1864* (New York: William C. Bryant and Co., 1864), p. 5.

They also attacked two trading posts belonging to Major James Savage, one of the pioneer traders and miners in the region. In a classic frontier response Savage and other miners formed the Mariposa Battalion, consisting of three volunteer companies that gave chase to the Indians. By late April 1851, one group of Indians had been defeated on the San Joaquin; others had been chased all the way into the Yosemite Valley, where those captured were brought to a reservation on the Fresno River. The battalion achieved lasting fame not as Indian fighters, however, but as the discoverers of Yosemite Valley. The battalion was mustered out on July 1, 1851, only two months after Perlot had begun to mine.

As we shall see in the following chapters Perlot had to make his way in a region in which most of the important gold discoveries had already been made. Further, while men of all nations penetrated both the northern and southern camps, the Southern Mines were rumored to be the place where miners from the American South and Mexican miners from Sonora had congregated. A more volatile situation could hardly be imagined when Texas argonauts found themselves mining side by side with Mexicans with whom they had been at war only two years before. Understandably Americans tried to impose a foreign miners' tax to drive both Mexicans and other foreigners out. There was, in fact, a major confrontation between Americans and Frenchmen and Mexicans at Sonora in 1850. But these tensions were eased when the California legislature repealed the miners' tax and substituted a more moderate license fee that, in fact, was seldom collected.

On the other hand there were many reasons Perlot went to the Mariposa region, for it was said that Europeans, especially Frenchmen, preferred the southern camps because they were largely placer diggings, which called for a minimum of capital investment and no elaborate company organization. Given Etienne Derbec's positive description of Mariposa in his first gold rush letters sent to the *Journal des debats* and Frémont's reputation in Paris, one can well understand why Perlot journeyed to Mariposa rather than some other region.

It is fascinating to watch Perlot become a miner and a frontiersman as well, for he chose to remain in the camps during the winter of 1851–52 rather than retreat to Stockton, where food and supplies were available. Perlot's daredevil nature was, in effect, the secret of his success. He emerged from the ordeal of winter not only confident that he could survive but relishing the rough life of the miner.

Chapter Eight

Learning to Be a Miner

Hornitos was a camp of thirty to thirty-five tents, all occupied by sellers of food, tools, and clothes; there was a butcher-shop, a bakery, besides a sort of inn.[1] Meat was sold at twenty-five sous an English pound, which is fourteen ounces, bread thirty sous. After having bought for our supper thirty-five francs worth of meat, bread, and grease, we set up our tent for the night.

All around Hornitos, in the creeks, in the gulches, we saw nothing but people occupied in seeking this precious metal. We watched them do it, while waiting to imitate them; many of them had only two or three feet of digging and, coming near the rock, washed the dirt at the bottom and found gold there; others had holes ten to twelve feet deep; they threw the water out of the bottom, if they found any there, broke up the earth in it, and washed it at the creek nearby.

In the evening, the work of the mines ended, there were many people in the camp; one came to buy supplies, another clothes, another tools: picks, shovels, crowbars, and pans. I estimate that there could have been at Hornitos from two hundred and fifty to three hundred persons, all men in the prime of life: I saw no women there, nor children, nor old people. In business, they spoke English and Spanish; in the street, still covered with brush, we heard all possible tongues spoken; we encountered there even the Indian, all flurried and much distressed because he was dressed, dressed in the sense that he had on either an old shirt, or old trousers, or an old coat or even simply a vest, sometimes only a hat; I have never seen one wearing two of these objects at a time.

We slept little that night. Although we dispensed with a guard, we were restless; we didn't have a very clear idea of what work in the mines was, and we were wondering how we would manage.

The next day, a group of us proposed to remain at Hornitos. Some Frenchmen returned from Mariposa were working there and were satisfied with their lot. They had left the Mariposa (river) because there was too much water; it was still running

1. Hornitos (little ovens) appears to have been founded by Mexican miners but the exact time seems obscure. Gold is said to have been found there in 1848; another source suggests that Hornitos was founded by a Frenchman in 1850. (Glasscock, *Golden Highway*, p. 305.) Gudde, *California Place Names*, p. 145, gives the date of founding as 1852, but it was certainly a camp when Perlot passed there in 1851. Hittell described it as "one of the richest localities for placer mining as well as one of the largest and most active towns in the Southern Mines" (*History of California*, 3: 135).

full, several days before, flooding the holes dug on the flats so that one could not work there comfortably. However, after having deliberated, we kept to the original project, and we set off on the road to Mariposa.

We had only nine miles to cover and the question of the road to follow no longer puzzled us. We saw people everywhere and in all directions, and there was on all the trails a continual coming and going. At each step we encountered someone, whether on foot, with pack and tools on his back, or on horseback, driving before him a loaded mule; each one had a five or six shot revolver hanging from his belt. Everybody seemed busy, spoke all kinds of languages, French rarely enough. Near Bear Valley, we encountered a train of thrity mules which were carrying all kinds of merchandise to Mariposa; it was conducted by four men, one of whom spoke French. We made the trip together and arrived at Mariposa about two o'clock in the afternoon, seventeen days after having left Monterey.

Our first care on arriving was to dine; the second to take inventory of the supplies we had left. It was established that we still had enough for supper that day, then just about enough to live on the next day. We therefore had no time to lose; from the next day on, we would have to hunt for gold and find it in order to buy supplies, for the company had little coined silver. It was agreed in consequence that we would go in a group of three, Messent, Schmutz, and I, to buy the tools that very day to put us to work the day following; the others, while waiting, would set up the tent, occupy themselves with the animals, and also later with supper, so that on our return there would be nothing to do but cook the beefsteaks which we should bring.

Mariposa was a camp in the course of becoming a city, for it included already, besides fifty to sixty tents, three adobe houses, among others that of General Frémont, who had been there for a year and was occupied with setting up a pounding-machine or stamp-mill to crush the quartz, of which he had discovered several very rich veins in the neighborhood.[2]

The camp or the city was already a relatively active commercial center. One found there on sale all the objects of prime necessity for the population of the placers: victuals, tools, clothes, arms, and household and cooking utensils. Almost everyone there was talking English, some Spanish; we heard no one speaking French. So there we were in the camp, inquiring the price of tools. Here is the tariff: a shovel, forty-five francs; a pick, thirty-five francs, independently of the handle, which cost six francs; a crowbar, a plain bar of iron with one end flattened and the other pointed, thirty-five francs; a pan, twenty francs.

Between the ten of us, we didn't have the money necessary to outfit completely a single one of us! Quite shame-faced, we turned on our heels, without buying

2. The town of Mariposa—some eighty miles from Stockton—owed its beginnings to the discovery of gold on Mariposa Creek in 1849, although rumors persist that Mexican miners were panning along the stream in 1848. Situated near the southeastern boundary of John C. Frémont's Mariposa Estate, it was the southern end of the Great Johnson Lode, discovered in 1850, which ran from Horseshoe Bend on the Merced River to Mt. Ophir. Sam Ward called it "the ultima Thule of the so-called Southern Mines" (Collins, *Sam Ward in the Gold Rush*, p. 41). Unlike so many other gold rush towns, Mariposa endured as a supply town, a county seat, and a major stopping point on the highway to Yosemite Park (Gudde, *California Place Names*, p. 193).

anything, naturally, and we took the path back to the tent. Our companions, seeing us from afar returning without tools, were amazed; on arriving, we told them what the trouble was, and there we were, looking each other in the eye without saying anything.

This silence lasted long enough; but, finally, someone made the judicious remark that we would have to decide on something, and we held council; it was now or never.

Some of us proposed to return to Hornitos and to hire ourselves out to the Frenchmen whom we had seen there; yes, but were they there still? If not, where to find them? Where were they working? The leader of the pack-train had spoken to us of Agua Fria (cold water), only three miles distant from Mariposa, where, he said, there should be some Frenchmen. There were some, doubtless, but where were they? and how to find them? We would have been just as distressed as at Mariposa, where perhaps there also were Frenchmen, for we had only just arrived and we had not had the time to make inquiries as to the situation. Therefore we had to remain, at least provisionally, where we were; only, what to do? Deprived of tools for lack of money, we could not work on our own account; therefore, while waiting for better, we would be forced to hire out to others, were it only to work for our board; that would be better than dying of hunger with our arms folded. In brief, it was decided that the next morning we would seek work under these conditions. The council broke up, we sat down to dinner, but the repast lacked gayety.

After supper, four of us, Duléry, Ragache, Braconnier, and Bigot, went to the camp and did not return until fairly late; the others occupied themselves with the animals, then went to bed.

The night seemed long to them, for they slept little and that a troubled sleep; each moment, one or another was heard turning in his blanket. The next day we were up early and breakfast was soon ready; moreover, it was one of the most frugal, composed of coffee, very little biscuit, and as little chocolate.

While breakfasting, the four who had gone to camp the evening before apprised us of the good fortune which had befallen them. They had encountered some Frenchmen who were working a mile lower down and who, their day ended, had come to camp to buy supplies. These Frenchmen, who formed a company, had hired them by the day and they were to join them immediately, for, that very evening, the company had bought them the necessary tools; they had contracted for a month at the rate of three piastres (fifteen francs) each per day's work, with tools furnished, and board and room. When I say room, it must be understood that they could sleep for nothing under an oak or, in case of rain, under a tent. They added, by way of justification, that they did not think it possible to remain a company of ten and that the best thing was for each one to try to take care of himself. They had managed to place themselves; it was for us to try to place ourselves the same way.

We settled our accounts immediately, which did not take long, considering the simplicity of the operations performed to date by the company.

The thing ended, our ex-associates shook hands and then they were gone. Six of us were left. We looked at each other some time without saying anything, but out of the six there were three whose eyes were moist. "I think," I said to one of them, "that you weep for the departure of these gentlemen? you are afflicted when you ought to be joyful to see the chance they have to earn their living immediately on arrival. Isn't it a good sign that they have succeeded so quickly? Why should we complain, anyway? from the ten unfortunates which we were, here we are reduced to six; a great evil!"—"No," replied one of them, "I cannot be happy seeing what happens," and saying this, he wept.

"Indeed! we are lost in a country whose language we don't know, where we don't know anyone, we have no work, not even tools, we have only enough food left for one meal, and because these four have the chance of finding work, they leave us in the lurch, and go to work for themselves, while forcing us to buy back their shares of the tent or to get along without it! If Perlot and Messent leave us, I don't know how we are going to eat tomorrow."

It must be observed that Messent and I were the only ones with a little money.

"Gentlemen," I said then, "if that is what is distressing you, save your tears for another occasion; I have a hundred and fifty francs, that represents a hundred loaves of bread. So we still won't die of hunger tomorrow; as long as there is any left, we'll eat; when there is no more, let us hope that God will provide or, better, will help us to provide; but we have some time ahead of us."

"As for me," said Messent, "I have only eighty francs, but the company may dispose of them."

"Well," I said, "that gives us two hundred and thirty, we have some bread on the board for several days. Heaven helps those who help themselves! and to help ourselves today, the only thing we have to do is to look for work; so let's look and let's look together.

"As I speak a little English and as Messent understands it a little, I will ask the questions and he will translate the answers. As he and I are the Croesuses of the company, we won't place ourselves until the others are placed. Is that understood, Messent?"—"Perfectly," he said, "and let's do better, let us stay united; if one alone has a chance of finding work, let it be for the six; everybody must eat!"

"Agreed, bravo!"

The pact was concluded, sanctioned by handshakes, and there we were, six brothers. The desertion of the four others succeeded only in tightening the cords which united us already. As a consequence, and without waiting longer, we leave for the camp.

First, I enter a supply store and, more or less, rather less than more, I explain that we are new arrivals, that we want to work by the day, and I ask where we may have a chance of finding work; they suggest a Mr. Mack.[3] We seek him out, he

3. This may have been J. W. Mack, who served as a juror during a special term held by the District Court of the Fifth Judicial District of the State of California for the County of Mariposa in August 1851. See "Minutes, Court of Sessions," p. 49, in Mariposa County Records. I am indebted to Helen Bretnor for this information. Mrs. Bretnor consulted the Mariposa County Records extensively to identify as fully as possible the names of Americans mentioned in Perlot's narrative. Hereafter this source is called Bretnor Notes.

doesn't need anyone, but he sends us to a Mr. De Lamare; that one didn't need anybody either, he was in partnership with two others and their labors were suspended because of too much water. This Mr. De Lamare was of French origin; his grandfather had been expelled from France as a Protestant, had taken refuge on the Isle of Guernsey and had become an Englishman.[4] This De Lamare, speaking the two languages equally well, was in consequence overwhelmed by our questions; he replied with complaisance, showed himself very obliging, and concerned himself with us as if he had owed us something; if he did not give us work, he procured it for us; he gave us a letter for a person called Dick, who was installed two miles lower down. We come to this Mr. Dick; after having read the letter and consulted his two associates, he asks us how much we want per day. Messent translates this question for me, I reply in as good English as is possible for me: "Not much to begin with; give us four dollars (20 francs) each per day, with board and tools"; seeing that he was considering, as it seemed to me, too long, and that perhaps he was going to say no, I add: "We will work under these conditions for a trial week; afterward, if we are satisfied on both sides, well, we will make arrangements for a longer time."— "Good," he says, "but I need only four workers and you are six."—"That makes no difference," I tell him, "we will work four at a time. When do you want us to begin?" He replies: "Tomorrow at noon," then adds: "See, lower down, if my neighbors might not need workers."

We go, in fact, to see the neighbors and we have the good luck to be engaged at the same wages and conditions as the others with Dick; only, work would not begin until Monday and it was Wednesday. But what did it matter? since we were immediately going to work by fours, the six were sure of having something to eat.

Our companions, who had listened to all of these conversations without understanding anything, did not tire of making me repeat both the price and conditions, and when they would begin. It seemed to them so miraculous to earn four dollars a day right away that they could not believe it, and if one of us two, Messent and I, spoke, they looked at the other to be sure it was serious. By dint of making us repeat everything, they ended, however, by believing it. To see us, while we were returning to our encampment, one would have sworn that we had already made our fortune—it was only that we had just escaped from a bad spot.

In going back up the river, I did not forget to stop at Mr. De Lamare's to shake his hand and thank him. After that, my path passing through the camp, I buy some beefsteaks for fifteen francs, some bread for the same sum and—what it is to be young!—three bottles of St.-Julien for forty-five francs; then, loaded with these victuals, I return to the tent. "Gentlemen," I say to my companions, "I treat today; here are the makings of a splendid banquet; we must celebrate our arrival. We have reached the end of our voyage, we are in good health, and we are going to earn our living; we have succeeded and so justified the device inscribed on the flag of La

4. This appears to have been J. G. De Lamare, whose name appears in the Quartz Claims, book A, p. 198 (Mariposa County Records [Bretnor Notes]).

Fortune: Audaces fortuna juvat [Fortune favors the bold]; it is Latin, it seems, and it means that with audacity one can always get oneself out of trouble. Therefore, we must be joyful and show it. You, Béranger, don't be jealous any more of the four others, who, by leaving us, have succeeded only in losing five francs a day, for they have only fifteen francs and we have twenty." That said, we prepare the feast and draw up to the table or, to be more exact, seat ourselves down on the grass around our beefsteaks, flanked by our three bottles. We eat, we drink, and in spite of the singularity of our menu, we banquet as joyfully as anyone in the world.

The fatigues of the route, the dangers we have run, the alarms we have experienced, all that is forgotten, or rather, we are happy to recall, in order to laugh over them, the most moving episodes of our odyssey. As for the miseries which the future can still reserve for us, we do not dream of them, we don't have the time.

Next day for breakfast we turned out our sacks of provisions, which had, moreover, become frightfully light; then, folding the tent, we prepared to report with our baggage to Camp Dick, as we called it. . . . But there was still a difficulty to resolve; in settling our account, the day before, with Duléry and associates, we had not been able to come to an agreement on the subject of the donkey and the mule, neither one side nor the other being in a state to buy them back. In short, they left them to us to keep, authorizing us to make use of them, on condition of paying them, in case of sale, the share they had coming to them. So, now that we were going to work by the day, these animals could no longer be useful to us; moreover, we no longer had the time to take care of them and, finally, we could not feed them, considering that there was no grass at the place where we were going to settle, nor in the surroundings. After having discussed it a long time, someone suggested setting them at liberty. We had bought them when they were not fat and they had not put on much weight during the trip; helped by blows, they had been able to carry our baggage as far as the placers, but it would have been difficult for them, I think, to go any farther.

Recognizing their good and loyal services and taking pity on their condition, we who felt ourselves so happy, we unanimously adopted the proposition which was made us to give them their liberty as compensation for the miseries which we had made them suffer during the trip. We immediately executed this decision, reserving the right to notify our former associates, less happy than we, that if they wanted their share, they had only to take it with ours, which we abandoned to them.

We had almost four miles to go to report to Camp Dick; but they seemed short to us and we were there well before noon. While waiting for dinner, we set ourselves to cutting from the bushes, with blows of the axe, what was needed to make us beds and a house, for the tent could serve us only as refuge in case of bad weather; it was too small for an establishment however little prolonged. By dint of piling long props against long props on both sides of a big, spreading branch of an oak, we had a fairly comfortable hut, twelve feet long and eight feet wide, where we could set up our four beds and install the six of us until the following Monday.

Our bosses, Macdonald, Thomson, and Dick, had built themselves a house for the season. [5] They had felled trees, they had cut them to the desired length, and, on a nicely leveled plot, had placed the two biggest, parallel and distant from one another by the width which they wanted to give their residence; on the flattened ends of these two first, and on the square in order to close the parallelogram, they had put two others, then on these, the ends always flattened, and crossing at right angles, they had placed the following, and so on until the edifice had reached the height of five feet. Two big poles forking at the height of ten feet were set outside the centers of two of the sides; these forks replaced the absent gables and supported a big pole running from one to the other and serving as ridge of the house, whose roof was a canvas which passed over this ridge-pole and was nailed to the walls; with branches, moss, and sod they had stuffed the interstices left in the walls. The hole serving as entrance to the house had been made by sawing two of the logs forming the wall at a distance of three feet from one of the four corners; finally a canvas nailed at the top of this opening, by falling naturally, blocked it and so served as door.

Cooking was done in the open air. The hearth was established at the foot of a big oak; a meter above the hearth they had drilled an auger-hole in which they had stuck an old pick which served as pothook; all around the trunk of this oak, nails half-driven in served to hang the kitchen utensils, which were of tin or wrought iron. About half-past ten, Thomson, who served as cook, returned from work to busy himself with dinner. He piles up the equivalent of six fagots and sets fire to it, then he goes to a neighboring oak where a quarter of beef is hanging with an enormous piece of fat, cuts a piece of one, a slice of the other, and returns to fry his fat in a pan as big as an ordinary round table; in a sheet-iron saucepan, he puts water and some potatoes just as they are—I think that they are not even washed—then lets it boil. During this time the fagots have been consumed and have produced a great mound of coals. Thomson takes an old shovel, opens this heap, then goes into the house to look for a sheet-iron pan full of a raised dough, probably prepared in the morning, throws his pan bottom-up in the hole which he has just made and covers it with the coals; there is his bread in the oven. That done, he occupies himself with the beefsteaks.

At noon, when Macdonald and Dick return from work, all is ready. Thomson then calls us to dinner. I say to Dick that all six of us should dine; my two comrades not starting work for the neighbors till the next Monday, I beg him to permit them to eat with us until then; he could retain from our wages what he thought it was worth. He replies: *all right* (très bien) and we sit down at table; the table, as I have said, was the grass. The bosses, in their character as bosses, ate at their house. They came to get on their wrought iron plates what they wanted to eat, cut from the pan

5. The identities of Perlot's first employers are difficult to establish. In the "Index to Locators of Mines" in Mariposa, there were four McDonalds, three Thompsons, and one Joseph Dick. In October 1851, however, Isaac McDonald and Isaac Thompson were listed as juror and witness, respectively, in "Minutes, Court of Sessions" (Mariposa County Records [Bretnor Notes]). In 1864 Joseph Dick is listed as having married Emma Jane Ashworth at Mariposa ("Record of Marriage Licenses," Mariposa County [Bretnor Notes]).

which Thomson had just extracted from the brazier as much bread as they wanted, then returned to their residence. On our side, we took from the skillet and from the pan what we wanted, then, seated majestically on the ground, and holding on our knees a plate well garnished and well irrigated with beefsteak juice, we devoured our dinner.

When Thomson had supposed that the potatoes were cooked, he had simply poured the contents of the saucepan out on the ground, the water had run off, and the potatoes had cooled somewhat. We gathered them from the ground, we peeled them, then we soaked them with the grease which we spooned from the frying-pan. Thomson, after having washed this saucepan, had refilled it with water; when the water had boiled, he had thrown into it a fistful of tea, and it was there that those who wanted to drink went to dip a mug (tin cup).

That was where the culinary art was on the banks of the Mariposa in 1851. But if the cuisine of Sir Dick was not refined, it was healthful and fortifying.

Hardly was the repast finished, when Dick came out of his cabin and said to us: "Gentlemen, to wark [sic] (Messieurs, au travail)." It was in the orders: we were mercenaries, we no longer belonged to ourselves; he had the right to command us; he commanded us.

We each took a pick and a shovel on our shoulders and descended as far as the river flat—that is, about fifty paces—then we proceeded to what our three bosses called the works. They consisted quite simply of a canal dug the length of the hillside, into which they had turned the river water, and, at the lowest part of their territory, of a ditch dug across the flat, that is, from one side to the other. They had taken care to touch bedrock all the length of this ditch, in such a way that they had exposed all the veins or channels which the water had cut when forming this alluvial flat. It was in these veins or ditches that was found the auriferous dirt which had to be washed.

The depth of the trench was eight feet, but only two feet of dirt at the bottom carried enough to be worked. There was thus an average of six feet of dirt to clear away, and it was to do this work that they had engaged us.

So they set all four of us to work on this excavation, indicating to us the manner of procedure. Two workers threw out the dirt, one to the right, the other to the left; the two others, placed in the middle, threw it from the other side of the trench which was only four feet wide; when a stone or a rock was too big, it was rolled to one side or else was allowed to fall into the trench.

Our bosses, on their side, were occupied in digging a drainage canal in the exposed bed of the river, and in the deepest ditch, so that the bottom of the trench was below the level of the water which filtered between the earth of the flat and the bedrock.

Needless to say that we picked and shoveled hard and fast. Twenty-four hours before, we were afraid of starving, and thought that perhaps we would be very lucky to find work for nothing but our board, and here we were fed and supplied with tools, and we were earning, besides, twenty francs a day. Enchanted by what we regarded as an unhoped-for favor of destiny, we did everything possible to deserve and preserve it.

In two days, we had finished our excavating, and as the drainage canal was finished, the bosses got ready to wash the earth at the bottom next day.

A miner had just invented a new process of washing which permitted performing the work in a much more expeditious manner than by the pan; going faster, one did more work and as a result one found more gold.

This new invention was called the long-tom; it consisted of three planks nine to twelve feet long, nailed together, one of which served as bottom for this sort of boat; one of the ends was cut in an elongated bevel, and a sheet-iron plaque pierced with fairly big holes was nailed on this bevel.

This boat was set at a slope, so that the iron sheet was horizontal. On it they threw the dirt to be washed (*balux*), which they stirred with a shovel whose end was cut square. Water was thrown on the upper part of the boat with a bucket, or else it was brought there, either by a canal, or by a hose of strong canvas. This long-tom was supported from below by a sort of square wooden box with a flange all around and inclined in the same direction as the boat.

Into this receptacle fell the water and all that which could pass through the holes of the plate; the remainder was thrown aside with the shovel. It was enough to wash in the pan, twice a day, the little gravel which was at the bottom, in order to gather all the gold which had been moved during the day.

Our bosses, therefore, having installed the long-tom, took charge of the washing; we dug the earth, put it in the buckets, and brought it to them.

Thus all the earth we had excavated was washed, after which they set us to excavating another ditch, which was washed in the same manner, and so on, from trench to trench, following back up the river as far as the barrier of the canal. Then the claim (concession) was exhausted, it was necessary to make another canal, dam the river again, and continue as before.

On Saturday evening, Dick paid us for the two and a half days which were due us, say about fifty francs to each one, which he weighed by taking the gold with a spoon from the dust gathered during the week, he counted the gold for us at the rate of sixteen dollars an ounce (84 francs). It goes without saying that we pocketed this gold gladly; we were at last quite convinced that the placers and their product were not a chimera, but a brilliant and ringing reality. For sure, we were all soon going to make our fortune, and Lord knows the castles we were building in Spain!

Chapter Nine

Laws and Customs

On Sunday morning, wanting to spend this day of rest agreeably, we dressed in our Sunday best and left for Mariposa. While going up the river, I noticed that each "Claim" (concession) was marked by notices nailed to the trees and signed by the claimants.

All that was in English and, having no one to explain it to me, I only half understood what it meant. I saw very clearly, according to the notices, that the right of working the claims belonged to those who had signed them, but I wondered on what they based the right to make these their territories, and what would happen if another came to work there.

We were edified on reaching the camp.

It seemed that the miners, gathered at the camp of Mariposa on the first of March, had agreed to give themselves some laws, for nothing was organized until then; there was neither law nor government nor police. Forthwith, on the public square, they had named a committee of five members charged with formulating the most necessary laws and, the following Sunday, all the multitude of the miners, assembled at the same place, had passed these laws, voting for them article by article.[1] Moreover, they had given to a resident of Mariposa the powers necessary to judge any case which might be presented, but in all, without exception, the cause should first be submitted to a jury accepted by the parties to the cause. The preamble of these laws said: "The white men (that is, the civilized European and American, which excluded negroes, still slaves at that time in the United States) gathered at Mariposa, wishing to replace the missing laws of the United States (that is, not yet promulgated in California), have resolved, as having the force of law, the following:"

There followed eighty articles which were adapted, as closely as possible, to the situation. One read there, among other provisions, these:

"Every man has the right to one claim (concession to mining land) of twenty-five

1. The Mariposa County Records indicate that the laws adopted on March 1, 1851, carried the signature of 215 miners and that similar codes continued to be adopted in mining camps throughout the county during 1851–52 (Bretnor Notes). The famous Quartzburg Convention, designed to adopt codes for quartz mining, was held in June 1851. The movement to establish rules for quartz mining is discussed in Paul, *California Gold*, pp. 217–19. An account of the Mariposa County convention may be found in the San Francisco *Daily Alta California*, June 30, 1851.

feet, along a watercourse, of whatever kind, and that from one ridge to the other. In default of a watercourse, the claim shall be a more or less rectangular space of six hundred and twenty-five square feet at the maximum. There shall be a notice at the top and another at the bottom of the claim, which will show the number and the names of the persons who have claimed it. These notices shall be made known to the neighbors if there are any, if not, the description of the claim and a copy of the notices shall be deposited in the hands of the sheriff (a sort of justice of the peace who united all powers). Three days of absence not caused by an instance of superior force, shall presuppose the voluntary abandonment of the claim, which may thereafter be taken by another person.

"The holder of a claim has the right to drain the water from the lowest part of the subsoil, etc., etc."

Then a penal code which was somewhat Draconian:

"Whoso willfully does wrong to anyone to the value of fifty dollars (250 francs), shall be hanged by the neck until death shall ensue. The penalty for a lesser wrong shall be from five to fifty strokes of a switch on the fleshy parts of the body, stripped. The number of lashes, within these limits, is left to the discretion of the judge.

"Any repetition of an offense carrying a penalty of twenty or more lashes, shall be punished by hanging. For any repetition of an offense of lesser importance, the guilty person shall receive twenty lashes, then shall be banished from the *County* (department or province). If he returns, whoever finds him there will have the right to arrest him, and he shall be hanged.

"Whoever kills except in self-defense shall be punished by death.

"If anyone, after sunset, approaches, without calling out, within fifty feet of a house, tent, or a fire indicating that someone lives there, the occupant has the right to shoot at him.

"It is forbidden to destroy needlessly; whoever is convicted of having, without a legitimate motive, killed a domestic animal, or destroyed anything of value, shall be punished by a fine of a third of that value. In default of payment, he shall receive from three to fifteen lashes, etc., etc."

A final article provided that these laws would remain in force until others had replaced them, or else until the government of the United States should be legally installed. In order to change them, add to them or subtract from them, it would require a petition signed by more than twenty-five persons, which petition should be posted for fifteen days in all business houses before being submitted to the assembled citizens. In order to promulgate new laws, the same formalities would have to be carried out with the same delays.

As for the cases not foreseen by the law—and naturally there were many of them—it was arranged that they should be submitted to a jury composed of nine members accepted by the two parties to the cause and judging without appeal.

This summary code carried the signatures of two hundred and fifteen persons.

There were many people at the camp who had come to supply their needs for the week. Every day, too, there arrived a great number of new emigrants. We met several Frenchmen there who were working two, four, even six miles from Mariposa. On all sides, the news was good, almost everybody was finding gold; it was easy to find claims where one could make a fairly good day's pay, that is, from four to ten dollars. We also saw our four ex-partners there. They were dragging their tails; their employers had given each of them only ten francs for three days of work which were due them, in order to be sure that they would stay with them the whole month as they had engaged to do. We, who had gold in our pockets, felt pity for them as we complaisantly compared their situation to ours. It is true that the work which paid us four dollars a day was well worth five or six, but our ex-partners, bound for a longer term, earned less than we. And then, what a difference in the manner in which we were considered and treated by our respective employers! Ours, who had our word, had full confidence in it and feared no desertion on our part; they had paid us our full due; while the others. . . . And, in observing this difference, we experienced a sweet satisfaction, a sentiment that was hardly charitable, certainly, but—isn't it true?—very human.

Toward evening, being well informed on all that could be useful to us to know, we returned to our encampment, in order to be ready and willing next morning to being the week. That same evening, our two comrades settled on the flat where they were to begin their work on Monday morning; I asked Mister Dick how much we owed him for their board. He replied: "Nothing." I insisted.—"Oh," he said, "they have rendered services: they have cut wood, and done the cooking, it is quite natural that cooks eat what they cook; no, I don't want anything, let's say no more about it." I thanked him and the matter was dropped.

Monday morning we went back to work, but it limped a little, and the expression is so much the more just—may I be pardoned this innocent play on words—as we hadn't a finger uncrippled by its blister (ça clochait un peu . . . nous n'avions pas un doight qui n'eût sa cloche); several even had them on the palm of their hand. It was also because we had lost, for longer or shorter periods, the habit of manual labor. It had been seven years, on my part, since I had had a shovel in my hands: in the trade of Calicot one is hardly exposed to calluses, in that of a laborer, it's another thing. Soon our hands were all covered with them, and when there were no more empty spots, new calluses grew on the first ones. It was especially these parasitic blisters which made us suffer. But one becomes inured to everything; at the end of several days the skin was hardened, the spirit too, and we thought no more about it, which is the best method, I think, of not feeling pain. While we were working, we were calculating the capital which we would have to dispose of at the end of the week. Taking everything into account, we decided that we would have, among the six of us, enough to establish ourselves. We could supply ourselves with tools, and procure enough supplies for a week, and we would still have gold left; though not much, to be sure. All during the week, we discussed the question of whether we should stake a claim in order to work it, or if it wouldn't be better to continue a little longer to work by the day, inasmuch as our two comrades, who were working farther down, were still engaged for a fortnight.

On Saturday evening, it was definitely decided that we would look for a claim the next day, would buy some tools on Monday, then we would establish ourselves on our own account. When Mister Dick had paid us, I informed him of our resolution. He seemed gravely disappointed; he was content with us, and as he needed workmen, he would rather, he said, keep us than look for others. If we were not satisfied with our salary, we had only to make known our demands and probably we could reach an agreement. He would have liked to keep us at least long enough to work the claim. "See your comrades," he said in closing, "and then let me know your conditions."

Messent and I—for we still had to stay together for parleying, one being the spokesman, the other translating the reply—we went back to find our four companions, and we submitted to them Mr. Dick's propositions. We took them under consideration.

The for and against were successively stated, examined, discussed. "Fortune knocks but once," said those who wished us to persist in the resolution taken—and I was of the number—"let us hasten to answer. We can still, at this time, find unoccupied claims easily enough, but this situation will not last long, in view of the ever-growing increase of immigrants to the placers. We know about ores, and already we know enough about the miner's trade to discover a vein of gold as well as anyone, in any terrain. Then, to sum up, did we come to California to work for wages for the gold seekers, and pass our time in extracting the precious metal for them? Our work produces more, apparently, than the salary they give us; the difference forms the profit of those who employ us. In working on our own account, we will have this profit for ourselves. And, who knows? soon perhaps we will have, in our turn, laborers who work for us by the day, and then we can, like our employers today, make ten to thirty ounces of gold each day of washing, that is, twice a week. Isn't the prospect tempting?"—"Yes," said the others, "but we only have just enough gold to pay the expenses of setting ourselves up. What will become of us, what will we do, if we don't find gold, which could happen, or if we don't find enough? Return to find our employers? They will doubtless have taken other workmen or, perhaps, will no longer need any. We can look elsewhere, but will we find anything? Aren't we, at the end of one or two weeks, going to find ourselves, as on our arrival, without supplies and without money?

"It is true we will have what we didn't have then—some tools, but it is not very certain that we will be good enough miners to be able to recognize and make the most of an auriferous terrain. The trade may seem simple and easy to us; but still it is a trade, and one must, to know it, have learned it. Is it enough to have worked eight days to know all its secrets? This work, done under the direction of experienced miners, does not present very great difficulties and, on the whole, is not very distressing; will it be the same when we are doing it on our own account? At present, our four dollars are assured us every day and we are urged to ask for more; we are promptly paid, well fed, well treated, for our employers hardly make us feel the weight of commands; why leave them? Moreover, would the procedure be quite correct? They saved us, after all, from misery; they have given us, without bargaining, the salary we asked for; and now that we have this salary in our pockets, we are going, without having warned them, to abandon them at a time when they, in their turn, need us! Wouldn't that be paying them with ingratitude?" The former responded, the latter replied. Having thus discussed it a long time, we went to bed without concluding anything. That is how discussions most often are terminated.

The next day, at breakfast, I told Dick that if we should leave him, it would not be with the intention of offering our services to others, but of working on our own account; that was why we had come to California, and he ought to understand. All the same, we did not intend to leave him in trouble; if he did not find replacements for us by the following Monday, we would still stay that day, and, if necessary, the day following, so that he would not be forced, for lack of help, to stop operations.

"Oh well," he said, "at that rate you will stay, because . . . I'll not find anyone."

Then, after a pause: "Let's do better," he said, "let's conclude an agreement. How much do you want for working another month, at the end of which you will be free?" On this, Messent left me and went to get the opinion of the others. He returned shortly after: the others gave me carte blanche. "Well," I said, "Pop Dick, give us six dollars a day."

It may be believed that while we were deliberating, our employers had deliberated too, for they did not need to confer long to accept the bargain.

The business concluded, we experienced a sort of relief. We were free from uncertainty and from a somewhat false position; now, we had a respite of a month, at the end of which we would be able to put into effect our project of establishing ourselves under more favorable conditions than we could have done at the moment. Just think, six dollars a day, that is, thirty-one francs fifty centimes, for the dollar is worth five francs twenty-five centimes, that is, six francs twenty-five centimes more than the indemnity for which the members of the Constituent Assembly were then so reproached!

Each of us was going, at the end of our engagement, to find himself on top of a little pile of money of nearly a thousand francs, altogether six thousand francs; that seemed magnificent to us. With such a capital, we could undertake anything, and we were, assuredly, on the road to fortune!

This does not contradict the fact that I would have preferred another solution. It was repugnant to me to work for others when I had gold in my pocket, and I would have felt more joy in earning four dollars by working on my own account than in receiving six from an employer. But I saw clearly that at bottom this was not the opinion of the others—it was necessary to renounce making mine prevail or else break our newly formed partnership, which I did not want at any price. I had to resign myself to it.

The month passed in digging and washing, then digging and washing some more.

While awaiting our liberation, I spent my Sundays in exploring the environs, with Messent's gun on my back. I had bought a livre of powder at two and a half dollars, the shot cost me a half-dollar the American pound (14 ounces). We ate, in company, the game I shot; that slightly varied our regular fare, which was composed solely of beef. While hunting, I studied the terrain, the places where people were working, and I tried to recognize those where one could still work profitably.

About the twentieth of the month, at Mariposa, we saw the arrival of the Provençaux, our companions of the trail, whom we had left at San Juan. . . .

[Without the benefit of Perlot's compass or leadership the Provençaux had taken twelve days longer to reach Mariposa. They were so exhausted that most had to rest for three or four days before taking jobs as laborers similar to those held by Perlot and his companions.]

Chapter Ten

Wintering in the Southern Mines

When the term of our engagement had expired, and we had become free again, we began the search for a claim to stake. The expedition of the Cagnade Blanche having made a certain gap among the miners, we had only the embarrassing variety of choice, but this embarrassment was serious, for all that.[1] We were not experienced enough as miners to know how to choose well, and we soon realized that we had presumed too much for ourselves in this regard. After many goings and comings, marches and counter-marches without result, to bring it to an end we fixed our choice, almost by chance, on just any claim. We bought tools, we provided ourselves with supplies, and there we were at work. At the end of the week, after having dug three times and washed three times, it was found that we had each earned three dollars a day and consumed a dollar and a half in supplies, net a dollar and a half; while as workers we had earned six! Discouraged in the presence of this pitiful result, two of the partners, Viot and Schmidt, went at once to find the Americans, our former employers, and contracted an engagement of three months at the rate of five dollars a day, besides board.

The others held fast and continued to work. During this second week, we each made four dollars a day; that was better, but we were finding that it was not enough. Perhaps we did not have a good vein; it was necessary to seek it a little more to the right or a little more to the left, make soundings, open trenches.

As we were occupied on Sunday morning in discussing the matter, one of our former employers arrived, accompanied by another person who knew both languages. He proposed that we return with him, promising us, like the others, for an engagement of three months, five dollars a day and food, tools, etc. I saw the time coming when I was going to be left alone, my three partners being of the opinion that they must accept these proposals.

"We have happened on a poor claim, doubtless, but were we capable," they said, "of finding a better? It would be preferable, whatever the reason, to keep to

1. Here Perlot is referring to a rumored gold strike at a location called Cañada Blanca [Cagnade Blanche] somewhere southeast of Mariposa which attracted 120 miners to the area, but they returned empty-handed.

110

the certain advantages which are offered us than to stick stubbornly with an enterprise whose success is at least doubtful."

"Gentlemen," I told them, "it may be that you are right, and I do not want to influence your decision in any way: let each one, then, do as he wants; as for me, I do not want to give myself a master when I can be free; I have tools and I still have some gold in my purse; I will work on my own account. If I do not succeed, when I have spent my last ounce of gold, I will go out again for hire to another, but only for the time necessary to put myself back in funds. I have a chance, like anyone else, of finding a claim which would bring me ten or fifteen dollars a day; in any case, I will not give up looking for it. Now, Gentlemen, let us settle our accounts! Take back the tent and the long-tom (we had bought it a fortnight before at the price of 75 dollars); alone, I no longer need these objects which would be an embarrassment to me; I would rather sleep under an oak than under a tent, and a pan or a rocker* suffices me for washing."

While we proceeded to the division of the different items composing the community property, one of the three, Béranger, said suddenly: "Oh well, let's make it only two shares, I'm staying with Perlot." So it was done; the two others took the tent, and the long-tom remained with us.

There were two of us left; so the famous Company of the Ten was definitely dissolved.

While Béranger was away at the camp to buy supplies for the week, I left in search of a richer claim than the one we had been working until then. I saw many places, but I was always faced by the same difficulty: How to distinguish the good from the bad? And in a good claim, how to know where the rich vein is? How, under six or ten feet of earth, to foresee where to find the most auriferous dirt, the *balux?* There certainly was a means of recognizing it, it was only a matter of finding it. I had observed the ways of three Mexicans who, shortly before, had settled in the neighborhood; they were miners in their own country, they should know the secrets of the craft; they had not established themselves by chance on the claim they were occupying. They had examined the rock at each turn of the river, had sounded it, had consulted among themselves, then by way of conclusion had started to dig a pit on the flat, at the foot of the hillside, and fairly far from the riverbed. They had come to a good conclusion, it seemed, for they were finding gold. Why, on what indications, had they dug this trench so far from the watercourse? There was only one way for me to find out, that was to ask them. I tried it, but, whether they did not understand me or did not want to understand me, I could draw nothing from them. I was forced to guide myself by my own lights, profiting by the observations I had already made, and by those which I might yet make. So I passed my time in

---

*So we called a machine for washing the dirt, which, in fact, resembled a cradle; it was a box, mounted on two feet cut in a half-moon, and covered with a sheet-iron plate pierced with holes.

coming and going among the diggings of others, without asking any more explanations, while waiting for Béranger's return.

I proposed to him, as soon as he had returned, that on the next morning, Monday, we dig a test hole, at the bottom of a big flat where I thought I had observed that the river, in times past, must have deposited the same alluvium as where the three Mexicans were working; there was, in fact, the same lay of the land. Béranger having consented, that very day we moved to the flat and staked a claim there to be able to begin work the next morning. Before proceeding any farther, we would be obliged to open a sort of pit in order to discover the nature of the ground, for we had to dig a drainage ditch to be able to work. That was a costly operation because it took a great deal of time. Hardly were we at work when already the passersby were laughing at us, beginning with our ex-partners. To be sure, they said, at the bottom of our pit we were going to find the big lump, that is, an ingot which would have assured our fortune, a thing which happened sometimes to miners. However, we continued to dig without paying attention to these remarks and, at the depth of six feet, we observed that the gravel contained gold; two feet lower, we found the rock.

We then tested the gravel; the first pan gave us the value of four dollars. What a windfall! Were we really going to find the *big lump*, as our good friends were ironically saying? We washed what we had extracted from the gold bed, counting on a marvelous result.

Alas, no! The result was nothing marvelous, it was only satisfactory. Farewell to our dream of speedy fortune! But at least there remained with us the hope of working profitably. We judged, in fact, from the size of the nuggets and also from the thickness of the *balux*, that we had struck a good vein. In three days our ditch was finished. Full of confidence and eagerness we began the regular working of our claim: four days of digging, then three days of washing; so it was that we proceeded ordinarily.

Fourteen days of this work gave us one hundred and seventy dollars, that is about twelve dollars per day of work. This result confirmed our predictions; we had a good vein. While the land beyond us was still free, I proposed to Béranger to hire four day-laborers, in order to be able to claim a hundred and fifty feet instead of fifty, each worker, according to the law, having the right to only twenty-five feet of land along and on each side of the river. But Béranger feared to commit himself to expenses which would be a little heavy if the vein happened to end. He was of the opinion that we should exhaust the land we had, then claim for ourselves the neighboring land, subject to establishing ourselves farther away if, during the interval, others came to locate beside us. That is what happened; ten days later we had neighbors on all sides. The Cagnade Blanche expedition having returned, that made one hundred and twenty miners more on the river.

We had exhausted our claim at the end of six weeks. It had brought us ten to fifteen dollars a day; we each had in our purse the value of 2,350 francs, expenses paid.

The Mariposa was claimed all along its course and, in order to get another place for ourselves, we had to go to another watercourse. On the other side of the mountain forming the ridge west of the Mariposa, there was a camp and a creek called Agua Fria (cold water).[2] We found a claim there situated two miles below the camp. Already the lack of water was making itself felt, as the month of September was approaching, so that we washed only with much difficulty and then we washed poorly. However, we were still making from seven to eight dollars apiece per day.

Shortly after, my partner fell ill. He went to board with a Frenchman who had just established himself at Mariposa as a baker and restaurateur; he was a man named Chanac, a shipboard companion, member of the defunct company of La Fortune, and also of the famous company of the Provençaux who, on leaving San Luis, had gone to take the air for several days on the plain of the Tulares.

I continued to work our claim alone; I made an average of eight dollars a day.

At the end of two weeks Béranger had recovered; but soon we lacked water to do the washing. So we had to look for a claim on another creek.

Moreover, it was the end of September and the rainy season was about to begin. During the five months that we had been on the placers, we had not seen a cloud in the sky; but as soon as the rain began, it would fall for five or six months. People stopped working because of the lack of water; when the rivers filled, it would become impossible to start working again because of the abundance of water. The season therefore was ended; those who employed workers released them; most of the miners were preparing to return to Stockton or San Francisco to spend the rainy season there and to return to the placers in the month of February or March. They were afraid, besides, that the same thing would happen to them as to those unfortunates who, the winter before, when surprised by the rains and lacking provisions, had died of hunger and hardship while trying, but too late, to return to the coast.

A certain number, however, appeared disposed to remain; they alleged that winters like that of the preceding year, when it had rained without stopping for three months, were the exception, continual rains lasting ordinarily four weeks; and then, last winter, after the rain, the snow had fallen abundantly and, according to the statements of the Indians, that occurrence was extremely unusual. If then, one were provided with supplies for only three months, one need not fear famine, and one could profit from the interruptions in the rain to dig for gold. In the meantime,

2. Agua Fria, sometimes spelled Agua Frio, was founded in 1849. Enos Christman found Frenchmen and Mexicans mining there in March 1850. Located on a creek noted for its very cold water, it became the first seat of Mariposa County in 1850 but eventually lost the title to Mariposa. Agua Fria is also associated with the California frontiersman James D. Savage, who moved his store there in 1850. See Raymond F. Wood, *California's Agua Fria: The Early History of Mariposa County* (Fresno: Academy Library Guild, 1954), p. 31, and Enos Christman, *One Man's Gold: The Letters and Journals of a Forty-Niner* (New York: Whittlesey House, McGraw-Hill, 1930), p. 128.

the merchants, not knowing whether the placers would be completely deserted, put in hardly any supplies.

Whatever the case might be, we decided, Béranger and I, that we would stay, would buy canvas to make a tent, and would provide ourselves with supplies for three months; when winter came, we would wait under our tent for the return of spring; that, in the interval, however little or much we could work, we would only be better off and more ready the following year. It would cost less, in any case, than to cover sixty leagues on foot, live three or four months in a hotel, and afterward make the same trip again. The only danger to fear was the return of the Indians, whom the snow would drive from the mountains and who, they said, coming down as far as Mariposa and even farther, would kill and steal every time they had a chance. But after all, Mariposa already numbered eighty to ninety houses or tents; if at least two or three persons remained in each dwelling, we would be strong enough to resist the Indians.

This resolution taken, and abandoned claims being numerous, we settled on the almost dry river, a mile below Mariposa, in order to work there while waiting for the water coming from the rains to drive us from the river.

In consequence of the departure of most of the miners, the water, being used less, had become a little less scarce and much clearer, and as it was more abundant and cleaner in the morning, we began the day by washing the gravel extracted the day before, which took us three hours, and the rest of the day we spent digging the dirt which we would have to wash the next morning. We managed, by proceeding this way, to make from seven to eight dollars each per day. We passed our Sundays in sewing the canvas of our tent so that we would not be caught unprepared when the bad weather began.

There came a time when the water was completely lacking; the season was ended. While waiting for the rain, I occupied myself with hunting; there was found in the environs an abundance of game of all kinds, hare, rabbits, wildcats, partridges, quail, wild geese, without counting the bear and the mountain lion. These last two, who little liked noise and disturbance, were beginning to stay away from the placers, but they would return when the flats had become peaceful again and when snow covered the mountains where they had withdrawn.

I bought a double-barreled shotgun, a six-shot revolver, five livres of powder and twenty livres of balls and small shot. We left in the morning, carrying on our backs the supplies for the day, one armed, the other bearing the miner's tools. At the same time we were hunting, we were exploring the country on this side and that, gathering observations, sometimes making assays, with the next campaign in view. Where were we going to establish ourselves? was a question which we wanted to settle before the coming of winter.

One day when we had headed east, we found ourselves not far from the banks of a river which the Indians call Chowchilla; it was near noon; I had just unloaded then reloaded my gun with small shot, with the intention of killing a rabbit for our dinner.

I was walking thirty or forty paces in advance of Béranger, hoping to surprise

Johnny Rabbit at the moment when he was passing from one bush to another, when I heard my partner calling me softly. I turned around, thinking that he saw some rabbits between him and me, for these animals seemed very numerous in this brush; consequently I had the gun at my shoulder, ready to fire, but I saw Béranger, terror painted on his visage, seeking which way to flee, at the same time pointing at a big oak blown down by the wind. I looked there and I perceived, fifteen paces away, an enormous bear; it had its back up like a cat in the presence of a dog, and was preparing, without doubt, to stand up against me if I should approach. At this sight, I admit that I thought no more of the rabbits and that I had no other preoccupation than to put the greatest distance possible between the monster and me. I think however, that I can do myself this justice, that I knew enough to keep up appearances before the beast; walking backward prudently but with dignity, my eye fixed on the enemy, little by little I approached Béranger, who, I was pleased to realize, was no more reassured than I. Once reunited and seeing ourselves at a good distance from the animal, we stopped and began to consider him, asking ourselves what was going to become of him and of us. All at once we saw him come out from behind the branches of the fallen oak which half hid him; he began to turn about, holding his head in the grass and rounding his back, which stood nearly four feet high. Each time he turned his hindquarters to us, he raised his head from the grass, looked at us for a moment, then, lowering it again, let a growl or two be heard, smacked his lips, and continued to turn around. I thought I observed, not without inquietude, that each circle he thus described brought him sensibly closer to us. Everything considered, we judged it expedient to augment the distance separating us from him by another few hundred meters. Having reached a part of the wood where the brush, less thick, was less favorable to surprises, we felt ourselves a little reassured and made the brave resolution of taking our repast on the bank of the creek, of that very creek from which probably came our bear. This encounter nevertheless having quite startled us, we had become wary; we advanced only on assuring ourselves, each time that we passed near a bush, that there was no bear hidden behind it. However, we reached the stream without having any unfortunate encounter; but there we saw that the sand, wherever there was any, was all covered with the prints of these terrible Plantigradas; it wasn't only the footprints of the one we had just seen, for they were there in all dimensions, big, little, medium. That made us suppose that we were surrounded by bears, and we concluded that the best thing for us to do, after having quenched our thirst, was to go farther away to dine, for fear that during our repast a thirsty—or perhaps hungry—bear might come to claim that we were troubling his drink. So it was done. Our dinner was not long. We placed ourselves about two hundred meters from the stream, on a small eminence where the bushes were comparatively scattered; for greater security we ate standing. I think it would have been difficult for no matter what man or animal to approach us without being seen. However, we saw, we heard nothing. The repast finished, I discharged my gun, then reloaded it with ball, and, unanimously, we decided that we would try to return directly to Mariposa. We walked with caution, avoiding the bushes as much as possible, and we had the happiness—unhoped for—of returning safe and sound to the camp.

Still quite upset, we recounted our adventure and, convinced that we had escaped from a great danger, we thought to interest our audience; they made fun of us, and we passed for very timid men or at least very inexperienced. We had been frightened by the encounter with an inoffensive animal and we had just missed a fine shot. In spite of all that they could tell us, we did not regret in the least having let this bear go on his way. Later we knew by experience that, in fact, the bear is not as dangerous as we had imagined him, that he does not attack and is content with defending himself; on the other hand, he defends himself furiously; it would not be good, for example, when walking in the wood, to stumble, even without bad intentions, on this inoffensive animal, because then he believes it a case of legitimate defense and acts accordingly.

The grizzly (gray bear) would be capable of lying in wait to seize a victim, man or beast, which might come within his reach, but no more than the brown bear does he pursue it; he has to be wounded and thus warned that he is being attacked, before he will dash upon a distant enemy.

This encounter, moreover, which indicated that these animals were beginning to come down from the mountains to approach the placers, warned us that winter was about to begin and that it was prudent thenceforth not to venture too far.

Meanwhile, we met with three shipboard companions, two of whom were members of the former company of La Fortune, in search like us of winter quarters; they were Huguet, Gaillot and Brillet. They were among those who, after our debarkation at Monterey, had become cultivators of the soil and had taken service with different farmers. But, since the month of July, they had left agriculture there and taken the road to the placers. They had even better reasons than we for not going to spend the winter in one of the coast cities where they would have had to live on their savings.

As much as we, moreover, they counted on profiting from the breaks in the rain to get a little gold. The two companies were reunited. After having tried a claim whose situation seemed promising, but where we found little gold, we resolved to settle on the claim I had had to abandon for lack of water in the month of September, and which was situated down the creek from the camp of Agua Fria and about half-way between this latter camp and the confluence of the Agua Fria with the Mariposa. Our three new companions set up their tent there too.

While we were occupied, Béranger and I, in finishing ours, two prospectors arrived. As they spoke French, we had an interview. For a month, they told us, they had been prospecting without being able to find a convenient spot to settle in for the winter. In the course of the conversation they learned with astonishment that we were of the unfortunate company of La Fortune, of which they had heard. I owned moreover that I was Belgian. "Well!" said one of them, "so am I. What province are you from?"—"From Luxembourg."—"Oh, not I; I am from Jemeppe, or if you prefer, from Vônèche, for I lived there a long time."—"I would have preferred that you were from Herbeumont, like me, but I am not less enchanted to encounter a compatriot." Then the conversation, begun in French, was continued in Walloon; each one spoke his dialect, which varied the dialogue and gave it an additional charm.

My compatriot was named Thomas; he had embarked at Le Havre, on the *Cachalot,* which had left the port a month before the *Courrier de Cherbourg.* He had gone at first to the Northern Mines, then, having fallen ill, had returned to San Francisco. He had formed a partnership with a man named Louvel, from Cahors (France), in company with whom he had been wandering for the last month in the environs of Mariposa. They decided to settle near us to work, and three days afterward, they came to set up their tent beside ours.

So we formed a little camp.

We had laid in supplies for two or three months. The placers being more and more depopulated, the bakers and butchers had had to shut up shop for lack of clients; however, the other business houses were still going. We worked every day, a matter of killing time, for we made nothing much because of the dryness. Three weeks after our installation, the rain began and we then saw how it rains in California. It fell at first in torrents for about twenty days, without stopping for as much as two hours a day. With that, there was a south wind strong enough to break a bull's horns, so much so that one fine day, or rather, in the middle of a frightful night, the three tents were lifted at once and thrown in a tangle into the branches of an oak growing more than a hundred paces away. Lord knows how we passed the rest of that night! When day came, we divided among ourselves the rags still hanging from the tree, and we began to construct a house of dirt and wood, although it was rare in this neighborhood; only the roof was of canvas. We finished it in spite of the rain; but that took us three days, although there were seven of us. Then only could we dry ourselves, us and our provisions; but they were lost anyway: they went moldy in a short time.

Some days later, the rain stopped; but the rivers and creeks ran full to the banks and it was only at the end of eight or ten days that we were able to go back to work. We made from five to six dollars each, but the work was difficult because of the water which flooded the trenches. While working the claim, we went up the river; as we took the precaution to throw nothing behind us, the worked ground, at the end of some weeks, served us as a drainage ditch and permitted us to work more comfortably; but shortly after, the rain began again more heavily, and the overflowing river came, alas, to fill up everything. When the rain stopped again, there remained no trace of the ditch; we had to begin all over as if on virgin ground. We set to work without being discouraged, and so arrived at the extreme limit of our claim.

We had to look for another.

But the rivers and creeks, full of water, made prospecting difficult. The Mariposa, which had become a veritable torrent, had leveled everything on the flats, and of the former diggings nothing remained. So it happened that after having painfully dug a trench on an apparently virgin claim, one discovered that one was working a vein already exhausted.

To remedy as much as possible the inconveniences of this situation, the miners remaining in Mariposa were in favor of modifying California legislation as it concerned the extent of claims. Naturally they modified it to suit their convenience. They enacted that each miner had the right thenceforth not to twenty-five but to one hundred and fifty feet of land along and on both banks of no matter what river or creek. Only, when the width of the watercourse exceeded eight yards, the claim was reduced by half in the sense that it could extend on only one bank. The claim without watercourse remained twenty-five feet. The result was that the exploitation on a grand scale of mining lands became possible. Companies were formed, claiming great extents of land along the rivers and creeks; during the winter they carried out preparatory works for the next campaign. At these works were employed a certain number of laborers recruited among the new arrivals, who, in spite of the season, continued to increase almost as in the autumn. Since, at that time, we were not working, Béranger left me and went to work by the day for one of these companies; he earned four dollars a day. I bought back from him his share of the provisions we had left; then I found myself alone.

It was at this period that the remnants of a company, formed at Liège to work the gold mines of California, arrived at Mariposa.[3] Whether from lack of funds, or from an entirely different cause, the company had not been slow to dissolve. Alone and reduced to inaction, I betook myself to Mariposa in the hope that perhaps one of these new-comers would bring me news of Herbeumont. But it happened that these Belgians, numbering twenty-five, were from Liège, Huy, Verviers, and other places in the vicinity. The ones nearest to Herbeumont were from Bellain, a locality on the grand-ducal frontier, not far from Houffalize, and were named Thill, Burgrave, and Kesch, but they were ignorant of all but the existence of my native place, and consequently could give me no news. However, my twenty-five compatriots, grouped around me, examined me like a curious beast; seeing my unkempt hair, my rough beard, my face the color of chestnuts from the effect of the California sun, my clothes in the state that a miner's costume might be in, they seemed stupefied that I should claim to be from their country.

A native of Verviers, named Colson, said in the dialect of Liège to a native of Huy, who responded to the name of Macorse: "He a Belgian! never in his life! what the devil! there is no savage like that in Belgium!" I approached him, and, holding out my hand to him, I said in the patois of Herbeumont: "I see that you have a high idea of the Belgians and I'm not the one to contradict you. But wait a bit. You arrived two days ago and you are staying at the hotel; you have a fine new

3. Les Mineurs Belges secured a quartz concession from Frémont and arrived in Mariposa in the early winter of 1851. "Frémont promised his business associate, George H. Wright, that he would 'put them immediately on a good vein,' as their 'report to France will be of great importance.'" I am grateful to Mary Lee Spence, Editor of the Papers of John Charles Frémont, for this information (Spence to Lamar, Nov. 8, 1977). See also Blumenthal, "California Societies in France," p. 258n.

greatcoat, nicely polished boots, neatly combed hair, and you are freshly shaven. But your company will hardly last and doubtless you will become a miner. Wait until you have led like me the life of the placers for nine months, spending the day in a ditch, your pick in your hand, the night under a live oak, cooking your own stew, yourself providing for all your needs; then you will see what will become of your greatcoat, your hair, your beard, your face. You will realize that under these conditions a man, even a Belgian, can well have some resemblance to a savage."

I should admit that Colson was quite excusable in refusing to see in me a civilized man. I entirely neglected the care of my person, absorbed as I was by a single passion: the love of gold.

This was going on in the middle of the street, opposite the hotel where these gentlemen were staying. "You are," I said to them, "the first Belgians whom I have met, it's really the least we can do to have a glass together; let's go in, I offer it to you." They accepted not without some hesitation, for most of them were not in a state to return my politeness, a glass of anything costing fifty sous! We entered a *Bar* (estaminet); we drank two glasses each and after having talked a long while about Belgium, we separated. Hardly was my back turned, when I heard one say to the others:

"Wat' bin stia din ses feurloques! il è d'lor din's'potch." ["Take a good look at this fellow in his rags! he has gold in his pocket."]

I took the path back to the camp of the three tents. The news had just reached Mariposa that in Bear Valley they had discovered extremely rich deposits of a new kind. A great number of the inhabitants of Mariposa had already gone there; many more were preparing to go. On arriving, I told the news to the inhabitants of the three tents, who had, throughout the day, scoured the area in search of a claim and had found nothing suitable. It was immediately decided that two of us would go to Bear Valley and, if it was expedient, would stake a claim for all. Thomas and I were designated for this mission. We set off on our way the next morning, after breakfast; we had only three leagues to cover, we had no need to ask the way; the news, spreading rapidly, of the discovery of the new mines, had produced among the population of the area an extraordinary effervescence. From all points of the horizon, men on foot and on horseback were heading for Bear Valley; it was necessary only to keep them in sight. The riders passed with all the speed of their mounts. Several, in the hurry of departure, had improperly cinched their mule and it sometimes happened that the saddle turned and so came to rest under the belly of the beast. We saw one, among others, to whom the accident happened, and who, resaddling his mule in haste, left at the end of the train without noticing that he had put the saddle on hindside beforemost.

As for us, we went on foot, but at a rapid pace, driving before us a mule which carried our tools and four days' supplies. We encountered three individuals who were already returning from the famous mines. They did not, however, have the air of having found the *big lump;* as they approached, I recognized them for French-men. "Well," I said to them, "did Fortune break her wheel back there?"—"Oh no," said one of them, "I even think that she has never passed that way"; then he explained to us that these mines were nothing at all, a pit and nothing more. We nevertheless continued on our way and soon arrived at Bear Valley.[4] All around the pit of which they had told us, and in a radius of a thousand paces, the land was claimed in the name of one or another; a square of twenty-five feet on a side indicated each claim. We saw, on all sides, miners, with pick or shovel in hand, occupied in digging.

We finally arrived at the famous pit. It could have been six feet in one direction, fifteen in the other, and ten in depth, of which three feet were of earth and seven or eight in the rock. It was beside a rivulet which came down from the mountain on a fifteen per cent grade, and emptied itself, fifty meters lower down, into a creek worked by some Mexicans. One of these had noticed that the fine gold of his claim stopped across from the said rivulet. This observation led him to assay the dirt there; he found powdered gold, a real flour. Guided by this lode, he climbed the rivulet and so succeeded in discovering the famous pocket under four feet of clay.

But it was a pocket in the rock and nothing more. The nearest neighbors had no more chance of finding one like it on their claims than the ones farthest away.

We were both of the opinion that there was nothing to do. It was a windfall for those who had found this sort of chimney filled with a very rich *balux;* but finding another was doubtful, even in the whole mountain.

Nevertheless, we wanted to get it out of our minds.

As soon as day appeared, we took our precautions, we put in play all of our auriscopic [*sic*] knowledge. We succeeded in staking a claim and in beginning a prospect hole there; at the end of two days of work we were fully convinced that there was nothing there and the third day we returned to inform our companions of our discomfiture.

Except for the happy proprietors of the famous pit, who had worked it as far as thirty feet in depth and had found twenty-two thousand dollars there, the others had been no luckier than we. Fifteen days after the discovery, there were more than four hundred miners occupied everywhere in turning the soil, and at the end of a month there remained twelve of them: those who were working in the pit in question.

4. Frémont is said to have named the area Bear Valley in 1848, but the mining camp that eventually bore that name was first called Haydensville for David, Charles, and Willard Hayden, who bought or leased mining rights to a portion of the Great Johnson Vein. It was the site of the famous Josephine Mine, one of the richest in the Southern Mines. As owners came and went, the camp was called Biddleville, Simpsonville, and Johnsonville, but by 1858 its official name became Bear Valley. When Mexican miners found at least $250,000 in gold in one hole—Perlot's "pit"—at Bear Valley in November 1851, a grand rush ensued in which it was estimated that 3,000 men arrived there in a month's time. See Gudde, *California Gold Camps,* pp. 29–30, and Glasscock, *Golden Highway,* pp. 301–02.

IV

INDIANS, POLITICS, AND SURVIVAL, 1852–1853

In our immediate neighborhood we had three classes of miners, Mexican, French and Chinese.

The French, among whom are many Parisians, will work in a quiet and tolerably steady manner if nothing unusual occurs to disturb them; but, if by chance a strange Frenchman should arrive in their camp, or an old copy of the "Moniteur" should reach them, the picks and spades are relinquished for the day and all devote themselves to discussion.

Frank Marryat
Mountains and Molehills or Recollections of a Burnt Journal (1855), p. 171.

In the following four chapters the overwhelming theme of Perlot's fascinating narrative is that of survival. Having lived through the winter of 1851–52, he felt cocky, and at one point condescendingly referred to "those poor fellows" who had to retreat to Sacramento and San Francisco and spend all their earnings in order to survive. But in the coming months the misfortunes that befell him and his companions—most of whom were fellow Belgians—add up to a realistic, even grim account of mining life in California. It is to Perlot's credit that he never complained of bad fortune or tried to describe himself as being heroic.

Perlot discovered first that in order to survive, he had to be a hunter as well as a miner, and, as noted in the introduction, he became a professional hunter of sorts by supplying game to a butcher at Mariposa. He was also extremely candid about the crudeness of life in the camps when it came to finding food and housing.

Perlot's own troubles were more than matched by those of the various Miwok Indian bands living in the valleys of the westward-flowing rivers of the region. Traditionally these bands moved from the foothills to the Sierra themselves in the spring and early summer to live, hunt, and collect edible seeds and roots. Then in the fall they returned to the foothills to collect acorns and more seed. As winter came on, they followed the game in its retreat from the higher snowbound areas all the way to the lush banks of the San Joaquin.

The intrusion of the miners seriously disturbed this delicate cycle of life when the whites tried to prevent the Indians from coming down from the hills to engage in their seasonal search for food. When hostilities broke out between miners and Indians in the so-called Mariposa War of 1850–51, the result was that the first peace treaty between the United States government and the California Indians was signed. It created six temporary reservations in the region and promised to supply the Indians with food and farming equipment. Confinement to a reservation, plus the lack of food for both those on the reservations and those still in the hills—who were afraid to come down into the white settlements—created an impossible situation.

Thus in the early spring of 1852, when Perlot decided to try his luck on the Chowchilla River to the south of Mariposa, he and other miners were attacked by Indians who were trying to steal their mules and donkeys for food. If Perlot's account is accurate, he and his companions experienced four such attacks. Several miners were hit by arrows and one died from his wounds. Although the miners gave chase to the Indians they were unable to catch them. Instead they persuaded the sheriff at Mariposa to "outlaw" the Indians, which meant giving miners the right to kill hostile Indians if they would bury the body and report their act to the sheriff. Before a second Mariposa War could break out, however, the government sent regular army troops (Perlot called them dragoons) stationed at Fort Miller on the San Joaquin to chastise the Indians and bring them down to the reservations.

Lieutenant Tredwell Moore, who was in command, chased the Indians—who appear to have been Yosemites located on a reservation near Fort Miller—all the way to Mono Lake but did not catch them.

While gold and Indian troubles dominated Perlot's life in 1852, he also recorded his impressions of local political events. Because of his poor command of English and his lack of familiarity with state and county political organization, his accounts of the local elections at Mariposa are not always accurate. Perlot believed, for example, that Mariposa County was being organized for the first time in 1852, whereas the California legislature was actually created in 1850, at which time Agua Fria, not Mariposa, became the first county seat. The election of 1852 was highlighted by efforts to move the county seat to Mariposa. Thus Perlot is confusing the annual spring election that occurred in April with county organization.

Understandably, Perlot also associated the fact that United States troops and Major James D. Savage were present during election time with an effort to organize local government. Actually the troops and Savage were there to work out the details of a treaty signed with local Indian groups the preceding year at the close of the Mariposa Indian War. The treaty was concluded in March 1851 by three federally appointed Indian commissioners, Redick McKee, George W. Barber, and O. M. Wozencroft, who had come to the Mariposa region for that purpose. It was, in fact, as William Henry Ellison has observed, the first treaty to be negotiated between the California Indians and the United States. The treaty guaranteed six tribes reservations between the Merced and Tuolumne, whereas others agreed to settle on the Fresno. By January 1852 Indian Agent Adam Johnston had identified five reservation sites, one each on the Stanislaus, the Tuolumne, the Merced, the Fresno, and King's River. (It should be noted that a second treaty had also been signed with sixteen tribes on the upper San Joaquin River on April 29, 1851.)[1]

The troops were there as a show of force, but Major Savage was playing a triple role in the post-treaty negotiations. On the one hand the Indians saw him as their friend and protector who had lived among them and had formed marriage alliances with women from several tribes; on the other the United States government was using him as an interpreter, for he was fluent in several Miwok dialects.

1. As far as the commissioners and agents in California were concerned, the treaties became effective upon signing and, forthwith, they spent some $50,000 in appropriations for the San Joaquin area and contracted for perhaps a million dollars in supplies for the remaining California Indians. The California legislature and the state's delegation in Congress, however, violently opposed the ratification of the treaties, saying they reserved too much land for the Indians. The United States Senate, in secret session, acceded to California's wishes and never ratified the treaties, although the disapproval was not known in California and it was not publicly revealed until this century. See Crampton, *Mariposa Indian War*, p. 79, n. 15; p. 108, n. 1; p. 109, n. 5; and William Henry Ellison, *A Self-Governing Dominion: California, 1849–1860* (Berkeley and Los Angeles: University of California Press, 1950), pp. 144–58.

And third, Savage was there as Colonel John C. Frémont's agent, for Frémont was seeking the contract to supply beef for the reservations under the provisions of the 1851 treaty.[2]

Perlot, of course, had little knowledge of these negotiations and soon left Mariposa when rumors that gold had been discovered on the Fresno led him and his partners to the banks of that river in the spring of 1852. Unfortunately a severe outbreak of malaria swept through the southern camps that summer. One by one Perlot's partners fell ill while scores of miners in nearby diggings became sick and some died. Perlot himself experienced three bouts of malaria. As grim as his account of illness and death in the camps is, it is valuable because it reveals the network of friendships that existed among foreign nationals, and how they supported one another in times of need.

After having been dogged by bad luck for the entire summer, Perlot found enough gold on Rich Creek to see him through the winter. But the specter of death continued to be everywhere—in the half-eaten corpse of a miner he found at Rich Creek, and in his discovery of the tomb of a Mexican woman who had been buried in a wilderness area. Then, during the winter of 1852–53, he and his partner Thill, who were living in Bear Valley, ran out of food. Although they had sufficient cash, there was no food to be found in the major camps around them, and in the end they had to depend on supplies rationed out to miners once a week at Oak Flat. Meanwhile some equally desperate Tuolumne Indians stole and ate Perlot's donkey. And finally, at a reunion of La Fortune company members at Mariposa in 1853, Perlot learned that fourteen of the forty-five members of the company had died since their arrival in California, and that none of the survivors had struck it rich.

Even so, Perlot's incredible vigor and unquenchable optimism, and his faith that knowledge and logic could overcome all things, led him to dwell on the future rather than on the past. He was still inordinately curious about the little known areas of the Sierra, and who the Indians were who appeared in the fall to gather acorns. Where did they come from? What were they like? Without knowing it, Perlot was preparing for the next evolution of his career. He would become an explorer of the Tuolumne and Yosemite valleys, and an amateur ethnologist as well, engaged in studying the lives and customs of the Yosemite Indians.

2. Glasscock, *Golden Highway*, pp. 309–10; Harris, *Gila Trail*, p. 116n; Crampton, *Mariposa Indian War*, pp. 109–11; Collins, *Sam Ward in the Gold Rush*, p. 51n; and Ellison, *Self-Governing Dominion*, pp. 157–58.

Chapter Eleven

Conflict on the Chowchilla

On the return from this expedition, finding myself alone and seeing that almost everywhere there was too much water for mining, I turned to hunting. The Mariposa butcher, who had closed his shop for lack of customers, nevertheless still killed a beef from time to time and sold the meat at thirty sous a livre; hunting therefore could be, for the moment, a lucrative enough occupation. The rains had brought back around Mariposa, along with lesser game, deer and bear; there was a chance of killing some and selling them; the meat was worth eighteen sous a livre.

In a few days, I had killed enough game—hares, partridges, rabbits and deer—for sixty-eight dollars; I was able to sell them easily, and often the butcher, for a slight commission, took charge of cutting them up and disposing of them.

I was not alone in hunting, far from it; many others were engaged in it, so that it was necessary to go far to be sure of encountering big game, I mean deer and elk; as for the bear, he was caught in traps or hunted with the pendulum.

This is how the traps were arranged: on level ground, one rolled pine logs, one foot in diameter and twenty-five feet long, against each other; on this kind of a floor, one raised a square room, from four to five feet high, whose sides were formed of logs similar to those of the base; they touched each other and were pegged to those of the adjacent side at the angle where they met and crossed. This big box was furnished with a lid formed of logs a little lighter than those of the base and fastened together by two other logs placed on top and across, to which they were pinned. This lid rested, on one side, on one of the walls of the room, on the other on a column formed by three or four pieces of wood placed upright on one another; this column was seven or eight feet high. Thus the trap was open on one side. At the foot of the column was attached the bait, which consisted of a piece of lard or pork.

The bear entered to seize the bait; as soon as he touched it, he shook and dislocated the column. The roof fell back on this kind of a cage and closed it completely. When the trapped bear was destined for the butcher or the miners, he was shot once or twice; then, on the back of an animal or on a wagon he was brought to camp.

It often happened that before he was killed, he was rented to a company of Spaniards who, on Sunday, in an improvised circus, presented one of these spectacles which the Spaniards, a somewhat ferocious people, dote on. The combat of the bull and the toreador was succeeded by the combat of the bull and the bear, after which victor and vanquished were delivered to the butcher.

Hunting with the pendulum is fairly original. Every morning the bear returns to the dense brush where he seeks repose during the day. It would be dangerous to go to look for him there; no more can one dream of tracking him, for he never flees.

The pendulum was devised to prevent him from returning to his fort before daylight and so to permit the hunter to shoot him.

To a strong branch diverging from a tree, one attaches a strong rope, at the end of which hangs a big stone of forty to sixty livres, which reaches to a foot from the ground. Just below, one buries a bucket, a box, or better yet a little cask whose bottom is removed, which contains a piece of pork big enough not to come out easily. The bear, coming out of the neighboring brush or else wanting to return to it, is enticed by the scent of the bait and comes to help himself. But at first, this is difficult for him, because his paw and the bait are too big to come out of the container at the same time. On the other hand, as the stone bothers him, he gives it a blow with his paw; the stone, knocked from the perpendicular, returns to it with more or less force, according to the violence of the blow; it hits the bear on the head, he becomes angry, replies with yet more violence, the stone in returning hits him with more force. Oh! then the bear becomes furious and he engages with the obstinate stone in a terrible, long, bloody struggle.

At more than half a league from the ring, one hears the tremendous growls of the wild beast; at length, however, his voice lowers and weakens, it is the moment for the hunter to show himself; he approaches within thirty or forty paces of the animal and finds him lying on his back, exhausted, out of breath, but gnawing with rage on the unlucky stone, turning and re-turning it in all directions between his four paws. As the battle has lasted one or two hours, ordinarily, day has come; the hunter shoots the bear at his ease. It happens sometimes, however, that one hears the noise of the struggle during the night, then when day comes the bear has disappeared. On still other occasions, he comes to the snare in the evening, and the shot is missed because the combat never lasts a whole night. It has happened that in the morning I have passed near a pendulum of this sort, which was still balancing; the bear, fatigued by the struggle, had returned to the brush.

As I was not hunting with a rifle (a *carabine* with a long rifled barrel), I avoided entering these bushes, and I went elsewhere to seek the hare, the rabbit, the partridge and the deer, for which my double-barreled shotgun was an adequate weapon.

When a bear suitable for circus combat was caught in a trap and they wanted to take him alive, he was left three, four, sometimes five days in this trap without food or water, then he was brought a ham which had been carefully saturated with salt; ordinarily, the bear devoured it whole, and two hours later he was given two or three litres of water mixed with one litre, at most, of brandy. Parched by the salt, he had soon drained the bucket, but soon too he fell, like an inert mass, dead drunk.

They profited from that moment to open the trap; then, with hooks and levers, they rolled him into a big, specially built cage, which they closed again very quickly, that goes without saying. They loaded this cage on a wagon and so the bear was driven to his destination.

I would have continued hunting if I had had a companion to help me carry the game; alone, it was too fatiguing. Often I had to go very far to encounter a deer, the game which paid me best; many times it happened that I covered four or five miles, carrying on my shoulders a deer which weighed from a hundred to a hundred and fifty livres, although it was reduced to its minimum, that is cleaned, the head and legs removed; I could not use a mule, because it would not have been able to go everywhere; to tie it somewhere, while I hunted in the neighborhood, was not to be thought of; I would not have been sure of finding it again at night. The Indians who, they said, were approaching the placers in pursuit of the bears and mountain lions, would have stolen it from me one day or another, and that would have been from two hundred to two hundred and fifty dollars lost.

So I gave up living from the hunt, picked up my miner's tools again and began to work here and there, where I could be the least troubled by the water. Each day brought its bread, or almost. At the end of eight days, I found a passably rich claim; only I had to carry the dirt three hundred paces to wash it; besides, I had more than a league to go, morning and evening, to get to work and to return. To settle alone in this place, far from all habitation, would have been imprudent; during the last six weeks, six or seven individuals, judged by right of lynch law, by the assembled people, had been hanged in Mariposa and its environs, for theft or murder.

The Mexicans, especially, were hungry, and, on my word, I was afraid of not sleeping peacefully every night. Under these circumstances, I decided to go to the camp of the three tents, which I had left to settle in Mariposa when my supplies were exhausted. I found Thomas there again, his partner Louvel, and my crossing companion, Brillet. Since my departure, they had been working, but at the moment they did not know where to dig. I told them about my find and proposed that we all go together to work this claim, representing to them that, being four in number, we could keep the respect of the Mexican prowlers; as these prowlers nevertheless were fairly numerous in the area, they hesitated at first, then at last let themselves be persuaded. Two days later, we were occupied in digging a ditch four hundred paces long, in order to bring water to work the claim. We stayed there four weeks and returned from it with a profit of six ounces of gold each, all expenses paid. Provisions, moreover, had cost us little: in one hour's hunting, morning or evening, before or after work, I killed one or two hares or rabbits, so that we ate hardly any other meat. The last week, it happened that I killed a deer, with the meat of which we made stew until the last day. Hardly was this claim exhausted, and we were preparing to seek another in the environs, when the rain, again beginning to fall, forced us to return to Mariposa. After two days of rain, in fact, it would have been impossible to leave our camp without having to swim two or three streams.

This rain lasted ten days, during which I boarded with Chanac, where I paid a dollar for each meal, for which this was the invariable menu: beans, pork, then some bread and water. I was lodged for nothing, that is to say that, like the others, at night, I rolled myself in my blanket on the ground, seeing that there was neither bed nor floor in the bakery. Those who were cold went to bed on top of the oven, which was made of mortar dried on the spot without lime. The building which contained this oven was of canvas mounted on a wooden frame; aside from the canvas, it was like an immense birdcage, which had for its base a piece of the surface of the terrestrial globe. This was not clean, it is true, but one was sheltered there from the rain; it was even dry, to such a point that dust flew throughout the apartment, except, however, a corner which everyone inundated to avoid getting wet at the door. The meal was served on two tables, built on each side of the entrance door; they were made of three planks, each a foot wide and twelve long, nailed on cross-pieces, themselves nailed to the top of stakes driven into the earth and serving as feet. These three planks originally, no doubt, touched each other and were placed on the level, but in my time that was no longer the case. On each side of these tables and at a varying distance, according to whether the consumer was big or little, a plank nailed to the top of stakes driven into the ground and eighteen inches high, served as a bench. This furniture, from necessity, was never washed, because the washing water would have dampened the earth underneath which, at night, served as mattress to the habitués of the hotel.

The service, suited to the premises, was all of the most rudimentary kind, inasmuch as each consumer brought his spoon, his fork, his knife, his plate, and his cup; the whole of metal, which had nothing in common, be it understood, with that which we were seeking in the bosom of the earth. It was reduced, this service, to big basins and little buckets, in which were served the comestibles listed above, and where we went to ladle them ourselves into our plates. The beverage was brought to us in a pail: each one, armed with his mug, dipped into it at will.

During this time Thomas left Louvel, his partner, and came to board with Chanac. I was preparing, after a few days of good weather, to begin again on the search for a claim, when Thomas proposed that we work together, pleading that he had a mule which carried his baggage and would find it no more trouble to carry mine. This arrangement was agreed upon. We left together for the Chowchilla, two leagues to the east of Mariposa, with a month's supplies on the back of the mule. There was too much water there to be able to work properly, but at last we succeeded in earning our day's wage. We had been there for three weeks when the Indians announced their presence to the white men by stealing at one stroke eighteen mules belonging to different miners.

The alarm given, the miners united and set off in pursuit of the thieves, in order to recapture the mules from them or at the very least to run them out of the country.

We left, numbering twenty-two, with six animals loaded with supplies, and eagerly followed the Indians. But they walked faster than we: almost every day, we found the carcass of a mule they had eaten. After nine days of pursuit, we arrived on the banks of a river which they had swum across and which it was impossible for us to cross. We were forced to retrace our route, after having waited two days on the watch, thinking that they perhaps would return to this side of the river. So we returned to the Chowchilla, where Thomas had stayed to guard our tent, our provisions and our mule, which, happily, was not one of the eighteen.

Eight days later, the rain began again with a vengeance. As it could fall for a long time still and cut off the road to Mariposa by making the rivers run over their banks, the greater part of the miners were preparing to break camp, when one fine day, at midnight, the Indians came suddenly to attack our neighbors. Happily, foreseeing an offensive on their return, we had devised a plan which allowed us to be assembled in a half-hour, to the number of thirty-five, at the point of attack. Our herded animals formed a square a hundred meters on a side, and we had to keep up our fire all around this square until the moment when, day approaching, we no longer heard the arrows whistling around us, nor the echoing of those raucous and plaintive cries which the Indians utter when fighting. They had disappeared.

With daylight, on counting up our losses, we had three men wounded, two of them lightly, one mule carried off and one tent pillaged. One of the wounded had received an arrow which had gone through the flesh of his right arm; he was stretched out without movement and, at first sight, we thought him dead; but, after examination, we realized that he had only fainted. Before he came to himself—and I think it was just that which made him come back more quickly—a man called Big Joseph, a former ship's mate, had extracted the wood of the arrow which was still in the flesh. Another had received the arrow full in his chest, but it had not penetrated and had fallen to earth. The third had merely had his face grazed by the shaft. I do not speak of those who pulled out arrows stuck in their coat or their blanket; almost all were in that state. However, I had not received any, although occupying a corner of the square and consequently having to face two sides.[1]

We decided to pursue the Indians, or rather to cut off their retreat, supposing that they would take refuge again on the other side of the river, which we had not been able to cross. In order to walk faster, we each brought supplies for four days and no animals. There were eighteen of us. Fifteen remained to guard the tents and the animals; two others were to take the two most severely wounded to Mariposa. The other, the one who had received the arrow full in the face, had wanted to accompany us.

1. It is difficult to identify the Indians involved in these raids. They may have been Chowchillas, but since a number of males from the Yosemite bands confined to a reservation near Fort Miller had escaped that spring and were making their way back to the mountains, it seems likely that they were Yosemite. At about the same time that these raids were taking place, two members of a prospecting party that had gone into Yosemite Valley were killed by Indians there. See *The Mariposa Indian War, 1850–51. Diaries of Robert Eccleston: The California Gold Rush, Yosemite, and the High Sierra*, ed. C. Gregory Crampton (Salt Lake City: University of Utah Press, 1957), p. 109, n. 5.

These arrangements made, we left, going in a straight line toward the river, not that we had any intention of going to that point, it was too far; we only wanted to reach a pass which we had observed during the first expedition, conceal ourselves there and await the arrival of the Indians. We marched at an accelerated pace until very late in the evening, without stopping, and the next day we left before it was daylight. Shortly after midday, we were lying in wait in the middle of the pass; great was our surprise to see, about three o'clock in the afternoon, some Indians arriving, but going in the opposite direction to those whom we were expecting, that is, instead of going away from the Chowchilla, they were approaching it. What to do under these circumstances? Attack them? Wouldn't we be putting innocents to death? Assuredly, these were not the ones we had just been fighting; it was even less admissible because they had women and children with them.

Big Joseph, our captain, had divided us into four platoons, had placed two of them on either side of the path and opposite each other. These two first groups were to let the enemy pass, then fire on the last ones, each one emptying his revolver before making use of his double-barreled gun. When these Indians appeared in our midst, the captain consulted us with a look and we were unanimously of the opinion that we would have to let them go. There were sixty of them, all counted, and they passed without seeing us. We stayed at our post all day without seeing anything come. In the evening, we approached the sort of path which the Indians had followed, and we stayed there uselessly ambushed all night. Next morning, about nine o'clock, no longer hoping to see the Indians arrive, we left, followed the path behind those who had passed the day before, but walking with caution, in order to surprise the enemy if he came from the opposite direction. Toward noon, having come to a place where the trail forked, we observed that the Indians who preceded us has taken the direction which went the farthest from the Chowchilla. We took the one which brought us back to camp.

About two o'clock, we arrived at a place where the burned and blackened earth indicated the spot where a big fire had been lighted. On looking all around, we saw that the ashes, cinders, and brands had been thrown to the wind. It was quite recent, for the floor of the immense hearth was still warm. We were about to ask ourselves what it could really mean, when in moving with my foot the few cinders left on this floor, I uncovered a lead plaque the size of a five franc piece. I showed it to my companions, all as astonished as I and as puzzled to explain the presence of this lead on this hearth. One of them made the remark that there was just the amount needed to make a ball. That was a ray of light; everyone shouted at once: "Oh! but it is a ball! It is here that our Indians have burned their dead; this melted ball was in one of the corpses." We looked in the ashes, and we found three more melted balls. On examining the residue with care and attention, we succeeded in finding here and there small fragments of calcined bones, which fully convinced us that our conjecture was right.

So we were on the track of the Indians—but we had only enough supplies for the day; we had to return to our tents. Those of us who had stayed to guard the animals had, after the night combat, examined the field of battle. They had found no dead, but, in many places, the earth was bloody, proof that the Indians had withdrawn carrying away their dead and wounded. If, instead of trying to cut them off, we had been content with pursuing them, we would certainly have reached them during the day, because, having their dead to carry and probably some wounded, who also retarded their march, they must not have made a very long stage. The sole difficulty would have been not to lose their tracks, for in withdrawing they had followed neither path nor definite direction.

However, as our provisions were becoming exhausted, we, with a certain number of miners, took the path to Mariposa. Only twenty, who were provided with supplies, remained and set up fortifications, that is, built some houses of tree-trunks.

The precaution was not superfluous. Soon the Indians, knowing, doubtless, that they now had business with only a small number of enemies, returned to the charge three nights in succession. The miners finally had to beat a retreat to Mariposa and, having no more bridges for crossing the streams, because the waters had carried everything away, they had to make a detour of eight leagues. The rains had begun again; they arrived soaked and covered with mud, with two wounded, one of them mortally; he had been hit in the chest by an arrow probably poisoned. The other had been wounded in the thigh; he had managed to withdraw the arrow from the wound, but his thigh had swelled enormously; he nevertheless had been able to reach Mariposa on horseback. Doctor Grandvoinet, who treated him, always claimed that this arrow was poisoned, without being able to determine with what kind of poison. This doctor, who was French, had arrived in Mariposa with the company from Liège mentioned above, of which he was a member. The company having dissolved, he had established himself as a doctor and surgeon at Mariposa. He had not been able to save poor Mr. Cahla, who died the day after his arrival; but he was happier with Mr. Henris, who recovered, except that for some time he remained lame.

In the presence of these Indian aggressions on the Chowchilla, the miners of the area called and held a meeting at Mariposa; on the spot, they drew up a petition which was covered with seventy-five signatures, demanding the outlawing of the Indian. It was posted for ten days throughout the county, nobody made any opposition to it; then the sheriff, sole civil and judiciary authority established in Mariposa, rendered this decree: "Whereas the Indian has openly made war on the miners and against all kinds of property, without their being in any way able to deliver the malefactors to justice: I pronounce the Indian outlawed. Consequently, everyone is permitted to kill the Indians he encounters anywhere in the county of Mariposa, on the sole condition of burying them and of letting the sheriff know where and how many of them he has killed."[2]

---

2. James Burney, who had been an officer in the Mariposa Battalion, became the first Sheriff of Mariposa County on April 1, 1850. He was succeeded by John Boling, also an officer in the Mariposa Battalion, April 6, 1852. See Crampton, *Mariposa Indian War*, pp. iii, 16, 18, 19, and throughout, for references to Burney; and pp. iv, v, 23–25, and throughout for Boling.

Two days after our return to Mariposa, the rain, as I have said, had begun again; it lasted fifteen days without stopping; after that, the weather improved very agreeably; that is, for ten or twelve days, it rained two or three hours every day. We profited, at the same time, both from the fair weather and the rain by working during these ten or twelve days. While out hunting, I had noticed a sort of false flat almost at the top of a hillside, two miles from Mariposa; thanks to the rain, there was enough water to work there. We tested the dirt; it was good; we worked it until the moment when the rain stopped alternating with the sun. Soon there was no longer enough water to wash the dirt. We had each made five ounces of gold there, board paid.

It was the first of March and already, for nearly three weeks, from San Francisco and from Stockton, the miners had been returning to the placers they had left in the fall. They returned to us with their pockets not exactly lined with gold, most of them having spent the winter in living well, in amusing themselves, and in losing more than their time in the gaming houses so numerous in San Francisco at that period.

It had hardly rained, it seemed, on the coast, and they were not expecting to find, at the placers, watercourses overflowing and the weather still rainy; nevertheless they went to work again, gay and eager, without letting themselves be stopped by these difficulties. One saw them, up at dawn, leaving for their claims, pick and shovel on their shoulder, pan under their arm, to pass the day in digging, shoveling, and washing the dirt in all the creeks, then, in the evening, returning, one can imagine in what state, often with not much, sometimes with nothing. They were at the height of joy if they had gathered enough to pay their board; and those were the lucky ones. We others, miners already full of knowledge, thanks to the experience which this long winter spent on the placers had given us, having our purse well enough filled to await the next day without anxiety, we took things at our ease, keeping sheltered from the rain, taking big puffs on the pipe of repose and smiling at the coming and going, at the agitation of these poor fellows.

Chapter Twelve

American Government and Indian Reservations

It was about this time that the government of the United States came to take official possession of Mariposa, that is, it sent a captain with his company, ordered to conduct an election for the appointment of judges and prosecutors, justice of the peace, lower court, court of sessions, policmen, etc., etc.; to establish, in a word, all the things which would make Mariposa the capital of a *County*. This installation was quickly accomplished.[1] After ten days of posting notices in English, German, French, and Spanish—all announcing that the official language was the English language—we proceeded to the vote. All were electors and could be candidates, except the Indian and the Negro—for at this time, they had not yet decided if California would or would not be a slave state.

One arrived at the polls, with or without a prepared ballot; in the first case one passed it to the chairman, who read it aloud; then the committee inscribed the vote. If there was no ballot, the elector voted verbally for each position, which was indicated to him in his language, the committee inscribed it, then the voter withdrew. They proceeded thus for three days, at the end of which the committee posted the names of those who, for each position, had obtained the most votes.

This new administration changed nothing, for the time being, of our laws, usages, and customs.

We soon learned that a delegate of the government, who knew the language of the Indians, and who for this reason was called Savage, was coming to conclude a treaty in due form with the greater part of their tribes. The peace was made and, thenceforth, one was going to mine in full security—that was, at least, the common hope. By this treaty, the United States undertook to feed the Indians for three years; to get them the necessary cattle, if they wanted to raise them; to furnish them tools, if they wanted to work; on the condition that they would remain, during this time, in what were called reservations. These were restricted areas, as big as cantons, on which the citizens did not have the right to settle without the consent of the Indians. Outside of these reservations, the Indian was under the same obliga-

1. For a more accurate version of the 1852 elections, see pp. 124ff.

tions as the American citizen, judged according to the same laws and by the same judges.[2]

These reservations were established, of course, in a way to leave the mining lands free as well as the sections where, no doubt, agriculture was soon going to be born and developed.

Most of the surrounding tribes having accepted this treaty, we found ourselves almost rid of the Indians.

Already many people had left for the Fresno (ash tree), a fairly big river which ran thirty miles to the east of Mariposa. The Indians who occupied this canton had just abandoned it on account of the treaty. Marvels were told of the metallic richness of this river.[3]

I resolved to go see what there was there and, if there was anything, stake a claim there for the summer. During this time, Thomas was to explore the environs of Mariposa in case there should be nothing to do on the Fresno. So, one fine morning, I left with our mule well saddled and bridled, accompanied by the hotelkeeper-baker Chanac and by three miners, none of whom knew any better than I the road to follow. But, as the Mexican says, "*Vamos* for the Fresno."

We first came to the Chowchilla, four miles lower down than the place where the Indians had attacked us during the winter; we crossed it in water as high as the bellies of our mules. Farther on, we swam across another river which could have been eight feet deep by thirty wide. Then, following the first Indian track encountered, we marched on, so that at dusk we reached a rather bigger river. There, we encountered three Americans who had left Mariposa three days before. They were searching for the Fresno and had not found it; they didn't even know where they were themselves, and they hadn't met anyone who could tell them. They seemed very happy to see us. They were on the other side of the river and invited us to cross over to join them immediately. But it was late, the water was cold and swift, and our mules were warm; the operation was put off until the next day. The Americans, who already were settled for the night, began to cut an enormous pine, which they made to fall across the river to serve us as bridge the next day. The tree broke in falling; nevertheless, it resisted the current and was able to serve for the use to which it was destined, although covered, toward its extremity, by two feet of water.

The next day, early, we began by crossing our animals on a rope. Here is how we proceeded with this operation: we attached a stone to the end of a strong string whose other end was tied to a rope which ended at the neck of a mule; we threw the stone to the Americans, who pulled the animal toward them. When all the mules had thus swum across, we ventured over, loaded with our saddles and our provisions, on the narrow, slippery, shaky bridge, formed by the cut pine. We ran a great risk of falling in the water and staying there, but heaven took pity on us, and

2. A context for Perlot's brief reference to Indian treaties may be found on pp. 124–125 and pp. 124–25, nn. 1 and 2.

3. Here Perlot is referring to the reservation on the Fresno near Fort Miller.

we arrived safe and sound on the other bank. Our union with the Americans being thus effected, we left all together in search of the Fresno. We had been told that it was the fourth river after leaving Mariposa; so we were about to reach it. About ten o'clock in the morning, in fact, we reached a river, but there was absolutely no one there.

As we were not far from the mountains where the said river had its source, we began to descend it and, around noon, we at last saw a tent. It was occupied by five Americans, who informed us that we were not on the Fresno but actually at Coarse Gold.[4] The Fresno was the river we had crossed the preceding night, but at a point almost ten miles higher than the miners' camp.

From the spot where we were, we had six miles to go, after wheeling about, to reach the camp.

Coarse Gold was a series of big alluvial flats, composed of big stones rounded like pebbles, of earth, and of sand; one would have said that a mighty river had passed over this land in other times, then had withdrawn, leaving its banks dry and its bed stony. The basin of Coarse Gold extended between two slightly elevated ridges, with a gentle slope, and consisted of flats fifty to a hundred meters in width, seven to eight feet in depth, which we followed for two hours in order to reach the first tent. These vast flats were watered only by a small creek which already at this season carried little water and which let it be guessed that soon it would be dry. We who, precisely, were seeking work for the summer, we could not dream of settling there just at the moment when the dry season was going to begin.

We rested there for a few moments, then we left for the camp on the Fresno, where, following the directions we had been given, we arrived toward evening, after having crossed the river exactly as we had done in the morning.

The camp was in the full course of construction.[5] We took temporary lodging with a Belgian, named Moret or Morhet, former builder in Chaudfontaine. He was occupied in building himself a house in which to keep a café-restaurant; he gave me the information I needed to direct me along the river in search of a claim.

Almost all the river was already staked for working when the water would permit it, that is, according to the experts, toward the month of June or, perhaps, the month of July. One could not dream of making assays; there was absolutely too much water, by reason of the slope, which was slight. It was therefore necessary to make a claim entirely by chance. So it was, in fact, that the next day I staked a claim about two miles lower than the camp. It was, apparently, a good enough flat,

4. Coarse Gold (Madera County) was a tributary creek to the Fresno River where five Texans are supposed to have discovered clearly identifiable nuggets (hence coarse gold) in 1849. A rush followed which attracted two of the most articulate miners in the region: Etienne Derbec, the French journalist in 1850, and Robert Eccleston, an American miner, who was there in 1851. Both described the area. See Nasatir, ed., *French Journalist in the California Gold Rush*, pp. 140–51; Crampton, *Mariposa Indian War*, pp. 96, 113ff.; and Gudde, *California Gold Camps*, p. 76.

5. The lower Fresno River attracted miners at the same time that Coarse Gold did, of whom Perlot and his friend, Thomas, were two (Gudde, *California Gold Camps*, p. 125).

which no one had yet taken up, doubtless because there was too much digging to do and too many bushes to pull up. In short, I staked it, put up the notices, then returned to camp. Shortly afterward my traveling companions arrived, who had also found places to claim, except, naturally, Chanac, who came to the Fresno only to establish a bakery.

We prepared, consequently, to leave together the next day for Mariposa.

About midnight the rain began to fall; in the morning, as it was comparatively clear, we got ready, breakfasted, and left. But we had hardly gone a league when the rain began again worse than ever and continued the whole day. We swam across the two rivers on our mules; it wasn't worth the trouble, truly, to seek to cross them on bridges, for we were hardly more soaked on leaving the water than on entering it. However, the crossing of the second was not effected without our suffering an accident which could have become a misfortune.

One of us had a rather small mule who had let herself be carried farther than she should below the ford; she wanted to come out of the water at a place where the submerged bank was high and difficult to climb, so that, mounting the edge, when her two hind feet plunged in ten feet of water, she fell backward and over on her rider. Being just about the youngest of the band and possessing the strongest mule, I had crossed the watercourse first, I had tied my mount to a bush and, on occasion, I was helping the others to find the fording place. When the accident happened, I found myself all prepared to lend my aid; I profited from a turning a little lower down where I got in the water up to my arms, I managed to seize with one hand the mule's ear, which was passing within reach, carried by the current, while, with the other, I kept hold of the branch of a bush which the water had tossed up on the flooded bank; thus I could pull the mule to me with the rider, and finally effect their rescue. The rider, who had remained completely submerged, was suffocated but fortunately not asphyxiated; he regained consciousness after a few moments and, when he had taken a good dram, showed no further sign of it.

We reached Mariposa about four o'clock in the afternoon, with it still raining. I told the news to Thomas and it was decided that we would go to spend the summer on the Fresno. While waiting, we worked here and there and gathered handsomely the wherewithal to pay for our supplies. The twenty-fifth of April arrived. The weather had remained fair for several days already; we left Mariposa and the evening of the same day arrived without difficulty at the Fresno. We set up our tent, bought provisions, and then, while waiting for the water, by receding, to permit us to dig our diversion ditch, in order to dry the riverbed, we began to work in the tributary creeks, thus making two or three dollars a day apiece. This lasted until the twentieth of May. We had no more water than was in the river, but there was still more than could be contained by a canal six feet wide; in all this part of the Fresno basin, the rock is granite and the terrain, in spite of some undulations, is almost flat, so that springs are very rare there; that is why, after three weeks of continued fair weather, all was dry, and if the river still had water, it was because it had its source in the high mountains where the snow melts very late.

Not finding a place to work elsewhere, unless we went too far away, we began our ditch, which was to be five hundred and twenty feet long and, most of the way, eight feet deep. We had for neighbors a company of six Frenchmen upstream, and downstream a company of fourteen Chinese.

The three companies were to make their canal on the same side, in order to bar the river only once, that is, above. The flat had very little slope; it extended between two cascades, about three thousand feet apart, that is to say, it included less land than would be allowed to the number of men who were going to work there, a claim being 150 feet per man. To be sure of keeping the 520 feet which we had claimed, we had to add two partners; we would have been able to take two day laborers, but the construction of the ditch was going to take us almost two months, during which we would not be able to wash nor, consequently, to gather any gold. Now, the salary of two workmen during these two unproductive months would have exhausted our finances. So we wrote to Mariposa, and Thill and Burgrave, those two Belgians from the neighborhood of Houffalize, came to join us. After six weeks' work, our ditch was finished, but our neighbors the Chinese still had enough work for ten days at least. In any case, it was necessary to wait, for even though the level of the river was beginning to lower, it was not yet time to bar it.

In the course of the month of May, the Yosemite Indians, who had refused to report to the reservations, had returned to the Chowchilla. They had killed several miners, taken many mules, and then had retired to the upper Merced, in almost inaccessible mountains.[6]

In the presence of this hostile attitude, the government had given the order to three companies of dragoons, camped on the plain of the Tulares, to march against them in order to obtain their submission or their retreat.

The dragoons, therefore, went back up the Fresno to go from there to the Merced, where the Indians were. To hear them, they were in for five days of marching, after which they would return by the same route; as we had ten or twelve days ahead of us without being able to work, we decided that three of us would follow them, leaving the fourth at the Fresno to guard the tent and the provisions. So, Thomas, Thill and I, with the mule loaded with supplies for ten days and with tools—we left on the trail of the military. On occasion, we tested the soil, hoping to find a place that would be worth the trouble of being worked, but during the first three days we hardly had the time to make our assays, because the soldiers, having good mules lightly loaded, made long stages. They were accompanied by some twenty pacified Indians who guided them during the day and kept guard during the

6. In May 1852 a party of miners from Coarse Gold Gulch "started for the upper Sierras on a prospecting trip. They had scarcely entered the Valley Yosemite?, when a large party of Indians, who had been lying in ambush, came suddenly upon them, and killed two of their number . . . and wounded a third." The miners appear to have fought back but retreated to seek reinforcements. Some forty volunteers appear to have marched toward Yosemite but were not able to find the Indians. Later that spring a company of U.S. infantry from Fort Miller on the upper San Joaquin, under Lieutenant Tredwell Moore, started for the Yosemite Valley to punish the Indians and to establish a post there, but the Yosemites had fled. See Hutchings, *California Magazine*, 1, no. 1 (July 1856), pp. 6–8.

night. But, beginning with the fourth day, I think that we made no more than two leagues in a day's march. At first, in the morning, patrols of fifteen to twenty men left in all directions, each one led by three or four Indians, and did not return to the camp until the end of two or three hours; it was only one hour later that we started our march, sometimes almost by turning our backs on our goal. We marched thus until three or four o'clock in the afternoon, then we camped, and the patrols left again in all directions, to return only toward evening.

After six days' march, we arrived at the edge of a very big river which, although it was not wide, carried a considerable volume of water, with a violence that would overthrow anything. I estimate that it had a good six or seven per cent slope; its bed was naked rock and its flats, when there were any, were composed of a mass of enormous stones.[7]

It was utterly impossible to cross it otherwise than on a bridge. We stopped on a sort of flat to camp there; half of the soldiers, instead of making reconnaissances to all points of the horizon, as on the preceding days, retraced their path, I don't know how far, and did not return until the next day at about ten o'clock in the morning. Those who had stayed began to cut down an enormous pine which fell across the river; they crossed on this first tree to do the same on the other bank. So they made a second pine fall alongside the first, but they took their measurements badly, so that the trees, instead of being parallel to each other, touched on one bank and were a dozen feet apart on the other. They cut other pines, which they brought in their arms, and put them across the first two to form a floor; the whole, covered with moss and leaves, offered a commodious road on which the mules set forth without the least hesitation. So we crossed the river and we regained the two days lost in awaiting the completion of the bridge, by making a long stage; we did not halt until nine o'clock in the evening. This rapidity of march was necessary, because we were going through a country absolutely destitute of water; not a creek, not a spring. We had been warned by the Indians, and Thill carried in a pot a supply of drinkable water which permitted us not to suffer too much from thirst. We gave, later, to the place where we had stopped, the name of the *Camp of the Dragoons*. In fact, as they expected to be stationed there fifteen days or three weeks, they built there a camp of shelters made of branches. As for us, after having explored and assayed the surrounding terrain, our supplies becoming exhausted, we again took the path to the Fresno. All along the route, we had found gold but in slight quantity, perhaps because the tests were not and could not be very thorough. The fact is that we did not dare remain too far in the rear, for fear of the Indians; very often, we had to abandon the hole we were digging without having gone as far as the bedrock.

We could therefore conclude nothing from the slight result we had obtained. On the return, we could hardly stop any more, no longer from fear of the Indians, but because of our lack of supplies. However, we took note of the places which seemed

7. Later Perlot concluded that they had come to the South Fork of the Merced River (see chap. 17).

to us to promise the most, in order to return to them if occasion offered. After five days of forced march, we got back to the camp.

A painful surprise awaited us. It was almost deserted; one man out of six perhaps had remained there, the others had taken flight, those, at least, who were not dead. It seemed that four days after our departure, the fever had appeared among the population settled on the river; at the end of four days, more than six hundred persons, out of the eight hundred who composed the colony, were shaking with the fever.

The only pharmacy there was in the whole country, was at Mariposa; moreover, it was poorly supplied, so that in a few days all the sulfate of quinine it possessed was exhausted. It was necessary to have some brought from Stockton, but, while waiting, the disease did its work, and when the first medicine arrived, there was a goodly number of the sick, alas, who suffered no longer. The appearance of the placer was most sad; each tent, out of five or six occupants, counted three or four shivering in their beds.

On the neighboring flats we saw, here and there, a newly raised mound, with two crossed sticks and a sign giving the names of those who were buried there. I have seen some graves whose cross bore as many as five names.

After the twenty-fifth of August, quinine was sold at twenty-two dollars an ounce (110 francs).

It was not only on the Fresno that the epidemic raged, it appeared along almost all the rivers where there were miners. That is why all the pharmacies were empty.

On arriving, we found Burgrave, who had only just got up after having been bedridden six days; he had been one of the first to fall ill. One of our neighbors, a German, had nursed him; he had been able to procure some quinine and, in three days, the fever had been cut.

Our neighbors up above were no more than four; the two others had left, sick. Those below, the Chinese, who had at last finished their ditch, now numbered twenty-two, another company composed of eight of their brothers of the celestial empire having come to join the first.

As the river was sufficiently lowered, the three companies, for greater speed, united to execute in common the work of diverting the stream. The first day, we made a third of the dam, from the opening of the ditch to a point well forward in the river; the second day a second third, from the other side of the river, thus leaving only the middle of the river for the third part to be made the third day; but it was, naturally, the most difficult part of the work. There was a great deal of water; our soil was a rather loose sand, and finally the water rose with greater speed than we could manage in building the dike. The result was that the moment the work was on the point of being finished, the water broke through the earth and carried away all the day's work. We had to begin this last third again. The next day, taking our measures a little better this time, we succeeded in turning all the river into the ditch, but the water, too abundant, filled it to the banks, so that it overflowed across the diggings, regained the riverbed, and impeded the work.

It was discouraging, and, in fact, our neighbors up above lost courage and abandoned the project; the Chinese set to work just the same, but they had absolutely too much water and did not do much.

As for us, we still hoped that the water level would go down, after which the difficulties would diminish. We decided, consequently, that we would wait eight or twelve days if necessary, and that then we would know if we could set to work or consider our campaign as lost. While waiting, in order not to remain unoccupied, we went to a place, one and a half day's march distant, where, on returning from our excursion following the dragoons, we had noticed and assayed a fairly rich location.

Not one of us wanted to stay to guard the tent; we entrusted it to one of our neighbors, the one who had nursed Burgrave, and, with our mule loaded with provisions and tools, we were on our way. On arriving at the placer in question, we installed ourselves under an oak, then we went to work with a cradle, not having enough water to work otherwise; each day, we washed four hundred buckets of dirt and extracted the value of twenty to twenty-five dollars. At the end of twelve days, all our supplies were exhausted. We returned to the Fresno, promising ourselves to return to spend the winter at the place we were leaving; pay dirt was not lacking and, assuredly, when one had enough water, one could work there profitably.

On our return to the Fresno, we found that the water had hardly gone down, but, after all, the season was advancing; it was necessary, cost what it might, to try to work there.

We began, at the lowest point of our claim, a drainage ditch, which we brought as far as a hundred and fifty feet higher without losing any elevation, seeing that the water was standing the full length of the ditch. This work had lowered the water by two feet; at the end of this ditch, we opened a trench big enough to permit all four of us to work in it at once, and so to try to reach the earth on the bedrock, if possible. We dug this trench down to two feet lower than the bottom of the drainage ditch; at this depth, it took two of us to throw out the water with buckets, while the other two were digging, and even so they dug while wading in a foot of water. Under these conditions, we washed the dirt at the bottom and found some gold, but not much, not being able to clean the rock; perhaps we didn't even touch it. This work seemed impossible to us without lowering the water another two feet. In order to lower it so much, we had to begin a new drainage ditch twelve hundred feet long, about the length of the flat below us, seeing that it was, so to speak, level to the cascade downstream. To do this new work or lose all the fruit of our previous work, such was the alternative which was placed before us. We would need a month or six weeks to execute it, and we were advancing into the month of September, and the rains could begin in November. We would have very little time left to work, to wash the pay dirt, and to gain the gold which we would need in order to live during the winter; for it must be noted that while we were on the Fresno, we were spending without earning. Finally, when the ditch was done, would there be enough gold to be worth the trouble of working it? that is what we didn't know. However, the indications were good and, in the last analysis, if it turned out that there was a great deal of gold, at least we would be settled for the next year, and we would be sure of waging a successful campaign when the month of May arrived.

All things considered, we decided to dig our ditch. We bought supplies for two months, and we bought them cheap, because all those who were sick, or who feared to become so, were leaving the Fresno en masse, and most of them were not taking their provisions with them, everything being less expensive at Mariposa; then we set to work.

In order not to lose any of the elevation, we dug the ditch very deep, at the same time making it very wide, which obliged us to work in the water up to our knees all day. In five days we had already done a good bit, when Thomas fell ill with the fever; we nursed him as well as we could, while continuing our work. Hardly had Thomas recovered, when Thill became sick in his turn, so that we were never more than three working at once. Thill's illness seemed to be growing worse from day to day when we heard the official news that the government had taken measures to come to the aid of the sick miners.

It had engaged, at its expense, forty doctors who were to travel over all the rivers to take care of the sick and leave everywhere in sufficient quantity the medicines needed to treat the fever and all the maladies to which miners are exposed; but it was necessary to let it be known at the camp, within four days, where the sick ones were and, in case it was too far, to send an express to guide the doctor there.

On this news, I reported to the camp and gave our address to M. Morhet, of Chaudfontaine, who informed me that in three days two doctors would go up the river and, consequently, would pass near our tent. They came, in fact; they visited Thill and gave us, to treat him, some medicines with a prescription and an ounce of quinine, all that gratis. Two days later, Thill was up and, although still weak, he was working.

Meanwhile our ditch progressed; there was only about a third of the work left to do when one morning a violent headache attacked me, so that I had to stop work. It lasted three days, after which the fever began, but that was nothing since we had an ounce of quinine with the directions for making use of it. Nevertheless, in spite of the quinine, the fever held me almost a week; then I stopped trembling and I could go back to work. Three days later, the headache attacked me again, and the next day, the fever. I had recourse to the quinine; I took two packets more than usual, in order to be sure of a good effect, and the following day I could work. The next day again, the fever reappeared, and, beginning with that day, for some time, it returned regularly every two days. So I, also, was working only one day in two. It was very necessary, however, to dig, if we were going to have done, if we were going to know whether there was any gold there and, consequently, if, ultimately, we should stay or go. This moment, which we asked for with every wish, was not to come; the fever, from being intermittent, became continuous, and so intense that it was no longer possible for me to leave what served me as bed, a pile of dry leaves on a pile of branches. In vain I fed myself quinine, it no longer had any effect on me, save a ringing in the ears which bothered me a lot; at the end of two days, as the sickness was getting worse, Thill left to go consult the doctors who, they said, could then be found twelve miles lower down, on the river. But Thill got lost on the way and could not return till the next day, in the afternoon. I did not recognize him, as it seems I was delirious and took Thill for my brother Nicolas-Joseph; I wanted to force him to tell me what they were doing at Herbeumont, and why my sister had not come to see me. It was my mother, doubtless, who had made him come, himself, but he should tell her that I was well, for fear that she would come, for she was too old to make such a trip. I had just awakened after fifteen hours of sleep. After Thill's departure, a neighbor had come to see me and had persuaded Thomas that if he made me take a packet of quinine in some porto, that would cure me. Thomas did it but he gave me too much of this white wine; I became dead drunk and fell into a sort of lethargy which, from what they told me afterward, lasted fifteen hours. Thill brought back a little phial of some sort of liquid, with a long prescription which explained that the contents of the phial should be administered so many drops at a time. By the next day, I was better and, at the end of two days, I could walk by helping myself with two sticks.

During this same time there passed a convoy of supplies destined for the dragoons; I bought some turnips for twenty francs, of which I had fifty; they were not big, but they were good. Thomas cooked some for me in bouillon, and it must be believed that this diet is strengthening, for in eight days I was in a condition to work.

Since I had been sick, my comrades had not done much; they were more or less unwell themselves, so that they had neglected to maintain the dike which held the diverted river. One morning they found it pierced; the river had retaken possession of its bed and had half filled our drainage ditch. We did not have the courage to begin again. Moreover, the Chinese, all as sick as we and reduced to eight, had left rather than rebuild the dam which was collapsing more and more. We had to decide to do the same. Thomas alone wanted to stay and begin seeking elsewhere than in the river, which decidedly had too much water. I left him my tent and the greater part of my effects, and we left, Burgrave, Thill, and I, taking with us only our blankets, our tools, and some supplies.

Chapter Thirteen

Searching for Gold

We headed for the upper Tchaoutchili [Chowchilla], where, at the time of our expedition against the Indians, I had observed a certain location which seemed to me to contain gold. We arrived there on the third day, but others than I doubtless had also observed this terrain, for we found that it had been worked; more than fifty miners, in fact, had spent the season there. We wanted to push farther, when Thill became sick, and so sick that he was unable to walk any more. We had to take the road back to Mariposa. It is difficult to give an idea of what Thill had to suffer during the two days we took to make the trip. He could hardly walk, even very slowly, for two hours together, after which we had to let him sleep another two hours, and so on during the whole trip.

We arrived nevertheless at Mariposa, which was much improved since our departure. The camp had, so to speak, become a city; one found there all comforts, all commodities which circumstances permitted.

Having put Thill in a boarding house and confided him to the care of Doctor Grandvoinet, we left, Burgrave and I, for the Merced; some Belgians who were working there had let us know that a claim was available beside them, and we were going to settle there, satisfied that Thill, cured, would come to join us there in a few days.

From Mariposa to the point on the course of the Merced that we were making for, was twenty-five miles. Hardly had we gone half the way, finding ourselves at Bear Valley, two miles from the famous hole, cause of the excitement of the previous winter, when Burgrave felt his strength flagging. At noon, he was put to bed in the tent of an American who sold provisions and who was found there just in time, for, without this tent, I would have had to leave Burgrave lying in the depths of the forest, and return to Mariposa to fetch a mule to bring him back. However, once installed for better or worse under this tent, Burgrave seemed less unwell, and as the American volunteered to take care of him, I was able to continue on my way to the Merced. It was understood with Burgrave that if he found himself better the next day, he would try to return to Mariposa, where he would go to bed beside Thill; if not, he would await my return. I would limit myself to finding and staking our claim and, that done, I would return immediately.

Even though I had hastened my steps, I didn't reach the Merced until very late, and I had to lodge with the ferryman. The next day, at eight o'clock, I was with the Belgians, who showed me the claim they had spoken of; I staked it, posted its limits, and set off immediately en route for Bear Valley, where I had left Burgrave sick. My compatriots had shown me a shorter road than that which I had taken to get there. Only, I no longer had a ferryboat for crossing the river; I had to undress, take all my clothes on my head, then enter a cold, swift stream which came to my armpits and threatened to carry me away; I was able, however, to reach the other bank. As soon as I was dressed, I began to run, thus regaining my lost warmth, while at the same time shortening the route. By taking this path, I gained a league and a half, a precious advantage in consideration of the circumstances. I found Burgrave sicker than I had left him. Even the American, seeing him worse, had gone to kill some partridges for him, a very common game in the vicinity, then a rabbit or two, in order to give him nourishment at once more delicate and more fortifying than that which formed his usual fare, that is, something other than pork and beans; moreover, he had decanted for him a bottle of Bordeaux, and this wine, weakened with much water, served him solely as drink. Finding him less well, I left immediately for Mariposa in order to send him the doctor; hardly had I gone five miles when I encountered the American doctor from the camp, who was going to see a sick person not far from there. I begged him to go and see Burgrave and to tell me that evening how he was, then I continued on my way.

Thill, on his side, was not much better; Doctor Grandvoinet assured me that he still had fifteen days, at least, before being able to work.[1] On the contrary, the American doctor, on returning, assured me that Burgrave's illness was nothing much, and gave me a prescription which I should take him the next morning.

But, at the moment of leaving, I felt a certain discomfort, a sort of lassitude in all my limbs; I sent the prescription by an express, thinking that a day's rest would suffice to put me back on my feet.

Of the three forming our company, two were sick, so that instead of making gold we were spending it.

On leaving the Fresno, improvident as I was, I had left what gold remained, buried in a place which only I knew and, in the position I was in, I was going to need it. It was therefore necessary for me to return to the Fresno to get my treasure.

Two Belgians from Verviers, who for that reason were called Verveux, also had to go there to see M. Morhet, whom they had known in Belgium, but not knowing the way, they did not dare go there alone, on account of the Indians. These, during the season, had killed or wounded several miners, simply to take their clothes from them, for often, beside the corpses, one found purses containing gold dust, which the assassins had thrown aside as things without value for them.

It hadn't yet been very long since hunters had seen some of them wandering in the neighborhood. I thought myself that it was not prudent to risk myself alone on this route; I proposed to these two Belgians to wait for me, and instead of leaving that very day, which was a Thursday, to wait until Sunday, the day when we would

---

1. J. Antoine Grandvoinet, whom Perlot mentioned earlier as someone who had come to Mariposa with Les Mineurs Belges and had abandoned mining for his original career as a physician, also continued to mine. He appears in the Quartz Claims, book A, pp. 60–61, of the Mariposa County Records (Bretnor Notes), as claiming a vein overlooking the north bank of the North Fork of the Merced River in 1852.

have the most chance of encountering travelers and, in case of need, of finding help. They accepted and, when the day arrived, we left Mariposa about three o'clock in the morning, in order to avoid having to walk during the worst heat, which, in spite of the advanced season, was still overwhelming around the middle of the day.

We had thirty miles to go. We had walked at first fairly fast; toward ten o'clock, I absolutely had to slow the pace. An hour later, I felt quite unwell; my vision was troubled, I stumbled at almost every step.

Then we stopped to eat a crust which we had in our pocket, with a piece of cold beef. I hoped that this repast, simple as it was, as well as the halt of an hour which followed it, were going to return my strength and put me in condition to continue on my way; but after two hours of rest, I found myself no better. However, time was passing; it was necessary to try to reach the end of the trip. We set off again en route, walking very slowly; nevertheless I soon had to stop—impossible to take another step. It was four o'clock in the afternoon; I urged my companions to continue on their way, giving them all the necessary directions for them to be able to find the Fresno; I begged them, on returning next day, to bring me a horse or a mule, adding that probably they would find me somewhere along the route, and that I would continue to the Fresno on the mount. That agreed on, they gave me what they had left of supplies, and went on. Hardly had they left me when I felt myself weaken. I was lying in the shade of a live oak; I got up in order to get a little away from the path, but I had trouble in standing. I staggered like a drunken man; I managed, however, to drag myself thirty or forty paces from the path and let myself fall in a thicket, hoping, if some Indians happened to pass, that they would not see me. In excess of caution, I renewed the caps of my revolver, but before having finished my preparations for defense, I fell into a deep slumber.

When I woke up, I was surprised to see that the light which shone on me was that of the moon; it was the cold which had awakened me. During my sleep, I had perspired abundantly and my clothes were soaked until water streamed from my flannel shirt; in order to warm myself again, I started walking; I felt much better, I walked easily, only I was thirsty. At the first spring I encountered, I dipped some bread in it and ate it; I was afraid to drink because the water seemed cold to me. After an hour and a half of walking, I perceived a tent of whose existence I had not until then been aware. I approached with a shout, as was the custom. A man came out, still very sleepy. I asked him to permit me to relight his fire, whose remains I saw beside the tent, in order to dry my clothes. He was quite surprised to see that I was wet; he himself made me a big fire, then went back to bed, telling me to come into the tent when I wanted to sleep; but after turning around the fire to dry myself, I lay down nearby and went to sleep.

This tent was occupied by six Americans who were working in the neighborhood. The next morning, they invited me to take coffee with them, an invitation which I accepted in order to drink something warm. Before leaving, they filled a bottle with it for me to drink along the way.

I had been walking for an hour when I encountered the two Verveux. They had not been able to find a mule; all that they had been able to do, was to get me a bottle of wine, some bread and a slice of venison. I took what they brought me, I paid them, then they continued on their way and I on mine; I had about six miles left to go. I arrived on the Fresno about three o'clock in the afternoon; I went to stay in my tent, which Thomas was still occupying. Shortly after our departure, he had fallen ill, had returned to the camp in order to nurse himself better, and, after four days of sickness, had started to work again here and there, but he had not piled up much. I absolutely had to leave the next day; seeing my state of weakness, Thomas saddled his mule, made me mount it, and brought me back to Mariposa.

I found the situation there somewhat improved: Thill was better, Burgrave had returned from Bear Valley almost recovered; seeing himself alone of the three in a state to work, he went to the Merced to take possession of the claim I had staked, but the legal delay had expired, our right had lapsed, and Burgrave, on arriving, found our claim occupied by others. To evict them, it was enough for us to establish before the sheriff the legitimate cause which had prevented us from taking possession of it, but Burgrave did not think he should begin this litigation. Instead of returning to Mariposa, believing that we would not soon be in a condition to rejoin him, he joined the company of the Belgians of the Merced.

After eight days of convalescence, I felt myself strong enough to go back to work. Thill and I bought a jenny, in order to travel more at our ease; then, having loaded her with supplies for a month, we left in search of a creek which had recently been discovered and where, they said, much gold was found; but that was all that they knew of it. How to reach it was a secret which the first occupants of the placer were very careful not to reveal; they went for provisions sometimes to one camp, sometimes to another, and returned during the night in order not to be followed.

It was almost a year before that one day, out hunting, I had perceived from afar a tent at the base of a sort of precipice, between the upper Mariposa, the Merced and Bear Valley: someone therefore was working there, and yet I had never heard mention of that placer.

It was in that direction that we turned our steps, and we were in some difficulty to know where we could descend to it when we saw three miners leaving from this same side. Thinking without doubt that we were in the secret, they took, without hiding themselves from us, all the desired precautions to disguise their trail and not break a path. They covered, in this fashion, about two kilometers, then they came to the true path which was fairly well marked. We kept them in sight while doing as they did, and we arrived, almost all at the same time, at the bottom of the funnel. I was not mistaken in my supposition: it was really there that the Ruisseau riche (Rich Creek) was found—that is the name it was given later.[2] Hardly had we arrived when we staked a claim and we set to work, but we no longer had the strength and courage of other times. With great trouble we did in one day the work which we would have done easily in six hours before having been sick.

In spite of that, we made from five to twenty-five dollars a day each, according

2. Although several Rich Creeks or Gulches or Bars appeared in the California mining region, none appears to have been in the location Perlot gives here.

to the state of the rock at the bottom of the trench. The terrain had a steep slope from which we excavated big stones which we had some trouble in removing; between these stones, we had little paydirt, but it was rich. This brought back a little of our courage; for a long time we had done nothing but spend and, my word! the purse was growing light: in the month of April, at the time I left for the Fresno, I had fifty-eight ounces of gold; now at the beginning of November, there remained to me no more than ten ounces. It was not too much, on the eve of winter; it was high time to stop expenses and to earn something to live on.

For almost three weeks, that went along pretty well; our strength, moreover, returned to us little by little. But then an unexpected rain occurred which lasted three days; this rain put too much water in the creek, so that, while giving us more trouble, we found less gold. Our neighbors, some Provençaux whom we had known only since we were on this creek, found themselves in the same situation, as well as many others. They proposed to conduct us to Pelon (baldy), claiming that there were some pretty good gold-bearing areas there.[3] These areas were dry in the summer, but there was just the amount of water needed in the winter; therefore one would not be long without working. On the other hand, if another day or two of rain occurred, the campaign would be terminated on the *rich creek*, and it still would be necessary to decamp to go and spend the winter elsewhere. These reasons seemed good to us, and we left with them and with two others who came to join us, namely: Kesch, of Diekirch, and one called Thomas, of Verviers, who must not be confused with Thomas, of Jemeppe.

Two days later, we were at Pelon, but we found already occupied all those good claims of which the Provençaux had told us. The three days of rain had somewhat replenished the water there; as a result, a number of miners had rushed there, because those who had stayed there the previous winter had all found gold. We therefore had to seek elsewhere. Now, while we were on the Fresno, Kesch, who was working on the Merced, had taken part in an expedition which the miners had had to make to repulse the Toualumné Indians, who came as far as the Merced to steal their animals; and, in the course of this expedition, which had taken place at the beginning of May, he remembered having made some soundings along a creek which seemed rich in auriferous deposits; but he had not been able to pursue his researches, because of the abundance of water. Some others of the expedition had also made assays in the vicinity, and had found not a little gold; only, they had not dared settle there, foreseeing a vengeful return of the Indians. He was not sure of being able to find this creek again; however, if we wanted to try the venture, he offered to lead us. It was decided that he and I would attempt it, while the others would wait for us at Pelon, at the same time seeking a placer where we could spend the winter.

So we left, Kesch and I, heading at first for the Merced; we arrived there

3. Pelon, or Baldy, remains somewhat obscure. It is possible that they had gone as far north as Bald Mountain (Tuolumne County) near Sonora. See Gudde, *California Gold Camps*, p. 25.

toward evening and supplied ourselves with food for five days. In order to be less laden, we took only rice with pepper, salt and lard, counting on procuring our meat with gun shots.

We left again the next day, walking always straight ahead, or almost. After two days, Kesch ended by admitting that he no longer knew in the least where we were. We nonetheless continued our forward march, assaying each watercourse we came upon and not wasting our efforts too much. Toward the end of the fourth day, we reached a fairly considerable stream, at least to judge it by the width and depth of its bed, for there was not a drop of water running in it; only some holes, probably filled by the last rain, held all the liquid that one could see there. In the hope of finding some kind of spring higher up, we climbed it. While we were walking over the stones with which it was strewn, one of those accidents happened which, under circumstances such as those in which we found ourselves, sometimes take almost the proportions of a misfortune; I let fall the iron pot in which we had put all our provisions in order to save ourselves a pack, and in which we cooked our rice; it hit, in falling, a stone which made a large hole in it, so that it could no longer serve us; we threw it away.

Toward evening, we came to a spring. After having quenched our thirst, we lit a good fire and cooked on the coals the hind-quarters of a hare killed along the way; then, our stomachs full and our consciences clear, we lay down in our blankets.

In the middle of the night, we were jolted awake by a frightful noise, so much the more frightful because we could not distinguish the cause. Soon, by the light of the moon, we saw coming out of the bushes two completely black monsters: they were two enormous bears. We soon realized that they were individuals of opposite sex, husband and wife! That was what was making those terrible cries with which the forest echoed, and these cries, we were able to assure ourselves, expressed not fury but tenderness!

We were lying under a very bushy tree which rose from a hillock a hundred and fifty paces from the spring where the two lovers came to drink. When they had quenched their thirst, they turned to us and examined us for a fairly long time, even a very long time, at least this examination seemed to us enormously long. They seemed, at a certain point, to consult each other. Were they deliberating, oh heavens! on what they should do with us? that is what we asked ourselves, in anguish. However, they ended by returning the way they had come, without occupying themselves any more with us. We breathed then, but we could not, neither one nor the other, shut our eyes again that night.

In the morning, at full daylight, we approached the spring and lit a big fire, so as to have a good coalbed to cook the rest of our hare.

Suddenly we saw coming out of the bushes, what?—a third bear who was coming directly toward us. To permit His Lordship to drink quite at his ease, we withdrew to a respectful distance from the fountain; the bear, then, perceived us— for I believe that he had not yet seen us and that is why he was advancing toward us with so much assurance—he stopped, hesitated a moment, then, turning on his heels, he beat a retreat, but with slow steps, while making his jaw clack as a pig does after having eaten, and letting us hear from time to time the rumbling growls which gave witness to his discontent.

Recovered from so great an alarm, we assayed the gravel of the creek by washing it at the spring, and so determined that this paydirt contained enough gold to pay our day's labor, if we settled there seriously in the wet season. After which, we continued to climb the creek while keeping ourselves as far as possible from the brush which we had seen the bears reenter.

No longer having a pot to cook our rice in, we decided to return to the Merced, while heading a little to the right in order to see if, from a mountain which was not very far off, Kesch would be able to recognize his surroundings. But when we had reached the summit of this mountain, in vain did Kesch look about on all sides: it was impossible for him to tell where we were; without my compass, he could not even have told me on which side lay the Merced. So then we continued on our way, always walking toward that river, testing the streams we came to when we had the luck to find water in them, which happened rarely enough. Toward evening, as we were climbing the bed of a dry creek, not hoping to be able to reach the Merced that day, we were looking for water to assay the ground and, in case we found it, planning to spend the night there, when by dint of climbing we found ourselves no longer in the creek-bed but on a big flat where the grass seemed abundant and fresh. We were running in all directions over this sort of a prairie, in the hope of uncovering there a damp spot indicating the existence of a spring, when a boot caught my attention. "Well!" I said to Kesch, "someone has already passed this way; maybe that boot belonged to one of the members of your expedition." I bent over to pick up this boot, which did not seem beyond usefulness; it was heavy; I looked inside: I saw a leg there. Kesch, on his part, found a red flannel shirt in rags, then the other boot, then what had been a pair of pants, farther away a hat, next two arms half eaten by a wild animal; five paces farther, in the trampled grass, the rest of the skeleton, whose head had recently been detached: the lower jaw was gone and the animal had eaten the brains; however, the hair still covered the whole head, the eye was hardly shriveled. When I took this head in my hands, I saw Kesch shudder and turn pale; he looked with a somber air and said not a word. I examined turn by turn the bones and what flesh was left, to determine if the man to whom these remains had belonged had not been killed by a shot or a knife-cut, but I discovered no trace of a wound of any kind. As a fancy to divert Kesch, who was becoming more and more absent-minded and who was letting me make my reflections out loud without replying, or perhaps myself feeling the need of reaction against the somber thoughts which were overwhelming me, I committed an atrocious joke: "Well!" I said to him, "here is just what we need."—"What?"—"We now have what we lacked and we can continue our enterprise."

"Come now, what? what do you mean?" Kesch gruffly interrupted.

"Well, here is something to cook our rice in, this skull. . . ."

Kesch looked at me for some time with both eyes inordinately wide open; then, without replying, made a half-turn and went away with long strides. I called him back. "Eh, Kesch," said I, "I didn't mean it, we'll have to bury this poor devil."—"Oh, yes," he said, retracing his steps, "yes, I'm willing, but, look, I don't like to hear you joking like that in such circumstances."—I promised not to joke any more and we set to work to dig a grave, where we deposited these sad remains. Kesch made a cross of two pieces of wood and we planted it on the grave to inform passersby that a man, a miner like them, had fallen at this spot. That done, Kesch put his pick on his shoulder and, without saying a word, started to walk in the direction of the Merced. He walked with such a speed that I had a lot of trouble following him. After having gone perhaps a mile this way, I said to him: "But, aren't we looking for water any more?"—"No," he said, "let's go farther, there isn't any here." However, night was approaching, it would soon be time to stop to cook two grouse which I had shot during the day, when, by chance, we fell upon a path which seemed somewhat frequented. As it went more or less in the direction of the Merced, we followed it. It led us to the top of a ridge; from there, but at a great distance from the trail, we saw a fire.

Who, in this desert, had lit a fire? Prospectors or Indians? Impossible to distinguish those who were seated around the hearth; it was already too dark. Most likely it was some prospectors, as, for a long while, the presence of Indians had not been reported in these parts. We decided to approach them; from prudence, I put some balls in my gun, we each took our revolver in hand, then we advanced with caution. At two hundred paces, Kesch heard German spoken, then we put our guns back in our belts and advanced boldly. There were eight men, as many Germans as Americans; they had just finished their supper and were preparing to go to bed at the moment we approached them. They were, in fact, some prospectors who had found a spring in this place and had stopped beside it to spend the night; the next day they would continue their route toward the Toualumné. Kesch told them our adventure, the misfortune we had had to lose our pot, and begged them to lend us theirs to cook our rice. They gave it to us still half full of pork and beans, telling us to eat that rather than cook our rice, which is what we did. Next morning we all took coffee together, then Kesch and I left, giving our hosts the two grouse. At two o'clock in the afternoon, we were on the Merced and toward evening at Pelon; as we had made a detour in going, we had almost a day less to travel in returning. During our absence, our companions remaining at Pelon had looked for and found a claim where they were all working together; this claim was very limited and could not occupy us for long. After several days' work, Thill and I abandoned it to our comrades, hoping to find elsewhere a location which would permit us to settle for the whole winter.

So we reloaded our burro (donkey) and returned to Bear Valley; hardly had we started when the rain began again. We got under shelter for a while, waiting for the return of fair weather; we waited in vain, and had to continue our journey in spite of the rain.

In order to go faster, we walked without following either path or trail, driving the donkey before us. The wood we were traversing was open, without obstacle to interfere with the march, and the sort of turf with which the ground was carpeted offered the feet of the poor animal a support that was more solid than the slippery surface of the path.

Evening came while we were climbing the last mountain which separated us from Bear Valley. We had the firm intention of walking without let-up, in spite of the rain and in spite of night which was coming, until the end of our journey; but, by degrees, as we climbed, the bushes became thicker, and soon the rain was falling harder. Then we found ourselves in a sort of thicket, soaked to the bone and unable to see ten paces in front of us.

The place where we were was completely unknown to us; nevertheless we were forced to stop, to set up our tent as well as we could, and so to wait until it was daylight. Already, at the same time we were slowly advancing, we were seeking a propitious spot, when we perceived, at some distance on our left, a feeble light; it came, doubtless, from a miners' camp. After that, we had only one decision to make: to enter there to spend the night.

We started therefore to make a beeline for the light, but we encountered, after the first steps, an unexpected obstacle: it was a creek whose existence we had not in the least suspected; the two banks, much steeper than the mountain, were covered with a thicket which, in the obscurity, became almost impenetrable, and it was at the price of unheard-of efforts that we succeeded at last in disentangling ourselves. It took us two hours to travel the kilometer which separated us from the place we wished to reach; the light seemed to flee before us. However, beyond the creek, the wood became thinner, and we soon stumbled on a path leading to our destination; at last we could approach it. At a respectful distance, we announced our presence in a loud voice; no reply. We shouted in Spanish, in English, in German, same silence; while crying out, we continued to advance. When we were within fifty paces, we observed that the light came to us through the canvas of a tent. Doubt-less, those who occupied this tent had gone to sleep, forgetting to blow out the candle. We shouted again—not possible to obtain a response. Thill, who ended by finding the time long, then said to me: "Let's go, by Gott! and if they shoot at us, I shoot at them the same." That said, he intoned, full-throated, the *Mar-seillaise*, and advanced in great strides. So we came up to the tent, which was of light cotton canvas; we looked all around; insofar as the obscurity permitted us to judge, there was no other. We began to shout again—always the same silence; it was the first time that we found miners so soundly asleep.

We didn't know quite what line of action to follow, when, having the idea of looking through a place where the canvas was unsewn, I saw, in the middle of the tent, a table on which a wax taper was burning; at one end of this table was a cross, and underneath it the earth was raised as if it covered a corpse. I lifted the cloth flap which served as door and I entered. The tent actually enclosed nothing but a table, a grave, a cross, and a candle, which must have been burning for at least ten days. An epitaph in the Spanish language said that Mrs. Pedro de Alquijo, dead at the age of twenty-three years, reposed in this spot; it recommended that passersby pray for her, respect her tomb, and have the charity to relight the taper if it was extinguished. I went out and said to Thill:

"Well! let's unload our burro, tie it where there is some grass, and try to sleep beside the Señora Pedro de Alquijo."—"Must not laugh," said Thill gravely, "but we go to bed in the tent all the same, and let it pour." We went to sleep, in fact, in a profound slumber, sheltered from the rain.

Next day we made a big fire, so well that while we were breakfasting, our clothes were able to dry. The rain having somewhat ceased, we left, but on the way it began to fall again and we were soaked on reaching Bear Valley.

This rain fell for three days; it put water back in all the creeks, so that we set off in search of a claim to profit from this windfall.

After two days' seeking, we found one that suited us. Wanting to proceed, after that, to a somewhat durable shelter, in order to be able in case of need to spend the winter in the same place, we began building a sort of cabin of tree trunks, topped with canvas to form a roof; this roof was double, that is, it was composed of two tightly stretched pieces of canvas, one six inches above the other. Thanks to this system, we had an interior which was sufficiently warm and dry. The single room of which the house was composed was just big enough to contain two beds separated by an interval of four feet. At one of the ends, beside the feet, was the door, at the other end a fireplace, that is, a place forming a half-moon outside, where we made our fire. Our habitation was entered through a door with two leaves; they were two widths of canvas sewn to the roof, then nailed all the way down to the ends of the logs which served as wall and at the same time as door-frame; these widths falling naturally closed the entrance.

Our building completed, we bought provisions for two months. They were not expensive: ten livres of flour for a dollar, same price for the ham, pork, lard; potatoes at four sous a livre; beans, peas, broad beans, etc., at twelve sous; coffee cost a dollar a livre, as did tea. Sugar (brown) six sous as well as the rice; beef cuts, a dollar for three livres.

So we had supplies and shelter; now we had to work. We began our labors. The claim chosen by us had hardly any water except when it rained, and, basing our plans on the experience of the past winter, we hoped to work there between showers, even during the rain. The claim, in fact, being almost at the top of the mountain, formed a steep slope, with a shallow soil; often even the bottom of the trenches was the bare rock, so that all the earth was paydirt, and so, having no excavation to make, we could wash every day without needing to dig a drainage ditch. The little creeks in the environs produced fairly well; utilizing the water of the last three days of rain, we made four to seven dollars each. We were therefore quite resolved to spend the winter there.

Few miners were leaving the placers; they had been able, the previous winter, to work and make money, and it was to be hoped that it would be the same this winter.

At the end of eight days, lacking water, we were forced to carry our dirt in sacks to a distance of almost three hundred meters, near a fairly small spring where we washed it; we used our donkey in this task. In spite of everything, we did well enough, while waiting for better.

We worked in this fashion until the sixth of December, the time when the rains came for good. Never in my life have I seen it rain more heavily or for a longer time. From the sixth of December to the first of March, the rain didn't stop for as much as three hours, unless it was during my sleep, which is hardly probable; how many times, during those three mortal months, how many times I awakened at some hour of the night! and always I heard the monotonous sound of the rain falling on the roof of our house. However, in spite of the weather, we worked sometimes two hours, sometimes four. In the smallest gullies a strong stream was running, and it was in these gullies, almost at the top of the mountain, that we found the most gold. We generally began our day, in rainy weather, at ten o'clock in the morning, dug hard until two o'clock in the afternoon, then returned to the house to change clothes and dry those we took off, that is, our shirts, pants, and hats, the only garments we wore to work. It often happened that, after a half-hour of work, we were soaked as if we had come out of the river; then we took off our flannel shirts, which had become too heavy, and continued to work, almost *in naturalibus*, two or three hours; then, in order not to catch cold, we ran to the cabin to warm and dry ourselves. The distance could have been five hundred meters. Often, when we went to work in the morning, we were soaked before lifting the pick. This work brought each of us from five to eight dollars a day. Beginning with the fifteenth of January, we had to moderate our ardor; the rain became cold, and, once penetrated, we shivered even while working. Nevertheless, we didn't miss working each day more or less; indeed, we took a good "drop" before and after the operation. At the end of January, we found ourselves short of supplies, a grave situation, for it was not very easy to procure them, even with gold.

At Mariposa everything had gone up in price; flour was selling for three francs a livre, beans at a half-dollar (50 sous), meat at three francs, the rest on the same scale. Even at this price, it did not do to bargain; Messieurs the merchants, knowing that it was impossible, considering the weather, the rivers and the state of the roads, to bring any more from the coast, were not too eager to sell their merchandise. In the first place, they did not have much left, and then, they hoped, if the rain continued, to obtain even higher prices in a short time. Luckily, they had competitors; in the month of October, many of the miners, getting settled for the winter, had bought provisions for four and five months when they were cheap; seeing them so dear in the month of January, they resold them at four times what they had cost them, saving only what they needed for their own food for fifteen days or a month. At the same time that they were realizing a fine profit, they lowered the soaring prices; they expected soon to be able to buy supplies cheaply when, after the rains stopped, the roads became passable again.

The latest news from San Francisco announced that everything there was very cheap; we ourselves bought provisions for only three weeks, hoping, after that time, to pay less for them. But, contrary to these expectations, the bad weather continued throughout the month of February; when the rain stopped falling, it was the snow which fell; there was almost a foot of it. It was the final blow. During the rain, it was still possible to replace butcher's meat by game, which was abundant enough; but the snow forced it to descend twenty-five or thirty miles lower down, to the plain, where it was not snowing. Instead of the fusillade which echoed all day, no more was heard than, from time to time, a shot fired at a belated hare or deer, or at a passing flight of partridges. Soon it was a general rout. On the roads one saw miners, their blankets rolled on their backs, mud to the knees, trying to reach the plain in order to walk, from there, to Stockton, the nearest place where they could hope to find anything to eat. However, since we still had some provisions, we held fast; we were even still working, though little enough, the snow being a serious obstacle; then, we did not dare leave the house too much, for fear that someone might come, during our absence, to steal our supplies which were as precious to us as—and more so than—our purse. After eight or ten days of snow, our donkey was dying of hunger; in order to prolong her sad existence, we had to empty our mattress of dry grass and admit her to the house. Every evening, before going to bed, we brought her in; she remained standing, between the two beds, her head turned to the side of the fire; in the morning, we made her back out, as there wasn't room enough for her to turn around. In short, we did so much and so well that after all the poor animal did not die of hunger.

Around the twentieth of February, as our supplies were consumed and the snow still covered the ground, I left to go after provisions but without taking the donkey, who was too feeble to carry anything, no matter what.

I went first to the camp at Bear Valley, the nearest; for more than fifteen days nothing had been sold there. Ten days before a store had been pillaged of supplies and the two proprietors killed. Since then, the eight inhabited houses composing the camp had been gathered in one, and had fortified themselves there; and these people, having only just enough supplies for themselves, were not selling any to anyone. I learned that at Mariposa all the stores were empty and closed. No more restaurant, no more baker, the butcher alone was still going; he had killed his last animals, which, perhaps, had eaten nothing for three weeks; he was selling the bones at three francs a livre. On hearing this news, I headed for Agua Fria. There I was still able to buy twelve livres of flour for twelve dollars (60 francs), six livres of beans for nine dollars, then three livres of potatoes, the biggest of which was like a nut, for a dollar and a quarter (seven francs). Even so it was necessary, in order to be able to conclude this bargain, that I had the luck to find five individuals who had no more than that and who, for fear of dying of hunger, were leaving next day for the plain.

I returned to find Thill with my purchases, recommending that he be economical when it was his turn to cook, because I was bringing back all that was left for us to eat from now to fair weather, that is, perhaps for eight days, perhaps for fifteen, perhaps for a month. "Good," said Thill with his German accent. "I know my business, and to you I will the product of my day show." So saying he presented me with an enormous hare and two crows which he had had the luck to kill while hunting.

As if on purpose, on the two or three days following, so much half-melted snow fell that it was impossible for us to leave the house. However, supplies were disappearing and there was no more hope of finding any in the region! We therefore had to go away; but where? It was useless to dream of turning in the direction of Mariposa, or of Agua Fria, everybody was getting away from there; the very ones who had sold us some supplies in the month of January were forced to leave, after having bought back at seven francs a livre the provisions which they had sold in the month of October at ten sous and sold again in the month of January at forty. In the opposite direction, we had the Merced river, which had not been crossed for almost two months because the ferry was no longer working, the water being so high and swift that it would have broken everything.

We would then, like the others, have to reach the plain and, from there Stockton; it was a hundred and twenty miles to go (40 leagues)! and God knew by what roads! And perhaps in three days, perhaps tomorrow, the sun would show itself at last, and we would have to return! While we were consulting each other without being able to come to a decision, my eyes fell on our burro. "Oh, well!" said I to Thill, "here we are, bewailing our fate, and we still have meat for at least fifteen days."—"How is that?" asked Thill. I showed him the donkey, occupied at that moment in devouring the rags of an old flannel shirt, which one of us had thrown away. Thill reflected a moment, then said to me: "No, she is too thin, and besides she is our companion, our friend, I love her, I do, this poor animal; she has suffered with us, let her be saved with us, if we are saved. We will not have eaten half of her, perhaps, when the bad weather will end; once the snow disappears, she will quickly recover; as we'll have to leave here anyway since the claim will soon be without water, we'll then need the services of our jenny, and we will be happy to find her." I found that Thill was right, and we decided to procure our meat by other means. Instead of working, we began to hunt, but, as I have said, game was scarce, and we had much trouble in killing what we needed.

One day however—it was the third after the deliberation of which I have spoken—having noticed the prints of rabbits in the neighborhood of some thick brush, two miles from our cabin, I went into it and I had the luck to shoot three. Thill, on his side, returned with two birds as big as thrushes, and a squirrel.

The next day, we returned together to beat the bushes and we killed five rabbits, very small, it is true, but we were not concerned with their size; we would have eaten rats, if we had had any.

On returning quite happy to the cabin, we were much astonished not to see our donkey under the roof of branches which we had built for her and where she habitually stayed. We entered our hut; everything was in disorder, someone had come to rob us. They had upset everything to find the cashbox. They had not found it, luckily! but they had taken our supplies, our linen and our donkey. Although it was almost night, we picked up the thieves' trail in the snow—there were two of them—and that of the donkey, and we set off quickly in their pursuit. At one place, we observed that the donkey had fallen; no doubt, they had forced her to get up again and to continue the march. Ten minutes later, the donkey had fallen anew; we could see it easily in the snow.

Five hundred paces farther on, we encountered the donkey, who was staggering back alone. She was at the end of her strength, she could hardly stay on her feet. We continued to follow the footprints of the thieves, until darkness forced us to stop. We returned without having seen anything and recaptured the donkey in passing. That evening, while we ourselves were eating, we gave her one of our pillows, not, that goes without saying, to rest her head on, but to eat the contents.

The unfortunate beast ate all that she could reach with her teeth; the bushes around the cabin were gnawed to the ground; of stems as big as a finger she made only a mouthful.

Next day we repaired, to the best of our ability, the havoc wreaked in our cabin; then, by means of a thread tied at one end to a plank adroitly hidden under the sill of the door, at the other to the trigger of a revolver, we took our precautions against our friends the thieves.

Chapter Fourteen

From Coultersville to Marble Spring

During the seven or eight days which followed, it did not stop raining or snowing, and often the rain and snow fell at the same time. The eighth day the rain, having no doubt become less cold, began to melt the snow. Three days later an American, the first whom we had seen in six months, passing on a mule behind our cabin, told us that the ferry on the Merced was working again; he himself had just crossed the river that way. He told us also that at Coultersville [Coulterville] one could still obtain ham.[1] We were only eighteen miles from there; now, we were growing short of game, the rain could recommence and the ferry be interrupted again; on the other hand, the convoys sent from San Francisco were not to arrive so early. We decided, in consequence, to leave immediately for Coultersville; we loaded the doneky with a pack-saddle, put fifty livres' weight on her back—she couldn't have carried any more—loaded ourselves with the rest, and there we were on our way.

The Merced was still flooding all the flats along its banks. It was frightening to see; while descending the hill we heard it roaring half a league away, and we saw it leaping from rock to rock. The ferry cable which, in summer, was eight or ten meters above the water, cleared it by not more than one or two meters. The boatman, however, dared to cross it; he came to get us from the other bank, and ferried us over.

We had some trouble in climbing the hill on the right bank; the rain had soaked the ground, and the path was slippery. We had to share the burro's load, and even though she now had no more than her saddle to carry, from time to time we had to stop to let her catch her breath; otherwise she trembled on her legs, then let herself

---

1. Perlot's "Coultersville" reflects the usual spelling of the town's name in the 1850s; later it became Coulterville and so remains today. Founded in 1849 by George W. Coulter, a Pennsylvanian who had come to the Southern Mines via Santa Fe, the area was known first as Maxwell's Creek. Coulter chose this tributary on the Merced River as the spot to pitch a blue canvas tent beneath an oak tree and to open a store. Coulter also raised an American flag over his establishment. Coultersville eventually replaced Maxwell Creek as the name of the mining camp, which soon became a supply center for the mines in the northern and northeastern sector of the Southern Mines. Eventually it became a way station for tourists visiting Yosemite Park; Coulter was, in fact, "one of the first commissioners for the Yosemite Valley grant." See Gudde, *California Place Names*, p. 77, and Catherine Coffin Phillips, *Coulterville Chronicle: The Annals of a Mother Lode Mining Town* (San Francisco: Grabhorn Press, 1942), pp. 60ff.

fall. When at last we reached the top of the hill, where, by good fortune, there was abundant grass, we permitted her to pasture at her ease, and we let her go the rest of the way without loading her.

It was night when we reached Coultersville. On entering the camp, we noticed right away this sign in French: "M. Rivet, restaurant. Lodgings."—It was exactly what we wanted, tired and famished as we were. After having put our donkey in a sort of stable made of planks, we entered the restaurant. "What time is supper?" I asked the master of the establishment. This person looked at me with astonishment; one would have thought that I was speaking Chinese.

"What!" said he, "what time is supper? you still eat supper, you two? Here, for two months we have lost the habit. When is supper!—At ten days after the rain; for three months now it has fallen; if only half of it has fallen, you will have supper here in three months and ten days, for I'll surely need those ten days to receive the provisions I ordered at the end of autumn. While waiting, if you have something to cook, there is the kitchen, there's the fire, do as you would at home since you still eat supper, and don't be afraid of bothering me, especially in the kitchen—it's at least fifteen days since a living soul has entered it."—"But," I said, "how do you pass your time, if you don't eat any more?"—"In waiting," he said, "till the rain has stopped. Only, from time to time, I go gnaw on a ham which I eat raw and which I mix with some ship's biscuit, of which I have one or two livres left."

I asked him if I couldn't find some provisions left in the camp to buy.—"Oh, no," he said. "It is useless for you to look; I myself sold the last ham, so that if it rains another eight days, I'll have to get out of here or else perish of hunger."

"Well," I said to Thill, "let's cook our game, and then, tomorrow, we'll go farther on; I don't insist on staying in a camp where there is nothing to eat."

We left, in fact, the next day for Oak Flat (*plateau de chêne*) [Big Oak Flat] where, they said, we could buy something to eat.[2] We had only twelve miles to go; we had gone nine when, having reached Spring Gulch (*ruisseau de source*), we encountered an American whom I recognized from having seen him at Mariposa.[3] He advised us not to go any farther, assuring us that it was easier to find gold at Spring Gulch than nearer to Oak Flat. As for supplies, he told us that we could have some on Sunday at Oak Flat. "How," I asked, "on Sunday?"—"Yes," he said, "the distribution is made only on that day."

"What, the distribution?"

"Oh, that's true, you don't know. Understand, then, that next Sunday, at Oak Flat, whether you have anything to pay with or not, they will give each of you four

2. The mining camp of Big Oak Flat, north of Coulterville, took its name from a giant oak near which miners found gold in 1849. Because one of the first to mine there was James D. Savage, it was also called "Savage Diggings." See Wood, *Agua Fria*, p. 41; Gudde, *California Place Names*, p. 29; and idem, *California Gold Camps*, p. 37.

3. This is not the Spring Gulch near Columbia where a Frenchman found a single nugget which it is said weighed twenty-five pounds (Hittell, *History of California*, 3: 144).

livres of flour and three livres of beans; the distribution will be made in person; each one has to go to get his share."

That was the case, and here is the explanation: In the month of January, a man named Mack, a supply merchant, having emptied his store, had left for Stockton, had hired thirty-six mules, had loaded them with flour and beans, then had tried to bring all that to Oak Flat.[4] But out of the thirty-six mules, only twenty-six had been able to withstand the fatigues of the road, so that, counting everything, these provisions had cost him almost a dollar a livre. This businessman, more astonishing in his way than St. Yves, *advocatus et non latro*, this businessman, I say, had doubled as a philanthropist: instead of speculating on the public misery—and he had a fine chance to do it since he alone in the camp had something to sell—he called a general meeting, showed his invoices, and asked that the public name a committee in charge of fixing the price of the provisions and of distributing them each week, in such a way that each one would have something to eat at least until the first of March. The committee was formed, it was installed about the fifteenth of January with the said Mack, and the distribution was still being made although it was the eighth of March; that was because many people had left the placer and, naturally, the number of joint partakers having diminished, the provisions lasted longer.

With this information, we settled at Spring Gulch. While waiting for Sunday, we ate the results of our hunting, which was more productive than at Bear Valley, for, in two days, we had killed three hares and some birds. The weather was turning fair; it still rained a lot, but less often, the earth was draining, and the game was returning from the plain.

When Sunday came, we went to the distribution of rations at Oak Flat; they gave each of us, in fact four livres of flour and three livres of beans, for which we paid twenty-eight dollars. The committee, after the first distribution, seeing that half the miners, more or less, did not have the gold needed to pay for their supplies to the first of March, had called a meeting of all those who could pay easily; they decided, so that Mister Mack could recover his expenses, to bring the price of supplies to two dollars a livre, instead of a dollar and a half; by this arrangement, the rich paid for the poor. At the distribution, whoever took an oath that he didn't have sixty dollars in his purse, was considered indigent, and received his ration of supplies free; he only placed his name on a register.

We, happy miners, forming a part of the well-to-do class—we paid without sulking too much. We were too happy to have at last something else to eat besides meat, pepper, and salt, for that had been our diet for almost two months.

This first week, we worked all the time we were not hunting. On weighing our gold on Saturday and adding our household accounts, we found that we had made

4. Gudde has noted that Big Oak Flat had a "strong German element," to whom August and Albert Mack, merchants, belonged. One of the major mines near Big Oak Flat was the "Mack." See Gudde, *California Gold Camps,* p. 37.

thirty-two dollars and had spent thirty of it to live. "Well!" said Thill, "there is some gain and I think that we are saved."

In fact, from week to week, the situation was improving: the weather was more favorable, and the days longer, game was becoming common again and, without losing much time, we had a hare or a rabbit to cook with our beans. A hunter, having killed an enormous bear, cut it up and, the following Sunday, sold the meat from it in the camp; his bear brought him three thousand, five hundred francs, at the rate of three francs, 75 centimes the livre.

We bought a good portion of it and with it made sometimes soup, sometimes stew. The stew and the steak were excellent; as for the soup . . . one had to be a miner and have been threatened with famine for four months to eat it.

M. Thibeau, son of the former manager of the company, La Fortune, happened to be, like us, at Spring Gulch. He asked to enter our company. The business was done and we were three. This Thibeau had a sort of a house like the one we had at Bear Valley, and he had just room for three. We went to settle there with him; our claim was beginning to bring in less, we had changed it and were working on an old claim—that is, in a place where others had already worked—but it had the advantage of being beside the cabin. Unfortunately, in the first week of April, it happened that I was overcome by weakness, so much that at the end of two days I had to stop working. The claim being difficult, my two partners, left alone, did little, and for this reason they decided to rest until I should recover. While waiting, they made a trip to Mariposa, Thibeau to find out what had become of his brother, and Thill to get news of Burgrave and Kesch, his two compatriots. It was agreed that they would return in eight or ten days.

The day after their departure, I was able to go as far as Oak Flat. People were no longer under rations, provisions were arriving from all sides and were generally being sold at three francs a livre; I went there with the intention of buying some cuts of beef, with the aim of being able at last to make what could be called, without derision, a soup. The butcher had just returned to the exercise of his functions, by killing several animals. I bought, at the same time, for twelve dollars, a case of a dozen bottles of Bordeaux wine, which I had to carry back to the cabin on my shoulders, for alas! our donkey, our poor donkey, which we had had so much trouble saving from famine, for three weeks had no longer been with us; she was eaten! The Indians of the Toualumné [Toulumne] (a river running fifteen miles farther to the north) had come during our absence, had seized her, had killed her on the spot, then had fled, leaving us the head and feet.

As soon as I returned to the cabin, I made a special soup, decanted a bottle of St.-Julien, and served myself a true Lucullan feast. The next day, I did as much; I found myself thriving on this diet—so much so that at the end of three days I recovered and could go back to work. When my case of wine was exhausted, I returned to get another, after that one, yet another, and I was soon on my fifth case. Seeing the marvelous effects of this medicine and supposing that it was a specific to prevent the sickness as well as to cure it, I promised myself to use it generously in the future and to make an ample provision of it. Besides, it was more economical than being sick every six months.

Having thus recovered before the return of my partners, I started to work here and there with the pan; I daily made two, three, sometimes four dollars. One day when I was working on an old claim (a claim already worked) and examining it attentively, it seemed to me that they must have passed to one side of the vein of gold, or, at the very least, had worked only one, since, according to my calculations, there should be two of them. Forthwith, I dug a hole in order to find out for myself. The next day, the paydirt extracted from the bottom of this hole produced twelve dollars. I immediately staked the claim for four, and two days later, my partners having returned, we made a canal to bring water to it; at the end of five days, we were working there with the long-tom, each making ten dollars a day. This claim lasted fifty days and always brought us as much; we worked it to the end without any neighbor coming to take the portion which we had left over.

Our partnership did not last longer than the exploitation of this marvelous claim. Thibeau, seeing himself in command of a little capital, wished to undertake some sort of business with his brother; Thill left me to go rejoin Kesch, his countryman; this latter, it seemed, with three others, had found a good claim which ought to last a long time and, in order to be able to monopolize it entirely, they took Thill in with them. Once more I found myself alone. As we were nearing the month of June and as the water would soon dry up in Spring Gulch, it was necessary for me to leave and seek another placer where I could spend the summer. But, first, I wanted to take an airing at Mariposa. I had written to Herbeumont, eighteen months before; perhaps there was a letter at the camp for me. Moreover, I was desirous of seeing my friends and of learning about the members of the former company of La Fortune, who all, or almost all, in the spring of the preceding year, had come to work at Mariposa and in the environs. I started on my way with a simple overnight bag. In passing through Coultersville, I did not miss entering the restaurant Rivet, where they had returned to the good habit of eating supper, since the rain had stopped; so it was very well supplied, and the kitchen smelled much better than it had in the month of March. Rivet had taken a partner, and this partner was none other than Badinier, the former lumber merchant of Orléans, the father of the people, the emulator of Mirabeau.

One can well imagine that as we had not seen each other for two years, we had many things to ask and to tell one another. He told me that he had just spent the winter in company with six others who were working with him on the lower part of the Mariposa River, without having suffered much, because in the month of October they had bought, at a low price, supplies which had lasted until the month of April, that is, until the return of fair weather. They had even had very little snow, being near the plain; but they were working on a flat claim, which the water had submerged, so that they had not been able to work at all in the winter. As this claim nevertheless was good, in the month of April he had sold his rights to another for a good price and had come to Coultersville to join with M. Rivet, a Canadian with whom he had made acquaintance on the Merced.

When he had finished telling his story, I told mine; then I left for Bear Valley, where I was to stay that day. I crossed the Merced, which had gone down a lot in three months, to such a point that some miners were beginning their preparations to take up the work which winter had interrupted. Bear Valley was full of people returned from Stockton and elsewhere; however, water was going to be short there and already many of the claims were unoccupied.

Out of curiosity I went to see again our cabin of the previous winter. It had been occupied by others, then abandoned, probably because of the lack of water; in fact, everything was completely dry in the vicinity—impossible even to find anything to drink there. I did not see again without emotion the places where we had suffered so much, and, in going away, I turned back more than once.

Two kilometers away was the camp. It was late, and I stopped there to spend the night. The population was still fairly numerous, in large part Mexican, like, for that matter, all of the placers where water was wanting, because the Mexican always works alone and with the pan, and thus can work with much less water than those who use the long-tom or even the cradle. The Mexican does not like to clear away the earth; he digs a well and, when he has reached the bottom, he washes the dirt from it, then continues to follow the vein by means of a drift in the form of a tunnel. It follows that, to do this work, he needs no water at the bottom or very little.

The following day, four hours after having left the camp of Bear Valley, I was at Mariposa, at Chanac the baker's. He was a little better set up than the preceding year; he had for partners a Swiss named Joseph, and a Norman named Henris. They had many boarders, some miners who were working not far from there, and who took all their meals at the hotel, claiming that they got off more cheaply than by feeding themselves.

Mariposa was on the way to becoming a city. There were already many brick houses; all the commerce of the region was concentrated there. Having arrived on Friday evening, I planned to leave again on Saturday morning; but some shipboard companions, whom I found there, decided that I would stay until Monday morning; most of them being occupied, they did not have the leisure to see me on another day. I invited them to dinner at Chanac's, in order to have an hour of fun together once again.

All were on time at the meeting, but no one wanted to let me pay for his dinner. We numbered eighteen, Latuy, Duléry, Béranger, Messent, Huguet, etc., etc., all former workers of the company of La Fortune, or passengers on board the *Courrier de Cherbourg*.

One can easily guess that the day passed gaily. The following Monday morning, a good number of the convivial souls, who had not been able to return to their tents, were still sleeping when I went to shake their hand, wish them good luck, and tell them goodbye. Each one, after dinner, had told his story; all, with minor variations, were condensed in this: "They had found gold, and they had spent it; they had been hungry, they had slept in the bushes, two, three, and sometimes six months in a row, without undressing, whether for lack of a bed, or from fear of the Indians, who had more chance against an undressed man.

At the final reckoning, not one had yet made a fortune, but all were still hoping to reach it—when I say all, I mean the eighteen present and the other survivors, for, alas! many of the comrades who arrived with us two years before, now were no more. Out of forty-five that we numbered on debarking at Monterey, only thirty-one survived; three were dead because man is mortal, especially in California, at least the two first years; two, because the Indians had killed them; three others, already for almost a year, had disappeared: were they dead? were they living? we did not know exactly, but there was reason to fear that they were dead, if we thought of the number of miners buried in the last two years without their identity having been determined. Two had been wounded in firearms accidents and had succumbed to their wounds; two had been drowned in crossing rivers, and finally two must have perished of hardship, or of violent death, while trying, the preceding winter, to reach Stockton; they had, with this aim, left Mariposa in the month of January and had been seen no more.

I found Thomas again at Mariposa, returned long since from the Fresno; he was thin, pale, haggard, and had aged ten years during the last winter. Useless to tell how he had passed it; let it suffice me to say that after having sold all that he had and even my tent, he found himself without supplies and without money and had nothing to eat, for several weeks, but the weeds which he went to look for in the woods and which he cooked in the manner of spinach.

Toward the end of January, he had looked for us for several days but had not been able to discover where we were.

He was, at that time, in partnership with a man called Bégon, of Liège, a former sergeant; they were not doing much and they, too, were preparing to abandon the claim they were working because it lacked water. Thomas proposed that we two become partners; I accepted, and we left together for Spring Gulch.

As soon as I returned, I started looking for a beast of the donkey species to carry our tools and supplies. After three days' search, I found some miners at Deer Flat (*plateau du daim*) who had just arrived and who had a little black donkey; they didn't need it any more because they had a claim quite near the camp: I bought it.[5]

Two days later, two men were traveling in the mountains which separate the North Fork (*fourche du nord*) of the Merced from the Toualumné; they were driving before them a donkey which carried supplies for a month; these two men were Thomas and I, in search of a placer to work during the summer.

When passing through Coultersville, we learned some interesting news:

5. Deer Flat, or Creek, was west of Garrote (present-day Groveland) and boasted rich placers (Gudde, *California Gold Camps*, p. 94).

In the month of September of the preceding year, some troops had been sent against the Indians entrenched in the mountains between the Merced and the Toualumné; they had killed many of them and had captured a greater number. Finally, the government had made a treaty with the Indians; it had put them in a reservation on the plain, where it fed them. It had thereby delivered the mountain region from them, always with the exception of the valley of the You-sé-miti [Yosemite], where some hundreds of Indians were holding out.[6] But winter having been excessively prolonged, these last, in their turn, had had to surrender to obtain the right to come down from the mountains and to show themselves in the lands occupied by the miners.

I remembered, indeed, that when I was on the Fresno, at the time when the government had sent the doctors, we had seen many Indians who were going down toward the plain and were conducting themselves peacefully enough. The troops spoken of were doubtless those dragoons whom we had followed for eight days, and who, having made their junction with another column, which had gone up the Toualumné while they had gone up the Fresno, had seized the big Indian camp established in these mountains.

Whatever might be the reason, many miners were going up the Merced very much higher than the preceding year, and it did not appear that they had been disturbed by the natives.

What was said of the richness of the auriferous lands of this region determined us, like many others, to go there.

Having left Coultersville in the morning, we arrived, toward evening, at the North Fork of the Merced, which had been discovered only six months before. There we found not many people and not much gold. Next day, we went on up to a point where the path, very little worn, ceased to be visible, then, bearing a little to the north, we walked haphazardly, seeking only the route that was most favorable for our donkey; we even had, from time to time, to remove his load and work him around the rocks which blocked our passage, having afterward to reload him and to continue on our way.

We were heading for an area which we had seen from the top of the mountain, before descending to the North Fork, an area which, seen from a distance, seemed to us to be, comparatively, not very uneven. If we did not find gold there, we had the resource of falling back on the Main Fork of the Merced, which this direction brought us close to. It was on the course of the Main Fork that the You-sé-miti Indians, it was said, had their camp.

We were climbing the hillside without following any kind of trail, consequently without being sure of being able to get out from among the rocks, when we suddenly found ourselves in the presence of three Indians who were hunting; as we were

---

6. Here Perlot seems to be referring to the Indian bands assigned to a reservation between the lower Merced and the lower Tuolumne that Sam Ward described in his "Incidents on the River of Grace," in Collins, ed., *Sam Ward in the Gold Rush*, pp. 51–64.

resting at that moment, the Indians had come quite close to us without seeing us, for otherwise it is probable that we would not have seen them at all. The surprise was equal on both sides. Without hesitating, however, they came to us under the protection of the word *Oualai*.[7] All at once, one of the three left the two others and came to salute me in his fashion, that is to say that he planted himself in front of me, holding out both his arms, as the priest does to say the *Orate fratres*, alternately raising and lowering them, but always holding the forearm in a vertical position. He observed, doubtless, that I had the appearance of not understanding him, and I swear that the appearance was not deceiving. Then he pointed first to his eye, then to me, and said: *Flesno, moula*, then made a sign of falling; afterward, he made a sign for drinking from a glass. These words, this pantomime, finally awakened my memory: *Flesno*, was the Fresno, for the Indian does not use the letter *r*, and replaces it with *l; moula* was a mule which, in Spanish, is written *mula* and pronounced *moula*.

I then remembered the circumstance, which was this: One day, when I was on the Fresno, I had gone after supplies with the mule. On the way back, the animal, tormented by flies, had rubbed against the bushes so vigorously that his load was leaning all on one side, and I had to take it off to put it straight; now, that is a job which is not easy when one is alone and when one has to deal with an animal who is shaking off flies and moves around a lot. In vain did I storm and bluster and swear; I was getting nowhere, when some Indians came by; not being able to speak to them, I took one by the arm; he was afraid and resisted, I used force, drew him near the mule, and put the bridle reins in his hand. Then he understood and ended by holding the mule, while I balanced the load again. That done, to recompense him and to help him recover from his emotion—for I had noticed that his look had been fixed on the revolver which hung at my side—I gave him a good dram to drink and a bit of bread which I had in my hunting bag. This Indian was without doubt the one whom I saw before me; my features, it seemed, were well engraved in his memory since after a year he recognized me at first sight. I did not recognize his, for nothing resembles one Indian more than another Indian, but, after his gestures, I had no doubt of his identity. I took my flask, poured a good dram for each Indian, then gave them each a piece of tortilla (a piece of paste flattened and cooked in a frying pan) which we had left from our breakfast. I asked them, making myself understood as best I could, if there was a road this way, if there was anyone there, Indians, etc. They proceeded to put us on a path, then they explained that farther on there were some miners; at least that is the way we interpreted their contortions. After which, having exchanged an amicable "oualai, oualai," they went off on their way and we on ours.

Toward evening, the path led us to a wagon road. We were not a little surprised to see that people could have gone into these mountains with wagons; this road had such steep grades that the wagons would necessarily, on the de-

7. See introduction to part 2.

scent, have had to be braked on all four wheels. But after all, people had passed here, and this road ought to lead us somewhere. It led us, in fact, to Marble Spring (*source de marbre*).[8] There was a vein of quartz being worked there, and the wagons, whose tracks we had seen and which had worn the road, had brought in a steam engine which was running the stamping-mill. There had been at this place, a year previously, a small camp of miners; the Indians had attacked them, had killed three of them and chased the others away, then stolen the provisions. On our arrival, there were, as far as miners were concerned, only six Irishmen; then, there were fifteen workmen employed in the exploitation of the quartz, exploitation which, it seemed, gave marvelous results.

Having found an unoccupied cabin, we settled in it, and there we were, lodged immediately on arriving. It was a house built of tree trunks; even the roof was formed of pines a foot in diameter, rolled one against another, then covered with two feet of earth; the door, which opened on a pivot, was made of boards pegged together. In short, it was a real fortress, eighteen feet long, fifteen feet wide and ten high; two windows, oppositie to each other and embrasured, gave it air and light. Opposite this cabin was another just like it, occupied by the Irish; the stamp-mill was five hundred meters farther down.

Once we were housed, all we had to do was find a claim where we could work. As water was becoming scarce, we hardly had a choice, and when we had found, a mile from our cabin, a creek where there still was enough water, we set to work there. The work was easy; we washed all the dirt and made very irregular wages, which varied, for each one, from two to eight dollars. As long as the water held out, that is, until the month of September, we stayed on this creek, which was called Lewis Gulch; we got our supplies at Coultersville, from which we were eighteen miles distant; we went there, every month or six weeks, to get a load for our Jack (our donkey). As for meat, we got that with a gun; it was a real preserve for game of all kinds: hare, partridge, quail, brown pheasant, grouse, pigeons, and gray squirrels abounded there in autumn and spring; it was a highway for deer and bear, who from the mountains higher up were going down to the plain, or else were going from the plain to the mountains, according to the season. Generally, Sunday sufficed for me to procure all the meat we could consume during the week.

Having no more water, we could no longer work. We were not disposed to go to a river where there still was water, which we would have had to deflect by means of a dam; the season was too far advanced. And then, we were so well settled, so tranquil, so well fed and for so little! So we decided to stay and wait until winter

8. Gold was discovered at Marble Springs (which Perlot always called Marble Spring), eighteen miles east of Coulterville, in 1851. Situations on the North Fork of the Merced River, very near Bower Cave, it became for Perlot as much of a home base as any camp he lived in during his nearly seven years in California. On July 27, 1855, Perlot filed a quartz claim on Marble Springs Gulch with the Mariposa County clerk in which he described the site as "between North and South Fork of the Merced River, in a certain ravine, which empites into Marble Spring gulch about one and a half miles above the mouth of Marble Spring gulch." See Quartz Claims, book A, p. 193, Mariposa County Records (Bretnor Notes).

gave us water. The Irish, who lacked water before we did, left, promising to be sure to come and keep us company all winter; but, to tell the truth, it was company for which we were hardly eager: our six neighbors equaled seven downright drunkards, including one of their friends, who lived at Coultersville and who often came to see them, each time carrying on his back a barrel of ten or fifteen litres of whiskey; the seven did not leave the Casa (house) until the barrel was dry as a bone.

During the season, many people had come to prospect in our section; several had worked there three or four days, then, with their supplies exhausted, they had gone and not returned, because there was too little water and also, sometimes, because they did not find enough gold. We alone had held firm.

The workmen on the quartz mill had left as soon as the water for washing the pulverized quartz had dried up; they were to return at the beginning of the rainy season. They had, however, left two men who spent their summer cutting cord wood, to fire the engine when it began to run again.

Although the regular working of the auriferous earth was forbidden us by the dryness, we utilized our forced leisure in prospecting the gulches of the Marble Spring basin.

We carried this paydirt in sacks to the spring of Marble Spring itself, two kilometers distance from our quarters, and washed it in a pan or in a sebilla.

Once we had determined on the gulch which seemed the richest, we began to prepare the ground in advance, that is, we dug it up, removed the stones and roots, then, with the shovel, we threw it up on the bank, so that there would be nothing more but the washing to do when the water returned. Naturally, there was nothing urgent about this work and we took our time to do it.

During the great heat of the day, we rested; we really worked only in the morning and evening.

We also wanted, before the return of the rains, to complete our establishment. We constructed a stable to house our *Jack* during the winter, then an oven to cook our bread, our roasts, our pies and stews, which we made with all kinds of game. We were in the midst of abundance and we felt the need, if not of luxury, at least of being comfortable; we had completely forgotten our hardships of the previous winter.

One day, while out hunting, almost two leagues from our dwelling, and seven or eight leagues, perhaps, from any other inhabited place, I saw a black and white animal running toward me; when he was within shooting distance, I recognized a dog. Without hesitation, he proceeded to lie down at my feet; he looked sad and miserable and he was certainly hungry; having brought in my knapsack several crusts as hard as crusts can become when aged in a sack, I presented them to him; he pounced on them avidly and swallowed them whole. I waited a long time, expecting to see his master arrive, but the master did not come.

I started on my way again, the dog followed me; I pretended to want to hit him, he lay down instead of running away. Then, supposing that his master was in the neighborhood, I shouted, then I shot off my gun, then I shouted again; I listened a moment and heard no response. The idea then came to me that, perhaps, his master was dead somewhere in the vicinity; I tried to make the dog guide me by going in the direction from which I had seen him come, but he seemed more concerned in following me than in seeking a lost master. Having given him what was left in my sack, I tried again to persuade him to lead me to the place he had come from, but instead of leading, he continued to follow me. After having beaten the surrounding country for two hours, and having found nothing, I climbed on a neighboring eminence, I shouted, shot off my gun, and, as always receiving no response, I thought I had done everything possible whether to inform the legitimate proprietor of the animal, or to find his corpse. I took the path back to the cabin, followed by the dog, who, after that, never left me. He was a cross of a griffon, a hound, and a spaniel, who might have been six months old; if he had belonged to me, I would certainly not have given him up for a hundred dollars, and I had him for nothing; he was never reclaimed from me. I succeeded, in a short time, in making him a model dog in all respects, a vigilant sentinel, especially against the Indians, and an incomparable hunter.

About the month of November, foreseeing the imminent return of the rains, for already it was freezing every morning at Marble Spring, we went to Coultersville to get our provisions for the entire winter. M. Rivet, who, while remaining a restaurateur, had become a food supply merchant, offered to send ours to our domicile. Three days later, we had in abundance all sorts of excellent victuals; there was enough for six months at least and we could wait for winter without stirring.

During the months of August and September, we often saw Indians coming and going. It was the time of their harvest; they came to our flats to gather all kinds of seeds, even hayseeds.

It is the Indian woman who does this work; she has a big hamper or very open basket, of very fine reeds, and coated with a starch made of powdered seeds and warm water. She holds this hamper with one hand under the grass in seed; then, with a sort of fan also made of reed and supplied with a handle, which she holds in the other hand, she pulls the grass over her hamper; the seeds, thanks to the shake given by the fan, are detatched and fall; the half-full hamper serves as winnowing-basket to clean them. After which, the Indian woman puts this grain in conical baskets; when she has her load, she puts the whole in her big cornucopia, which serves her as basket, then she returns to the camp to come back again some days later.[9]

9. The food of the Miwok bands is described briefly in Barrett, "Geography and Dialects of the Miwok Indians," pp. 335–37; A. L. Kroeber, "The Food Problem in California," in R. F. Heizer and M. A. Whipple, eds., *The California Indians: A Source Book* (Berkeley and Los Angeles: University of California Press, 1971), pp. 297–300; and E. W. Gifford, "Californian Balanophagy," in ibid., pp. 301–05. See also Phillips, *Coulterville*, p. 15.

Watching from Belt's Ferry and Store on the Merced, Sam Ward observed: "In the autumn, for several weeks preceding the deluge, I had admired the ceaseless activity of the crones who went forth into the forest to gather acorns, and upon the hill sides to strip the rarer grasses of their seeds, and were often several days absent before having filled their baskets" (Collins, ed., *Sam Ward in the Gold Rush*, p. 136).

So it was that in the month of October, we were still surrounded by a crowd of Indians and especially of Indian women occupied in gathering all kinds of fruits, of seeds and grasses, when one fine morning we were awakened by these Indians, men and women, who were going by again, singing, and running with all the speed of which they were capable in the direction of the Merced. They kept passing this way for two days and two nights. They were singing in voices which lacked a little in precision and harmony: "Metta ette accaégnème." We had never seen them so noisy and eager. Seeing that the movement was general, not knowing and not suspecting the cause of it, we nevertheless said to ourselves that there was one, and as it could very well be that it concerned us somewhat, we stayed on our guard.

However, their attitude in regard to us had nothing hostile in it; rather it was friendly. We were scratching our heads to discover what all this could mean, when two Mexicans who were passing explained it to us: "Metta ette accaégnème" meant quite simply: *The acorn has fallen.* The falling of the first acorn is, indeed, an event which the Indians celebrate with a festival. The oldest man in the tribe spends his whole summer in choosing an oak; on this oak, he chooses a branch, and on that branch, an acorn; when this acorn falls, he lets the whole tribe know. Those who are away, leave their occupations and hasten to return to the camp; when everybody is reunited, the festival begins. Those whom we saw passing by Marble Spring, so noisy and joyful, were therefore not animated by the bellicose intentions we supposed; they were going to celebrate the acorn festival.[10]

10. Gifford, "California Balanophagy," pp. 301–05.

V

ENCOUNTERS WITH THE TUOLUMNE AND YOSEMITE INDIANS, 1853–1854

The Nang-à on the Toualumné have come to take our salmon and have killed two of my brothers; they are numerous and strong. If you consent to drive them away, we will be friends of the whites, we will never take anything from them, we will not get drunk any more, we will sleep at night, and we won't eat your mules any more except when they have died. I, Juan, have spoken; it is enough.

Juan, a Yosemite,
to Perlot on the eve of a
battle against the Tuolumne

The following chapters record Perlot's increasing curiosity about, and his eventual alliance with, the Yosemite Indians whom he encountered in the foothills and mountains of the Central Sierra. Because he and his Belgian companions, Thill and Thomas, chose to spend the winter in their log cabin at Marble Springs (which was in the northeast quadrant of the Southern Mines and east of Coulterville), they had many opportunities to observe Indians as they passed their cabin on their way to buy flour and other supplies from Coulterville or the Garrotes.[1] It was not lost on Perlot that somehow the Indians had found gold to pay for American goods and staples. At first it was largely for selfish reasons—that is, to find out where the natives were mining—that Perlot befriended two Yosemite Indians named Flesno and Juan.

Flesno was so named because Perlot had met him a year before on the Fresno River, where the young Indian had assisted Perlot in loading a mule. Quite by accident Perlot encountered Flesno again at Marble Spring. The latter became a frequent visitor to Perlot's cabin, where he could always find food and drink. Eventually Perlot learned that Flesno (which was Perlot's phonetic rendition of the way Indians pronounced the word Fresno) could not communicate in Spanish or English and thus was unable to tell him much about the region. But Flesno, in a sincere attempt to answer Perlot's persistent questions, introduced him to Juan, a Yosemite Indian who had learned Spanish while living at a California mission. From Juan Perlot learned that Juan and his brother Scipiano were the sons of a Yosemite chief named José, who lived somewhere in the mountains to the east.

Perlot's imagination appears to have run wild as he dreamed of visiting the unknown region in which Chief José lived and in which he might find new sources of gold. His eventual penetration of the Yosemite regions via the upper Merced River accompanied only by Juan and Flesno, and his historic meeting with Chief José, form one of the most dramatic episodes of Perlot's stay in California. Perlot's careful, observant, and generally objective description of Chief José and his camp again demonstrates his skill as a reporter.

The meeting was not without its ironies since José mistook Perlot for a representative of the United States government and therefore was careful to recite his treaty rights from memory. The encounter is all the more valuable for historians because it revealed—in this instance at least—that Indians not only understood their treaty rights but asserted them. One can only surmise that James Savage, that master of Indian tongues, had explained the treaty of 1851 to José.

1. According to Gudde, the mining camp of Garrote(s) [cudgels] was so named because in 1850 a thief had been executed there by strangulation or by clubbing. When a second execution took place a few miles away, the original site became First Garrote and the other Second Garrote. By 1879, however, First Garrote had adopted the more peaceful name of Groveland, which exists today as a town on one of the major routes to Yosemite. See Gudde, *California Place Names*, p. 129.

After his visit to Chief José, whose camp appears to have been within a few miles of Pilot Knob, Perlot decided to leave his mining companions and take a shortcut back to Marble Springs. He became lost in the wild and seemingly impassable regions of the Merced River area. Fighting back panic as his food ran out, Perlot used his compass to get his bearing and eventually reached Marble Springs nearly a week later than he had intended. There he found that some of his companions had mounted a search party for his rescue. Yet Perlot had no sooner had a good night's rest than he began to try to fathom the mystery of the region he had seen. As he put it: if they were to mine gold so far up the Merced, "we still had to study the question of communication, for it would be necessary to bring in provisions and, in order to do that, to have a practicable road for animals."

Perlot then remembered that when he was mining on the Chowchilla in 1852 and had pursued marauding Indians into the mountains with a group of volunteer miners, he had encountered a large westward-flowing river that he now believed to be the South Fork of the Merced, perhaps the very stream on which he had seen members of José's tribe panning for gold when he made his visit to the chief. He knew that the Chowchilla, or more southern, route to the Merced was passable because Captain John Boling had penetrated the region with a company during the Mariposa War in 1851, and Lieutenant Tredwell Moore had chased Indians all the way to Mono Lake in 1852.

In the summer of 1854, after many false starts, Perlot and a group of miners—mostly from France and Germany—reached the South Fork of the Merced by going up the Chowchilla River, where he joined Juan and his Yosemite tribesmen to dig gold. There Indians and whites worked together from June until late September perhaps no more than twenty miles from the entrance of Yosemite Valley.

Always inquisitive, Perlot began to write down his observations of the Yosemites. He witnessed an Indian burial ceremony, recorded Indian words and speeches, and joined the Yosemites in a fight against a Tuolumne raiding party that was trying to seize the salmon that the Yosemite had caught as part of their food supply. This act of comradeship on the part of Perlot and his fellow miners so impressed Chief José's elder son, Scipiano, that he began to confide in Perlot. Among other things, Scipiano complained that his band had been wrongly accused of conducting the raids that led to the Mariposa War of 1851 and had, as a consequence, been forced by white soldiers to sign a treaty with Major James Savage forbidding them to enter the area between the Fresno and Merced rivers. That banishment forced a hardship on the band because they had always left the mountains in the fall to collect acorns and grass seed and to live and hunt in snow-free hills closer to the San Joaquin. Scipiano even showed Perlot the order or the treaty which he kept tightly furled in his quiver. Perlot now understood why José, on the occasion of their first meeting, stated that Scipiano had a paper that allowed him to travel in the Tuolumne Valley, for that region was still accessible to them.

Perhaps it also explains why the tribe panned gold for flour, for they were short of native foods, given their restricted right to move from place to place.

Scipiano's protestations of his tribe's innocence were so convincing that Perlot was moved to take him to Mariposa, where he, in turn, persuaded Sheriff L. V. Bills to allow the Yosemites to circulate throughout Mariposa County on the condition that they wear clothing and be of good conduct.

Perlot's memorable summer with the Yosemite band developed in him a much greater respect fo the Indians. "We had built a false idea, certainly of the Indian when we considered and treated him as a wild beast. He is a being naturally sweet and inoffensive. Having few needs, consequently few desires, he is easy to please."

Perlot's new respect, combined with his insatiable curiosity, led him to interview Juan and Scipiano, and others of the band, about their customs and beliefs. Perlot's remarkably detached explanation of the cosmology of the Yosemites is of immense value, as are his accounts of marriage customs, childbirth ceremonies, family life, divisions of labor, and their material culture. His record of Juan's interpretation of the meaning of death for the Yosemite must stand as one of the most stoic comments ever to come from an American Indian.

> I asked Juan, who was explaining his theodicy to me, if the Indians were happier up above, after their death, than here in the mountains. "Oh," he said, "I don't know, I don't think so; we are happy here, and when we die, if we have been good Indians, we are still happy up above, that's all; isn't that enough?"

Taken together, Perlot's observations constitute one of the most moving and vibrant recitals of California Indian life that one can find. In the end Perlot himself was so affected by what he had learned that he was not at all sure that white civilization had much to offer the Indian. "Alas!" he exclaimed. "What have they gained."

In evaluating Perlot's observations one can see clearly that he belongs with J. Ross Browne and James D. Savage as one of those few sojourners in gold rush California who came to respect the native inhabitants.[2] After Perlot had feared and fought Indians in his first two years in America, his move toward tolerance was yet another example of his remarkable sense of logic and fair play.

2. See J. Ross Browne, *The Indians of California* (San Francisco: Colt Press, 1944), and Annie R. Mitchell, *King of the Tulares and Other Tales of the San Joaquin Valley, 1772–1852* (Visalia, Calif., 1941), as well as "Major James D. Savage and the Tularenos," *California Historical Society Quarterly*, 28 (Dec. 1949), 323–41.

Chapter Fifteen

Befriending the Indians

In the month of November, three companies composed of Americans and Germans settled not far from us, at Marble Spring, to pass the winter there. They had spent their summer at a dam on the Toualumné, had not done much and hoped to do better at Marble Spring, when the rains came. They were twelve in all; Marble Spring therefore had sixteen inhabitants from then on; it was enough to remove all our worries on the subject of the Indians, who, in spite of their peaceful manners, were always more or less to be feared by isolated miners. The newcomers, lacking water as we did, occupied themselves, like us, in preparing the dirt and in hunting.

Six of these miners proposed to me that before the rains we should make an exploring trip between Marble Spring and the Garrotes (clubs, cudgels), not far from the Toualumné, where they had just spent the summer. According to them, there was a chance of finding some rich and unoccupied claims in that direction.[1] I accepted.

So seven of us left, with supplies for six days. We had two donkeys to carry supplies, tools, and tents, for already the nights were too cold for sleeping in the open air with impunity. After the second day, the expedition separated into two groups composed, one of three, the other of four, men; the object of this division was to cover more country and to shorten the time of the expedition. By means of an itinerary planned in advance, each group knew where the other was spending the night.

We had been walking separated this way for two days when, on reaching the point marked on the itinerary for us to spend the third night, we found the four others waiting for us. They were forced to rejoin us because they had lost their provisions as the result of a series of fairly amusing misadventures.

The first night following our separation, these four had camped forty paces from a spring.

After supper, beside a good bed of coals, they had put ham and beans to cook in one pot in order to have their breakfast already cooked and warm when they got up in the morning. Hardly had they settled themselves in their tent, ready to taste the sweets of sleep, when they heard the sound of steps accompanied by growling; one of them opened the tent a little and saw a bear with two cubs, already quite large,

1. See p. 173, n. 1.

who were coming up the flat; he called his comrades, and all four, poking their heads out through the half-open tent flap, contemplated in astonishment and some disquiet this interesting family which was coming to drink at the fountain. The mother came to the spring, drank along with her little ones, then, probably attracted by the odor of cooking ham, approached the fire still followed by her cubs; after having walked around it several times, she perceived, doubtless, that whatever smelt so good was in the pot; with one blow of her paw she made it roll some distance from the fire. That done, she sat herself down beside the ham which had fallen from the pot, and prevented her little ones from touching it until she judged that this dainty morsel had sufficiently cooled. Then she divided it equally among the guests, and all three set to without further ceremony. During the whole time the meal lasted, the four Amphitryons had been silent witnesses, hardly daring to breathe for fear of making a noise and attracting the attention of their guests, but holding their revolvers in hand in case the celebrants might not be contented with ham and beans—these revolvers were all they had for arms. However, the feast concluded, the bear sniffed a moment around the fire, then went back where she came from, accompanied by her cubs, and without having deigned to pay the slightest attention to her hosts. These then came out of their tent, and in going to pick up their pot, observed that their donkey, probably frightened by the sight of the bears, had made an effort, pulled out the stake to which he was attached, and had run away, trailing behind him the rope and stake. The darkness was too deep to be able to follow his track; it was only the following morning that they found him again three hundred paces away: the stake, caught in a bush, had forced him to stop. In sum, the misfortune, limited to the loss of the breakfast, was not too bad. Recovered from their emotion, our men proceeded to the usual operations, then continued on their way; they stopped, for the night, on another creek, which they found near ours. After having supped, they put beans only on to cook for the next day, for fear that the odor of ham might attract another bear and her cubs who would regale themselves again at their expense; that done, they went to bed in their tent, which they took care to close. As this tent was a little small for four, they had stowed their provisions in one stack, under a live oak, just outside; they had covered this pile with the packsaddle and the donkey's blanket. During the night, one of them awakened and heard something; he listened, and heard distinctly the step of one or of several animals who, it seemed to him, were approaching the tent. What was it? a bear, evidently, and perhaps three, like the night before. Without losing time, and especially without any noise, he awakened one after another of his companions and announced that a bear was wandering around the tent; they lent an ear and heard, in fact, tha animal approaching. They silently seized their re-volvers, each one sitting on his bed because the tent was too low for them to stand upright, and they waited.

The bear approached the fire, then the tent, went away for a moment, returned, and ended by heading for the pile of provisions. They heard all this coming and going very clearly, but they could see nothing, considering that the tent was closed and that they were careful not to open it, for fear of making noise and attracting the attention of the terrible visitor. Shortly afterward, they heard him upset the provisions, and tear up the sack of potatoes and eat them; soon it was the turn of the flour sack, and he shook it, tore it, and devoured the contents.

As for the inhabitants of the tent, although threatened with famine, they didn't even dream of intervening to put a stop to it; they said to themselves in petto that, after all, if the bear, after having eaten the victuals, went away without trying to make their acquaintance personally, they should consider themselves very lucky to get off so cheaply. The glutton, poking his nose into the flour sack, doubtless had breathed some of it, for he began to sneeze. "Well!" one said very low, "it sounds like a donkey with a cold!" The suggestion was unanimously rejected; it really was a bear; therefore they had to be quiet and not move. Again the animal sneezed; this time it did not seem natural to one of our men, who took the risk of half-opening the tent flap. What were not his surprise and his indignation on observing their donkey finish devouring what was still left of their provisions! They all four came out of the tent, threw themselves at once upon Master Aliboron, and gave him a good drubbing. The one who had tied him up that evening had not taken the precaution of making sure that the stake was firmly fixed in the ground; the donkey, taught by the experience of the night before, had pulled out the stake and, finding himself free, had naturally headed for the tent; hunger, opportunity, and doubtless some devil too, pushing him, he had attempted the little hoax for which he had just paid so dearly.

Next day, after having made the usual observations, they had done their day's work with what was left of their provisions, but for supper, they had had no other resource than to go and wait for us at the place where they knew we should camp that night. This circumstance considerably reduced our provisions and, after having continued our prospecting the next day together, we had to return to Marble Spring.

We had found some places where one could work profitably, no doubt, but not rich enough to cause us to leave our camp.

After our return, the dry and rather cold weather continued, and by the end of November we had hardly had two days of rain. That wasn't enough; the dust had disappeared, mushrooms were growing, the springs were beginning to flow again a little, but all that did not give us the water we needed to wash the paydirt we had prepared; we needed a good rain and it did not come. Tired of waiting, we decided to go back to work anyway, by making the best of the little bit of water which was beginning to flow again in Lewis Gulch. That hardly gained us anything but the advantage of escaping inaction, but that was something. At last, on the 25th of December, it rained abundantly enough to let us begin washing the dirt extracted. But, at the end of five days, the weather turned fair again, and soon we no longer had enough water to treat this prepared dirt, while there was too much water in Lewis Gulch to be able to work there without a diversion ditch. Was it worth the trouble to begin to dig one? perhaps tomorrow or the next day, the rain would begin to come in abundance, like the two preceding winters, and then we would really have enough to do with the dirt we had extracted, without having to occupy ourselves with a claim on Lewis Gulch.[2]

We remained undecided a whole week, having no resource but hunting to pass our time.

Thomas was not a hunter, and the time seemed much longer to him than to me; for that reason, we decided to begin a ditch and to turn Lewis Gulch from its bed, leaving us free, in case of rain, to suspend this work in order to apply ourselves to washing the dirt extracted during the summer. As there was nothing urgent about this work, I often let Thomas dig alone, while I went out to get, by shooting it, something from which to make a hare-ragout or a pâté of some sort.

Our neighbors across the way, Captain Chaive and Sir Moore, were both excellent shots; armed with rifles (guns with rifled barrels), they hunted bear and deer. Having only my double-barreled shotgun, I limited myself to hare and rabbit, to feathered game, to all that can be killed with shot.

As I killed more game that we could eat and as these gentlemen were in the same situation, we exchanged our surplus; that was how we could, from time to time, regale ourselves with deer soup and eat excellent bear steaks.

Compared to them I was, surely, only a very amateur sort of hunter as far as big game was concerned, and still, it is certain that they were more afraid than I of a bear.

On occasion I might, perhaps, have shot at a bear with my shotgun; they, with such a gun, wouldn't have risked it for anything in the world.

Armed with their rifle, indeed, they had neither fear nor hesitation; they approached within thirty or forty paces of the bear, often even closer, and aimed while supporting the weapon on a forked stick which they carried like a cane. They were sure of their shot; when the bear wasn't blasted on the spot, he would fall in a few steps; I say they were sure of it because they never shot except from the flank and when the bear was standing; the ball always hit within two inches of the heart. During the winter they killed nine of them; all were hit in this manner. I must add that every day, at noon or in the evening, they took two or three shots at a target to keep their hand in. In a pine, a hundred and fifty paces from their cabin, they had made a hole with a big auger; in this they stuck the neck of a bottle, the bottom of which made the center, the bull's eye, of their target; when they didn't break it with the first or second ball, they claimed that their rifle needed repairing and dismounted it.

Meanwhile the month of January was passing, and we had no rain. We had nearly three hundred livres of salted bear and almost as much of deer meat; we were living in abundance, we were growing fat, but we were not getting any gold,

2. Lewis Gulch probably refers to Lewis or Lewisville (Tuolumne County), or Lewis Ferry below the junction of Moccasin Creek and the Tuolumne River near Stevens Bar. See Gudde, *California Gold Camps*, p. 193, and Trask's map, 1853, in Wheat, *Maps of the California Gold Region*, p. 114.

although the ditch on Lewis Gulch was finished. It was because, every morning, or almost, the overcast weather, which promised rain, prevented us from leaving for Lewis Gulch; if it rained, we should be there and all prepared to start washing our dirt; now, the best happened to be situated clear at the top of a ravine where we could wash only in the rain. Not to have water at that season astonished us, for, since we had been in the country, the California winters had rather sinned by excess of dampness. It rained, however, from the fifteenth to the twentieth; then the weather once more became fair. To complete our bad luck, it began to freeze in a way to prevent all kinds of work; it finally happened that, out of about fifteen days, it rained one day, then it was fair, then it froze, then it snowed, then it rained a little, etc., so that we came to the month of April, that is, to the end of the rainy season, without having succeeded in entirely washing the dirt we had extracted. However, it "paid well," as the miners say, for often, in four or five hours of rain, we had made from twenty to twenty-two dollars each; it was because, the dirt being all prepared, we could wash four times as much in the same period, but also we needed four times as much water.

We could therefore consider the season ended, for from then on we could no longer hope for much rain. Already our neighbors were going to leave Marble Spring to return to the Toualumné, where they had come from, and we were soon going to find ourselves alone again on the placer, for, as water was lacking for the quartz mill too, the workmen as well were preparing to leave the place. We therefore had to decide to look for a likely spot to spend the summer; but we promised ourselves to return in the month of October or November, in order first to finish our dirt, then to work, as much as the rain would allow us, in the surrounding gulches, where the deposits seemed as rich as any to us.

Since the month of January, the Indians had reappeared; we even saw them quite often. They did nothing but pass, to go to Coultersville, or to the Garrotes (cudgels), in other words, to the nearest camps. They returned from them loaded with flour, the only provision they bought. They paid for this flour with gold; did they work in the mines somewhere and find it? I had, unfortunately, some leisure during that cursed winter; I wanted to make use of it and so I got in touch with them: I had taken it into my head to learn or at least to study their language. *Flesno*—that is how I had baptized the Indian I had known on the Fresno, for lack of any other name to call him by—Flesno never passed by Marble Spring without coming to see us because, each time, he got something to eat. Sometimes even, he arrived in the evening with two or three comrades; on such occasions we made them sleep in the cabin. I must admit that we treated them this way, not only to fulfill the duties of humanity, but above all to be sure that they would not get away with our Jack (donkey) during the night.

This Flesno, then, who could teach me nothing, because he knew absolutely nothing but the language of his childhood, had once brought me one of his comrades called Juan, who spoke a little Spanish; thanks to this language, we could almost understand each other, and I had made this Juan my instructor. Each time he passed, he gave me a lesson in the Indian tongue. This language is very simple; I don't think it's composed of more than a thousand words, but its simplicity is itself a difficulty when one wishes to learn it. It has no verbs; the art of making oneself understood consists in the manner of placing the words and of pronouncing them. Mimicry, moreover, supplies at need the deficiency of the language; the Indian expresses his thought as much and more by gestures and by the play of expression as by words.[3]

Without letting myself be discouraged, I eagerly applied myself to the study, and by the month of April I had made some progress: I understood and I made myself understood well enough.

Juan was one of the sons of "the old man," that is, of the chief of the tribe of the Yo-sé-miti (American translation of these Indian words: èchè-mèti, big waterfall). He had given me to understand that his father and mother were still living and that they were very old; that his brother Scipiano was the elder, that it was he who would be "Capitano" (chief) of the tribe after his father, that Nang-Oua (God, the ruling spirit) had favored him, that he had come into the world after seven moons (seven months), in so great a hurry was Nang-Oua to produce him in order to give the tribe of Echè-mèti a chief capable of leading them.[4]

Scipiano, soon after he was born, had been taken to a mission where his father and mother had stayed three snow moons (three winter months). They had returned *hidden* (clothed). He, Juan, had come into the world two years after Scipiano, and he still clearly remembered his stay at the mission, without being able to name it to me. It was there that he had learned Spanish, but his brother Scipiano knew it much better than he, having stayed longer at the mission. At each lesson I took, I tried to get him to indicate to me where their camp was, and where they found gold, but José (Joseph), Juan's father, had expressly forbidden him ever to reveal to the palefaces where their camp was. I was anxious, however, to obtain this last information, because the Indian is less to be feared by him who knows his refuge. When Juan and his friend offered to take me where they found gold, I always accepted, but I had never called upon them to do so, because I had reason

3. The Miwok Indians whom Perlot encountered in the Merced and Tuolumne valleys spoke either Tuolumne or a Central Sierra dialect, or Mariposa or a Southern Sierra dialect. Barrett observed that although "the language in Yosemite Valley and that spoken in the lower foothills about Mariposa were slightly different . . . this difference did not amount to more than a sub-dialectic one . . ." ("Geography and Dialects of the Miwok Indians," p. 354).

Some of Perlot's assertions, such as his statement that the Miwok bands he encountered had no verbs in their vocabulary, seem quite dubious. Barrett has eight verbs in his Mariposa vocabulary: eat, drink, run, dance, sing, shoot, kill, and shout (ibid., p. 367). James D. Savage's command of many Indian languages or dialects inspired Sam Ward to try to learn that of the Potoyensee band, whose rancheria was near Belt's Ferry Crossing. Ward claimed to have learned the verbs for "to sleep" and "to know." See Collins, ed., *Sam Ward in the Gold Rush*, p. 63.

4. In some instances it has been impossible to correlate Perlot's phonetic renditions with known words in the Mariposa dialect, but there is enough correspondence in the case of key words to realize that he was accurately informed.

to believe that it was very far; in the first place, Juan told me so, and I had no reason to believe that he was not speaking the truth; on the contrary. The Indian's habit is always to say he is your neighbor; you ask him where he lives, he invariably replies, "here, nearby"; go to see him, you never arrive, so that, from lack of supplies, you have to retrace your path without having found his home; one does not take eight days' supplies with him to go see a neighbor! But here, Juan told me it was far "nè-ouine-otto" (way up there), and this probably was true. On the other hand, I had noticed that an Indian going east, that is, in the direction I supposed their camp to be, stayed ten to fifteen days before passing by again; if, on the contrary, he was going west, that is, toward Oak Flat and the Toualumné, he passed again after three to five days; therefore, supposing the same stopping-time at one end as at the other, the camp to the east was much farther from us than the one to the west. Also, while hunting, I had gone in that direction as far as one could go and return the same day, and I had observed no trace, no indication, of miner or Indian.

I decided to go explore this region, which could very well be a virgin territory. But, fearing for my skin as much as anyone, I did not wish to risk myself alone or even with too few companions. I wrote about it to Thill, by means of a German who happened to be at Coultersville and was returning to Mariposa; I informed him of my intention of going prospecting among the Indians; I invited him to try to recruit ten or fifteen men in Mariposa and, if he succeeded, to let me know; I would then show up at Coultersville to conduct him to Marble Spring with his men, supposing that he did not know the way; from this last place, I undertook to guide them, helped by the Indians, to an auriferous region where no miner had yet appeared.

My letter had its effect, and in a week, Rivet took the first opportunity to send me a letter from Thill, which gave me a rendezvous at Coultersville for the evening of the 20th of April.

On the day indicated, I went to Coultersville; there I found Thill with nineteen miners, as many German as French, well armed, each one having a mule. The next day we all left for Marble Spring with supplies for three weeks.

The last time I had seen Juan, I had told him to return on *domingo otîco* (Sunday two—in two weeks) to lead me with my comrades to the region where he found gold; that if there was enough of it, we would make a road to bring flour there, so that he would no longer need to go so far for it.

When the Indian went to get flour at Coultersville, it was the Indian woman who brought it back to camp, thus walking, as I was later able to determine, nearly eighteen leagues (56 miles) with a load of fifty livres on her head, after having covered the same road unburdened. Juan had counted: "Semana, otîco (week, two), ouatou, tolôcote (sun, three—three days)"; then, turning around without moving his feet, he had said: "nè m̄ (Note: To pronounce m̄, say *un*, with the mouth entirely closed) (I am here)."[5] Which meant that, after this time elapsed, he would

5. Here Perlot's translation of Mariposa words was quite accurate. See "Vocabulary" in Barrett, "Geography and Dialects of the Miwok Indians," pp. 362–67.

be at Marble Spring. In fact, two days after the arrival of our caravan, he arrived with Flesno and three others.

We fêted them in fine style, always taking care to dilute, in ten times its volume of water, the brandy they drank, because the Indian, once drunk, no longer thinks of anything but fighting.

The next morning we were on the march, preceded by three Indians who formed the advance guard, and followed by two others, who, incidentally, kept close to me and carried half of my load. This load was composed of supplies, rolled in a blanket, and a pair of socks and a fresh flannel shirt; the whole wrapped in a sort of hammock or net of heavy twine, which I had fashioned myself and in which I made my bed on certain occasions, for example when the ground was damp or else when there was reason to fear being attacked at night by the Indians. I chose, in that case, a promising tree, then, two or three meters from the ground, I hung my hammock, which was six feet long and three wide. Thus finding myself out of reach of dangerous animals and of Indians, I was able to sleep tranquilly. This hammock, hanging from the four corners by means of four ropes, not very heavy, not very troublesome, was really convenient and was very useful to me in my distant expeditions.

We walked in good order, but slowly; I don't think that, on arriving at the camp site on the evening of the first day, we had made more than four leagues, despite having walked almost all day. The next day, we started off early on our way; after having walked until almost two o'clock in the afternoon, we had to stop; it was absolutely impossible for us to go any farther with the animals. We had reached the top of a precipitous hillside quite dizzy in height, at whose foot ran the Merced, which we did not see, but which we could hear roaring; from the way the noise reached us, we guessed that it came from very far below.

At a turn of the river, well up the stream, we saw it fall in a cascade and throw itself into rapids from which the water burst forth all white with foam. The Indians, when questioned, pointed at the bank and said: "There is the path."

The trail, in fact, seemed to descend into this gulf. I asked Juan: "Isn't there some other way?"—"Yes."—"Where?"—"Toualumné nè-ouine, etc. etc."— "How long does it take?" Juan thought a little, then told me: "Semana, otîco (two weeks)." It was necessary to return to the Toualumné, go up it, then from above reach the Merced, descend it a little, and there you were.

Such was the outline of the directions supplied by Juan, but the details of the itinerary so traced had something that made us stop and think.

When one asks the route of an Indian, he puts one of his hands against his chest and holds the other arm out horizontally; when the trail rises or descends, he raises or lowers his arm; if the path changes direction, he moves the indicating arm to right or left; each time his hand beats his breast, that shows the path forks or crosses a watercourse; if he turns around, it means that the path crosses another.

Now, Juan had raised and lowered his arm perhaps sixty times; twenty-five to thirty times he had beaten his breast, twice he had turned around. It was frightening and at the same time very complex.

Despite all my care in following his motions, I lost my Latin, or if you wish, my Indian. I turned to my comrades and said to them: "Gentlemen, Juan here has just described our itinerary; but considering the time it would take to follow it to the end, and the difficulties it involves, seeing also that I have not understood any great part of the explanations of this aforesaid Juan, I think that we would do well to give up making this long detour." Everyone was of this opinion.

But then, what to do? Must we give up the pursuit of our enterprise, because of the animals, who could not follow us? The Indians passed that way, therefore we could pass too! Night came before we had ended the discussion; we lay down on the spot. Next day, we had to make a decision; of the twenty-one in our party, only eight decided to venture into these mountain defiles, where there was no other trace of living beings than the track of the bear and the print of the bare foot of the Indian. The others were to return to Marble Spring with the animals and wait for us.

We each brought five days' supplies, a revolver, a double shotgun and forty balls. Four had shovels, the other four had picks, pans, and an axe to make a bridge in case of need. We left, this time having two Indians at the head and three at the tail; this first day, we hardly advanced, for the path was something to frighten the Indians themselves. We went up the Merced to a place where the hill is precipitous and rocky; we advanced only by jumping from one rock's point to another. Three or four hundred feet perpendicularly below us was the river, which fell in whirlpools from cascade to cascade; each stone we displaced in walking rolled into the gulf. We had to cover this stretch with a thirty-livre sack on our back and a shotgun in hand, serving as counterweight each time we had to jump. Happily, toward evening, rock gave way to earth and the path began to become practicable. We reached, at nightfall, the first flat of the river. After supper, we drew numbers to determine the order of watches, each of which was to last two hours, a precaution which seemed necessary to assure us that our guides would not abandon us during the night.

During the day and at different times, I had asked Juan to take us to their camp, assuring him that I had an eager desire to see his father, that I would make him a present; but always he had made evasive replies, saying that we would have to make a long detour, that it would lose too much time, that the gold region was not in that direction; at last, that his father forbade him to do it.

As I had actively insisted, we had reason to fear that our Indians, to escape these importunities, might have conceived the project of furtively leaving us, which we would have found very embarrassing; we really had confidence in them, but no more than the Indians deserved. The next day, we were on the march again. We had a comparatively easy path and were going at a good rate, but toward three o'clock in the afternoon, the rain forced us to stop; the fairly thick brush we had to go through was loaded with water and made walking difficult.

We made ourselves a tent of our blankets and, sheltered under it, taking care to keep our powder dry, we waited for fair weather, which did not return until the next morning. After having dried our clothing, our packs, and our blankets beside an enormous fire, we set off again on our way.

Shortly afterward, we reached the confluence of the South Fork with the
Merced.[6] Juan said, showing it to me, "è nè ouine olo" (there, up high, gold). Olo
is the Indian pronunciation of the Spanish word *oro* (gold); in the Indian language
neither gold, nor, for that matter, any other metal, has a name.

We therefore knew already on what river they found gold; there was nothing
more left to do but to climb it to the exact spot where they found it.

But we were ascending the Merced along its right bank and the South Fork
poured in from the left bank, so that we had to cross the Merced. It was impossible
where we were then; perhaps, if necessary, one could have cut down one of those
enormous pines which were found on the flat and have made a bridge of it; but it
was precisely the absence of a bridge which made us suppose that the Indians
crossed the river in some other place. Meanwhile, our guides had seated themselves
and didn't seem in the least disposed to lead us any farther. I asked Juan what way
they went to the mines, where they crossed the Merced? After letting these
questions be repeated, he consulted a moment with the four others, then he made us
a sign to follow them.

After having walked for an hour on the flats, going up the river, we left it to
climb a mountain so high that we had to walk until one o'clock in the afternoon to
reach its summit. On descending it at an angle, in order to return to the Merced, we
came in sight of a valley whose existence we would never have suspected in the
middle of these perpendicular mountains. It extended before us, as far as we could
see, angling off to our left; it was almost two kilometers wide; some hills did not
permit us to see the end of it nearest us. Far away on our left, we thought we saw
smoke; we supposed that it indicated the location of the Indians' camp. Juan said,
showing me the valley: "è tollette auttau" (there, earth, big). Having arrived at the
bottom of the hill, we found ourselves on a very big stream which we descended to
its mouth. In this place, the Merced was crowded between two very steep cliffs.
An enormous pine, probably carried down by the water in the rainy season, had
been placed across the river so that its two extremities rested on the rocks which
formed the two banks—that served as bridge for the Indians. Juan showed it to us
and made us understand that we had to cross over by it, then climb the opposite
cliff, then descend it, after which we would reach the place where he found gold. In
crossing the bridge, we would turn our backs on the valley we had seen from the top
of the mountain and, consequently, according to our guess, on the Indian camp;
that called for consideration. I stuck to my idea of making the acquaintance of the
chief of the Yo-sé-miti tribe, for, if, having succeeded in our search, we should
come to work around here, we were going to be surrounded all year by these
Indians, and it could not be a matter of indifference to us to know exactly where we
could go to find them, and, in case of need, to drive them away. Moreover, night
was about to fall, the weather was becoming overcast; in case of rain, we would be

6. Without knowing it, they were more or less at the site at which James D. Savage had maintained a store
in 1849 (see map following p. 34).

more sheltered in the valley where we were then; it was therefore decided that we would stay where we were.

My companions were not of a mind to go to the Indian camp: "What is the use? They were perhaps more afraid than we; it would be better to leave them alone. Moreover, our supplies were becoming exhausted, and we were not yet at the placer; in this situation, why lose our time in looking at some huts? The bridge to be crossed was a more serious problem than the search for the camp of these savages; above all, the problem was to find out how we were going to cross the Merced on the morrow."

We went to bed, luckily without rain, and also without deciding anything. Next morning, after having breakfasted early, it was resolved that while the seven others considered the means of crossing the river, I would go to the camp. According to Juan, it was a league away; consequently, in two hours we would have returned and, if the seven who remained wished, as several among them suggested, to cut a pine to make another bridge, so short an absence could not retard the crossing.

This agreed upon, I called Juan and said to him: "Let's go to the camp." He did not reply; I made a sign to Flesno; he came, I said to him: "Otcho-nomi-ni-ouaksos" (let's go, on the march, to the camp), and I started to climb the stream which we had descended the day before.

Flesno followed me and, shortly afterward, Juan silently decided to do the same.

Since our departure from Marble Spring, according to my compass, we had made a grand tour, almost a half-circle, to reach the point where we were. Our supplies were becoming exhausted, and, while going to the camp to ascertain how the Indians were disposed, I wanted, at the same time, to inquire if there were not another path by which to go home than that which we had followed, for if, on our return, we could take a straight line, we would thereby gain a day's march, which deserved consideration.

So we climbed again, Juan, Flesno, and I, the path which had brought us to the river the day before. After a half-hour's walking, and quickened walking, for this time I had nothing to carry but my revolver hung from my belt, we turned to the right, leaving the previous day's path on the left; we were far from being at the top, and we seemed to be going around the mountain without either climbing or descending it. After an hour's walking, we were returning, it seemed to me, toward the river; I asked Juan if we would arrive soon: "médio tiempo," he said shortly, in Spanish, *half time*, that is, we were half-way there. — "Why, then, did you say that it was only one league?" — "So that the others wouldn't come." — "But they could have come, since you said it was close?" — "Yes; then, here, I would have said a league again, and they would have returned without going to the camp." — "Why?" — "Because they wouldn't have believed me."

He knew psychology, that Indian.

Shortly afterward, we descended into the valley seen the day before, and soon we were surrounded by Indians who probably had run from the camp. I was, without doubt, the first paleface they had seen, for they examined me like some strange beast; the most agile, placing themselves at my right and left, walked abreast with me, constantly keeping their eyes fixed on my person; those who had not been able to place themselves at my side, preceded me, and went to plant themselves five paces ahead of me, so that they could see me well when I passed before them; I had somewhat the appearance of being their prisoner.

A moment before, Flesno had gone on ahead; so, foreseeing that I would need, not an hour and a half, but four or five hours for going and coming, I took a piece of paper from my game-bag, then wrote some words in pencil to warn my companions that they should not expect me in less than five hours, the camp being farther than we had supposed, and that they should not, at any price, allow the three Indians who had stayed with them to leave before my return. I asked them also to take my extra shirt from my pack and give it to the bearer. Then I told Juan that I had forgotten to bring a shirt I wanted to give his father, and requested him to ask an Indian to take this paper to my friends, who would give him the thing. He immediately found a willing messenger, who left at full speed with the missive. Shortly after, leaving the valley on the right, we climbed a swift stream, and, in a few minutes, we arrived in sight of the camp.

It was situated at the head of a little sloping valley, which led into the big one. It consisted of three villages, whose huts, scattered as if at random, resembled enormous beehives.

On our approach, everyone, especially the children, fled, then returned to escape again, each one in his house. Juan conducted me to his father, who was in front of his hut, seated on the ground as tailors sit on their worktable. I said "good day" to him; without getting up, he saluted me with his two hands, holding them closed, except the thumb and index finger—the gesture of the priest when he turns to the faithful, saying: *Dominus vobiscum*. I held out my hand to him; he looked at it without giving me his, but Juan having said some words to him in Indian, he presented it to me; it seemed to me it trembled a little, but this could have been from age; I told Juan to inform him that that was a sign of friendship with the whites, that one never gave his hand to those he didn't like. He didn't let go of my hand, I had to withdraw it.

This old chief appeared to be about eighty; he doubtless was not, since Juan, who was not the youngest of his children, was only twenty-three.[7] The mother, who arrived shortly after, seemed quite as old, and nevertheless she was accompanied by a little girl who had not reached the nubile age, for she was not yet wearing a waistband, being completely naked. At that moment Flesno arrived, who had disappeared more than an hour before; he was followed by men, probably his relatives, and women and children; these last hid themselves or tried to hide themselves behind him. Flesno brought all these people to let them see me close up; he recounted to them, Juan told me, the story of the Fresno, and in order,

7. Because it is difficult to establish exactly where the Indian village was, it is impossible to identify Chief José with with any certainty.

doubtless, to prove to everybody that he and I were good friends, he happened, during his harangue, to take my hand perhaps more than ten times, so that I was there, at Flesno's disposition, almost like a dog whom one is teaching to give his paw. During this time, the old man began to talk with his son Juan. I couldn't understand what the father was saying, because he mixed with his Indian no word of Spanish, except the word *Olo* which, as I said, had no equivalent in the Indian language. Around me, the Indian men and women took up their occupations, which our arrival had interrupted for a moment; these latter were constructing, with split osiers and with the bark of certain trees, the huts, winnowing-baskets, and all sorts of panniers which served them as vessels. The men were making bows, arrows, and especially instruments for fishing. While I was examining them, I saw come out of a hut two Indians who carried a third from it, and then seated him on a sort of a mat; then they applied their lips like cupping to his chest and back. Juan, who had come back close to me, said: "sick, doctors, working," then, putting on a serious air: "My father," he said, "asks me to tell you that Scipiano is on the Toualumné with the paper which gives the Indians the right to be here and to go and get flour from the whites who occupy the rivers, in exchange for *olo*.

"The acorns are for the Indians and so is the manchineel-tree. On condition that the Indian hide himself (dress), he may go anywhere he wants, leaving where he finds it what belongs to the whites; there is only fishing which is shared. The Indians also have the right to get sugar and cloth for their *olo*, and he who has killed will be killed, etc., etc." Juan continued to report all the terms of the treaty which the government had concluded with the Indians, a treaty which the *old man* knew from memory; what was also in this treaty, and which he did not mention, was that the Indian must never be drunk, nor possess a gun, etc. I told Juan to assure his father that, when the whites concluded a treaty, they always observed the things agreed upon, and the Indians should do the same.

I soon saw that I had acquired, in the eyes of the old chief, an importance which I had not sought to give myself: he evidently took me for an envoy of the government, of which he was afraid since he had seen the dragoons. I wanted to reassure him; I asked Juan to explain to his father that we were the friends of the Indians, and that we wanted to remain so; that it was enough for the Indians to leave us in peace, in order to have nothing to fear from us. On this, I offered my hand to the old man, still seated, who gave me his, and I took leave.

As I was leaving the camp, accompanied by Juan, we encountered the messenger who was returning with my old flannel shirt rolled in a packet and tied with a string; I took the packet, opened it and examined it to assure myself that my comrades had written me nothing. I next told Juan to take it to his father, then to return, which he did. We were accompanied by thirty to forty Indian men and women who walked two hundred paces in front of us; as we approached our encampment, my companions, fearing an attack, put themselves on the defensive, but on seeing me they put down their breastplates.

What we called our "breastplate" was simply our blanket folded double and attached to the neck by a cord; in our combats with the Indians it protected us from arrows shot from a distance. I reported on my mission: in sum, all the observations I had been able to make, when in the Indian camp and on the way, did not teach me much; I had seen no path leading to Marble Spring. As for the population of the camp, I estimated it at two hundred and fifty persons, men, women, and children; Scipiano, his father had told me, was on the Toualumné; they therefore had another camp which they called by this name, for the Toualumné river which we knew was more than twenty-five leagues from there. One could hardly suppose that Scipiano had gone to camp so far from his tribe. Whatever the case might be, we were, according to all appearances, entirely reconciled with the Indians, and that somewhat calmed my companions, who, at Mariposa, had not been accustomed to seeing them so close. Shortly after my arrival, we dined.

Chapter Sixteen

Lost in the Sierras

During my absence, my comrades had scoured the bank of the Merced above and below the encampment, with the intention of choosing a tree and cutting it to make a bridge easier to cross than that used by the Indians; but, after the propositions, oppositions, and contestations customary in similar cases, they had decided nothing, unless that they would wait to have my opinion. They had therefore waited. During dinner, it was decided that we would break camp and try to cross to the other bank by using the Indian bridge. This tree, fallen from one bank to the other, as I mentioned above, was not an easy bridge. The enormous pine—it was at least ten feet in diameter—rested, for a hundred and twenty feet from the bank, that is, for two thirds of its length, on rocks emerging above the water; what went beyond was in the air eight feet from the ground, which was covered, at that time, with standing water two feet deep.

We therefore had to risk ourselves on this pine, then, having reached the end, leap from a height of eight feet and take another eight or ten steps in the water; after which, the crossing was done. Now, the river, in this place, was extremely rapid: beginning at five hundred meters upstream from the bridge, the water leaped rather than ran; it was all white with foam. One would have thought it a flock of sheep descending a mountainside at a gallop, leaping over each other; these sheep, on reaching the bridge, generally passed beneath it, but sometimes they leaped so high that they hit the tree, and rebounded as much as ten feet above it. The bridge therefore was always damp and slippery; it was one more difficulty and danger.

However, the tree was massive, solid; it seemed that by walking barefoot, like the Indian, we would have been able, like him, to cross without too much trouble, but perhaps it would also have been necessary to be able to close our eyes. Whatever it was, the problem placed before us was this: being given a tree thrown across an abyss and eight men accustomed to walking on terra firma, how will they cross this abyss?

My companions, who had had time to meditate during the six hours my absence had lasted, had ended, I think, by deciding that it was insoluble.

On my arrival, nevertheless, the question was raised again. Only three or four consented to cross over—if the others crossed. Only one had already resolved the difficulty on his own account, and that was a Lorrain from the neighborhood of Toul, named Manet, a former military man, a retired gymnast. He had crossed over the bridge and had made sure that the Indians crossed it, by recognizing on the flat, on the other side of the river, the path they had worn. I determined to try in my turn; I passed over the bridge, went to measure the depth of water in the part that had to be waded through, and then I returned. I next induced the Indians to cross; they formed a line, and took each other by the hand so as to form a chain; then men and women, their backs turned to the upstream side of the river, ventured without hesitation onto the tree; by walking sideways like this and, I think, with most of them shutting their eyes, they arrived without hindrance on the other bank. It was our turn to cross. I said to Manet: "Let's not have these Indians laughing at us any longer; the two of us can take the packs; I am going to cross to the other side, and you can bring me one pack after another; then I'll carry them the same way to the flat, so that you won't have to jump down from the tree each time. I like to think that these Gentlemen, having nothing to carry, will decide to cross on all fours or astride." Manet accepted the proposition; a German by the name of Bill, a carpenter by trade, joined him.

In half an hour, all the packs, guns, etc. were transported to the other bank. Then, two others dared to cross by straddling the tree, but that was all.

We could sooner have cut the heads off the other three than persuade them to risk themselves on this narrow, slippery, and shaking bridge. Naturally, we could not leave them there; they wouldn't have dared, being only three, to return to Marble Spring.

It was agreed that we would camp on the bank and that the three others would employ the rest of the day in cutting a suitable pine which was some six hundred meters lower down, and would cross over on that. Five hours later, they crossed, in fact, on their pine, the end of which, being broken, was four feet under water where it touched the bank; but after all they had perferred to go in the water than to risk themselves above it. Manet and Bill, who had gone to help them, returned over the Indians' bridge rather than put themselves in the water up to their armpits.

The Indian men and women did not wait for the morrow; in spite of the advanced hour, they climbed the hill and went to the place where they found gold: Juan and Flesno with four women, of whom two belonged to Juan, one to his brother Scipiano, and the fourth to Flesno. The Indians, in fact, are polygamous, or rather, several Indian women can have the same husband; the family belongs to the mother, and the man can be the father of several families. Juan, as son of the chief of the tribe, had three wives; the third had stayed at the camp to watch the household.

As for us, when evening came, after a meager supper—for supplies were diminishing—we rolled ourselves in our blankets to go to sleep, without taking the ordinary precautions with a view to preventing the flight of the Indians; now that we knew their camp, we had no more reasons to fear their desertion.

Next morning, we got up early; in order to have something else still left for the following day, we contented ourselves with a tortilla and coffee for breakfast; then we began to climb the hill, which was very high and very precipitous. In three hours' time, we were at the summit. Before reaching it, we hoped that, from this height, we could discover either the valley where the Indian camp was, or Pilot Hill, a very high peak which was not far from there, to the northeast of Marble Spring, or else, again, the course of the Merced, or finally, a point already known which could serve to orient us. We were completely disappointed in our expectation; the horizon, though far-reaching, was closed on all sides by mountains or peaks which we did not know. We were on a fairly wide plateau, so that we went almost two kilometers to reach the top of the second hillside, the one we had to descend to reach the river where the Indians were working. This hill was long, but comparatively easy. Around two o'clock in the afternoon, we were on the banks of the river, where we found all the Indian men and women of the day before in the midst of washing the sand in pans. They found enough gold, although washing only the surface; we therefore had a chance of finding a lot by working seriously, when the water would permit. At the moment, it was too abundant; it was not possible to dig a hole on any flat whatever and reach bedrock. It was therefore judged that, to have made our way to the placer, to have identified its situation, and to have ascertained that there was gold there, was, for the time being, all that could be done, and that the best thing, considering the few supplies we had left (just enough for three light meals), was to return to Marble Spring. We proposed going to camp, that very evening, near the bridge we had left that morning, thinking we would be able to arrive shortly after nightfall.

After having just about assured ourselves that we really were on the South Fork, whose confluence with the Merced the Indians had shown us in passing, but twenty or twenty-five leagues higher than the known portion of this last river, we left. We had no guide, as all the Indians had remained at work. Shortly before dusk, we reached the top of the hillside and were heading toward the descent to the bridge, when, great surprise! we saw ten men, probably Americans, who were following our trail, conducted by three Indians. Surely they, too, were going to discover the placer where the Indians found gold. They were at the top of the hill which we were soon going to descend, and it was to be supposed that they intended to spend the night near the Indians.

We had not imagined that we could be followed by human beings in these unknown and almost inaccessible places. We had therefore taken no precaution, we had staked no claim, and these newcomers were perhaps going to seize the best flats! Immediately, we decided that I would retrace my steps, that I would go to claim some good flats we had observed, and would spend the night near the Indians; the next day, instead of climbing and descending the two hillsides, I would go down the river. My comrades, having almost a day's head start, would arrive well before me at the junction of the two rivers, and would make me a bridge while waiting. This agreed on, I retraced my steps and arrived two hours after sunset at the Indian encampment.

I immediately wrote my notices by the light of the fire; I boiled the rest of my flour in a handle-less frying-pan, which served me at the same time as a plate, reserving for the next day the sole tortilla that remained. I ate half of this mush, then passed the plate to my dog Miraud, who cleaned it for me to perfection. The meal ended, I lit a pipe, spread my blanket, and lay down. However, I had no wish to sleep, I was impatient to see the arrival of the ten men in question. After an hour's wait, seeing and hearing nothing come, and the Indians having gone to bed, I was going to sleep when Miraud, tied to my pack which served me for pillow, warned me by low growls that someone was approaching.

Indeed, shortly afterward I saw two Indians who came to rejoin the others. Hearing them speak to Juan, I approached, and learned from him that the two Indians came from Coultersville, and that they had brought ten men who were in search of me. These ten men had not wanted to descend to the river today, because it was too dark, but they would come tomorrow morning. On that I went to bed, counting on getting up early to go and stake the ground before their arrival. It wasn't yet day when my dog, disturbed by the comings and goings of the *oualais*, woke me. Well before the arrival of the Americans, my duty was done. I returned to the Indians, who were preparing to take their morning repast. The Indian women had been cooking, since dawn, some wild clover, a sort of cress, and wild corn salad; they pounded the whole, put it in a big conical basket, added flour and all kinds of seeds pounded together, then poured water into it. They had heated stones, which they knew how to choose, till they were red-hot, without breaking them; they plunged them successively into the pot until they obtained a sort of mush or glue, which they next poured out, to cool, into as many small conical baskets as they wanted to make helpings. This small basketful is the portion for each; when it is empty, they refill it anew, if any is left in the pot, with what is, in the big basket. Having nothing to prepare, not even my breakfast, for I wanted to be economical and keep for the day the two meals I had left, I came to watch the Indians' breakfast, knowing very well that my presence would embarrass them no more than I embarrassed Miraud by watching him eat. But Juan had better manners than I supposed; he asked me if I was hungry and, on my affirmative response, he spoke to one of his wives, who, hesitating and with a visible repugnance, came to place herself beside me. Shortly afterward, she began to cry, and she trembled throughout her body; then Juan spoke to her, but so brusquely and so fast that I could understand nothing of what he said. I asked the reason for these tears: "It is," said Juan, "because I told her to bring you something to eat, and as she has only one *agné* (basket) to eat from, she is afraid of being your wife."—"If that prospect afflicts her so much," I told him, "let her keep her *agné*, I will eat from the pot."

Suiting the action to the word, I flattened a piece of wood, then with this sort of dipper—and not like them, with the index finger and thumb—I began to eat from the basket-pot, which amused the Indian men and women very much, especially the one who thus avoided becoming my fiancée; according to their customs, in fact, if a man eats from the same *agné* as a young girl or even a woman, he can consider her as his fiancée.

The repast lasted no time at all, and really I felt, on leaving the table, that my appetite had scarcely diminished.

This mush was not good, to my taste, but it seemed to be enough to the taste of Miraud, for he gathered, without losing a drop, what I had poured for him on a stone; it is true that, for several days, the poor beast had been reduced to a similar allowance, and it was apparent in his fleshless flanks. For the rest, I had tasted this abominable cooking, not to appease my hunger, but to perform a gracious act to our friends the Indians, to whom I knew this would give pleasure.

Meanwhile, the Americans did not come, although it was already late. Toward seven o'clock, an Indian who had camped with them, came to tell Juan that they were on the river, but two flats farther up. Not knowing if they intended to come soon to the camp, I went to find them. They were in the middle of breakfast, one kilometer away; they too had left without taking many provisions and found themselves short. Nevertheless, they offered me a piece of biscuit and a cup of coffee, which I accepted.

These gentlemen came from Oak Flat and from Coultersville; they had had wind, after our departure from this latter place, of the aim of our expedition, and two days later they had set off in search of us. Having learned at Marble Spring that the paths were impassable for animals, they had immediately started off on the way, their packs on their backs. As, on the other hand, they had not gone to the Indian camp and had found the bridges ready made, they had gained two days on us.

I explained to them where I had staked our claims, where the Indians were working, etc.; then I left them, telling them that I was going to descend the river as far as its confluence with the Merced, where I counted on finding my comrades again. I accelerated my pace in order to reach the meeting-place as quickly as possible.

It was eight days since we had left Marble Spring. We had strolled along the way; the rain had stopped us, we had lost a day to go to the Indian camp, to throw a bridge across the river and pass over it; in short, we had lost a lot of time. I concluded from it that we should not be so far from Marble Spring, and it was conceivable that we could very well return there in three or four days of uninterrupted march. Only, four days is still long, when only enough provisions are left for two more meals. It wasn't that each one had not brought a sufficient quantity of supplies for himself, but he had had to feed the Indians along the way.

Happily, I had my gun, powder, and shot, and, at the worst, one does not die of hunger while eating birds and squirrels. It is true that we saw them rarely since we had come down to the Merced, but after all there was a chance of encountering at least two or three a day, and that was enough.

To go down the river was not an easy thing; there was, after all, almost always a sort of path along the bank, but the water, which was high, often came almost to the foot of the hill, which ended in vertical rock. Then I had to climb the hillside to the top of this rock, then redescend to the river-flat, as soon as there was a flat. Finally, by dint of climbing and descending, and hanging on to rocks when the way was too narrow, I arrived about three o'clock in the afternoon at the confluence of the two rivers. My comrades had already been there for several hours; they had busied themselves with cutting a suitable pine to make me a bridge, but the tree, instead of falling across, had fallen along the river. On my arrival, they were occupied in cutting another; at the end of two hours, that one fell, and fell well across, but it broke, so that, on my side, it plunged entirely into the water. After having struggled bravely, for some moments, against the current, it ended by going down it. This discouraged us entirely. Cutting a third one would have kept us until evening; and again, wouldn't it break? My comrades, after having held council, addressed me, but I could not understand them because of the noise of the river; we could only use sign language. As I knew that they too were short on supplies (they had enough for four meals), I signaled to them to go along, and that I would go up the river to the Indian bridge. Thereupon, they seemed to consult a moment, then prepared to leave. Before that, Colson, of Verviers, with whom I had shared supplies and who knew that I was threatened with famine, showed me a tortilla, then, by main force, tried to throw it to me over the river. Alas! the tortilla fell in the water ten meters from the edge. Colson, then, took another and showed me where he hid it, in order that I might find it the next day when I passed; two others put some biscuits in the same place, then all went away. I then started to go up this river as I had gone down the other. Night surprised me some hours later; I found myself on a big flat watered by several springs; I noticed there a lot of the cress and clover which the Indians ate; I gathered a supply of it before it was entirely dark, then I lighted a good fire and cooked these grasses in my frying pan, like spinach. There was very little butter in my spinach, but, on the other hand, I had put in a passable amount of pepper and a little too much salt; nevertheless, it made me a supper which I found delicious. Miraud, who for two days had not been running— he contented himself with following me step by step—Miraud refused outright to touch my spinach; I had to give him a biscuit and a piece of beef cooked eight days before.

The repast ended, I hung my hammock from an enormous and very branchy tree, which rather resembled a beech tree but which wasn't one. I placed it as high as possible, no longer from distrust of the Indians, but in order that, knowing myself out of the reach of wild animals, I could sleep peacefully. I really needed it: I had got up at two o'clock in the morning, I had walked all day, almost always without a path, in a precipitous and rocky country, and it was ten o'clock at night; one can believe without trouble that I was exhausted from fatigue and quite ready to sleep.

However, next day I was on my way at the first crack of dawn. I had the luck to pull down a sort of woodpecker and a gray squirrel before reaching the Indian bridge; having crossed it without difficulty, I lighted a fire and cooked the results of my hunt.

I hoped to see, from one moment to another, the ten Americans descending the hill, supposing that they had, the day before, occupied their time in exploring the river where the Indians were working.

But after having breakfasted well, my dog and I, not seeing anyone appear, I thought that the best thing was not to lose any time, and I started on my way. I went up the stream which we had descended four days before, then I climbed obliquely up that immense hill from the top of which we had discovered the long valley. It was two o'clock in the afternoon when I reached the point where the path comes closest to the summit.

I went as far as the summit, and, examining all the neighboring country from the top of this observatory, I could determine the direction we had followed to come from Marble Spring. I observed that we had described a very pronounced arc of a circle—if I went again by the same route, I should, according to the readings of my compass, walk until evening to the south-southeast, the next day the whole stage almost to the south, the following day to the south and to the southwest, and finally for a day, at least, to the northwest.

I did not succeed in understanding the reason for this long circuit. It was not, to be sure, in order to have an easier route since that one was detestable; nor could it be, it seemed to me, in order to have water, since we found that almost everywhere. No, the real reason was that the Indians had no notion of geometry and did not know that universal indicator which bears the name of compass. So I reasoned, and from regard for geometry as much as to shorten my route by almost a day's march, I left the road and headed almost to the southwest, the direction in which, according to my compass, Marble Spring should be found.

It was scarcely two hours since I had left the path when, contrary to my expectation, as I was not very far from a large watercourse (the Merced), I found myself constrained to descend to another river, which ran on my right and whose right bank I would probably, for the time being, have to climb. It was, of course, less powerful than the Merced, but bigger than any of the streams which we had had to cross in coming, which made me suppose that it was the Merced itself or at least one of its principal branches, whose confluence with the other branch occurred above the Indian camp. On this supposition, Merced or branch of it, it should form a sort of peninsula, in the middle of which was the Indian camp, and whose isthmus I was crossing. Whatever it might be, I continued to walk, following the crest of the heights and shortly afterward I encountered a path beaten by the Indians, which went in the same direction I was following; this path led me to a point where a big stream emptied itself into this river. As it was getting late, I stopped there to spend the night, the more so as the weather was overcast and as on arriving at the stream I found three Indian huts on the flat of its junction with the river.

These huts seemed abandoned for a long time. Nevertheless, from fear of surprise, I didn't settle there until very late and then without tying Miraud, who would not have missed warning me if any being, man or beast, had approached.

I had spent the day with my gun on my arm, thinking to have the luck to bring down some sort of game; but nothing, absolutely nothing had appeared, except an eagle, of the kind whose head is bare of feathers. He had come to circle above me, takine me, doubtless, the rogue, for some prey which his lucky star sent him; I wished to remove this idea from his head and by a providential chance, I think, I had broken a wing with a charge of buckshot. Afterward, cutting off his neck, feet,

and wings, I had attached the remainder to my pack in the hope of making a good
supper.

However, in sight of the Indian huts, I did not dare make a fire at night, for fear
of attracting the attention of the Indians, if there were any in the vicinity; for, if the
Yo-sé-miti were our friends, it must be noted that not all Indians were Yo-sé-miti. I
contented myself with eating a biscuit and finishing with Miraud what meat I had
left. After which, I lay down.

Toward midnight, rain began to fall. I had to move and settle myself in one of the
huts, choosing the least permeable to rain. I placed my dog near the hole which
served as a door and I slept a profound sleep until the next morning; I had gone to
bed fairly tired. On waking up at dawn, I heard that it was still raining and went
back to sleep, so that it was full daylight when I got up to light my fire. While the
coals were forming, I determined to pluck the beast that was to serve as my
breakfast; impossible! I had to skin it, that is, take off the skin with the feathers. It
was far from being fat, I think too that it was no longer in its first youth; the flesh
was red and hard and, to tell the truth, unsavory; but whether it was savory or not,
I had to breakfast.

Once my bed of coals was formed, I spread it out and I roasted the two legs; I
turned and turned them over the brasier, according to the rules of the art, then,
after the proper time, I withdrew them and I bit into them. Then I perceived that
nothing was cooked; what was not burned was warm and nothing more. However,
I bit and bit again with all my strength, I extracted all I could draw from them, then
I passed them to Miraud, who sniffed them a moment with a disdainful air, then
turned away his head; one would have said that, witness of the efforts I had had to
make to get down this meat, he had simply wanted to assure himself that it was not a
sham and that, having perceived it was serious, he gave up attempting the enterprise on his own account. However, really determined to breakfast, I cut the two
fleshy parts of the breast, I began the roasting again, and arrived at almost the same
result as with the legs; but this part of the beast having no bone, I cut it in little
pieces on my pan and by dint of chewing, mixing them with a little biscuit, I
succeeded in eating them, as probably one would succeed, with a little resolution, in
eating rubber. As for Miraud, I had to give him some biscuit rather than see him
leave with an empty stomach.

As the day before I had made my journey without seeing any kind of game, the
same thing could happen again to me and, in fear of having absolutely nothing for
dinner, I cut the flesh as well as I could from the skeleton of my eagle and put the
meat in my pack, then broke camp. The rain had ceased bit by bit and it seemed the
day should be fair enough; the brush, agitated by the wind, was shaking off the
water with which it was loaded, so that I had lost nothing by waiting. To cross the
stream, I had to take off my trousers; I had water up to my chest for a distance of
several meters, moreover I had Miraud on my shoulders; I saw that he was too tired
and too weak to let him swim in this cold and swift water; I don't know even if he
could have crossed it, so exhausted did he seem. After crossing the stream, the path

went for some time up the river, which I had on my right, then it started up the hillside; as it did not absolutely depart from my route, I continued to follow it. The hill was not difficult to climb, inasmuch as I was climbing obliquely and as it was covered only with occasional bushes; even the grass was scattered and, though damp, it hardly wet my feet. I had the luck to encounter three birds, a kind of thrush, and to kill one. A fact which seemed strange to me, was that in shooting my gun, I had almost not heard the detonation; it had not hung fire, however, since a thrush had fallen. For fear that the other lead might be as damp, for I attributed this effect to the humidity, I discharged it in the air; the same phenomenon was produced: I heard no echo.

Well then, I dried my gun as best I could and then reloaded it with care. The hill was long to climb; I did not reach the plain until about ten o'clock in the morning. There, I had to abandon the path, which went too much to the right and which, moreover, was hardly visible for the reason that scarcely anyone passed that way; besides, there was almost no brush, and what I was treading underfoot was rather stones than dirt. I was astonished even to see that trees—scattered, it is true— could grow in so thin a soil. The summit on which I found myself was far from being as high as the neighboring summits, so that the horizon around me was rather restricted; I could not, consequently, judge whether I was far from the Merced or realize, even approximately, where I was. However, it was not the forest which prevented me from seeing; there were hardly any trees and no bushes at all. I walked, so to speak, on the bare rock, a rock of black granite which must have been covered with snow during the winter, for when by chance I encountered a tuft of grass, it was bruised otherwise than it would have been by the wind; then too, when there was a little hollow in the ground, I saw water which was absolutely too clear to come only from the rain of the night before.

The path having ended, I had recourse to my compass: I took my direction, and it bore exactly on a rather high peak which I had on the horizon and fairly far off. It seemed to me that I could not be better placed than on this peak to observe the country. Not seeing any obstacle to arriving there, neither bush nor stream, I walked in a straight line at least until one o'clock in the afternoon. I then found myself unexpectedly on the edge of a very swift stream very deeply embanked. It ran in a sort of enormous crevasse which seemed to me to be almost a thousand feet deep; the rock, on the two sides, made walls, so to speak, so that it took me some time to seek out a place where I could descend and to assure myself that I could climb up the other side again. I succeeded without too much trouble and without accident. I have always thought that this stream was the same I had crossed in the morning near its confluence with the river.

This stream crossed, and to avoid too rocky a terrain, I had to bear a little to the right and to head toward a group of trees which I saw some kilometers ahead of me. The country was still rising but with an easy slope; I did not reach the trees until nearly three o'clock in the afternoon. The horizon then opening around me offered me a spectacle which struck me with astonishment and fright. These trees formed a little wood which was in a sort of very open funnel, about five hundred meters in diameter, whose base was occupied by a lake. Around this funnel, as far as the eye could reach, one could see not a bush, not a tree; nothing appeared but the bare rock.

While climbing, I thought that the forest, which had almost disappeared since morning, was going to begin again, but it was quite to the contrary; I had reached what one could call the last bush. What would become of me! useless to hope to encounter game of any kind on this desolate terrain where life was absent. I understood then that if the Indians made so long a detour to reach the Merced, ignorance of geometry had nothing to do with it; for a moment, I thought I was lost and I despaired.

Retracing my steps meant too much ground to cover, and it would lead me away from my goal. I had no more supplies, it was three o'clock, and night was going to fall before I was on the other side of this arid plain, abhorred, it seemed, by all living beings. But on the other side! where was that? what was there? These peaks which festooned the horizon were too far away for one to judge by the naked eye whether or not they were covered with timber; perhaps it was the same kind of country as this I was in, and then, after tomorrow, I would succumb to fatigue and to hunger. However, the Merced, whose banks were wooded, could not be very far on my left, a day's walk perhaps, although the horizon, on that side, looked the same as that before me. Reasoning by analogy, I said to myself that if the forest was on my left, it ought also to be in front of me, for I should be approaching Marble Spring and, surely, well before getting there, I would find game again. It remained to be seen if may compass was out of order and if I really was walking to the southwest; I set the instrument on the ground, I took all possible precautions, I removed my gun, my revolver, in short all the metal I had about me, and I found that the direction I was following should be the right one. These indications agreed exactly enough with those furnished me by the course of the sun. That gave me back my courage; I comforted my body with the thrush and a bit of the eagle; I abandoned to Miraud all but one of the remaining biscuits, and without losing time, I continued on my way across this terrain, which, as I said, was pure granite, without an atom of mold. In spite of some undulations, it looked enough like a plain, where enormous boulders, more or less round in form, were scattered as if by chance. At a distance, these blocks, of which several had a diameter of not less than five or six meters, resembled houses and, what seemed strange to me, they were not of the same granite as the bedrock; that was of a blacker granite. How did they get there? where did they come from? that is what I could not guess; when later I asked the savants, I learned that these gentlemen knew no more than the common people on this subject, they were content to consider these blocks as *vagabonds;* that is the exact translation, I think, of the word *erratic*, which explains nothing.

The sun went down without my having been able to judge if the horizon was wooded or not; I profited by the occasion to verify the indications of my compass and I had the pleasure of determining that they were exact: I was correct in the direction. The setting sun indicated west-north-west; it was the fourth or sixth of May; therefore, my compass informed me well, I was walking straight west-south-west by south. Once persuaded that I was on the right route, I found my strength return with hope, I scarcely felt any more fatigue, I continued to walk as long as the twilight permitted me to perceive the peak behind which the sun had set and which I left a little to the right. As the wind was making itself felt, I gained the shelter of one of these erratic blocks scattered over the plateau, and rolled myself in my blanket after having lit a pipe; supper must not be thought of.

It was nine o'clock in the evening. Since three o'clock in the afternoon, when I had set foot on this granite plain, I had seen not a tree, not a shrub, not a blade of grass; on the earth, in the air, not the smallest animal, not even flies, which are said to exist everywhere. Animal and vegetable life was completely absent from this cursed spot; everywhere, a more or less disintegrated rock, without the least appearance of soil. One would have said that I had before my eyes a sample of the earth's surface as it must have been before life had appeared on it.

I was cold and I could not make a fire; I was forced, as some sort of substitute for it, to light a second pipe while waiting for sleep to come. While I was following with my eyes, by the uncertain light of the stars, the smoke which rose slowly in the air, it seemed to me I heard the detonation of a gunshot. From what side did it come? I did not know, but it was very far off. However Miraud, to whom I had just given my last biscuit and who was lying at my feet, Miraud slept peacefully; it was enough to make me doubt that I had heard anything; in spite of that, I began to listen attentively, holding my breath in order to hear better, and I heard it again. It was one of those indistinct noises which could just as well be a cannon shot at a very great distance, as a gunshot; sometimes they were produced shot after shot, sometimes they succeeded one another at long intervals. Sometimes too, I seemed to see the fugitive glow of lightning cutting the horizon, sometimes to hear the whistle of will-o'-the wisps moving through the air; a little longer and I would have heard the stars marching over my head. I heard, as someone said—I no longer know who—"I heard the silence."

All of that really existed only in my imagination; the true cause of these noises, of these visions, was that for fourteen days I had walked from fourteen to fifteen hours a day and that for two days I had walked almost without eating; my stomach being empty, my head was too.

Finally, I slept, so profound a sleep that I was awakened the next day only by the morning freshness. The sun was not up, but already dawn was fading the east to a milky white. I was cold; I got up immediately, rolled my blanket, and left.

Miraud looked at me, astonished by this sudden departure, not preceded, as usual, by the morning meal. Alas! the pack was empty, and our breakfast awaited us in the next forest—all it took was to get there. Miraud seemed to understand the situation, for he began to follow me without asking for anything more.

The movement had sufficed to warm me again, and I was walking as briskly as a tired and hungry man can. Soon, the rising sun showed me the peak toward which I was directing my march. It was always the same terrain; it descended doubtless in an imperceptible slope, for at the end of some hours of walking, the peak which I had in sight disappeared below the horizon. I had to replace it with the top of the mountain behind which I had seen it disappear, in order to keep on in the same direction.

Toward ten o'clock in the morning, I found myself on a hill at the bottom of which ran a fairly swift stream; I then perceived that it was the hill on the other side which prevented me from seeing the peak. Although this stream was rather steeply banked, I crossed it easily; I then made use of the bed of a torrent or ravine which came down to it from the hill I had to climb; I climbed it to the top of a mountain of sorts where it had its source. Toward noon, I was at the summit; I could, from there, reconnoiter the surrounding country. O happiness! in front of me, to the west, the horizon was cut off by a forest, and it was nearer than I had supposed. I was saved! I had only to descend to reach the first trees, which I did by taking advantage of a ridge* which, I saw, went on a long way and would spare me from crossing many creeks which would have forced me to descend and to climb. At three o'clock in the afternoon, I reached the first trees, and soon I came to the junction of the stream on the right with that of the left, where my *ridge* ended. I crossed the creek on the right by taking off my shoes and rolling my trousers over my knees; then I climbed the hill on the other side, which wasn't too high. It was only then that I found myself in the real forest. While walking, I kept my gun ready for the first opportunity that might present itself; I had hardly gone a kilometer when Miraud encountered a squirrel which quickly took refuge in a pine; I fired, the animal fell. I lost no time, one can well believe; I lit a big fire at the foot of that very tree and cooked the squirrel on the coals. I ate a good half of it and gave the other to Miraud, who had already devoured the skin and feet.

This operation completed, I felt better, my step was firmer and my gait more assured; the pipe I smoked as a form of dessert seemed delicious to me.

A little farther on, I again had the luck to shoot a sort of jay; as I did not want to stop any more until near evening, I put it in my bag and continued walking. Soon afterward, I encountered a poorly marked Indian path; I followed it nevertheless because it did not wander too far from the right direction. It brought me, about six or seven o'clock, onto a big grassy flat, where I recognized the marks of a former Indian encampment. There, paths crossed each other in all directions, to take any one I had only too many to choose from; I took the one which led to the south-south-west, hoping thus to encounter more quickly the path by which we had come to the Merced. Scarcely had I left this prairie when Miraud started a hare; I fired and missed. What a pity! I would have pulled out my hair from vexation if I had had the time. He had started it a few steps from the path, behind me, and he pursued it a

---

*I call a ridge the succession of crests formed by the hills which separate two streams having about the same direction.

moment before he returned to me; he was at the end of his strength, he could hardly walk.

I was climbing a gentle slope which I thought was going to last a long time, when the path, turning away, led me onto a fairly high and steep hillside. It was covered with very big pines, my foot slid on the thick bed of needles in a way that made walking, tired as I was, very troublesome. It took me more than an hour to go three kilometers; arrived at the top, I could not reconnoiter the terrain ahead of me, because the pines were too close together. The path led me to the descent of a ridge which ended, the creek on the right angling off from that on the left, in a flat covered with thorny bushes, where I arrived toward evening. Ordinarily, in these thorny bushes which abounded around Marble Spring, I found plenty of hares and plenty of rabbits; as night was approaching and as my jay could not suffice for my supper and that of my dog, I thought that it was more urgent to look for a bit of game of some kind than to look for my path. Without doubt Providence intervened, for no sooner had I arrived near these bushes than I made a double shot on two rabbits; one was torn by the buckshot, but the other was properly killed. At the gunshots, Miraud darted forward—he was going to devour the rabbits for sure! no, he brought them to my feet. I embraced him effusively; this deed had touched me. The poor animal had hardly eaten for three days, he was falling from fatigue, he was dying of hunger, and the first nourishment which was presented to him in almost three days, he tried to find some strength to fetch it and place it at my feet; wasn't that sublime? How many men would have been capable of this act of honesty, of fidelity, and of abnegation? He had gone to get them one after the other, had put them beside me, then he sat down on his haunches, looking at me. By his ears, which he drooped and raised alternately, he seemed to be saying to me: "Well, there they are . . . after you, if there's any left." That was not the way I understood it; I thought that he deserved being served first: I took a rabbit by the two hind feet, tore it in two and gave it to him. To be sure, he did not have to be begged; while I was putting in my bag the one that was left, he had already eaten his.

I reloaded my gun, then regained the path in the hope of finding a creek on the edge of which I could light a fire and settle down for the night; for the sun had set and darkness would soon gather under the tall pines, which I doubtless still had to go through.

Two kilometers from there, in a place where the path forked, I did indeed find a spring and I halted. Needless to say, the supper, although very simple, was found good.

Miraud helping, everything went, jay and rabbit; as for what was left of the eagle—for some still remained which I had not been able to cook the night before for lack of wood—I threw it away with disdain; only to look at that reddish and repugnant flesh nauseated me.

It was because, for more than five hours, I had been walking on earth and no longer on the bare rock; that was enough for me to become particular again and to disdain that which, twenty-four hours before, had seemed acceptable and good to me.

I was less cold that night than the previous night, and I would have slept much better if the *coyotes* (jackals) had not come, on two occasions, to trouble my sleep with their discordant cries.

It was scarcely daylight when I was in search of my breakfast. I had ordered Miraud to stay on my blanket and I had gone off alone. I had not prowled for forty minutes around my headquarters before I had a hare. It happened that it was a big one, consequently an old one, and was therefore a little tough, but, as I was too pressed to choose, I had shot the firstcomer.

Half of the hind-quarters sufficed for my breakfast, and I put the other half in my bag; as for the fore-part, it fell to Miraud's share. I left. I had hardly covered six kilometers when I came to the path from Marble Spring to the Merced; there, I knew my way.

The sight of this trail made my heart beat; I had been almost sure of finding it, but nothing is as good as reality in such a case; therefore, my legs, which were beginning to have trouble carrying me, took on a new vigor. But I had no longer to push myself, I had barely twelve miles to go (four leagues), and the day was little advanced; I was therefore sure of reaching Marble Spring at least by evening.

I had gone hardly seven kilometers, when I perceived a man in the distance, coming to meet me; he saw me in his turn, stopped, looked at me attentively, then fired two shots into the air. I was wondering what that could mean, when I saw him continue his march and advance or rather run toward me.

At two hundred paces, I recognized Thill. Well before joining me, he drew from his pack a piece of bread, which he held in his hand. "Where do you think you're going?" I asked him. — "Take it," he replied, "and eat. We were leaving to look for you." — "What! to look for me! where are the others?" — "At Marble Spring." — "Why did you shoot?" — "To inform Van Ghen, who took the other path." Then he brought me up to date on the situation.

This is what had happened, beginning with the moment when my companions had left me at the confluence of the two rivers. Having no more than half the supplies they would have needed, they had to regain Marble Spring by a forced march; they started off at three o'clock in the morning and did not stop until nine or ten o'clock at night. That way they were able to reach Marble Spring at midnight on the third day; the third day was Monday, and it was Wednesday, at eight o'clock in the morning, that Thill met me. The Americans, who had not stopped at all on the river near the Indians, had had to march in the same way. While I was going down the river, they had returned to the Indians' bridge and so had gained almost thirty hours over me: they had reached Marble Spring on Tuesday, toward noon. My comrades had gone to see them to get news of me; they were content to tell them that they had not seen me since I had left them near the Indian encampment, and that they did not know what had become of me. This strangely surprised my comrades; they could not understand that the Americans had not encountered me along the way, neither me nor my dog. Someone expressed the idea that, perhaps, I was lost. Thomas, my partner, who had seen me at work, swore not, that I would not get lost, that he was sure of it; if I had had no accident, if the Indians had not killed me, if, while walking at night along the difficult path which bordered the cascades of the Merced, I had not fallen into the water, he wagered his head that I would return. "But," suggested another, "mightn't he have had a quarrel while staking a claim? Couldn't it be that the Americans have killed him in order to seize the flats he had claimed?" They looked at each other; nobody replied. From that moment on, there had been, at Marble Spring, two camps all ready to become enemies, two parties which looked at each other with mistrust. When the Americans, who until then had attached but little importance to the incident, had understood the suspicion of the Frenchmen, they began to reflect; then nobody laughed any more.

Night came, and no one saw me appear. It was then that two men, one from each camp, offered to leave in search of me the next morning, if I had not returned during the night. These two men were Thill and Van Ghen (a Hollander).

In the morning, as they had promised, they started on their way. As there were two trails from Marble Spring to the Merced, each had taken one in order to be sure of meeting me. The one who found me was to notify the other by firing two shots, one after the other. That is what Thill had done. Twenty minutes later, we saw, in fact, Van Ghen running at full speed through the brush.

The most general idea was that I had committed the imprudence of following by night the path which bordered the Merced. Now, this path, for a distance of two leagues, was barely practicable during the day; my foot had slipped in climbing one or another of the hundred precipices which had to be crossed and, infallibly, I must have rolled all the way down to the river; if I had not been killed in my fall, I was, at the very least, drowned. All that Thill and Van Ghen proposed to do, was to go that day to the presumed theater of the catastrophe, where they hoped to arrive for the night; then, the next day, to try to discover some sure signs, beginning with my dog, who should not have slipped as easily as I into the abyss.

In my turn, I explained my tardy arrival, and how I had been neither killed nor assassinated, nor torn to bits by falling on the rocks, nor drowned in the Merced, but had run the risk of dying an even more lamentable death.

Then, one having relieved me of my gun, the other of my pack and my blanket, we all three gaily took the trail to Marble Spring, where we arrived about two o'clock in the afternoon. Twenty minutes later, I was at table, savoring a splendid dinner.

Miraud, stretched at full length under the table, seemed more interested in sleeping than in banqueting; he hardly got up to take the bones I threw him from time to time.

My arrival had naturally reconciled everybody. The Americans had come to

Marble Spring in the number of fifteen, although only ten had taken part in the expedition to the Merced. Among them was Mr. De Lamare, the same to whom we had owed finding work on arriving at Mariposa.[1]

He had not recognized me, but I, I was not unwilling to recognize him; I have never been able to forget those who have done me a favor or wished me well, and we renewed our acquaintance.

1. J. G. De Lamare, Perlot's friend of 1851, is mentioned in Quartz Claims, book A, p. 198, Mariposa County Records (Bretnor Notes), as being from Coulterville, and renewing a claim first discovered by Franklin Runyon in 1851, on September 14, 1855.

Chapter Seventeen

Invading the Indian Placers

When I had finished dinner, we all held council together on what was to be done about this new placer on the Merced. First, everyone was of the opinion that there should be enough gold there to be able to work it profitably, though not until later when the season was more advanced; for the moment, there was absolutely too much water.

This first point resolved, we still had to study the question of communications, for it would be necessary to bring in provisions and, in order to do that, to have a practicable road for pack animals. Now, those who had made the trip were unanimous in admitting that it was utterly impossible to have such a road in going back up the Merced, as we had done.

The best thing that we could do, was to explore the left bank of the river where the Indians were working, in order to reconnoiter the most propitious route for descending the hills which bordered the river at that place; for once having descended to any flat whatsoever, it was no more than play to pass to another, especially in summer, when the water would have gone down. Now, I remembered that at the time Thomas and I were working on the Tchaoutchili [Chowchilla], being in pursuit of the Indians, we had followed them to the crossing of a swift river which flowed toward the west. Considering the situation of the Tchaoutchili in relation to Marble Spring, it seemed to me that the river in question could very well be the branch of the Merced where the Indians were working, and which we would have reached two or three leagues higher than the place where we happened to see them at work.

On this hypothesis, I proposed a return to Mariposa, then, gaining the Tchaoutchili from there, to go up it until from the top of some mountain we recognized the confluence of the two branches of the Merced. To attain the goal of our trip from there, we would only have to go up the left bank, as I had descended the right bank after having left the Indians. Out of the thirty-seven of us, only three, a Frenchman named Serf, Thomas, and I, knew the Tchaoutchili. Hardly had I finished speaking when Serf got up and declared that I was right, and better than that, that he would now undertake then and there to guide us directly to the place where the Indians were; he knew the way, and, already, he had gone as far as the top of the ridge at the foot of which flows the Merced. After that, everybody was of the opinion that nothing remained but to disband the meeting; we had the solution we were seeking. Before separating, we agreed to meet again in Mariposa in six days; from there, we would all leave together for the upper Tchaoutchili and the Merced, with animals loaded with supplies for a month. Once on the banks of this river, we would study the terrain and, without the slightest doubt, before long we would be on the way to making a fortune.

Each one promised to maintain the most absolute secrecy; otherwise, on our arrival we could have found invaded those placers whose discovery had cost us so much trouble. We had set the rendezvous six days from then at Mariposa, in order to leave everyone time to rest, for the trip took only two and a half days' walking, going by way of Coultersville.

We had held council in the open air, sitting or lying on the grass. Was it the effect of fatigue or of too generous a dinner? in any case, my head was heavy and I would have fallen asleep on my feet if I had not made the wise decision to go to bed.

It was about five o'clock in the afternoon and I did not awaken until the next day at eight o'clock in the morning; everybody was busy with breakfast or in making his preparations for the departure for Coultersville. An hour later, of all the band no-one remained on the spot but Thomas and I.

Once left to ourselves, we began to make a sort of inventory by setting apart the objects we had to take with us, and those we had to leave; we had a fair amount of supplies left, such as coffee, sugar, beans, peas, rice, etc., besides a number of tools. We packed up as well as possible the objects we were not taking with us, and entrusted them to the caretaker of the quartz mill, who willingly agreed to guard them for us till autumn or the next winter. Moreover, we staked our claim and the dirt we had readied, putting up the necessary notices so people would know it had not been abandoned; we did the same for the cabin, which had become ours from having been in our possession more than a year. On the door I nailed the notice: *Not abandoned.* By the next day all preparations for departure were made, and the following day, early in the morning, we broke camp, our intention being to reach Mariposa by short stages. In fact, the next day we lodged at Coultersville after having done our eighteen miles. As we had left almost everything at Marble Spring, our Jack was lightly loaded; he had only our blankets to carry. Leaving Coultersville fairly late the next day, we put up for the night at Bear Valley, two kilometers from the cabin where we had spent, Thill and I, the famous winter of 1853. Next day we arrived at Mariposa at one o'clock in the afternoon, after having gone fifteen miles. We stayed with Chanac, who still had his partners, and who still baked bread and sold meat at the same time; he was a little better settled than at that time, in the sense that his house, instead of being entirely of canvas, was now half built of wood; by degrees as the canvas disintegrated, he replaced it with boards.

The day after our arrival, toward evening, most of our partners rejoined us there. We said nothing in the presence of strangers, in order not to betray the secret; so that we could make arrangements and consult with each other, we gathered together in a big tent set up across the way, which served as a café and bore the pompous name of "Eldorado." We decided to leave the next day, at five o'clock in the morning. Each one, as had been agreed, brought supplies for a month; those who did not have animals joined those whose donkey or mule could carry an increase in its load.

Next day, the departure was made without noise. Each group, as soon as its preparations were finished, left separately on the ordinary road to Tchaoutchili; then, halfway, in the depths of the forest, turned to the left and proceeded in such a way as to arrive about mid-day at that river, nearly a league higher up than the last worker, therefore at a place where we were almost sure of meeting no miner.

Toward noon, in fact, all eighteen of us reassembled around a spring, near a big meadow, where our animals grazed while we dined. Shortly afterward, we left together, going up the north fork of the Tchaoutchili. We followed a path that Serf and I knew, from having followed it two years before while pursuing the Indians; it brought us, toward nightfall, to a big flat which seemed to us to be the highest point of the mountains which separated Mariposa from the basin of the Merced. There was thick and succulent grass for the animals and some very good water for us. This plateau, of fifty to sixty hectares, was a meadow surrounded by a forest of enormous pines, all struck, topped, and slashed by lightning. I have never seen anywhere else more beautiful grouse (*coqs de bruyère*), nor in such quantity; nor ever as many bear tracks: one would have sworn that they had been holding a ball there, if one did not know that these heavy plantigrades practiced the dance only in a state of domesticity. Those of us who were walking at the head of the caravan saw three of them when we arrived, whom our presence annoyed, no doubt, for, very quietly, they ceded us the place. The grouse, themselves, did not have this discretion; in the morning we were positively deafened by the grave and gutteral song of these birds.

Having broken camp, we continued to follow the path, but, soon afterward, it became difficult; it went down a fairly steep slope over a rocky terrain, although the base was of schist. After having crossed a swift stream, it led us along the crest of a ridge, where it forked at almost a right angle, or better, met another perpendicularly. Neither of the two paths could suit us: that on the right climbed, it was the one we had taken when pursuing the Indians; the other, which descended, would deviate too far to the west. As it seemed to us that we should not be very far from the top of the hill whose foot was bathed by the Merced, and as the terrain offered no difficulties, we went straight between the two paths; soon afterward we came down to the source of a creek which, in everyone's opinion, must flow into the Merced.

Finding there, in abundance, both water and grass, we made a halt to eat, contenting ourselves with unloading our animals without taking off their pack-saddles. After that, having gone on our way again, it was not long before we encountered an Indian path which came from our right and which we followed until evening, that is, until sunset; then this path got involved in a rocky and tortuous terrain, with so steep a slope that it was impossible for us to descend it with our animals loaded, and we had to climb back up as far as the flat where it began. As there was grass and water, we camped there. We decided that evening that, before entering this enormous chasm which opened before us, whose bottom could not be the Merced because the opposite hill was too near, four of us, provided with supplies for the day, would descend into it, would follow the path far enough to reconnoiter where it led, then would return to inform the company. It was better, assuredly, to lose a day where we were than to proceed on this path with our animals without being sure that they could follow us there. What we could already foresee, was that the opposite hill was impracticable for them. The next morning, therefore, four left, following the path as had been agreed. At the same time, Serf went to the right, that is, to the southeast; he headed, accompanied by another, toward a peak which we had in sight, in order to see whether from there he could locate the valley of the Merced, where he said he had already been once. On my part, I was to head to the left, that is, to the northwest, getting out, if possible, from among those big pines which prevented us from finding out where we were, and I was to try also to discover the Merced or else to reconnoiter a peak which I had been able to single out during the expedition at the beginning of the month. I left therefore; retracing our steps for several kilometers, I found myself at the top of the hill; I then angled to my right and followed its crest as long as it lasted. After having descended the bank of a little creek and then climbed up the opposite side, I found myself on the crest of another ridge which I followed, still in the direction of west to northwest, so that I arrived, about one o'clock in the afternoon, on a peak a little more elevated than those around it.

No visible path led to it and, an astonishing thing, I found there a piece of a French newspaper and an empty sardine tin. I was mortified; I had flattered myself that, the first of all mortals, I had climbed it: this tin can and this fragment of newspaper proved the contrary to me.

Be that as it may, from the top of this observatory I thought I could recognize the course of the Merced, but still fairly far to the north. Then, taking a sheet of paper and a pencil, I sketched a map where I indicated the location of Coultersville, of Bear Valley, of Marble Spring, and of Mariposa, and the path which we had taken with the Indians and that which we had just followed on leaving Mariposa, the whole on a scale of two inches for a day's march; I found that the two extremities of this curved line would be joined in about two inches. If my sketch was exact, we were a day's march too far to the east; in order to reach the Merced, we would have to march yet another whole day, heading to the north.

I retraced the path to the camp, where I arrived in the evening. Serf and his companion had already returned; they had discovered nothing and recognized nothing. I then told them about the find I had made on the peak. Serf cried out: "That's it, that's the peak where I stopped; I was with Pinoto, my partner, a Provençal, a former ship's mate like me, and who has since died. I remember now that we had dinner there and that we ate sardines. That's it, that takes care of it: the Merced is ahead of us, we'll have to go that way tomorrow."

While we were having supper, the four who had gone down the hill returned from their expedition. They had followed their path, which had taken them to a place where two fairly big streams came together; they had gone down the combination of these two watercourses until they were in sight of a river which could only be the Merced. We could go that way.

The hill to be descended was frightful and long, but once on the stream there were no more difficulties; there even was, not far from the river, a fine flat where we could camp with the animals.

On this report, we decided to take this route. It was agreed that in the morning the animals would carry only half-loads, that we would go down the hill, then that we would return the next day to get the baggage and provisions left on the flat.

This agreed, we went to bed.

As soon as day dawned, we set off, leaving six men to guard what we did not take. The hill was, in fact, difficult to descend; however, we reached the bottom without accident. Continuing our route by descending the stream, we reached the Merced toward evening, and we set up our tents.

The next day, three men went back up with the unloaded animals and returned the evening of the following day, with all we had left there.

The problem now was whether to go down or up the Merced, for we did not know if we were higher or lower than the place where the Indians were working. It seemed to me that I did not recognize this part of the river's course, yet I had gone down it from the place in question as far as its confluence with the middle fork; I did not remember having seen the flat we were on, which made me suppose that we must be higher up.

However, I could be wrong; to clarify these doubts, three of us left, going up the river, while three others went down. While waiting, those who remained occupied themselves in cutting a pine to make a bridge.

Those who went up the river did not go far; they reached a place where the rocks on the bank plunged into the water—impossible to pass, even on foot, without crossing the river. Those who descended the current covered more ground; after having been absent the whole day, they returned to announce that they had not seen any Indians and that they had not come to any flat similar to that which I had described to them. They, moreover, offered the opinion that it was impossible to descend this bank and perhaps even the other with the animals. To clear a path for them, it would have been necessary, in many places, to blast the rock away, and we could hardly think of that. As for us who had remained at the camp, we had tested, as much as the water permitted, the surrounding territory, and had found it fairly rich—less so, however, than we expected. Having succeeded in throwing a bridge over the river, we had crossed to the other bank; there too, in different prospect holes, we had found enough gold to suppose that, once the water had gone down, one could work there profitably. Two of my companions had followed that bank up the river, had gone as far as they could go and return the same day, and they had not seen the Indians either or anything which indicated their presence on the flats.

What should we do? We passed the evening in discussing this question.

Should we settle where we were, occupying both banks, and spend the summer there? or else go back up the hill, then try to come down again to the Merced at the place where the Indians were? The greater number inclined toward this latter choice; they supposed that the Indians had chosen this place to work because of the richness of the deposits; for another thing, because of the difficulties and the dangers presented by the path coming down the hill, we exposed ourselves, by remaining where we were, to paying very dearly for our provisions. The others replied that we could, by means of a little work, improve the path or perhaps find another, easier one; and as for the Indians, how should we know that they had been influenced by the value of the land they occupied? These novice miners assuredly were hardly competent judges in such a matter; it was rather more likely that they had settled in the place which had seemed to them the most convenient to work. In sum, we debated much without deciding and we went to sleep without having been able to come to an agreement.

The next day, on getting up, we were much astonished to see our bridge no longer; the water, during the night, had carried it away. This fact having aroused our attention, we began to study the river a little. We first observed that it was at least three feet higher in the morning than in the evening—that is why our bridge had gone with the current during the night. Should we build another? Yes, on the hypothesis that we would stay, for, in that case, we would have to occupy both banks; but, after full consideration, we decided not to, and this incident had the result, which our long discussion of the evening before did not have, that we came to a decision. We resolved to go and rejoin the Indians. We broke camp and we climbed the stream as far as the foot of the hill in question. If it was difficult to descend, it was even more difficult to climb: we had to take the baggage and provisions in two installments and still, in order to ease the animals, we had to carry a part of the load ourselves; each took on his shoulders a sack weighing from fifty to seventy livres, according to his strength. Five men remained at the bottom to guard the provisions left at the foot of the hill; then the loaded men and animals began to scale this hill. Hardly had we gone three hundred paces on this zig-zag trail, when a mule, whose load had brushed a bush, put her foot off the trail, stumbled, fell and rolled to the bottom with all she carried; she was thrown against a tree and was instantly killed. Except for this accident, the ascent was performed successfully, but it was almost night when we reached the top of the hill. We were out of breath, covered with sweat, and falling from fatigue.

Nevertheless we still were able to reach our former encampment at not too late an hour of the night.

The next day, three men descended again with the animals, and at three o'clock in the afternoon the full caravan, personnel and matériel, was reunited at the camp.

That day, we rested, and we set off on our way the morning of the following day.

In order to avoid a ravine very difficult to cross, we followed for some time the path by which we had come. We took the ridge I had followed to go and reconnoiter the Merced; we left it toward noon to take another which seemed to me to come closer to the river and, toward three o'clock in the afternoon, we made a halt at the head of a creek in a field which seemed to us to be favorable for camping.

We did not want to go farther that day, in order not to drive our animals too hard; for lack of water, we had not stopped at noon; men and beasts were dying of hunger and thirst. Having at the same time dined and supped, we passed the rest of the day in setting up the tents and resting. The next morning, early, following a plan settled on the evening before, four or five men, with supplies for the day, took the ridge on the right of the creek whose source was near the camp. Thill, Colson and I took the ridge on the left, and there we were, the two groups, on our way as scouts.

It was agreed that the first who arrived on the Merced or who recognized it from near enough to be certain of reaching it, would fire several shots to inform the others, and that all would then return to camp.

By following our ridge, Thill, Colson and I, we determined in a short time that it did not continue as far as the Merced; it separated two creeks which joined well before reaching the river. We therefore went more to the left and going from the head of one creek to another, we arrived at a point from which we saw the confluence of the two watercourses.

From then on we knew where we were. Nothing remained but to choose the most favorable point for descending the hill and rejoining the Indians, whom we did not see, but who I knew were at the foot of a peak which we had on our right, that is, opposite to the country which separated us from our comrades. We chose the ridge which seemed to us to go most nearly in that direction. Arrived half-way, we became certain that no obstacle prevented us from gaining the river; Thill therefore fired a shot, then a second. These shots thundered like veritable cannon-fire, so many echoes there were among all these rocks. Shortly afterward, we heard the shot with which they replied to us, but faintly, because the other troop was very distant and there was, between them and us, a high hill forming the elbow in a bend of the river. However, we continued to descend our ridge as far as this river, then went up it for two kilometers; then, at a turn it made, we saw the Indian men and women on the opposite hill and on the other bank, running here and there, frightened, and trying to climb the hill at full speed.

I understood then that our gunshots, by awakening the surrounding echoes, had thrown them into a flurry; not knowing what this musketry could mean, they had judged that the best they could do was to flee first—and they were fleeing.

I climbed onto a very high rock, which was quite near us, and there, being in full sight, I shouted with all my strength: "Oualai! oualai! mènèt to ouauksosse? (Friend, friend, where are you going?)" Some of them stopped; I made myself hoarse by repeating my appeals; they gathered in a group, consulted each other, then descended the hill and came to the shore, across from us, to pay us their ordinary addresses. I saw among them neither Juan nor Flesno.

We followed the bank as far as the foot of the ridge by which we had descended.

We began to climb it, while looking for the most propitious place to build a road, as it was absolutely impossible for a man to descend it while laden, therefore so much the more so for animals.

That evening, at about the same time, we all returned to the camp.

The others had seen nothing good; to hear them, it was almost useless to try to build a road on these ridges; the enterprise was beyond our strength. I foresaw the moment when everyone was going to go off his own way, without anyone taking that of the river.

However, the next morning, I proposed that we all go, less three who would remain to guard the animals and supplies, to reconnoiter a ridge which we had noticed the day before while climbing the one beside it.

As it was not very far, the proposition was accepted. Arrived on this hill, we found rocks, bushes, enough difficulties to surmount or avoid, but finally we judged that it was not impossible to clear a road there; starting the next day we went to work.

For twelve days, all eighteen of us worked there, employing the pick, the shovel, the axe, and—when all that was insufficient—fire. Finally, the thirteenth day, we set up our tents on a river flat, and we settled there with supplies and animals. In a few hours, a pine was cut and thrown across the river in order to go and see if the Americans had respected the notices I had posted some kilometers higher up, on the other bank; I went there and determined that they were still there.

Before going to bed, I marked the water's height on a stone. The next day, on our awakening, no more bridge: the water had carried it away; the mark I had made the night before was three feet under water. Each day we threw across the river a bridge which disappeared each night. Soon pines tall enough to serve us as bridges were lacking. We had made the observation that the water went down until ten o'clock in the morning and began to rise at five o'clock in the evening. The explanation of the phenomenon was simple: the sun, during the day, melted the snow on the Sierra Nevada (snowy range), a chain of mountains always covered with snow, in which the Merced, like all the California rivers, had its source. This melted snow took ten hours to come to us, therefore the nocturnal crest. Naturally the bridges reached by the crest were carried off by the force of the current; the main thing was to know the extreme limit of the high waters. The river began to rise at five o'clock in the evening; it was therefore the effect of the snow melted at seven o'clock in the morning, for the sun could hardly melt it before that moment.

Now, if the snow melted at seven o'clock in the morning produced its effects for us at five o'clock in the evening, the biggest melting of the day, which took place at one o'clock in the afternoon, must necessarily correspond to the crest which was produced at eleven o'clock.

We therefore measured the height of the water at eleven o'clock in the evening, and we observed between this high water mark and that of low water a difference of four and a half feet. It was evident that, in these conditions, a pine put across the river was necessarily carried off, and we knew it anyway.

We had to make a real bridge, that is, a bridge which would stay constantly above the water. Having chosen for this purpose the place which seemed the most propitious to us as much by reason of the arrangement of the banks as by the abundance of the necessary materials, stones and wood, we went by pairs into the water up to our waist; the others passed stones to us, and so we raised a wall or pier which passed high water by a foot. Then we threw across the river a pine on which ten of us crossed to the other side. They were supplied with provisions, knowing very well that the tree would be carried off by the current the following night. They constructed a second pier opposite the first. We cut four pines a hundred feet long, which were placed two by two on each pier at a distance of two feet from each other. The big ends which rested on the piers for a length of twenty feet were loaded with a wall of big stones as counterweight. These trees, which extended only eighty feet beyond the piers, reached above the river toward each other, leaving between their extremities an interval of twenty feet. We pegged cross-pieces on the extremities; on these cross-pieces we put lighter pines, and the bridge was finished. It passed by a foot, as I have said, the highest level which the water had reached until then; but fifteen days later, it rose above this level, battered the bridge, and before long would have carried it away like the others. We had to maintain it by means of lashings.

As soon as the bridge was constructed, we settled ourselves on the other bank and took possession of our flats. That day, I think there were at least two hundred Indians on the bank watching us.

I said to Juan: "Are these the Nang-à (the Indians) who would build some of these bridges?"—"Oh," he said, "the Nang-à would build them well if they had that," and he indicated an axe.—"Well," I said, "work, find gold, and with your gold you will have axes."—"I think," he said, "that gold costs more trouble than it's worth."

I did not undertake to demonstrate to the Indian that he was wrong, not being fully persuaded of it myself.

So we were on the river, we had a bridge to cross it on, and we were settled on our flats.

We first formed three companies, each of which had its flat, but, the work being difficult, one of the two others asked to amalgamate with ours, which was composed of Thomas, Thill, Burgrave, Colson, Manet, and me; Green, Bills, Wolfram and Busch came to join us, while continuing to do their cooking separately.

We all ran short of supplies; it was agreed that three men, one from each company, would go, by rotation, with all the animals, to obtain them at Mariposa. Three men therefore left and took two days to get there and, after a day of rest, three days to return. When they returned, for two days we had been nourishing ourselves exclusively on fish we caught on the line; luckily they were abundant, and, when all was told, we had lived, even quite well.

In spite of the advanced season (June 10), the water stayed high. We could not begin serious construction; we were working, while waiting, here and there, singly or two by two. We each made two, three, or four dollars a day; not much.

When our men who had gone for supplies returned, they were followed by thirty to forty miners who camped above and below us. It was a laughable spectacle to see the newcomers when they wanted to cross the river. They started bravely over the bridge, pack on back, took ten or twelve steps on the pines, then hesitated, then stopped, finally turned heel, prudently regained the bank and, putting down the pack, sat on a stone. They remained, for an hour or two, in contemplation before this masterpiece of hydraulic architecture before risking themselves again. It is easy to understand that this bridge, being without support for a space of a hundred and eighty feet, balanced in a disquieting manner under the feet of the traveler, and that he who did not know the manner of effecting the passage, ran great risk of taking a bath in the icy waves of the Merced.

When it was finished, only five out of our eighteen had dared to cross it without using some other artifice than leaning on two forked sticks by way of staffs. The greatest difficulty for those who crossed came from the fact that the two pines forming the bridge, being naturally flexible toward their extremity, dropped and rose alternately under his feet, as do the two footboards of a weaver at work.

Some, straddling one of the pines, had made this fatiguing and dangerous passage with their legs in the water. At last, a Norwegian, named Geen, had thought of a very simple expedient, very easy and very ingenious, thanks to which everybody could cross.

Taking an empty barrel which had contained our supply of biscuits, he had pushed it in front of himself—that was the whole invention. This barrel, which the passenger rolled in front of himself while leaning heavily on it, forced the two pines to descend and to rise simultaneously, and at the same time served as a point of solid support for the two hands. Naturally, when anyone had a bundle to transport, instead of leaving it on his back, he put it in the barrel which was closed by means of canvas and string. We had procured two barrels so that there would always be, as nearly as possible, one at each end of the bridge. When an uninitiated traveler presented himself for the passage, we shouted to him, from the other bank, to roll the barrel; nine out of ten took this advice for a joke and did not decide to follow it until they saw the tenth cross.

Eventually, when we had a saw to cut boards, we nailed cleats to the bridge and we supported it from place to place on trestles; it thus represented an immense ladder on its back.

The secret of our discovery had not been guarded, as you have seen above. From Mariposa, where it had been divulged at first, the news had spread afar and, as always happens, had been enlarged and embellished on its way; at Mariposa, we had discovered rich placers on the Merced; at a certain distance, it was Eldorado, no more and no less. In two months, we saw the arrival of more than six hundred people who wanted to profit from the windfall. I saw some who came from places fifty or sixty leagues away by crow-flight, convinced that they were going to make a fortune in a few months. They had been told that we had made up to fifty dollars per bucket of dirt, taken only on the surface, because the water prevented us from going to the bottom. At this rate we should each make a thousand dollars a day when the lowered water would permit regular work.

These poor people, when they arrived, learned that we found, sometimes, not fifty dollars, but fifty sous in a bucket of dirt.

Imagine their discomfiture! Many had left much better placers.

For the month of August, all the claims, for a distance of two leagues, were occupied and, in spite of everything, each miner had a reasonable hope of having a good season. Once the water began to diminish, it went down rapidly. At the end of eight days, we could begin the main operation and work altogether instead of remaining isolated, or almost, as before. The washing was done by means of *sluices*, troughs made of three boards, one of which served as bottom, and open at both ends so one could make a sort of wooden canal by placing them end to end. We gave these troughs a steep slope (six inches in ten feet), so that the water, having a strong current, carried away the earth while leaving the gold at the bottom, where some cleats held back a little dirt. But it was necessary first to bring the water to the flat, which could not be done by means of a simple canal, since this flat was higher than the riverbed at the place where we had to take the water.

We had, among us, a German carpenter, named Bills. He volunteered to make us a wheel to raise the water.

We had the necessary tools brought, principally a long saw. Some sawed the boards and joists, while others constructed on the river a dam furnished with a gate, so as to produce sufficient force to turn our wheel. This was fifteen feet in diameter; buckets attached to the felly drew the water from below, moved up to pour it into a trough or reservoir above, whence it was carried by a wooden channel into the first *sluice*. Thus we had all the water we needed to do the washing. There were, one after another, six sluices each eight feet long, which gave us enough space to work all at once, half of the workers on each side; one of us was occupied in throwing the big stones out of the sluices, by means of a quadrangular fork with seven teeth, which let pass only what the current could carry away. At the end of the day, we only had to wash what sand one or two cleats nailed to the end of the last trough had been able to retain. It went on this way until the month of October, at which time we had to stop work for lack of water.

The river which, in the month of May, was as large as the Meuse is at Sedan, then no longer had enough water to turn a simple mill-wheel.

Our flat, in sum, was not rich. Nevertheless, thanks to our installation, we had worked there profitably enough, for we had made an average of eighteen ounces of gold a week for the ten of us, and it should be noted that we were never all at work together, I mean at the washing; one or two were ordinarily occupied in maintaining or repairing the dike, etc. Besides, beginning with the last days of the month of August, one or another was always sick, and it was fully understood that we would work for the absent, the sick, as was just, naturally.

It also happened that Thomas and Bills, our German carpenter, could not endure it and left us definitely after having sold their shares to two others.

It was doubtless the bad water, helped by the poor nourishment, which engendered these maladies. For my part, I had boils on my legs and arms which more than once prevented me from working, and the same happened to almost all my partners, so that, once or twice a month, the flat rather resembled an infirmary. Busch claimed to have an infallible remedy for boils; it was a mixture of fat and turpentine. One day, returning from Mariposa, where he had been after supplies, he had brought back this unguent; I annointed my leg with it at a place where a boil was beginning to show. The next day, instead of having a simple redness on my thigh, it was the whole leg which was like a single boil. After this trial, the unguent was discredited, as one may well believe, and was no more employed. I let nature take its course and, at the end of several days, the boil had grown, burst, and disappeared. All these maladies were perhaps not very dangerous, but they were very inconvenient and especially very troublesome because they returned often. It is true that in the season some miners died along the river, but people died everywhere; even two Indians succumbed. I was curious enough to witness the funeral of one of them. I have already said that the Indians, like the Greeks and Romans, burned their dead; they did not wish to use our fire to light the pyre, they obtained it by rubbing the end of a piece of wood obliquely in a groove gouged the length of another piece of wood; these two pieces of wood are prepared, I think, to serve this purpose. The pyre was formed of branches gathered and not broken, for it would not do if the wood had been uprooted or torn from the tree; branches shivered by lightning should be used exclusively if that were always possible and it is, I think, in order to find this combustible more easily that they always establish the pyre on a wooded height. When this pile of wood has the desired height, let's say about four feet, the oldest man in the tribe sets fire to it in four places, then withdraws. Then the Indians form a circle, turn all around it, at first slowly, then, as the fire mounts, in a more lively manner; soon they are running as fast as their legs will go. When they reach the point where the circling can no longer be accelerated, they dance, and that lasts until everything has been consumed. Then they throw on the coals all that belonged to the dead man. His hut goes on first, the rest is generally not much. Then, they watch the fire for a long time, throwing back on it everything which served to feed it and which ought to be entirely burned. Nobody has the right to take from this fire, it has to cool by itself; they then cast the ashes to the four winds.

Until about the twentieth of September, the Indians had worked constantly around us. All the companies let them go freely where it seemed good to them, even in our ditches, to gather the paydirt in their pans, carry it on their heads and go to wash it at the river. The women especially did this work; the occupation of the men consisted almost entirely in watching the women's work; however, I have never seen an Indian woman cede to her husband the gold she gathered, which made me suppose that each one worked for herself. But, at that time, at least half left us to go salmon-fishing on the other fork of the river, which, in spite of the season, always had a fair amount of water. As soon as the salmon had arrived, the Indian women came to sell them to us at a dollar apiece, big or little, so that a salmon of twenty livres did not cost any more than one of five livres. It is true that they sold them always two at a time and chose in a way that the smallness of one compensated for the bigness of the other. This salmon came at a good time to vary our diet, which, since the month of May, had been composed of salt pork, salted beef, sardines, beans, peas, with the bread we made ourselves; at 36 to 40° [Centigrade] of heat, these salted meats hardly formed a hygienic diet. During the months of June, July, and August, the heat had been really overwhelming; we went to work at three o'clock in the morning, and we had to stop at nine o'clock to rest until four o'clock in the afternoon. After nine o'clock, when we had breakfasted, each one sought a shelter, to sleep there, if possible, until four o'clock; I say shelter, not against the sun, but against the wind, which burned our faces as if it had come out of an oven.

My place of repose was a simple canvas nailed to four pieces of wood forming a frame; above, a light cloth stretched horizontally to make a shadow, then a part of this same cloth stretched vertically to stop the wind.

I lay down entirely naked and I threw my shirt over my hips to cover myself. In this state, I perspired in such a way that my bed dripped with it; even at night, the wind remained hot.

At the beginning, I had hung my hammock from the branches of a live oak, eight or nine feet from the ground; I climbed to it by means of a rickety ladder. I was at my ease, nothing could trouble my repose at night; when day came, I threw my dog in it, who kept good guard there all day. But, from the end of June, it was impossible for me to stay there, the wind burned me; I had to move and it was then that I installed myself on the canvas bed which I have just described.

For work, we wore only a light pair of pants without suspenders and a flannel shirt which we pulled out of the pants. Often enough, at two o'clock in the morning, we plunged fully clothed in our pond, then we went to work that way; at the end of half an hour the shirt was dry, after another half-hour, it was soaked again, but, this time, with sweat. At work, if one or the other had some water to throw out to reach bedrock, he gave great pleasure to his comrades by pouring this water over their backs, because coming from the bottom, under eight feet of earth, it was a little less warm than the river water. We had, moreover, in the matter of exposure, the most poorly endowed flat; the sun shone on it from eight o'clock in the morning and did not leave it again until four o'clock in the afternoon.

Chapter Eighteen

War between the Tuolumnes and the Yosemites

One morning, toward the end of September—it was at the time of the salmon run—we were awakened at two o'clock, by the Indians' war cry; I recognized this cry from having heard it at close quarters on the Tchaoutchili. It was uttered by five or six natives who were coming down the hill, not far from our flat. At once all the Indian men and women who were staying around us were on their feet; their hasty coming and going made me guess their inquietude and increased my own. In a few moments they all were gathered. I awakened my partners, who were not disturbed by so little a thing, for the Indians often had noisy, clamorous meetings, by night as well as by day; but I told them that, this time, it must be serious, because it was while making this same cry that they had attacked us, two years ago. At that everybody got up, much disturbed; a war with the natives! that was all we needed!

While waiting, each one dressed, folded his blanket double, passed a cord through it to make a breastplate of it in case of need; then we awaited events.

Shortly afterward, the Indians who had called out the alarm came near the others and spoke to them. Suddenly these latter broke camp and began to go down the river at a running pace. Soon I saw Juan and four other Indians armed for war approaching me; they had a sort of vest of untanned deerskin folded over the chest, then another deerskin in the form of an apron, rather like that worn by farriers; with that, the quiver full of arrows on the back or under the arm, then an arrow between each finger of the left hand or the right hand—the Indians are ambidextrous—the bow in the other hand. Their long black hair, gathered and tied, formed a sort of horsetail on the top of the head. In short, they were hideous.

Juan said to me: "Oualai, the Nang-à are fighting, and my father has sent these men to ask if you would go to his aid. The Nang-à of the Toualumné have come to take our salmon and have killed two of my brothers; they are numerous and strong.[1] If you consent to drive them away, we will be friends of the Whites, we will never take anything from them, we will not get drunk any more, we will sleep at night, and we won't eat your mules any more except when they have died. I, Juan, have

1. Perlot used the term *Nang-à* to mean chiefs. Juan appears to have been using the word *naña*, meaning man (or men) in the Mariposa and Tuolumne dialects. See Perlot, Index—mots indien, MS in Bancroft Library.

220

spoken; it is enough." I then asked my partners, after having acquainted them with the matter, if they wanted to go to the aid of our friends the Indians; all consented, urged as much by curiosity as by the taste for adventure. So I took a piece of paper and a pencil, then I wrote in English:

"The Indians of the Toualumné have come to attack the Yau-Sé-miti, our friends; they have killed several of them and taken all of their salmon so that we won't have any more. Would it not be good to go and show ourselves and thus save our provisions of fresh fish? Let those who wish to help repel the aggressors sign this paper and show up on Round-Flat at nine o'clock in the morning; we will leave for two days." Our signatures followed. I said to Juan: "Give this paper to a *Nang-à*, tell him to show it at all the tents from here to the fork of the river and to bring it back to me afterward." Juan gave this paper to an Indian who, as soon as Juan's gibberish was ended, left at full speed to go down the river. I wrote another note couched in the same terms as the first, and an Indian took it the same way to the miners upstream.

At the end of three hours, the messengers brought the two notes back to me, covered with forty-five signatures. Two hours later, we all were gathered on Round Flat—for so we called a flat through which passed the shortest Indian trail to their camp.

Two of our company would have to stay to guard our tents. I foresaw that we would have to choose them by lot; in the end, however, two let themselves be persuaded and devoted themselves to it. About nine o'clock, we were climbing the hill, numbering forty-eight out of eighty to ninety who occupied that part of the river; at one o'clock in the afternoon, we were having dinner on the bank of the other river, surrounded by a crowd of Indians, among whom a great agitation reigned.

We left there, guided by Juan, who took us by a much shorter path than the one we knew. Behind each bush, we saw an Indian armed with arrows or with that sort of club they call a "tomahawk"; others had long tapering poles which probably served as lances. The women and children were running here and there on the hills and on the mountaintops; there was general confusion. I think that everybody had camped that night in the woods and hills, for they all were carrying something.

As we approached, their cries were silenced and they came in a crowd around us; our presence seemed to reassure them.

We found ourselves, toward evening, I do not know how, on the river again. There were more than a hundred Indians gathered there, all armed with something, but principally with bows and arrows, and more than a hundred and fifty salmon which the women had spread out in good order to dry.

These salmon exhaled an infectious odor, which forced us to go and camp a kilometer farther on. Juan did not seem pleased to see us camp, he wanted to march all night in order to bypass the enemy and, the next morning, catch them in the rear, so as to cut their retreat, an easy thing, according to Juan. But as we did not see too clearly into his strategy, and as, for another thing, we were feeling the need of rest, I induced him to make this maneuver with his Indians, leaving only thirty [*sic*, i.e., three] of them to guide us; in the morning, we would form an ambush on the path of the enemy and would welcome them by a well-sustained fusillade, on condition, to be sure, that the Indians staying with us would warn us, for we could not distinguish between the Toualumné and the Yau-Sé-miti. Then Juan gave several shouts, which the nearest ones repeated, and shortly afterward fifteen to twenty Indians ran up. After a rather long conference with Juan, all left in different directions; Juan and two others only stayed near us.

Some of us wanted to establish a guard post, but it was judged a useless precaution, and we slept, in fact, as peacefully as could be, well knowing that we were guarded by a cordon of sentinels for three kilometers around us. Hardly was it day when the Indian women brought us twelve or fifteen salmon, quite fresh. Juan came to wake me by telling me to prepare to eat, that there were salmon for us. I got up and shouted: "To arms." In ten seconds, everybody was up, gun in hand, except me. I said: "Gentlemen, you've made a mistake in the arms, it's the arms one uses at table that we need, and as they are absent (we had not brought any cooking utensils), how are we going to attack these salmon which the Indians, accustomed to feeding their troops, graciously offer us?" Some tried to roast them on the coals; others cooked them on a spit, that is, at the end of a switch stuck in the ground. After all this, we couldn't make use of our salmon and had to fall back on the cooked meat we had in our packs.

As soon as our meal was ended, we left. Juan made us march almost in a circle, in order, he said, to be able to approach the Toualumnés without being seen. We were advancing in silence, as well as it could be done, when we encountered a crowd of Indians, who were running in all directions, at least that is what our advance-guard informed us. We went into ambush thirty paces from the path; Juan as well as our two other guides were to give us the signal by waving the rags of red shirts which a joker had fastened for them to the ends of sticks, to serve as flags. But it was found that the Indians seen were Yau-Sé-miti, our friends. It seemed that the night before, Juan, seeing us determined to camp, had sent the most vigorous of his men in pursuit of the Toualumnés, who were withdrawing with their booty. They were ordered to make a surprise attack about two o'clock in the morning, to try to take one of them, dead or alive, and to carry him away while promptly beating a retreat. As the Indians never abandoned their own when captured, the Toualumnés, in order to rescue him, would surely all come rushing and fall into the ambush where we were waiting. The Yau-Sé-miti had, in fact, attacked at the intended time; but they had not succeeded in taking a Toualumné; I think, on the contrary, that they had left some of theirs.

This was a major reason that they should decide to retreat because, when the Indians are at war, they make their prisoners suffer in all sorts of ways, as long as peace is not made. Nevertheless, the ruse had half-succeeded; the Toualumnés, seeing the Yau-Sé-miti retire, had pursued them, and it was these fugitives whom we saw running toward the place where we were in ambush.

Juan, after having obtained intelligence from them, came to warn us to be ready, that the Toualumnés were climbing the mountain and that we soon would see them descending. We waited, but at the end of two hours, seeing nothing come, we decided to climb the hill. We advanced all abreast, five to ten meters apart; knowing that all of our friends among the Indians were behind our line, we could, in complete security, fire on those whom we might see in front of us. We reached the top of the hill without seeing anything—it was only on the descent, almost halfway, that we encountered some Indians, who fled.

While we were in ambush on one side of the mountain, I think that the Toualumnés were in ambush on the other side. Having had less patience than the Indians, we had exposed ourselves first; now, as soon as they saw that they no longer had to do with the *Nang-à*, they promptly scuttled away: it would have been easier for us to catch a running deer than one of these Indians.

The first who saw us gave a strange and terrible cry which made the entire hillside shake. Those of us who were in advance fired rather to frighten them than to hit them, for, except one or two, they were already out of range; then our Indians, who were keeping behind us, ran down the hill at full speed and pursued their enemies as far as the flat at the bottom. The war was ended for us, for we hadn't the strength to follow those lads.

In returning, we again passed by the camp of our allies, which was already beginning to be reoccupied although it had been completely devastated. "The old man," Juan's father, had already returned; you should have seen him trying with hands and feet to express his gratitude to us. Juan attempted to translate the thanks which his father addressed to us: "As long as Ouatou (the sun) would turn before his eyes, as long as he would see the Merced flow with water and plunge in waterfalls, as long as these mountains, witnesses of this favor, would rise above the plain of the Tulares, he would remember the service rendered. . . ." But as it was growing late and as we wanted to try to cover half the road that day, we cut short the thanks of the old man, and left.

The next day, at three o'clock in the afternoon, we had returned to our flats. Two days later, Scipiano, Juan's brother, arrived; he came to thank us in his turn. Scipiano spoke Spanish very well and English very little; he informed us that he had arrived at the Indian camp some hours after our departure, that he had left immediately with all his warriors for an encounter with the Toualumnés and that he had found them bringing back the booty.

After our shots, they had been afraid that we were going to burn their camp and they came to meet us to make their submission. He, Scipiano, had negotiated with them, and finally peace was made. Now, Scipiano, on his side, had an account to settle with the palefaces: he and his tribe had been outlawed for three years, that is, since the battle of Tchaoutchili. He profited by the occasion to state his grievances in that respect: he claimed that "his Indians were innocent of that deed; it was the *Nang-à* of Red Volcano (name of the chief of the tribe camped on the San Joaquin) who had come to steal the mules and kill the miners; but as for him, he had always forbidden his people to do those things, and since then, they had already killed thirty of his men who were innocent; they no longer dared to cross the river* and they found themselves deprived of the big flats covered with oaks which surround Mariposa and which belonged to them, so that they were forced to go to seek their winter provisions among the Monos, who lived on the plains on the other side of the sky (on the other side of the Sierra Nevada). † If the Big Chief (sheriff) wished, he would swear, he Scipiano, upon his wives and upon his bow, that his Indians would behave well, like true "*Oualai*," as they had been doing, moreover, during all the days of sun (the summer). At least, let them go to gather the acorns on their flats, where *Nangoua* (God) calls them, since he plants their food there, for, he said, the *nang-à* (the man, the Indian) is not a *hin-hin-mèti* (bear) of the mountains, he is born in the plains and flats which you now take from him. He has had to take refuge in the mountains, where he never came except during the days of sun (summer) to refresh himself; our women that *Nangoua* gave us so that we could remain without end (so that our race could perpetuate itself) have more trouble remaking us (giving us children), because they have to give birth in the cold (the snow), and the *piquini* (the child) perishes. Look for *l'olo* (gold) where you want, let the *Ochà* (Indian woman) seek her seeds where they are and *Oualai Nang-à Blanco* (and the Indian will be the friend of the White)."

This long harangue, which I abridge, had been pronounced in a language compounded of Spanish and Indian.

With what pride had this savage expressed himself! His illustrious namesake had a less haughty tone, I think, when he dictated to the conquered Carthaginians the conditions of peace. As, from this time on, we believed it necessary to distinguish between these two personages, and in order not to confuse this one with the conqueror of Zama, we designated him under the name of "Scipio Americanus."

I said to him: "Where is your *paper?*" He was speechless a moment, doubtless asking himself how I could have learned that he had one. He emptied his quiver and drew out a paper carefully rolled in oilcloth; this paper contained the treaty which Savage, in the name of the government, had concluded with the tribe of the Yau-Sé-miti, and which Scipiano had signed in the name of all his people. It was the same treaty which the old man, the father of Scipiano and Juan, knew by heart and had recited so well to me on my first visit to the camp.

"Well," I told him, "you should go to Mariposa to show your paper to the Big Chief, and if you repeat to him all that you have just told me, he will permit you to go and gather acorns where you want."—"Ah yes," he said, "that is what I want, but I don't dare go to Mariposa, they will kill me."—"Well, get ready, the two of us will go, and I will swear on my gun that they will not kill you. I will take you to

---

*The interdict forbade the Indians to appear between the Merced and the Fresno.

†The Indians believed that the sky rested on the chain of mountains of the Sierra Nevada; beyond that, another sky supported on one side by the same mountains extended to another chain of mountains and so on indefinitely.

the Big Chief, and I will tell him to let the *Ocha* go to gather acorns."[2]—"The truth comes out of your mouth," he said, "you have never lied, Juan has told me, and José (his father) calls you *Oualai;* I will go as you have said."

Never had I seen an Indian more joyous than Scipiano, when he heard me pronounce the words I have just reported, but he let his joy be seen only by the whites. Drawing himself up with all his hauteur, like a drum major preparing to give the signal to his drummers, he turned majestically toward the Indians who accompanied him and announced to them that he was going to make known his wishes to the Big Chief of the whites.

Two days afterward, as a miner was going for supplies, I charged him with a letter for Mr. L. V. Bills, who had just been elected Sheriff at Mariposa. In my letter, I explained to him our situation with respect to the Indians, how these latter had behaved all summer, what they asked and what they promised. I ended by asking him if it would not be equitable and prudent to raise the interdict which weighed on the Indians at Mariposa; we who had let them work beside us all summer, although they were within the County limits—we had had nothing, in any way whatsoever, to complain of from them. Moreover, to push them back beyond us, would be as much as to exterminate them entirely; in fact, we were almost at the foot of the snow-covered mountains, where the Indians could find nothing to live on; to drive them back there was to lay ourselves open to continual attacks by them, for, urged by hunger, they would come to steal our provisions. Instead of which, if one let them settle in the environs of Mariposa, where they all would be eager to stay, they then, lacking nothing, would necessarily be peaceful; though if they nevertheless became turbulent, it would be easy to surround them and to be in the right.

Five days afterward, I received a most flattering letter from Mr. Bills. He knew me, he said, perfectly; he had been my neighbor at Bear Valley, and, moreover, he had seen my name in three verdicts returned on the river. We had, in fact, during the course of the summer, judged, by virtue of the lynch law, three men of whom two, at least, had deserved the rope; on my advice, they had been banished instead of hanged. As the copy of each verdict had to be deposited in the hands of the Sheriff, Bills had seen my opinions explained and signed. Mr. Bills, seeing in me a decided adversary of the death penalty, especially of that inflicted by hanging, the most degrading punishment, according to me, which one can inflict on a human being, had concluded, it seemed, that I was a rare man, an excellent judge; and that, quite simply, because my manner of thinking was also his. He ended by begging me to bring Scipiano to him in order to succeed this time, if possible, in concluding a general peace. In the interval, Scipiano had come to see me two or three times each day. I invariably said to him: "We will leave tomorrow or the day

2. While Perlot used the term *ocha* for women, Barrett spells it *osa* for the Tuolumne dialect, and *oha* for the Mariposa (Yosemite) dialect. See Perlot, Index—mots indien, and Barrett, "Geography and Dialects of the Miwok Indians," p. 362.

after tomorrow," reserving to myself the right to deny it if the Sheriff's response was not favorable. As soon as I had received it, I gave Scipiano a rendezvous for the next day at five o'clock in the morning, enjoining him not to forget to wear, for this solemnity, his pants and shirt, because very often he had on only the one or the other; moreover, to carry a fat purse, because, at Mariposa, there was nothing to eat but for those who had gold.

He went around to all the Indian men and women, and at four o'clock in the morning, he came to wake me to show me his purse, which was sufficiently filled. "Good!" I told him, "now we can leave."

One hour afterward, we were en route. As we approached Mariposa, the brave Scipiano lost his assurance; he had, certainly, at that moment, nothing in common but the name with the other Scipio: this was no longer the captain who spoke of going to impose his conditions on the Big Chief of the whites, and I thought for a moment that I would not be able to persuade him to go on to the end. From time to time, we encountered a miner on the path; Scipiano, always on watch, saw him well before I did, and maneuvered in such a way that I found myself, at the moment of meeting, between him and the passerby.

On entering Mariposa, where we arrived the second day at three o'clock in the afternoon, he was trembling in all his limbs; the encounters being too frequent, no longer knowing how to place himself quickly enough on my left or on my right to put me between him and the passersby, he put himself behind me, following me very closely. However, seeing that, all considered, they seemed not to pay much attention to him, he was reassured a little.

All along the way, he had asked me at least a hundred times what he was going to say to the Big Chief. I replied each time: "You will tell him all that you told me."

We entered Chanac's and I asked for dinner. Scipiano would not have left me for all the gold in California. When I was served, I said to give this Indian something to eat in the kitchen, that is, near the stoves, separated by a canvas from the dining-room. But Scipiano would rather not have eaten than have left me to go by himself into that room; it was necessary to bring him something to eat where I was. I then had to let Chanac know who this Indian was, and why he came to Mariposa, because the Indian, clothed or not, had no more right than the negro to be found, no matter where, next to a white.

They brought him a bowl of soup; they had also brought him a spoon, but not knowing the way to use this utensil, which he doubtless saw for the first time, he put the plate to his lips and drank the contents from it without losing a single drop. As he had done without the spoon, he did without the knife and fork—he ate the meat and vegetables by taking them in his fingers; that done, he ate his piece of bread as dessert.—"Well," I asked him, "is it good?"—"Oh yes," he said, "but it's little."

I think that he could really have eaten three times as much; I shared my dinner with him and told him that later we would begin again. Now let's go, I said, to find the Big Chief. Shortly after, I presented him to Mr. Bills; the latter knew Spanish perfectly. When these two personages were face to face, I lost all my importance, I did not even have to fill the role of interpreter. Scipiano, forsaking me, spoke directly with the Sheriff, who for him was the Scipiano of the whites. I soon perceived that Scipiano, who had just dined well, was casting in Bills' face some belches as loud as the puffs of a locomotive. I said to Bills: "Sheriff, I beg you to excuse my having brought you this King of the Merced too soon after his dinner, for I begin to believe that he is going to asphyxiate you with its returns before he finishes with his harangue."

The magistrate, without answering me, began to laugh gravely, as a magistrate ought to laugh, indicated a chair to me, and seated himself; Scipiano, left standing, decided to go and look out of the window, bumped his head against the pane, and, passing his hand over the glass, perceived only then that something separated him from the street.

This new incident provoked a new fit of gaiety, in which Scipiano himself took part with good grace. After which, their visages returning to the serious air which the circumstance demanded, an interview, which lasted a long time, began between the two diplomats. They succeeded, however, in agreeing; Scipiano promised everything that was asked of him. It was arranged that to distinguish the good Indians from the bad, he would see to it that his Indian men and women were decently clad, that is, covered by a shirt which came down at least to the knees. Scipiano, in conceding this last point, could not prevent himself from casting a glance at his own, which came down by no means as far; but the thing was hardly improper because, on my recommendation, he had given himself the luxury of a pair of pants. The agreement attained, Bills gave Scipiano a certificate of permission to travel, in virtue of which Scipiano, as well as his subjects of both sexes, had the right to circulate throughout the County of Mariposa. All and sundry were ordered to let them pass in peace, to protect them in case of need, but to inform Justice of any act contrary to law or morality which they might commit.

"The interdict against the natives being raised," added the document, "it is henceforth forbidden to take the law into one's own hands; regular Justice, which must be informed of all grievances charged to them, will know how to punish them in conformity with the laws."

This paper thus drawn up and set down, to Scipiano's great satisfaction, in all its width and length, for I think that he attributed value to it in direct ratio to its area—set down, I say, on all the grandeur of the sheet of paper, the Sheriff impressed the County seal thereon, then rolled it as carefully as one could a precious parchment, and gave it to Scipiano. Yes, gave it to him, but with all the solemnity which suited this great act, this grand deed which should have its place in history. Bills, as serious as Scipiano himself, and that is saying a great deal, had the chief of the Yau-Sé-miti approach him, and ordered him to stand upright in the center of the room. The Sheriff, then, with the roll of paper containing the treaty in his right hand, came and placed himself in front of the Indian; with his left hand, he took the right hand of his opposite, who, with his left hand, grasped the paper which the Chief of the whites presented, but did not yet abandon, to him.

While these two men, rather these two powers, were standing thus hand in hand, both in possession of the scroll symbolizing the peace, the union which was going to begin between the White and the *Nang-à*, I received from the Sheriff an invitation to circle the group three times; and, at the same time, he delivered a discourse to Scipiano which doubtless would have impressed me strongly if I had understood Spanish better, so grave was the essence of it and so solemn the tone, without reckoning that the imprecations it contained against the party who did not observe the treaty were, as far as I could comprehend, absolutely terrifying.

When the Sheriff had finished speaking, he abandoned the paper to Scipiano, I stopped parading around them, and they separated.

We next had a rather long conversation, and at last, after the customary thanks, we took leave of Sir Bills.

In order not to have to weigh my gold dust for each payment I had to make, I went to exchange it for money; Scipiano did the same, but wanted all silver pieces, doubtless because they seemed more beautiful to him and because they were bigger than gold pieces.

I saw some friends, then I returned to Chanac's for supper, without Scipiano's having left me as far as a step and without his having stopped holding his roll of paper in his hand; he had already been able to prove the virtue of this sort of paper and, to be sure, he would not have given this one for a white horse.

Next day, we returned to the camp on the Merced. Our return was a festival for the Indians; one would have said that Scipiano, with his paper attached to the two ends of a string and slung over his shoulder, was bringing them a treasure.

The returning Scipiano was no longer the Scipiano whom I had had so much trouble taking as far as Mariposa; this was no longer the Indian whom the Sheriff of the County had seen before him, three days before, humble, fearful, and trembling. This was rather a cock who, mounted on his dung-heap and raising his head as high as his legs, his body, and the length of his neck permit him, flaps both wings to sing of his recent victory over one of his neighbors.

Our stay among the Indians during a whole season had had this result, that we had recovered from our prejudices in their respect. Previously, the native was, in the general opinion, a dangerous animal which it was lawful to destroy. So whoever had occasion to kill one did not avoid it, and thought he had done a useful and praiseworthy deed. After having worked with them, side by side, during the entire summer, peacefully or at least without too many quarrels, after having exchanged services and sometimes perhaps a few thumps, knowing them better, we judged them more favorably. They themselves seemed to have come to a better feeling with regard to us: it was from lack of understanding each other that we had exchanged tomahawk blows and gunshots. This habit of judging without knowing each other is, I think, most of the time, the source of the wars which break out between peoples, whether they are savage or civilized.

We had built a false idea, certainly, of the Indian when we considered and treated him as a wild beast: he is a being naturally sweet and inoffensive. Having few needs, consequently few desires, he is easy to please. He is called savage, I hardly know why; whether by this word one means a ferocious, unsociable being, or simply living in a state of nature, it belongs in no way to the Indian.

He has, just like us, his customs, his laws, his religion; only, they differ from ours, they constitute at the very least the beginning of civilization, unless they may be the final goal, or else the remnant of an extinct civilization; assuredly, they do not belong to a people who have recently left a state of nature.

Doubtless, there is an institution which forms for so-called civilized peoples one of the bases—some of them say simply the base—of society, and which the Indian does not know: property. Is this a sign of inferiority? I will not decide the question. But who can tell us that the progress of civilization will not bring us, in this respect, to the point where the Indian is? In the meantime, the latter owes to this ignorance his living in peace in his tribe—and in his family: he does not know law-suits.

His laws and his customs proceed from his religious beliefs: the Great Spirit (God) himself is his legislator and his judge; but his action is exerted without any intermediary whatsoever. A theocracy without priests—there, truly, is the government of the Indians.

An attentive observer of nature, the Indian sees in the mighty phenomena it presents to him, the manifestation of the will of *Nang-Oua*, the Great Spirit, and endeavors to make his conduct conform to it; he obeys him and offers no other worship to him: the precepts of this religion, which the old teach the young, constitute his civil code and his penal code.

If the Indian commits a crime, it is God whom he offends, it is God who will punish him. Others avoid him, for fear of being punished because of him; they leave him in his isolation until they are persuaded that by his good works he has succeeded in appeasing the Great Spirit. Thus, the Indian who has fought with another member of his tribe, who has refused to share his food with one more feeble than himself, who has broken his bow, his arrows or his fishing tackle, has to exile himself from his tribe and not reappear until the moon has returned to the same phase and to the same point of the sky where it was at the moment of the sin, that is, at the end of a month. Each day of this month, when the moon again passes the point of the meridian where it was at the moment of the sin, the Indian is on his guard, persuaded that the Spirit is going to punish him, by depriving him of health or of food or of sleep; it is ordinarily of this last blessing that he is deprived. If it is a murder he has committed, he expects to be killed, even by his relatives or his friends, especially by them, for they are convinced that by giving him death, they are rendering him a supreme service. In fact, if the Spirit lets him live, it is in order to kill him where the Spirit kills, that is, when he will be where the Indians go after death, above the vault which rests on the mountains. Then he will exist no more, he will be annihilated, instead of which, if he is killed on earth, he will go above with the others to live there forever.

I asked Juan, who was explaining this theodicy to me, if the Indians were happier up above, after their death, than here in the mountains. "Oh," he said, "I don't know, I don't think so; we are happy here, and when we die, if we have been good Indians, we are still happy up above, that's all; isn't that enough?"

The Indian marries at whatever age he pleases, provided that his wife is younger than he and that she has reached puberty; one of the worst crimes he can commit is to approach a girl who does not yet wear an apron. Now, the Indian woman does not put on this light and minimum costume until the phenomenon has manifested itself by which she knows that the Spirit permits her to belong to a husband.

The Indian can marry at any time, but his wife will not herself be approached while *Ouatou* (the sun) is climbing, that is before the 25th of June, because the Indian who bears a child before having seen the moon of March is dishonored; the other women refuse to help her, the Spirit forbids it, and often she dies in childbed; but if she survives, it is because the Spirit has pardoned her, and the sort of excommunication which has weighed upon her is lifted.[3]

I wanted to know why children should be born between the month of March and the month of June. "It is," Juan told me, "because the Spirit wishes it, and the proof that he wishes it is that *Ouatou* is climbing then, and that beginning with the *great turn* (summer solstice), he descends again."—"But," I said to him, "*Ouatou* climbs in the months of January and February too; why cannot children come into the world in those months?"—"Because," he said, "at that time it is *Commè* (the moon) who rules, she is superior to Ouatou, but she makes nothing grow, consequently, she can nourish nothing. Instead of which *Ouatou*, when he is superior in his turn, makes everything grow, the birds in the air, terrestrial animals, and plants.

"It is when the Spirit gives existence to everything, that the *Oscha* (woman) should also give existence—one cannot do wrong in doing what the Spirit does." I interrupted Juan again: "But it's Ouatou who climbs and descends and who makes everything grow. How does it happen that you believe that in imitating *Ouatou* you imitate *Nang-oua* (God)?

"Do you think, then, that *Ouatou* is *Nang-oua?*"

"No, *Ouatou* climbs, *Nang-oua* remains, Ouatou descends, *Nang-oua* remains; *Ouatou* goes away, *Nang-oua* remains; *Ouatou* acts and *Nang-oua* thinks; to do as *Ouatou* does, is to do what *Nang-oua* thinks, is to do well."—"But *Commé*, doesn't she do as *Nang-oua* thinks?"

"No, and she is punished for it; that is why she is called *Commè* (*Commè* means

3. Perlot uses the correct Indian words for sun, moon, and so on, but understandably as they would be phonetically spelled in French. Thus the word for sun, *watu* is "ouatou" and the word for moon, *kōme*, is "comme." Barrett, "Geography and Dialects of the Miwok Indians." p. 364.

changing, punished, sick, crippled, suffering, unsubdued, etc.), and why she governs those who are punished like herself."

"Who is it who punished her?"

"It's *Ouatou*."

"How is that?"

"*E ouatou-ni-ni otto*," Juan began. . . .

—But some grammatical explanations are necessary here: *Ouatou* means day, light, sun, etc; *Ouatou-ni*, a year, a return; this word, moreover, also signifies: good and bad together, to go and return (to make the circuit), the past, etc. When the Indian wishes to express the idea of number, he repeats the last syllable of the word which designates the object multiplied. *Ouatou-ni-ni* therefore means year-year, or several years. Moreover, in pronouncing *ni-ni*, Juan closed his eyes, which means that the speaker does not know the number, he has forgotten it, he no longer sees it; but as Juan had added *otto*, which means very, much, numerous, too much, to close the eyes meant incalculable, infinite (out of sight).

These three words therefore meant approximately: An infinite number of years ago—in principio, say the Scriptures. Juan continued: "*Nang-oua ouana-m*"— and for fear that I might not understand, he immediately added in Spanish: "*Dios piensa il movimiento*," which can be translated by: "God thought of motion." Motion made two suns: *Nang-oua* left them the care of making and directing everything that moved, as long as they should last, and they would last as long as motion lasted.

One of these two suns made the Indian man, the other the Indian woman; each maintained that what he had made was worth more than what the other had made, and the quarrel becoming warm, they hit each other with strokes of *î-attissa* (arrow, lightning, ray, spark, will-o'-the-wisp, light). One having hit his adversary very hard, he detached thousands and thousands of pieces from him. These pieces spread everywhere, they preserved their rays, but they lost the faculty of reuniting.

The *Ouatou* thus struck preserved the power to move himself, but he lost his light—deprived of his *î-attissa*, he became *Commè* (the moon).

The conqueror alone remained *Ouatou;* when he is not there (when it is night), one sees the pieces of the conquered *Ouatou* (the stars), which are still trying to approach each other in order to restore him, but when the conqueror reappears, he disperses them and makes them flee, and *Commè* having no more arrows (rays), cannot fight advantageously against him.

However, she tries to avenge herself: when she is behind *Ouatou*, she gathers her strength, grows and becomes powerful again because during the fifteen days she has remained hidden behind *Ouatou*, she has gathered many of her pieces. Then she presents herself before *Ouatou* again and gives him battle, but *Ouatou*, hitting her with his arrows, reduces her again to pieces, so that he obliges her to disappear. Always *Commè* begins the fight again and always, up to the present, she is beaten. See *Commè* when she is behind *Ouatou*, how she hurries to gather her pieces! How she hurries to grow! But when she is quite big, when she wants to present herself before *Ouatou*, one sees her diminish each day and, in the distances behind her, one sees all the pieces that *Ouatou* has detached from her. It even happens sometimes that they fall this far and one sees them passing with great speed, heading in all directions (shooting stars, meteors, will-o'-the-wisps).

"Well," I said to Juan, "do you think that in the end *Commè* will succeed in beating *Ouatou* and that she herself will become a *Ouatou* again?"

"Oh yes," he said, "I believe it, for already the *î-attissa* of *Ouatou* are diminishing; already, in spite of him, the snows are appearing on the mountains, and *Commè*, who gathers her *î-attissa* and who does not throw them, is keeping them to make use of them when she has enough. Look carefully when she has grown big and you will see a large bundle of *î-attissa* she is hiding so that *Ouatou* doesn't see them, but she lets them be seen enough so that *Oscha* always hopes that *Ouatou* will be conquered at last. Then it will be so much the worse for *Nang-à* (man), that *Ouatou* made, and so much the better for *Oscha* (woman), who is the work of *Commè;* then the latter will rule the world, which will begin again, and the *Oscha* will rule the *Nang-à*, and she will avenge herself on him, if he has mistreated her."

Such is the cosmogonic system of the California Indians.

Certainly, we are stronger than that in astronomy, and we know very well that the stars are not pieces of the moon, but they have other advantages over us: we would be wrong to despise men who have neither judges, nor police, nor priests, nor even ministers or legislators, and who do very well without them.

The Indian who wants to marry, whether he be a young man, widower, or already with a wife, must carry off the young girl or the widow whom he wants to make his wife. It is made a point of honor to go and take her from another tribe; a rape in his own, without being absolutely illegal, would be frowned upon. Relations between tribes make these marriages easy. If a young girl permits a young man to eat with her from the same *a-gné*, it is . . . permission to call, it means that she consents to become his wife (the *a-gné* is a little basket in the form of a truncated cone from which Indian men and women eat mush). Then she indicates a place of meeting, where the young man goes to await her. If other claimants can guess the place, they go there, there is a battle and, ordinarily, it is the one whom she loves who succeeds in carrying her off; the others retire. The happy conqueror takes her to his people and puts her under the protection of the old women of his tribe.

The next day, his mother or an old woman who still has her husband, celebrates the marriage. The whole ceremony consists in attaching a sort of garter above the left ankle of the bride; this garter, perhaps originally a symbol of slavery, announces that the young woman has henceforth a husband for whom she will work all her life, to whom she owes *fidelity and obedience*. For this provision of the Napoleonic Code seems borrowed from that of our Indians; only, with them it is better observed than with civilized people. Often an Indian carries off in this fashion two or three young girls and consequently finds himself with two or three wives. The bride cannot go to see her relatives again until a month after her abduction, that is, when the moon has returned to the same point where it was then.

When she is pregnant, the Indian women of the tribe never leave her alone, night and day other women keep her company; on the march, she is never the first nor the last; the others serve her and spare her all work and all fatigue. In a word, she is sacrosanct to everybody and, if someone permitted himself to annoy her no matter how little, he would, I think, be forced to leave the tribe because everybody would flee from him or would be hostile to him. We never saw the Indian women in this state, and I, for my part, saw them only during my visit to the big camp, in the month of May; several even at that time already had their new-born babes in their arms or on their backs.

When the Indian woman is in labor, the women who are helping her keep her awake after the birth by singing and dancing, while the sun makes half his round (12 hours), then they let her rest. She does not give birth in her hut, she fixes a sort of nest somewhere else and there awaits her delivery. After the birth, she stays there another *na-atcha-ni*—that is, ten days, as I understand it, for *na-atch-a* means ten—then returns to live with her family.[4]

Once she is up again, she detaches from a medium-sized tree, always with the sap rising at this season, a strip of bark eighteen inches long and eight inches wide, spreads on this band some soft moss (lichen) or squirrel skins or bird skins with the feathers on, according to her wealth, then lays the new-born baby on it, covers him with the same material and swaddles him by means of thongs made of the inner bark of the willow; the baby's arms remain entirely free. Two holes made at the two corners of the band of bark near the baby's head, serve to attach to it the two ends of a thong which performs the office of a suspending strap. Through these same two holes passes a flexible stick which forms an arch in front of the baby's head and which protects him in case of need; from this arch hang little pieces of wood, or— when the mother is rich, doubtless—nacreous shells, which amuse the child by their movement.

When the mother moves from one place to another, she tosses her offspring thus swaddled on her back and keeps it there by means of the strap which she passes across her forehead. When she stops, she hangs the swaddle from a convenient branch of a tree and goes about her business; if the child cries, she rocks the branch in all directions, and ordinarily this movement quiets it. She washes it every day in the river water.

The children belong to the mother, she is the one who raises them. Juan had three wives, all of whom had children; that made three families of which he was the chief (the *Nang-à*), but it was a purely honorific title; he paid no attention to any of them and did not seem to inquire if his wives went elsewhere than home to get their babies. The Indian, for that matter, seldom lustful, is seldom jealous, and, moreover, has no reason to be.

Every Indian capable of having a wife, has one or several; he has not the right to dispose of his wife or wives; these, although giving themselves to him, belong to

4. The Mariposa word is *naatca*.

themselves. But when an Indian woman has joined her destiny to that of a man, whether he has one wife or whether he has several, she can no longer, during his lifetime, unite with another. The most difficult thing for the Indian is to obtain his first wife; as soon as he has one, he easily finds a second, and even more easily a third. He rarely goes beyond these to the fourth; he even has to be a chief to have three.

Outside of fishing and hunting, he does absolutely nothing, it is the woman who does everything. It follows that she has a lot to do, from all points of view, when she is the only wife of her husband; therefore a young girl looks twice before marrying a bachelor; she has to be really smitten with him to make up her mind to it; she prefers, generally, a man already married. That also is why, when an Indian loves his wife very much, he finds nothing better, to show his love for her, than to take a second; he thus lightens her task: the two wives attend together to the cares of the household and are, moreover, on a footing of perfect equality in a house then divided into two compartments, or rather, they each have a house, contiguous or not to each other; they are each at home, and they each prepare to have a family by the same *Nang-à;* this last, who often lives with his relatives, visits these ladies only when he is called.

If the husband is a chief, from love for his wives or from ostentation, he takes a third, and then there reigns in his harem an unalloyed happiness; domestic cares are reduced to a minimum for each of them, and they have the time to attend to their children; that is, I think, the greatest happiness of the Indian woman.

But, one will say, how does the husband of three wives succeed in keeping the peace in his ménage or ménages? By what art does he settle quarrels, or by what miracle does he prevent them? He has nothing to do with that; discord does not reign in the Indian's hut or huts. His companions are sweet creatures, who live together without quarreling; they never have an attack of nerves and cry only when they are afflicted.

But, if that's the way it is, why does the Indian—when he is a chief, of course—hold himself down to three wives? Why doesn't he take a fourth? Oh, there is a reason for that: four would be too many; if, by misfortune, when *Ouatou* climbs again, he didn't see his wives pregnant, it would be a great mortification to him and that would hurt his prestige considerably. Moreover, *Nang-oua*, speaking to him with the voice of experience, has said to him: "Have as many wives as you want, but know well that the more you have, the fewer children they will have and the less happy you will be, for I will measure your happiness by that of your wives."

Among a people who have few needs, who live solely on hunting, fishing, and the seeds produced naturally by their forests and wild fields, who live in a climate warm enough to permit them to do without clothes, industry is reduced to very little. The Indian makes his bow, his arrows, his equipment for hunting and fishing: that is all; the wives make the conical baskets of all sizes, which serve them for carrying things, as furniture and as vessels.

I have seen them also making small covers of fur and of bird-feathers, that is, of hair and drawn feathers, with the woof composed of twisted gut and sinews. The finest piece that I saw, which I could not buy at any price, was five feet by three; it was of duck's down and very artistically made.

The Indian man is entirely naked. If sometimes he wears a loin-cloth of a sort, or rather a little apron hanging down to mid-thigh, it is pure ostentation on his part: this clothing serves less to hide him than to distinguish him, for it often happens that he lends it to another.

However, if he does not know the use of clothes, he does not disdain ornament. He paints his brown skin with blue and red, in other terms, he tattoos himself; I ought to say, however, that this is not a general custom. It is especially the young people of both sexes who use tattooing; men and women pierce the ear-lobe and pass through it a feather of some bird or other; they pierce as well the cartilage which separates the nostrils in order to pass through it a piece of wood six to eight inches long: this wood has a penetrating odor which recalls that of the laurel and it is, I think, in order to smell this odor continually that they attach it thus under the nose. Finally, their long black hair, coarse as a horse-tail, is gathered and tied on the top of the head.

The Indian women, aside from tattooing and feathers, have for all ornament the nacreous shells they gather along the watercourses; by means of twisted gut or sinews, they make collars, bracelets, and belts of them.

They let their hair fall naturally, keeping it short in front of the face beginning with the eyebrows.

All this refers to the redskins of California, such as they were at the already remote time when I knew them and associated with them. Already then, their commerce with the palefaces had inoculated them with two vices, the thirst for gold and the love of *firewater;* it could be that today, by virtue of the law of progress, they dress, live, speak, and think like us: they would then have succeeded in becoming civilized, or rather would have exchanged their civilization for ours. If that is the case, alas! what have they gained?

VI

EXPLORING THE UNKNOWN: FROM MARBLE SPRING TO YOSEMITE, 1854–1857

Be it enacted by the Senate and House of Representatives of the United States of America, in Congress assembled, *That there shall be, and is hereby, granted to the State of California, the "Cleft" or "Gorge" in the Granite Peak of the Sierra Nevada Mountain, situated in the county of Mariposa, in the State aforesaid, and the headwaters of the Merced River, and known as the Yosemite Valley, with its branches and spurs, in estimated length fifteen miles, and in average width one mile back from the main edge of the precipice, on each side of the valley, with the stipulation, nevertheless, that the said State shall accept this grant upon the express conditions that the premises shall be held for public use, resort and recreation; shall be inalienable for all time; but leases not exceeding ten years may be granted for portions of said premises.*

Act of Congress, June 30, 1864

[Yosemite] The only spot that I have ever found that came up to the brag.

Ralph Waldo Emerson

Having spent the summer and early fall of 1854 mining with the Chief José's Yosemite band on the South Fork of the Merced, Perlot and his fellow miners slowly worked their way back to Mariposa. Exploring and placer mining all the way, they visited the mining camp of Sherlock northwest of Mariposa. There Perlot befriended a gentle French miner named Louvel, who eventually agreed to share Perlot's cabin at Marble Spring for the coming winter.

The two men could not have been more different. Louvel, who spoke no English, was convinced that foreigners in American California were persons without rights, and so he behaved in a circumspect and deferential manner. Perlot, on the other hand, was now completely bilingual and had begun to learn Spanish as well. He was certain of his legal rights and expansive, even aggressive, in dealing with people and problems. As the following chapters demonstrate, Perlot did not hesitate to fight bullying Irishmen who tried to interfere with his mining rights at Marble Spring, or to take his case before a camp meeting run by Americans. On another occasion he summoned the Coulterville sheriff to force a claim jumper to decamp.

Compared to most individual miners, Perlot was now relatively well off and hired other miners to assist him in building flumes or digging for ore. With time on his hands once again he began to explore the region around Marble Spring. He soon became intrigued with the upper reaches of the Tuolumne River and its forks. Eventually he penetrated the terrifying Grand Canyon of the Tuolumne above the present-day Hetch Hetchy Reservoir. It seemed an almost symbolic event that for the first time he encountered a California mountain lion in this dangerous wilderness.

Although it is sometimes difficult to follow Perlot's movements it appears that he then explored the North Fork of the Merced and mined from time to time on Bull Creek. Without quite realizing what he was doing, he was defining and traversing, with uncanny accuracy, the future Coulterville route to Yosemite Valley. Indeed Perlot used the famous landmark, Pilot Peak (which he called Pilot Hill) as both a base point and an observation post to spy out the surrounding terrain. He drew crude maps in his notebook and, as always, depended on his compass.

As he kept up his explorations for gold he also came closer and closer to the entrance to the Lower Valley of the Yosemite, which he had actually visited when he had his historic meeting with Chief José. By this time Perlot had undoubtedly heard of the visit of the Mariposa Battalion to the great valley, but appears not to have realized until 1856 that he already knew the location of the outer valley and thus that the scenic marvels could be found in the inner or upper valley. He now knew that Yosemite could be reached from Coulterville and Marble Spring. By 1857 his reputation as a seasoned explorer was so impressive and so well known that George Coulter, founder of Coulterville and a future commissioner of Yosemite Park, and a group of San Francisco businessmen hired Perlot to open a trail between Coulterville and Yosemite.

As is evident from the text Perlot was greatly flattered by this invitation and wrote a charming account of the opening of the trail: an operation witnessed by some 200 tourists, a band of musicians, and an indeterminate number of friendly Indians. Perlot then described his own response to the mysterious valley with its roaring waterfalls and awesome cliffs. The whole episode was a fitting climax to seven adventure laden years in the foothills and mountains of the central Sierra Nevada.

Because Perlot's own role in the opening of the Coulterville Free Trail and his own descriptions of the valley are virtually unknown to American scholars, it seems appropriate to place his activities in context by summarizing the visits of both earlier and contemporary explorers and curiosity seekers.

The American discovery and penetration of the great valley embraced by present-day Yosemite Park form an intriguing story of rumors and claims that go back to 1833, when Joseph Rutherford Walker and a party of mountain men passed near Yosemite and may well have seen a portion of it from the top of one of the cliffs.[1] Although proof of a sighting by the Walker party is lacking, the diary of William P. Abrams, a worker for Major James D. Savage, confirms the fact that Abrams and a friend, U. N. Reamer, wandered into the valley in 1849, while on a grizzly hunt, and described its features.[2] Because Abrams worked for Savage, it seems likely that the major himself learned about the valley. Indeed Savage actually established a trading post near the mouth of the South Fork of the Merced less than twenty miles from El Portal in the same year.[3] James Hutchings, an early chronicler and promoter of tourism in Yosemite, asserts that in 1850 Colonel G. W. Whitman, an early miner in the Mariposa region, saw Yosemite Falls from the top of one of the cliffs while looking for lost stock.

The first verifiable sighting, however, was in March 1851, when the Mariposa Battalion, commanded by Captain John Boling, in pursuit of raiding Indians, entered the valley via present-day Wawona, descended the South Fork of the Merced for a time before going up Bishop's Creek, and then traveled due north to Old Inspiration Point and the valley itself.[4]

The weather conditions under which Boling's company saw the canyon do not appear to have been favorable, and the remarkable "natural wonder chasm"—as Hutchings was later to call it—appears to have impressed most of the volunteer soldiers less than it did a romantic Ohio physician, Dr. Lafayette H. Bunnell, who

1. Bil Gilbert, *Westering Man: The Life of Joseph Walker, Master of the Frontier* (New York: Atheneum, 1983), pp. 135–36, asserts that Walker did see the Yosemite Valley in 1833.

2. Shirley Sargent, *Galen Clark: Yosemite Guardian* (Berkeley, Calif.: Sierra Club, 1964), p. 47.

3. Annie R. Mitchell, *King of the Tulares and Other Tales from the San Joaquin Valley* (Visalia, Calif., 1941), p. 98; Crampton, *Mariposa Indian War*, p. iii.

4. Crampton, *Mariposa Indian War*, p. v.

had come to Mariposa to seek gold and had joined the battalion.[5] Bunnell was so overwhelmed by Yosemite, in fact, that he spent the remainder of his life talking and writing about the valley and making periodic visits there.

It was Bunnell who proposed the name *Yosemite* for the valley, an Indian word that meant "grizzly." The Indians themselves referred to the valley as "Ahwahnee": the Valley of Deep Grass. Meanwhile other visitors suggested the name *Paradise Valley* and Hutchings tried to popularize the spelling "Yo-ham-ite," which he thought was a more accurate phonetic rendition of the Indian word for grizzly.[6]

Later in May 1851, Major Boling returned to Yosemite and camped there a second time with the intention of cowing the Indian bands there. A year later Lieutenant Tredwell Moore found himself pursuing Yosemite tribesmen who had been placed on reservations near Fort Miller on the San Joaquin but who had decided to return to their summer camps in Yosemite. Moore established a military outpost in the valley, but the majority of the Yosemites themselves fled eastward over Mono Pass to live with the Mono Indians. Perlot, who was working on the Fresno that summer, actually followed Moore's troops to the Chowchilla or the Merced but no farther. Had he persevered he would have seen Yosemite in 1852.

After 1852 it is impossible to say exactly who visited Yosemite Valley. It appears that James Capen Adams, a hunter of grizzly bears, and Robert Bruce Lamon and five friends visited it in 1854. But the first genuine tourists did not come until 1855, when James M. Hutchings, an architect turned journalist, who founded the *California Magazine*, joined Thomas Ayres, an artist and illustrator, and some businessmen to explore the valley and to decide on the best route for a trail or wagon road into Yosemite.[7]

Hutchings and his party first visited the Big Trees of Calaveras and then proceeded to Coulterville, where he asked George Coulter for advice as to who could guide the party to Yosemite. Alexander Stair and Wesley Millard joined the party at that time and a short time later the Mann brothers, mining engineers from Sherlock, joined Hutchings. Hutchings then tried to persuade Captain Boling to guide him to Yosemite, but he declined, and in the end he was forced to recruit two Yosemite Indians who lived near Hunt's store on the Fresno. They led the party up the divide between the Fresno and Chowchilla valleys and to the fork of the Merced River and into what is now Yosemite Park.[8]

During their stay Ayres made the first sketches of the valley and other members

5. Lafayette H. Bunnell, *The Discovery of the Yosemite and the Indian War of 1851* (Chicago: F. H. Revell, 1880), p. 301; Sargent, *Clark*, p. 47.

6. *Hutchings' California Magazine*, vol. 1, no. 1, July 1856 (San Francisco: J. M. Hutchings and Rosenfield), p. 6. See also 1857 issues and later volumes entitled *Hutchings' Illustrated California Magazine*, as well as his *In the Heart of the Sierras: The Yo-Semite Valley, Both Historical and Descriptive . . .* (Oakland, Calif.: Pacific Press Publishing House, 1886).

7. Sargent, *Clark*, p. 47.

8. Ibid., pp. 47–48; Bunnell, *Yosemite*, p. 303.

of the party took measurements of the heights of the cliffs and domes and waterfalls. Upon his return to Mariposa, Hutchings asked L. A. Holmes, editor of the *Mariposa Gazette,* to write a description of the valley based on Hutchings's notes and to interview those who had gone there. Holmes was ill, however, and Hutchings himself wrote the first famous description of the valley for the July 12 issue of the *Gazette.* Almost immediately thereafter, Hutchings's article or variations thereof were repeated in his *California Magazine,* while Ayres's lithographs of Yosemite Falls appeared in the fall issue. Hutchings, like Bunnell, was so overwhelmed that he spent the rest of his life promoting Yosemite, where he ran a hotel.[9]

No one had followed the news that Yosemite was destined to be a tourist resort with more interest than George W. Coulter, for the town of Coulterville, which he had founded, seemed to be a logical stopping place for tourists and a natural supply base for the camps and hotels that might be built in the park. He had wanted to join Hutchings on his 1855 trip into Yosemite but had been unable to do so. Such was the condition of things when Perlot received an invitation to cut a trail from Coulterville to Yosemite in the spring of 1857.

It is difficult to say with precision exactly who was in the trail-blazing party. Coulter and Dr. Bunnell appear to have been present, as perhaps was Thomas Ayres the artist.[10] Several surveyors or engineers were also there, for Perlot made a point of imitating their activities by making his own measurements with homemade instruments that he had brought along.

The description of the route Perlot helped blaze, which ran from Coulterville to Bull Creek, to Deer Flat, Hazel Green, Crane Flat, and Tamarack Flat, coincides with that noted by Bunnell.[11] It came to be called the Coulterville Free Trail, and though Yosemite continued to be accessible only by horseback or on foot, it helped guarantee Coulterville's future. In 1874 a wagon road was completed between that town and Yosemite, but it had competition from one built that same year from Big Oak Flat and from one completed from Mariposa in 1875.[12]

Whereas Perlot's description of events—especially of the way the Indian members of the 1857 party behaved—is quite valuable, his own response to the coming of tourists was almost that of a mountain man watching settlers overrun the wilderness. The country was becoming too tame; digging gold for someone else in a known country was not adventure but mere labor. It was time to move on.

9. Sargent, *Clark,* pp. 47–48; Clark P. Russell, *One Hundred Years in Yosemite* (Berkeley and Los Angeles: University of California Press, 1974), pp. 50, 57–60.

10. Some writers disagree about the year the Coulterville Trail was opened. Bunnell, *Yosemite,* p. 315, states that it was 1856, but that was also the year the Mann brothers completed a trail to Yosemite via Mariposa. Russell, *One Hundred Years,* pp. 51–52 and 181, notes that construction on the Coulterville Trail began in 1856 but does not suggest that it was completed that year. Sargent, *Clark,* p. 58, agrees with Perlot's journal that the trail was opened in 1857.

11. Bunnell, *Yosemite,* pp. 315–16; Russell, *One Hundred Years,* pp. 52, 62–63.

12. Russell, *One Hundred Years,* pp. 63, 183.

☛ Chapter Nineteen

Marble Spring: "Americans" versus Irishmen

As I said, we had lacked water since the month of October and we could no longer wash in the sluices. Our company was disintegrating; they left in bands of two or three, so that at the end of a few days, there were only three of us left on the flat, Thill, Burgrave, and I. The season was still too little advanced to take to our winter quarters; so we stayed and, while waiting, we worked here and there, where we thought we could best make our day's pay without carrying out large preparatory works which would have taken our precious time.

About the 15th, Kesch came to find us; he induced us to go with him to test a creek, where, he said, there was a lot to do when the water had returned. Two German friends of his had worked there, but had not been able to stay because they had fallen ill and had had, on the advice of the doctor, to give up working in the mines. There would have to be several to work there, because there were many bears and panthers in the neighborhood.

We had just about exhausted our provisions and we had no desire to have a new supply brought where we were; therefore nothing held us; we loaded the two remaining donkeys and there we were, on our way with Kesch.

The creek in question was to be found between our camp on the Merced and Mariposa, but much to the left of the path coming from the latter place.

On this subject, Kesch had some information which his friends had given him in writing, but he had already, with two others, tried to make use of it to find the aforesaid creek and had not succeeded. Now, we remembered that in the month of May, at the time of our arrival on the Merced, we had noticed a place where bear abounded; perhaps the creek ran not far from there. Following this indication, we again took the path from Mariposa to the famous flat of the bears; we spent the night there and, next day, bearing to the right, we followed the longest ridge. Toward noon, leaving our ridge, we went down the right side and followed the creek at the bottom of this hillside, in the hope of finding water for dinner; but water was rare there, we had to walk almost three hours more to find any; even this spring, hardly abundant, was fouled by the birds who came to bathe there; however, we had to be content with it, for lack of better. No trace of work on this creek; it therefore was not the one we were seeking, unless the Germans had worked

243

even farther down, for we were descending it almost from its source. As we had taken the right-hand creek on leaving the ridge, the idea came to us to go back up the hill, for that matter not very high, then to descend to the other creek—which was done; but we got there only toward evening and we followed it until night without finding a drop of water. We had to make a dry camp; the night seemed long to us, and we shortened it by leaving at the crack of dawn. It wasn't until nearly nine o'clock that we came to a spring which gave forth fresh and abundant water and had thick, high grass all around it.

We rested in this place and made a copious repast, so we would be able to walk until evening without stopping again, then we continued to descend the creek; the water from the spring was lost little by little and, at the end of a quarter of an hour's march, the earth was dry again. Around three o'clock in the afternoon, we saw that we were approaching so near the Merced that we could not be on the right track. We climbed the hill on the left, then, from above, descended to the next creek and began to climb it; about six o'clock in the evening, we were camped near a fine spring and we were eating supper. Our animals, tied so that they had food and drink within reach, were doing the same when, passing near them, one of us heard one of the two donkeys who, his nose in the air, was blowing hard; he approached and saw that the donkey had his lips so swollen, as well as the front part of the head, that he could hardly breathe and could no longer see. We ran to the shout of our companion, and with the help of a candle, for it was already dark, we found that the poor animal had been struck by a rattlesnake: the holes from the fangs were perfectly visible. Without losing time, we burned his upper lip with the contents of two bottles of alkali which we carried with us as a precaution; the remedy, applied a little late, had small effect; then we pounded together some garlic and onion with a lot of pepper and salt, and, moistening the whole with vinegar, we put it in a piece of flannel shirt and vigorously rubbed the affected part. We worked in relays to perform this operation, and did not quit the game until eleven o'clock at night, when we were sure that the animal had recovered his sight, and that his lips were sufficiently unswollen to permit him to drink and eat. Next morning, we looked for the rattlesnake around the place where he had committed his misdeed, but, whether he had decamped or was staying hidden, we did not find him.

After having tested the soil on this creek, which seemed rich enough to us, we reloaded our animals and continued to climb the creek. Toward noon, we came to a place where the earth had been worked; Kesch consulted his writing, verified the information it contained: no more doubt, it really was the place which the Germans had indicated to him.

Consequently, we settled there and tested the soil; there was, in fact, some gold, and I think that the place was good. We stayed there eight days, that is, as long as our supplies lasted.

We had, unfortunately, very little water, just enough to work with the pan; even that became too dirty, consequently too thick and too heavy toward evening. Each one worked for himself. We went to get the dirt in sacks and carried it to the spring to wash it; the whole thing was to choose one's paydirt well, otherwise the contents of the sack paid little. However, we made five to twelve dollars a day each. I think that we could have worked profitably there all winter, but having left the ground all prepared and a claim at Marble Spring, I insisted on returning; I had, with that intention, arranged a rendezvous with Thomas at Mariposa for the fifteenth of November.

When our supplies were exhausted, we all left, but the three others, thinking to return, staked the claim.

As it would have been too long a detour to go back along the Mariposa trail to the flat of the bears, we headed toward the west, hoping to reach Sheer-lock before evening, a little camp six miles northeast of Mariposa; but the path we took was difficult: many of these hills were covered with impenetrable brush which we had to force aside in order to pass through.

We camped quite early, in order to profit from a spring which we had found on our path. Around this spring, the dirt seemed to be promising, but it wasn't deep enough; the auriferous bed was rarely more than six inches deep under three feet of earth. Nevertheless, the paydirt was rich, and, had I not had to return to Marble Spring, I would have returned to the neighborhood. It was not the same with my companions, who found the country hardly reassuring, because of the bears. It is true that we saw many tracks, but, in the final reckoning, we saw not a single one of these animals; this made me suppose that it was their passage-way at certain times, but that they did not stay there.

We left, and eight hours later we were at Sheer-lock; we found many people there, but few were working, because water was lacking.[1] They were there, guarding their claims and waiting to work when the rains came.

As we found at Sheer-lock, as well as at Mariposa, all sorts of provisions, we set up our tent there in order to rest and restore our strength by a reviving regimen. Some days afterward, Thill and Kesch left us; they went to settle not far from there, on a claim of which they had bought two shares out of five, where they counted on spending the winter.

I wrote to Thomas to let him know that I was at Sheer-lock and that when he was ready, he would find me on the lower part of the creek of that name, where I intended going to work while waiting for him. I was going to move into the cabin belonging to a man named Louvel, whom Thomas knew from having come with him to California on the same ship (the *Cachalot*), and also from having had him as a partner, and with whom we had worked during the winter which had followed our arrival on the placers.[2] This Louvel having come for provisions, on Sunday, to

1. Perlot's Sheer-lock was Sherlock's Diggings, named after a miner who formed a partnership with seventy Mexicans in 1849 to exploit gold found in a gulch "northeast of Bullion Mountain" (Gudde, *California Place Names*, p. 307).

2. A person named "Lovel" had come to California on the *Cachalot* in 1850 and had accompanied Etienne Derbec to the Southern Mines in March 1850. It seems possible that Derbec's partner "Lovel" and Perlot's "Louvel" were one and the same person. See Nasatir, ed., *French Journalist in the Gold Rush*, p. 31.

Sheer-lock, we had encountered each other; he had offered me the hospitality of his house, situated three miles lower than the camp, and I had accepted. Working with the pan, he persuaded me that I would have more chance of making money in that place, where, moreover, there was more water than around the camp. I went there the next day.

As for Burgrave, who did not want to return to Marble Spring with me as I suggested to him, he helped me move, then left for Mariposa, where he planned to rejoin two of his comrades with whom he had worked the past winter.

Louvel had a cabin of tree-trunks (Log-house), spacious enough to lodge six, and there were only two; Louvel's tenant was a Gascon called Rocq, who had been sick for two weeks and Louvel, son of a pharmacist of Cahors and a bit of a pharmacist himself, was nursing him—it is well to know that the fairer half of humankind had made her appearance at the placers and that Rocq had a tender heart . . . that is why he was sick.

At that time, until we were entering the year 1855, not a woman had yet appeared on the placers; we were all men, neither too young nor too old, and in our rude and often miserable life, we were comparatively happy; we knew only one passion, that for gold; on the physical side, we felt only one need, to eat: it was our principal and, very often, our sole preoccupation.

The miner who found gold and who could procure his provisions, entertained no other wish; so, when after a day of labor he returned to his tent or cabin, he sang of his happiness while accompanying himself on some sort of instrument: violin, flute, accordion, cornet. In the evening, wandering through the streets of a camp, one could have thought oneself in an Arcadian vale. But at last the day arrived, as was inevitable, when the blonde Eve presented herself to the miners. Eve or Pandora! She brought them ineffable joys and exquisite sorrows, the latter, I think, in a greater proportion.

From that moment, everything changed. Farewell to the peaceful life of the placers! Farewell to the concerts and songs! Farewell, too, to the concord which until then had reigned among us.

People worked less and spent more; illnesses were more frequent, more numerous, more deadly.

Love, it was thee who lost Troy!

I had been with Louvel two days when I received a letter from Thomas; he informed me that he was in partnership with two others; they had a fine, fair house for the winter, a claim which they thought would be profitable as soon as the water had returned, and he, Thomas, thought he would do well to stay there. He abandoned to me all that we had left at Marble Spring and . . . wished me good luck.

Once again, I found myself alone. After that, I was so much the less pressed to return to Marble Spring, where I knew that there was no water yet; I resolved to stay until the first rains. While waiting, I worked with the pan now here, now there; that way I had days which varied from one to twelve dollars, according to luck and the prospect. Louvel made less than I, although doing regular work on his claim; he had too much excavation before reaching the auriferous bed, which made too much work for him and took too much time for the little dirt he had to wash.

At the end of the ten to fifteen days that I was with Louvel, I thought I observed a change in his demeanor with regard to me: in the evening, after supper, instead of taking his flute, on which he played very well, and playing us a few pieces, as he had the habit of doing, he lit his pipe and kept silent. As soon as I entered, Rocq and he interrupted their conversation, which often was animated and accompanied by loud outbursts, and became silent again; I concluded from this that I was one too many and I was annoyed that I had not perceived it sooner or had not guessed it. However, these ways of behaving, on the part of Louvel, astonished me extraordinarily; I had known him for a long time, I knew his frank and open character and his unalterable evenness of temper; I could not explain to myself this sudden change of attitude toward me.

Having decided to leave, I bought supplies—a full load for my donkey—then returned toward the house; just at the instant of my arrival, I encountered Louvel, who was returning from his work for dinner. "Well!" he said, "is it because you want to leave us that you buy so many provisions at once, or, better, is it that you have decided to spend the winter with us? In that case, we'll buy our provisions together and make a common table, that will be at once more economical and more convenient for you."

"I think," I told him, "that I am going back to Marble Spring; it will rain soon, I hope, and, while waiting, I will have the time to get settled. Moreover, I cannot always stay with you; after all, everyone wants his own home." Louvel looked at me fixedly, then said: "I don't know what you mean, unless you are annoyed because you are in my house. That is not very nice of you; myself, in such a case, I would not find myself annoyed in your house. But it isn't that, admit it, you will have observed that I am no longer in agreement with Rocq, and you think it's your fault in some way; disabuse yourself, you have nothing to do with our quarrel. Here is the cause of it: Somebody stole three ounces of gold from me, I'm sure of it, for I had weighed my purse Saturday night, and there were eleven ounces; the following Saturday, when adding the week's gold, I noticed that different nuggets which I had marked and stamped were missing; I re-weighed my purse, and there were three ounces less. There are only three of us in the house; I am sure of you—and anyway you didn't know where my gold was; consequently it's Rocq, who, besides, never leaves the house and who has already seen me go to my hiding place; I told him that I knew it was he, and I conjured him to return what he had taken from me, and no more would be said.

"He insists on maintaining that it wasn't he; I think that he will reflect and that he will return my gold to me."—"And if he does not return it to you," I asked, "how will you be really convinced that it is he, since we are three?"

And without awaiting his response, I entered the cabin and found Rocq lying fully dressed on his bed. It seemed that I had a villainous expression, for Rocq, seeing me, was frightened; he got up and tried to leave: "No," I told him, "no one leaves any more." Louvel entered on my signal, then I fastened the door on the inside. "Rocq," I said, "Louvel has just told me that somebody has stolen three ounces of gold from him, that somebody must be one or the other of us; the one who took them will have to return them, and that before the door is opened again." Saying this, I took my revolver and cocked it, then said to Louvel: "You are free, begin your search; if no one wants to give back your gold, take it where you find it."

Louvel hesitated a moment, he was trembling. However, he soon decided, and made to begin with Rocq's bed, but he reflected and began with mine, upset everything, dug everywhere, found my purse four inches under the earth at the head of my bed; he poured the contents on a plate, looked for his nuggets, then put my gold back in my purse and the purse in my carpet-bag, which served me as valise and pillow and which he had just done his best to turn topsy-turvy.

He next came to search me, examined my pocket purse, and returned it to me.

He then passed to Rocq, who all the time had been trying to weep without succeeding, and, as if he suffered much, had lain down on one of the unoccupied beds. Louvel looked everywhere and found nothing; he asked Rocq where his gold was; the latter, slowly, pointed out an auger-hole two inches in diameter, sunk in one of the logs of which the cabin walls were composed. A stick which he used to hang his linen on, corked the hole.

Louvel removed the stick and saw the purse. He took it, poured the gold onto a plate, looked for his nuggets, and found them there no more than he had found them in mine. He put this gold back in Rocq's purse, then replaced it in its hole without putting back the stick. He took apart all the pieces that made the frame of Rocq's bed, then prodded the earth a foot deep wherever he could suspect a hiding place. All that took him at least two and a half hours' time, without any results whatever.

He was warm and sat down to rest. During all this time, not a word had been exchanged between us, and all three of us were livid. Louvel, after having rested, said: "I am going to begin again, and if I find nothing, I will not be any the less convinced that Rocq is a thief; that will prove that he has hidden my nuggets outside the house, that is all."

Louvel looked again, pulled his own bed apart, prodded the earth underneath and found nothing but his purse, which he showed us. In putting Rocq's bed back in place, he knocked over the block on which we cut meat, and in the end which stood on the ground I noticed a big peg. "Well, " said I to Louvel, "there's a peg the size of the one that hid his purse, pull it out to look." He pulled it out with difficulty because it was short as the bung of a barrel.

In the hole it covered, he found a tin box and, in this box, some gold. He poured it out on a plate. Then I stopped Louvel and asked Rocq: "Whose gold is that?"—"What gold?"—"The gold hidden in the block?"—"I don't know what you mean," he said, "I didn't know that there was any gold hidden in the block."

However, Louvel investigated and recognized his nuggets. He had marked four or five with an L, with the point of a knife, and showed me the blows of the stamp on the others; it was by these marks that he recognized them. He weighed the whole and found it three ounces. I said to him: "Put that in your purse and let's get it over with; as for you, Rocq, you are going to leave at once for Sheer-lock and I forbid you to show yourself here or in the neighborhood in the next twenty-four hours, or if I see you, I'll take a shot at you, so watch out; tomorrow you can return because I will leave in the morning for Marble Spring."

Rocq left without any more explanations, and so precipitately that he forgot to take his purse. I said to him: "Take your purse with you and don't forget this: never let yourself be found where I am, or you will pay for it; get out!"

When Rocq had been gone a moment: "I didn't think you were so mean," Louvel said to me, "you frightened me; I thought that you were going to kill him."—"No," I said, "I cocked my revolver because I supposed that he had one too and I wanted, in case of need, to be ready first." Louvel assured me that he had no arms. When I had recovered a little of my self-possession, I communed with myself and examined my conscience. I had shown a man the door of his own house, in any case a house which wasn't mine; if this man was sick, had I acted properly? I was not sure and I felt a sort of remorse. I could not prevent myself from sharing these reflections with Louvel. "Let your conscience be at rest," he said, "you have not chased a man out of his own home, for it was Rocq who was in my house, he came when I was already here and I let him in so as not to be alone; no, no, he was only my guest in this house. He is sick, that's possible, but if you had not thrown him out the door, I would have done it, myself, and right away. He is a thief, you see, and a cunning thief; what precautions he had taken to hide his theft and to allay my suspicions! No, I tell you, don't regret anything."

Evening came while we were still discussing this painful incident.

I supped without appetite, then I felt a general discomfort which was succeeded by a most violent headache. I did not worry about it too much; I knew what it was, I had been angry and I have never been able to get really angry without being sick soon after.

I took my gun and went out to walk in the woods, seeking distraction rather than game. I returned an hour after nightfall and went to bed, but I could not sleep, nor could Louvel. Next morning, I got up early in order to depart; I was better. While we were having breakfast, Louvel, who had risen at the same time as I, proposed that we leave together for Marble Spring, saying that he could not make up his mind to see Rocq again and that, for that matter, his claim was nothing wonderful. The thing was soon decided. Louvel asked for two hours to finish his preparations; he stored with a German merchant, our neighbor, all that he did not want to take with him and, at the moment of leaving, also took him the key of the house, recommending that he lend the cabin to anyone, except Rocq.

During the summer, they had built a road from Sheer-lock to the Merced; after crossing the river, according to the information given by our neighbor the merchant, one could climb the opposite hill easily enough with loaded animals. We resolved to take this road rather than make the trip by Bear Valley: we could thus gain two days' march. We descended the bank of the Merced without difficulty.

At this place, the river was fairly rapid, but one could, nevertheless, in this season, ford it easily.

The hill to be climbed was very long; it was about three o'clock in the afternoon, and we climbed until evening without being able to reach the summit; we chose to spend the night at the place where there was the most grass for our *Jack* [sic]. We also had water, but only what was necessary; having dug a hole, we had to wait twenty minutes to fill a bucket which our donkey emptied three times before quenching her thirst. The next day, by ten o'clock, we were at last at the top of the hill. We made a halt for dinner and also to let our poor burro rest; she had a load of two hundred livres on her back and although she had climbed the hill very slowly and we had helped her a lot, she was jaded, but having grass and water at will, she soon recovered her strength. At one o'clock in the afternoon, we set off on the march again.

We zig-zagged over an undulating terrain, completely covered with small thick bushes, five feet high, through which it would have been impossible for us to pass, considering the extent of the terrain, if the path had not been cleared. In the evening, we came to a place which was known to me, five miles distant from Marble Spring, but as it was late, as we had all we needed, and as nothing, consequently, was pressing us, we pitched our tent to camp there, finding that it would be better for us to rest than to march unnecessarily during the night. Next day, at ten o'clock, we were at Marble Spring. All the houses were occupied, including ours; they had even built new ones, so that Marble Spring was taking on the appearance and the animation of a veritable camp. A certain Black, an Irishman, had established a supply-store there and, naturally, among these supplies strong liquors figured in the front rank.

Three Scotsmen were settled in my cabin. At noon, I went to see them; thinking that I came to tell them to leave this house of which they knew I was the legitimate proprietor, they asked me for a delay of three days to pack up, but I had no intention of evicting them. This cabin, too much below ground level, was damp in the winter; we had resolved, Louvel and I, to build a new one.

I said to the Scotsmen: "You can keep this house, if you want, on condition that you help us to build another."

The proposition was accepted at once; they gained by it at least the expense of moving.

Manet, Patrick and Le Basque, three neighbors we had when we were working on the Merced, and who were now living in a brand-new cabin at Marble Spring, came to help us build ours, and some Americans, who also came from the Merced and whose acquaintance I had made at the time of the expedition against the Toualumnés, joined the three Scotsmen, so that we were fourteen to build a log cabin six meters long by four wide. So it was finished in three days: shingle roof, fireplace, door and window (everything in the singular)—nothing was lacking, save a few minor details: nails to put in, chinks to stop up with moss; that was our business. In short, the fourth day, which was a Saturday, we were getting settled in our establishment; nothing more was left but to have a house-warming.

Black, the merchant, having gone on Friday to Coultersville to make his purchases, I had given him a commission to bring back all that I judged necessary, except the meats, to offer a banquet to those who had so generously lent their aid. Moore, the hunter, who had returned like us to Marble Spring, offered to furnish some hares, a deer, perhaps a bear, but surely two at least of these three kinds of game. Manet and Patrick were content to promise grouse and partridge; I set out to hunt on my own part, proposing to bring . . . what I could. That was that for the solid part of the feast; as for liquids, we had two cases (24 bottles) of St.-Julien, a hamper (12 bottles) of champagne, and sufficient cognac.

On Sunday, you should have seen Louvel, transformed into chief cook, struggling in the midst of an incalculable number of pots borrowed from all the barracks and tents of the camp and giving his orders to Manet, invested with the functions of kitchen helper! What activity, what calmness, what prudence, and what courage under fire!

It is enough, to eulogize the chef and his assistant, to say that they were equal to their task. Therefore success crowned their efforts; everything was cooked to a nicety!

The table had been set under an enormous live oak whose thick foliage protected us against the sun's too ardent rays. I will not describe the feast by the menu; it is enough for me to say that it was splendid. There were sixteen good fellows at table; they spoke nine different languages, from Erse to the idiom of the rivermen of the Semois. What interest would not this polyglot assembly have offered to a philologist or an ethnologist, if there had been any savants in California! But there were none.

In spite of the difference of race and of language, we talked a lot and we understood each other very well, although after a certain point we could hardly hear. Certainly, if heaven heard the prayers of poor mortals, it would not have been our fault if humanity did not enjoy an unmixed happiness. How many toasts to the brotherhood of man and the independence of the world! After eloquence, came poetry and music in the guise of song. When each one, in his turn, had sung one or two songs in the idiom of his country, one of the guests had an idea: he climbed on the table and proposed that we all sing together, but each in his own language, two couplets of an ad libitum song; he offered to beat the measure, from the table where he was perched. After not a few glasses of champagne, the idea was too ridiculous not to be adopted unanimously. A-one, a-two, a-three: all mouths were opened at once. . . . It was a most successful charivari; the dogs howled in the camp and the frightened birds took flight with all possible speed.

We had sat down to the table at four o'clock in the afternoon; the next day, at eight o'clock in the morning, there was still a certain number of guests, but these were no longer at table; they had rolled under.

It took us only a few days to finish getting settled comfortably, after which we thought of going to work; with some boards bought and added to those which Thomas and I had left the previous year, we had all we needed to work with at the return of favorable weather, that is, of rain. While waiting, I went to look at the dirt we had extracted the year before. It had not been touched; it could not be otherwise, since we had left it, Thomas and I, when there was no more water to wash it, and since I returned with Louvel before the water had come back to the dried-up creeks. It was not the same for the claim: three Americans had dug a ditch to bring water from a neighboring creek (Lewis Gulch), which had retained a little water. It was their right, but the claim remained mine; I had left it for lack of water to work it, I returned to exploit it as soon as the water flowing there naturally would have returned; that was also my right. If, during the temporary abandonment of a claim, a third party, by his industry, brought or carried water there, he could work there by using his water, but no other: such was the law.

I went, accompanied by two witnesses, to notify these Gentlemen that I had returned to take possession again of my claim and to continue working it as soon as the water would permit me. They knew the law as well as I and did not contest my right, only they represented to me: "as this ditch by means of which they had washed very little dirt, in view of the small amount of water, had cost them fifteen days' work, were they going to lose the fruit of it? should they, when the rain came, prevent the water from coming to me by their ditch? It was the law; was it equity? Without doubt, the work on the ditch had been done without my consent, even to my detriment. But after all wasn't there some means of arranging things in a way that both parties might utilize at the same time the water of the ditch and that of the sky?"

Everything considered, and finding the basis of their proposition just, I accepted it. The claim was divided between us and we had the common use of the ditch; they had the upper part, we the lower. Louvel had pushed for this arrangement; he feared the Americans, because each time he had a bone to pick with them, a misunderstanding had arisen. At the Fourcades [Forks] even, on the Calavéras River, there had been gunshots exchanged; it is true that Louvel did not know English.

Whatever it was, since then, he wanted to have nothing more to do with them. Very much astonished to find, in the present case, some reasonable and accommodating Americans, he had been so much the more disposed to come to terms.

Thanks to the harmony achieved, we were able to set to work immediately.

In the beginning we gathered very little gold, because there was little water; but the flow of Lewis Gulch grew in proportion as the nights became longer, the ditch gave more water, and we succeeded in making from four to five dollars each a day, in spite of the dry weather.

Soon it began to rain and then only began the serious working of our claim, which was exhausted in two months' time. It had not yet rained enough for us to start washing the dirt extracted the previous year. We went to settle on Lewis Gulch, which we had to dry up by means of a diversion ditch; when the ditch was made and the creek-water turned aside, we worked there eight days; then the rain began to fall in earnest. We had to begin washing the prepared dirt; as half of this dirt belonged to Thomas, although he had given it to me, we decided, considering the circumstances in which this donation had been made, that half of the gold produced would be shared between him and Louvel; the other half would return to me. We set to work washing this dirt under a beating rain; in order to go more quickly and to profit by the opportunity—for two hours after the rain had stopped, there was no longer enough water—we had accepted the help Manet and Patrick had offered us, averaging a dollar per hour of work; we worked a five-hour day without stopping.

In four days, the dirt was washed: it produced 432 dollars (2289 francs). Louvel paid the workmen, paid for a treat, and, at the first opportunity, sent half of the surplus, augmented by half of the price of the supplies reclaimed at the quartz mill, to Thomas, who did not know what it meant, and who wanted to send back the whole, saying that he did not understand how Louvel could have owed him anything.

The rain lasted several days more and ended by putting too much water in Lewis Gulch, so that we could no longer work there. We left our tools on the claim to preserve our rights. In the intervals between showers, we worked here and there with the pan, mainly to keep from being lazy.

At the end of eight or ten days, as the rain had stopped, three Irishmen, profiting from the fact that the water in overflowing had broken our dike or *dam*, settled above us in the place left dry by this break, but which our dike flooded when it was full, in order to raise the water to the mouth of the ditch which, because of a rock, could not be made on the level of the creek itself. They claimed to make their own this land which the backwater of our dam flooded. Naturally, in rebuilding the dam we flooded them; thence came a quarrel which nearly degenerated into a bloody battle. At first, I thought that these gentlemen were joking; I soon perceived that they were speaking seriously. While we were occupied in rebuilding our dike, one of them came to make objection, claiming that we would flood his land. "Why," I asked him, "did you stake a flooded claim? my dam was made before your arrival and I had the right, since this claim was free, to use it to bring the water to the desired height so it would run in my ditch; you *claim* this land, it is your right since it is outside our concession; but you'd better wait to work there until my dam becomes useless, until I no longer need my ditch: you do not have the right to prevent me from using it, since otherwise I cannot work."

The Irishman had nothing to answer to that, so he did not reply; he contented himself with rushing toward me to throw me in my own ditch; he missed his aim; in my turn, I threw myself on him, and there we were, pounding each other in earnest.

Then his two companions, who until then had not taken part in the discussion, advanced toward us; I thought, naturally, that they were coming to the rescue of their comrade and I saw that I was going to have plenty to do. Then vigorously shaking my adversary, I succeeded in stretching him at my feet, then breaking my shovel with a stamp of my foot, I tore out the handle, dealt a good blow with it to my Irishman who was trying to get up, and resolutely advanced on the other two. At the same moment, Louvel, with a pick-handle in his hand, was running to my aid. What was my astonishment to hear the two Irishmen shout to me: "Bravo, Perlot, you've done well, we were coming to help you; he's an imbecile, an ass, he deserves to have you break his head." While speaking, they were approaching and offering me a hand; the other, who had risen, was approaching too, rubbing one of his shoulders, which had luckily received my blow with the shovel-handle, instead of the head I aimed at. I ordered him to keep his distance; holding in his hand his shovel, which he had let fall in order to grab me and which he had just retrieved, he placed himself so that the two other Irishmen were between him and me. A long conversation followed, and the affair stopped there for the moment. We began again to rebuild our dam.

However, I foresaw that the Irishman would return to the charge. That same evening, I took two witnesses with me and went to each house, to each tent, to call the inhabitants of the camp to a meeting, at Black's, for the next evening at six o'clock, in order to have the question judged properly; then I sent my two witnesses to Raley, my opposing party, in order to let him know that I was convoking this meeting and that he would have to be there to maintain his rights if he thought he had any. That day, on the advice of Louvel, we excused ourselves from working there. In the evening, twenty-eight were gathered at Black's to judge the affair; I arrived shortly before six o'clock; I gave Black, the president of the meeting, my convocation list signed by forty-two inhabitants of the camp; then we awaited the hour. Moore, who was returning from Coulterville and had heard nothing about it, entered and, astonished to see so many people said: "Well! one would think that there was a meeting here."—"It is a meeting, indeed," said another, "and Perlot is calling it to settle his quarrel with Raley."—"What! Perlot has a quarrel with Raley? Well!" throwing a twenty dollar piece on the table, "I bet this piece that Perlot is right."—"At least wait," someone said to him, "until you know what it's about."—"That doesn't matter," said Moore: "if Perlot weren't right, he would not quarrel, there wouldn't be a meeting, and you would not be here; I have known Perlot for a long time, I have often seen him keep quiet when he would have been right to speak, but I have never seen him speak when he should keep quiet." Soon after, Black opened the meeting; in a few words I explained the affair, which had the issue it should have: a judgment, rendered unanimously, gave me the decision. On the spot, I took a copy and had it given to Raley by the two witnesses who had summoned him, for he, Raley, had seen fit not to attend the meeting and not to have himself represented. When the sitting ended, Moore came, smiling, to shake my hand. "I am happy," he said, "to have arrived in time; it is true that, this time, you didn't need a lawyer, so I will ask nothing of you for having defended you, on condition that, in your next case, you will take me to defend you, but then you will pay me my honorarium, for you have seen I am a good lawyer."—"I thank you," I told him, "for this time and for the next which, I hope, will not come too soon; I am going, in anticipation of your honorarium to come, to treat you today, and at the same time treat these Gentlemen to thank them for having been so good as to take the trouble this evening to come here and decide in my favor." This said, I spoke to Black, who had returned behind his counter, and asked him to serve, at my expense, each one of these Gentlemen a glass of the liquor he thought best to order.

The evening ended soon afterward. I returned to the casa, where I found Louvel, his revolver at his belt, in the midst of cleaning our guns; he was convinced that there was going to be a battle.

I added up my expenses, for the witnesses on the previous evening as well as for the entertainment after the meeting; I found forty-four glasses of liquor at twenty-five sous, total 55 francs, which Louvel wanted to pay out of his own purse, he was so happy with the ending.

The next day we were at work, armed, on Louvel's advice, with our revolvers.

The claim brought us each five to six dollars per working day; the trouble was that it took only one day of rain to force us to a standstill for two, sometimes three, days, because of the excess of water. However, as I had a perfect knowledge of the diggings, we always found a way to make our day's pay here or there by washing with the cradle.

On the whole, the beginning of the year 1855 was dry, so that our claim was rather promptly exhausted.

When we reached our ridge going up the creek, we had to make a new ditch higher up and [beyond?] the claim which had given rise to the litigation between the Irishmen and us. They had properly claimed it and had posted their notices, but they had omitted renewing them every week as the law required.

For this reason, we had the right to *jump* it (*sauter dessus*) and to put our papers there. To do it legally, I took two witnesses, had them determine the state of the Irishmen's notices and observe ours. We next set to work on the new ditch; hardly were we half-way through this labor when Raley came to renew his notices, but he was fifteen days late. Thereupon, explanations began again; I soon saw that to make my Irishman listen to reason was an enterprise beyond the power of my rhetoric; losing patience, I said to him: "Raley, are you a civilized man or a savage? If you are civilized, you know that there are laws, obey them; if you want to evict me from this claim which I say I have the right to occupy, prove to me, the law in your hand, that I am wrong, I will withdraw; but if you are a savage, if you recognize no other right than brute force, because you know that you are stronger than I, well, then, I will treat you as a savage, and you may learn very well that the powder in my revolver is as good as the powder in yours."—"But," he said, "I staked this claim before you, I . . ."—"No explanations, they are wasted words; be at Black's tonight and I will prove that this claim is mine; if you aren't there, I'll call a second meeting which will give me a second decision against you, and you know, I think, that I need only three to have you banished from the country at your own expense. Take care."

The conversation ended there.

Raley nevertheless renewed his notices without, however, removing mine, then went away.

That evening, he was at Black's before me; he had already told his story to all who were present, omitting, naturally, to say that his notices had not been renewed, a circumstance which authorized me to consider this claim as abandoned.

On entering, I took from my pocket the declaration of the witnesses who had observed the posting of my notices and who mentioned the last date seen on those of Raley; I gave it to Black, asking him to read it aloud, which he did. Black, though he was Raley's friend and compatriot, addressed him rudely, reproaching him for his quarrelsome behavior; "it is individuals of your kind," he said, "who excite quarrels and disturb the public tranquillity;" then, seeing that others wanted to get mixed up in it, Black ended by throwing him out the door. Three days later, Raley left Marble Spring; finding myself at Black's, I learned this news from friends of the Irishman, or at least from people who associated with him. "There you give me some good news," I told them; "I was afraid that that unfortunate man would someday force me to kill him. If the law is bad, let's change it, but as long as it exists, let's follow it; as for me, I will fight, if necessary, to see that it's observed. Yes, I repeat, you give me some welcome news, and that deserves a drop, and I'm the one to offer it to you." That said, I treated each of the seven or eight Irishmen who were present to a glass, and among them were the witnesses I had used in my suits; for I should add here that, from prudence, in order not to divide the camp into two parties, I had approached Irishmen by preference for everything, taking care at the same time to choose those whom I had never seen drunk, or loafing.

When our ditch was finished, we worked our new claim until it was exhausted, claimed the land above and made a new ditch without anybody's coming to offer us competition. That is not surprising; there was land at Marble Spring for a hundred and fifty miners, and there were barely fifty of us.

We worked in this manner all winter, making very good pay. About the month of April, this claim being exhausted, we settled two kilometers from there, on the creek which gave its name to the diggings and which, itself, received it from a spring which flowed into its bed, the Marble Spring (*source de marbre*). It was a very powerful fountain which gave the same volume of water all year. Its spring leaped from the marble rock (hence its name), and was extremely clear and cold. What astonished me, was that this water flowed, from its issuing out of the rock to the creek bed, a distance of eight meters, over a bed of pebbles and the débris of stones, without leaving any apparent deposit, so that there appeared no trace of vegetation, nor green grass, nor water-cress, nor mud. This bed, throughout its length, seemed to have been dug but the day before, although it certainly dated from the creation of the gulch. About two hundred meters up from the spring and fifty meters above its level, one saw, in the hillside, the opening of a grotto or cavern.[3] An almost vertical hole, which could be ten meters long with a width varying from one to five feet, left this opening to end in an immense cavity whose extent it was impossible to measure or to calculate. A pistol-shot fired in this sort of well had a tremendous and prolonged echo; if one threw a stone into it, it fell, for an appreciable time, into the void, then one heard it hit the rock, roll a long time on an inclined plane, take a new leap and, an instant later, fall into the water. That made us suppose that the whole mountain was more or less hollow, which often happens in limestone formations, and that the spring-water came from these caverns. For two kilometers below the spring and four kilometers above, there were, along the same creek, other caverns into which one could penetrate; but the water, almost touching the roofs of these vast grottos, prevented traversing them to the end.

3. The grotto Perlot describes was Bower Cave, later a tourist stop for those taking the Coulterville route to Yosemite. See J. D. Whitney, *The Yosemite Guide-Book* (Cambridge, Mass.: University Press: Welch, Bigelow, & Co., 1871), p. 48.

Chapter Twenty

Venture into Tuolumne and Yosemite Valleys

On arriving at the aforesaid Marble Spring, we settled, after having repaired it, in a house that had been abandoned for a long time; then we went to work at washing with a Long Tom.

After a while we made wages of six to eight dollars a day at it. This claim had already been worked, but they must have passed to one side of the auriferous vein, or, at the least, have taken only half its width; what was left sufficed to make our day's pay. But while we were using this claim, we were not slow to observe that, contrary to the general rule, it scarcely corresponded to the alluvial deposit of the creek we were following; it was enormously enlarged and at the same time was buried well below the natural level of the watercourse. Having made this observation, we dug a shaft which took us four feet below the creek bed, still finding the same formation, which still brought as much to be washed; but the water coming from the bottom prevented us from going any farther.

Sixty feet higher we dug another trial shaft and, after having removed six feet of surface dirt, we found the same depth of paydirt as farther down, as well as the same quantity of water at the bottom.

These observations made, we believed ourselves rich; we had enough paydirt to keep four washing for at least three years. This dirt, once we were properly set up, could bring us each eight dollars per workday. A fine prospect!

We resolved to keep this claim for ourselves alone and to work it by hiring day-laborers, but all that was only for the next winter, as the water would soon dry up.

On this understanding, we continued to work as long as the water lasted, and all the time we found as much gold as the small amount of water we had would permit.

About sixty feet downstream from our establishment, there was a waterfall six feet high. In order not to be bothered by the water the following winter, we spent the summer blowing up the rock which separated our work from the bottom of the waterfall; this rock was of white marble veined in blue and rust-red.

In three months, we had dug a channel four feet wide by five deep, but in order to achieve this result, how much powder did we have to burn and how many steel bars did we have to wear out!

Our inexperience in the art of digging rock and blowing it up had something to do with it. However, we acquired the necessary skill promptly enough; the greatest difficulty for us, neither one of us being a smith, was to sharpen our mining bars. When, with the coming of summer, the horse-shoer employed at the quartz mill had left, we had to go six leagues to reach the nearest forge. This trip would have to be repeated too often; I got it into my head to have a forge of our own. I concocted a canvas bellows, whose mouth was a pistol-barrel; I made some charcoal, bought a specially made hammer, some tongs, a few files, and my forge was set up. It happened at first that I tempered things a little too hard because all our mining bars were cast steel, whose temper, I know now, requires less heat and not such cold water as ordinary steel. So I had an apprenticeship to put in; it took me several days to see that I should heat it less and use water that was less cold, but once this discovery was made, everything went beautifully; only, I hadn't properly covered the canvas of the bellows with pitch, so that, an hour before using it, I had to plunge it in water, but aside from that it worked well enough.

When our work was finished, we were at the end of July. We couldn't work, not yet having water, and the season was too far advanced for us to go and settle elsewhere, without reckoning that we would have had to go too far from Marble Spring.

Now, a few hundred meters below our claim, a fairly large creek flowed into the one on which we were working; we had noticed that this creek had had water two months longer than ours. This suggested to us the idea of studying the terrain with a view to catching this water, if possible, by means of a diversion ditch, and of having longer to work when the period of high water had come. We recognized that this ditch could be made but that it would cost us a great deal; we had first to dig it a distance of two thousand feet in a steep hillside, next, as we then came to the bare rock, we had to continue it by a wooden conduit three hundred feet long; we had to drill holes in the rock in order to fasten the iron bars supporting the flume. When this bad section was passed, it remained for us to dig the ditch in the earth of the hillside for a distance of three to four hundred feet; the ditch thus constructed brought the water to a certain height above the claim we had to work, but it was not possible for us to make it come any lower. Everything considered, we decided to undertake the project and we engaged two men, good sawyers, to prepare boards for us, while we ourselves would dig the ditch in the ground.

With a rod placed squarely on another, and a string with a lead weight, we had a level by means of which we laid out our ditch, according to the rules of the art; after which, we excavated it.

It was not entirely finished until about the month of October. It cost us very dear, as much because of the time it had taken as because of the quantity of boards used (three thousand feet at twenty-five sous a foot); but, after all, it was done, all was prepared, we had nothing more to do but wait for rain; it is true that it wouldn't come for another two or three months. This time seemed too long to Louvel, who, doing no hunting, had nothing for distraction but his culinary occupations.

He resolved, after some weeks of inaction, to go and rejoin one of his countrymen, who was working in the north, on the Clamath [Klamath] River; he offered to cede me his share of the claim and equipment. After some days of reflection, the bargain was concluded, and I found myself alone once more.

For almost a year that I had been with Louvel, we had bought beef only once or twice a month in order to make soup, and because we could not eat venison eternally. The hunt had always furnished in abundance all the meat we could eat. Louvel, with a rather refined palate, was a very good cook, and I very mediocre; this had brought us to abrogate the rule generally observed between miners in partnership, which was to do the cooking by turns of a week. Louvel had consented to do it alone, on condition that I would go hunting every Sunday. He concocted the stew, I furnished the hare; each one found his satisfaction in this arrangement, for if Louvel especially appreciated good cooking, I found hunting more agreeable than occupying myself with the stew-pot.

It was rare that the Sunday hunt did not furnish us enough meat for the whole week, often even on Monday we still had some left from the week before; we then threw it out, however little the hunt of the day before had produced. It was because game of all kinds was very abundant in the environs, with the possible exception of deer, which was particularly sought after and pursued by the Indians. It often happened to me, when hunting, to see my dog return to me, his hair standing up on his back, because on the hillside he had smelled, instead of game, the scent of an Indian; generally I encountered, shortly afterward, the latter covered with an untanned deerskin, whose head, well enough preserved, was arranged so that it could serve as a hat. Thus costumed, and holding himself bent over, the Indian succeeded in fooling the deer and in approaching near enough to shoot, without fail, his arrow into its flank. The animal thus hit flees with the arrow and dies, a day or two later, in some thicket, but the Indian knows how to find him.

Once, at the top of a hill, I saw my dog returning like that, with his tail dragging and a thwarted air. I kept him near me and, approaching the brush with precaution, I discovered three Indians disguised as deer, with enormous horns on their heads; there really was reason to be fooled when one saw them from behind, and the deer could very well be excused for letting themselves be taken. It was only when one of them turned around that, seeing that the forefeet were not resting on the ground, I recognized bipeds of my own species. Then, exposing myself and pretending to be the dupe of their deceit, I took aim at them. It took them less than two seconds, when they had seen me, to throw their disguise to earth, jump aside and cry "oualai, oualai" loudly enough to make themselves heard by the deaf. I then raised my gun, approached them and played astonishment with an art which duped the poor Indians in their turn; it was easy to read on their faces that they thought they had had a narrow escape, and they would assuredly have been very pale, if the coppery tint with which nature had provided them had been able to lend itself to this alteration of their physiognomy.

Thereafter, this farce which I had played to amuse myself, had, for me, a useful result which I had not expected. The Indians, warned by this adventure of the danger to which they were exposing themselves, left me the field. The rest of the hunting season passed without my encountering ever again these false deer; on the other hand, I more frequently encountered the genuine article.

At the end of some weeks, alone and lazy, I became bored; I had hunted, I had almost a thousand livres of venison which were being salted, so that the hunt had lost any useful goal for me. I had several neighbors, five or six, who had stayed all summer to prepare dirt and wash, but they lived four or five miles from my cabin and fairly far from one another, without considering that the paths were hardly passable. I therefore saw nobody, so to speak; I felt the need of distraction and I left for Mariposa. Moreover, for two years I had been writing regularly to Herbeumont without having received any news; I wanted to make sure that there wasn't a letter at the post office for me, and then write anew.

I took again the trail by which I had come with Louvel a year before. No longer having a donkey to drive before me, nothing but my dog and my gun, I made good time; the evening of the same day, but a little late, I was lodged on the Merced, in the tent of four Americans who had spent the preceding winter at Marble Spring and who were preparing to return there. They had done a great deal of work on the Merced which had occupied them all summer, but they had found little gold. The next day I arrived at Mariposa; having left Sheer-lock on the left and gone cross country, I had cut the way short and had gained a half day.

Mariposa had been partly destroyed by a fire, and was already rebuilt. This city, if city it was, had gained by being burned in this sense that it was better built than before; at the same time, it seemed less populated to me.

I found nothing at the post office; I mailed a long letter and the next day I returned to Marble Spring, passing through Coultersville. This detour took me almost two days more, but I was not in enough of a hurry to take account of this delay.

At Coultersville, I engaged three workmen for the winter; they were to report to Marble Spring by the fifteenth of December at the very latest; before, if it had rained. Quite naturally, I went to stay at Rivet's. I was not a little surprised, in the evening, to see that my arrival had made a sensation and that a gathering of the miners of the camp and the surrounding country was going to take place at my hotel. I learned then that I owed having become an important personage to the famous expedition of the past spring. Badinier (the father of his people) had recounted this odyssey to everyone so well that all those who—like Badinier himself—had done nothing but hear of it, were as eager to see me as if I had been a strange beast. During this evening, I had to give the same recitation more than twenty times to twenty different groups; hardly had I finished giving it in French when others obliged me to begin again in English.

Next morning, I was preparing to return to Marble Spring, when I encountered five or six Indians, among others Flesno, who was no longer recognizable, so handsome was he; so handsome that at first I did not recognize him, but he recognized me readily enough. He told me that, on Scipiano's orders, all the Indian men and women were working at the mines, were finding gold, and that this gold served to buy clothes, so that everybody was dressed.

In fact, shortly afterward I had proof of this last assertion. Thirty to forty Indians, men and women, passed through the camp itself, more or less loaded with tools and, worth noting, all of them clothed. It is true that their toilette presented a good many incongruities and a good many gaps.

They gave me the explanation of this fact. It wasn't at the price of gold, as Flesno affirmed, that most of them procured the clothes with which they were more or less covered; the miners didn't throw away the least bit of worn-out clothing without its soon being gathered by an Indian who covered himself with it on the spot; he who had found the most, was necessarily the most, if not the best, dressed. Some had shirt and trousers, or rather the remnants of what had been shirt or trousers; they were the best endowed. Others had nothing but a shirt, so much the better if it was long enough; others, only the trousers, but ordinarily these trousers were too long. They had found a very ingenious method of wearing them without cutting off the ends: they ripped them at the fork almost half-way down the legs and so could raise them to the arm-pits, even as far as over the shoulders, so that this single garment covered the whole body, save precisely that which civilized man wants especially to cover. I have seen those who had for entire costume an old overcoat, whose skirts they fastened together in front, thus uncovering St. Peter to cover St. Paul. I saw one who had nothing but a vest, which he had taken the precaution, 'tis true, of buttoning from top to bottom; and another decked out solely in a dress-coat!

The Indian woman, very often, clothed herself with what she found and, naturally, she could not find woman's clothing since civilization, in California, was still represented only by men, but, although having only the same rags to cover herself with as the Indian man, she knew how to make use of them with more ingenuity. The first dress that she imagined was extremely simple: it consisted of a piece of calico having in the middle of its length a tear through which she passed her head. This sort of chasuble covered her well enough in front and behind; it was drawn in at the waist by a belt ordinarily consisting of a simple rope or string. Not having been slow to learn about needle and thread, she began to sew the sides of her chasuble; soon after, she added sleeves to it and the dress was complete.

He who, not having lived in the torrid zone, has never had a close view of man left in a so-called state of nature, like the natives of California, might imagine that decency and modesty are unknown to these people who go naked. That could be true of the Indian man, who, especially in his old age, hides himself little and restrains himself less. It is otherwise with his companion; modesty, that supreme grace of woman, is not unknown to the female Indian. I have often seen these women, who are completely naked, who do not even keep on the narrow band which is their sole garment when they are outdoors; I have seen them walking, bending, seating themselves, squatting, getting up, and I have always admired the extreme decency with which they accomplish all these movements, without ever exposing what they want to hide.

Yet another thing worthy of note: I have sometimes seen Indian men or women disputing, quarreling, even fighting among themselves, without ever hearing issue from their mouth an oath, a blasphemy, or any of those insults, those violent or filthy expressions which the contending parties would not have failed to cast in each other's face in a civilized country; these children of nature know how to remain dignified even in anger. While observing such traits of customs and character, and without denying, as do certain embittered philosophers, the advantages of civilization, above all without wanting to renounce them, I could not, however, prevent myself from wondering if it is all profit for man to cease being savage. . . .

Pardon, civilized reader, this little digression, I will again take up the thread of my recital.

Having ordered the provisions which I lacked and which Rivet offered to have brought to me the next day, I left for Marble Spring, which I reached that same evening.

After some days given to rest, I resolved to undertake the exploration, from the mining point of view, of all the creeks surrounding my residence in a radius of ten or twelve miles. Every day or almost every day, I left in the morning for the day, sometimes in one direction, sometimes in another; everywhere that I could hope to find a little water, I tested the soil and took my notes.

There existed, to the north-east of Marble Spring, and at the distance of just ten or twelve miles, a sort of big valley: it wasn't a plain, it missed that by a good deal, it was a vast space situated much lower than the base of the mountains which surrounded it on all sides, and scattered with little hillocks which made it resemble from a distance the environs of Marble Spring. When I was hunting and happened to climb to the top of Pilot Hill (*mont Pilote*), which enclosed the southwest corner, I could not prevent myself from admiring the truly impressive spectacle which this vast enclosure presented. To the north, it was closed by rock forming a wall, of a prodigious height, from which several streams fell in cascades into the Toualumné, which ran all white with foam at the foot of this wall. To the east, almost opposite Pilot Hill, the slope, although steep, was covered by a forest of pines of enormous girth and proportionate height; this forest broke into the northeast corner of the enclosure to open a passage for the Toualumné, which, seen from a distance, seemed to throw itself from the top of the pines. This river, big as the Meuse, arrived in the valley as if it had descended a circular stair; it was not, properly speaking, a series of cascades or rapids, it was a mass of water rolling in monstrous whirlpools which, when it reached the valley, formed an almost peaceful river. To the south, the valley must have been, as on the north, closed by a rocky wall or at least by a very steep slope; from my observation post, seeing it in profile, I could hardly judge it, but I saw very well that, on this side, the terrain mounted suddenly to a height of two thousand feet; the thick forest which covered it seemed to continue that which grew on the eastern slope, whose summit seemed to extend into a large plateau. As for the west side, which was at my feet, Pilot Hill rising at its southern extremity, it was impossible for me to say what it could be. Pilot Hill, on the summit of which I found myself, is a high wooded mountain, with steep sides;

although the terrain which extends to the base of the mountain was almost under my feet, I saw it from such a height that it appeared to me as objects can appear in the haze of a distant horizon.

How to penetrate into this valley which was so well enclosed? The sole means of managing it, it seemed to me, was to go around it, that is to go south while heading toward the region I had traversed alone when returning from the expedition to the upper Merced, then in a way retracing my steps, to descend by the pine forest which bordered the valley on the east. But this trip required eight days; I therefore could not risk myself there alone. However, it was impossible to suppose that the Indians did not live or had not lived in this place and, without any doubt, they must have found a means of avoiding the immense detour I have just described. There was a shorter route, I must look for it. As I found that I had some time to myself, I took supplies for three days on my back, and started off. Leaving Marble Spring, I took a northeast direction, keeping Pilot Hill on the right in order to have less to climb; I walked all day without stopping, hoping that way to reach the hill by evening and still be able, before nightfall, to explore on the other side the terrain I would have to descend the next day. Indeed, at four o'clock in the afternoon I was at the top of the hill which bordered the mysterious valley on the west; I had it in view, but I saw no means of descending into it; I had climbed the hill with great trouble, and the opposite slope was even steeper; moreover it was a rocky terrain; if I had undertaken to descend it, supposing that I might succeed, I was not at all certain that it would be possible for me to climb it again. Was the cliff like that everywhere? did it present an easier descent farther on? that is what I could not determine, the thick brush with which it was covered not permitting investigations. This obliged me to bear to the left, keeping myself, as much as possible, on the ridge which led me toward the Toualumné. Shortly before nightfall, I wandered somewhat from my route in order to find water for supper; I encountered it in time and hastened to drink from it, for I saw that otherwise I would have to dispute it with the bears and coyotes whose tracks furrowed the earth around the spring. These tracks astonished me; I did not think that the bears had already come down from the mountains again, from which the snow chases them every winter. But not being able to doubt the fact, since the proof was there, and as night was approaching, I hastened to make way for them, for assuredly my presence would irritate them and an irritated bear does not have an easy temper. Therefore, having drunk first at my ease, then supped, then swallowed a few more mouthfuls of water to aid digestion, I withdrew in order to seek a shelter for the night; five hundred meters from there, I found a promising oak, that is to say, it presented two parallel branches at the same height; I hung my hammock from them, three meters above the ground, then climbing up, with my dog on my shoulders, I settled myself there and spent the night tranquilly. I left the next day, as soon as it was dawn, and breakfasted while walking, in order not to lose any time.

I was not slow in finding a ridge with steep sides, of which I availed myself in order to descend to the plain; but after having followed it for a long time, and still being far from the foot of the mountain, I found myself at the confluence of the two creeks it separated, which, when joined, entered a gulch which the rocks and brush prevented me from following. I had to cross the creek on the left and gain the hillside which bordered this gulch.

One would have said that the deer and coyotes had established their general headquarters in these parts, for at every moment I encountered one of their runs, which formed paths going in all directions, except however toward the bottom of the hill. That was a bad sign, for if the animals never descended it, it was doubtless because it could not be descended.

The hill becoming steeper and steeper, I chose the most pronounced tracks and used them as a path. From time to time, a frightened deer fled at my approach, always along or up the hill; I had trouble restraining the ardor of Miraud, who seemed greatly surprised and even scandalized to see my gun remain on my shoulder.

Well before noon, I arrived, to my great surprise, at a perfectly marked trail; as it went in the right direction, I followed it. This path was trampled, it neither climbed nor descended, but followed the zigzags described by the edges of the gullies which cut into the hill. All at once, a new surprise! I came upon some mule dung. After having stopped several minutes in contemplation of this unexpected object, I continued on my way; soon I perceived on the sand—for frequently there was no grass on the path—the prints of shoes, mule tracks, etc. It was not necessary to be a profound logician to conclude from all this that I was in a region already known, and I expected to encounter miners before evening.

However, when hunting on Pilot Hill, I had never noticed either fire or smoke in the valley, nor heard, from this hill, any gunshot; so I had not in the least expected to find it populated.

Toward noon, at the bottom of a short, steep slope, I came to the banks of a river which must have had lots of water in winter, but which, at the moment, was almost dry. This watercourse, which ran toward the Toualumné on the left, came consequently from the right and, from all appearances, upstream it ran between Pilot Hill and the valley; it apparently was the western limit of the valley in question. The path ended just at the top of a cascade formed by the river in question, or rather at the top of an immense crevasse which widened as it went and in which the river was engulfed. The difference in its level above and below the cascade must have been enormous, but the rocks, the brush, the drifted tree trunks accumulated at this point by the high waters, all were obstructions and prevented one from seeing the bottom of the falls. The river, formed again at the base, could not be seen for a kilometer farther down, and seemed then to have fallen from a height of two thousand feet. The tree trunks heaped up across the river formed a bridge five hundred feet wide joining the two banks of the crevasse; beyond that, it was suddenly widened and its sides formed the two banks of the river which, for at least a kilometer, resembled two walls drawing farther and farther from each other; four kilometers farther on, the river reached the Toualumné, flowing in a deep cut whose meanders I perceived in the distance on my left. The bridge of which I have spoken was formed, as I have said, by the piling up of trees which the high waters carried away each winter, and which, being presented more or less crossways, could not penetrate within the narrow crevasse and so remained suspended across the abyss.

For centuries this had been going on, as one saw from the hundreds of tree trunks five to eight feet in diameter which had had time to rot and to be replaced by others which had suffered the same fate.

With an axe, somebody had opened a wide and commodious path across these trees, and animals as well as men crossed easily from one bank to the other.

At the end of the bridge, the path climbed a low hill, doubtless because the water in the flood season did not permit walking along the river, whose banks, at the moment, were dry.

Half a league farther on, however, the path descended to the right toward this river, which began to have high flats on its right bank. On going down the hill, not very high, I saw three tents on the nearest of these flats, toward which I directed my steps. On arriving, I noticed a spirit-level, a graphometer, a chain, a surveyor's plane table, then finally some men, occupied in sawing joists; there were twenty or twenty-five of them, with beasts of burden and supplies. They had worked there all summer, not at the extraction of gold, but at opening a ditch which was to carry water from the river I have spoken of, to Oak Flat, that is, eight or ten leagues away. They were all Americans or Germans, except one Frenchman from the Département du Nord, of the name of Debrai. He told me that a company had been formed at Oak Flat (*plateau du chêne*) with the aim of digging the ditch in question, which should bring to Oak Flat and its environs the water necessary to be able to wash paydirt at all times at placers where water was lacking. I asked if there were any miners in the area; Debrai told me that, during the whole summer, only two men had come, had prospected for a few days, then had gone away again; that there was not to his knowledge one miner or one Indian in the valley, but in return, it was filled with all kinds of game. After having visited the mill-dam where their ditch was to begin, I put my pack on my back again and went back up the river, provided with a crowbar and a pan which Debrai had been good enough to lend me.

Some miles higher up, I came upon an old Indian path which went almost parallel to the river, and at nightfall I halted to camp on a vast flat or small plain four or five miles above the dam. As soon as we got there, my dog, without saying anything, dashed into the brush which bordered the path. In vain did I whistle and call: Miraud, so docile—Miraud, whom I had kept near me all day without trouble—no longer heard me. Rather puzzled, I advanced with my gun at the ready; hardly had I taken a hundred steps from the path, when I saw Miraud, who was running around a tree; from the ardor of his pursuit, I immediately conjectured that he had business with a hereditary enemy of his race. In fact, on raising my eyes, I saw, perched in the tree, an enormous feline, something like an ocelot. I shot, the animal fell to the foot of the tree, it writhed some seconds more before dying; I prudently stayed fifteen paces away, ready to fire my second shot, if it was needed. When it no longer moved, I at last hazarded an approach: it was enormous, it was a good three feet from the nose to the base of the tail, which was cylindrical and comparatively short. All that I could do with this game was to take from it its coat, which was superb, then to roast a quarter for my supper; it was edible without being very good, but not at all to Miraud's taste, who did not want to touch it. On examining this animal attentively, I ended by being afraid of it; the more I looked at it, the bigger I found it. It was not, however, a panther or a jaguar, for I had already seen them running, and they were, it seemed to me, bigger and differently marked; nor could it be a California lion: this lion without a mane has a dark sandy coat, while this animal was striped; whatever it was, it could well be a redoubtable animal, first because it belonged to the feline race, having retractible claws, as long as fingers, and then by reason of its size; it was perhaps thanks to the offensive resolutely taken by my dog that it had not launched itself onto my back; what astonished me was that it had deigned to flee before Miraud. It was a female, another hardly reassuring circumstance, for perhaps the male was not far away and, as night was approaching, perhaps he would come in search of her. Finding her dead, what would he do to her murderer? This thought made me anxious; I first reloaded my gun, then, in spite of that, I judged it prudent to decamp. I therefore went to settle farther away for the night; I did almost another kilometer, and suspended my hammock from a tree at a sufficient height so that the big cat, or the small tiger, whose visit I expected, couldn't reach me without climbing the tree; in this last case, I counted on the vigilant Miraud to warn me.

I was installed in my nest without being able to sleep, when the idea came to me that I had committed an imprudence in leaving the skin with my tools at the foot of the tree; the male would smell it, approach, and then. . . .

I descended at once, dragged the skin three hundred paces farther and threw it onto a bush. I then returned to lie down, and I was able to sleep, but it was a disturbed sleep; I had frightening dreams in which appeared my dying victim and her terrible spouse thirsting for vengeance. The next morning, on waking up, I ascertained with a real satisfaction that the latter had not strangled me.

After having breakfasted, I left in a pile hammock, blanket, and provisions, and, armed with my gun, my revolver, and my tools, I explored the surroundings in a radius of two or three kilometers; I surveyed the country rather than prospected it, for water, generally, was lacking. However, it was promising, and I carried with me on leaving the conviction that during the season one could make his day's wage there. Before quitting the area, I had examined the country from the top of a knoll like a sugar-loaf, elevated enough to enable me to orient myself: I realized that Pilot Hill should be found between Marble Spring and the point where I found myself, and that, in taking a ridge which from a distance seemed propitious to me, I could shorten my route considerably, for the Oak Flat road, by which I had come, made a big detour; it seemed to me that I was in the middle of the valley, from east to west, but nearer the south than the north. This point established, I regained the place where I had left my pack, and dined there, then slowly took the path to the camp at the dam; having left at one o'clock in the afternoon, I arrived at four o'clock.

I don't know now if this day was a Sunday or if there was another reason to take a holiday; anyway the workmen on the ditch had not labored all day and were occupied in amusing themselves; they were playing cards, draughts, chess, skittles; above all it was the last kind of diversion which seemed to please them most. The cook of the outfit had become a café-keeper that day; he sold a glass of brandy at twenty-five cents and those who were the most drunk by evening were doubtless those who had won the most during the day.

Their engineer, a thoroughbred gentleman, admired my catskin, which I was showing to Debrai, and proposed that I let him have it for five dollars; I consented on the condition that he would take a glass with me and with Debrai, to whom I owed this proof of gratitude for having lent me his tools. The bargain concluded, we went to take our drop, which I paid for; then the engineer, from politeness, offered his round, which we accepted; Debrai next made the same offer, which received the same welcome. The engineer paid me my twenty-five francs; on receiving all that money, I felt myself obliged to offer another round, and my two companions did not want to be in my debt, so that what with round following round, bedtime came while we were still at table with glass in hand and our heads somewhat heavy; we went to bed without supper. In the morning, after having breakfasted with these gentlemen and paid for the farewell round, I had nothing more left of my catskin.

After having gone up the river for half an hour, I crossed it and, leaving the valley, began to climb the ridge which, the day before, had seemed the most promising to me.

All these hills were covered with enormous pines which, interlacing their branches, let no underbrush grow at their feet. I think that the sun had never been able to pierce through to the ground, so that almost nothing grew there, except feathery ferns, which grew to a height of seven or eight feet; when I came to a place where these ferns were thick, I had to make a detour as I would have had to do around bushes that were too close together. By walking easily along, I reached the top of the ridge at about two o'clock in the afternoon.

From this height, situated to the south of Pilot Hill, which I had not far on my right, I discovered Marble Spring and its surroundings; but I was still too far from it to be able to get there that evening. That is what decided me to stop for dinner and to rest before descending.

The crest of the mountain on which I found myself was composed of rocky points which rose to a height of ten, twenty, and thirty feet; these rocks rather resembled a wall forty feet thick in which, at irregular intervals, breaches had been opened by cannonfire. These breaches, which gave access from one slope to the other, were singular and of bizarre shapes; sometimes what rock remained between two of these breaches was raised like a high, thin column, but a column which had been raised in defiance of the laws of statics, so far had it left the perpendicular.

What astonished me most, was that these fragments of wall and these columns were polished as if they had long been rubbed by some other body; as I scratched my head to seek the cause of this effect, I noticed that all these polished surfaces were in the same direction, from south to north: a rapid watercourse running to the east in which these stones had been submerged could have polished them thus.

But how to admit such an hypothesis? no river, surely, had ever passed that way, especially in the direction I have just indicated, since at the east there rises, three thousand feet higher than Pilot Hill, the Nevada range; as for the San Joaquin, it flows three thousand feet lower than this same peak and twenty leagues farther south, parallel to the range of which the peak forms a part. In the impossibility of finding another cause for the phenomenon, I concluded that clouds alone had been able to produce it and, in fact, when it rains in California, it is always with the south wind, and the summit of the mountain is, after a fashion, immersed in the clouds.

After having rested a long time on this summit, I chose the ridge that seemed to me most promising for the descent, and set off on my way; I arrived about five o'clock in the evening on the first flats of which the terrain around Marble Spring is formed. While descending and without wandering from my route, I had killed two grouse, one of which, cooked on the spit, made a most delectable supper for me, which Miraud seemed to place well above that which I had offered him two days before. I said: "cooked on the spit;" you will perhaps ask me where I procured such a complicated culinary instrument. The one I used was of the simplest, and here is how I proceeded: after having started a good bed of coals, I had attached a string to a branch of the tree at whose foot I had lit the fire. This string came within two feet of the ground and ended in a Paris point, curved in a hook; when my plucked cock was cleaned, turned, and sewn according to the rules of the art, I had hooked it to the aforesaid string, then I had twisted the latter, which, by twisting and re-twisting, made my bird turn slowly before the coals at a proper distance. The juice was carefully gathered in a pan; by means of a piece of linen serving as sponge which I had attached to the end of a switch, I poured it back over the beast. After having, by the same procedure, exposed all the parts of the animal successively to the fire, I had obtained a roast cooked to a turn, with a delicious flavor, from which there would have been nothing lacking if I had had some truffles; alas, there is no complete happiness in this world!

As I was in the middle of digesting my grouse and of preparing my bed for the night, two Indian men and five Indian women, perhaps attracted by the odor, came up to me. It was impossible for me to determine if I knew them; they called themselves "èch-è-mèti," but they seemed to me rather to belong to another tribe. Seeing that they were preparing to spend the night near me, I thought it more prudent to continue on my way than to sleep beside these ladies and gentlemen. I left, saying to them that I wanted to walk all night. Rounding a knoll, I stopped and lay in wait to assure myself that they were not following me; but no, I saw them, soon after, relight the fire, then lie down. I went on another kilometer, avoiding the paths, then I settled myself in a live oak. In the morning, prodded by curiosity, I retraced my path and returned to look around my fire of the night before. The Indians were no longer there; they had spent the night there and had left in the direction of the Merced. So it could be that they were èch-è-mèti, that is, friends, but, being in doubt, I had still taken the precaution, all the time I had stayed with them, of leaving my revolver hung on my belt and my gun within reach; I poked up the fire, which had not been extinguished, and breakfasted there before taking the path to Marble Spring.

As I was in no special haste to return, I ended the journey in hunting, in order to have some fresh meat for a day or two. Shortly after noon, I reentered my casa with a young partridge, four quail, and a rabbit, which, added to the grouse shot the day before, assured me of provisions for some days.

On opening my door I noticed, by certain indications, that someone had tried to open it; proceeding to a more attentive examination, I determined that someone must have slept beside my cabin; however, no depredation had been committed, except that someone had burned all the wood prepared for my fuel.

It is agreed among miners that when one encounters on his way a lodging not abandoned but whose master is temporarily absent, he may make use of all he finds there, even and especially of the provisions, but that, before leaving, the visitor inscribes his name and address, with the date, on a piece of paper which he places in plain sight. It was this piece of paper which I was astonished not to find; as I was seated before my door, occupied in digesting my dinner and reflecting on this incident, I saw a man coming down the hill as if he was coming from Black's; soon I recognized Colson, from Verviers, who had worked near us, on the Merced, the preceding season: it was he who had tried to open my door; for two nights he had lodged near my casa, while waiting for me.

Black, who had moved and was now settled on Bull Creek (ruisseau de taureau), two miles farther south, had pointed out my cabin to him, but naturally had not been able to tell him where I was, nor if I was gone for a long time.[1]

Colson had heard that as soon as the rains came, I was going to take on some workmen, and he came to offer me his services. I accepted them, though I had already engaged three workmen, for Colson was a good digger, and besides he was a fellow countryman.

He left me to go and get his baggage and tools, which he had left at Black's.

While waiting for his return, I made preparations for an extra feast, for I wanted to celebrate his coming. It had been so long that I had had no other companion than Miraud, and I was so happy to find a human being with whom I could talk!

---

1. Bull Creek District in Mariposa County was, according to Gudde, "about twelve miles east of Coulterville." It had a longer history than most mining districts because its placer mines were succeeded by lode mining. Beginning in 1896, the official name came to be Kingsley, which soon evolved into the name Kinsley. See Gudde, *California Gold Camps*, p. 187.

One must have lived, like me, in solitude, entirely cut off from commerce with his fellows, in order to understand to what point man is a sociable being and how much he suffers from being alone. *Voe soli!* said the wise King Solomon, who knew men well. To live alone is the hardest punishment one can inflict on a man, and the inventors of the cell-system know it well; those who wish to maintain the death penalty in our codes because they consider it as the hardest of punishments, are under a grave error.

How many times have I happened to address my dog as if he could understand and reply to me! How many times have I surprised myself conversing aloud with an imaginary interlocutor! Often it was only at the end of a quarter of an hour that I realized that this conversation was nothing but a soliloquy. Sometimes sadness overcame me to the point where it would have drawn tears if reason had not intervened to oblige me to master my emotion. In the end, I was afraid of going crazy, and when these attacks of melancholy were repeated too often, I took my miner's tools and went to prospect some creek, or else, my gun on my shoulder, I set off ardently in pursuit of hares, deer, and partridge, who were not responsible for my trouble. The most remarkable effect which isolation had produced in me, was the singular acuteness it had given to my senses, especially to sight and hearing. My sight did not reach farther than before, but it was marvelously clear and nothing escaped it. When I was passing through a wood, if a mouse, if a bird moved, if a branch or a leaf quivered, however slight might be the movement, I perceived it and related it immediately to its cause, and that with no effort of attention and without even turning my head when the movement occurred to one side. This result astonished me the more as I had in no way sought to obtain it.

It wasn't quite the same as far as hearing was concerned. I had exercised it in this sense, that in my peregrinations, in hunting especially, I had to listen very often and for very long periods, but it must also be admitted that in my solitude, being deprived of sustenance, it was, so to speak, famished, and seized avidly on the feeblest sounds: an insect walking on the ground, I would have heard; a fly, buzzing near my bed, woke me; in the evening, I heard very distinctly the flight of a bat, a thing that had never happened to me before; lying on the ground, sleeping a deep sleep, a fox, a hare, a cat would have awakened me by passing at a walk fifty meters from me, especially if, instead of my pack, I had for my pillow a piece of wood or a stone, objects which I always placed under my head when I had to listen. Isn't it for this same reason that a hare beats its resting place before lying down? Is the following fact explained by a refinement of hearing or does it pertain to that order of mysterious phenomena which constitute hypnotism? it has happened more than once that I have been awakened by the step of some animal; on raising my head, I saw the animal and no longer heard it.

About five o'clock, Colson returned with [an] *Asor* (pack) on his back; he found me stretched out on my bed happily playing *Lisette* on the flute which Louvel on departure had left me as a souvenir; I know very well that I played it badly, but my audience, which habitually was composed of Miraud alone, was indulgent, and although Miraud perhaps was not a fine connoisseur, his approbation sufficed me.

We sat down to table and I served a succulent supper. I noticed that Colson's attention was drawn especially to a salad composed of young cabbage and turnip leaves, of cress, etc., which I had dressed with lard fried in the pan, having no other oil; but as he said nothing, I explained nothing. The soup of herbs and venison seemed good to him, so did the quail, but it was the salad he kept returning to; I thought for a moment that he wouldn't leave me any. When, the meal over, we were smoking a pipe and having coffee, Colson suddenly got up without saying a word, walked around the spring, then went twenty paces farther, examined the fountain where I got my water, and returned to me: "Where the devil," said he, "is your garden then?" I wanted to amuse myself a little with his astonishment: "My garden?" I asked him, "it's all of California; my vegetables grow wild on all the hillsides around here."—"Even your cabbages?"—"Ah, my cabbages, that's different, one must believe that the great gardener, when he was sowing his seeds, found himself short of that kind of vegetable when he was sowing hereabouts, and I had to supply it by sowing it myself. . . . But the lesser vegetables, such as chervil, parsley, cress, artichoke—it is providence, doubtless. . . ."—"Don't tell me that, let's settle it: Here for two hours I scratch my head to guess how you can provide yourself with all that greenery I have been deprived of for more than four years and which you don't seem to hoard; do you have much of that salad there?"—"Well," I told him, "come, you will judge for yourself; let's go to the garden, we'll gather what we need for tomorrow." Saying this, I led him a hundred paces from the house, into the deep woods, where I gathered chervil; a few steps farther to a place where cress was growing well, I cut it; a little farther, I found lamb's lettuce and added that to my handful of herbs, as well as a celery plant which I encountered shortly after; Colson was following me without saying a word when, walking as if by chance, I came to a place where Louvel, the autumn before, had dug, raked, and scattered seeds of all kinds of vegetables which had grown, gone to seed, and formed, so to speak, a grass patch around each mother-plant. "It is useless," I said to Colson, "to go any farther, this probably is where Providence has sown all these seeds on behalf of the poor miner"; and, in fact, there were, in a space not more than ten meters square, all the vegetables one could cultivate in a garden, except, that goes without saying, beans, sugar beets, cucumbers, and, in short, all those which need special cultivation in order to grow. Colson opened two eyes as big as those of the cat I had killed three days before, he was lost in astonishment; after having stayed some time without saying anything: "My God," he said at last, "how stupid can you be! to suffer four years as I have, without having had an idea as simple as that!"

Considering the resources we had to dispose of, Colson willingly took on the duties of cook. Three days later, he was watering a mass of plants which he had transplanted to a part of the flat which he had had the patience to burn, dig, and clear; in spite of the advanced season, all these vegetables came along very well.

The rain, itself, did not come; Colson, while waiting for it, having sought and found a promising place, began to prepare the dirt for washing; I had ordered from

Rivet's, for Colson and me, provisions for about three months, I had prepared everything so as to have nothing to do but to dig and wash when we had water; I then went, in order not to lose my time, to work with the pan, on a creek four miles to the southeast of Marble Spring. While going to work in the morning and returning in the evening, I hunted; my day's labors brought me a bare three dollars because I had very little water.

About the first of December, Langlois, Moquet, and Payen, my three workmen, arrived from Coultersville.

They settled down in an old abandoned cabin, which they restored, mine being too small to hold all five of us. These gentlemen fed themselves and furnished their tools, and I paid them at the rate of forty cents per working hour. Colson was hired on the same conditions, except that our supplies, like our lodging, were in common. Once installed and furnished with provisions, the three newcomers, like Colson, began to prepare the dirt while waiting for the rain.

Already people were leaving the big rivers, and they were seeking to settle on dry claims in preparation for the winter which was approaching. They descended in crowds on Marble Spring and its environs, so that before the first of January, 1856, this camp numbered nearly two hundred miners. Business had followed the movement, and Black no longer had the monopoly on the sale of supplies.

So it was that a man named Nicolas, butcher by estate and Swiss by nation, brought us fresh meat twice a week. Moreover, as a result of a petition which the miners, as practical men, being gathered in a meeting, had addressed to the county seat, mein herr Nicolas, the butcher, was charged with carrying the mail between Coultersville and Marble Spring.

The rain was late, but it ended by falling and, thanks to the ditch, we could work at last.

The first two weeks brought me three livres of gold, so that, after expenses were paid, I had left about thirty-six ounces profit. A fine result! At this rate, I had a well-founded hope of making my fortune, a modest fortune if you wish, in two years.

Soon the rain fell too hard, so that we had to suspend all work; my laborers washed the dirt they had extracted in advance, then . . . they let it rain; the modest creek where we were working had become a veritable river.

In order to take advantage of the current, with the help of a dam I turned as much water as I could onto the ground I had to excavate, then, in this water up to my knees, I dug and churned so as to make it carry off as much dirt as possible. In a week I thus made it lower the ground by an average of three feet. A few days without rain decreased the volume of water enough to permit us to begin washing the paydirt again, from which the return was no less than before. So I was making gold in quantity, when the frost came to shorten the working hours. In fact, every morning, the ice in our sluice-boxes forced us to wait until ten or eleven o'clock and sometimes until noon before we could begin operations. The frost had yet another effect: the water lowered rapidly so that at the end of seven or eight days I had to restore to the ditch the flow I had turned off as too abundant. Finally, the weather changed; it snowed, then the temperature became milder and the rain began again, so that we could work only four or five hours a day. That lasted until the twentieth of February; the weather then returned to fair and soon forced me to take recourse to the water in the ditch. But, alas! a quite unexpected catastrophe soon came to take this resource from me.

One day when we were at work, at about ten o'clock in the morning, we heard a dull noise like a distant clap of thunder, and at the same time we felt the earth shake; we were terrified and we were asking ourselves what it could be, when all at once we ran out of water. One of us left work and went up the ditch, thinking it was only a matter, as usual, of going to stop up a mole-hole which, on being enlarged, had allowed the water to run out; he climbed the hill, followed the ditch, and suddenly stopped, stupefied: the hill had disappeared; in its place there opened a yawning chasm into which the ditch water was falling in a cascade. Running to his cry, we found that, in fact, the ditch, for a distance of a hundred feet, had disappeared into a hole forty feet deep; into this hole were piled pell mell the pines, oaks, and bushes which covered the hill, the hill itself was at the bottom of the excavation; it doubtless covered a great cave, whose vault, mined by frost, rain and especially, I think, by the ditch water, had collapsed. Whatever it was, it was useless labor and above all dangerous to try to suspend our wooden flume around the walls of this abyss; we judged that the misfortune was irreparable and that we would have to resign ourselves to it. In fact, to build the ditch again, it would have been necessary to raise it thirty feet above this collapse and, to establish it at this height on the hill, to prime it two thousand feet farther up than the head of the first ditch; as the terrain was rocky almost everywhere, we would have had to make it entirely of wood, an impossible thing. From then on, we could work only when the creek furnished us the necessary water. It was a run of bad luck, for we were approaching March, the time when the rainy season ended, and the lack of water was going to suspend all work. While waiting, a little still fell from time to time, but by the tenth of March, I already kept no more than two workmen, and even that was because I, myself, was working only half time, occupied as I was in building a reservoir above my claim.

By means of the boards which had served for the construction of the flume, I had built a dike twelve feet high; I closed this reservoir at night, and in the morning I opened a sluice in the bottom which gave us until noon a third more water than the creek ordinarily furnished. In spite of that, by the first of April, there were only two of us, Colson and I, and ten days later I was alone.

I had in my strong box somewhat more gold than in the month of November, the place therefore was good; I calculated that I had left more already extracted dirt that I could wash the following winter. But until then, there was nothing more to do here, because water was absolutely lacking.

I therefore suggested to Colson, Moquet, Langlois and Payen, who were running around here and there to no great advantage, that we go to the branch of Bull Creek where I had spent the previous month of December, and that we work there all together as long as the water might last, whether for a month or six weeks. This proposition was accepted at once and the more willingly as I offered to furnish free the boards necessary for our installation down there, on the sole condition that they would take care of the transportation; the distance was four miles. These boards were those which had served me in building the ditch which had collapsed a few weeks before. Four days later, we were on the north fork of Bull Creek, where we were each making two to four dollars per working day—the working day was ten or twelve hours. We had been there three weeks when Thomas and two others arrived at our flat; they had just left their winter claim and were in search of another for the summer.

Thomas brought me a letter from Europe which he had claimed from the post office at Mariposa. It was from my older brother and was dated at Chartres (France); it was the reply to my letter of the month of December last. My brothers, from what I then learned, received my letters fairly regularly and, it seemed, replied the same way, but their replies, until now, had not reached me. This letter, the first I had received from my family for more than five years, was an event for me; it told me that he, the elder, who was writing to me, had left the country three years ago to seek his fortune in Paris, had joined the Western Railway and at present was attached to the station at Chartres as merchandise examiner; he had just married. The other had stayed at Herbeumont, and was living with our mother, who was still in good health. As he, too, had been married for two years, I could no longer hope to see either one of them come out to join me.

In each of my letters, I invited them to come and join me and, in order not to leave our old mother alone, I had suggested to them to arrange matters with our brother-in-law Mouzon and, in case of need, to make the necessary sacrifices, to persuade him to leave Thonne-la-long (France) and come to live with her at Herbeumont.

I thought that my mother and my sister, living together, would be happy. There had been some difficulties, it seemed, and the combination could not be worked out. I really think that the principal difficulty was that my brothers did not care enough to come and join me; it was too far, they were afraid they would not find me, or else that I would be dead when they arrived, believing themselves lost, doubtless, if they found themselves alone in California; in short, they had preferred to remain. The good news this letter brought me was that my mother was in good health.

He who has never left his relatives, his village, his country, can have no idea of the sorrows of exile, whether it be voluntary or forced; one must be far from those he loves to feel how strong is the cord which ties us to them, and the farther apart we are the more we feel it. All the miners, moreover, were in that situation. In any camp, the arrival of the mail was always an event; work was suspended, everyone ran, hoping to find a letter addressed to him. When the distribution was over, one saw the happy ones, those whose hope had not been disappointed, some seated on a rock or tree trunk, others leaning against an oak, others squatting, still others standing, everywhere one saw them, without taking a step farther, breaking the seal and devouring with their eyes the welcome missive which came, without any doubt, from the native village. The poor miner, lost in the rocks of California, was not then forgotten! The strongest ones, those least accessible to the tender emotions, rarely reached the end of the letter without wiping away a furtive tear.

How many times, in the last five years, I had found myself at the arrival of the mail, without ever having a seal to break! I had finally cured myself, and dry-eyed I saw the mail come and go, but before having achieved that control, I had suffered for a long time from that terrible scourge, homesickness; then I had reacted and had armored myself with indifference. The words "my country," sweet to pronounce in a foreign land, seemed to have no more meaning for me; I had arrived at that detachment which finds every country good to live in and every place suitable to die in.

I had sought to make myself a soul of bronze; I had succeeded, at least I thought so. I was mistaken; this letter which came to me from my homeland, from which I had had no news for five years, had suddenly awakened and revived all the sentiments which seemed extinguished in my heart. I, too, let fall a tear on the precious paper. My mother lived, she was in good helath, I could therefore hope to see her again!

I wrote a long letter to each of my brothers, intending that they should share it with my sister; I urged them especially to be sure to convince my mother that I was happy, very happy, and that in a few years I would go to embrace her.

I begged them earnestly to write to me often. California was being organized at last, the postal service was being handled in a regular and sure way, already even newspapers were coming to us from America and Europe; they cost us fifty cents a copy, which we paid willingly in order to learn what was happening back there and especially what was becoming of the French who were fighting under the walls of Sebastopol.[2]

2. Here Perlot is referring to the siege of the Russian port city of Sebastopol during the Crimean War. British and French troops, acting in alliance against the Russians, began the siege in October 1854, but Sebastopol was not taken by the two allies until the fall of 1855. Its surrender marked, for all practical purposes, the end of one of the most senseless wars in modern history. A treaty of peace was signed in February 1856 in Paris.

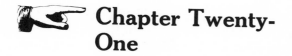 # Chapter Twenty-One

Making Do: Mining at Oak Flat, Bull Creek, and Marble Spring

Thomas and his companions had a month's supplies with them. They had no intention of settling where we were; it wasn't worth the trouble, in fact, because the water was going to be gone; they had come to find us, simply because they did not know where to go.

Thomas, knowing Marble Spring, where he had counted on finding me, knew that I would be without water, and he came to propose that we leave it together. . . . where? he did not know, but he supposed that I myself would.

It was, in truth, showing a great deal of confidence in me, but in the end he landed on his feet; already, for several weeks, I had been nursing the idea of returning where I had killed my wildcat in the fall of the preceding year, but, not having a pack animal to carry my supplies, I did not know too well how I could transport myself there. Now, Thomas and his companions, Louis and Létang, had two animals; so they couldn't have come at a better time.

I offered to guide them there, without however assuring them that we would make a fortune there; they accepted at once. I returned to my cabin at Marble Spring, I put everything in order, as I wished to find it again next November; I posted the necessary notices to keep the claim, had them witnessed by Black and Schréder, who each had a business house on Bull Creek, then went to find my traveling companions.

The next day all four of us left; the others were to come and join us later, if we found enough gold to spend the season there; it was agreed that if we had not returned in two weeks, that would indicate that they could come.

I had the hope that in going up Bull Creek and leaving Pilot Hill far to the left, we could find a way to descend into the valley with the animals and so gain the two days it would have taken us to go by the Oak Flat road and reach the sluice for the ditch, which was still at least a league lower than the place where we wanted to go prospecting. For the rest, my companions, knowing nothing of the terrain, gave me carte blanche in this regard.

I decided to try to enter the valley at the same place where I had left it in autumn, while avoiding, to be sure, the mountain which I had climbed to the south of Pilot Hill, well knowing that our animals could not cross it. All day we went up the hill bordering Bull Creek, profiting from an Indian path known to me, which led us up beyond the source of this creek; in the evening we camped in a natural meadow, a sort of lake half filled and dried, where thousands of frogs were playing and croaking and where I could have killed as many ducks as I might have wanted. I fired one shot, five fell from it; there were only four of us to eat them, and everyone was of the opinion that we should stop there, for our animals and we ourselves were already sufficiently laden. The next morning, after two hours' walking in the same direction as the day before, we turned to the left in order to profit from a ridge which seemed slightly wooded, and which promised to take us in the right direction, for it seemed to bring us behind the chain of mountains of which Pilot Hill was the principal peak. In fact, this path was passably easy until two o'clock in the afternoon; but, at that time the rocks which abruptly ended this ridge stopped us short, I foresaw the time when we would have to retrace our steps; we had arrived at the confluence of two deeply cut creeks which the ridge separated, and we were still far from the river. We therefore had to cross one of the two creeks, but which? It wasn't until after three hours of marches and counter-marches that we decided to pass over the one on the left.

For about five hundred meters, the path was difficult; sometimes it presented such bad footing that all four of us were busy supporting the same animal. Nevertheless, we came out of it without accident; then, after having followed the bank of the creek long enough without experiencing any very great difficulties, we arrived near the bottom of the ridge which I had followed in the autumn; as night was near, we camped there.

Next day, we set out on our way early. The hill was easy but steep; we went down it in a zig-zag to the river, which was running then with a volume of water twenty times more considerable than in the month of November. We had to cut a pine to make a bridge which permitted us to transport our provisions to the other bank; after which, we swam the animals over. In spite of the time this work took, we were camped by three o'clock in the afternoon at the foot of the sugarloaf peak which, the autumn before, I had climbed to orient myself.

We agreed to set up camp there provisionally, and while two of us raised the tent, the other two looked for a claim where we could work the next day.

The following day, as soon as it was morning, we went to work, two with the pan and two at the cradle, the sole means of washing which we had available at the moment.

We made barely two dollars each. Doubtless, our means of washing were very imperfect; it was no less true, considering the quantity of earth to excavate and the shallowness of the paydirt, that there wasn't great profit to hope for there. Moreover, the water was lowering rapidly; the state of the banks showed us that; and the creek would be dry in less than a month. We resolved, consequently, to seek another, and in this search we lost a whole week without too much result.

Everywhere we found gold, but not in a sufficient quantity; moreover the river-banks themselves were what gave the best promise, but there was absolutely too much water; we had to wait. A creek flowing three miles farther down, on the sluice side, seemed to promise better than all the claims we had tried during the week. Nevertheless, before going to settle there and leaving the head of this valley without intending to return, we decided that two of us would go to find out if the terrain we were leaving continued to be auriferous on the high pine-flat, to the east, which I had noticed from the summit of Pilot Hill and, if so, they would spend some days in prospecting it. During this time, the two others would return to the sluice to see if there was still anyone there and, in case there was, if we could buy provisions there. The morning of the following day, Létang and I left with two days' supplies, going up the valley. The day was passed in walking and in testing little creeks here and there; before the end of the day, we had been able to convince ourselves that the pine-flat was not what I had thought at first: it was less a flat than a slightly inclined hillside, but which, from afar, seemed flattened. On reaching the crest we saw, on the other side, in the distance, a big river which seemed to us to flow toward the north; this could be, according to us, nothing but the Toualumné or one of its principal forks, which, a league farther on, having joined other branches, fell in a cascade into the valley, flowing to the west. Having determined this, as we still had a little daylight left, we retraced our steps as fast as we could and returned to the tent about ten o'clock at night. The two others, long since returned from the sluice, were in bed; they told us they had found people at the head of the ditch and, moreover, two companies of miners who were working a mile higher than the sluice. As for supplies, there were no means of procuring any. The next morning, early, we broke up camp and went to establish ourselves near the river, a little above the point where I had crossed in the fall. There, we were within reach both of the river where we proposed to work as soon as the water permitted us, and of the creek I spoke of earlier.

Having decided to spend the season in this new camp, we had to plan to settle there for a prolonged sojourn. We went to borrow a long saw from the workmen at the flume, who were quite willing to lend it to us, but only on Sunday, that is, while they were resting, for none of us knew exactly what day of the week it was, a thing, moreover, to which we were quite indifferent. They were pressed and had only that one saw; they were on their fourth day of work and, out of habit, rested on the seventh; we should therefore come to get the saw on the morning of the third day following.

We needed three days to get the saw-pit ready and to load it with three logs all prepared to be sawed; Létang, although not much of a carpenter, took charge of directing this preliminary work.

Sunday arrived, and before the sun had risen, Létang was on his log and I was below. I wasn't any kind of a carpenter, but the two others, after some fruitless attempts, had definitely excused themselves, and I alone had dared to try to help Létang, who, it is true, had promised to explain to me what there was to do. The logs were planed with the axe above and below, with guides for the saw traced in black lines, and everything was ready, there was nothing left but to saw.

Alas, it isn't an easy thing to follow a trade, for one who hasn't learned it! It took me incredible efforts of intelligence and also not a few muscular efforts to succeed in making the saw cut without being caught and especially to make it cut on the black line, and not beside it; but finally I succeeded. *Labor improbus omnia vincit*, appropriately I remembered this copy-book maxim.

In order to make as many boards as possible, we took little rest at noon; you needn't ask if I was soaking, but, by evening, we had three hundred square feet of boards. To be sure, it was impossible for me to work the next day: pain in the loins, pain in the side, and a stiff neck, kept me in my bed, and for all the gold the river contained I would not have wanted to begin again; my consolation was that Létang had as much of a pain in the side as I had.

But after all we had our boards, and by means of nails which the flume-men obligingly lent us, we could build a sluice. In a few days, we had made a canal which gave our installation the water necessary to wash conveniently the unsubmerged part of the river-bank.

We made three to five dollars each, according to whether we were washing the surface or the bottom of the earth on the flat; in a few weeks we exhausted this claim, which was only the steep river-bank.

The water lowered in the watercourse, but slowly. However, as the paydirt seemed to grow richer as we approached the river-bed, rather than seeking another place on the bank and moving our installation, we resolved to wait till the water had lowered, in order to turn the river aside and work the bed itself.

While waiting, we went, each one for himself, to work with the pan on the creek of such fair promise which we had discovered before leaving the head of the valley. Gold was found only here and there—it was, as the miner says, pocketed, so that the days were very unequal; here I would have several two-ounce days; there, right beside it, I would have to work very hard to make two dollars. We sometimes found nuggets big as beans, and when we stumbled into a good pocket, five or six buckets of dirt gave us one or two ounces of gold; but too often, under four feet of excavation, we reached smooth rock without any dirt to wash. As long as there was water in this creek, we worked there; then we started to turn the river aside in order to work the bed.

We had been living for three weeks on provisions which we had bought from six miners who had come to prospect in the environs and who, having found nothing to their taste, had unloaded themselves in order to return faster and more easily to Oak Flat. As these supplies were reaching their end, Thomas and I left with the animals to get a new load; it took us a full day, walking at a good rate, to reach Oak

Flat; the road was clear and easy, hardly any mountains, simply undulations of the terrain whose contours it followed when they could not be climbed.

The camp was much changed in the three years since I had seen it, it was now almost a city; the miners, very numerous in the area, came from three leagues around to get provisions there, and they elbowed each other in the streets. We were surprised to see so many people installed on these old claims which we had worked in our time and which we had disdained. However, they managed to live there more comfortably than we had done, because if we made wages of five to ten dollars, we had to spend from three to five to live and still we lived poorly; now they got off with fifty cents a day. On the other hand, a day's wage of two dollars was a very rare thing; many miners worked claims which produced only a dollar a day, and they still needed, for that, improved equipment unknown in our time, and then had to make use of mercury in order to extract all the gold the dirt contained. Therefore the set-up became more considerable, more costly, and consequently more difficult.

It was easy to foresee that before long the work of the mines would have to be abandoned to enterprises raised on shares, that is, to the capitalists; according to reports, they were being formed already on various sides.

It was no longer, in fact, like the first days, when one passed from one claim to another, taking the cream, so to speak, and leaving all the gold whose extraction would have cost too much time and trouble. Now, the crowds were such on the placers that it was becoming very difficult to find unoccupied claims.

The newcomers, who were innumerable, considered themselves very lucky if they could, by working hard, earn a little more than a living; that is what we other old miners could not resolve to do. The neighborhood of the camps and centers of population, where life was easy and distractions numerous, but where one had to be content with earning a dollar, to see half a dollar a day, had no attraction for us; we preferred to bury ourselves in the solitudes, to gain the mountains where one endured many privations, but where one still made a day's wages of four or five dollars.

After having rested a day, we left with six mules and our donkeys laden with provisions. The merchant consented to take care of the transport, on condition that we would help his muleteer, who accompanied us, to bring back the mules in three days; we were back at our camp the second day after, a little past noon.

Létang and Louis, during our absence, had bravely begun to dig the diversion ditch; they had made their plans so poorly that their ditch would have taken water to the river rather than from it. We had to begin the whole work over again; in spite of that, eight days later, we started to wash. The claim wasn't very rich, but having no excavation, for gold was found in the full depth of the earth (three feet), we washed every day and thus made twenty to thirty dollars each per week. This lasted all through the season, that is, until the twentieth of October. A little rain came during the last weeks, not enough to give water where there hadn't been any, but, from the natural resurgence of the springs, the water rose in the river; soon our ditch was not going to be able to hold it, it was going to chase us out of the river-bed, and we thought the time had come to settle for the winter. Our claim was not exahusted; we abandoned it to Louis, a Frenchman of Saintonge, and to two others of his compatriots, who had worked on the Oak Flat ditch all summer and who proposed to spend the winter in the valley. I would have made the same decision, if I had not had Marble Spring.

All the time that I had stayed in this valley, I had spent my Sundays, I mean to say my days of rest, in hunting; the hare, the partridge, the tufted quail abounded there, but the deer, the grouse and the pheasant were rare. Very rarely too I encountered the tracks of the bear and the wildcat, that terrible wildcat which had caused me so much emotion the preceding year. One ran the risk of meeting them in these parts, about as one risks meeting a wolf in the forest of the Ardennes.

It had happened too, when I had . . . some hares on the shelf, that I took a fancy to fishing, and great had been my surprise to see that this river, big as the Semois at Bouillon, contained no kind of fish whatsoever, not the least white-bait, not the smallest gudgeon. What was the cause of this phenomenon, which certainly seemed so much the stranger to me as in all the watercourses of California where I had fished, in the smallest as well as the greatest, I had until then found fish of all kinds in abundance? Doubtless the cascade downstream from the dam had at all times been an insurmountable obstacle for the fish, which abound in the Toualumné; a naturalist, in my place, would not have missed invoking this fact to prove that the watercourses are populated only by their communication with the sea; and Darwin, in his *Origin of Species*, would have been able to quote it to establish that fresh water fish are nothing but transmutations undergone by the inhabitants of salt water.

Before leaving the area, I wanted to visit the bottom of that cascade of which I knew only the upper part, where too many obstacles and dangers prevented the approach from above.

Debrai, the laborer on the ditch, wanted to accompany me. We left one day early in the morning, and followed the valley on the right bank of the river, keeping always fairly far from the stream in order to avoid the hills and the bends, and to take advantage of the flats; then, having come in sight of the Toualumné, we began to descend the hill which ended at that river, reached it a kilometer higher than its confluence with our watercourse and, turning to the left, descended it. There was no kind of a path, but, as the water was low, although its course was still rapid, we were able to follow the bank without too much difficulty. We arrived a little before noon at the confluence of the two rivers which, after their union, ran, urged on with great speed, between cliff-like rocky hills, like walls two or three thousand feet high, whose sides were battered by the river in the high-water season. The only thing we could do was to go up the course of our river to the foot of the falls; our progress, at first easy, became more and more difficult.

From time to time, enormous stones, veritable blocks of rock, six to ten feet high, barred our path; we had to go around them unless we found means of sliding ourselves under them. One can understand at the price of what hardship we succeeded in covering three to four kilometers in that fashion.

The slopes on both banks of the river, already very steep, drew together proportionately as we mounted; soon they seemed two almost vertical walls, which were separated by a trench a hundred and fifty feet wide and two thousand feet deep, the bottom of which was occupied by the river.

This river, which at its confluence with the Toualumné, carried a fairly large volume of water, and which still kept it for the distance of one or two kilometers upstream, afterward imperceptibly lost it, and the water began to be no longer seen except between the big blocks of stone with which the river-bed was scattered; finally, a little higher, it disappeared entirely. We were then walking in the dry river-bed, whose slope, which was increasing, was from eight to ten percent, and which consisted of a paving composed of enormous boulders irregularly placed, often fairly distant from one another, whose intervals were filled with smaller detached boulders, on which we walked and under which, very distinctly, we heard the water running with a monotonous roar; we walked with caution in order not to slip into the openings, yawning gulfs under our feet where the water, doubtless, filled the depths.

Here and there, occasional bushes clinging, at different heights, to the sides of the two rows of rock I mentioned, gave them rather the appearance of old walls in ruins.

We were advancing; these almost parallel walls approached each other, and soon, at their foot, there were only twenty meters between one and the other; the great height made them seem almost to touch at the top. We continued to advance in silence, and soon the dimness prevented us from seeing more than eighty or a hundred meters ahead of us; farther on, it was night. Some blocks, big as houses, suspended at different heights above the void and forming a vault pierced to the day at intervals, were the cause of this obscurity.

It was soon no more than a dark passage where sight penetrated with difficulty. Doubtless, these monstrous blocks, precipitated into this abyss, had encountered each other in their fall and, leaning one against another, had remained thus suspended in the void; or, perhaps composed in their upper portion of less soluble elements, had resisted the action of the water, which had dissolved and carried away their base. Some were suspended this way two hundred feet above the floor, others farther forward were lower, yet others, upstream, still higher; a colossal stairway which we were looking at from below. I noticed, among others, three enormous masses of granite, of which two, leaning against the walls of the crevasse, supported the third in the void; they seemed suspended above our heads in spite of the law of gravity, and held there by a supernatural force.

We went on almost below the vault they formed, in order to see beyond. As far as the eye could reach in the immense and somber passage, one saw these rocks suspended which, from the first leap of the falls to the bottom, doubtless formed a succession of steps, of which the uppermost must have been immediately below the bridge of tree trunks which joined the two banks of the abyss up above, and which we could not see from below.

A dull noise, continuous, loud enough to drown our voices and prevent us from speaking to each other, came out of this chaos and seemed as much to come from under our feet as from the immense crevasse which we had before us; the atmosphere was damp and misty. In the presence of this spectacle, the sublime horror of which nothing equals, we had remained with our eyes popping, our mouths hanging open, our ears straining, without speaking, without even looking at each other; when at last our glances met, Debrai had to admire the size of my eyes—as I admired the size of his. "I'm getting out," he said all at once, making a half-turn, "for, devil take me, I'm afraid; if there were the least shake, these rocks would fall and there we would be, buried more than a thousand feet deep." Saying that, he departed. As for me . . . I followed him. Miraud, who, for some time, had already been advancing only slowly, turning a worried ear to the noise he heard coming out from under his feet, and who, with a pitiful air, had remained seated on a stone, more than fifty paces from us, passing his time in following with his eyes the bats which were taking wing, frightened no doubt by our presence, Miraud, I say, seemed to feel a lively satisfaction in seeing us return toward him.

"Look," said Debrai, "your dog is more reasonable than we are, for one must be really crazy to go adventuring here, at the risk of remaining, and that in order to see the water fall, which, parenthetically, we have not seen."

"No matter," I replied, "I don't regret having come."—"I'll wait," he said to me, "to say as much, till I'm in a place where there's more security than here."

We went back down, considering what we had seen, and trying to see if the cliff didn't offer somewhere a ramp which might permit us to climb it and to reach the top; but we realized very quickly that that was possible only in a balloon; we were forced to continue to descend as far as the confluence of the two rivers and to go up the hill along the Toualumné. It seemed to me far to climb, much farther than it had seemed to me when descending it in the morning; night came while we were still climbing it; it was not until after we had walked on half an hour by the light of the moon that we arrived at last at the first flat, where we made a halt to spend the night.

We had not brought any supplies, expecting to return the same day; we had to be content, for our supper, with a crust and a little piece of cold meat, remains of our dinner, after which we lay down and tried to sleep. Setting off again on our way early the next day, we returned to the camp for breakfast with the others.

I returned with Thomas and Létang to Marble Spring. A disagreeable surprise awaited me there: six individuals were in the midst of working my claim. They had made a wagon road and brought the dirt in a cart to wash it near the spring, two hundred meters lower down. For two months they had been working this way; they had the right to do it: they had, by making the necessary outlay, found the means of utilizing the claim.

It was perfectly legal, but what was not was that they had thrown their tailings in the ditch which I would have to reopen in order to work when the water returned.

That gave me right there a hundred cartloads of stones to move. The day after my arrival I went, accompanied by two witnesses, to see these Gentlemen, and informed them that I had come back to begin my work when returning water would permit it, and called on them at the same time to reopen my ditch before that period, on pain, if they were late, of having to indemnify me: ten dollars per man and per day of delay. I left them a copy of this demand; in the said paper, I declared that our company was composed of six workmen.

This other company was managed by a man named Watson, who had with him his wife and children. His wife, the first whom I saw at Marble Spring, kept a boarding-house, that is, she gave meals to the miners of the area.

These Gentlemen did not seem too disposed to submit. For fear that they might sell the two mules and the carts they were using, and might leave Marble Spring, I went to register with the Sheriff of Coultersville the papers which I had had signed by Black and Schréder at the time of my departure, then I invited the Sheriff to come and seize everything these Gentlemen possessed, in order to have a guarantee in case, through their fault, my ditch might not be opened in time. I am sure that Watson had the firm intention of continuing to work as long as the water had not returned, then of leaving me there with my ditch filled; but, when he saw the Sheriff and the attachment put on everything he possessed, he was humanized. He sent one of his friends to find out if I wouldn't want to sell him my rights to this claim as well as all the apparatus which served me to work it and which was stored in my cabin.

On reflection, and better appreciating the value of this claim, I accepted the proposal.

By this sale, I recovered a part of the outlay made with Louvel, and this was no small thing. The work that Watson had done had allowed me to determine that the claim was far from being what we had judged it to be. The paydirt diminished greatly in extent and depth as it went up the creek and, by an extraordinary chance, our sample shaft marked just the limit of the good dirt.

It was easy to see from the shafts that Watson had dug there that the claim was drawing to an end, but not having explored the claim lower down, he could not perceive it; otherwise, he would certainly have reopened my ditch and gone away. He expected, on the contrary, to have paydirt for a long time and to get gold when the water had returned; for with the carts, as there were six of them working, they hardly made wages of two dollars a day each.

As soon as the bargain was concluded, they paid me a pound and a quarter of gold (20 ounces), then, stopping work, they reopened the ditch and waited for the rain.

As for us, we went back to the branch of Bull Creek where we had left Moquet, Payen and Colson. They, having no more water shortly after our departure in the spring, instead of coming to rejoin us, had left for the lower Merced.

We cut down some trees, and built a cabin from them; we had Rivet bring us some supplies in almost sufficient quantity to spend the winter, then we waited until the water deigned to return. But then Létang found it worth while to leave us to hire out as carpenter at the quartz mill at Marble Spring. It had been, however, implicitly agreed among the three of us that we would stay together all winter, because I would not have wanted, unless we were three, to settle there to undertake the difficult work there was to be done; not counting that, if there were only two of us, when one had to be absent, as happened frequently, the other would be left alone, which was not without inconvenience in the isolation in which we found ourselves. When it had been a question of forming our partnership, my Norman had not said yes or no: without our knowledge, he had taken steps to enter the quartz mill, reserving the right, according to whether he succeeded or failed, to accept or reject our proposition, and, while waiting, he had moved in with us again.

We had just begun a ditch to divert a part of the water which the next crest of the river would naturally bring; we therefore had in prospect three or four weeks of work during which we would consume much and would earn nothing: Létang had judged that this was the moment to withdraw. One fine morning, after breakfast, he rolled his effects in his blanket and there he was, ready to leave.

We did not judge it appropriate, Thomas and I, to protest against this procedure, preferring to recognize his right to profit by the chance he thought he had found to improve his position.

His share of the provisions was paid to him and his place in the cabin which he had helped to build was reserved to him, in case it pleased him to return.

He left.

Eight or ten days later the water returned.

We went to work; it paid fairly well. But the enormous stones for the two of us to remove, the trees on our claim to uproot and roll aside, the equipment too heavy to transfer—all that discouraged Thomas, who found that at his age (he was fifty) it was impossible to continue this work. He loaded his donkey and left.

This departure left me alone with a storehouse full of provisions. We had bought back Létang's share, I had had to buy back that of Thomas, so I had for myself alone almost two thousand francs worth of supplies; I was at least without worry on that score. What saddened me in advance, was the thought that I was going to spend five months absolutely alone, in a remote spot, a real solitude where the nearest neighbor was three miles away. I had stayed alone at Marble Spring too, but that was in summer, and still I had found the time long. Now, I was going to suffer, besides boredom and isolation, the torture of confinement, for one hardly leaves his house in the winter in California. But what could be done about it? I had to resign myself. Happily, I had water, I could work, and nothing makes the time pass better.

Soon after, several days of rain put too much water in the creek and completely inundated my works; and the diversion ditch was not finished, I had to wait until the water had lowered to get back on the job. While waiting, I labored on the ditch between floods, but as soon as it was possible, I eagerly returned to the search for the precious metal; I succeeded in making fairly good wages. Whenever the water came anew to interrupt this occupation, which happened too often, I returned to the ditch, already half finished.

Every week, I went down to the camp on Bull Creek to buy the Sunday stew-beef from the Swiss; I was afraid that satiety would disgust me with deer and hare, which I never lacked; as far as grouse and pheasant are concerned, I think that I would have been able to eat them perpetually without ever tiring of them, but as these birds, in winter, no longer descended from the trees, they became more rare in my casa.

The earth was covered with snow, which lasted fairly long and chilled the temperature; frost followed. As it was difficult to work under these conditions, I spent my time in hunting.

One day I came upon the track of a wild beast in which I thought I recognized a near relative of the terrible cat which had caused me so much disquiet.

However, the print was much too big to be that of a wildcat! It could as well be that of a panther or a California lion, that lion without a mane and of medium size, which although less redoubtable than its African cousin, is none the less provided with claws and teeth.[1] The print was fairly recent, for it was not covered although it had snowed the night before.

Miraud, whom I had called for consultation, put his nose to this print, reflected a bit and seemed disposed to follow the scent, but I held him back.

I was almost at the top of a hill; the tracks headed toward a group of rocks which were ahead of me. The snow permitted me to see the direction well enough, the bushes at that place being scattered; as I advanced toward these rocks in order to see the hillside better, well before arriving I heard, in front of me, a rustling of leaves; I quickly shouldered my gun, but at the same moment I saw, already far from me, a panther which was descending the hill with the rapidity of a bird in flight; I raised my gun again and took a breath.

A panther makes a fine shot, and that one was truly a superb beast; I admit however that I was not annoyed by the dénouement of the adventure. Miraud seemed to share my appreciation, for he did not try to follow the beast.

It descended the hill and began to climb the opposite side with the same rapidity, then having reached the top, stopped and began to look attentively at me. Was it going to change its mind? happily it did nothing. At the end of a few seconds, which seemed hours to me, it left at a trot and disappeared behind the hill. I continued to advance, and at the end of eighty meters, I found its lair established under a rock, where it was dry. It was a sort of enormous nest, and I judged that it was in the habit of staying there, on noticing the prints left by its muddy feet one day when it had rained; for more than ten days, in fact, the snow had covered the ground, and these prints were therefore already fairly old. I

1. See Maurice G. Hornocker, "Mountain Lion" in Lamar, ed., *Reader's Encyclopedia of the American West*, pp. 777–79.

returned to the cabin, well satisfied that my imprudence had not had a distressing result.

Moore, the hunter, had assured me that there were two panthers in the environs of Pilot Hill, that he had seen them and that they had fled before him. That was of a nature to reassure me, doubtless; in spite of this, I did not depend on it, for I was persuaded that when an animal of that strength cedes the game to a creature as puny as man, it is pure condescension on its part, and thereafter I went to hunt elsewhere than around its nest.

Three days later, having gone to the camp to get my supplies, I told my adventure to a man named Carter, the cleverest rifle shot that I had ever seen; he begged me to lead him to the beast's lair, saying that he would try to kill it; it was agreed. The next day, Carter, with two others, arrived at my casa and all four of us left in search of the panther, taking the necessary precautions. My three companions posted themselves on the path I had seen it take, while I headed, like the first time, for the rocks where it had its retreat: by degrees as I approached, I felt my apprehensions rising again . . . if the panther is in the lair, will it flee this time? if it does not flee, I will shoot, but if I miss . . . I did not feel strong enough, after all, to strangle a panther with my hands. I went close to the nest, then I sent Miraud . . . it was not there; my footprints and those of the beast, in spite of a little fallen snow, were still visible.

I was able to explain to my companions which way it had fled and where it had stopped.

As it was beginning to rain, we separated, planning to meet in three days. Rain, not heavy but continual, fell during these three days; it was still raining when Carter, prompt at the rendezvous, presented himself at my cabin, this time with three companions. Three placed themselves on the presumed passageway of the beast; accompanied by the other hunter, I went, as the first time, to start it again from its lair. I now had more assurance; on my observation that I was alone to face a possible attack by the animal, Carter had given me this companion, and, this time, there were two of us!

The rain had melted the snow, and we could not see the panther's tracks; but when we came to a hundred meters from the lair, we saw it suddenly start and descend the hill, following exactly the path which it had taken the first time. Like the first time too, it stopped on the other hill; at the same instant, three shots echoed; the panther, in a few bounds, reached the summit of the hill and disappeared.

On going to verify the shots, we found, forty meters from the place where it had stopped, some traces of blood; farther on, the blood was even more abundant. But then it had entered some brush too thick to permit us to walk ahead and see each other; we had to consider it as being at home and so renounce the pursuit. We returned to verify the shots; it had been shot at sixty paces; it had, it seemed to me, climbed farther up the hill, before stopping, than the first time. Two balls must have reached it, for only one could be found; Carter affirmed that he had hit it, the two others affirmed nothing, it only seemed to them that they had aimed well. What was sure, was that the beast had not stayed on the spot, and it was a hazardous enterprise to go and start it again from its refuge, if it was only wounded; but Carter swore by Nimrod that it was dead and insisted so strongly that we go in search of it, that we decided to accord him that satisfaction. We separated into two troops which made, each on its own account, the tour of the bushes forming a thicket of about two hectares, and we thus assured ourselves that our wounded one was no longer there; we were not slow to come upon the traces of blood which indicated the passage by which it had left; we joined forces again and followed these tracks, walking cautiously. At the end of three or four hundred meters, we found it dead and already cold; on examination, the three balls had hit it, one, probably Carter's had gone through the sides without tearing them, another had traversed the flanks, and the third, aimed too low, had taken some skin off the chest. It was not as big as it had seemed to me when alive; however, it was almost four feet from the eye to the base of the tail, which was almost three feet long and of the same thickness from one end to the other. The pelt, of a uniform reddish tawny color, was not beautiful; Carter skinned it on the spot. It was a female, pregnant with three little ones.

These gentlemen insisted that I return with them to the camp, in order to celebrate the victory. We arrived at Bull Creek drenched to the bone; after having dried ourselves as best we could, and having had a proper spree, we presented Carter with the skin, on condition that he pay the score. I returned home very late in the evening, stumbling somewhat and again well soaked, for the rain did not stop falling.

This rain on the snow had made all the watercourses overflow, so that, for almost eight days, it was impossible for me to work, except in spurts, on my ditch.

Some three or four weeks later, one evening, returning from the hunt, I found, leaning against my door, a pick, a shovel, and a rolled and tied blanket; I entered and prepared supper for two, being sure that the proprietor of these three objects would not be slow to come, and that I could not dispense with giving him food and shelter.

In fact, soon afterward I saw Margraff appear in person, the former shipboard companion whom I have already presented to the reader; he came, he said, to wish me good day on the part of Mr. Thomas, whom he had just seen at Mariposa.

Then, taking a somewhat solemn tone, he addressed me approximately as follows: "Thomas, in his recital, aroused in me a philanthropical emotion; he avowed to me that he was still sorry to have been forced to leave you, to have, so to speak, abandoned you; for he left you alone in the midst of the desert.

"You, great heart that you are, did not permit him to take his share of the tribulations that overwhelmed your company; in calamities, you forget yourself and think only of others. You have saved him by permitting him to go back to an inhabited land, and that without any sacrifice on his part, for you insisted on reimbursing him, as the two of you had done to Létang, for his quota of the expenses paid, which he offered to abandon to you, in order to compensate, if possible, for the annoyance which he was forced to cause you; yes, this recital moved me, and I said to myself: I will go and find Perlot, I will go to sweeten with my presence the bitterness of his isolation; he, who always sacrifices himself for others, will learn, by this act, that he is not alone in feeling these good sentiments. Having said that, I started on my way, and here I am."

Thus spoke Margraff. He continued:

"Thomas told me that your cabin was big, that you were provided and somewhat encumbered with a mass of supplies, but I can assure you that this did not turn me from my resolution."

So Margraff came to see me out of pure charity, in order not to leave me alone, and to help me use up my provisions. I found that very admirable and I asked Margraff how much all these advantages were going to cost me. "Oh!" he said, "the best part of the story is that this will cost you nothing at all; I will eat your provisions, I will work with you, and I will do the cooking for the two of us, because I know that you don't like to do it, and all that at my expense; at my expense too, I will use your claim, on the sole condition that you will give me half of the gold which we find, for, otherwise, I could not pay you either for half of your claim, which you can value as you want, or for half of your provisions, which we will inventory tomorrow, or for half of your equipment, which I have seen just now, or for half of your cabin, which I am going to live in, for I come here because you are here, and you can see all I possess: a blanket, a pick and a shovel, which I have no desire to sell you. I have just drunk up my last sou as I went by Schréder's, because I thought that it would be useless to me here and because I don't like to keep any unproductive capital; I needed a drop to comfort me and to strengthen my legs. I also had to show my gratitude to Nicolas (the Swiss), for the information he gave me, thanks to which I was able to find you."

Margraff came from the lower Merced, where he had spent the summer. He formed a part, himself one-fifteenth, of a company which employed thirty day-laborers; instead of making money, they had spent it; moreover, the manager had run off with the strongbox before paying the workmen. He had been followed, found, arrested, judged, and hanged; but as the strong-box, also found, was empty, his fourteen partners were condemned to pay the laborers. Margraff had had, for a month, to work by the day in order to have the necessary gold to pay his quota; after having paid, he had ten dollars left, which he had eaten and especially drunk while coming to find me.

For Margraff, while remaining the finest man in the world, was a frank drinker, although he was not a drunkard: I mean that he was very rarely intoxicated in spite of the considerable number of little glasses that he drank on occasion. He was a former military man; he had served in the artillery; having reached the rank of lieutenant, he had renounced it to go to Africa, lieutenants, it seems, not being able to go except on that condition. He had promptly regained his rank on the fields of battle, then, surfeited with military glory, had turned in his resignation and obtained a concession in Algeria. But at the news that gold mines had been discovered in California, he had sold that concession and had come to Paris to ask the advice of his brother-in-law, representative of the Lower Rhine at the Constituent Assembly. Finally, he had hired out as working standard-bearer in the company of La Fortune and, as I said in the proper place, had made the crossing with us.

Like me and the majority of the other partners, he had come to the placers shortly after our debarkation at Monterey, seeking gold and, when he had found it, hurrying to spend it, for it was the spirit of adventure which pushed him even more than the desire of making a fortune; fortune, according to him, had to be waited for and not run after.

And then, having faith in his splendid destiny, he scarcely worried about the future: he was the son of the doctor and chemist Margraff, younger brother and regal brother of the grand duke of Baden, who, on the fall of Napoleon, had established himself in France, near Strasbourg, all his wealth having been confiscated by his said brother, reinstated in his grand duchy by the Holy Alliance. That is what Margraff recounted, he who came to help me consume my provisions. He calculated that some day or other a new revolution would inevitably return to him all that a revolution had taken from him: he would ascend the throne of his fathers and would enter again into possession of his goods. Now, that represented a large sum; what was the use, until then, of hoarding? and that is why all the gold that he could gain was promptly and conscientiously spent.

In the agreement entered into between us, as it was necessary to foresee the possibility that we might consume all my provisions without finding gold, it had been stipulated that I would have as guarantee of my debt, with interest added, a mortgage on all his confiscated wealth in the Grand Duchy of Baden. Thus having full security and especially seduced by the promise he made me of receiving me as an intimate—and without making me feel too much the distance separating us—in the grand-ducal palace, when he was reinstated there, in consideration also of the fact that we had always been good friends, I could not hesitate an instant to accept him as partner.

While awaiting this restoration, inevitable according to him, we went to work digging hard each time the weather permitted it, and succeeded in finishing the ditch, which was a great help to us because after each rain we diverted the excess water the river contained, and so were able to continue working. This work was passably productive, although it was not sufficiently so to realize my dream of fortune; for I, who had not the prospect of ascending a throne, I would have liked to become rich, inasmuch as I had come to California only for that.

From time to time, companies of four, five, or six miners came to prospect in the area, then returned, and a few days later, came back to settle, so that by spring a large part of the creek was occupied.

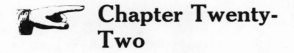 # Chapter Twenty-Two

Opening the Way to Yosemite, 1857

About the month of March, I received a letter from San Francisco, by a person unknown to me who signed himself: A friend of Mr. Huguet.

Huguet, a former hatter in Paris, was one of my shipboard friends and I had remained on terms of intimacy with him. On his arrival in California he, with two others from our ship, had hired out as a farmer near Monterey, but distaste for his new trade had promptly overcome him; he had quitted it and had come to the placers, where fortune had rarely smiled on him, for he was no more miner by vocation than he was farmer. As there could be no question of making hats there, he had become a cook, and it was in that capacity that he had gone to work for a man named Coulter, who kept a hotel on Maxwell Creek; around this hotel had risen a camp destined to become a city, which had taken from him the name of Coultersville.[1] Coulter having sold his establishment, Huguet had renounced the culinary art and had set himself up as a butcher; he returned to San Francisco, on business, at a moment when a stock company was being organized there with the intention of claiming the falls of the Merced in the valley of the Yausémiti, and of laying out, if possible, a road where mules and horses could go.

The dragoons, four years before, had gone to dislodge the Indians settled in this valley of Yausémite; moreover, prospecting miners had seen it from a distance: miners and dragoons had told everywhere of its marvels. Some tourists had gone there, had admired its beauties and had claimed them; on their return to San Francisco, they tried to form the company I mentioned. Now, I had told Huguet, two years before, that at the time of the famous expedition of the *Eight* to the upper Merced, returning alone from the camp of our friends the Indians, I had seen from afar the lower part of this valley, of which I could say nothing more, not having had the leisure to penetrate it; but if I did not know the famous falls, I at least knew the path which led to them and I was the man needed by the company to guide it and inform it. Thus reasoned Huguet and he had spoken in this sense to one of the

1. See chap. 14, n. 1, for a description of Coulterville.

292

organizers of the aforesaid company. The letter in question said that they counted on me to indicate the direction to take and path to follow in order to lose the least time possible, and that about the fifteenth or the twentieth of March, some members of the company would report to Marble Spring to confer with me.

Nicolas, who brought me this letter, informed me at the same time that the rumor was running around Coultersville that they were going to make a road to go to Yausémite, that they would build hotels, and that already a crowd of tourists was preparing to go there in the spring.

About the 15th of March, three gentlemen accompanied by a dozen workmen arrived, indeed, at Bull Creek; they had with them six mules loaded with supplies. Although they might have had, if they had wanted, fifty Indians to guide them to Yausémite, they came to find me and gave me a letter from Huguet which insistently begged me not to refuse my co-operation, because he had guaranteed that I would grant it; it was only a matter of indicating the route of the road to be built to reach the valley; for that I would have an indemnity of ten dollars a day, payable in free shares in the company. I decided to accept and, the next day, we set off on our way.

My three companions were supplied with a newly drawn-up map of the country, and drawn up in such fashion that a blank paper would have been preferable; however, two of them were, it seemed to me, expert cartographers, for, when I had shown them in my notebook the paths I had followed at the time of the expedition to the Indian camp, immediately, with red pencil, they corrected their map and indicated there the differences in level which I gave them—approximately, that goes without saying. These corrections made, I had them make a mark where I supposed that the falls would be found.

We first went up Bull Creek, taking advantage of an Indian path which we had followed, Thomas, Louis, Létang, and I, at the time of our departure for the valley of the flume.

We followed it as far as the lake of frogs and ducks; there, we turned to the right; with an axe, I blazed a mark on the trees along my route; behind me the workmen, with pick and shovel, smoothed and enlarged the path which I marked this way, so as to open an easy passage to the mules which carried our supplies. Ten Indians, who accompanied us and thought they were helping us a great deal because they indulged in a great deal of movement, ran ahead and returned to warn me of the kind of terrain we had before us. We had to trace an easy path, however long it might be; for this, it was necessary to avoid, as much as possible, crossing the watercourses and consequently the hills, which ordinarily were difficult to descend and to climb. So, once arrived on the summit of the ridges drained by the Merced, we stayed on them almost constantly, making use of the flats where the tributary creeks had their source.

The greatest difficulty was to descend the hill which bordered the valley in question; of the fifteen days' work which the road demanded, we spent eight on this hill, which was hardly two kilometers in a straight line; our road going down it was at least five. Each day, the curious came on horseback from one camp or another, impatient to see where we were in our work, in order to be among those who were the first to enter the valley on horseback; one would have said, seeing the excitement caused by our enterprise, that it was a matter of solving some of those great problems which stir the world, such as reaching the North Pole.

Four days before the completion of the job, we let it be known that on such a day at such an hour we would leave Bull Creek to inaugurate the road.

On the eve of the day indicated, from all sides there came men mounted on horses, mules, or donkeys, others on foot, all with beasts of burden and provisions; there were a good hundred and fifty, of whom five were musicians with their instruments, a horn, two violins, a flute, and an accordion. In the morning, as soon as it was dawn, the horn sounded reveillé; an hour later, everyone had had breakfast, saddled his horse or his mule, loaded his donkey or packed his haversack, and was ready to leave.

It was a curious spectacle to see the camp moving, assembling, then forming in a long file on a narrow path, where two people could not pass at a time. We were to make a halt on a flat situated a little more than half way there, but the first had had time to get bored before the last had rejoined them, so that some were preparing for departure while others were unpacking for the rest period.

The head of the caravan reached the valley a little before the end of day and the tail arrived only well along in the evening. The best part was that no accident happened, nothing came to trouble the joy which animated this crowd.

They made during this single day the trip which we had taken three days to make when we had come to the valley the first time, guided by five Indians. This road which we had just followed was placed between that by which the Indians had guided us then and that by which I had returned alone and where, without my eagle, I would have died of hunger. These two last crossed at the top of the ridge which I had descended to the three abandoned Indian huts.

We happened therefore to enter the valley about a league higher than the Indian bridge on the Main Fork of the Merced and, I think, a half league higher than the place where we had encountered the Toualumnés, so that our road reached to the very end of the little valley, where we found the Indian camp three years before, though in the upper part. This camp no longer existed; the Indians were settled higher up, at the very entrance to the big valley, more than a kilometer from the point where the road came in.

The pack animals which carried the camping equipment and supplies walked in the lead; we were able, as soon as we arrived in the valley, to set up the tents, prepare the beds and busy ourselves with the supper, so that the last arrivals would only have to sit down at table, then go to bed.

Next day, early in the morning, we discussed, while breakfasting, the question of knowing who was going to guard the camp, for it was understood that we would cover on foot the whole length of the valley. Nobody wanted to stay; we were constrained to choose the guardians of the camp from among the Indians themselves; we chose five of them, of whom I knew three personally. After a great many promises of supplies, of shirts, and especially of brandy, I told them, taking them aside to make them understand that it was serious: "Wâlais, listen, you must be faithful, or let all the Nang-à beware! For if ever these people have any complaint against you, what will they do to your camp? and what will Scipiano say when he learns that his Nang-à are no longer Wâlais for us? We have promised you much, and if you are faithful guardians, you will have more yet." The Indians extended both their arms horizontally; it is their manner of taking an oath, and that meant that they would be responsible for everything on their own heads.

At the exit from the valley, the river has a slope of five to seven per cent, which probably continues for some distance; it is too rapid, even when it makes a detour, to have any flats.

As far as the eye could reach, it resembled a canal whose banks, two thousand feet high and of a sixty degree inclination, were joined almost at the bottom without leaving the narrowest ledge along the water.

Immediately after breakfast, we were on the march, having at our head our five musicians, who tried with much vigor and more or less success to perform *God save the Queen*. For the distance of almost five hundred meters, the path crossed, in almost a straight line, the meadow which ended at the new Indian camp. At this last point, the marvels of the valley began. It narrowed suddenly; it was then four or five hundred meters wide and the river wound slowly through it without ever approaching near enough to the sides to prevent one's passage. The two sides, at first slightly inclined, closed in little by little and, at the height of six hundred meters, formed two absolutely vertical walls. Stationed at the entrance and at the valley's center, one could believe that one had before him the boulevards of Paris seen through a magnifying glass, in a way to make the houses seem two thousand feet high.

To the right and to the left, there rose two enormous semi-circular towers a hundred to a hundred and twenty meters in diameter, surmounted by a dome or platform of turf on which rose huge trees.[2] Two thousand feet high, fifteen hundred feet distant from each other, one would have called it the entrance gate of a city built and inhabited by giants. At the distance of six hundred meters, we already had to raise our heads to look at the domes; they were not simply perpendicular, for they hung over the valley, so that the rain-water running from the turf of the dome fell fifteen or twenty feet from the base. At the angle formed downstream from the tower by the thrust of the one before us, there fell a cascade eighteen hundred feet high. During the first third of its fall, the cascade formed a cylinder like the water from a full vase which one inclines; then, it was no more than an avalanche of whirlpools half water, half vapor, which now plunged downward, now seemed

2. The "domes" of Yosemite are described in Whitney, *Yosemite Guide-Book*, pp. 59–60. Among the famous domes in Yosemite are the Washington Column, the Royal Arches, the North Dome, and Half Dome.

suspended in the air, and finally reached earth in a fine, brisk rain.[3] The water fell on a sort of meadow with uneven grass, which sloped to the river; but it was only at a hundred meters from the fall that it formed a stream a dozen feet wide.

By degrees as we approached, the towers seemed higher to us. An eagle, probably within sight, but which we had not seen until then, left the dome of the one ahead of us and, after having planed and turned above the valley, alighted on the dome of the tower opposite. During his flight, he seemed to be in the region of the clouds and nevertheless we saw him beat his wings, as a bird does when it climbs, to reach the height of the grassy platform.

The inhabitants of the Indian camp, numbering perhaps a hundred, themselves appeared to marvel, not at the beauties of their valley, but at the spectacle which we offered them. All standing, big and little, men and women, ranged in line, immobile as statues, their eyes wide open and their jaws hanging, they contemplated us! An anchorite contemplating the glories of Paradise, would not fall, I think, into a more profound ecstasy. Although they were on our path, they let us come without making the least movement, so that our musicians, who were walking at the head, bumped into them; they had to push to open a passage for themselves.

From that moment and as far as the top of the valley, the Indians followed or rather accompanied the musicians on the right and on the left, in order to lose sight of neither men nor instruments; they flanked them, stumbling, climbing over each other, falling, getting up, then running to regain their post, without an instant's interruption of their profoundly attentive and imperturbably serious contemplation of the objects of their admiration.

If what we were experiencing ourselves at sight of this astonishing valley did not make us stumble, it had at least tired our eyes and heads; on reaching the foot of the tower, we all had stiff necks. However, we were not at the end.

From the other side of the river, there was also a waterfall which the jutting mass of the tower had hidden from us until then; it was not as high as the first, but twice as big a volume of water flowed there; a deep crevasse, a steep slope, brought this water to a point about five hundred feet above the valley.

It was only at this moment that we could enjoy completely the view of the valley properly speaking, which the tower had hidden from us until then.

I then understood how I had come, three years before, as far as the Indian camp without even dreaming that this existed: it was because this same tower, at the foot of which we found ourselves, hides the view from those who look either from the lower part of the first valley, or from the mountain which one descends to reach this one; it breaks the direct line and divides, after a fashion, the valley in two, letting one see only the lower part. Whatever it might be, from this point, the prospect was

---

3. Here Perlot is referring to Bridalveil Falls, which Whitney states is "unquestionably one of the most beautiful objects in the Yosemite. It is formed by the creek of the same name, which rises a few miles east of Empire Camp, runs through the meadows at Westfall's, and is finally precipitated over the cliffs, on the west side of Cathedral Rock, into the Yosemite, in one leap of 630 feet perpendicular." See ibid., p. 55.

splendid; the valley extended almost out of sight and seemed to end at such a distance that the top of the cliff appeared to merge with the bottom of the valley.

From distance to distance, towers similar to these and almost as high detached themselves from the line of the walls and seemed to do duty as buttresses destined to solidify and contain it. Before or behind these towers, there fell a cascade more or less high pouring more or less water into the valley.

We were walking without being too conscious of the distance we were covering, when our march was interrupted by a mass of débris which seemed to come from a recently collapsed tower; however, the Indians, whom I consulted on this subject, could not tell me when the collapse had taken place. The river, in its wanderings, came to touch it, and we had to cross over it. It was not without trouble that we got ourselves out of this mass of disordered fragments which covered a space a hundred meters in length. The obstacle overcome, we enjoyed the view of the valley's great cataract, whose dull sound, in spite of the distance, already drowned out our voices to the point where it was difficult for us to hear each other. On our left, about four hundred meters away, or a third of the distance which separated us from the head of the valley, the Merced threw itself from such a height that it seemed to fall from the clouds.[4] Imposing spectacle! we were overwhelmed, fascinated, motionless; we remained some time as in an ecstasy, and the Indians, at whom we had laughed so much in the morning, could have taken their revenge, if Indians laughed.

At last we set off again, desirous of seeing the marvel from nearby. We went the whole way gaping at the waterfall; we stumbled, we fell on each other, we got up and continued on our way without paying any attention to our neighbors, with our eyes always fixed on the same object—absolutely like the Indians.

The cataract is composed of two cascades.

On our left, as we climbed, the wall of the valley, beginning at a height of three hundred feet, recedes and slopes by degrees, while the base remains perpendicular; then, the upper part returns to a right angle to form with the lower part, as before, the wall of the valley. It is in the recess formed by this offset and this projection of the upper part of the wall, that the cascade is found, and it is from the very top of the projection of the wall that the Merced is launched. The water, precipitated into the void from the height of two thousand two hundred feet, falls at first into an immense basin which has been, without doubt, worn into the lower part of the wall of which I have spoken, then from this basin, through several outlets worn in the wall, it falls again into the valley from a height of two to three hundred feet.

We stayed a hundred meters from the cataract in order better to encompass it in our sight; we could not hear each other except by speaking into the ear and shouting very loudly.

The water, in its first fall, forms at the beginning a cylinder of two or three hundred meters, then divides into great whirlpools, which resolve into a multitude

4. The most famous of the falls is nicely described in ibid., pp. 57–58, in which Whitney declares that Yosemite Falls, "if not the most stupendous," is "at least the most attractive feature of the Yosemite."

of white balloons animated by a rapid gyratory movement which tends to make them rise again; but as soon as they touch the column of falling water, they are carried away, tearing themselves to shreds and ending by forming a mass with the immense whirlpool of foam and white vapor which is perpetually raised above the intermediate basin.

From this vast receptacle, the water escapes through several outlets or canals ten to fifteen meters long, then launches itself anew into space, all white with foam, and is not slow to disappear in a cloud of vapors which rises from the bottom of the valley, similar to that which floats above the upper basin. Thousands and thousands of rainbows color it with tints at once dazzling and harmonious, which give it the aspect of a rose, but of a rose of immeasurable dimensions. From the bottom of this cloud comes the Merced, four to five feet deep, sixty feet wide; it runs rapidly for a hundred meters, then slows down and flows lazily, describing capricious meanders in the valley.

We would have wanted to cross the river to continue our exploration as far as the end of the valley, but we did not find near the water a tree tall enough to serve as bridge if made to fall across the river; and there could be no question of swimming across it: its waters were colder than those of Cydnus; that is at least what we were assured by the savants of the expedition, although they had never bathed in the Cydnus, and had never seen it.

What excited our curiosity, was a small river which joined the Merced and whose course we would have wanted to trace, in order to know how it penetrated into the valley.[5] From the point where we were, the two walls of the valley, without decreasing in height in any way, seemed to approach each other suddenly and to leave between them nothing but a sort of narrow gorge which doubtless gave passage to the river in question. The Indians, whom I consulted, declared to me that there was no more valley there, no more cascade, that it was *oxh-otto-è-nètte*, that is to say, "bad, abandoned, punished, fallen." I concluded from that that the valley actually ended in a crevasse more or less deep, more or less long, and that the small watercourse which intrigued us penetrated it from this opening.

At the end of an hour during which we remained in contemplation before the cataract and although we had kept ourselves at a respectful distance, we were soaked as if we had been exposed for a whole day to a pounding rain. It was because we were still too close to it; unless one withdrew to a great distance, one was enveloped in a fog thick enough to cut out the sight of the sun, although there was not a cloud in the sky; one saw even the nearest objects only confusedly; one felt his clothes becoming heavy and one did not see the rain, so fine and penetrating it was. As, moreover, our eyes were sated with the spectacle, we took the path back to the camp to prepare our dinner and dry our clothes. But the Indians, themselves, who had not paid the least attention in the world to the waterfall, had not tired an

5. Ibid., pp. 61ff.

instant of watching our musicians and the strange objects which produced so agreeable a noise.

We were crossing again, not without difficulty, over that mass of débris which had already stopped us in the morning when, approaching me, they said to me: "Walai, Sôlème-à-doum-doum (Friend, there is no more music)." I transmitted to the musicians the desire expressed by our friends the Indians; as soon as we were out of the bad passage, the musicians began to play some tune or other; but, o surprise! the accordion made no sound, the two violins only scratched: the water of the cataract had penetrated there too and put, momentarily at least, these instruments out of service; happily, we had the horn and the flute left, and we could regain the camp to the sounds of the *Marseillaise*.

The Indians charged with its guarding had faithfully accomplished their mission; they each received in recompense a shirt more or less new, and as much to eat as they wanted, and lord knows they were not sparing. The Indian, generally, is very temperate, but when one offers him something he likes, he gorges himself, then goes to bed and sleeps.

After dinner the scientific operations began. Our three gentlemen had brought the necessary instruments to measure heights, distances, etc. While one of them, a very good draughtsman, sketched the principal views of the valley, the other two, with the aid of the transit, triangulated and surveyed.[6]

For my part, to show my knowledge as well as for my personal satisfaction, and also to give myself the pleasure of demonstrating the uselessness of bringing so far so many very encumbering precision instruments, I set myself to taking heights, widths and distances, and I succeeded in it, I think, almost as well as they. While I was proceeding with my operations, I had more of the curious around me than the engineers and the draughtsman together. By means of plane-tables and the compass which the latter was willing to lend me, I constructed a right-angled triangle, like the half of a perfect square, cut diagonally; I had made this triangle as big as possible with the arms coming from a biscuit-box. Three nails driven halfway into the top of the three angles defined the triangle and served as sights; with the help of this instrument so constructed I could determine the point of the valley which would be touched by the diagonal of the square which would have the height of the waterfall for one of its sides; once this point was found, it was enough for me to measure the distance which separated it from the foot of the falls to have at the same stroke the height of the latter; the same for a rock, a tree, etc. Of course, to take the width of the river or else that of the valley, I used my instrument in the horizontal direction instead of holding it vertically; so, to determine the width of the river, I had only to trace a right angle of which one side crossed the river and the other followed the bank, then back up along the latter, until my diagonal reached the opposite shore, at the point where the other touched: I thus obtained the heights and

6. Perlot appears to be referring to Thomas Ayres, the artist, and two engineers.

the widths of the principal objects of the valley, with the exception of the great cataract. It would have been necessary to find, beginning at its foot, a length equal to its height; now, on one side the river, and on the other the fallen rocks of which I have spoken, prevented me from withdrawing to the desired distance, and moreover the foot itself of the cataract was inaccessible. We had to be contented with an approximate estimate, leaving to the engineers the trouble of doing better. According to us, there could be two thousand feet of débris at the foot of the waterfall; the hypotenuse of my triangle leaving the first of these points was still far from reaching the top of the cataract.

We estimated this difference at three hundred feet, which gave two thousand three hundred feet for the total height. We measured the horizontal distances by walking, the step being estimated at two and a half feet; it was always the same person who measured, and his step, verified several times, had seemed regular enough to us to make our calculations an adequate approximation.

The whole afternoon was employed by some in proceeding with these operations, by others in watching them done, by yet others in returning to gape at the cataract. A certain number, however, less curious or more fatigued, remained in their tents and slept while waiting for the others to finish measuring or looking.

Toward evening, a new caravan composed of about thirty miners arrived at the camp; as soon as their tents were set up, in spite of the advanced hour, they wanted to go and see the waterfall; the darkness soon forced them to return without having seen anything.

The next day, about half of our expedition—and I made a part of this half—took the road back to Bull Creek. The others wished to stay to begin looking and admiring again or to construct a raft which would carry them to the other side of the river.

As for me, on the evening of that same day, about nine o'clock, I was supping beside Margraff. It took me a good hour to recount to my partner, in detail, the marvels of the valley of Yausémite. When I had finished, he contented himself with saying that he did not believe that all that was worth the grand-ducal palace of Baden.

All the people from Mariposa, from Bear Valley, from Coultersville and from Oak Flat whom I had seen at Yausémite, while bringing me up to date on what was happening on their respective placers, had much weakened my faith in the future reserved for the gold-hunters, and for the first time in seven years, the idea was presented to my mind that perhaps, the moment would arrive when I should renounce digging fortune out of the earth with pick and shovel.

They had told me that everywhere, on the placers they knew, people were shoving and elbowing each other; everywhere there was a great number of people who did not find enough to pay for their labor, who did not earn enough, often, to pay for the supplies they consumed. They saw some, they said, who were working for a dollar a day. This gave me something to think about.

The moment that the price of the day's labor went down, it meant that the chances of finding gold were decreased. It therefore would soon be necessary to renounce the hope of becoming rich, whether suddenly by a happy find, a stroke of fortune, or in the long run by means of seeking and finding a claim where one could have good days for a long time. Now, it was this hope which had sustained me until then. How resign oneself to lead the miserable life of the placers, with no prospect other than that of not dying of hunger?

Under these conditions, the miner ceased to be a man pursuing fortune, and was no more than a laborer seeking work, and, in fact, almost everywhere he was already reduced to the condition of a mercenary.

Everything was changing on the placers; companies raised on shares exploited them on a large scale with the perfected procedures and equipment which science places at the service of big industry; from then on, in order to have gold, it would be necessary to begin by having much silver.

The isolated worker could not struggle against the capitalists, from the moment that they intervened. So he did not struggle; he conformed to circumstances and made himself, if his means permitted it, a shareholder; if he possessed only a hundred dollars, he bought a share, then hired out as a laborer, and so his capital worked with him. If, instead of one share, he could acquire ten, fifteen, or twenty, the dividends formed a considerable addition to his salary; it even happened, when the shares brought a good return, that he could live on his investments.

In that case, it was easy to find lands where life was more agreeable than in this one where we happened to be. To stay on the placers under such conditions, it was necessary to like to live in complete savagery or else to feel oneself incapable of getting along in a civilized country. Moreover, it seemed to me that I myself could turn my money to account without having recourse to a third party who too often would not succeed, and who sometimes would even abscond with the money which had been confided to him.

In this case, it is true, the police entered into it, and pursued him, but they did not always catch him, or reached him when he was no longer supplied with funds. The thief was hanged, but the victim was none the less ruined.

There reflections were bound to have their result.

While waiting, not wishing to run the risk, by keeping and burying the little gold I had, of finding it missing one day—for there were, in the last analysis, other thieves than the capitalists—I had decided to lend it on mortgages to a man named Wheeler, who paid me 2% a month interest, capital demandable every three months. So that you won't shout usury, so that you won't be too sorry for the fate of my borrower, I think that this Wheeler, when he didn't miss his shot—and he hardly ever missed it—made my money bring 4% a month. He had houses in San Francisco, in Stockton, in Coultersville, and had given me mortgages on all. He had indeed written me that he did not want to keep my money any more unless the interest was reduced to 1 ½% a month, being able, he said, to obtain all he neded at this rate; but I knew that at Mariposa, and Coultersville too, the rate was always maintained at 2, very often at 3%, and I turned a deaf ear to him.

Already, on my return from Yausémite, the water was not too much in our way, as our diversion ditch easily contained the excess which would have bothered us in the creek bed. We were working at our own speed and making our wages regularly; it was then that Létang left the quartz mill and returned to occupy the cabin with us, as it belonged partly to him.

He paid for his share of the ditch, his share of the provisions, and there we were again, three in the company. As long, almost, as the water lasted, we remained on the same claim.

About the tenth of May, Nicolas the butcher, knowing that we would soon be leaving, came to propose that we sell it to him with the cabin and equipment. He made the proposal because he knew a company of nine Chinese to whom he hoped to resell the whole outfit. Naturally, the butcher preferred this company of nine consumers who would eat only butcher's meat, to a company of three poor clients, like us, who fed themselves principally on game; as everybody gained by this sale, it was quickly concluded. The three of us left immediately with one of the butcher's horses, which we had included in the bargain, in order to have an animal to carry our supplies and our tools.

VII

HO! FOR OREGON
1857–1858

I concluded that Portland was nothing but a warehouse, a sort of terminus where outside commerce came to deposit the merchandise which was distributed throughout the country, and where, on the other hand, there flowed the products of Oregon to be exchanged against this merchandise; it was the double movement of commerce which made the importance of the place and gave it so much animation.

Jean-Nicolas Perlot
1857

Portland seemed old even when it was young, respectable when it was still crude.

Earl S. Pomeroy,
*The Pacific Slope: A
History of California,
Oregon, Washington, Idaho,
Utah and Nevada* (New York,
1965), p. 136

In the remaining chapters of his narrative Perlot is so articulate and so candid that few added explanations are needed to clarify the text. Similarly, because much of his account focuses on his career in Portland it becomes more the story of an immigrant's adjustment to an American city than one of wilderness exploration and adventure. Nevertheless it seems worthwhile to note that once he had settled in Portland, Perlot had to start from the bottom again, first as a woodcutter, then as a garden digger and worker in a pigsty, and only after that, did he achieve the status of a landscape gardener and nurseryman. In each of these jobs he discovered that he had to work for or please other people, a fact he found extremely difficult to accept after nearly seven years of being his own master in the Southern Mines. That a Belgian immigrant would voice the same sentiments that we would expect a Daniel Boone or a mountain man to express, again suggests that the impact of a frontier or wilderness experience is not unique to Americans but is universal.

During the initial period of personal adjustment and self-discovery that Perlot went through when he arrived in Portland, he was fortunate to have as his mentor and friend, Captain Alexander Ankeny, a Yankee sea captain turned businessman. Ankeny was perhaps the first person since the death of his own father for whom he had total respect and admiration. The way in which the shrewd, no-nonsense Yankee entrepreneur guided—and sometimes manipulated—the hard-working, rational Belgian ex-miner is one of the most amusing and heartwarming episodes in Perlot's entire life. The following chapters tell us much about the character of early Portland, but they reveal even more about the Americanization of Perlot and his rediscovery of the society of men and women.

Portland, the small town of 2,000 souls, 100 shops, and a thriving port, that Perlot saw in the summer of 1857, was, as he and many others observed, not so much a city as it was a vast warehouse where goods from the farms and settlements along the Columbia and Willamette rivers were deposited until they came to be transshipped to San Francisco. Although Portland was only twelve years old in 1857, having been founded in 1845 by two New England merchants, Amos L. Lovejoy of Massachusetts and Francis W. Pettygrove of Maine, the California gold rush provided such a fabulous market for the tiny port town that it was incorporated as a city in 1854.[1] Appropriately one of the first steamers to carry goods and passengers between San Francisco and Portland was named *The Gold Hunter*. At the same time, Portland served as the entrepôt for goods going up the Columbia to interior settlements and the Idaho mines.

By the time Perlot arrived the great merchant families of Portland—the Ainsworths, the Corbetts, the Failings, the Ladds, and the Reeds—were beginning to

1. A delightful brief portrait of Portland's early years may be found in Terence O'Donnell and Thomas Vaughan, *Portland: A Historical Sketch and Guide* (Portland: Oregon Historical Society, 1976), pp. 3–17.

amass fortunes, for the city was, in fact, the largest port and urban center on the Pacific Coast north of San Francisco.[2] Nevertheless, it remained a curious mixture of the virtuous, churchgoing New England town—for a majority of its merchants and settlers came from the American Northeast—and a frontier port city with saloons and brothels where heavy-booted miners and rough lumberjacks could be found.

As the following chapters demonstrate, Perlot, always energetic and restless, soon embraced the Yankee enterpreneurial spirit of Portland and eventually accumulated enough of a fortune to retire to his native Belgium at the age of forty-nine!

2. Ibid., p. 14; Arthur L. Throckmorton, *Oregon Argonauts: Merchant Adventurers on the Western Frontier* (Portland: Oregon Historical Society, 1961). pp. 124–244.

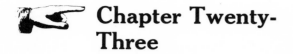

Chapter Twenty-Three

California Transformed

We left with the intention of going to revisit the valley of the flume which we had left the previous fall, and of trying to settle, for the season, on some claim on the river which had paid so well the year before.

On leaving Bull Creek, we passed by Marble Spring and I cast a last look on the claim which I had occupied with Louvel. Watson had not done much there; he had worked there during the winter as long as the water had lasted, then had completely abandoned it. A few isolated Chinese were scratching it, searching for the gold which, probably, was no longer there; they carried the dirt in sacks and went to wash it at the spring.

Without stopping any longer, we descended the creek as far as its confluence with the North Fork of the Merced. Having crossed this last watercourse, we followed a succession of flats bringing us to the Oak Flat ditch; we kept this direction all day, which we made a long one in order to reach, before night the next day, the point where we had left Louis the Saintongeois. It was night and we were still walking, when from afar we perceived a campfire. We approached it to spend the night near it; we found there two companies of six miners each, as many Germans as Americans, who having passed the winter in the valley of the flume and finding themselves without water, were going back near the camp of Sonora, to take up again their old diggings on the Calaveras River, where they hoped that the crest would soon come to permit them to begin again. We learned from them that almost two hundred miners had just spent the winter in the valley, that already there was hardly any water except in the river and that, for a great distance, this was occupied by a large number of miners, who were waiting for the water to lower even more so they could work.

They advised us not to go there, saying that we would have small chance of finding a free claim there. That gave us cause for reflection: by entering this valley on the Oak Flat road, we would, in case of failure, have to retrace our path to Oak Flat, then probably descend to the Toualumné and perhaps even cross it and go prospecting farther on. This required eight to ten days which would be expended in a complete loss. We made the decision to follow our German-Americans and, the next day, toward evening, we were crossing the Toualumné at Don Pedro Bar, where there was the ferry nearest Oak Flat.[1] We spent the night there. This river still flowed full to the banks; the miners were working on the highest flats and did not think they would be able to touch the riverbed before the fifteenth of August.

Early the next morning we left for Sonora, which we entered toward evening after a long day of forced march.

This camp was already a city; several streets had houses of brick, wood, iron, or adobe, in one and two stories.[2] Since morning, we had been traversing a thickly populated region; on all sides we saw villages, farms, gardens, cultivated fields, everywhere fruit trees and especially those which we knew: apple trees, pear trees, prune and cherry trees; beeves and cows were pasturing in the meadows; flocks of sheep covered the fallow lands; pigs wandered on the roads, and the cackling of hens was heard around the houses. We could not believe our eyes: were we in the land of the placers or in one of the rich cantons of Belgium?

The papers had been telling us clearly enough, and that for four years, that the immigrants were crowding from everywhere to California. The miners coming from the north whom we had happened to encounter, had spoken much of the transformations which were being accomplished on the Yuba, the Calaveras, and on the right bank of the Toualumné, where we were at that time; but we were far from expecting to find ourselves, on crossing the Toualumné, in complete civilization.

On seeing these milling, noisy streets of Sonora where a dense crowd of men, women, and children circulated in all directions, as in any European city, I could not get it into my head that I was only thirty leagues from Bull Creek; it seemed to me that I was coming out of a long dream, a seven years' dream, during which I had seen only Indians, rivers, precipitous mountains, sterile rocks, and brush.

After we had put our horse in the stable of the inn—pardon, of the hotel—

---

1. Don Pedro's Bar was actually named for a Frenchman, Pierre Sainsevain, an early California pioneer who came to the Southern Mines as early as July 1848. Located in Tuolumne County, it survived as a mining town until the 1860s. It is now under the waters of a reservoir. See Gudde, *California Gold Camps*, p. 98.

2. Sonora, one of the largest towns in the Southern Mines, was first settled in 1848 by Sonorans who had come to California after hearing of the discovery of gold at Coloma. From the outset, Sonora appears to have been a town rather than a camp, and boasted a population of 5,000 as early as 1849, although the number declined after that. "In the early part of 1849," writes Theodore Hittell, "the travel from Stockton to Sonora was so continuous, that the camp fires along the route were near enough together to show the traveler his way, even at night."

Sonora had more than its share of troubles: the foreign miners' tax of 1850 fell heavily on its largely non-American population (until it was moderated in 1853), and led to open conflict between French and Mexican miners on one side and Americans on the other; but the town survived. In 1851 Frank Marryat found "booths and barns lighted by chandeliers" that made the gold, "piled high on each monte table," glitter while both American and Mexican bands played for the miners.

When Sonora became the county seat of Tuolumne in 1850, Americans tried to change its name to Stewart, but, as Gudde notes, local pressure resulted in the return to the official name of Sonora. See Gudde, *California Place Names*, p. 317; Glasscock, *Golden Highway*, pp. 288–93; Hittell, *History of California*, 3: 125, 128, 262–64; and John Heckendorf and W. A. Wilson, *Miners' and Business Men's Directory* (Columbia, 1856), p. 35.

where we had stopped, after we had supped, quite amazed to have a meal which we had ordered, instead of making it ourselves, as we had had to do for so long, I went out to see the town; I took as much pleasure in it as if I had never seen one. However, I did not go very far; each step I took among the passersby, gave me the occasion to make an observation that was mortifying to my self-respect. I saw no one who had shoes as old and as broken as mine; everybody had finer trousers than mine; I was in a flannel shirt, and those whom I met were wearing a white shirt and a coat. My hat, in its time, had had its stiffening, but long since I had had to replace it by a false base; and those whom I met had well brushed and shining hats; mine shone too—from being greasy, alas!

In spite of that, I held out. For some time I continued to promenade while admiring the marvels which civilization had brought to Sonora, until at last I entered a billiard saloon; I came to the bar and ordered a cocktail (mixture of different liquors); I was standing then, waiting for them to serve me, when my glance, falling on a mirror of large dimensions, was arrested by a rather displeasing object, a mannequin, it seemed, put there expressly to amuse the customers; I thought I noticed that it imitated my motions. To make sure of the matter, I leaned on my left leg, then on my right leg—and I saw, not without surprise, that the object in question did exactly the same thing. No more doubt, the mannequin was I! I frightened myself; I represented negligence carried to its last extreme. I then recalled that I had spent four years without undressing to go to bed, without combing my hair, and without cutting either my hair or my beard or my nails; I certainly did not imagine that I could be very beautiful, but I did not think myself that hideous. However, the barkeeper (*le cafetier*), doubtless hardly enchanted to have such a customer in his establishment, surveyed me as if he wished to memorize my description, for I do not suppose that he dreamed of using my outfit as a model. After having composed the mixture which I had ordered, he pushed the glass toward me while keeping as far from me as possible, doubtless saying to himself, in an aside, "This mountebank must be over-run by vermin." He was mistaken, however; I was only negligent and untidy.

The next day, at three o'clock in the afternoon, in the same café, one could see, playing a game of billiards with two other individuals, a sort of Mirliflore [fop or dandy] who had just hung a new dress-hat on the coat-rack; he wore a silk shirt with an embroidered front, superb trousers whose bottoms were tucked into the legs of polished boots fresh from the hands of the cobbler; he had a well trimmed beard and his hair, combed, pomaded, shining, was cut in the style of the day.

The Mirliflore was I.

To be thus transformed had cost me two hundred and fifty francs! What I could not rejuvenate as easily as the rest of my person, was my arm; I had never had any great skill at billiards, although in Paris I had managed satisfactorily, but at Sonora I shot altogether badly, and it was rare that I succeeded in cannoning. It was not for lack of application; this study absorbed me so much that I did not see that a great number of curious people had made a circle around the billiard table and were watching us play. Several had passed and repassed before me while examining me attentively, although without distracting me from my play, when I heard Margraff say: "But you told a lie, it is he, you did not recognize him, that's all!" I turned and I saw Margraff surrounded by six or seven persons, whom I did not remember ever having seen. One of them detached himself from the group and came to offer me his hand, saying to me: "Well! Oualai, how goes it?" I took the hand which was offered me, and replied that the Oualai was well; then looking more attentively at my interlocutor, I recognized Serf, who had been on the first expedition from Marble Spring to the upper Merced. "My word," he said, "without Margraff, I would not have recognized you, nor would any of these gentlemen," and he indicated the other members of the group, who came immediately to shake my hand. They were, among others, three Germans who had also formed a part of the same expedition, but whose names I did not remember, except one named Wolfram, who had spent the summer on the same flat as we after the expedition in question.

Serf, a former ship's mate, was now a horse dealer at Sonora, passing, according to his custom, through the hotels and inns, where he tried to buy or to sell his merchandise to the travelers; he had entered our hotel, had there encountered Margraff, and this reunion in the café had followed. Wolfram, a former cigar merchant in Germany, was a gardener and milkman; on going to offer the products of his garden and his barn to our inn, he had encountered the nephew of the duke of Baden, who had informed him of our arrival; another, a former notary's clerk in Alsace, had become a brickmaker: all seemed happy and were earning, they said, as much gold as when they were working on the placers; all the others, French and German, whom I did not know, had come to see "Oualai," of whom they had heard from the members of the expedition.

These Gentlemen, in their accounts, had exaggerated the facts and incidents of this promenade across the mountains; they had embroidered our stay among the Indians with extraordinary stories. They had made me especially the hero of all sorts of completely improbable adventures, so that I had become, without suspecting it, almost a celebrity, and people were curious to see me. They designated me by the name of "Oualai" the Belgian, because the Indians always saluted me by that word. Several of the people who came to the café to see me called me Mr. Oualai very seriously, thinking that it was my name.

According to Serf, I had lost by having my hair cut and my beard trimmed; he claimed that these two things left in the natural state, as I was wearing them, inspired respect in the Indians and that this, doubtless, was the cause of their often selecting me as judge of their differences.

Our expedition was known by the name of the *Hike-or-bust* company. Here is the incident which had given cause for this appellation: the day after the day when my companions had left me at the confluence of the two Merceds, and while I was trying to eat my eagle, they were devouring their last provisions—some of them hadn't even enough to make a meal. Then, one of the band made the suggestion, unanimously accepted, of eating together, fraternally, all the supplies that remained. Everything was put in a common store and eaten on the spot. "Now," said one of them, "that we are at once ballasted and unloaded, we must *hike or bust.*" It wasn't yet day and the rain was falling fast; someone suggested waiting to leave until the rain stopped. "No," said another, "there are no more supplies, *hike or bust,*" and they set off on the way, repeating this cry. The name stuck to our company.

As we were too numerous to play billiards all together, as, moreover, we had a lot of things to ask each other and to tell each other, we sat down at table and talked.

All were agreed in saying that the situation was profoundly changed in California: as the placers were exhausted, the immigrants increased; one had to dig hard now to find a little gold, and the chances of enjoying, through some happy find, a stroke of fortune, were diminishing every day.

In short, it was a thankless task, and there was nothing better to do than to throw away pick and shovel, and to seek another employment for one's activity and one's intelligence. From then on it was necessary to turn to commerce or industry. That is what my interlocutors had done: each one of them had undertaken one thing or the other, while living by the profession he had embraced.

Those who had amassed some capital had bought shares in the numerous companies which had been formed to exploit the placers on a grand scale; these shares brought them more or less and constituted a stake on which they could borrow at need.

They were unanimous in declaring to us that we must renounce the hope of finding an unoccupied claim where we might have some chance of working fruitfully.

"They knew," they said, "the country for ten leagues around, they had covered it, explored it, excavated it, and had lost their time there. If we wanted to continue the work of the mines, we would have either to buy a claim in the environs which, perhaps, would produce nothing, or cross to the other side of the Tuoalumné."

A German, owner of an agricultural property, suggested that we buy it from him; he had been naturalized as an American and, like all Americans of age, he had the right to a hundred and sixty acres (the acre equals forty ares and a half). He had surrounded his homestead with a fence, cultivated a part of it, left the rest in pasture, and rented it to people passing through who had horses to feed, at the rate of a dollar a week per horse; at the same time, he kept hens and cows, and made money from eggs and milk. I think that his position was good. All the land around Sonora was, just about, occupied; the population was growing from day to day; the value of the land was increasing in the same proportion. The question was to decide if we wanted to become farmers and at what price the German would cede his homestead to us. A brother of his, who was on the Kootenay, near Lake Pend d'Oreille, in the northern part of Oregon, had written to him to go and join him, for he was finding much gold and hoped to do so for a long time; that was why he was trying to sell his property. As he had had many expenses, he wanted to sell it for a good price: he asked three thousand dollars for it, cows, hens, etc. included. This price seemed too high to us, the more so as our desire to become farmers was not too strong. At Sonora itself, a butcher's shop, all set up, was for sale; the butcher was retiring after having made his fortune. At the time of our arrival, two amateurs were buying it; we could, the three of us, join them and exploit it together. The rumored receipts were fifty dollars a day, the expenses assessed at thirty, there remained twenty dollars to share among five; it was, perhaps, an honest living, but the butcher demanded twelve thousand dollars investment from us; it was too much, and we left the field free to the two amateurs.

During this single afternoon, which was prolonged, it is true, until two o'clock in the morning, it was successively proposed that we become farmers, butchers, brickmakers, milkmen, sawyers, café owners, grocers, hotel keepers, to say nothing of business agents, and we were not at the end! The propositions kept coming, but we no longer heard them, we had, while discussing them, opened and emptied so many bottles that our heavy heads were dropping to the table. At last, by way of conclusion, we decided to retire, and everyone gained his bed.

We spent a whole week in visiting first one, then another, in calculating, in planning, in reflecting. It was embarrassing; we wished neither to remain lazy, nor to take up the work of the mines again. But to what other work were we suited? We ended by deciding to go, provisionally, to reflect on all this in San Francisco.

Every three days, a stagecoach drawn by five horses left Sonora for Stockton, not traveling at night; it took two days to make this trip of eighty miles. At Stockton, one took the steamboat and descended the San Joaquin to San Francisco, a hundred and seventeen miles distant. Having sold our horse to Serf and our tools to the highest bidder, we reserved our places on the stagecoach, which left the next day. Several people gave us letters for their relatives or friends in San Francisco. At five o'clock in the morning, after having exchanged a good number of hand-clasps, all four of us left—all four including Miraud, whom I had not wished to sell at any price, for I had faithfully promised myself never to be separated from him.

From Sonora, the road went to the southwest and wound around many mountains as far as Knight's Ferry (passage du chevalier), where it crossed the Stanislaus River on a wooden bridge; we arrived there about two o'clock in the afternoon.[3] Shortly afterward, we found ourselves in a flat country, sparsely wooded and uninhabited, perhaps because of the lack of water. I could prove this

3. Knight's Ferry in Stanislaus County was founded in 1849 by William Knight. After his death the brothers of Julia Dent, Ulysses S. Grant's wife, assumed ownership with James Vantine. "Situated midway between Stockton and the central portion of the Southern Mines," it was a major crossing in the gold rush years. See Heckendorf and Wilson, *Miners' and Business Men's Directory*, p. 100; Gudde, *California Place Names*, p. 167; and idem, *1000 California Place Names* (Berkeley and Los Angeles: University of California Press, 1947), p. 41.

dryness of the soil, when, at evening, the stagecoach deposited us at the station where we were to spend the night: it was a group of five houses, which were supplied with water from a well at least a hundred and fifty feet deep; the wheel of a windmill, around which rolled a chaplet of mugs, brought the water to the troughs where men and animals came to quench their thirst.

Next day, at three in the afternoon, we entered Stockton after having spent all day, since four o'clock in the morning, crossing a sort of lightly undulating plain, much populated, of which Stockton marked, on the west, the extreme limit.

We stopped at a restaurant kept by a Frenchman. The departure of the steamboat (fresh water steamer) was announced for eight o'clock. After dinner, having three to four hours before me, I spent them in wandering around the city. It was already populated by twenty to twenty-five thousand inhabitants, had superb streets, drawn on the square [tirées au cardeau], cutting each other at right angles, sixty feet wide with sidewalks twelve feet wide, and bordered by houses of two and three stories. But all this was of wood, even the sidewalks, even the pavements; some houses, however, formed an exception: some were of brick, others of iron. In the evening, gas lighted everything; the telegraph tied the city on one side to Sacramento, on the other to San Francisco. I marveled at everything I saw there: how many changes in seven years!

I was as if ashamed of myself. During this period, in fact, I had returned, in some fashion, to the savage state, while California was becoming civilized and was being transformed. It was, seven years before, a desert designated on the maps by the words *Unknown land;* now it was a populous country, fertile, covered with farms, villages, rich and prosperous cities, or it was becoming that. The rivers which the Indian, formerly, crossed by swimming, were ploughed by steamboats and craft of all kinds which served to supply a population of more than three hundred thousand inhabitants. Instead of the barely traced paths which it formerly offered to the rare nomads who traversed them, the country was covered with fine surfaced roads, where there passed in all directions, without counting horsemen and pedestrians, carts, wagons, stagecoaches, and even luxurious carriages. The sole habitations which were seen there before were Indian huts, four feet high, which, when seen from afar, resembled hives; today, there rose populous cities, full of noise and movement, with spacious streets, tall houses, great edifices. Seven years ago, the wild horse, the elk, the deer were crossing the plains in peace; one now heard nothing but the bellowing of cattle and the bleating of sheep, and the horse, now become as everywhere the servant of man, drew the cart there.

The mountains themselves were no longer the inviolate refuge of the bear and the panther; these wild beasts had fled before the motley army of miners who penetrated to the most inaccessible retreats, leaving no stone unturned.

The rivers, it is true, no longer flowed, impetuous or peaceful, in the beds which nature had dug for them; imprisoned in canals of wood or of earth, they now flowed only with troubled and muddy water.

This reminded me, appropriately, that they flowed at the same time with gold—
that is what explained everything.

It was gold, in fact, which in such a short time had performed this marvelous
metamorphosis which struck me with astonishment, I, a savage from the mountains
come down to the plains. It was gold, that vile metal, if one wishes, but that all-
powerful mover, which had here accomplished the work of civilization; religion,
this time, had nothing to do with it. The missionaries, during the almost two
centuries [!] that they had been established in California and indoctrinating the
Indians, had cultivated neither land nor souls; at that moment, the sole cultivation,
to tell the truth, which was practiced in California was that of gold. Could it be that
religion is not, as some think, the essential bond of society?

And gold, on the contrary, could it not be the great initiator of all progress, the
creator of the arts, of the sciences, of industry? in a word, the benefactor of
humanity, until the moment when it escapes from the hands which have extracted it
from the earth to pass to the hands of those who monopolize it?

As I was asking myself these questions, I perceived that it was going to be eight
o'clock and, without giving myself the time to resolve them, I hastened to regain my
hotel, and from there, followed by my companions, the landing where the steamboat was warming up.

This boat was as long as the turns of the river permitted, which facilitated
running aground. As it was the season of high waters, the San Joaquin was wider
than ordinary, so that the trip between Stockton and San Francisco was made with
less difficulty and more speed. Soon after having left the landing, night came; when
we woke up, we were going down the Sacramento and were not far from San
Francisco; we arrived there about five o'clock in the morning. We went to put up at
the What Cheer House, a vast hotel like a barracks, in which more than six
hundred people could lodge.

San Francisco, although burned three times in seven years, or perhaps for that
very reason, was a fine city of a hundred and twenty thousand inhabitants; today it
counts three hundred and thirty thousand; but in 1857 it already had its paved
streets, its underground sewers, its gas and its tramways, just like an old city; eight
years before, it was composed of fifteen adobe houses and some tents. The bay
which served it as port, a sort of small inland sea, contained, on our arrival, more
than three thousand ships which occupied barely the hundredth part of it. The
streets, the wharves, three kilometers long, the public squares, the avenues, and the
promenades were encumbered with people and merchandise; a compact and busy
crowd was moving or rather was rushing in all directions.

An ant-heap stirred up by a kick, in warm weather, can give an idea of this
agitation which seems characteristic of the cities of America. The crowd which
gathers, on Sunday in Paris, between the Madelaine and the Place de la Bastille,
would perhaps give an idea of it if this crowd were going about its business and not
its pleasure.

Should I settle in San Francisco? As a businessman, impossible; I did not have enough money; as a clerk, I would have had a salary of sixty to a hundred dollars a month, and I would have been able very easily to place the little that Mr. Wheeler was going to repay me, in sure mortgages, at an interest of 2% a month. After having seriously reflected on it for several days, I abandoned this idea; for several years I had been independent and free; no kind of subjection, I had been absolutely my own master. It was a poor preparation for the life of a clerk and, moreover, I had never had any great fund of docility.

I remembered that at Paris, I had needed the unalterable sweetness and the unequaled goodness of Mr. Dupont to make bearable the subordinate position I occupied with him; I was younger then, and age did not soften character as far as I knew; it was natural to suppose that I now would be less than ever inclined to submit myself to the will of an employer and that, from then on, I would make but a poor employee, and consequently an unhappy one. I sought therefore at any price to remain my own master. I felt that if I succeeded only in earning my living by working for myself, I would be happier than if I enriched myself in the service of another. After all, contentment is better than wealth, and who knows? the country offered so many resources! Who would prevent me from having both the one and the other?

In any case, I was a few dollars ahead; I owed it to myself to tempt fortune.

Ah! if I had been a mason, I would have remained in San Francisco; I would have earned eight dollars a day; I would have made the same wages if I had been a carpenter; I would have remained, in short, if I had known any kind of trade. All these artisans earned a generous living. I would have amassed some money; before long I would have established myself on my own account, earning much and spending little, seeing that the animal life was comparatively cheap there (three dollars for three meals in a hotel). But I was good for nothing but a day-laborer: that is why I made the choice of leaving San Francisco quickly and going to tempt fortune elsewhere. Where? I did not yet know.

Was I going to take up again, in despair of doing better, the free but difficult life of the miner? or become a settler? In the latter case, I had only to return to Sonora and buy the farm I had priced. After having weighed the reasons for and against for a long time, I still was not able to come to a decision, when Margraff appeared.

He had taken charge, with Létang, of distributing the letters which our friends in Sonora had confided to us. There was, among others, one from the German of Sonora addressed to another German, a house painter in San Francisco. This painter, to mention it in passing, earned twelve dollars a day, without furnishing either paint or brush. Margraff learned from him that he had received a letter from the German who was on the Kootenay and who was calling his brother there, the one at Sonora. This letter, although written in very bad German, as Margraff assured me, contained some very fine things about the country from which it came.

It let it be known, for example, that Oregon had just ended by a peace treaty the war which it had sustained against the Chinook Indians (Schenooks), the Snakes, the Nez-percés, the Coeurs-d'alêne and the Pend'oreilles; that by virtue of this treaty, all the country between the Rocky Mountains, the Pacific, the Fraser, and Salt Lake, was open to miners; that they found gold everywhere and that there were still few people; he, like all those who were working between Fort Colville and the Kootenay, was finding as much gold as was found in California at the moment of the discovery of the mines; with that, the climate was much less hot than that of California, and consequently work was much less difficult. Margraff, as a conclusion to his report, opined that we must, without delay, leave for Oregon. The mines, he said, could not be very far from the point where the steamer stopped, for this German proposed to come and get his brother from the steamer; only, he was to write three months before leaving because, as the mail delivery was performed only by wagon-trains, the letter could suffer delays. As for the painter, he had not been able to give information other than that contained in the letter.

Considering Margraff's tone of assurance, we quickly made our decision.

The steamer the *Commodore* was leaving in two days for Portland (Oregon): we immediately took our tickets: the price of the passage was twenty-five dollars.

We were going into an unknown land, of which we had very vague ideas. What did it matter? There were people in that country, since someone wrote from there, and if the author of the letter, who knew California, called his brother to Oregon, one had to admit, at the worst, that Oregon was as good as California.

Reassured on this point, we awaited with impatience the moment of leaving. We saw everything in rosy tints and we passed these two days in thanking the gods for having permitted us the lucky encounter with the German of Sonora.

I profited by the delay to write to some friends at Mariposa, at Coultersville, etc. I informed them that I was leaving California for Oregon, begging them to take from the post all letters which might arrive for me and to keep them until the time when I could let them know my new address.

The day and the hour arrived. The *Commodore* raised anchor, a cannon shot gave the signal of departure and the voyage began. [16 May 1857]

Chapter Twenty-Four

Learning to Live in Portland

The Pacific deserves its name; we made the trip from San Francisco to the mouth of the Columbia, call it seven degrees of latitude, in three days and two nights, gliding gently over the smooth surface of the vast sea with as much security as if we had been descending a peaceful river. Two or three times each day we saw land on the starboard hand, that is, each time we doubled a promontory; the steamer was heading north-north-west and was going thus from one promontory to another, but staying three or four leagues offshore; the third day before evening, they discovered land ahead and before sunset we were floating on the waters of the Columbia. This river is three or four leagues wide at its mouth; this width is maintained as far as Astoria, a city composed of sixty to eighty wooden houses, situated three leagues from salt water; soon after, the river assumes its average width, which is from twelve to fifteen hundred meters.[1] We then found ourselves between two slightly elevated banks, with irregular contours and, most of the time, descending in a gentle slope to the river. Everywhere the eye could reach, whether on the two banks, or in the extension of the valleys which opened to the stream, one saw nothing but a vast forest composed of enormous pines, two or three hundred feet high; the mountains, which seemed to rise and to take on a more rapid slope by degrees as we mounted, are doubtless covered with a thick bed of earth, for, in spite of their precipitousness, one sees the bare rock only along the banks. From Astoria to Portland, there are a hundred and ten miles (37 leagues), but soon after having passed the first of these two cities, night had come, and when morning awoke us, *The Commodore* was fast to the wharf at Portland and had already extinguished its fires.

We debarked and went to stay at "Howard House."[2] It was a boarding house

1. When John Jacob Astor organized the Pacific Fur Company in 1810, he hoped to sell furs collected in the Pacific Northwest to the Chinese. To realize his plans, he sent a ship with supplies to the Oregon coast that year, and a year later dispatched Wilson Price Hunt on an overland expedition to the mouth of the Columbia, where both groups established Astoria. The whole enterprise was fraught with many problems, and upon the outbreak of the War of 1812, Astoria was sold to the Hudson's Bay Company. It exists today as a small coastal town in Oregon.

2. The Howard House, located at 3 North Front Street, was operated by James W. Going. *Portland Directory for 1863, Embracing a General Directory of Citizens, A Business Directory, and Other Statistical Information* (Portland [compiled and published by S. J. McCormick], 1863), p. 48.

where one was lodged and fed at the rate of eight dollars a week. After breakfast, we left to go see what Portland was like: we saw that it was a street one kilometer long, having on one side the wharves (quais) and the river, on the other, some more or less contiguous houses. The land for the city, if one could call it that, had been conquered, blow by blow of the axe, from the forest, and enormous pine stumps still impeded traffic in this unique street. Moreover, the woodcutters were always at work there, and, from time to time, one heard the crash of a pine which, in falling, increased by so much the clearing which Portland occupied in the forest. The city contained two thousand inhabitants, three steam sawmills, two flour mills, a distillery, a foundry, several furniture factories, and the press of the newspaper, "The Oregonian."[3] Everybody seemed occupied; however, seeing nothing but forest everywhere, I could not at first explain to myself with whom these people, merchants all, could do business. I understood it when I approached the river: there I saw a crowd of steamboats, here made fast, there arriving or leaving; among these last, some were going down the river, others were going upstream, loaded with passengers, and taking away the merchandise which the steamer from San Francisco had just unloaded.

I concluded from this that Portland was nothing but a warehouse, a sort of terminus where outside commerce came to deposit the merchandise which was distributed throughout the country, and where, on the other hand, there flowed the products of Oregon to be exchanged against this merchandise: it was this double movement of commerce which made the importance of the place and gave it so much animation.

At noon, we were numerous at table, all workmen and, except us, all employed. We learned that Portland was situated on the left bank of the Willamette, a tributary of the Columbia, six miles south of this latter, sixty miles north of Salem, the capital of Oregon, and seven hundred and sixty miles north of San Francisco.

Portland was in the midst of being built; everything was cheap there, except manpower, for labor was lacking. The day's work (ten hours) of the laborer was for three dollars; as for skilled workmen, they were paid as at San Francisco, that is, at the rate of eight to twelve dollars a day.

The reverse of the medal was that they had to be idle for four months in winter, because it rained there almost continually. That hardly mattered to us, anyway, it wasn't there that we were going—it was to the mines; we asked information on the road to follow.

Great was our surprise and our dismay to learn that we had four hundred and fifty miles to cover (150 leagues), we who had counted on four or five days' walking! We had to take the steamboat which in one day would transport us to the

3. The *Oregonian*, founded in 1850 as a Whig newspaper, was noted in its early years for its invective, but when Harvey W. Scott assumed the editorship in 1865, it developed into the leading journal of the Northwest. See Sidney Warren, *Farthest Frontier: The Pacific Northwest* (New York: Macmillan, 1949), pp. 192, 205–08.

cascades of the Columbia, from there, to go on foot to The Dalles, forty-five miles higher, then get on a boat again which, in three days, would unload us at Walla Walla, situated two hundred miles east of Portland.

On reaching there, you bought as best you might a mule . . . loaded with provisions which you drove before yourself for ten or twelve days; after having thus covered two hundred and forty miles (80 leagues), one arrived at last at Calville [Colville], near the mines. It was now the 25th of June, and perhaps we would not be at the placers in less than a month. Now, the 25th of July is too late to begin the work of the mines, so much the more so as, the Kootenay being between the 48th and 49th degrees of northern latitude, it was very probable that winter began there early; perhaps it would have been necessary, as soon as we arrived, to return to spend the winter in Portland; last fall, they told us, many miners had done it and had returned to the placers in the month of April. So we were constrained to postpone the trip to the next spring, but this contretemps took on for us the propositions of a calamity, for two out of three would soon be at the end of their resources. How could we have committed this enormous blunder? Had Margraff misread the German's letter? No, Margraff had read it well, he had even read it too well, but that rascal of a German, instead of writing that he would go to look for his brother at the *steamboat*, had written that he would go to look for him at the *steamer*. Now, the steamer only went as far as Portland, while the steamboat went clear to Walla Walla; the error was one of two hundred and ten miles (70 leagues). It was enough to prevent us, that year, from continuing our trip; sighing, we resigned ourselves to wait for the month of March next. We had to occupy ourselves until then, for, to pay board for nine months and do nothing was out of the question.

It was decided that we would seek work immediately. Létang, something of a mechanic, something of a carpenter, looked for it in the sawmills, [and] in the flour mills; he did not find any. Everywhere, as if on purpose, they had the number of workmen wanted for the season.

Each one, at the moment, was at his post and was staying there; we arrived too late. One day, however, at breakfast, we heard it said that a workman was needed in a sawmill, to replace a sick man; immediately, Létang left and went to present himself. At the end of two hours, not seeing him return, we supposed, Margraff and I, that he was hired and already at work; at that, we got up and went to find him. On approaching the river, we saw him seated on the bank, his elbows on his knees, holding his head between both hands, his fingers threading through his disordered hair. A painter or a sculptor in search of a model to represent Despair could not have found a better. Laughingly I asked him if that was all the duty he was charged with, and how much did they give him for that? He raised his head, showing us, with a tragic gesture, an innumerable quantity of tree trunks floating on the river, and explained to us, in a few words, what the work consisted of that they proposed for him and for which they offered him four dollars a day. It was a matter of bringing them, one after another, near the sawmill; to do this, it was necessary, leaping from one log to another, to seek the one they asked for, open a passage for it through all the others, drawing it, pushing it, and finally to bring it to the place where, by means of a chain to which he fastened it, the motive force of the sawmill made it slip on an inclined plane, then drew it onto the slide of the saw. Armed with a pole fifteen feet long, terminated by a pick and a hook, the workman charged with the work had first to embark on one of these logs, which were from twelve to twenty feet long and three to four feet in diameter. To maneuver this raft through the dangers to right and left, it was enough to have dexterity, a sharp eye, strength, calmness, and especially audacity; one had to take care, for example, not to place his foot beside the center of gravity, for then this piece, round in form, turned, and its guide must leap promptly to another if he found one in reach; if not, he fell in the water: forty feet deep. One could get out of it hale and whole, if one was a first class swimmer and if one was endowed with a strong constitution. "My word!" I said to Margraff, "you like to drink, here is your chance."—"No!" replied Margraff in the same tone, "one must avoid excess; I give it up."—"I give it up too," I said to him, "I have not made my will." In short, it was unanimously decided that this work was not our style and that we would have to look for something else. And we began to look again.

Margraff was content to follow us, saying to himself that if we found work, there would probably be enough for three, and that, consequently, he would have his share. As for me, I looked, without hope of finding, for I was a stranger to all the jobs which I saw being done around me, and I realized it with bitterness; in civilized life, I saw clearly, I was good for nothing, and I aspired all the more ardently to return to the vagabond existence of the gold seekers.

After three or four days of useless applications, Létang met a Mr. Bell who was looking for woodcutters, and brought him to me. The problem was to cut two hundred cords of firewood for him and, considering our inexperience, Bell offered to choose for us the trees that were easiest to split; he would pay us two dollars and a half per cord (Spanish cord: a six-foot base, four high, the wood being four feet long; the English foot is thirty and a half centimeters).

After being informed, we accepted these conditions and the bargain was concluded.

Two days later, we were woodcutters; having acquired all the necessary tools, axes, wedges, saw and maul (*mailloche*), we were at work.

We had to begin by building a log cabin, not to move into it ourselves—it was too warm—but to store our provisions and to preserve them from the ardor of the sun as well as from the voracity of the animals. I do not speak here of wild animals, but of the domestic animals, dogs, pigs, cows, etc., which wandered everywhere in full liberty, and who willingly extended it to license. We were operating a few hundred meters from the last houses; while enlarging the hole made in the forest, we were doubtless going to prepare for the growth of the city and, at the same time, cut wood to fire the innumerable steamboats which plowed the river. Well and good! That raised us in our own eyes, we were no more the simple woodcutters, but the agents of a work of civilization. We had been in Oregon only six days and we were already rendering eminent services to society; it remained to be seen how society would pay us for our pains. . . .

After having built our storehouse, we really had to build ourselves some kind of a shelter. From the first logs of the first tree cut down, I made laths of a sort, for the wood was very easy to work, and from these laths, a trellis eight feet long by five wide; a plain canvas thrown over it served as roof. Such was my lodging; I set up my bed there on four stakes serving as feet, whose forked heads supported two poles long and strong enough—with my hammock placed on this frame, I slept above and Miraud below. Margraff and Létang didn't take so much trouble; less opulent than I, they were necessarily less refined, so they slept on the hard ground.

According to Létang, who knew it himself only by hearsay, a woodcutter, without too much trouble, could cut two cords a day: at this rate, we were going to make five dollars each. That was fine; thereupon, full of ardor, we cut down several trees, recut them in four-foot lengths, split them, then corded them; that gave us eighteen cords after five days' work.

We were far from our five dollars and yet we had worked hard, but we had set about it wrong, which was not astonishing on the part of novice woodcutters such as we were. We had cut down trees that were too big, thinking to gain thereby, while the contrary was the case; next we had recut them with the saw without notching them with the axe on each side; it was a loss of time because the sap-wood alone was difficult to saw: with the axe, one came more easily and quickly to the end.

Finally, we had made our trees fall by cutting them with the axe, and that was, of all the procedures, the least expeditious; but once in possession of the technical knowledge which we lacked at the beginning, we were going to do better.

To fell our trees, we used an auger instead of the axe. We bored a horizontal hole a foot deep, eighteen or twenty inches higher, we dug obliquely a second hole which was going to join the first. This latter was a hearth to which the other served as chimney; we introduced a few coals into it, which soon set fire to the walls, the hole being hollowed into an oven, the tree fell at the end of two or three days.

There were continually ten or twelve of these trees on fire, while we were cutting up those which had fallen. The precaution which we had to take was to beware of the trees which fell without warning us, and to prevent the stock from being caught, for we would have had to pay for it.

One day Margraff ran a great danger; he was in the midst of accelerating, by strokes of the axe, the fall of one of these trees, trying to make it fall on the most advantageous side for cutting it up, when a person passing a hundred paces from him asked for some information. Margraff, the better to explain, put his axe down near the tree and approached this individual; hardly had he taken twenty steps, when he suddenly saw him fleeing, shouting that the pine was falling; Margraff, who had his back turned to this tree, could see nothing, but he just heard a cracking whose cause he understood perfectly, and without losing time in turning around, he began to run as fast as he could in the direction he saw the other taking. All at once he heard above his head that whistling which a falling tree produces when it has almost reached the ground; Margraff, gathering all the strength he had left, made a prodigious leap: at the moment he touched ground, the top of the falling tree tore the shirt from his back.

I really believe that the air violently displaced by the tree pushed Margraff and saved him, for it would otherwise have been impossible, without believing in a miracle, to explain, considering his corpulence, the inordinate length of the leap he performed.

By this adventure Margraff acquired one of the four cardinal virtues; beginning with that moment, in fact, he became extremely prudent, and he never lost sight for a second of trees ready to fall.

After fifteen days of work according to the new method, it was found that we had done sixty-five cords of wood, or four and a third cords a day; there was progress there and we were pleased enough with ourselves. But, whether because we had worked too hard, or because of the heat, which was great, we suffered a sort of languor accompanied by a very pronounced loss of weight; perhaps too it was from being unused to it, for we had as neighbors some Canadians who each did two cords a day and seemed less tired than we. For them, it was their trade: they knew how to prepare and care for their tools, and then, a thing which was not within our scope, each one of them worked at his own tree, cutting it down, sawing it and splitting it, while we had to join our efforts.

We spent Sunday in repairing our tools: Létang, most used to handling them, sharpened the axes and filed the saw, while I was occupied with the wedges and the maul, and Margraff was occupied with the cooking. Mr. Bell came, at diminishing intervals, with a cart drawn by two horses, and took into the city the wood which we had prepared and which he sold at six dollars a cord, which constituted an honest profit for him.

Létang had noticed, the last few times, that every Monday Mr. Bell arrived, loaded his wagon, and went away without saying good day to us. We were wondering what could be the cause of this whim when, one Sunday morning while we were, according to custom, in the midst of preparing our tools for the next day, Mr. Bell came to complain that we were working on the day of the lord; from his house, which was not far distant, his children saw us working, and were scandalized; it was a shame, according to him, to work on Sunday, and he came to beg us to put a stop to this scandal.[4]

We looked at each other, all three overwhelmed, then there followed between him and me the following colloquy:

"So, Mr. Bell, your religion tells you not to work on Sunday?"

"Yes, sir."

"And if it told you to work on that day?"

"I would obey."

---

4. Unfortunately, neither the Portland city directories nor the list of the ministers of the five Protestant churches of Portland identifies Mr. Bell with whom Perlot dealt.

"Well, Mr. Bell, I do as you do; my own religion tells me: work—and I obey."

"Oh! it is written that man cannot work all the time."

"It was perfectly useless to write that, for anyone who wishes to be informed in that respect has only to come here and do our job; he would perceive very clearly, at the end of five or six hours, that man cannot and, consequently, ought not to work all the time; whether it be written or not, he would be quite content to rest."

"What is your religion?"

"The religion of duty, and you will not say, doubtless, that it is not a duty to work."

"Oh, surely not."

"Well then, permit me to do my duty on Sunday as on any other day; be as tolerant of my religion as I am of yours."

"Well! But man should not think only of this world, and Sunday is the day when he ought to occupy himself with the other."

"Mr. Bell, I came into this world without my having previously occupied myself with it, and similarly, before occupying myself with the other, I will wait until I am there; I defy you to prove to me that, beyond the accomplishment of my duty in this world, I could do anything in advance for the other."

"I think you do not believe in God?"

"I believe so well in God, that I believe only in him; but you, Mr. Bell, I doubt that you believe in him?"

"I, not believe in God? But, I am a Preacher!" (prêcheur, prédicateur, ministre protestant).

"Oh, I admit your good faith; you are convinced, I don't doubt, that you believe in God, but if you would really analyze what you believe, you would end, I think, by recognizing that you believe simply what men have said of God; now, I do not call that believing in God, I call that believing in men."

"Well, if you believe in God, yourself, why do you work on Sunday? He has said: Thou shalt keep holy the Sabbath day."

"Pardon me, Mr. Bell, the one who said that was Moses, they say; now, I don't have faith in Moses, but in God alone; and then you say: *the Sabbath day;* the Sabbath day was yesterday and you worked; today is Sunday, the first day of the week, the day itself that God, according to you, began to work, and you are lazy! Moses tells me to rest on Saturday, you tell me to rest on Sunday: which to believe? I will believe neither one of you, I work every day and rest when I feel the need; on this point as on others, I prefer to rely on God himself, who, each day, whatever they say, accomplished his work. Do you claim the contrary?"

"If you do not believe Moses, if you do not believe anyone, I do not see how you expect to save your soul?"

"Mr. Bell, I don't believe that my soul is in danger; consequently, I don't have to save it, I don't believe that mankind has ever been lost; God, who created everything, has never destroyed anything; to believe that the devil, by his guile, had succeeded in fooling him, is to suppose more intelligence in the creature than in the creator; it is absurd."

"If that's the way it is, then tell me what was the use of the death of Jesus Christ?"

"None."

"Then you don't believe that Jesus Christ is God?"

"No, I don't believe that any man has been God, nor that God has ever become a man."

There followed a little discussion on the incarnation to which . . . Mr. Bell put an end by declaring that I touched with great lightness on an august mystery, and that I scandalized him very much.

"Mr. Perlot," he continued, "I see that you do not allow of mysteries, you judge everything through the eyes of human reason."

"Alas, Mr. Bell, I know no other; as for the word *mystery*, it is, for me, synonymous with ignorance: everything is a mystery for the one who knows nothing."

Mr. Bell then asked me if, in what I called my religion, there was a profession of faith, a credo?

"Yes," I said, "Mr. Bell, there is one."

"What is it?"

"*Credo in unum Deum;* that is all."

At that Mr. Bell contented himself with replying that I was an infidel of the worst kind and that he did not believe that I was speaking seriously; he added that, moreover, it was not to convert us that he had come, but to inform us that, from the moment we worked on Sunday, his principles did not permit him to maintain any kind of relations with us, and that consequently he would no longer take our wood. He humbly begged us not to hold it against him, if his character made it a duty for him to break all agreement with us, assuring us that nevertheless he loved us as every man should love his kind.

He recognized our right to act as we thought fit, but no doubt we would also recognize his right to do business with whoever seemed good to him.

"That is," I said to him, "Mr. Bell, while recognizing our right to act as seems fit to us, you reserve for yourself, if we use it, the right to make us repent it; you claim to love us as a man should love his kind, yet it seems to me, according to the sample you have given us, that the love you bear your kind is very luke-warm."

Mr. Bell, while listening, had half turned his back, as if to go away, and no longer replied. "Let's see," I said to him, "Mr. Bell, your principles forbid you to buy wood from us, that's all very well, but you know that we are strangers in the locality; do your principles also forbid you to suggest where we could offer it?"

"Not in the least," he said, "it is my duty to render service when needed, and I would be wrong not to do it. Speak to Mr. Hollman, at such and such a place, he's in the wood business like me, and very probably you will make arrangements with him."[5] That said, Mr. Bell, still half turned away, saluted and left.

5. Although the Holman family was prominent in early Oregon, it is difficult to identify precisely to whom Perlot refers. It could have been Joseph D. Holman, an early settler who tried to develop Pacific City with

"Well," I said to my partners, "here we are in a fine state: if all the woodsellers here are preachers, if all are dumbbells like this one, we have only to decamp as quickly as possible, especially me, an infidel of the worst kind. However, I would rather believe that it is Mr. Bell who is a preacher of the worst kind and that we will find some who are more accommodating than he."

"Before anything else," said Létang, "I am going to find this Hollman, we'll see if he is a Bell."

Létang dressed and left; he returned three hours later to tell us that he had not found Hollman at home, but that the latter, informed of his visit, would probably come on Monday morning to see our wood.

He came, in fact, and bought from us all the wood that we had prepared, leaving us to hope that he would take still more, and that, in any case, he would pay for it as he took it.

We continued in this way for fifteen days. But then, whether because of the heat, which was overwhelming, or because our strength was exhausted, Margraff found himself out of condition to work; he asked to rest a few days. Soon after, Létang fell ill to the point of having to stay in bed, not his, since he didn't have any, but mine; as for me, I slept on the ground, in his place. At the end of two or three days, seeing that Létang was getting no better, I went to the city in search of a doctor and brought back Doctor Wilson, whom they pointed out to me as the best in the place; then I went back with him to the city, in order to go to the pharmacy to get what was needed.[6]

Two days later, Létang got up and could take a walk. The doctor told him that the weakness of his chest did not permit him to stand the hardships of the rough trade of woodcutter, and advised him to take up another.

In the meantime, Margraff had made the acquaintance of a German farmer, who needed laborers to begin his harvest. He went to work for him for the season, at the rate of two dollars a day, or rather at the rate of twenty cents per working hour, with board and room; he had set as an express condition that he would begin his day when it seemed good to him and would end it when it pleased him.

Margraff one fine morning folded up his blankets and went to move in with his compatriot, who had the seat of his operations near Salem, on the banks of the Willamette, sixty miles upstream from Portland. As for me, I finished putting up

Dr. Elijah White and Alonzo Skinner, or Albert Holman, who was associated with *The Oregonian*, or Captain Charles Holman, who came to Oregon in 1852. See Dorothy O. Johansen and Charles M. Gates, *Empire on the Columbia: A History of the Pacific Northwest* (New York: Harper & Brothers, 1957), p. 335; and Joseph Gaston, *Portland, Oregon: Its History and Builders* (Chicago and Portland: S. J. Clarke, 1911), vol. 1, p. 656.

6. Robert Bruce Wilson, "Physician, Surgeon and Accoucher," had an office in Cree's Building on Stark Street and lived at Fourth and B streets (*Portland Directory, 1863*, p. 110). Wilson came to Portland in 1850 and married Caroline E. Couch, daughter of Captain John Couch.

Perlot could have patronized one of three pharmacies or druggists in Portland: Hodge and Calef at 97 Front Street; Smith and Davis, Wholesale and Retail Druggists at 71 Front Street; or W. Weatherford, 139 Front Street. See *Portland Directory, 1863*.

our last cut trees in cords, and sold little by little what wood we had left; at the same time I took care of Létang, who was getting better, but could not yet do anything more than walk around.

I went every other day to take news of the invalid to the doctor, in order to avoid his visit, which cost five dollars (25 francs). I had noticed that his house, newly built, was in the middle of an uncultivated block—so they called the land included between four streets meeting at right angles. In Portland, the block was two hundred feet on a side and the streets sixty feet wide; I asked him one day why he left his property in this state, when he could make such a fine garden for both pleasure and produce.

"Oh," he said, "that would cost me too much; moreover, it would require a professional and I don't know any in the city."

"Well," I said, "I'll take charge of it if you want."

"Could you really do it?"

"At least, I can try. Make me the plan of your garden; if I don't succeed in executing it, you won't pay me for it and, in any case, I won't have done any harm, so you have nothing to risk."

Wilson reflected a moment, then said to me: "I'll see—I don't say no. I will have to consult my wife and I'll give you an answer in a few days."

Three days later, having finished cutting up our trees and having sold our last cords of wood, I was walking in the city, when I encountered Doctor Wilson; he brought me to his office, that is, a room which he had in the city where he received his patients, and talked to me about his garden. He told me that he had looked for someone to make him a plan for it, and had found only Mr. Burage, a mathematician (surveyor), who asked fifty dollars for this work; Wilson thought that it was expensive.[7]

I offered to make him one for which he would pay me what he wanted, if I was not asked to execute it; on the contrary, if I was, I would do it gratis. He accepted. The same day I bought pens, rulers, pencils, ink, five sheets of paper for the plan, and a compass; the whole cost me five dollars; I thought that it was a lot to risk for an uncertain result, for I was much afraid of not succeeding.

Be that as it may, I carried off my purchase and returned to care for my invalid, for whom, besides, I did the cooking, for the least fatigue was still forbidden him.

The next evening, I had two plans spoiled and the third half done; the following day, I went down to the city with a roll of plans under my arm and I went to the office; Wilson wasn't there. That astonished me, for it was the hour when he habitually was to be found there; I went to his house, where Mrs. Wilson told me that the doctor had just taken the steamer for San Francisco, and that he would return by the next steamer, that is, in ten days. Annoying setback! to wait ten days,

7. C. W. Burrage was one of three civil engineers listed in the *Portland Directory*. He was also county surveyor and maintained an office at the corner of Stark and Sixth Streets. See *Portland Directory, 1863*, p. 28.

perhaps twelve, I could not remain so long in idleness, I had to make a decision and make it promptly.

Then I was again presented with this embarrassing question: what to do? I could not dream of continuing the trade of woodcutter alone, and moreover this trade was not my sort of thing.

I ended, in desperation, by settling on the idea of seeking a livelihood from that which had hardly been for me, until then, but a pastime: the hunt. It remained to be seen if this trade could be lucrative enough in a country where food of all kinds was abundant and, consequently, low in price. It seemed, moreover, full of game: grouse, pheasants, geese and wild ducks, deer abounded there; the bear too was not lacking, but this redoubtable plantigrade was not yet game for me; it was rather an enemy and an obstacle. In these woods full of thickets, where there was no path marked, one took a great risk of stumbling on Martin before having seen him—and then Martin [facetious French term for an armed person], with his teeth and his claws, tore you in pieces. . . .

So I reflected while returning from Doctor Wilson's, where I had left my plans, explaining to his wife what it was all about. As I was passing before the butcher shop where we got our supplies, I entered and inquired of Captain Ankeny, head of the place, the prices I could get for the game I might bring him.[8] He told me that he would pay me twenty-five to forty cents apiece for ducks, depending on the kind and size, fifty cents for grouse and pheasants; as for deer, he could take that from me only at the rate of eight cents a livre and then on condition that I not bring them often; but he offered me twenty-five cents a livre for bear, gross weight; there were even three of these animals for which he promised to pay me at the rate of a dollar a livre, not because their flesh had a particular savor, but because they were his personal enemies: these three individuals came to steal his pigs in his slaughterhouse, and he was eager to get rid of them.

"But," said I, "Captain, how will I be able to prove to you, if I bring you a bear, that it is one of these?"—"Bring me," he said, "a bear with pork in his stomach and I will pay you a dollar a livre for him."—"Well," I said, "I accept, but on that account, it will cost you dear; I'm going to buy pork from you and I will make the bear eat it before killing him."

"As you please, but look: be careful; I'm not hiring you at all to hunt bear; I'm only telling you the price I will pay you for them, and I warn you that you are playing for big stakes. Since I have been here, two hunters, to my knowledge, have

8. Alexander P. Ankeny, a former sea captain, was engaged in many enterprises. Besides working as a merchant and a butcher, he joined H. W. Corbett and others to form an independent transportation line to operate on the Columbia. Unable to compete with the Oregon Steam Navigation Company, headed by Simeon G. Reed, the firm failed, but Ankeny continued to make money in other enterprises. Portland's New Market, opened in 1872, was built by Ankeny. This multiple-use building had stalls or concessions on the ground floor and a 1,200-seat theater on the second. The latter was described as the most elegant north of San Francisco. In recognition of his contributions, A Street in Portland was named Ankeny Street. Throckmorton, *Oregon Argonauts*, pp. 253–54, and Snyder, *Skidmore's Portland*, pp. 139–40.

been victims of their own daring. In any case," he added, "it is still too early for you to bother with that; it is now the month of August and I will not be able to use your game and, consequently, buy it from you until the month of October."—"The devil! that won't take care of me from now to then, what will I do? I'm no longer cutting wood, because I am alone; I was in the midst of discussions with Doctor Wilson on the subject of making a garden of the block around his house; but before concluding anything, he left for San Francisco on the last steamer, which gives me ten days at least to wait; now, I cannot keep on doing nothing like this, that is why I thought of hunting and of making it my trade."—"So you are a gardener?"— "Not precisely, but I think that I can make a garden, that is, level the land, mark the paths, plant trees, etc."—"But then, you are the man Portland lacks; the city does not have a man capable of properly leveling a lot suitable for making a garden. I have employed at this work, around my house, five or six individuals in succession who could do nothing but receive my money."

"It is true, Captain," I said, "that that is the point, but what would you want to do around your dwelling?"—"Two years ago, I planted fruit trees there; they are not doing well; I would like, however, to make something grow there, to cultivate it (*le fumer*), in short to make it something other than a wild land disagreeable to the eye; none of those whom I employ in my five butcher shops has any skill at it. Listen, give up the hunt, that can be an agreeable pastime, but here it is a poor trade; observe that this beefsteak which I sell you for five cents, costs me only three, I pay four cents for pork, same price for mutton; when I sell a chicken for twenty-five cents, it is selling well, and then, to get that price for it, it must have been killed and plucked properly. Under such conditions, what do you expect should become of the sale of game? I would have bought yours, from time to time, intending it for a few fine palates I know, for whom it would have varied the ordinary fare and who would have paid me a good price for it; but don't go and think that you would have earned your living at that trade; no, become a gardener and you will make money. Listen to me, for fifteen years now I have lived in Oregon, and I have passed half that time in Portland, that is, I have been here since it first existed; I know the country, and I guarantee you that I, in your place, would not budge from here and I would not hunt, I would make gardens; it's at that trade that you will earn money. In any case, try to do my block while waiting for better, come to see me Sunday at my house, I think that we will be able to come to an agreement." Note here that in America, the tradesman never lives in the building where he has his shop or his store; Ankeny had, in different quarters of the city, five shops where he retailed his meat, then a house where he lived with his family.

Somewhat comforted, I took the road back to our camp. On entering, I found Létang gay, radiant, almost disposed to sing; I expressed my astonishment to him. "I have," he said, "good news to tell you: I now have a trade, I am a tanner. Mr. Field, who has a tannery lower down here, came to see me in passing; in the course of the conversation, I learned that he needed an extra worker in September, I offered myself, and the bargain was concluded; I am to start with him in fifteen days.[9]

"I have four hundred dollars a year, with board and room, and, at the same time, he is to teach me to cure leather. I think my bargain is good, in a year I will more or less know the trade, then I will earn more. Field told me that if I knew how to cure properly, he would give me sixty dollars a month; what better could I wish? I have what I need.

"And you," he said to me, "what will you do?"

I brought him up to date on my projects and told him that if I could not succeed in making a gardener of myself or in living by the hunt, before long I would go back to California, not wishing to expose myself to spending the winter in a country where I would find nothing more to do with myself, since in that season it rained, they said, continually.

Planning to hunt the next day in order to assure myself that I had lost none of my cynegetic aptitudes, and also to determine if the country was as full of game as it seemed, I took my gun, long neglected, and began to clean it. Miraud, at sight of this, could not contain his joy; he began to bark, to frisk, to perform a million follies; then finding the preparations a little long, he did not stop stretching and yawning to signify his impatience. It was necessary, however, to wait until the next morning; I believe he hardly slept that night. Dawn had scarcely started to open the doors of the East, when he was afoot in seeming reproach of my laziness, but he did not wait long; I went out early, heading toward the hill which rises on the west of the city and separates it from the Tualatin basin. Miraud, then, abandoned his worried attitude, stopped his disordered movements, and assumed a serious air on following me; he was going to enter into the exercise of his functions and he felt his importance. I saw, going up, quite a few tracks of rabbits and grouse or prairie hens which I could not shoot, but it was a good augury to have seen them. On reaching the top of the hill, I found myself in a sort of clearing. There was a farm there, already abandoned for several years. With fire and axe they had made a certain opening in the forest and more or less cleared it; in particular, the farmer had planted some fruit trees and, although left to themselves, they had grown and at that moment were bearing much fruit; but little by little the forest was regaining possession of its domain, bushes were springing up everywhere, even in the stables of the farm, where the roof, half fallen in, allowed the air, the sun, and the rain to penetrate.

From the culminating point where I found myself, the view embraced a very extended horizon, but the spectacle was little varied because the whole surrounding country was nothing but an immense forest. At one point and another, there rose,

9. Two "Fields" are listed in the 1863 directory: H. G. Field, butcher, and D. C. Field, clerk. Since D. H. Lownsdale was the foremost tanner in Portland, it is possible that one of the Fields, most likely the butcher, worked for Lownsdale and hired Létang. See *Portland Directory, 1863*, p. 27.

above this sea of verdure, a column of smoke, indicating, doubtless, the location of a farm. Far off to the north, I discovered the palisaded walls of Fort Vancouver, built on the right bank of the Columbia; the distance is six miles.

In the interval which separates this locality from Portland, there extends a plain, in the western part of which the Columbia and the Willamette come to mix their waters; it is prolonged to the east as far as the Sandy, eighteen miles distant. Then there begins a series of hills which, rising gradually, come to an end in Mount Hood, an enormous peak, eighteen thousand feet high, they say: one sees it distinctly from Portland, sixty miles away.

Its immense base is entirely covered with a thick forest, which rises to the point where all vegetation ceases; above this verdure, and plunging into the clouds, appears the head of the peak, eternally covered with snow. The plain is continued to the south with slight interruption as far as the Clakamas, a river which flows twelve miles from Portland in the direction of the west and joins the Willamette below Oregon City, where the latter drops abruptly in a cascade twenty feet high. On the west as well there extends a vast plain, but lightly undulating; after fifteen miles this terrain, gradually mounting, ends by hiding the horizon. This plain is watered by the Tualatin, which flows in the opposite direction to the Willamette, that is, from the north to the south, and comes, by a very gentle slope, to throw itself into that river some miles above Oregon City.

I shot two grouse on this plateau, then Miraud raised a deer, whose tracks only I could see. As the underbrush became somewhat thinner toward the west and as the dog seemed to bring the game from that side, I went into it; twice, a deer pursued by Miraud passed by me without my being able to see either one or the other.

After two hours lost in marches and countermarches, I shouted out to recall the dog, then began to walk through the woods to reach a path which I knew and which ought to be at my right. The brushy terrain permitted me to advance only slowly; often an enormous pine, fallen for a hundred years perhaps, barred my passage and obliged me to make a long detour at least to be able to pass under it, or else, by helping myself by bushes already growing over it, to succeed in climbing it; but it was not always easy to cross in this way trees which often were six to eight feet in diameter. I spent almost three hours in making a few kilometers; from time to time, Miraud flushed a grouse or pheasant, which I did not always have the luck to shoot.

At last I found my path and I returned to Portland toward evening. I brought back three grouse and a pheasant; that was the result of my day and I was exhausted by fatigue! I began to share the opinion of Ankeny: hunting in this country, at least in the environs of Portland, could be a relaxation, but not a trade.

I needed something else to make my fortune, or simply to earn my living in Oregon. In spite of all the good that Ankeny had said of it to me, I regretted having come there, and if there had been at that moment a steamer leaving for San Francisco, I think that I would have returned very quickly to California; one was sure in the first place of finding work there, and then one was more free there, or, if one wishes, more independent. The Bell incident gave me something to think about; so from then on I would have to find out and worry about what my neighbor thought! I could no longer live according to my fancy under pain of scandalizing and estranging him; I would be forced to watch myself, to control myself, I who was so unaccustomed to it! There was enough to make me regret the half-wild life I had led on the placers.

However, when Sunday came, I reported to Captain Ankeny. He lived in the lower part of the city in a great house—of wood, naturally, but spacious and comfortable; he had bought it for eight thousand dollars with the block which surrounded it. On my arrival, he was walking in his garden and gathering fruits for dessert; he had some fine pears and some fine peaches, but he had few of them, the whole block having been planted with trees only two years before.

We began to talk business:

"I have reflected," he said, "on what we were speaking of the other day. To make it short, here is what I propose: I will give you this block to cultivate; you will make the humps and holes you see disappear from it; I will furnish tools for you, fertilizer, and seeds; and all the vegetables which you make grow here, except what I need for my kitchen, will be yours. There are only three of us, my wife, a laborer, and me—I do not count four children, the eldest of whom is twelve. You will enjoy the land under these conditions for three years. If that does not suit you, here is another combination: You will clear my block so that it can be properly leveled and spaded, between now and the 20th of September, that is, before it rains; I will pay you three dollars a day, with board and room. Or else again, let's discuss a contract, you look at the work there is to do, and tell me how much you ask to do it; if we come to an agreement, I will pay you the price decided on when you have finished. You will work when you want, how you want, and as much as you want."

As I was going to reply, Ankeny stopped me and told me that he wanted no answer that day. "Here," he said, "for three days I have thought of it, you think it over for three days too, we will find ourselves on the same footing. You see, no surprise, let each of us really know what he's getting into, because I myself do not like to go explain things before the justice of the peace; one goes there, ordinarily, only for lack of sufficient explanation before coming to terms. Moreover, you, a stranger to the locality, you cannot appreciate whether the offers I make you are advantageous before informing yourself of many of the things you do not know; so find out in town the price of vegetables, of manure, of a day's labor, etc. I could tell you myself, but I would rather that others did it. Return in two or three days, perhaps we will do business."

On that, and without leaving me time to say a word, he gave me his hand, then we parted. I had not yet had enough to do with the Yankees to have learned that that was their way of doing business, and I thought that Ankeny had so brusquely put an end to our interview only because he was in a hurry to sit down to table or because he had business elsewhere. On leaving, I made a circuit of the block which was to be cleared; a rapid examination was enough for me to decide on the choice I had to make; I had no wish to work by the day any time when I was free to work by the job; I estimated as a month the time I would need to finish the work and I fixed the price for it at a hundred and fifty dollars.

Ankeny seemed to me to be a man positive in business, as he was clear and precise in his words: he would not like to bargain. If my price had been too far from his, he was no doubt the man to break it off right there: so I must not show myself too demanding. As for cultivating his block and selling its produce, I had not thought of that for an instant. A gardener? I who had never planted a radish and who didn't even recognize its seed! Ankeny could be right when he said that there was lots of money to be earned by raising and selling vegetables, but one would have had to know the trade. Good enough, if only I had had a partner who knew how to sow and who knew seeds; might as well be a gardener as work in the mines or as a laborer; but alone, once again, I could not think of it.

While making these reflections, I had crossed the town without noticing it, and I was surprised to find myself all at once face to face with Létang, occupied in plucking a pheasant and a grouse. "You have done nothing," he said to me, "I read that on your face; if you had succeeded, you would have a less pensive air."— "Nothing is decided," I told him. "We shall see, in two days, if we can come to an agreement. I have to go to town tomorrow to find out the price of vegetables; wouldn't it be funny if I were going to become a gardener?"

"My word," said Létang, "now that I am a tanner, I'm no longer surprised at anything. As for the price of vegetables," he added, "I can already give you some information: here is a head of cabbage which, yesterday, cost us twenty-five cents (it weighed three pounds); these carrots (one pound) cost me ten cents, these turnips (three little ones) as much. I have not bought any other vegetables, because there were no others on the market, but they told me that there would be some soon; from day to day they're expecting the steamer which brings them from California; then you can get full information on the prices."

This revelation that the vegetables came from San Francisco plunged me into new perplexities; so the soil of Portland was unsuited to this kind of cultivation! I did not want to wait till the next day to find out about this: I immediately took the road back to the city and spent the rest of the day in wandering around it to see what they cultivated in the gardens, and how it grew.

I observed at once that vegetables were very seldom and very badly cultivated there, and yet they grew. The inhabitants of Portland, preoccupied above all in beautifying their residences, subordinated the useful to the agreeable, that is, vegetables to flowers; before almost every house, there was a garden-plot, more or less big, more or less well-arranged, but generally poorly kept up. Ankeny might be right, there was money to be earned by whoever knew how to do it better. Should I try it? But the mines? Was I going to give them up? And to these questions I replied, not without having heaved some sighs: "Why not? Provided that I earn my living, I might as well dig here as spade the sands of the gold-bearing rivers; besides, in any case I have to spend the fall here; let's use it in making gardens; if I do not succeed, the mines will still be there."

That is how I decided to do business with Ankeny, but Caesar, at the moment of crossing the Rubicon, had been less perplexed than I. It was not the image of the weeping Homeland which was raised before me, it was Fortune, deceptive Fortune, showing me, in the sands of a creek, a golden ingot of a hundred kilos.

"Well," Ankeny said to me, when on Monday, in the afternoon, he saw me come into his house, "well, where are we?"

"Captain," I replied, "you pay me a hundred and fifty dollars when I have finished leveling and spading your block, and I will start the work immediately."— "The devil," he said, "you want to make it pretty fine to ask that much?"— "Perhaps; if I couldn't claim to do better than what I've seen in the town, I wouldn't get mixed up in it."

"I accept then, but on one condition, that is that you begin by laying out a good garden-plot in front of my house; I had forgotten to speak of it to you and it isn't in our bargain, but that doesn't matter, if I give you a hundred and fifty dollars, that will go along with the rest, especially as that is what my wife wants most."— "So be it, I will begin tomorrow. Prepare a plan of your garden so that I may see more or less what you want."— "Ah, as for that, you still will have to give us your ideas; make some sketches yourself, then my wife will choose what will be most to her taste; as for me, I decline to give an opinion, I know nothing of it."

I returned to my hut, immediately set to work, and made three different designs.

Early the next day, I was spading and leveling the ground, while Mrs. Ankeny was choosing between my three plans.

In two days, during which I worked at least thirty hours, that plot was leveled and spaded; then, with the chosen plan in my hand, I marked the paths, the circles, the kidneys, and the hearts; by Saturday, before evening, this garden was prepared; there only remained the planting and sowing, but for that it was necessary to wait for the rain, which should not come until about the month of October. The next day, Sunday, there was a crowd all day in front of the Ankeny house; strollers of both sexes were passing and repassing to admire my work. You can imagine if I was proud!

The following Monday, I began to level the block. I began my day at four o'clock in the morning, at ten o'clock I returned to the house, I dined, then slept until three o'clock, after which I worked until eight.

Létang, at the end of a few days, left to move in at the tannery, and I lived alone, forced to do my own cooking. The menu for my meals, always the same, was of the simplest: beefsteak and bread, bread and beefsteak, then a glass of beer, which I went to get at the neighboring brewery; a half-liter cost me ten cents.

The following Tuesday, when hardly off the steamer which had brought him from San Francisco, Doctor Wilson sent for me; I thought it was to ask me for news of Létang, whom he had left convalescent, but no, it was to talk to me about his garden. Someone had told him that I was clearing the Ankeny block and he was afraid, I think, that I would not do his. "I have seen your plans," he said; "we have chosen this one. How much do you ask to carry it out?"— "Doctor," I said to him, "first take into consideration the importance of the work, which you have not had the time to do as yet, and you will tell me tomorrow or the next day if it is too much to ask you for three hundred and twenty dollars. Ankeny is giving me a hundred and fifty and there is practically nothing to do there but to spade, while at your place there is a lot to level, plus fourteen stumps to pull up and burn."

"I consent," he said, "to pay this price, on condition that the work be finished by the fifteenth of November."

I accepted the condition and, the bargain concluded, I returned to my work, but, on the way, I reflected that I had promised a little lightly; it was now the fifteenth of August; I had enough for four weeks' work at Ankeny's and I would need a good two months to level the Wilson block; that brought me to the fifteenth of November, but, supposing my labors were interrupted, even if it rained only ten or twelve days, it would then become impossible for me to fill my engagements and perhaps I would not be paid for what I would have done.

The result of my reflections was that I wrote to Margraff to have him return to Portland, offering him to work for me at the same rate that they were paying him back there.

The following day, a man named Reed came to find me at work, asking me to make him a garden-plot in front of his house similar to the one I had made for Ankeny. [10] He showed me a lot and asked what that would cost him. On the spot, I estimated the work at sixty dollars. "All right," he said, "do it at once and I will give you sixty-five." I accepted, subject to Ankeny's consent, as I was promised to him. This latter, to whom I spoke of it that same evening, authorized me and even made me promise to conclude this arrangement, assuring me that if his block was finished by the month of March, he would count himself satisfied.

The next day, I went to work at Reed's and in six days I had earned the sixty-five dollars—it is true that I made my workdays fifteen hours long.

I was still working at Reed's when Ankeny brought me a new client, a Mr. Birdseye, who had two blocks to clear. [11] He gave me time enough for that, provided only that his land would be available by the following June, for he wished to build. He showed me his blocks, explained what he wanted, left me two days to

10. Probably Simeon Gannett Reed (1830–95), who came to Oregon in 1852 and soon became the business partner of William S. Ladd. Their shrewd investments in river steamboats led to the creation of a powerful transportation monopoly in Oregon and Washington that eventually included railroads as well. The Oregon Steam Navigation Company became even more powerful under a remarkable triumvirate, Reed, John C. Ainsworth, and R. R. Thompson, in later years. Reed was also a successful investor in Idaho mines, real estate, and livestock ventures. A devout Unitarian who was always interested in education and the arts, he and his wife eventually left a large bequest which was used to found Reed College. His ornate mansion at First and Harrison streets was not built until 1871. There is no evidence in Perlot's memoir that he had a role in its landscaping although he was in Portland until 1872. See Lamar, ed., *Reader's Encyclopedia of the American West*, p. 1007; Snyder, *Skidmore's Portland*, pp. 47, 71; and Throckmorton, *Oregon Argonauts*, pp. 148, 250–343 passim.

11. Perlot later identified Birdseye as the proprietor of a hotel, but I have been unable to determine which hotel he owned.

make my estimate and tell him my price. But when I saw Ankeny alone again, I told him that I did not dare treat with Birdseye because that job would keep me too long in Portland; I had enough on hand to keep me busy until the month of April, and that was the time to leave for the mines. Ankeny looked fixedly at me, and shrugged his shoulders without saying anything; he was in the midst of arranging his display and continued as if nothing had happened. I took a chair and seated myself, thinking that the captain was too busy at the moment and that probably, when his display was arranged, he would answer me. But, at the end of a few minutes, passing in front of me, he said, showing me the door: "Get along now, go talk to that man and don't return until that's settled."

"What!" I said, "but if, as you tell me yourself, it rains so much in winter, I will not have finished this work before May, and it will then be too late for me to go to the placers."—"Well, so much the better, that means you won't go, you will stay on the placers you have discovered and are exploiting here. Haven't you a good placer in my block, where you are earning four dollars a day? and in Wilson's, where you are earning as much, and in Reed's, where you earned ten? What placer in Oregon or in California will bring you more? Listen to me, establish yourself in Portland, in four or five years you will have amassed enough to live in comfort.

"Quickly, 'le temps c'est de l'argent (time is money)', don't lose any, go talk it over with Birdseye; I knew what I was doing when I brought him to you: when you have cleared his blocks, that will make you known in the city and it will depend only on you to have clients. Go see what there is to do, make your price and stick to it; don't let him beat you down, keep that well in mind."

I was irresolute, Ankeny spoke with conviction and moreover I knew him to be a man of good counsel. That caused me to get up and go immediately to look at Birdseye's land; I calculated that there was a hundred days' work; estimating my day at three and a half dollars, then adding ten or twelve percent for unforeseen difficulties, I fixed the round sum of four hundred dollars as the price of my work.

From that moment my decision was made: Ankeny had won. For nearly fifteen days, I was wondering what I could do in Portland and how I could earn my living there. The question was thorny for me, who knew no trade and who wanted to remain my own master; it seemed to me, however, that it should not be insoluble. It was important first of all that the industry I undertook was a new thing in Portland; by that I avoided competition which I was not in a state to sustain, knowing nothing.

Now, Ankeny had, at different times, called my attention to the fact that Portland lacked what he called a garden-digger. I listened to his suggestions, contesting them enough to force him to explain himself, not enough to discourage him; this way I had obtained from him information which, joined to my own observations, had permitted me to weigh the pro and con, and put me at last in a position to make a decision with due knowledge of the situation. This decision I had just made: I was settling in Portland and I was becoming a garden-digger.

I went immediately to find Birdseye, who kept a hotel; I told him my price, he put off his reply until the next day; when I returned on the morrow, he presented a contract all drawn up for me to sign. This contract already bore the signature of Ankeny, who, without telling me of it, had not hesitated to be surety for me by guaranteeing to a sum of four hundred dollars that I would execute the conditions of the contract, if I signed it.

Birdseye wanted to have full security in this regard, because he was going to leave Portland, not to return until the month of April, and in order to be able to occupy himself exclusively with the houses he intended to build on the two blocks.

Once having decided to remain and to establish myself in Portland, I felt the need of going to settle on land belonging to me; I had, moreover, another reason for changing quarters.

My present residence was too near the Bell house, and I was eager to get away from it, as much for my personal satisfaction as for his; my proximity must have displeased this devout character, and his hardly agreed with me; I felt that we would never be good neighbors.

It isn't that Bell was a bad man, no, at least he didn't have the air of it, he was amiable insofar as his nature allowed, he spoke well and unctuously; it could even be that in our discussion of the other day, he had had the advantage over me by the propriety of his language if not by the strength of his arguments; it was perhaps one of the reasons which made me wish to have him for a neighbor no longer.

The following Sunday I explored the environs of Portland. I noticed, a kilometer northwest of the city, some land which seemed propitious for the establishment of a truck-garden; it was crossed by a stream which had water at all times and was entirely covered by trees and bushes. I informed Ankeny of my intention of buying this land, and asked him to whom it belonged. He named Captain Couch to me, and assured me that I would have dealings with a loyal and conscientious man; at once, I went to find Captain Couch, who sent me to Captain Flanders, his brother-in-law, in charge of negotiating the sale of land belonging to the family.[12] This last being absent just that day, I returned to find Captain Couch, begging him to consider the block no. 72 as sold; as for the price, I declared that I would accept whatever Captain Flanders found it good to ask me.

On the next day, I went to settle on my estate. Mr. Bell had obligingly lent me his wagon to effect the transfer of my goods; never, I think, had he rendered a

12. Ankeny referred Perlot to Captain John H. Couch, one of the earliest founders of Portland, who had come to the West Coast in the 1840s with his brother-in-law, Captain George H. Flanders. In addition to building the "wharf which extended from Ankeny to Davis Street," and Greenwich wharf, Couch constructed the first Masonic temple in the city. He and his family owned land in the northwest portion of the city called Couch's Addition. It was in this area that Perlot decided to buy property. See *Portrait and Biographical Record of Portland and Vicinity* (Chicago: Chapman, 1903), pp. 116–19, and Throckmorton, *Oregon Argonauts*, pp. 29–30. See also maps in *Portland Directory, 1866*.

Perlot purchased block 72 because it was traversed by Tanner's Creek, from which he could get water for his plants and seedlings. See front of *Portland Directory, 1867* (Portland, 1867), for map of Portland and Couch's Addition.

service so joyfully; so we parted good friends, but without the slightest tear being spilled on either side.

I spent the week in building myself a house, such as it was, with the materials of the old one, which I had moved to my block. Nevertheless, for months yet, I had to consecrate my Sundays to putting the last touches to it.

Moreover, it was nothing but a temporary lodging, for before building for good, I had to cut down nearly fifty enormous pines of which one alone, falling, would have been enough to crush my establishment. As soon as I was lodged, it was my occupation in the mornings and evenings to eliminate one after another these fifty pines of Damocles suspended over my head.

All this retarded the execution of the works which I had undertaken. To crown the bad luck, Margraff, whose reply I had at last received, could not come to join me before the month of January: he had undertaken the construction of a canal which would not be finished until that time.

Happily, a helper came to me; a Frenchman of the name of Abadie, a baker by trade, arrived one fine morning with the steamer which gave service between San Francisco and Portland. As he did not know English, they sent him to me. His bakery had burned, that had been followed by a suit with his neighbors, and his lawyer had advised him to get out of San Francisco for some time. He had nothing more left and he asked only to work. Such was his story. After a short exchange of words, I hired him; I gave him fifty dollars a month, board and room, on condition that he help me in my gardening work, do the cooking, and bake my bread, which until then I had bought at the bakery at the rate of six cents a pound, although wheat was sold for only two cents.

Thanks to this reinforcement, I was able to finish, before the first of November, the garden of Ankeny, that of Wilson, and one of Birdseye's two blocks. While we were working on the second, Mr. Lewis, brother-in-law of Doctor Wilson, came to ask me to clear his block and make him a garden like that of the doctor, which he had found beautiful; he gave me two years to do this work, but, profiting by the presence of Abadie, I set at it immediately and finished it in fifteen days.[13]

The rain came then, which stopped the works of terracing until the end of autumn; in the intervals which it left me, I employed my time in clearing my own block; I had begun by enclosing it, for which it was enough to cut down on the sides four pines which were each two hundred feet long; the walls extended another eighty feet beyond the limits of the block.

Abadie, who had helped me in this work, having received in the first days of the month of December a letter from San Francisco, was eager to return to that city,

---

13. Perlot is probably referring to Cicero H. Lewis, who came to Portland in 1851 and started a grocery business. He soon entered into partnership with a San Francisco merchant and eventually Allen and Lewis became "one of the foremost wholesale houses not only in Portland but of the entire West Coast." Lewis lived at North Fourth Street between D and C. See *Portland Directory, 1863*, p. 37, and Throckmorton, *Oregon Argonauts*, pp. 126–27.

where he was going, he said, to take up again his bakery trade. So I found myself alone to spend the winter.

Here I must chronicle a sad event, the tragic end of my poor Miraud. I had the habit of tying him in the morning to the door of my cabin and of untying him in the evening, but since I was working near the house, I let him free early. One day, when I had untied him, he had taken his run toward the town; shortly after, I heard three revolver shots and the plaintive cries of a wounded dog, and soon I saw Miraud returning, all covered with blood, and dragging himself with difficulty; I took him, made him lie down, and found that he had been hit by two balls. I did everything I could to stop the blood—grease, bandage, clay, each was employed and each was useless: at the end of an hour, Miraud expired. He was dead on my bed, wrapped in all the pocket-handkerchiefs I had. While he was receiving my attentions, and already in the agony of death, he let himself be turned and turned again without making any cry, without letting any complaint be heard, but he looked sadly at me as if he understood that he was done for, that all was ended and that we had to say farewell forever; there was nothing but his dim eyes still fixed on me.

Such was the end of Miraud, this devoted friend, this faithful companion of good and bad days, the sole being in the world, perhaps, who loved me. Never had I felt myself as alone as in that moment!

At first when I saw him stretched lifeless before me, I felt a great anguish in my heart, then sorrow gave place to anger, and sinister thoughts invaded me.

I loaded my revolver and, having hung it on my belt, I left, guided by the blood my dog had lost along the road. This way I covered six hundred steps, then I stopped and reflected; mistrusting myself, I returned to the house and deposited my weapon, cast on Miraud's corpse a sad look and set off again to follow the bloody trail. On arriving where the wood ended and where the town began, I encountered a lad of fourteen or fifteen years who, guessing what preoccupied me, said: "Those are the tracks of a dog you are following, it was Mr. Wolf who shot him; I think that he was yours."[14]—"Where was he?" I asked, "when Mr. Wolf shot?"— "He was in Mr. Colman's garden, where he was chasing a bitch in heat. Wolf shot your dog because he was fighting with Colman's."—"Were you alone when Wolf shot?"—"No, I was with that man there," and he pointed at a man who was cutting wood not far from us. I went to him, followed by the lad; he confirmed the other's report: so I had two witnesses. After having taken their names and address, I went to Mr. Colman's. Wolf was his clerk; they told me that he had just left to return to the store, located in the town. Without losing time, I entered the town and inquired for Mr. Colman's store; they pointed out a crockery-store; I entered and found two people in the midst of labeling some newly unpacked glasses and putting them on the shelf. I asked for Mr. Wolf; one of the two said to me: "It is I, sir."— "Ah!" I said, "you are Mr. Wolf? Well, then, you are the man who just killed my

14. Wolf does not appear in any of the Portland City directories available to me.

dog."—"Indeed! as a matter of fact," he replied as calm as could be in the world, "I shot at a dog; I shot three times, he cried out, it was probably because I hit him; well, so what?"—"Well," I said, "he is dead and I come to demand satisfaction."

"What! satisfaction? For a dog? are you speaking seriously?"

"Let me tell you that this dog was for four years my faithful companion, that he followed me everywhere in California, that he fed me by accompanying me on the hunt, that he saved my life more than once among the Indians; he was my only friend, my only consolation in my solitude. You kill him and you ask me if it's seriously that I demand satisfaction from you! Oh yes, it *is* seriously, and let me tell you that I'm not leaving here before knowing what to count on as to your intentions in this matter."—"Well, after all, what an idea! What sort of satisfaction do you want me to give you for a dog?"—"You have a revolver, I have one too, I didn't bring it with me for fear of using it too soon. Well, we shall see if you have a hand as firm and an eye as sharp in shooting at the master as in shooting at the dog."— "Oh, as for me, I don't fight for a dog."—"Well, then," I said, controlling myself no longer, "if you aren't a coward, you will fight at least to avenge an insult"—at the same time, I let loose with all the strength of my arm a slap which made him stagger into a hamper full of glasses; the man and the hamper rolled under the table serving as counter. The other clerk, who had said nothing yet, approached me with some hesitation, and said to me: "Sir, if you fight in the store, you are going to break more crystal than your dog is worth."—"What!" I said, "is this imbecile going to come kill my dog and think that that is the end of it? that it isn't worth the trouble to do anything about it? Well then, I myself will take charge of teaching him what a dog is worth." Then Wolf, getting up from the other side of the table and approaching the other man, said: "If his dog is worth something, I'll pay him for it; I don't want to get into a fight."

Meanwhile, the passersby, attracted by the noise of the quarrel and the broken crystal, stopped before the door and blocked the sidewalk; the other clerk, very gently approaching me, said to me: "Let's see! I beg you, no scandal; let's settle this business instead; fighting gains nothing. How much was your dog worth?"

"It isn't for me," I said, "to fix the price; to me he was worth a great deal, and if it had to depend on my estimate, he would pay dearly."

"Well, appoint someone to estimate it and Wolf will pay you. Who, among the people in the city, knew your dog?"

"Captain Ankeny, Doctor Wilson, Mr. Bell, Mr. Field the tanner," I said, "have seen my dog and can, I think, judge how much he is worth."

"Well" [the other clerk continued], "name three men who will judge the value of the dog."—"Yes," said Wolf, "I will agree with what they decide."

"In that case," I said, "that's all right, let's see who will be these three men," and addressing Wolf: "do you accept Captain Ankeny?"—"Yes."—"Doctor Wilson?"—"Yes. And you," he asked me, "do you accept Mr. Higgins, he is a man of law and capable of judging the matter?"—"I do not know him, but that doesn't matter. Tell him to be here tomorrow at nine o'clock, I am going to tell

Messrs. Ankeny and Wilson; I like to think that they will not refuse me this service." On that, I left and went to convoke my two men for the jury next day.

The following day, at ten o'clock, I had in my hand the verdict of these three gentlemen directing that Wolf had to pay me the sum of fifty-five dollars; I gave this verdict to Wolf and I waited. He read it, then told me that at the moment, he did not have fifty-five dollars, that I should return tomorrow and that he would pay me. "No," I said, "I don't leave here before being paid, I'm not at all eager to see you again, pay me." Then Wolf went out of the store without saying anything. Not knowing what he planned, I settled myself between two shelves where there was the bookkeeper's table, three feet high, on which I could seat myself almost without bending my knees. I had chosen this place after having noticed, beside it, two brooms whose sticks seemed to be solid; it could be that I might soon need to make use of them; moreover, no one could pass behind me nor even approach me without disturbing two hampers full of crystal which were right next to me and so served me as rampart. But these precautions were needless; Wolf, at the end of a few moments, returned and paid me. "You will observe," he said, showing me the verdict, "that once it is paid and you have received the fifty-five dollars, you are to consider yourself satisfied."—"Very well," I said to him, "since the judgment says that I ought to be satisfied, I am; but the judgment does not say that I ought to shake your hand or bid you goodbye." With that, turning my back on him, I left and went first to thank my experts. I learned then that I had come close to losing my suit; I had won it thanks especially to the circumstance that my dog had a collar and that Wolf had not been able to affirm that my name was not written on it; thanks also to the fact that Wolf was not on his own land when he shot.

I then returned to the house and dug poor Miraud's grave in my garden. I buried him wrapped in the linens I had used in trying to save his life.

The next day, a man came and knocked on my door; I opened it, I showed him a seat, that is, a fragment of plank nailed to three long sticks serving as feet. He offered me his hand, a sign of friendship rather than simple politeness, according to American usage; "My name," he said, "is Colman; you can guess, I imagine, what brings me here?"[15] "Ah," I said, "you are Mr. Colman, the employer of Mr. Wolf; I can guess very well what you want to discuss, but I don't know what you want of me."—"It is so you can tell me yourself," he said, "how things happened. I returned last night from Oregon City; they told me about the affair; I would like very much now to hear you tell about it yourself, if such is your pleasure."— "Willingly," I replied, and I told him my story.

After having listened attentively, he said to me:

"Now look, here is the situation: Wolf is a poor devil whom I took in with me so that he would have something to eat; however big and fat he is, his health isn't very

15. A D. C. Coleman is listed in the *Portland Directory, 1863*, p. 23, but his occupation is not identified. Edmund T. Coleman climbed Mount Baker in 1868. See Harvey W. Scott, *History of Portland, Oregon* (Syracuse: D. Mason, 1890), 2: 304.

good, he isn't very strong; he works little, and I keep him for not much more than his board. Now, after examination, between the two of you, you have broken forty dollars worth of crystal in the store; if Wolf must pay for it, I am going to lose it; he already had to borrow thirty dollars yesterday to pay you. Now, I don't imagine that it's me whom you want to punish for his fault? what do you say, if we divide this loss between the two of us?"

After having thought it over a little, finding the thing fair enough, I reached in my purse and gave twenty dollars to Colman. "I take it to be true," I told him, "what you tell me; if this Wolf has broken your crystal, I don't deny having helped him a little; here is half of the sum at which you estimate it; only be good enough to recommend to your clerk that he be more circumspect in future and remind him that he ought to respect at least, in a poor inoffensive animal, the property of another."—"I think," he said, "that the lesson will do him good; I thank you for the good will you have shown in the settlement of this affair; I do not wish," he added, rising, "to keep you longer; you look unwell."

In fact, I had a violent headache, a thing that invariably happened to me each time I had had a fit of anger.

Colman went away after shaking my hand; I lay down again and stayed in my bed almost all day.

VIII

THE FRENCH GARDENER
1858–1867

*Between the colonist, who came full of
knowledge of an artistic precedent, and the later
traveler, who rediscovered it, there was a gap in
which little contact was maintained with the older
culture of Europe, and little thought given to
developing culture here. Lest this seem
unappreciative of a century which produced
Irving, Emerson and Cooper, let us say it was a
century the very conditions of which focused the
minds of the people upon politics, letters, industry
and invention, rather than upon art. . . . Save
for the efforts of Andrew Jackson Downing to
introduce into this country the romantic,
naturalistic expression of landscape design, as
expressed in England by the works of Sir
Humphrey Repton, no attempt was made to
produce examples of garden art of any
significance.*

James Bush-Brown and Louise Bush-Brown,
America's Garden Book (New York, 1967),
pp. 4–5

Household 1333, Family no. 1207
Perlot, John N., age 47, m. born Belgium
Occ: gardener
Perlot, Catherine, age 33, wife, born Belgium
Occ: Keeps house
Perlot, Eugenia F., age 2, born in Oregon
Lamot, Joseph, age 20, born in Belgium,
gardener
Berlangie, Joseph, age 28, born in Belgium,
gardener

U.S. Census for 1870, Oregon

In the following chapters it is clear that Perlot has begun to enjoy his new identity as "the French Gardener" of Portland, as much as he had once relished being "Mr. Oualai," the rugged miner from Marble Spring and friend of the Yosemite Indians. His new sense of dignity and status surfaced when Captain Ankeny asked him to assist in the operation of his pigsty and abbatoir, for he strongly resented the fact that he might be considered a mere workman. Even so, the historian must be grateful for Perlot's vivid description of Ankeny's business, which bought, killed and processed 8,000 hogs—one of Oregon's chief exports to California—all within a three-month period.

Meanwhile Perlot's very success as a nurseryman and gardener created a cruel dilemma for him: Should he invite his younger brother—who had always wanted to come to America—to join him in the business, or should he join the thousands of miners, most of them Californians, who were setting out for the Fraser River diggings in British Columbia in the spring of 1858?[1] In the end Perlot resisted the siren call of gold, possibly because the Fraser River placers were both remote and hard to exploit, and, as he put it, "again took up my ordinary way of life."

Having made that decision, Perlot became all the more frustrated when he learned of the gold strikes in Idaho a year later. But the appearance of his brother with his family, and the continued prosperity of Portland finally persuaded him that he had made the right decision. Indeed, despite the flooding of the Willamette, an unusually cold winter which killed most of his plants, and competition from farmers who were now specializing in market produce for the Portland market, Perlot continued to prosper. As various of his former shipmates or acquaintances from Mariposa passed through the city on the way to or from the Salmon River mines or the brief Rogue River rush, Perlot must have realized that they were still itinerants without fortune or family. Perlot, now forty-four, began to think of returning to Belgium to take a wife.

1. The Fraser River gold rush, writes Rodman Paul, was a "case of inaccurate reporting rather than pure humbug. The gold was there but there was less of it than expected, and the river could not be worked effectively until September because of the late melting of the mountain snows in British Columbia. In the meantime life was too expensive and difficult in the overcrowded settlements. The disappointed began returning in July, and by late October most of those who had rushed there were back in California, Oregon, or Washington." See Paul, *Mining Frontiers of the Far West, 1848–1880* (New York: Holt, Rinehart and Company, 1963), p. 38.

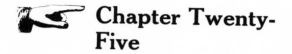 # Chapter Twenty-Five

Nurseryman and Landscape Gardener

One evening, as I was getting my meat at the butcher-shop, Ankeny told me that he had another job to offer me: his block was cleared, that was fine; now he wanted to cultivate it for two or three years to make his trees grow. He hardly had the time or the desire to take care of it himself. "Now let's see," he said, "help me to find a way we can arrange that."—"The thing," I said, "is easy: I will take up your first conditions again, you will furnish the manure, the bushes, and, instead of tools—which I don't need now since I have some—some glassed frames for hotbeds. I will cultivate your garden at my expense and will pay myself with what I grow there."—"Ah! you ask too much; let's share the crop, give me a third, I will help you to sell your part, I will take charge of selling mine."— "All right, so be it; make the contract, we will sign it tomorrow."

The next day all was concluded and signed, and already I was at the carpenter's to order eight frames five feet long by two and a half wide. Moreover, I had a load of hay delivered and from it made straw mats or sieves in order to be all ready to go to work as soon as spring came, that is, about the twentieth of February.

The weather had been superb, it permitted me to finish Birdseye's garden with the end of the year. I spent my evenings in studying the principles of the art I was practicing, and already horticulture had almost no more mysteries for me. I had not found in Portland, which, however, possessed two bookstores, the books which I needed for this study, but Abadie, as soon as he reached San Francisco, had sent me a treatise in French on the culture of flowers, a botanical dictionary in Spanish, and finally, a priceless book for me, the *American Gardener*, in English, which treated of the culture of vegetables, fruits, and flowers; this last I had not had fifteen days before I had read and reread it so many times that I knew it almost by heart.[1]

How many things just before had been mysteries for me, which now I understood perfectly and could explain to others! and I didn't hesitate to do so. Formerly, when people talked gardening to me, when they interrogated me on any fact of

1. Perlot may have been referring to Bernard M'Mahon, *The American Gardener's Calendar* (Philadelphia, 1819), which went through many later editions.

botany, I was very circumspect, very sober with my explanations, and those which I gave, ordinarily, did not explain very much; now, I was loquacious, tremendously proud of my knowledge of recent date, I loved to spread it; I explained things methodically, wisely, scientifically, employing technical names and terms. This raised me in the eyes of my clients and did no harm to my business.

When my preliminary works were nearly at an end, I composed a list of seedlings which I needed and gave it to Ankeny, in order that he might have them brought in time from San Francisco. In fact, as there was no seedsman in Portland, one could procure them only by the intermediacy of people who were going down to San Francisco, then returning to Portland.

While I was waiting for my seeds, Ankeny arrived one evening at my casa all out of breath, and told me that he expected a great service of me; he had no one but me at hand, he told me, and counted on my friendship for him to spare him a great loss of time and money. "Well, Captain," I said, "here is my coffee ready, let's take it together; you seem to be beside yourself; it will calm you, then you can tell me what it's about."

We took the coffee, then the Captain said to me: "I have just thrown three of my men out the door, I found all three of them so drunk that they were absolutely incapable of doing anything whatever, and that at the moment when I was the most pressed; I have just fought with them, I put them out with a beating; I am therefore alone, you will have to help me to get out of the affair; I will expect you very early tomorrow at the upper butcher-shop, I will explain to you what you have to do. — "All right, that's agreed, but I think, Captain, that it isn't for very long."—"Oh no, a few days only, the time to find someone, then you will return to your garden."

The next day, at five o'clock in the morning, I arrived at the butcher-shop, where I found Ankeny, who was waiting for me. Immediately, he gave his orders and handed me a list of the houses where I was to go, with a special cart, to look for what I would find all ready in buckets placed at certain spots. A man was to help me in this duty and show me the way to handle it. "This done," said Ankeny, "you will bring me the cart at the distillery, below the town, where I will await you to explain the rest to you."

I started my horse and there I was a carter. Everywhere we went with this cart, or rather with this box fastened any old way to two wheels, it was a restaurant or hotel, or else a middle-class boarding-house; we found there one or two buckets containing the kitchen refuse and we threw this into our box. When it was full, I brought it faithfully back to Ankeny, below the city, as had been agreed; I found him occupied with two or three workmen in feeding his *gentlemen*—so he called two or three hundred pigs which he had moved in beside the distillery.

The pigsty consisted of an immense plank roof, rather badly built, covering a lot divided in stalls or compartments, each of which contained from fifty to sixty of these interesting animals.

Ankeny did not need to give me ample explanations; at the distance of a hundred

paces, my olfactory organ had announced his pensioners and the species to which
they belonged.

On my arrival, all this population was awakened, aroused even; it was also very
noisy, especially in the compartments where they had omitted setting the table: it
was these whose guests were to be sacrificed that day.

Ankeny took my horse, guided my cart to the desired place, took out a pin and
the box, turning over, poured its contents all by itself into a big reservoir which was
found at a lower level. That done, Ankeny put back the pin, then said to me:
"Return to the city, go to the houses where you have not yet been, and return at
once with another load; after which you will help us in the killing."

Without having it repeated, I got back on my seat and whipped the horse, happy
to get away from this pestilential dwelling. While going back up to the town, I said
to myself that I had taken on a job beyond my strength: impossible to stand these
mephitic exhalations! How did the Captain and his men stand it? That is what I
could not explain to myself, but, assuredly, I would have to give up lending him my
help much longer. As I could not, in any case, leave him without warning him, I
went to reload my cart in the city, then brought it to the pig-farm. Not finding the
Captain there, I turned the cart, pulled the pin and emptied the load, then I waited;
I was much astonished not to fall down asphyxiated; now one could hardly even
perceive the proximity of Ankeny's *gentlemen!* Whence came this change? Before I
was able to find the answer, a man came to tell me: "take back the cart where you
got it this morning, then return." That is what I did. It was only on my return that,
having entered the pigsty, I had the key to the enigma: as the whole establishment
rested on piles, this permitted the river to pass beneath it; now, by means of the
pump and the steam engine of the distillery, which drew up the river-water in a long
rubber hose, two men, in an hour's time, had just washed the whole thing, board
and boarders too. Ordinarily, this washing took place each morning and it was
quickly done, for it was necessary only to turn a key and direct the end of the hose
properly; but, for the last eight days, the distillery had been stopped; in order to put
the pump in motion, it was necessary to light the furnace for the steam-engine, and
wait until it had built up pressure. For all these reasons, the cleaning was done only
every two or three days; it had not yet taken place that morning on my arrival; from
that came the aroma which had so disagreeably affected my sense of smell. I
recovered, after that, from my prejudices; I saw the others, beginning with the
Captain, splashing about in the pigsty as if there were nothing to it, smoking their
pipe, chewing their quid, all as tranquilly as a notary could do it in his office. "I
think," said Ankeny, "that it's clean," and he called the two others. "You ought,"
I said to him, "to suggest to your workmen not to chew that way; see, when they
spit, they soil even worse what they have just cleaned." The Captain looked at me,
smiling; "Fine!" he said, "tomorrow or the next day, when it will be your turn to
wash, you can do as you want. The job will soon be done regularly, for the
distillery will be put back in action before long; what you call my workmen," he

added, "are my two partners; abandoned by our workmen, we have to do the work ourselves."

While talking, we were going toward a big house situated across from the distillery.[2] On arriving, Ankeny said to me: "Since you don't have a costume, you will take one of mine here, it isn't worthwhile making you one." Saying this, he showed me a pair of pants and a jacket made of canvas, tarred and oiled.

It was seven o'clock in the morning; fifteen individuals entered the sort of hall where we were. All these men, young men for the most part, who seemed to me well set-up for workmen, took off their coats on entering, tucked the bottom of their pants in their boots and, over all their clothes, put on a jacket and pants similar to those which Ankeny had just given me. The toilette finished, each one went to turn the tap of a barrel placed in a corner and served himself with a good slug of whiskey; then the work began.

Two went to open a compartment whose guests threw themselves into a corridor in the form of a very acute angle, much extended, whose top ended in a see-saw or trap. This corridor then contained sixty to seventy porkers, which, necessarily, considering the narrowing of the walls, came one by one to the trap; their fall brought them on ropes stretched especially, where they received a hammer-blow. They were raised on the instant and dragged away by two men on an inclined plank where they bled them immediately.

As soon as they were dead, they were thrown on the ropes which plunged them into a trough full of boiling water; by means of two opposed ropes they turned and returned them in this boiling bath for a minute, after which, they were withdrawn from it and put on a table. Three men around each hog, washed it by hand and knife in a few minutes, then cut off its head; the decapitated body was attached to two hooks by the two hind feet, and a man opened the body from top to bottom, emptied it, cleaned it with cold water, then carried it not far from a cutting table formed by two pieces of wood, where six others, with big blows of their chopping-knives, were dismembering the pigs killed the day before. This table, twenty feet long, was a pine log seven feet in diameter and six feet long, which they had sawn in half down the middle [sciée en long par le milieu], and the two parts of which had been placed end to end, the cut edge forming the table. On each of the two sides there were three wheelbarrows on which the butchers threw the cut pieces; each full barrow was taken into a store next door, where some workmen were dividing the pieces by categories, and piling them up after having salted them. In the middle of the room, which was vast, they had set up, resting on the ground, a platform thirty feet square; the pieces of pork were placed and ranged there in such fine order, with such symmetry, that one would have called it a brick wall three meters high.

2. It seems likely that Perlot was referring to the Portland Distillery on the "North City Limits," which was owned by A. W. and L. M. Starr (*Portland Directory, 1863*, p. 63).

They left them piled this way long enough to take the salt, then, with the exception of the hams, they were taken up, put in casks, and finally sent to the mines or to San Francisco.

The hams were smoked in a square tower ten feet on a side by forty in height, built of boards; this tower, which had no other opening than a door cut in its base, was filled with hams in all its height.

They kept up, at the bottom, with wood scraps, a fire which should smoke rather than flame; in a few days, the operation was finished.

All the waste, head and feet included, was thrown into a huge boiler to extract the fat, which they sent away in tin cans hermetically sealed. The residue of this boiler served to nourish the unexecuted hogs. It was in this manner that a hundred to a hundred and twenty of these animals were disposed of every day.

From time to time, one or two men left their occupations to go to receive the new boarders which the farmers brought on wagons, or else which a steamboat unloaded at the pigsty itself; it was these which I was going to have to feed for a day or two while waiting till their turn came to be transformed into hams and half-salted pork.

At the stroke of noon, each one took off his costume and went to eat. Armed with a card which Ankeny gave me, I myself went to dine at the restaurant; to return to my house to make dinner, eat it, then return would have taken much too much time. At one o'clock, everybody was found at his post again and occupied it until six o'clock, the time when they closed the slaughterhouse. Three men only remained to hose everything off and prepare the place for the next day.

I did a lot of moving around, this first day, to do, on the whole, very little work; I ran, I hurried, and rarely did I find myself where I could be useful.

It was I, however, most of the time, who gave the hot-water bath. — "Well, new butcher," Ankeny said to me, "how is it going?" — "Captain," said I to him, "it's up to you to tell me if it's going well." — "But, it isn't going badly; keep coming and tomorrow it will go better, after tomorrow better yet. I think," Ankeny added, "that you would do well to go tell them up there to harness Jamey (the name of the horse) for you; you will bring a load this evening, that will put you ahead for tomorrow morning."

I got back on my seat, brought a load of supplies to the pigsty and helped Ankeny and company to distribute it. In the evening, at eight o'clock, I took the horse back to the upper butcher-shop.

"There," said Ankeny, "one day is done; tomorrow another begins again, it will pass like this one, and so with the others. They will harness your horse for you every day at five o'clock, they will care for it, and unharness it; you will have only to drive him as you have done today; only you will help me in the killing for a few more days, after which you will be occupied only with the wagon; in three hours' time, you will have finished your day's work."

"Captain," I said, "you speak as if I were going to stay a pig-man for a long time yet, and you asked my help for only a few days."

"No doubt; I am going to look for someone and will relieve you before long of your new functions."

"I'm counting on it, for, to speak frankly to you, and whatever pleasure I might find in feeding your interesting boarders, I still prefer to occupy myself with my garden."

"All right, all right, keep coming."

That went so well that I continued this trade another ten days without new protestations, getting up at four o'clock in the morning and ending my day at six or eight o'clock at night. Happily, the repugnance of the first days did not last, thanks to habit, so that soon I did my job, sometimes in blood to my ankles [ayant parfois du sang jusqu'à las cheville], with the same indifference as my collaborators.

Soon after, the distillery was put back in action and my task became easier.

Some pipes put the distillery reservoirs in communication with the troughs or boxes from which the hogs ate and drank; it was enough, three times a day, to raise or lower some plugs, and the distribution of the sort of black broth which composed their food and drink, took care of itself. In spite of everything, I would have preferred to return to my garden, and, after the ten days I spoke of had passed, I said to Ankeny: "Captain, you are playing me a dirty trick, you're not looking for anyone to replace me, spring is coming, my garden will be late."—"Oh," he said, "now you know the job it isn't worth replacing you; the distillery no longer has grain for more than ten or twelve days, then we'll stop killing and you can return to your vegetables. Wait, here is what I propose to you: You will stay with us until we have finished killing, then you will make, at my expense, the trip to San Francisco; you will go to choose your seeds yourself and will bring me back some shrubs for my garden. Is it agreed?"—"So be it, but on condition that it stops there and you don't make me any other propositions; otherwise, I get out."

I was not annoyed to go myself to look for my seeds at San Francisco; Ankeny was responsible for supplying them, but I knew how he could get them; they would have been good or bad, I had no guarantee whatever in that respect.

At the beginning of February, Margraff returned to Portland; he had finished his canal and came to see if I had work to give him. I hired him at forty dollars a month, but to begin after my return from San Francisco; until then, I would feed and lodge him on condition that he move into my casa and do the cooking for the two of us. Some days later, the steamer arrived; I stopped being a wagoner, being a butcher, and Ankeny himself stopped killing, because the season was no longer propitious for salting.

From the tenth of November to the fifth of February Ankeny and company had killed eight thousand pigs, which they bought at four cents a pound, live weight, and which they had resold in barrels at the rate of eighteen cents.

Before leaving for San Francisco, I went to see Dr. Wilson, who asked me to bring him what he needed to decorate his garden. I left aboard the *Commodore*, which took four days to make the trip. I had only two days to make my purchases. By a happy chance, on the morning of my arrival, as I was visiting the flower market to get information, I encountered Viot, one of my former companions on board ship and on the trip to the placers. He would not have recognized me if I had not accosted him, but at the first word, he remembered my name and my face; for a long time settled in San Francisco, he delivered newspapers and appeared content with his lot.[3] We entered a saloon and, in ten minutes, I had in my note-book the addresses of all our old shipboard friends who were living in the city, then, an essential thing, the address of Mr. Cuvreau, seedsman and gardener for flowers and vegetables, who lived at the Mission, three kilometers from the city. Soon after, Viot left me to continue his rounds, the newspapers under his arm, not without having made me an appointment for five o'clock in the evening at the Café de la Rotonde, kept by a friend, a passenger like us on the *Courrier de Cherbourg* but an independent passenger, whose name I do not remember. He was from Orléans and a hatter by trade.

I lunched with Mr. Cuvreau; I had just bought from him almost as many flower and vegetable seeds as I needed for two years. He was to bring me the case containing everything, plus an enormous bundle of shrubs, that same evening, at Mr. Vénard's, another shipboard companion, at present a wholesale dealer in ground coffee, then rejoin me at the Café de la Rotonde.[4]

My whole afternoon was spent in visiting friends, in shaking them by the hand and in giving them a rendezvous at the aforesaid café. Four only, out of eight, could report there; the others for the most part excused themselves by letter: pressing business had come up and, on my word, in America, business came before everything, but they promised me that they would be at the steamer next day to shake my hand at the departure. I none the less spent some good moments with those who came to the rendezvous. They exchanged the news they had of the former members of the company of La Fortune; in sum total, fortune had not smiled on them: nine or ten only, out of forty-five, seemed to prosper and, to my great surprise, they counted me among them. Salomon, the same one who, on board, charmed away the ennuis of the crossing by declaiming to us the recitation of Théramène or of the Battle of Waterloo, took pleasure in recounting to me the good each one had done since we were scattered; the evil, he had not learned, or the excellent man preferred to forget what he knew of it. He was married and he insisted on showing me his wife; after having drunk several glasses, we all went, except Mr. Cuvreau, who had to return to the Mission, to dine with our friend. This was a sort of small family feast for which Mrs. Salomon did the honors with a

3. The *San Francisco Directory, 1856* (San Francisco, 1856) lists Viot and Pons as maintaining a "French Library."

4. G. Venard is listed as a coffee manufacturer in ibid., p. 41. E. Venard, possibly a relative, is identified as Vice-President of the French Benevolent Society in San Franciso (ibid., p. 129).

perfect grace; two other ladies of their acquaintance were there for dinner too, which was only the gayer for it. When they had served the tea, which often, in America as in England, replaces coffee, these ladies sang some songs which reminded us of the absent homeland.

The party was prolonged well into the night; it was a long time since I had spent so agreeable an evening. These few hours flowing by so pleasantly in the middle of a small circle of friends made me regret very sharply the absence of a French colony in Portland. The Frenchman, more than any other, thanks to his sociable temperament and his communicative gayety, understands, in whatever position he finds himself, how to make life bearable.

It was not until very late that we were able to separate to go our different ways.

The departure of the steamer was announced for the next day, at two o'clock in the afternoon; I spent all the time I still had available in going through the bookstores, in order to get for myself the books about gardening which could be useful to me.

All the friends were waiting for me at the steamer when I arrived, but we had only time to take a farewell glass and shake each other's hand; some of them promised me to do all they could to come to see me in Portland . . . if business allowed!

On the 17th of February, at ten o'clock in the evening, the *Commodore* was moored to the wharf at Portland. I debarked, put my box and my bundle of shrubs in the house of Mr. Hibert, one of my friends living near the wharf, then, with my pile of books under my arm, I regained my home, where I found Margraff sleeping, as he usually did, very noisily.[5] I entered, lit the candle, had another supper, lit a pipe, smoked it, went to bed—without interrupting for an instant his formidable snoring. We didn't shake hands until the next day when we got up.

After breakfast, having gone to get my box and bundle, we spent our day in planting in Ankeny's and Wilson's gardens the ornamental shrubs I had brought. After which, and every day, we spaded to mix with earth the dung which Ankeny had had brought for his garden. I set up my hotbed, where I set all the shrubs I supposed I would need.

Doctor Wilson, whom I encountered by chance, asked if there wouldn't be a way I might undertake to cultivate his block by the year, taking charge of all the work to be done there during the season, in order, he said, not to have to bother with it himself; that his garden be kept neat, well set off with ornamental trees, and decorated with some flowers, was all that he asked. In a few words, the bargain was concluded: I took charge of everything at the rate of a hundred and fifty dollars and the use of about half of the block which was behind his house.

From time to time, someone came to look for me, whether to create a garden-plot, to clean it up, or to transform it. The one with which I had ornamented the front of Ankeny's house was invariably taken as model; it had been done the first,

5. P. Hibert lived at 13 North Front Street (*Portland Directory, 1863*, p. 33).

people had gone to see it, they had found it beautiful: they had to have the same, a more beautiful one would have pleased less because it would have been something else. I saw many lots more promising than Ankeny's and from which one could have made a more beautiful garden than his, but there was no way of making their proprietors listen to reason: I had to tear out everything, upset everything, and exactly reproduce this masterpiece.

In the month of March, I had so much work that I thought I would lose my head. I had continually hanging on my arms three or four owners of gardens, each more impatient than the other. I had to take [on] two workmen to help Margraff do my work, while I went to take care of a neighboring garden. In the month of April, I had four of them, including Margraff; I paid the three others at the rate of three dollars each per ten-hour work-day, without board or room. I employed them to move dirt, to dig and level, I had only to trace the plan of the gardens and to determine the place where each tree, each bank of flowers should be planted. The work went faster, but not enough yet to satisfy my clientele, which kept growing; I had to take two new workmen, which made seven, counting me. My first vegetables had come out, radishes, lettuces, and green onions; I sold them for a penny a radish, a penny an onion, and ten cents a handful of the lettuce-plants I pulled out of the seed-plat. I got up at three o'clock in the morning, I made my bundles, then filled two or three champagne-hampers with them: I went to sell them to the hotels, restaurants, etc. On my return, I planted and sowed until six o'clock, then went to take breakfast; so much the better, if Margraff had not forgotten it! At seven only, the day began, properly speaking: I distributed the work to my men, according to the ability of each one, gave the last touch to the job, then passed to something else. At noon, not having the time to return to the house (fifteen hundred meters to go), I devoured my dinner as quickly as possible at the neighboring restaurant, then I completed what had not been finished in the morning. At one o'clock, the workmen returned from dinner; I had to give a new occupation to those who had finished their task and see if the others were acquitting themselves properly with theirs. At six o'clock, the day was done, at least for the others; as for me, I began again to transplant, to sow, and very often to water. I still had to find the time to sell my heads of cabbage, cauliflower, and lettuce. It's unbelievable, but I sold, perhaps, in a month, at a cent apiece, more than forty thousand of these plants.

When I couldn't see any more, I returned for supper, went to bed, and began again the next day at three o'clock.

Ankeny, who had noticed that I was in the garden before he was up, and that I was still there when he went to bed, he who flattered himself that he had already earned his day's pay when others were getting up, said to me one day: "*Engineer* (ingénieur), you can't last long this way; you will have to take someone to help you, otherwise, fatigue will overtake you and break your arms right off."—"Captain," I said, "if you will find me someone to begin my work at four o'clock in the morning, continue it until nine, then begin again at four o'clock in the afternoon and finish at nine, I will pay him on the same footing that you paid me to care for your boarders (four dollars a day)."—"You won't find anyone to replace you at those hours, because the prejudice, here, is that it's the morning and evening fog that causes the fever, and nobody but you and I will risk it."

Ankeny was right, I was exhausted. How many times I woke up in the morning my nose on the table where I had gone to sleep the night before, beside the remains of my supper. Soon, I had to reinforce the bell of my alarm clock, which no longer awakened me.

But, toward the middle of June, work was less abundant, vegetables were coming down in price. A good number of farmers in the environs of Portland had started market-gardening; they came off badly, it is true, and their produce arrived on the market only when the season was already advanced, but at last they had arrived. The result was a competition which could have become disastrous if they had had, like me, a complete assortment of vegetables; happily, they missed it by far.

As the work decreased, I released my workmen. On the 25th of July, I found myself alone again; Margraff, who was the last remaining and whom I asked to stay all year with me, had just left; boredom had overcome him; he had taken the pedestrian path to California, proposing to spend the rest of the season in making this trip of seven hundred and sixty miles (253 leagues). It is true that he undertook it especially from the point of view of pleasure, quite resolved to stop where pleasure ended. "I'll write to you," he had said to me, "I will send you my impressions of the trip, I will describe to you the two hundred leagues of country which separate us from the Sacramento."

Here I should go back a bit.

In the month of May (the 27th), I received a letter from Herbeumont, which reached me very late, having been addressed to me at Mariposa; Chanac had picked it up at the post-office and had sent it to Huguet, still a butcher at Coultersville; the latter had forwarded it to me at Portland. This letter I had been expecting for several years: I opened it hastily, joyfully; it fell from my hands as soon as I had read the first lines—for four years, my mother was no more!

It was a hard blow; I fell into extreme dejection, I had lost strength and courage, I worked little and I worked poorly, sometimes I didn't work at all. What was the use? wasn't the mainstay of my life broken? If I had crossed the seas, if for eight years I had been intent, at the price of unheard-of fatigues and innumerable perils, on the pursuit of fortune, it was because I cherished the hope, if I became rich, of returning to my native village, to my old mother, to ease the last days she had left to live. It is a cruel thing to have a fair dream go up in smoke!

This letter, moreover, received after four years of waiting, seemed very short to me; it brought me very succinctly, besides the fatal news, the changes which had come in the family. My sister was still at Thonne-la-long and had no children; my elder brother was no longer at Chartres, he was at Rennes; Nicolas-Joseph, the one who wrote to me, had two children; as for the rest, no illness in the family; that was all in the way of news. He reminded me of several letters which he said he had written me and which I had not received; as a result of these letters, naturally remaining unanswered, and of information whose source he didn't give, he had believed me dead. But, recently, he had had knowledge of a letter written from California by a man named Gillet to his relatives living in Rossart, a little village near Neufchâteau, in which he mentioned that I was complaining of not receiving any news from Herbeumont for a long time; it was as a result of this communication that my brother had written. He added that, although married, he was still ready to come to join me; wasn't that telling me that he was not happy?

Since 1851, each letter I wrote to my brothers contained the same refrain: "Come and join me, or, at least, let one of you come."

I added to that all the necessary information on the route to follow and the means of making the voyage; but these explanations were never sufficient. When they judged it appropriate to reply to me, it was not to announce their arrival, but to inform me that they were staying, and to address new questions to me: there was a point to clarify, a difficulty to raise, some new information they needed; one would have said truly that for them it was a matter of migrating to another planet.

Sometimes their letter strayed, did not reach me, and it was only on receiving the following one, that I knew their questions; but, in the interval, a year had rolled by. Other times, my letter did not arrive; there was another year lost.

While waiting, I, persuaded that they had seriously decided to come, I thought them on their way, and every two or three months, I covered twenty or thirty leagues on foot to go to Mariposa to look for the letter announcing their coming, but always in vain. However, I awaited their arrival before undertaking anything serious.

I had learned at last by a letter from this same Gillet of whom I spoke earlier, that my brothers were married. Then they had given up coming to California; had they ever thought of it? I was left to doubt it. Whatever it was, from that moment, I stopped expecting them and I no longer wrote to them except to give them my news and try to receive theirs; but, for four years, I had not received any. And in this letter, which I received at last on the 29th of May 1858, I read this sentence, which seemed singular to me: "I am still ready to come and join you." That replied to an invitation which I had made him in a letter written in the month of April in the year 1851! Wasn't it enough to lose patience? So I replied with some temper to my brother, inviting him a last time to leave immediately after receipt of my letter and to write no more except to announce his arrival, being quite resolved to answer his questions no more. I sent on, moreover, although I had given them four or five times, all the necessary directions for making the trip from Herbeumont to Portland without trouble. I urged him to bring with him his wife and children, for how have heart for the job when one has left his family three thousand leagues behind him? But then the voyage was going to become costly; would he have the necessary funds to pay for it? I had reason to doubt it, after having read his letter. I therefore authorized him to sell my share of the paternal heritage to the amount of the sum he needed, and even to sell all, if he had to.

Would he come? I doubted it, but at last it was not impossible. He had had seven years to reflect, after all, and then, it was easy to see, cares ruled in his household. Perhaps he was going to decide to look and would realize that when all was said, to go to America, was not to drink the sea—since there was only to cross it.

Chapter Twenty-Six

The Fraser River Rush

The previous fall, some explorers had discovered gold in the beds or rivers tributary to the Fraser, a river in British Columbia, at 49° north. This news, which reached California during the winter, had produced a great sensation there.[1] Miners, crowded on the placers which were becoming exhausted, when they learned that somewhere, in a sparsely inhabited country, there were unexploited and abundant mines, rushed en masse to this happy land. On all the roads leading to it, one saw the numerous trains of the emigrants, piled into wagons or walking accompanied by beasts of burden, or alone on foot, carrying their baggage and tools on their backs. Some of them reached the nearby coast, and flotillas of steamers transported them, passing by Victoria, to the mouth of the Fraser, in the Gulf of Georgia; thence, embarking as best they could, they went up the river to the new placers; others, going by way of Oregon, went up the Columbia and so reached the country of the Shuswaps, where, they said, gold was especially abundant. It was this route which was taken by the miners from northern California and Oregon. So it was that we saw, from the first of April to the first of June, passing through Portland, more than twenty thousand emigrants going to the Fraser. During this same time, the steamers carried nearly a hundred thousand by sea to Victoria, then an insignificant village, which suddenly became a city peopled by forty thousand inhabitants. I thought, for a moment, that all Portland was going to emigrate; so many stores were closed in the city, so many farms, in the surrounding area, were abandoned! At the same time, great activity reigned on the wharves; they were loading provisions of all kinds to feed all the people who were flowing into Victoria; wheat rose from two cents to eighteen cents a livre, and the price of everything was increased in the same proportion. It was a general debacle.

A good many times, the idea came to me to follow the torrent, and to go again to try to make a fortune by digging the sands of gold-bearing rivers. Certainly, it

---

1. Although the Fraser River gold rush of 1858 lasted only four or five months, Rodman W. Paul estimates that between 25,000 and 30,000 persons started for the Fraser River and that "most of the adventurers came from California." See Paul, *Mining Frontiers of the Far West*, p. 38, and William J. Trimble, *Mining Advance into the Inland Empire* (Madison: Bulletin of the University of Wisconsin, no. 638, 1914).

would have been perfectly unreasonable to abandon the position which I had made myself at Portland, at that moment especially when I was earning more money than I would have been able to make, without doubt, by scratching the bed of the Fraser. The month of April had been worth three hundred dollars to me, all expenses paid; the month of May was perhaps going to be worth even more. But what was going to become of Portland? would it be repopulated? And I was hesitating, when I received my brother's letter. That changed the course of my ideas. Resolved to make him come, if it was possible, and having written to him in that sense, I had to wait for him. That decided, I again took up my ordinary way of life, and let events take care of themselves.

In the month of July, finding myself alone and not being pressed by work, so that often even I lacked it, I thought at last of clearing my block. I profited by the dry season to cut down the trees, pull out the stumps, and burn the whole, in order, if possible, after the following year, to make some vegetables or flowers grow there. I could occupy myself with this work almost without stopping. Every eight days, I went to spend a day or two in Wilson's garden to keep it neat; as for Ankeny's, three hours a day sufficed me to cut and prepare what ought to be taken to market, then to reseed and plant what was to be gathered later in the season. In this way I came to the time of the first autumn rains; September and October had been almost dry, it was only in November that the soil was found in good condition to be worked. Then I could take up again, with my clients, the work interrupted for several months; I was no longer reduced, to earn my day's wage, to digging in my block, which, moreover, was almost finished. At that moment, a good number of those who, in the spring, had left Portland to go to look for gold on the Fraser, returned less enthusiastic and less rich than they had left.

It appeared that rumor, according to its praiseworthy habit, had greatly exaggerated things; there was gold all right in this river and its tributaries, but there wasn't enough for everybody.

One day, in town, I encountered a man called Joseph, Chanac's Swiss partner at Mariposa. He came down from the Thompson river, a tributary of the Fraser, where he was established as a butcher; he came to Portland to buy beefs for his butcher shop. He told me that at the first news of the discovery of the Columbia gold mines, the year before, half of the population of Mariposa had left, abandoning a mass of things which they could not sell or which were sold at cut prices, as always happens in such cases, by virtue of the law of supply and demand. He himself had sold his share to Chanac almost for nothing, and had gone to settle as butcher, with two others, on the Thompson river, where they did a good enough business. Lacking, for the moment, the primary material, he had come to try to get some; I put him in touch with Ankeny, who sold him two hundred and fifty beefs, to be delivered in three weeks.

One day when I was in the garden, occupied in planting cabbages which I should gather as early vegetables in the spring, a man came to lean on the garden fence and, without saying anything, watched me work. As, in doing my job, I had approached the fence, he at last addressed a word to me: "They tell me you are Bezhian."—"Yes, sir."—"Me too, I'm from Bezhium."—"From what province?"[2] On that question he began to think a bit, then said to me: "from the province of Bruzes, province of Ghent, province of Flande."—"Ah, I have heard of those provinces, but I have never had the toothache there; it's all the same, we are countrymen and that is worth the trouble of shaking each other's hand." On that, I approached him and we gave each other a good handclasp. "Well," I said, "go around to the gate and come in, so we can talk together a bit, perhaps you too know how to work in a garden?"—"But," he said, "naturally I know about it, have you ever seen a Bezhian who didn't know about it?" And on that, he went around and came to smoke a pipe beside me.

My compatriot was named Ivon Voet; he was from Knesselaere, between Bruges and Ghent, eastern Flanders. He spoke English much better than French. He had been in America since 1850, in Oregon for seven years; he had come in one of those wagon trains which every year, in April, crossed the Missouri at St. Louis or at Omaha, traveled to the west, crossed the Rocky Mountains, descended the Snake River, then the Columbia, and ordinarily reached Portland in the month of September. He had always lived in the environs of Salem, which he had left six months before to settle in Brooklyn, a place situated almost opposite Portland, on the right bank of the river; he had bought some land there, he had built and he was fixed there. Carpenter and joiner by trade, he was building houses, running a grocery business and, altogether, making a very good living. After being mutually informed on our situations, we left each other promising ourselves to see each other often.

About this time, I received the letter which I had been expecting from Herbeumont; my brother announced that he had decided to leave with all his family, and without asking me any more questions, all the same, he could not start off on the way immediately: he had undertaken the construction of a schoolhouse at Herbeumont and ought to wait till it was finished. When would that be? he did not know exactly, but once free on that side, he would lose no time, would have a sale of everything it took to procure the funds necessary, and would leave. He promised to write me two or three letters more before his departure.

In spite of these assurances, I was in no way reassured; I feared, after so many tergiversations, a new change in my brother's intentions. However, I set to work to extend my cultivation, in order that, should the case occur, there would be work for two. A certain Captain Farnum, builder of steamboats, had two adjoining blocks cleared, surrounded by a fence, and very well situated.[3] He did not want at first either to give them on shares or to rent them; however, by dint of negotiating, I succeeded in obtaining the concession for two years, on condition that Farnum

---

2. Here Perlot seems to be playing on the phonetic spelling of the pronunciation of the word *Belgium*.
3. Possibly a reference to Samuel Farman (Farnum, Farnan?), a ship's carpenter listed in the *Portland Director, 1864*, p. 43.

would have the right to take, in the month of August, a third of all the vegetables which had then come to maturity. I was obliged to seed the ground with all kinds of vegetables. Having to seed, in the spring, these two blocks, mine, Ankeny's, and a third of Wilson's, that seemed sufficient to me; I spent my time, while waiting for the desired season, in preparing my ground and my seeds.

About this time, a man named Justin Demange, who, in 1852, was a gardener and milkman near Mariposa, came to see me. He assured me that I had seen and known him in California, but I did not recognize him and I had no memory of him; I recalled, however, having bought vegetables from his partner. Finally, since he recognized me very well, as he gave me all sorts of details on my Mariposa friends and on myself, I ended by persuading myself that I recognized him too. He was returning from the Fraser well before having made his fortune there, in proof of which he found himself stopped at Portland, for lack of money. As soon as he had heard my name pronounced, he had inquired my address and had come. He had, before leaving Mariposa, sold his garden and his cows and had left with half of the sum he had realized this way; having spent all this money, he was forced to leave the gold mines of the Fraser to regain Mariposa.

He had been able, by turning out his purse, to reach Portland, but he arrived there no longer having the least dollar left in his pocket. He had written to his ex-partner to bet him to send him the money necessary to continue on his way, and counted on receiving it before long; while waiting, he was living at the hotel on his watch, which he had given as guarantee. "Well," I said, "here's Margraff's bed, which is unoccupied, it is at your disposal; we will eat together, that will cost you less than at the hotel, and you will pay me when you have received your funds."—"I accept," he said, "with pleasure, you render me a true service; I gladly leave the hotel, because I haven't anything in which to be properly dressed, but I would like, on leaving it, to be able to redeem my watch for fear that some misfortune might happen to it." I returned to town with him and paid fifteen dollars at the hotel in exchange for his watch, which I immediately gave back to him. Demange, while waiting for his money, did our cooking and, in his spare moments, worked with me.

In the month of November, some young people engaged in the editing of a newspaper which was published in English in Portland, came to find me so I could teach them to translate French. They received quite a few papers written in French, and could reproduce none of it, for lack of a translator. Having little to do in that season as gardener, I saw no inconvenience in leaving for a while the spade for the pen. I was hired to translate two articles a week for them, that is, I would give them the word-for-word or not much more, leaving them the trouble of making it into good English, a thing for which I did not want to be responsible and for good reason. Moreover, I gave these Gentlemen French lessons three times a week. In order to simplify my job, I made them buy a Robertson method. It did not go badly; I had begun with six pupils, soon I had a dozen of them, of whom four were Germans. They gave me twenty-five cents each per lesson, and the paper two dollars per article. I thus remained journalist and professor until about the end of

February, a time when gardening work kept me occupied all day. One can understand that after a day's labor, I was not tempted to dress myself to go in town to become hoarse by repeating all evening into Anglo-saxon ears the diphthongs of the French language; I preferred to rest.

Fifteen days after the installation of Demange in my casa, he received the money he was expecting from California. The letter which accompanied the package informed him at the same time that their garden had just been sold again to six Chinese. This disturbed Demange's plans, who had intended to take up his business again with his partner and his own brother, to whom he had returned his share; renouncing therefore the return to Mariposa, where he would not have known what to do, he proposed that we become partners. I accepted, on condition that, if my brother came, he would enter the partnership by paying a third of all which might comprise, at that time, the community property. This agreed on, we made an inventory of all that I had to put into the partnership, Demange having to reimburse me for half of it; he acquired, at his own expense, a block beside mine; this block belonged to him and mine was left to me, but the two were put in community use for cultivation. We worked, in our spare moments, on Demange's block, so that it could be cleared and enclosed by the following year.

As soon as the weather permitted us, we got busy preparing for the work of the springtime. We had divided the job: Demange was to occupy himself especially with the cultivation of the market-garden; as for me, I had taken charge of selling its produce and I would, besides, as in the past, if occasion presented, lay out gardens and terraces, on others' account. Now, considering the quantity of plots which we were going to have under cultivation, we had to anticipate five or six times as much produce as I had had the preceding year, and I would no longer be able to manage by going to town with a few baskets: we would have to buy a horse and wagon.

The spring began well; I had work in town, and Demange was acquitting himself marvelously in his duties as gardener. Vegetables were selling as in the past year; we were hoping therefore to have a good season, but, before the end of May, once the movement of business which spring ordinarily produced was ended, there arose a crisis which increased from day to day, so that, after the fifteenth of June, business was in an absolute calm. Never, since Portland existed, had such a situation been produced; without any doubt, the fever of emigration of the preceding year was the cause of it.

All that the city had of carpenters, mason, joiners, etc., had left for Victoria, which was growing and prospering at the expense of Portland. The hotels, here, were empty, the boarding houses deserted; it was becoming evident that, for us, the season was lost.

However, far from closing shop, we thought of building, for our hut was absolutely lacking in comfort. No longer having to fear the crash of a tree, we addressed ourselves to Voet the *Bèze*, who built us a wooden house, spacious and comfortable; it comprised, on the ground floor, three rooms fourteen feet long by twelve feet wide, one of which served as kitchen, and an upper floor with two rooms; a flight of stairs to the ground floor and a balcony on the upper. Thanks to the leisure which business left us, we could help construct it and the house was finished in a short time; without being carpeted, without chimney, without well, it cost us eight hundred dollars (4240 francs). The brick chimney cost us sixty and the well forty; which well was thirty feet deep. Instead of walling it up with bricks, which cost too much, we had supported its walls by means of planks which were worth two cents a square foot.

In the month of August, the farmers established three or four miles from Portland came to find me and taking me for a surveyor, proposed to me to measure and divide their lands, then to study the means of draining the marshes which were found there; they were from old beaver dams which time had crumbled; these lands, generally very productive once they were dried, could not be given up to cultivation, inundated as they were by a water which had no drainage. These farmers therefore had twenty to thirty hectares of lands producing nothing, and rather harmful than useful. Having examined the land and recognized the possibility of doing the job asked, I set to work. The farmers, four in number, each furnished five workmen to cut the willows, the alders, and to dig the canals, so that I had only to draw up the plan of works. Sir Thompson, one of the farmers, who lived in Portland with his family, furnished me a horse to take me every day to the place and return.[4] By the fifteenth of October, that is, before the rains, the work was done; these gentlemen were well pleased with it and, in witness of their satisfaction, made me a present of a compass and a graphometer which, however bad it was, was still worth more than the plane-table I had made for myself. Moreover, they made me a reputation as an inexpensive surveyor, which brought me new clients: I worked, in fact, at the rate of sixty cents an hour, while Leland, the official surveyor, would not be bothered for less than a dollar.[5]

About the month of November, business picked up a little; people returned and money too, so that interest at 3% a month fell to 2%. But provisions fell to a ridiculous price: meat at three cents a pound, potatoes at twenty-five cents for sixty livres, wheat at three dollars and a half for two hundred livres, and so on—one spent little to live, but also one earned hardly anything.

At that moment, the news came that there had just been discovered, to the east of Oregon, some mines richer than all those which were known before then. Some explorers who had spent the season with the Coeurs d'âlène, the Flatheads, the Kootenays and the Nez-percés, came down to Portland, to spend the winter, with purses full of gold. They had worked in the same placers for which we had come to

4. Perlot often used the spelling "Tomson" for Thompson. It is unclear as to whether or not he was referring to D. P. Thompson, who was later mayor of Portland and governor of Idaho Territory, 1875–76, or Robert R. Thompson, a major business figure in Portland and a director of the Oregon Steam Navigation Company in 1875. It is also possible that Perlot referred to Thomas W. Thompson, who came to Oregon in 1857 and moved to Portland in 1863 but farmed outside of the city. See Johansen and Gates, *Empire of the Columbia*, p. 331; *Portrait and Biographical Record*, pp. 619–20; and *Portland Directory, 1863*, p. 51.

5. A. Leland is listed as a civil engineer in the *Portland Directory, 1863*, p. 63.

Oregon, and which we had not been able to reach because we arrived at Portland too late. What bad luck! Everybody was going to make a fortune in those mines, and I, I was vegetating in Portland! It was discouraging. However, I couldn't leave that city at any price, for I had received a letter from my brother telling me that he had just made a sale and that he was starting off on the way. This letter was written in the month of August.

The market-garden season having passed, I became a professor again; four of my pupils had left for the Fraser, but they were replaced by six new ones: I spent my winter in teaching them to translate from French into English. My pupils were apt and they did honor to their teacher.

In the month of December, Huguet came to cause me a very pleasant surprise; he had boarded the *Commodore* in San Francisco and arrived in Portland expressly to see me. He had just sold his butcher shop in Coultersville at the price of twenty thousand dollars; having to invest his funds, he proposed to go to see Paris again, where he had been a journeyman hatter for four years, and to return afterward to settle in California or in Oregon.

We amused ourselves the best we could for two days, then he took the steamer which had brought him, promising to write to me from time to time and especially to give me his address as soon as, on his return from Europe, he would be settled somewhere in America.

The news which he had brought me, was not of a nature to make me regret having left California; in the first place, our former companions from down there were leaving; many were dead, others had gone to Mexico, some of them, fallen into misery or who had never got out of it, had been repatriated at the expense of the government. The old placers were very crowded, but especially with Chinese; there had been a veritable invasion of sons of the Middle Empire, before which the Europeans had been forced to withdraw. It was for this reason that he, Huguet, had sold his butcher shop, which was bringing in less and less.

They talked a lot, in California, of Oregon, of the new mines, etc., and Huguet urged me strongly to remain where I was, assuring me that Portland could not fail to become, in the more or less near future, an important city.

With this news and on this assurance, we regained courage, Demange and I, and we went back to work with more eagerness.

The spring of 1860 came early; well before the month of March, everything, in the gardens, began to grow.

We undertook to make a hotbed two hundred feet long by six wide. For that we had to have an enormous amount of fresh manure, which we went to get in stables and barns at a very high price, two dollars per horse-cart.

We soon perceived that this hotbed was going to cost us more than it would bring us, and we were going to give it up, although already having had the expense of acquiring the glass, when Demange suggested using half manure and half sawdust, which we were able to procure gratis by hauling it ourselves.

I hardly believed in the efficacy of this means of increasing the temperature of a green-house, but as Demange believed in it and affirmed it and as, moreover, he took charge of going to get the sawdust himself with our horse and our wagon, I had no reason to object to the experiment's being made. The sawmill where we had to go to look for it was situated above the town; the pile of sawdust rose on the bank of the river.

To approach it with a wagon, it was necessary to follow a road cut in the bank, where they went to water the horses and carry away floating objects. Now, to turn the vehicle after having loaded it, and to return by the same road, it was necessary to take precautions, the edge was narrow, the slope rapid and, a short distance from the bank, the water was forty feet deep. These difficulties did not stop Demange; in two days, he brought eight loads of sawdust; but, the third day, while I was working in Ankeny's garden, I saw him pass on the horse at full speed. Where was the wagon? at the bottom of the river. Demange explained to me that, at the moment of turning and when the thing was already half done, he had taken the wrong rein, so that the horse, instead of continuing to turn and the wagon with him, had backed up; when he had realized his mistake, the wagon was already under six feet of water, rapidly pulling after itself both horse and driver.

From the box of the wagon, which was floating, Demange leaped quickly on the horse, then into the water; he was in it almost to his neck.

He had, however, the time to unfasten the collar of the horse, who immediately found himself freed, the strap of the wagon-bed which held the breech luckily having broken; wagon and harness continued to descend the current while horse and driver tried to reach the bank by swimming and succeeded only after unheard-of efforts. We fished up, first, without great difficulty, the box of the wagon, then, by means of a hook of three branches attached to the end of a forty-foot rope, holding ourselves in a wherry [rowboat], we succeeded in pulling out of the water the harness and the fore-carriage. As for the two back wheels with the binding-rope, which had been separated from the front, in consequence of the displacement of the pole-bolt, we could not find them; after eight days of fruitless search, we had to renounce the hope of reconstituting our vehicle.

This carriage, of which we had only half left, had just cost us two hundred and sixty dollars, and as it was absolutely indispensible to us, we had to replace it or complete it, at any cost. It was, considering our modest resources, a considerable loss that we had just suffered: poor Demange almost lost his head over it, he was quite demoralized. The results of the preceding season were not encouraging; on the other hand, news from the Oregon placers was good; then my brother was going to come, there would be three of us; perhaps it was too much. In short, he proposed to break our partnership; on my side, I wanted as much to give the place to Demange as to keep it alone. We agreed to stay together until my brother's arrival; then each of us would appraise in writing the joint property; the one whose estimate would be the higher, would pay the other his share and keep the establishment. While waiting, we continued to work together as if nothing had happened, without however rebuilding our wagon, which we didn't yet absolutely need; we paid a wagoner to bring us the manure we had to have.

The Perlot Brothers and
Gaillard

My brother, if I could trust his last letter, had been at sea since the month of
October, and ought, according to all probability, to arrive in San Francisco at the
beginning of March. I was awaiting the steamer to take me to that city, in order to
receive him on his arrival as had been agreed, when I received a letter from Huguet.

He had gone to Europe and had returned in twelve weeks; he was bored in
Auvergne, his native region, and was no more pleased in Paris.

France was then enjoying the sweets of the imperial regime; he, accustomed for
nine years to the free and easy life one leads in America, judged that it was not safe
for him to live in a country where everyone spoke of liberty without daring to speak
freely; where they lived tranquilly, moreover, under the paternal surveillance of the
police; tranquil, in the phrase of P. L. Courier, as one is on the eve of going to
prison.[1]

Foreseeing that he would be forced, sooner or later, to flee from the sweet land of
France, he had preferred to leave it at once; at the end of eight days, had quitted
Paris and had embarked at Le Havre—he wrote to me from San Francisco. His
letter came very conveniently; instead of going down with the steamer which had
brought it to me, I wrote to Huguet to ask him to go, in my stead and place, to
receive my brother at the moment of his debarkation, giving him the necessary
information on the probable time of arrival of the ship, the *Jean-Baptiste*, which
was bringing him. He should, as soon as my brother arrived, send him to Oregon.

For extra safety, I wrote in almost the same terms to Venard, in case Huguet
was absent or occupied.

This done, I went back tranquilly to work, knowing that I could count on these
two friends.

---

1. Paul Louis Courier (1773–1825), a well-known Hellenist and political writer whose lifetime devotion
to Greek literature was interrupted, first by service in the Revolutionary War of 1793–1809, and later by his
opposition to the regime of Louis XVIII (1814–24). His use of political pamphlets to expose the extrava-
gance of the Restoration Government resulted in fine and imprisonment for a brief time. In 1825 he was found
shot near his home. Eventually it was established that his servants had killed him. See *Encyclopedia Britannica*
6 (Chicago, London, Toronto: Encyclopedia Britannica, 1957), 601.

On the fifth of March, I received a letter from Huguet, announcing the arrival of my brother and his family. Everybody was well and, in three days, he was going to put them aboard the steamer which went to Portland, where, very probably, they would arrive on the eleventh or twelfth.

On the twelfth, at ten in the evening, I was in the midst of my pupils, gravely giving my French lesson, when a cannon-shot which seemed to me to echo more loudly than usual, announced that the expected steamer was in sight of Portland.

This cannon-shot put an end to the lesson, put an end even to my career as professor. I explained to my pupils that my brother was on board the steamer which was arriving, that I had not seen him since 1849; I asked their permission to leave them to go to receive him; I added that it was probably the last lesson of the season, the moment having come to leave the toga of the professor for the smock of the gardener. I released them, in consequence, making an appointment with them for the next year; then we all went down to the café to empty a farewell glass together; but, instead of one glass, we drank several, the result of which was that when I arrived at the steamer, it was fast and already emptied of the passengers who knew where to find lodging in the city; the others had gone to bed: they were, for the most part, Chinese come from California, fore-runners of an army which was preparing to invade Oregon.

I was running over the deck, lantern in hand, when at last I encountered my sister-in-law, whom, naturally, I did not know, but whom I recognized at the first word; I gave my name, we embraced each other, then she showed me her two children, who were sleeping together on a bed in a cabin. She told me that my brother had gone into town, guided by an Italian who said he knew me very well and knew where to find me. On that, I left the steamer swarming with Chinese, and climbed back up into the city, in search of my brother, surmising that Sposito (the Italian) was going to take him to the café which I had just left.[2]

I had not gone three hundred steps when I saw in front of me, in the half-obscurity of the darkness, three men talking politics; I heard one of them say that to all the demands of reform which Napoleon had made to the Pope, the latter had invariably responded "Non possumus." I had recognized my brother's voice. "The Pope is wrong," I said, interrupting, "he is infallible, he should be all-knowing, all-powerful." The three men turned sharply, and I found myself facing my brother, a man named Prosper Gaillard, come from Herbeumont with him, and Sposito, the Italian.

It was ten years since I had seen the two natives of Herbeumont; I found them exactly as I had left them, having gained nothing, lost nothing, learned nothing and forgotten nothing; physically and morally, not the least change, I recognized them as if I had left them the day before.

After the embraces, we returned aboard the steamer and, shortly after, we installed ourselves in a liquor shop, not far from the port.

2. Paul Sposito is listed as a fruit dealer in the *Portland Directory, 1867*.

We came out of it about three o'clock in the morning. What could we have said to each other during all that time? I do not know, probably not much, precisely because we had too much to tell each other.

The next day, early, I betook myself with a dray (*haquet*) to the steamer, and moved my brother's family to my house. He and Prosper settled as well as they could in the house, whose interior arrangements were not entirely finished. Demange and I executed our agreement, and as it was found that my estimate was the higher, I stayed and he left. I paid him six hundred dollars, in consideration of which he abandoned to me his share of the community property, each of us keeping his own block. This affair settled, I concluded another with my brother and Prosper; I ceded them two thirds of the whole at the price which I had just paid Demange for the half; the block and the house alone were reserved.

So we were three; my sister-in-law kept house and did the cooking. We all seemed content with this arrangement, all desirous of doing well and it seemed that we were going to live happily in our work.

To crown my happiness, I recovered, at that time, the two back wheels of my wagon, left in the Willamette. A sailor, a deserter from a French ship, offered to fish them up for a consideration of thirty dollars; the bargain was concluded. Mounted on a craft which I furnished him, he set to work and did not delay in bringing me the after-carriage of my vehicle, which therefore was rebuilt at small expense and very opportunely.

I undertook as much work as possible, for it was necessary to occupy the hands of three vigorous workers. It was to me, naturally, that fell the task of negotiating with the proprietors of lands and of directing their exploitation, for my two partners did not know a word of English and were not yet acquainted with the work there was to do; good workmen, otherwise, and full of good will.

The month of April had come and the season was announced under favorable auspices. The news of the mines was so encouraging that one saw being renewed, in yet more considerable proportions, the movement of emigration to the placers which had characterized the preceding years; but, this time, Portland, far from suffering from it, profited; it served as place of passage for the mass of emigrants, and many, giving up going any farther, sought to establish themselves there.

The hotels, the middle-class boarding-houses, and the restaurants were crowded. Commerce with Colville, the Kootenay, and the country of the Nez-percés, via the Columbia, took on an extraordinary development.

Finally, they were clearing all around the city and many new houses were being built; the result was that the price of property had doubled in Portland, provisions had gone up and were being sold more easily. So everything made us hope for a happy season, and I thought, on my own account, that the year 1858 was going to be repeated. Unfortunately, the month of June was humid; we had to take a lot of trouble and lost lots of time to maintain the gardens and grounds we had undertaken. In sum total, the year was not as good as we had hoped, better however than the year before.

I bought, in the month of October, a new block beside and to the west of mine; that of Demange had passed into the hands of a Mr. Hibert, who had given him, in exchange, two other blocks situated across from Portland, on the other side of the river. Demange had had a house built there for him by Voet, then had left for the Kootenay.

The block which I had bought was entirely in the flat crossed by a creek which ran into the Willamette. The soil was sufficiently mixed with sand to make a productive garden; moreover, by means of a simple reservoir on the upper part, it could be watered at any season. This block, although bought in my name, belonged to the company; it was the first part of the domain which it was going to acquire (in proportion) as it had the necessary funds to grow in size. This purchase was the more urgent as Captain Farnum had sold, as building lands, the two blocks which he was renting me, which had decreased our cultivation by that much; besides that, Captain Ankeny was finding that his trees were coming along well and was also preparing to withdraw his block from us. We had then, with the utmost necessity, to procure land to plant for the next year; we decided that the best [course] was still to buy some land and to raise our produce on our own property.

We hadn't the necessary funds to pay for this first acquisition, but Captain Flanders, the seller, was satisfied with my promise; he had known me for several years previously, and was good enough to have confidence in me.

But wasn't I going at the job a little quickly? Wasn't I pledging myself a little rashly? Already, I had bought Demange's share and had paid for it from my savings; I had ceded two shares to my brother and to Gaillard with a sixth loss, and had not received an obolus.

In review, here is what my situation was: instead of one partner, I had two; I took in no more than a third instead of half of the profits realized.

Moreover, I had made all of the advances and ran all the risks! In fact, if business made a bad turn, I alone would have to pay for the acquisitions made in common, for I alone would have been in a state to do so.

In spite of everything, we had to establish and increase our domain there where we had our residence, unless we went to settle somewhere else; but it was far from being proved that we would have been better elsewhere, and these moves are always costly. I would have gained personally from it because I would have been able to rent my house and block for twenty or twenty-five dollars a month.

But these small calculations were no longer in season; after all, if I had had in view only my personal interest, my brother would have remained in Herbeumont. Now that he had come on my urging, I could not limit myself to paying his passage; my duty was to put him in the way, if possible, of making himself an independent position; we were all three, it seemed, in good agreement, it was presumable that we were together for a long time, and it seemed impossible to me, being all three filled with good will, not to succeed in the business.

Everything indicated for us, moreover, a prosperous future. Portland was taking on importance, was being built up, extended; we could hope to be soon, if not in the interior, at least at the gates of a real city.

In spite of the snow which fell in the autumn, the winter having been clement, we found the time to level and enclose the land we had bought, so as to be able to cultivate and sow it as soon as spring came. In spite of that, we still lacked land. I seized the occasion, when it was presented, to rent some land around us; this way we were going to have five blocks under cultivation, but only our two would produce enough to pay our labor; the others, poorly cleared and never having been cultivated, demanded a great deal of work for an uncertain and in any case a meager harvest.

Spring came, it was promising, everything was growing at will, vegetables were cheap but were selling well. Without doubt, the market-gardeners of San Francisco were doing us damage; the steamers which, for a year, had been making the trip every five days from that city to Portland, were loaded with vegetables which lacked freshness, perhaps, but which, after all, were sold. Moreover, two German gardeners came to settle at the gates of the town and gave us an even more serious rivalry.[3] So there were three of us, to argue over customers every morning. Yes, it was true, we no longer had the monopoly of the market, but our industry hardly suffered from it, because, from day to day, the consumers became more numerous; it was even that—and it was inevitable—which had brought the competition. I said it, Portland was becoming populated, was growing, and commerce took on, from day to day, more importance.

Oregon itself, moreover, was becoming populated, thanks to its gold mines, which continued to attract a strong movement of emigration from the banks of the Fraser. In 1859, it had 49,000 inhabitants, and the census taken in 1860 acknowledged 57,000, without counting the floating population, which was very numerous. It had therefore been admitted as a State, and the constellated banner of the United States counted one star more.

Although the summer had not kept all the promises of the spring, the year was good. When the month of September came and our accounts were settled, we appeared satisfied with the results of this first season—but then a light cloud rose on our peaceful horizon.

My brother was not perhaps of a very sociable disposition, but Gaillard was even less so: I had not been slow to perceive that they did not feel for each other a lively sympathy; the work suffered from it in my absence, because, not liking each other, they did not understand each other. As they said nothing to me, I pretended to see nothing. For all that, the result was that one fine day, Gaillard came to ask

3. It is difficult to identify Perlot's competition. Not until 1865 does the Portland Directory list gardeners as a category. In that year W. Casey, G. Hummell, and Perlot were so listed. Louis Pfunder, an emigrant from Baden, Germany, became one of Portland's most successful florists and horticulturalists, but he did not settle in the city until 1870. By 1875, however, Portland had several nurserymen: Frank Hackeney and E. J. W. Stemme, proprietors of the Oregon Seed Depot; Pfunder; H. Hansen, who advertised "Feed, Garden and Flower Seeds, Fruit and Ornamental Trees, etc.;" and Henry Miller, Florist and Horticulturalist; Limeroth & Co.; and Kiernan's Floral Gardens—Roses, the latter in East Portland. See [Leo] Samuel's *Directory, Portland and East Portland, 1875* (Portland: George W. Hunter, 1875), pp. 14, 27, 64, 69, 290, 325.

me to make an inventory of the company and to return his share to him, leaving it entirely to me, however, to settle the accounts. That said, he left and went to hire himself out in a newly established sawmill below the city. He earned forty dollars a month, that is, much more than we would have been able to earn apiece by remaining together during the winter. He was to return in eight days, to get what was coming to him; three days after his departure, I encountered him in town; he told me that he would like to come in with us again, if there were any way of doing so. "Well," I said, "return, but, in the future, no more childishness, because I, in business, I allow only seriousness."—"But," he said, "what shall I say on returning?"—"Tell my brother that you find my estimate too low and that you prefer to remain with us rather than to sell at that price."—"But I don't know your estimate!"—"What does it matter? you can always find it too low." Two hours later, Gaillard had returned to the house and was no longer talking of liquidating the company. This escapade was forgotten little by little and we continued our ordinary way of life.

In the autumn, a crowd of miners came down from the mines; they all were rich. All these mines in Oregon brought in a great deal, and quite recently they had just discovered new ones which brought in even more.

The placers of the Salmon and the Boise River were, they said, the richest that had ever been seen; but the season was too far advanced at the moment of their discovery; they had not yet begun to work them properly.[4]

Tucked away as they were between very high mountains, winter began there early and did not permit working before the month of April.

The news of these mines always caused me some vexation. For two years, I had abandoned the idea of going there, and I am so made that I do not go back on a decision once taken, but I could not prevent myself from thinking of what would have happened if, in 1857, instead of arriving in Portland in the month of June, when it was too late for us to go to the placers, we had come, Margraff, Létang and I, in the month of April. I consoled myself, however, by making this very simple reflection that after all, if they extracted the gold of these fabulous mines without me, a good part of it came back to me by an indirect route. In fact, the more they would produce, the greater chance Portland had of prospering and growing, for its situation was such that it ought to profit especially from the increase in wealth and in population which resulted for the country. Therefore I had not been so ill-inspired in establishing myself at the approach to this town, for, if it was enriched, why should I remain poor? From then on, the best thing was to stay and continue to dig my garden and those of others.

4. Gold was first discovered on the Clearwater at Oro Fino Creek in 1860. A year later the Salmon River rush began and Florence became its center. By the fall of 1862, still another rush to the great placers in the Boise Basin was under way. Then in 1863 a rush to Silver City on the Owyhee occurred. As a result, writes Earl Pomeroy, "Portland in its relation to the interior became a kind of Northwestern San Francisco." See Pomeroy, *Pacific Slope*, p. 50, and Paul, *Mining Frontiers of the Far West*, p. 138.

The autumn was quite wet; it rained as I did not remember seeing it rain since 1853 in California and in Oregon. It was a real deluge.

The peaceful Willamette became, by the fifth of December, an impetuous torrent; leaving its bed, it upset and carried away the establishments which bordered its banks. It was, for two days, a curious and heart-rending spectacle: the river was covered with strays of all kinds, trees, animals, fences, provisions, houses, sawmills, flour mills, all that was floating pellmell, and passed before Portland with a speed of three leagues an hour. Portland, however, was spared, or suffered little; it got off with a few walls destroyed, a few gardens devastated.

It was at Oregon City that the houses had been knocked down and carried away by the current, among others two mills with their stores of grain and wheat. The river, at that place, was frightful to see: a cascade twenty-five feet high had completely disappeared; one no longer saw anything but an enormous mass of water which, in its ungoverned course, smashed and carried away everything it encountered.

At Champoeg, situated twenty-five miles upstream from Portland, only two houses, out of eighteen, remained standing; the land itself on which the village was built, had been carried away by the waters; afterward one could no longer see, in the place where the village had been, anything but some holes, full of water, from ten to twenty feet in depth.

A few days of sun sufficed to put the river back in its bed, but it still took some time to carry off to the sea the overflow of its waters.

After the big rains, there came the big freeze.

The year 1862 had begun with pleasant weather, but, about the tenth of January, under the influence of a strong wind from the East, the temperature dropped rapidly; in six days everything was frozen in the gardens we were cultivating and, shortly afterward, the river was caught: men and horses crossed it on the ice.

It had been, they said, thirty-two years since anything like it had happened to the Willamette. During the five years that I had been in Portland, I had hardly seen ice in the ruts of the streets. Some Canadians who had lived in Oregon since 1817, affirmed that they had never seen so rigorous a winter before.

When the ice had melted, the snow fell; it reached fourteen inches in depth in a short time and disappeared only under the rays of the March sun. The spring brought us, with the swallows, a host of Californian emigrants. It seemed that California had been even more tried by the rains of the last fall than Oregon: everywhere, the rivers, the streams, the creeks had burst their banks, destroying the agricultural enterprises, drowning cattle and even men, destroying the works of the mines. These disasters, coinciding with the announcement of the discovery of the Salmon mines, determined an almost general movement of emigration: farmers, businessmen, miners took the road to Oregon. Each steamer arriving from San Francisco brought from three to five hundred passengers, who waited in Portland until the snow was melted, to reach the placers; the city was jammed.

There resulted a sort of famine. In the rough winter which we had just gone through, the cattle had perished in large part from hunger and cold.

Captain Ankeny, in his part, had lost on the plains of Walla Walla fifteen hundred head of beef which he was driving to the mines; he had lost them in that sense that he had had to butcher them and salt the meat.

At Portland, the price of meat rose from five cents a pound to twenty-five; communication by the river being interrupted, because of the ice, other commodities became expensive in the same proportions. The last bundle of hay that I bought for our horse, cost me the same price as oats, five cents a pound. A cow we had bought in order to have milk for my brother's children, had had to be butchered because we no longer had anything to give her to eat and in order ourselves to have something to eat. It is thanks to this reserve that we were able, without dying of hunger, to await the good season.

As soon as the snow had disappeared, we went to work. As I have said, everything had perished in our gardens; we had to begin everything over again; we were working so much more eagerly as everything was selling very high. In spite of that, the city continued to be built, to be populated, and everything seemed to promise us an exceptionally fruitful season. In a short time, the weather helping, the garden was soon in a good state. But it was said that this year of misfortune would be excessive in everything; beginning with the 20th of May and until the end of June, the heat was extreme, so much that, suddenly, the Willamette flooded and, anew, left its bed, flooding almost all our gardens, which it covered with three to four feet of water, and making us lose three quarters of our vegetables. So, the extreme dryness, like the abundant rains, in the basin of the Willamette produced the same result, the flood. Here is the explanation:

The Willamette flows into the Columbia, two leagues to the north of Portland; now, between the plain where Portland is built and that where rolls the Columbia, there is only an insignificant difference in level; when the Willamette is lower than Portland, it flows no longer, it appears stagnant, and although separated by thirty leagues from the sea, submits to the influence of the tide, which goes up the Columbia and stems it; its crest is raised then by two feet every twelve hours. In the rainy years, it is more or less high, according to the quantity of rain which has fallen and according to the season; it then rises from eight to fourteen feet above the low-water mark and flows with a certain speed because its crest surpasses by so much that of the Columbia, which no rain has caused to rise.

In fact, the Columbia takes its source two or three hundred leagues farther, to the northwest, in the Rocky Mountains, where the rains are rare and the snow always abundant; by degrees, as the season advances, the sun melts the snow, and the Columbia rises; it rises more or less according to the quantity of melted snow and according to the time it takes to melt. Ordinarily, the rising begins at Portland on the tenth of May and continues almost to the 25th of June, then the river decreases until the 20th of July, after which it returns to its average crest. These periods can be advanced or delayed by five days, according to whether it is the south wind or the north wind which is blowing in the mountains.

As soon as the Columbia rises, the Willamette, at Portland, stops flowing, and the water of the Columbia backs up there if the water of the little river is not abundant enough to fill its bed and cover its low flats in proportion as the crest of the waters of the Columbia rises, so that, every year, in the months of May and June, the water is high at Portland; the Willamette is full to the banks there, often even it overflows and covers, as I have said, the lowlands with a stagnant and warm water. Its crest which, in ordinary years, rises by twelve to eighteen feet above low-water mark, rose to twenty-four in 1862, a height which it had not reached for a hundred and fifty years. So it was that our gardens were flooded as well as all the streets in the lower part of town.

The following year, on the flats which the scalding water had reached and covered for several weeks, all the coniferous trees, of which several were a hundred and fifty years old, died, a certain proof that, never, during this lapse of time, had a similar inundation been produced. This reassured, at least, the inhabitants of Portland: they had nothing more to fear than the return of the disaster for their great-grand-nephews. The town continued to grow in population and extent.

While waiting, all our works were destroyed. But what to do about it? We had to resign ourselves, to wait for the flood to recede, and begin again with new expenses.

Happily, the produce of market-gardening was sold at higher prices and moved easily, so that in the end there was some compensation.

A good understanding had seemed reestablished, for some time, among us; that did not last.

My brother, ordinarily loquacious enough, all at once became taciturn; Gaillard ceased being expansive. No more chatting in the evening, in the corner by the fire, at table no more gay jests, no more animated conversation, each one seemed to spy on his neighbor and, if by chance one opened his mouth, to try to penetrate the hidden meaning of his words. My brother no longer addressed me except with ridiculous questions, and misinterpreted my replies. He rose brusquely, returned to his room, then came out again to put new questions to me, of which I could catch neither the sense nor the hearing. Gaillard's conduct was no less strange nor less inexplicable: finally, the conduct of both of them was, for me, an enigma whose key I sought in vain.

When that had lasted eight days, I had had enough.

"Gentlemen," I said to them, "there is no more harmony among us, as it appears; a company cannot function under these conditons, let us liquidate. Besides, neither one of you is sociable enough, to speak frankly, to rebuild it on other bases; each one, from now on, will work on his own account."

So it was done. We settled our accounts, I mean those of the company; there could be no question, for the moment, of settling the special account I had with my brother.

The cultivation of the lands which we had, including that of my block with the house, was divided in three equal parts, and each one worked on his own side.

The horse, the wagon, the provisions were in common. It was agreed that I would continue, on condition of compensation, to take charge of the sale of the vegetables of my former partners, who did not understand English.

I bought back the block which we possessed in common, situated in the ravine where the creek ran, which made me proprietor of two blocks whose cultivation was shared between the three of us.

Three days later, my brother, advised by me, bought one in the neighborhood and eagerly set to clearing; he was a good worker, but he had to work alone.

Shortly afterward, Gaillard came to propose that I form a partnership with him, offering me a fifth of the benefits before division.

The result of this partnership would have been that my brother would have had to leave the house where I had offered him hospitality, that I could not have continued to sell his vegetables and that, moreover, I would have given him competition. I resolved, consequently, to remain alone, although that obliged me to employ workmen whom I had not the time to supervise and I was thus exposed to working at a loss, instead of making profits.

For the rest, beginning with the day when we stopped being partners, we began to be united, and the most perfect accord ruled among us; each one worked in his own way, but we lived together and we found ourselves happy; we had therefore made, on the whole, the right decision.

Portland continued to grow, the forest moved back and the city came near, so that its first houses were no longer very distant from ours. I foresaw that the value of the land, already relatively high, would continue to increase, and I bought a third block; as it was half situated in the gully of the creek, consequently more difficult to work and to level, Flanders let me have it for a thousand dollars; I would have paid more than double on the plateau. So I had my work assured; then, the spirit of speculation helping, I counted on reselling, in the end, this land for much more than I had paid for it.

In the spring of 1863, Gaillard, having made the acquaintance of a company of French miners who had spent the winter in cutting wood, not far from us, left with them for the mines of the Salmon. He sold me back his share of what had remained in common and, his work done, settled his account; he left with me, on deposit, on departing, the sum which was paid him.

Among the miners who went through Portland to reach the banks of the Salmon, I saw again several members of the old company of La Fortune; first Duléry, Béranger and Lemériel. Since I had seen them, they had successively given themselves, after having renounced the trade of miner, to business and to agriculture; discouraged by the first flood, which had destroyed their crops, they hoped to restore their fortune in Oregon mines.

One day, at last, I saw coming a colossal Alsatian, driving in front of him a donkey which carried his baggage and provisions: one has already recognized Margraff. He arrived on foot from Jacksonville, situated on the Rogue River [sic] (*rivière du coquin*), two hundred and twenty miles south of Portland, and was going almost three hundred miles farther to the Salmon river. Only, wishing to arrive there in the season, he proposed, on leaving Portland, to use for his and his animal's transportation the steamboats which went up the Columbia.

He told me his story. On leaving me in 1858, walking somewhat by chance and without pushing himself too much, he had reached Jacksonville; there, he had joined a company raised on shares which was interested in all kinds of things, sawmills, flour mills, business, exploitation of mines, etc. It was doing business, but the bookkeeper having just died, they found that he had fraudulently placed in his name half of the company funds. Hence, a case and, in America as elsewhere, cases are long and especially they are costly; but, in the end, the company had won it.

Margraff then wrote me three letters, none of which had reached me. In each letter, he urged me to come join him and told me that he had had me named bookkeeper and cashier of the company at a salary of a hundred and fifty dollars a month, on condition that I put what I had in the company. He had guaranteed me on his own responsibility—I must say that the company, composed in large part of Germans, had already been robbed twice by its administrative counsel, which had the management of funds. These letters should have been brought to the post-office, four kilometers from there, but the postman, instead of sending them to me, left them in his pocket. It seems that he was paid to do that.

Margraff had his suspicions, uncovered the fraud, and made it known to his partners. There followed an internecine war, even a bloody war, for the cashier and another lost their lives in it; then came the case in the court of assizes, then failure.

Margraff had come out of the brawl safe and sound. He had returned to the north and was working in a blanket factory, in Salem, when he learned that they were finding much gold in the sands of the Salmon and that, luck permitting, one could make a fortune there in one blow. That was the dream of Margraff; he had immediately taken up his miner's tools and had left. All the entreaties, all the offers I made him to keep him in Portland were useless; he left me. What became of him, poor Margraff? I did not see him again and heard no more of him.

A great number of farmers had come to settle in the environs of Portland; almost all took up market-gardening. The result was that in the month of July, harvest time, vegetables were sold at a vile price. We got ourselves out of the difficulty, however, thanks to the early vegetables, for which we had no competition yet.

IX

RETURN TO HERBEUMONT
1867–1868

*Every man has a lurking wish to appear
considerable in his native place.*
Samuel Johnson
(quoted in Boswell's *Life
of Samuel Johnson*, July 17,
1771)

Jean-Nicolas Perlot's decision to return to Belgium to visit his relatives and possibly take a wife, as detailed in the following chapters, is simultaneously a lighthearted, witty travelogue and a frank discussion of the shock he felt when he returned to his village of Herbeumont. He had felt like a latter-day Rip Van Winkle when he left the Southern Mines after seven years to find that enormous changes had taken place in San Francisco and all over California. Portland, too, had changed every year that he had lived there. But back at Herbeumont he believed that time had stood still and he had changed.

Perlot was convinced that the main reason for this lack of change and the confined and fearful lives his family and fellow villagers were living, could be blamed on the Catholic church. Indeed, he soon discovered that his old enemy, the Curé Mangin, was still hostile to him, so much so that the priest had persuaded both Perlot's aged bachelor uncle and Perlot's only sister, who was childless, to disinherit him and give the properties, instead, to church charities. His bitterness over this news was somewhat dissipated by the pleasure Perlot took in exposing the ignorance and prejudices of the local clergy about America. His conversation with the local curate, M. François, is almost on a par with Mark Twain's hilarious story of the meeting of a miner with a minister from the East in *Roughing It* (see pp. 414–16).

In effect Perlot's experiences at Herbeumont were those of a soldier used to years of military campaigns in foreign countries trying to adjust to civilian life. European immigrants to America returning to their homeland for a visit obviously had similar feelings and in that sense Perlot's story is a universal one. But seldom have the crises and tensions involved been described in such a sensitive, articulate way. In the end Perlot discovered that in America he was "the French gardener" and in Belgium, "Monsieur Perlot," an American.

In his original narrative Perlot devoted three chapters to his return trip and to his sojourn in Europe. Although these chapters are interesting and reflect Perlot's charming anecdotal style, they are padded with travel descriptions and chance meetings that have little to do with his American experience or his family. Where it has seemed logical to do so, those less pertinent portions of his adventures have been omitted.

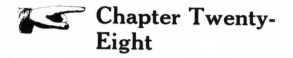 # Chapter Twenty-Eight

Thinking of Belgium

I was known in Portland under the name of the *French gardener;* the natives of California and Oregon could not understand that people coming from Europe and speaking the same language were not of the same country; they sent to me, as my compatriots, all the Frenchmen who wished to work or to be understood.

One day when I was busy in my garden, two of them, recently landed in Portland, came to me. I recognized one of them from having encountered him two days before in the following circumstances: while walking, near the forest, on ground covered with bushes, I thought I heard something like muffled cries. I went toward the place they seemed to come from, and I saw, seated on a stump, a man who, his head in his hands, was weeping silently. He was properly dressed, seemed neither sick nor tired. Judging that he did not need my help, and that the presence of a stranger could only annoy him, I had gone away without being seen.

It was he who, accompanied by one of his countrymen, came today to ask me to tell them about the country and the resources it could offer.

I understood the cause of his sadness, when he had explained to me the object of his visit. He and his companion, after having left the eastern states, had gone to California, where they had not found a way of earning a living; they had hoped to be happier in Oregon, of which they had been given a favorable report. They were quite disillusioned; not finding work, meeting few compatriots, they thought themselves in a wild country and hoped only to leave it to return to California, although not knowing too well what to do there.

But their resources were almost exhausted, and it was becoming almost as difficult for them to leave Oregon as to live there; hence, the discouragement.

They expressed themselves well, had an honest appearance, and seemed full of good will. To restore their courage with hope, I made of Oregon's situation a picture more flattering, perhaps, than exact; I told them what I, who knew the country, would do in their place, and finally offered them my services. On that, they decided to stay.

Two days later, one of them entered as apprentice in the principal bakery of the town; the other, following my advice, left for The Dalles, a budding little town, situated on the left bank of the Columbia, eighty miles to the east of Portland, where the government was having certain work done on the road by which the troop-wagons were to pass, and where they lacked workmen.

This latter wrote to me, at the end of a few weeks, that he had been hired at first as laborer, then as cook—although he was a simple commission merchant by trade—and that he was well satisfied.

Shortly after, I received a new letter from him, telling me that he had written to his two brothers he had left in the east, to have them come to him, and asking me to shelter them on their arrival in Portland, then to direct them to The Dalles. They arrived a month later, lodged two nights with me, then left to find their brother again.

About the same time, another Frenchman, named Cambet, native of the neighborhood of Lyons, came to ask me to act as his intermediary in negotiating the purchase of a block beside mine. He was of a certain age and knew English very imperfectly; it was, doubtless, to have someone with whom to talk that he wanted to settle beside me. Having bought the block, he cleared it, cultivated it, and grew some vegetables there, but that was in his spare moments; he continued to work for others. When spring came, I hired him with another Frenchman, the one from Franche-Comté, and I could, thanks to them, have a fairly good season.

I have already made the remark that my brother, since he was no longer my partner, had become sociable. Had he recovered from his errors? had his character suddenly been modified? or was it Gaillard's presence which offended him, and his departure which had returned his good humor? Whatever it was, he was quite another person, and I observed with surprise and pleasure that it was possible to live in harmony with him.

It isn't that, from time to time, there did not rise up between us some fairly lively dispute, but then it did not concern questions of interest or of personal grievances, it was in purely speculative discussions on rain or fair weather, politics, philosophy, or what not. We warmed up, we threw high words at each other's head, but that, happily, did not lead to any consequence; once the discussion was ended, we forgot everything.

My brother was so made that he could get angry, say and hear himself say the most disagreeable things without keeping the least memory of them, nor the least resentment of the insults said or received; I think he would have been capable, after an exchange of fisticuffs, of tranquilly pulling his tobacco pouch from his pocket and of offering a pinch to his adversary; when the occasion arose, he would have obliged him. One can conceive that with such a happy character, our quarrels were hardly more than discordant music.

In the month of September 1863, the three brothers reappeared in Portland, coming, I think, from the mines of Orofino, a placer to the north of the Salmon River; they stayed a few days with us; then, taking the trunks they had stored with me during their absence, they went across the river, settled near Voet, who having come to see me during their stay at my house, had indicated to them where they could be occupied during the whole winter in cutting cordword.

My connection with Ivon Voet had become one of intimacy; a fortnight rarely passed without one paying a visit to the other; I loved this loyal and good man, and I think that, on his side, he bore me affection. Since he had built our house, he had his bed in it. He came to spend the night there when he happened to be delayed in the city; now, for some time, his health had worried me; it was declining visibly, so much so that at last one of the three brothers came to tell me that he had been in bed for two days. I went to see him, I found him very weak. I came the next day to get him in a carriage to take him to my house; he hadn't enough strength to make the trip on foot. I closed his house, which I left to the care of the three brothers. When he arrived, he no longer knew anyone, the trip doubtless having fatigued him. However, after having received the ministrations of Doctor Wilson, he became better and, at the end of fifteen days, he returned to his house almost convalescent. Shortly after, he came to tell me that he was going to take a trip to Victoria, on Vancouver Island. He was convinced that the sea air would do him good and, then, he wanted to eat fish; at Victoria, the fish is excellent and it is never lacking there. I urged him instead to return, at least for a time, to Belgium, assuring him that the native air would soon cure him, while his illness could be aggravated if he did not take it out of the country. It was in vain; he left for Victoria. Ten days later, he came to knock on my door, at midnight, sicker, it seemed to me, than when leaving. I then persuaded him to return to his country; he left me the next day, promising me that he would leave as soon as he was a little better. I had invited him to stay with me until then, but he refused, on account, I think, of my brother, with whom he was not sympathetic; he preferred to take someone to do his cooking and keep his house. As soon as he felt better, he persuaded himself that the spring, which was about to begin, would complete his cure and he waited for it.

The spring came; Voet's situation grew no worse, nor did it improve. I went to see him each week. One day I found him more depressed than usual, a persistent dyspepsia afflicted him and discouraged him. I insisted anew that he come to stay with me; he thanked me, assuring me that he was very well cared for by his domestic. I left him after he had promised me that he would come to spend a few days with us. The next day, one of the three brothers came to tell me that he was dead, not naturally, but killed by a shot. Was there a crime, accident, or suicide?

I accompanied the Coroner who came to remove the corpse; we were able to prove that Voet was alone in his house at the time of the event. He had received the shot in the head, and death must have been instantaneous. His gun, ordinarily placed upright at the head of his bed, was on the floor, beside him; it had evidently served to give him his death. Was it voluntary or accidental? either hypothesis was admissible, that of a crime having been removed: how many men have killed themselves while handling their gun! and if the deed happens without witness, how to affirm accident or suicide?

The next day, we carried poor Voet to the cemetery. I announced the sad news to Knesselaere; Ivon's father and his other heirs sent the Belgian consul, in San Francisco, a blank power of attorney which he put in my name.

Too busy, at the moment, to be able to accept being administrator of the property which the deceased left, I had had the court designate for these functions a man named Kern, his neighbor. Once in possession of the power of attorney, I had this latter give me the sum total of the sale of the personal property which he had made as administrator, then I proceeded to the sale of the real estate, and sent the whole to Mr. Grisar, Belgian consul at San Francisco. At the same time, I wrote to the family's notary to bring him up to date on the situation and to inform him that I would come to Knesselaere probably in the following year. Voet had made me promise, during his illness, that if he came to die, and if I returned to Belgium, I would go to embrace, in his behalf, his father, his brothers and sisters, and take them his portrait which he had given me; moreover, he had charged me with telling one of his sisters a family secret to which he attached some importance. The agreement was, moreover, reciprocal; if I had died and Voet had survived me, he was to go and fulfill the same mission to my family.

The brothers X . . . were intelligent and enterprising. They had worked all winter as woodcutters in the neighboring forest; having a little money, they wanted to try a trade that was less difficult and more lucrative. In the month of March 1864, they came to ask me to point out to them the place in the city which seemed to me the most advantageous for establishing a grocery. I was, in truth, more so even than anyone else, the one to inform them in this respect: although I had never done this kind of business, I knew Portland. I suggested a house which they rented, then I took them to a wholesale house, kept by a French Jew and a German Jew, to whom I was particularly known. They procured eight hundred dollars worth of merchandise, for which they paid half on account, and were thus able to begin their business immediately. As, in Portland, the grocer is also a merchant of the four seasons (*marchand des quatre saisons*), as soon as I had my early vegetables, I brought them to them, [and] they would pay me after the sale was made. An easy sale, moreover, for I was the only truck-gardener in the city who sold the early vegetables, and I never had as many as I would have been able to sell.

Wishing to see them prosper and knowing the difficulties which sometimes attend beginners, as much in the career of the grocer as in any other, it often happened that I thought less of my interests than of theirs. I insisted that they always be supplied, and they often were to the detriment of my ordinary clientele. Finally, seeing that they were taking on very well, I abandoned the retail business in their favor and no longer occupied myself with anything but the wholesale, that is, sale in groceries, hotels, restaurants, boarding houses, and on board ship. They came, every day, to fill their wagon with the produce of my garden and went to deliver it to my clients under the name of the *French gardener*, or else I let it be believed that they were my partners, so that in a short time they were known and patronized.

I insist on these details because the story of my relations with these three brothers carries, like all stories, a moral which it is proper to bring out.

There was soon presented a new occasion for me to manifest the feelings of benevolence with which I was animated in respect to them. I read in the *Courrier de*

San Francisco, a French newspaper, to which I was, at the time, the sole subscriber in Portland, that the French consul wished to have correspondents on the whole Pacific coast, and was making, to this end, an appeal to his nationals; it was in virtue of instructions which had come from Paris. It especially concerned the furnishing of statistical information on the French population of California and Oregon. I had the article read to the eldest of the three brothers and engaged him to convoke, in a meeting, the Frenchmen established in the city and environs, in order that they might designate, as was asked of them, the correspondent of the Consul in San Francisco, promising to do all I could that he himself might be designated. I gave him to understand that the Consul's correspondent necessarily had every chance of arriving sooner or later at the vice-consulate.

The prospect was of a nature to seduce him, for he was not lacking in ambition, and nevertheless, in spite of my urging, he did not dare take the initiative as I advised him; he wasn't widely enough known and feared the ridicule of a failure. The objection did not lack justice.

As for me, I was known in Portland and the environs, and the French settled in the country thought me their compatriot; I decided to call them together myself.

Ten days after my appeal, thirty-eight Frenchmen, presided over by a Belgian, were gathered at the three brothers' house. When the assembly was regularly constituted according to American usage, I explained the object of the convocation, made known the reason which put me out of the running and, finally, the eldest of the three brothers, in whose home we were gathered, authentic Frenchmen themselves, was elected by a very strong majority. I congratulated myself on this result, not only because I had contributed to it, not only because I took an interest in the one elected, but also because the choice was good. The man they had just named had the qualities which suited the employment: probity, intelligence, a conciliatory mind, an obliging character.

He and his two brothers knew, moreover, that I wished them well, and when they could furnish me an occasion to be agreeable to them by rendering them some little service, knowing that they gave me pleasure, they did not miss the opportunity.

The eldest having fallen ill, as the house they occupied was hardly comfortable and as the noise of the street troubled his rest, he asked to be brought to my house; I gave him my room, and, finding more space there, more tranquillity and a healthier air, he was on his feet at the end of ten days.

The season that year had been good for me as well as for my brother, that of 1865 no less so. Our gardens, well cultivated, produced much and all was sold easily; we obtained, certainly, fine results, but at the price of what labors?

It was not without a secret satisfaction that I saw the time arriving for the dead season, which lasted four months, from October to February. During the eight other months of the year, the sun never rose before me, and it set well before my day was ended. That is how we were able to gather and sell, each year, three to four thousand dollars worth of fruits and vegetables.

In the month of September 1865, Gaillard returned from the mines of the Salmon. He was wounded in a hand, and stayed a whole month with me without being able to work. I then made an agreement with him, in virtue of which he was to work for me for two years, at the rate of forty dollars a month, with room, board, and tools. He replaced Cambet, who found that he had enough work to do on his own land.

With the savings he had left in my hands, and the gold which he brought back from the mines, Gaillard found himself possessed of a small capital which he was seeking to place. We bought, on joint and equal account, the old block which we had cleared with Demange.

Mr. Hibert, who had bought it from him, sold it back to us for two thousand dollars. It was somewhat with the object of speculation that we made this acquisition; we divided the block in eight lots to resell them as building sites, and in a short time we had sold two of them at the rate of four hundred dollars each. But then one fine day, in the month of June 1866, Gaillard came to tell me that he had ceded his share of the said block to the three brothers already mentioned, and that he was leaving the next day for Herbeumont.

This resolution, taken so brusquely, without any dissent having occurred between us, and in full season, at the moment when I had the most need of his services, must have seemed to me the more inexplicable in that it was agreed that we would go together to our country as soon as the term of his engagement had expired.

It was, in fact, a dream which I had cherished for some time, but which one circumstance or another had always prevented me from realizing until now.

Why did Gaillard leave me at the precise moment when this abandonment could cause me the greatest injury? Perhaps, alas, for this very reason, for it is impossible for me to discover any others, and he did not judge it proper, moreover, to give any. Whatever it might be, I did not think I should take advantage of the bilateral contract which bound us, for what could one expect of a laborer working against his will? I settled his account without making any observation, and he left the next morning.

It was impossible for me to replace him: I found only unskilled or lazy workers, whom I soon had to fire. Working alone the greater part of the time, I did not have a brilliant season. In this situation, the help of my brother would have been very precious to me if he had wished to sacrifice to me a day from time to time, which would have cost him little; but, doubtless, he did not realize that I needed his aid.

The season of 1867 was happier.

In the month of June, the annual inundation rose higher than ordinarily and I feared for a moment that it would flood the lands I was working; happily, it stopped at a crest a little bit lower, but the block of my neighbor Cambet, situated only two feet lower, was completely inundated and all the crop was lost. This disaster indirectly brought about an even more fatal event; the tragic death of poor Cambet. While waiting for the water to recede, finding himself without occupation, he took his gun and left for Oregon City, where he had worked before settling at Portland.

At the end of eight days, his little dog who never left him, returned alone to the house; he was sad, rubbed against no one, not even me, with whom he was familiar, and refused all nourishment; he stayed constantly on the door-sill, his nose in the air, howling, as does a lost or weary dog. Only on the fifth day, he ceased his plaints and decided to leave his master's house. As I was in the garden, he came to lie at my feet and remained motionless, without responding to my caresses, without manifesting any satisfaction. I entered the house, calling him; he followed me with his head down, refused to eat and finally went to bed in the stable where, the past year, when his master was working for me, he had the habit of staying. Some days later, they found not far from Oregon City the body of a dead man; although it was badly decomposed—for the death went back almost twenty days—it was recognized to be that of the unhappy Cambet. He had climbed the fence of an enclosure, and doubtless while wishing to draw up his gun which had remained on the other side, the shot had been fired and had hit him full in the face; death must have been instantaneous.

I was named administrator of the property Cambet left; I sent the French consul in San Francisco his death certificate with the address of his relatives, which I had found on his passport.

Three months afterward, a certain Mr. Delorme, curé at St. Louis near Salem, came to file, at the record-office of the Portland court, a testament by which the defunct willed him three quarters of his possessions; it happened that Cambet, on his arrival in Oregon, after having worked here and there, had become gardener to the convent of the *Soeurs de Marie*, placed under the direction of the Curé Delorme. On the advice of this latter, and in order to assure himself, in case of death, of a religious service and the prayers of the Church, he had made, or rather had had made, or perhaps even allowed to be made, in due form, the testament under consideration, which he had signed by marking his cross on it, for he could neither read nor write. Mr. Delorme returned to France to settle this affair with the natural heirs.

Some time after, Mr. Fearens [Fierens], Catholic curé of Portland, came to tell me that he had just received the power of attorney of the brother and sisters of Cambet and that he also had that of Mr. Delorme, which he had left on his departure.[1] Thus armed with the powers of all those having rights, he proposed to dispose of the block and the house, but not yet having settled on the day of sale, he asked me to keep administering the property of the estate.

The town was continuing to grow, especially on our side. Already, a great number of houses were built and occupied between the city and the stream which watered our gardens; for us to be in the town it was necessary only to tie them to the

1. The Reverend John F. Fierens is listed as pastor of the Roman Catholic Church in the *Portland Directory, 1864*, p. 20. Gaston describes Father Fierens as "about the most forceful, effective and popular priest that ever served the church in this city." He had a "bluff exterior and rather brusque manner," but underneath was very warm. On Sundays it was said that half the city came to hear him preach. See Joseph Gaston, *Portland, Oregon: Its History and Builders*, vol. I (Chicago and Portland: S. J. Clarke, 1911), 434.

houses beyond the stream, but this last ran in a ravine eighteen feet deep and two hundred feet wide. A street could not go down into this gully; I had the idea of making it pass over a bridge. I gathered, by means of a subscription, the necessary funds to construct it; I made a bargain for three hundred and twenty dollars with the Canadian carpenters, who set to work immediately and, in less than two months, built a bridge two hundred feet long by twenty wide. This bridge, although of timber-work, did not fail to produce a fine effect, but it produced especially good results: the street, on the side of the town, was rapidly built and property, in our section, immediately acquired a considerable increase in value.

I had engaged in the spring, as assistant gardeners, the man from Franche-Comté of whom I have already spoken, then his brother, steady men and good workers. They had done their job perfectly; I had only had to sow, cut, and sell, and I was well satisfied this time with the result of the season. I therefore had two men there on whom I could count; now, we were in the month of October, the bridge was finished, I was free until the next spring. Nothing prevented me from satisfying at last the desire which had tormented me for some time, to see again my natal village. I thought that four months would suffice me to go to Herbeumont and return.

On the 4th of October 1867, I left Portland on board the steamer *Oriflamme*, which gave service between that city and San Francisco, where I debarked three days later. I counted on boarding, the very next day, a steamer leaving for Panama; but that was counting without my friends Venard, Salomon and Chénot, who held me three days in San Francisco, Chénot especially, a childhood comrade, whom I had not seen again since 1850. Born at Conques near Herbeumont, he was my age, we had spent our first youth together, together learned to read at the community school of the village; then a little later, he had left for Paris, where I went to find him again; we saw each other often there until 1848, when he left for America, whence he sent me his address. Two years later, I left for California and, hardly arrived, I learned from someone who knew him and who gave me his address, that Chénot was there too.

I wrote to him at once; and so we had been for seventeen years in correspondence without having the chance of being able to shake each other by the hand.

Chénot had been married for four years; I could not, without impropriety, pass so near his home without going to make the acquaintance of his family. He kept me three days in San Francisco, so that instead of taking the boat which was going to Panama, I had to embark on a steamer with the destination of Nicaragua; which probably saved my life, as we shall see later.

[Perlot's itinerary took him from San Francisco to San Juan del Sur on the west coast of Nicaragua. From there he traveled across Lake Nicaragua and down the San Juan River to San Juan del Norte, or Greytown, on the eastern coast. Because he had prolonged his stay with old friends in San Francisco, he arrived at San Juan too late to board the steamer on which he was booked. That vessel was lost at sea in a storm. Instead Perlot took *The Fulton* for New York.

As soon as Perlot had boarded his steamer at San Francisco, he encountered two refugees from Mexico who had been associated with the ill-fated regime of Emperor Maximilian, which fell in June 1867. The first refugee, one Madame Cuvelier, was a Mexican national who had married a French military officer. She was on her way to join her husband, Captain Cuvelier, who had returned to France in great haste. Perlot was smitten by this beautiful, voluble, and temperamental woman who addressed him throughout the trip as Señor Peloto. At her request he became her *cavalcadour*, or squire. Although the flirtation appears to have been an innocent one, throughout the trip Perlot was half convinced that she was an adventuress who intended to seduce him.

Partly for self-protection and partly because Madame Cuvelier was so demanding and unpredictable—at one point he asked himself was she "crazy or just a comedienne"—he sought the help of a second refugee, a young Frenchman named DeMarcel, who had abandoned his business in Mazatlán at the approach of Juaréz's troops and was also returning to France. The three remained constant companions throughout the journey from San Francisco to Paris. At the same time, Perlot befriended a fellow Belgian named Van der Noot.

After a short stopover in New York Perlot and his friends boarded the *Denmark* for Liverpool and from there traveled by train to London. After touring the city, which he compared unfavorably to Paris, he journeyed to New Haven, crossed the channel to Dieppe and took the train to Paris. There, somewhat to his relief he delivered the effervescent Madame Cuvelier to her husband.

Perlot then paid a sentimental visit to Monsieur Dupont's store in the Rue de Bac, where Leborgne, one of the clerks, recognized Perlot and invited him to his home for a visit. Perlot remembered that the Leborgnes pummeled him with questions about California and Oregon. Impatient to reach home, Perlot immediately took the train to Sedan, the city from which he had first begun his travels in 1845, and then rented a one-horse carriage to reach Herbeumont.

The effect he was to have on his relatives and his fellow villagers, and they on him, certainly constitutes one of the most poignant passages in Perlot's long and interesting life.]

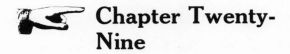 **Chapter Twenty-Nine**

From Portland to Herbeumont

It was twenty-three years since I had left my native village, aside from the short appearance I had made there in 1849. Naturally, except for the inevitable changes which time brings everywhere, I found it just as I had left it, with its houses grouped picturesquely on the high hill whose foot is bathed by the Semois and whose head is crowned by its old ruined donjon. What I was not to find there again, alas! was my family, all the members of which, except for an old uncle, were dead or scattered; I still had a reasonable number of more distant relatives there, but—they had told me at Sedan—these relatives no longer lived on good terms. I say "no longer lived," for after my departure in 1845, all the family was united. What was the cause of the change that had taken place? Here it is: My uncle Jean-Jacques died in 1859, leaving by will to his surviving brother all that he possessed. This brother was now eighty-four years old. His will was made, people were convinced, but they did not know what it contained; in order to know, they would have had to ask M. le curé Mangin, who had made it, but M. le curé Mangin wasn't saying a word. He was, moreover, no longer at Herbeumont; he was then serving the parish of Jamoigne. Only, from the fact that he was the spiritual and temporal director of the old man, they concluded, with a certain logic, that the natural heirs would be disappointed. Whose would be the profit? That was the question and that was the apple of discord. All the covetous were on watch; and whoever, among the claimants to the succession, came a little too close to my uncle, was looked at askance and put under surveillance by all the others.

Knowing all these things, I had myself deposited at Uncle Baptiste's door, ready to go next to the hotel if the welcome he reserved for me was not what I ought to expect.

But no, he received me with open arms. After the first effusions, the first news exchanged, I absented myself a few moments to take the driver to the hotel, with the carriage which had brought me. As soon as I was in the house again, I saw myself surrounded and as if assailed by all the cousins, both male and female, I had in the village; I supposed that only the pleasure of seeing me had brought them and as I had left them all good friends, I embraced them with good heart. They retired discreetly at the approach of evening. After dinner, my uncle on his bed, I on a chair, we talked tranquilly of one thing and another.

When the time came that he was in the habit of going to bed, he said to me, "Nephew, you have your bed on the upper floor, in front. I will give you a key so you can go out and return when you please, but don't say anything to Josephine (the servant); don't worry about me; I go to bed early and get up late, if I get up, for there are days when I don't leave my bed. I am going to try to sleep; if you are not too tired, go and spend your evening somewhere, for you must have a lot to tell. Since the receipt of your letter from Liverpool, you are impatiently expected in the village, and it is unlikely that you will return alone to America. Good night."

Josephine, who treated me as a cousin (*gros comme le bras*), and who with coming and going, managed to lose as little as possible of the conversation, secretly gave me a key to the house, recommending that I say nothing of it to my uncle; so that I had two of them.

I went to the hotel. In less than twenty minutes, the room was full of inhabitants of the village—principally young people who had run to see me. Only some of them, my elders or my contemporaries, still called me familiarly Jean Kâ—the name or nickname with which, in virtue of an immemorial usage in the country, I had been gratified in my youth: from my name of Jean-Nicolas they had made, by abbreviating it, Jean-Kâ. But the others, when they timidly risked addressing a word to me, called me respectfully: "Monsieur Perlot."

When I had finished replying to the numerous questions which were asked me and which were renewed by each new wave of arrivals, it was late. I went to bed and tried to sleep; not being able to succeed, I got up at four o'clock in the morning and went out without noise. I made the tour of the village, which was plunged in a profound sleep; only from time to time, a vigilant dog, disturbed by the noise of my steps, troubled the silence of the night by the noise of his barking. I stopped a long time before the house where I was born, where my childhood had been unfolded, and where strangers now lived. From there, instinctively, I turned, in spite of the darkness, toward the place where my people rested; I entered, so to speak, groping my way into the cemetery.

"Nephew," my uncle said to me after breakfast, "if you are ready, we will go to see the relatives; you owe them a visit, and I will take pleasure in accompanying you, on condition of not going too fast, for my time of running is past."

The visits were made correctly, methodically, beginning with the most aged.

Everywhere, the welcome was perfect, and everywhere, it was necessary to accept, for one of the following days, an invitation to dinner. On all sides, too, old friends, seeing me pass in the street, came out of their houses to shake my hand and show me where they lived, in the hope that I would go one of these days to take coffee with them.

It was past noon when we returned for dinner, and our visits were not yet ended, although they had been short everywhere! I went alone, in the afternoon, to the relatives whose houses were the farthest away, my uncle being too fatigued to accompany me there. I made six visits, and six times I had to take some coffee and eat some cakes.

I went in the evening to a saloon kept by a relative, and it was the repetition of the evening before, except that the number of the auditors was tripled and that the meeting lasted much longer.

The third day, which was a Sunday, my uncle said to me: "Nephew, I know very well that you have not returned from so far expressly to go to mass, the more so as I believe that you are scarcely devout; it would give me pain, however, if they came to tell me that they had not seen you there."—"So that won't happen, Uncle," I replied, "just give me a book." And arming myself with an enormous book of hours, I left for the church, passing by a house where I was expected for breakfast. On the big square, I fell into the midst of all the workers in their Sunday best, and received their vigorous handshakes. When the mass ended, they did not let me go; I had to take with them an incalculable number of mugs of beer (*chopes*) and of *baignons* (glasses of brandy with a foot-bath [*bain de pied*]). The result was that I did not return to my uncle's house until two o'clock in the morning, still armed with the enormous psalter which I had had to hold under my arm all day.

It was past time I went to see my sister; I had written to her the day after my arrival to announce my visit to her. I rented a cart in the village and had myself taken to Thonne-la-long, a village on the French frontier where she lived. We arrived there very late, having been detained at Florenville longer than was necessary.

As the villages, at night, are lighted only by the moon and as there wasn't any that evening, as my guide did not know the locality and as I myself had gone there only once, and that was eighteen years before, I was much perplexed to find my brother-in-law's house. Observing nevertheless a still-lighted window, I went to knock on a door which seemed to me to belong to the same house as the aforesaid window. Someone came to open to me; it was Demouzon, my brother-in-law. But it was not at his home that he received me, it was at his mother's, where he had gone to spend the evening. His house was a little farther on. He took me there and sent to find my sister, who was sitting up with a neighbor. She arrived while I was occupied, with her husband, in unharnessing the horse; she put her spinning-wheel on the ground, took her lantern in both hands and raised it to the height of my face. "I have to see," she said in a voice which seemed changed to me, "if it is really you."—"Yes," I said, embracing her, "it's really I, your brother Jean-Kâ doesn't die." She hugged me convulsively, then, picking up her spinning-wheel, entered the house and spoke no more that evening. While she prepared supper for me, her husband talked with me about his affairs; he had been a farmer for a long time and had succeeded well enough, so that he had been able, from time to time, to buy a field with the profits he realized.

Finally, as both of them were growing old, they had retired from the farm and, for four or five years, they had been living on their savings (*bien*). They kept a cow, some chickens, some pigs, to keep busy, and they rented a part of their lands: they almost had an independent living and they found that they were happy.

When I had eaten, we went on talking around the stove. My sister had her eyes fixed almost constantly on me, but remained silent. "Well," I said to her, "you say nothing—do you recognize me at last? Is it really I? One would say that you still doubt it. Well, come and make sure," and, so saying, I took her by the hand. She got up, kissed me on both cheeks, and without having said a word, left the room. I looked at my brother-in-law, he raised his shoulders.—"She is so odd!" he said; "the day before yesterday when she received your letter, she was already like that; she read it more than twenty times and did not want to believe that it was from you. Fifteen days ago your uncle had written to her that you had debarked at . . . I don't remember where, and that you would shortly be at Herbeumont. This letter was fairly long, she tore it up, I think, without reading it to the end, and without having read it to me—for, you know, she reads better than I, and it is always she who reads my letters. She claimed that there was nothing in this letter but lies, that you were on the other side of China and that, from there, one never returned. Where had she picked that up? who put those ideas in her head? I know absolutely nothing of it.

"Once, but it was already a long time ago, she wanted to order a service for you, claiming that you were dead, and that moreover, dead or not, you would return no more, that she knew it from a *reliable source.*"

Soon after, my sister came back to sit beside us. I continued to talk with her husband, without trying any more to draw her from her reverie.

The next day, she was relatively gay, she joined in, from time to time, with the conversation.

I went out with my brother-in-law, who wanted to show me his acquisitions, of which he was proud. While chatting, he said to me: "You know that Marie-Josèphe has been *troubled?*" "Yes," I said, "my uncle told me, and according to him, you are somewhat the cause of it; it seems that you are sometimes a little hard on her and that. . . ."—"What are you saying?" cried Demouzon with accents of indignation. "But that is infamous; ask your sister, when you are alone with her, you will see what she answers you. Who could have said that to your uncle, who never comes to see us? I want to know. . . . It isn't she, that's sure."

"Fine, fine, let's drop it; I wanted only to let you know the rumor that's going around; tell me, now, how she is?"

"Oh, quite well, only, you saw her yesterday, your arrival turned her topsy-turvy, but that will pass.

"As for her trouble, this, according to my recollection, is how it happened. When we had stopped working, not having any children, we said to ourselves that we would have to arrange our affairs so that, if one were gone, the other would have the enjoyment of everything, for after all, what we had, we had built up together and it is only just that we should enjoy it all our life; after us, my word, what we leave will return to the two families. We were both in full agreement on that, and we each made a sort of will with that intention.

"Fine, we were the happiest people in the world, when one day Uncle Baptiste wrote to my wife to come to Herbeumont, that he wanted to see her. She went there and returned at the end of two or three days, but she wasn't the same any more; she had a sad air, one saw that something was tormenting her. I questioned her, but she assured me that there wasn't anything wrong, that I was mistaken. All the same, she still was worried.

"Then the idea came to me that, perhaps, the paper we had executed was the cause of it and that she was repenting of it. 'Listen,' I said to her one day, 'you don't need to say so, I see very well that something is bothering you; if it is the paper we executed, well! let's go to the notary's and tear it up, we'll make another if you want and we'll do it the way you want it.'

"She assured me again that there was nothing wrong, added that she did not want to change what we had done and asked me to leave her alone, not to talk any more about all that. Then the curé here, a good old priest, who is a Belgian, began to pay her frequent visits and she seemed calmer. Easter time came; she wanted to receive the sacraments at Herbeumont; Curé Mangin, it seemed, had told her that it was a good deed to take communion in the village where one was born, and her uncle had been of that opinion too. She went therefore to Herbeumont, but that did not prevent her, after her return, from taking the sacrament again here. Then, after two or three months, there she was again, wanting to return to Herbeumont. One would have said that she was bored at Thonne-la-long; I took her to Herbeumont, we stayed there two days; on our return, I became aware that my wife was losing her mind.

"I had the doctors come from Montmedy. They told me that her trouble was very small, that she had a worry and nothing more, and that she should have a change of scene for a time; they advised me to put her in a rest home. I took her to an establishment they recommended, near Bar-le-Duc; at the end of some months, she was entirely recovered. Now, it doesn't show any more. However, since your uncle's letter announced your return to her, she is quite odd, but that can be explained, she loves you so much! The two other brothers, that isn't the same thing; you know, they annoyed us pretty much during the settlement of the family affairs after the death of your mother, and she is still bitter about it."

As I had to go to see my elder brother, employed by the Western railroad at Rennes, I had the idea of taking my sister there to try to distract her, and my brother-in-law approved. When I made the proposition to my sister, she welcomed it with pleasure. We left the next day. The trip was fairly long, for it was to last a day and a night on the railway; to be comfortable and better heated, we traveled in first class.

My sister seemed enchanted with this trip, she was gay and expansive. She told me first about her quarrels with our two brothers; her grievances seemed to me just a little exaggerated and, knowing her good character, it was easy for me to see that a third party had given himself the task of embittering things. Whatever it was, I needed few words to appease what resentment she might still feel for them, and to bring her to admit that, in spite of everything, she would be happy to see them again and to learn that they were prospering.

We passed to other subjects of conversation, carrying ourselves back to the days, already distant, when we lived together under the paternal roof; we took pleasure in recalling those thousand nothings which fill so large a place in life, and we laughed heartily at the memory of our childish tricks.

The greater part of the trip was passed this way, but there came a moment when my sister became taciturn and thoughtful; she replied no more than a *yes* or *no* to my questions. Was she going to fall back into that mournful sadness which was habitual to her and from which I had wanted to save her? I supposed rather that she was tired and needed sleep; it was about one o'clock in the morning. As she had not wanted to spend the night in Paris, where we had arrived at ten o'clock in the evening, we had taken the train leaving at eleven o'clock on the Brest line and already we were running at full steam toward Rennes. I urged her to sit in a corner and to try to sleep. She would have none of it. At the end of some time, she seemed to make an effort with herself and brusquely addressed me:

"What did they tell you at Herbeumont?"

"About what?"

"About the family . . . about our two brothers," then without waiting for my reply, she continued:

"So, you stopped at Uncle's?"—"Yes."

"How did he receive you?"—"Very well, better even than I expected."

"Did he talk to you about me?"

"He gave me news of you, at the same time telling me that he saw you but rarely any more."

"Did he talk to you of Uncle Jean-Jacques?"

"He told me about his last moments, but brother Nicolas-Joseph had already given me those details on his arrival out there."

"Ah, yes, that's true. Still, it's very astonishing that you could come home from those wild lands and go back there again."

"Not more astonishing than going to Rennes and returning afterward to Thonne-la-long, only the distance is greater."

"It's on the other side of China, isn't it, that country?"

"Yes, no doubt, if you want to go by way of China, but the shortest is to go to America and to cross it."

"Then, it's on the other side of America, and anyway, on consulting the map, one reads there, at the place you show me: *Pays inconnus*. When they explained that to me," she added sadly, "I really thought that you would never return, and I considered you as lost."

Seeing her overcome, I suggested that we get off at Le Mans, to take another train the next day by daylight.

"No, no," she replied quickly, "it isn't that. I'm not tired, I'm not sleepy; no, you see, I must come to it, I cannot keep quiet any longer. . . . Oh! if you knew . . ." and suddenly, she dissolved in tears. That lasted a long time. Moved myself more than I knew how to express, in the presence of this profound sorrow of whose cause I was yet ignorant, I tried vainly to calm her.

When my poor sister had at last returned to herself, looking at me fixedly and putting her hand on my arm, she made me swear never to say a word to anyone, as long as she lived, of what she was going to reveal to me. It was a secret of confession and it concerned her salvation, but she did not believe that God would punish her for unveiling a black plot and the most infamous betrayal.

"Listen," she said, "Uncle Jean-Baptiste has made his will, as M. le curé Mangin dictated it to him. He leaves you nothing, no more for Nicolas-Joseph. It's cousin Jacques Henrotte, the little Jacques, and my uncle's servant who have almost everything. Well, I have made the same will, I have disinherited you, me too!! . . . The curé, and my uncle, have forced me to it; in refusing, I would commit, they said, a mortal sin, for which I would never be able to obtain absolution; the Pope himself could not relieve me of it. I was terrified, distracted; however, I resisted a long time, I could not resolve to disinherit my family. Then M. le curé explained to me how it was that you would never return, that that could not be, short of a miracle.

"Now, God, he said to me, does not make miracles for impious people like you; as for Nicolas-Joseph, if he had been able to rejoin you, a truly astonishing thing, it was because, without doubt, God had so permitted him to punish him and to make him go through his purgatory in this world—He is so good, even to the bad ones! In any case, neither you, nor he, nor his family, would ever return, it was an impossibility; what was the use, after that, to leave you anything? It was simply to give a pretext to the government to keep in suspension, for thirty years, the execution of the will. For the law, he said, is so made, that at the end of that time the government would make off with my property. Since, in any case, my brothers would have nothing, would it not be better to make my will in favor of relatives or even strangers who would be present, themselves, at the opening of the testament. Tired of the struggle, I signed.

"So then, the *Ligneux*, the *Chic Chac*, the *Couvresse*, and all those others he had me put in my will, will have the property which came to me from my father and mother. You, my brother, you will have nothing!!"

These gracious appelations, *Ligneux*, *Chic Chac*, *Couvresse*, were, that goes without saying, the sobriquets of Curé Mangin's favorites; my sister was too much excited, at that moment, to give them Christian names.

She continued:

"I believed what Curé Mangin said to me. However, here you are back again! So he lied to me! Oh! my God, pardon me for speaking thus of one of your ministers, but that is infamous! infamous!

"And my poor Pierre," she continued, "who is not bad, whatever they say, for I have never had any serious complaint to make of him, my poor Pierre is their victim too, and I wrong him undeservedly. We had made a paper by which the survivor was to enjoy, during his lifetime, all the property we had amassed together. Well! they made me change that, he will have nothing but his share. The miserable ones! They have bewitched me, surely. It was following that that I had to leave my house and go to rest at Bar-le-Duc. A priest did that and my uncle helped him! My God! My God! is it possible? would you have believed it?"

I was stunned, but I did not want my trouble to be seen by my sister, already overexcited, and I said to her, affecting calmness:

"Alas, my poor sister, don't accuse our uncle, we have to expect everything on the part of a man who no longer belongs to himself; it isn't at him that we have to be angry for the evil he does, but at the one who has made away with his mind, and who imposes his will on him. And how could this poor old man, at the edge of the grave, avoid the yoke of a man who disposes of all the means of influence furnished him by heaven and hell? See for what purpose some men make their religion serve; don't make it the text to accuse their dupes, let that teach you quite simply not to confound God with those who speak in his name. He is not always in agreement with them, as you can see from my own example; while here, Curé Mangin and his aides were working to despoil me of my uncle's heritage and of yours, God, back there, was blessing my efforts; he returned to me a hundredfold what they had taken from me, which, after all, did not belong to me. But, believe me, let us forget these miseries, it is no doubt in the order of things that knaves exploit the weak.

"Let us pity the one and the other and behave so that we fall into neither of the two categories. Before finally leaving America, I wanted to see you, in order to tell you that I count on you to make my stew for me, from then on, when I return to our country. I have piled up enough back there to live on in relative ease; you haven't any children, I won't have any, for I am too old to marry, and besides I don't know anyone; I will come, if you find it a good idea, to move in with you, I think that I will sympathize with your husband, you will see that we'll live together well; we will try to forget the worthy Curé Mangin and his friends, or if we think of them, it will be to congratulate ourselves on not resembling them and on having other sentiments than theirs. We will prove to them, in any case, that one can live happily without swindling the heritage of the uncles or sisters of others."

"No, no, no," my sister interrupted eagerly, "believe me, give up this project; get married, and especially, have children; it is a great misfortune not to have any, I know something about it. You think that you will agree with my husband; what do you know of it? And then, what kind of existence is that of an old bachelor! look at our uncle, you will have the same fate: you will be surrounded by relatives who will show you the same friendship they have for him. They will await your death impatiently, they will take you quickly to the cemetery in order to return in haste to see how your will is made; and do it however you want, you will have made but malcontents and ingrates. Does that prospect seem very attractive to you? Get married, I tell you, you aren't too old; if you have some children, you will not see, at least, the collateral relatives disputing your inheritance during your lifetime."

Our conversation remained there, for the train had just entered the station of Le Mans, where there was a stop of twenty minutes. When we got back in the car, seeing my sister a little calmed, I urged her to try to sleep this time, for it was evident that she needed rest. She did not decide to until after I had promised to awaken her when we had arrived at Rennes; she was obsessed with the fear of passing that station during her sleep. She settled in a corner of the coach, but it was not until after long efforts that she succeeded in drowsing.

As for me, it would have been trouble lost to try it; I continued to smoke like a dragon, in spite of the rule, and I began to reflect. Certainly, there was rich material for reflections in the revelations my sister had just made to me. I sought to decipher that living puzzle, the Curé Mangin! Why, since my childhood, had that minister of the God of misery pursued me so implacably? what was the motive of that hatred which neither time nor distance had been able to extinguish nor even to dull? what vengeance had he to draw from me?

Before I had been able to find the reply to any of these questions, the train entered the station of Rennes.

It was eight o'clock in the morning. We breakfasted at the hotel, then we set off in search of *the old man*, as we called our elder brother; they pointed out his house. After having crossed a court and climbed a flight of stairs, we saw his name written on a door, so we were sure of the matter. The poorly closed door allowed us to hear the noise of a heated discussion between the two spouses. One claimed that it was half-past ten, therefore too late, the other affirmed that it was only past nine, and that it was therefore possible to arrive in time by hurrying a little. My brother was stubborn, as all good men of the Ardennes ought to be; my sister-in-law, in her double quality of daughter of Eve and child of Brittany, was no less so, without doubt, and, moreover, she was quick with the retort. The discussion could have continued a long time more; I did not think I ought to wait for the end, so I rang. A little girl seven or eight years old came to open to us. I passed by without asking her to announce us, entered a vast room and saluted. The mistress of the hearth was engaged in preparing coffee on a stove, at the same time skimming her pot-au-feu. At sight of me, she was thunderstruck, half turned toward the door and holding her skimmer in her hand, almost as one holds a taper. At the back of the room, my brother, in just a pair of drawers, seated on his bed, his night-cap on his head, one sock on and the other in his hand, looking with a frown at the intruder who had penetrated into his home without permission. When he saw my sister, who followed four steps behind me, he suddenly brought his eyes back to me, saying: "It's my brother!" We embraced, we made introductions; then, my brother having finished dressing, we began to talk. "Well," I said, laughing, "if you want to take up again the debate which our arrival interrupted, my sister and I will judge it."

"Ah, there," said my brother, "I went to bed at six o'clock, asking my wife to wake me up at half-past nine; I had an appointment this morning to bottle some wine; now, she let me sleep until ten o'clock, it is too late to dress, breakfast, and go to find my man, who, not seeing me come, will leave."

"Yes," said the sister-in-law, "but I saw him sleeping so soundly that I thought I was doing well in letting him sleep another half-hour, the more so as he is tired and as this week he has his night-duty and cannot sleep in the daytime; but in any case, he cannot go to his appointment, since you have arrived; let's forget it and have breakfast."

This was reasoning wisely; we explained, however, that having taken the precaution of breakfasting at the Hôtel du Cerf, before going in search of them, we would have to limit ourselves for the moment to watching them eat.

I found my brother aged, which was natural enough, not having seen him for nineteen years, but he rejoiced in an honest stoutness and a flourishing health.

He seemed happy. He had rented the whole of the house he was living in, which was composed of twenty rooms. By degrees as he made savings, he bought furniture and decorated his bedrooms, which he rented to the employees of the station and to the officers of the garrison; this industry, joined to his salary, permitted him to live in a certain ease. He had reserved only four rooms for himself. Four days before our arrival, he had given up two of these for ten days to one of his tenants, an officer, whose relatives had come to see him, and he had had to take refuge in the rather vast room where we found ourselves and which served him, at once, as kitchen, dining-room, and, thanks to an alcove built into the back, as bedroom. He wanted to take back his two rooms immediately for us to move in, and I had some trouble in persuading him to leave us at the hotel, where we found ourselves well off, and which moreover was not far from his house.

Rennes had on me the effect of one of those old cities where modern life has not yet penetrated. It is built on a hill sloping toward the southwest; at the summit of this hill there are the cathedral, the botanical garden, the bishop's palace, and some rather beautiful avenues and promenades; it is the most presentable part of the town; the rest, composed of long, narrow, tortuous streets, which are never washed—ordinarily deserted, moreover—could offer interest to an antiquarian, but not to a man accustomed to the large streets, regularly laid out and full of movement, of the American cities.

It seemed to me that the city contained few inhabitants, many priests and an enormous number of *petits-frères*. These latter, to mention it in passing, seemed charged with the direction of the local police; in fact, when the bells of the numerous convents of the city make themselves heard, all movement ceases, business establishments close and everyone goes home. So, having conducted my sister back to the hotel, at nine o'clock, after supper, as she needed the rest, I went out again immediately with the intention of going to read the papers at the café and of drinking a bowl of cider, [the] drink of the country; but already everything was closed, the streets were deserted and I had to go to bed like my sister. This silence of the streets, which is undisturbed by the sandals of the religious who come, go, meet, speak in a low voice, interrupted only at distant intervals by the noise which some delayed passerby with big sabots makes on the pavement, has something lugubrious about it; it lacks only the cry of the owl.

The next day was Christmas. One can imagine with what pomp such a festival would be celebrated in such a city. We had planned to meet at half-past nine in the morning at my brother's house, to go all together to—one can imagine where; one couldn't go anywhere else that day but to church. We were joined by my sister-in-law's mother: she was a person who still seemed vigorous, although she had been a widow for a long time. She had only two children, my sister-in-law and a son, who was a lay brother devoted to the instruction of the poor at Le Havre. She lived on her income, much reduced in consequence of the flight of her notary, who had just gone to England, taking twelve thousand francs from her; she bore this disaster philosophically enough, had settled at Rennes since the marriage of her daughter and lived there alone. Altogether, as far as I could tell, she was a good old woman, having no other fault than being a little curious.

The parish church was unapproachable, we had to give up trying to get in. So we resolved to try to enter the cathedral; the seats, which already were fairly expensive, on such a day, in other churches, would be beyond price, but then it would be so beautiful!

We began to climb slowly, on account of the crowd, up a steep street, which ended at the portico of the sacred edifice. Beginning at a hundred meters, approximately, from the church, we found ourselves between a double row of beggars, ranged symmetrically along the sidewalk, on each side of the street. They were the old people, the infirm, the children, the women, half naked, half covered with rags, shod with big sabots which often were cracked, without stockings in spite of the snow, and bareheaded. They held out to the passerby, in default of a hat, a hand chapped and reddened by the cold. In all this crowd, I did not see one hand, not a single one, respond to their appeal. At this spectacle, I felt myself moved by pity and I put in the trembling hand of an old man the few big sous I had in my pocket.

By dint of elbow-play, we ended by reaching the area in front of the entrance to the church; in the first glance, I saw a high, vast, splendid nave!

The Swiss, a man of fine presence improved even more by a magnificent costume and a plumed hat, was stationed opposite the entrance, from time to time making the flagstones resound under the stock of his halberd, and seeming preoccupied above all in forbidding the entrance into the holy place of poorly dressed people.

The interior of the cathedral was dazzling: everywhere shone gold and silver. A numerous clergy, also covered with gold and silver, circulated majestically in the choir and had just begun a mass with eight priests. The bishop in person officiated.

Above our heads, an immense organ filled the nave with its solemn tones and covered all the others, even that of the bells. The Saints, in festival garments, motionless in their niches, did not fail to heighten the splendor of the ceremony. It was beautiful, and I was not surprised, for they had warned me sufficiently.

However, I had not seen everything yet. As my dazzled glances wandered in all directions, I spied in a corner, toward my left, on an inclined plane, some sheep, goats, oxen, donkeys, men and women; all that, it's understood, in wood or in plaster and more or less cleverly imitated; that represented an encampment on a plain. In back, overhanging a little, in order to distinguish it better from the earth, the blue sky, sprinkled with golden stars; on the horizon, an infant, resplendent as the sun. The shepherds, on the plain, seemed absorbed in contemplation of this spectacle, I did as they did, and, after having looked at it carefully, I began to wonder if the painter had wished to represent the birth of Jesus or symbolize the winter solstice.

As we were standing and tightly pressed by the crowd, I suggested to my brother that we go to take a bowl of cider in the neighborhood. We left. At that moment, a gentleman was going through the church, a purse in his hand, preceded by the magnificent Swiss, who, to announce him, knocked the tiles with the wood of his halberd. All hands were stretched out to the seeker, and the sound made by his purse, when he shook it, indicated a copious receipt. I thought involuntarily of the poor devils whom I had seen outside the church, vainly stretching their hands to the passerby, and that suggested to me some reflections which I could not prevent myself from communicating to my brother. "Be careful," he said, "they are fanatical here, more than you can imagine. If they heard you, they would think ill of you (*on vous ferait un mauvais parti*), and you would do me harm; here, one has to go to church, or be sick; I get out of it by managing so that my illnesses fall, as much as possible, on Sunday. Once this tribute is paid to religious intolerance, one can live in peace in this country, and, for my part, I am happy enough here."

We entered the café. At Rennes, in the cafés, they sell nothing but cider and brandy, poor enough, to mention it in passing.

We approached a wooden table, on which they served us two bowls of cider full to the brim. I admired the dexterity of the consumers of the local stuff, who, taking their bowl in a single hand, emptied it without spilling a drop of the contents and without plunging their finger in the vase. I had to use both hands and take a good many precautions to achieve the same result.

I don't wish to establish any comparison between cider and the juice of the grape,

Heaven preserve me from having the thought
(*Me préserve le ciel d'en avoir la pensée*)

no, but finally I observed that the drink of the Normans, without disparaging the Burgundian, has its merit: it is light, sparkling, and flatters the palate; it goes to the head, too, I saw right away by the red faces of the drinkers, and by their uncertain walk when they left the establishment. I used it therefore with discretion.

The effect of the perfidious liquor on my brother was to make him serious; that is understood, he was not of the country, after all.

After having asked me the news of relatives in America and in Herbeumont, he wanted to talk to me of our family arrangements, and inquired about an account which Nicolas-Joseph should have repaid me. Family arrangements are ordinarily enough occasions of hatred and discord in families. I did not care to touch this chord with my brother; I cut him short, assuring him that I had come solely to see him and not to talk business with him. He adhered to it as said (*Il se le tint pour dit*) and there was no more question, between us, of account or arrangement, so that I was able to leave Rennes without having exchanged the least word of bitterness with him.

The interval between the mass and vespers (vespers were also obligatory) was employed in visiting the sights of the city; then my sister-in-law took us to the establishment of the *petit-frères* [lay brothers]; she insisted on showing it to us: it was so well kept!

Unfortunately, we were not able to enter, the superiors being absent. But that evening, while we were still at table, the Director arrived. They had told him of Mme. Perlot's visit, and he came at once to apologize for not having been there to receive her.

He was a little man, stocky, as his compatriots ordinarily are, with an agreeable exterior, moreover, and a fine talker. He stayed a part of the evening with us and I had the honor of conversing and even of arguing a little with him. When he had left, my sister-in-law and her mother hastened to inform me that I had just been talking to the greatest genius of contemporary France. "Ah! he was a savant, he was a philosopher, he was a great man!" I was careful not to contradict it, not knowing the exact value these terms might have in Brittany.

It could be that the Director of the *petit-frères* of Rennes was a learned pedant, but he was surely and above all a pedant. He had the decisive tone, he knew everything, he was always sure of his fact; he had some formulas to pull himself out of the situation when the discussion embarrassed him. "That, you see, I have that at my finger-tips, I speak pertinently—it's a settled thing, useless to contest it, let us pass on." How can one discuss with a man who knows so well how to cut short the discussion? draped in his infallibility, he has no trouble in triumphing over his adversary, and so it is that on all the points where we were not in accord, that is to say on almost all points, he was constantly right and I invariably wrong. This claim to speak of everything pertinently, and so to close the mouth of his adversary, seemed to me, however, somewhat impertinent.

The next morning on getting up, my sister declared to me that she wanted to leave that very day. She had a heavy head, an oppressed chest, and she was afraid of becoming ill.

The train for Paris left at ten o'clock in the morning; we had only the time to fasten our bags and to make our farewells; my brother and his wife were struck with amazement when we informed them of our resolution. They counted on keeping us at least eight more days, and the next day we should move in with them. Then a more serious thing, our sudden departure spoiled a project cherished by the mother-in-law: she had taken it into her head to present us to her acquaintances, among whom figured a widow with two children of tender years. This widow was independent and spoke English very well, I spoke it passably and I was unmarried; if they brought us together, did anyone know what might come of this interview? one would see. . . .

Naturally, I was supposed to know nothing, suspect nothing. My brother had revealed the plot to me, but . . . under the seal of secrecy.

It may be imagined that the widow was in exactly the same ignorance as I of what was going on. All those who were in the secret had good hope, the most hasty saw the thing as done already. The interview was to take place that very day, at three o'clock in the afternoon, while taking coffee. One can imagine if entreaties were made to my sister to persuade her to adjourn her departure, if only for twenty-four hours. But she was unshaken. I promised faithfully to return to Rennes before recrossing the Atlantic; but it was written that this marriage, so much desired, would come to nothing.

My sister had noticed that the *old man,* as we called our elder brother, had on his finger our mother's wedding ring; she insisted that I have it, claiming that it came to me as the youngest. She wanted to see it in my possession—I obtained it without difficulty and she left happy.

X

MARRIAGE AND RETURN TO PORTLAND, 1868–1872

Ah, Nephew, believe me, get married, get married—it is a sad thing to grow old and be alone. It's your Uncle, your uncle eighty-four years old who tells you.

Jean-Jacques Perlot to
Jean-Nicolas Perlot
Herbeumont, 1868

Some people said that the American had thrown a spell over her.

Perlot, *Vie et aventures*
(Arlon, 1897), p. 520

 # Chapter Thirty

Relatives and Friends

The next evening, we were at Thonne-la-long. Demouzon did not expect us. "It was Marie-Josèphe who wanted to return," he said, holding out his hand to me, "otherwise you would not have returned so early."—"Yes," she said, getting down from the carriage, "I had enough of that country, it is nothing like our Ardennes."

The following day, at the moment of leaving for Herbeumont, I made my adieux while telling my sister that perhaps I would return to see her before returning to America. For four days, she had not stopped repeating: "You are going to go back there, then it will be finished, we'll never see each other again." I replied to her: "You said that to me in 1844, you said it again in 1850, and nevertheless we have seen each other again. We will see each other again in five or six years, when I return for good."

She let herself be embraced without manifesting any emotion.

My brother-in-law accompanied me to the edge of the village.

"Marie-Josèphe astonishes me," he said, "and worries me. She lets you leave almost without saying a word to you, without spilling a single tear; I know how much your departure hurts her and I would have preferred to see her cry. . . ."

Not until evening did I reach Florenville, where I slept. The next day, a hired carriage deposited me near the Epioux forge, in the forest of Chiny. From there, I regained Herbeumont on foot, through the wood.

I took a lot of time to make this short trip; twenty times I sat down at the foot of an oak, my pipe in my mouth, thinking I was smoking and not perceiving that for a long time it had been out. I was absorbed in my reflections and these reflections were not gay. What I had learned in these ten days, obliged me to make a decision and, in truth, I did not know what to decide. I would have been happy then to possess a friend to give me advice, but, after so long an absence, I was no more than a stranger in my natal village. I still had some relatives, but I knew now that in them I had as many enemies. However, everybody, on my return to Herbeumont, had given me a kind reception, everybody had come to shake my hand; but that was because they remembered my father, who, while he was directing the works at the quarry, had done some good. "Ah! your father was so good and fine a man," the old people said to me, "that you cannot miss being well regarded in the village."

Shall I say it? my uncle, instead of being flattered by those praises which it was so sweet for me to hear, my uncle felt for them a spite which he did not succeed in dissimulating. It seemed that he took them for reproaches addressed to himself. Alas! I had observed, in fact, that he was neither loved nor considered in the village, where they accused him of being egoistic, avaricious, hard on the poor. It was judging him wrongly, moreover; he was naturally good and human, and he would have done good if those who surrounded him had let him. Whatever it was, he knew or guessed what they said of him and he suffered from it. Hence, that posthumous jealousy which until then I had only suspected but which was no longer doubtful for me now that I had the explanation of it.

However, I understood, I almost excused, this jealousy, although it wounded my filial sentiments. What could be neither comprehended nor justified, was the conduct of my uncle toward my sister. Was it not he who had struck the blow from which she was dying? for I could no longer delude myself, her days were counted, and the trouble with her reason was nothing but the sad forerunner of her approaching end. And it was he, my uncle, who had killed her! for it was he who, by lending his cooperation to the shady scheme of the Curé Mangin, had assured its success.

The good and simple creature, as incapable of suspecting evil as of doing it, had allowed herself to be easily wronged by those whom she had learned to cherish and to respect; and, disillusioned, she had conceived from it this profound, mournful, incurable despair, which was preying upon her and leading her slowly but surely to the grave.

Now that I knew all, it seemed impossible to me to accept any longer my uncle's hospitality! but, on the other hand, my sister had made me promise, had made me swear even, to maintain secrecy for her on what she had revealed to me, and I should keep quiet. I would have to seek a plausible pretext to leave my uncle's house and not to let him suspect the veritable motive of my departure. I was counting on circumstances to furnish me this pretext. I rose finally, having taken a resolution but not knowing yet how I would execute it.

It was eight o'clock when I returned to my uncle's house; he had already gone to bed, but was not sleeping. If he had not been so old, he no doubt would have noticed, like the people I had already met, my pale and dejected countenance, but he saw nothing. I told him briefly about my trip, but he seemed above all desirous of knowing what had passed between my sister and me; he addressed me, on this subject, with numerous questions to which I made evasive answers. After standing for several moments, thinking him asleep, I was preparing to leave, when he brusquely addressed me with this question: "Did Marie-Josèphe tell you that she had made a will? . . . you know, they haven't any children. . . ."

"Demouzon," I replied, "dropped a word of the arrangements which they had made on this subject. I didn't make any observation; they have done, I think, about what I would have done in their place. Moreover, it's their business. As for my sister, when she wanted to turn the conversation on this subject, I cut her short."

"And why didn't you let her talk?"

"Because the subject hardly pleased me, and, moreover, what she had to say to me, Demouzon had already told me."

He then inquired about *the one at Rennes*, about his wife, a right-thinking person, he said, and very religious, and about her brother, the *petit-frère* whom I had not seen, which seemed to annoy him. After which, he released me.

The next day, I went to see a relative whom my sister had made me promise to call on with her compliments.

It was the widow, Mme. Gaupin. I found her occupied in caring for her livestock; she gave me a very kind reception and seemed happy to see me again. She inquired with interest about my sister, whom she seemed to love very much. "Poor cousin," she said, "what a misfortune that she guessed so badly! One would have said that these Demouzons were worth more than that."

"And who told you," I interrupted, "that she had any complaints of her husband?"

"Oh, surely, it wasn't she, I have never heard her complain. But all the relatives say, here, that it is the bad treatment of her husband which made her lose her mind, and she so good, too!"

"Cousin, make no mistake: with his inequalities of character, Demouzon is a good husband, he loves his wife and is loved by her, and, notwithstanding some insignificant conflicts, it is a united household; if the rumors you tell me about have been spread here, it is perhaps because there are people who have an interest in accrediting them. No, Cousin, believe that the evil from which my poor sister suffers must have another cause."

"But," said Mme. Gaupin, astonished, "if there is another cause, she must have told you, for she has a great deal of affection for you."

I made an evasive response and I admired with what cleverness certain people know how to ruin the reputation of those whom they wish to despoil.

Mme. Gaupin asked me the news of my brother at Rennes. "Do you know," she said, "that he returned once to the village festival?"

"Yes," I said, "he told me that he had come with his wife, and that my uncle had not wanted to receive him."

"In fact, my cousin had written to him to warn him that he proposed to return to visit his old home; my uncle replied to him that he had the right to do it, and that he would find a good hotel at the village, but that, as for him, he never received anyone in his house, which was small. My cousin came and stayed at the hotel. You understand that if I had been warned, I would have written to him to stay with me, my house is big and I would have received him with pleasure, him and his family; but once at the hotel, he wanted to stay there.

"However, when our uncle saw that all the relatives and even strangers were inviting his nephew, who is also his godson, he could not do otherwise than to invite him in his turn. I must say too that his wife, who is, I think, a very religious person, had gone to see M. le curé, and I think that that contributed a great deal to bring about the reconciliation between godfather and the godson. Knowing the character of the uncle, I am astonished that he should so easily have received you and installed you in his house."

At that moment, a young girl entered with a book in her hand; she was returning, I think, from mass. Mme. Gaupin presented her daughter Victorine; I saluted, she made a pretty curtsy, asked me the news of my sister and brother, then passed into the next room.

Naturally, I did not leave my cousin without having accepted an invitation to dine.

I returned to my uncle's; my two cousins were awaiting me there. One had come first; the other, seeing him enter, had come running. Things, it seemed, always happened that way, my uncle never seeing his heirs separately. It was New Year's Eve; from time immemorial, the Perlot family gathered on that day, at the home of its oldest member, but, for several years already, my uncle had given up this custom, alleging that the members of the family were too disunited and that he could not invite some without the others. My cousins, therefore, had resolved, each on his own account, to profit from the happy circumstance of my return to revive the ancient tradition, and they came to invite us, my uncle and me, to dinner for the next day. Each one insisted eagerly that my uncle accept; as for me, they did not allow me the right to refuse. "Cousins! and it was so long since we had seen each other!" They had not importuned me until now, I had so many friends, I was so surrounded. They had been patient, trusting that surely their turn would come; now, their turn had come. I could not do otherwise than leave it to the decision of my uncle, which was that we would go to dine one day at the home of the one and the next day at the home of the other.

However, I had decided to leave my uncle's house and, encountering my cousin the *bourgmestre* in the street that same day, I begged him to come to plead my cause.

"What cause?" he asked.

"My uncle is old, a valetudinarian—I receive frequent visits, even from people whom I don't know. There is a continual coming and going in his house which disturbs his rest and changes his habits; I would like to take my trunk and go stay in the hotel. It's a matter of making him understand that it is in his interest and in mine; would you help me?"

The idea, as I hoped, seemed to please my cousin, and I found him well disposed to render me the service I asked of him.

We entered my uncle's house, I presented my request to him, and my cousin, warmly seconded by Mlle. Joséphine, respectfully supported it. My uncle who, at the first words, had knit his brows, brusquely cut short their words. "My nephew," he said to me, "you don't bother me in the least; you are in my house and I wish that you remain there; you won't be there, anyway, for very long, since you are going to leave again soon. Let there be no more question about it."

That was said in a tone which did not permit us to insist. I left and went, as usual, to spend my evening in the home of another cousin, the tavern-keeper, where I arranged meetings with the people who wished to speak to me.

When I returned, about midnight, I found my uncle in the corridor. "I heard you come," he said to me, "and I waited for you to tell you to come warm yourself a little beside my stove before going up to your room."

I entered, my uncle went back to bed.

"What does that mean," he said to me; "how does *that one* come with you to make me promise to throw you out of my house?"

"My uncle, it was I myself who begged him to do it."

"Ta ta ta ta! Look, Nephew, it isn't I whom you bother here, it's those people. You must have noticed already that we cannot be alone a moment; if you enter, one or the other is behind you. They would be well pleased to see you out of here. — Well, then, no, you will remain, were it only to enrage them. — There are things, you see, that I cannot tell you. . . . No, I cannot. . . . Divine goodness! I live too long. . . . My brother Jean-Jacques was right. . . . If only I were dead in his place! If he had survived me, he would have managed better than I have. . . . Ah, nephew, believe me, get married, get married—it is a sad thing to grow old and be alone. It's your uncle, your uncle eighty-four years old who tells you. . . . My God, what a misfortune to be ignorant and not to be able to guide oneself except by the counsel of another! You have to put your faith in a man who, often, does not deserve it; one meets so many schemers along the way! And I have been guided all my life. Ah! if it were all to begin over again! . . . But it doesn't begin again. . . . You realize that you are on the wrong road, you want to retrace your steps. . . . It is too late! . . ."

He continued a long, long time this way.

These incoherent words, these unfinished sentences, would have been absolutely unintelligible to me if I had not had, thanks to the revelations of my sister, the secret of the thoughts which obsessed him.

Touched by his sorrow, I forgot all my griefs; I stopped accusing him and felt no longer any sentiment but a profound pity for this unhappy old man, victim himself of the machinations to which, through weakness, he had lent his hands.

He ended with these words, pronounced with a melting sadness: "Happy he who has an untroubled conscience!"

After some instants of silence, he said to me: "I keep you here, when you must feel the need of sleep. Go put yourself to bed, we'll see each other again tomorrow."

I got up and said to him: "Uncle, I wish you good night, permit me also to wish you a happy new year, for now it is two o'clock, the year 1868 has begun."

I approached the bed, he raised himself a little, and I embraced him. When his head fell back on the pillow, I saw that he was weeping. . . .

As I went back up to my room, I heard, on the upper floor, a door which was closed discreetly. I concluded from that that Mlle. Joséphine found herself—by chance, no doubt—on the stairway during our conversation, and had not lost a word of it.

My uncle having a small account to settle with the curate of the parish, M. François, he asked me to accompany him to the parsonage.

I consented. As soon as we were in the street, we did not fail to encounter cousin Henrotte, whom we invited to accompany us, an invitation which he hastened to accept.

It seemed to me that our visit was not unexpected. The presentation made, my uncle's account settled, conversation began.

"So," said M. le curé, "you come from America?"

"Yes, M. le curé."

"From what part?"

"From Oregon, to the north of California."

"A beautiful country?"

"Beautiful and excellent."

"Peopled?"

"It is only beginning to be populated."

"It is at Portland that you are established?"

"Yes, at Portland, State of Oregon, not far from the Columbia River."

"The Columbia! ah, yes, I think that they also call the river Oregon; well, there is a question of it in the missionary journal. It is in that journal that I have seen these two names; do you have them, where you are, the missionaries?"

"Many of them."

"Portland is a city?"

"Which counts five thousand souls; a settlement of 5,000 souls, in a new country, is a city."

"Are there many Indians there?"

"There aren't any. One sees, from time to time, a troop going through the city; they do not live there."

"What is the religion of the country?"

"It doesn't lack religions. Portland, for its part, counts eleven different ones, without mentioning those of the Chinese, who have two."

At this response, my uncle opened his eyes wide, but M. le curé frankly laughed at it.

He continued: "In this great number of religions, there is at least one good one?"

"They all are in the eyes of the law, for it tolerates all."

"The Catholic religion is not, I presume, professed in the country?"

"Pardon, what would the missionaries be doing there, then? Portland even possessed a Catholic bishop, Monseigneur Blanchet, who is French; the dean is a Belgian, a Fleming, M. Fierens."

"But the missionaries, themselves, have nothing to do at Portland; they catechize the savages, no doubt."

"Pardon, they serve the parishes. Mgr. Blanchet receives the missionaries whom the bishops of France and Belgium send him, and then sends them off to different points in the country.

"The State being strictly neutral in religious matters, the faithful make direct payments to the ministers of their cult. Besides that, the bishop distributes to his curés the money sent from Europe to the missionaries."

"Ah!" said M. François, who seemed astonished, "would it really be like that?"

"I can certify to you, M. le curé, that in the eighteen years that I have lived on the Pacific coast, I have never seen other missions than those."

"Who are those who frequent the Catholic church?"

"The Irish, the Saxons, the Bavarians and the French, those in small numbers; the Frenchmen, once away from home, ordinarily practices no cult."

"Truly, I do not understand how they can find themselves there in all that hodge podge of religious sects. It must happen sometimes that the Protestant minister, for example, attacks the curé, and that consequently, the latter has to reply to him; what disorder must result from it!"

"But, M. le curé, if that happened, no discord would result; the world, as long as it has existed, has been given up to controversy. But that does not even happen; it has never come to my knowledge, at least, that that has happened.

"That is understood, in a country where several religions live side by side, all equally free, under the protection of the law, which favors none of them, that they are necessarily tolerant.

"The minister of each cult is shut up in his church, preaches to his flock morality such as he conceives it: on that ground, there is no place for controversy. If, supposing an impossibility, the morality which he preaches, did not conform to the universal morality, and he wanted to put it in practice, it would be the police who would intervene and not the minister across the way."

"So that in that land of liberty, religion is submitted to the police?"

"Not at all; religious associations, like all associations, enjoy a complete liberty; but it is not permitted to infringe the law under the pretext of religious opinion; if the public exercise of a cult involved acts contrary to good order or to good morals, the police would not tolerate them."

"And in matters of morals, who then is the judge?"

"The law and those who are charged with executing it."

"They must be very busy then; for in truth, I don't see how good order, how good morals are compatible with such a system, the liberty to do everything!"

"That liberty, M. le curé, exists no more in the United States than elsewhere; there as everywhere liberty consists, in the last analysis, in doing all that is not forbidden by the law; only the law, in the United States, imposes no other restrictions on natural liberty than those which social life renders necessary; moreover, it is equal for all; it neither establishes nor admits privilege of any sort. It is this which distinguished it from the laws which still, in old Europe, rule even the states which believe themselves the most advanced."

"Morals, in that country, must be frightfully dissolute?"

"They are more austere than here."

This assertion seemed, no doubt, completely extravagant to M. le curé François, for he began to laugh and my cousin Henrotte could do no otherwise than to burst out laughing. I cited some facts, explained to them that certain acts which seem lawful here and which everybody is permitted, are considered, back there, as

reprehensible and constitute sins punished by police regulations. But M. le curé
had his opinion set on this unfortunate republic which had no state religion, and I
left him persuaded that it would perish in a short time, if it did not give itself as
quickly as possible a king or an emperor, with state religion and privileged clergy.
How many people think themselves more enlightened, on these matters, than a
village curé can be, who do not judge more sanely the things of America!

New Year's Day and even the day following, were passed in numerous visits to
relatives and friends and in interminable meals. After these days of merriment, I
remembered the promise I had made to poor Ivon Voet to go to see his family, and
so there I was on the way to Knesselaere, passing by Jamoigne, where the mail
collector was the brother of Eugène Chénot; the latter had given me a letter for him
which I had had to promise to take myself. Jamoigne was the present parish of the
curé Mangin.

My uncle, knowing that I had to stop there, begged me to go, on his part, to wish
good day to M. le curé; and seeing my hesitation: "You know," he said, "I do not
ask you to pay him a visit on your own account. It is a commission with which I
charge you, you will give me pleasure by performing it, since you pass that way, as
it won't disturb you and as you have the time for it." After a moment of reflection, I
replied: "I will go." I was not annoyed, after all, to have an interview with the curé
Mangin.

I arrived late at Jamoigne: after having supped and having seen M. Chénot, I
hastened to go ring at the door of the parsonage. A woman with a loud voice, with
a bold look, came to open to me: it was the servant.

She had me enter a fairly sumptuous salon, where I found several people at table
whom my arrival seemed to disturb and annoy considerably; there were first four
laymen, big shots [*gros bonnets*] of the parish, no doubt, who were playing cards
with a remarkable determination. Then I perceived, a little to the side, stretched
out in an armchair, an enormous mass, almost formless, covered by a cassock: this
could be only the master of the house. Thanks, I presume, to the benedictions from
on high and a clear conscience, he had become big and fat; that had changed him a
little for me; but I would have recognized him anyway by his sanctimonious face and
his false look.

He did not recognize me, or perhaps made a pretense. I named myself: "Ah!
yes," he said, "I know now, ah! yes, it is you; they told me, in fact, some days ago,
that you had returned from America *and that you would go back there soon.*" He
seemed to pronounce these last words with a visible satisfaction. I briefly explained
to him the motive of my visit, motive which, for me, was only the pretext; I had
come, I told him, with the intention of having a long talk with him, but I saw, right
away and not without surprise that he did not care at all to have the least explanation with me and that it would be impossible for me to bring him to it. He did not
inquire about my uncle, nor about my sister, nor about my brothers; to all of my
attempts to engage him in conversation, he replied by yes or no. His friends, for the
rest, did not seem disposed to give up the place to me: they awaited impatiently, no
doubt for my departure in order to take up their game again, which my arrival had

interrupted. After that, I had no reason to remain longer in the presence of the Curé Mangin. I got up, he raised himself painfully and accompanied me to the doorstep; we left each other without giving each other our hand. I have seen him no more.

I took the train for Brussels, then for Ghent, then for Aalter, a small station on the Bruges line. Nothing more remained for me but to get, from there to Knesselaere, on foot or in a carriage; but when I wanted to ask my way, it was impossible to make myself understood either by the travelers male and female who got off the train with me, or by the personnel of the station. In vain did I speak to them, in turn, in French and in English; all, men and women, replied to me invariably: "niet, mein Heer." Now, night had come, and it was already very black; I did not have a map of the province with me and I did not find it in the station, I did not know how far I was from Knesselaere and I had not been able to obtain any indication of the direction to take. The travelers, for that matter not many, were leaving, I was going to find myself alone, and I was much troubled when I saw, near the station, a one-horse carriage; it was unharnessed, but supposing that it could not have come alone and that those whom it had brought ought to be found still in the waiting-room, I entered and saw there two men and a woman; I said to them, joining the gesture to the word: "Carriage for Knesselaere?"—"Niet, mein Heer." I was exasperated. "Sacrebleu," I said to them, "miladies and gentlemen, let me tell you that I come from the end of the world where I have lived twenty years in the middle of people who came from everywhere, English, Irish, Arabs, Mexicans, Chinese, Germans, Spanish, and that I made myself understood by them, and now, in my country, I cannot get my compatriots to show me the way! it's a shame, it is, do you hear?" Certainly, they heard—I spoke loudly enough for that—but they barely understood; after having listened, their eyes wide open, to this eloquent apostrophe, gentlemen and ladies began to repeat in chorus their irritating refrain: "Niet, mein Heer." "Go to the devil," I told them, and they replied again: "Niet, mein Heer." Then, taking one of the gentlemen by the arm, I guided him to the carriage and, showing it to him with my finger, I cried in a formidable voice and carefully marking the interrogation: "Knesselaere?" He reentered the station and spoke to his companion; the latter came out, and I wished to follow him, but, as he went considerably away from the railroad and as the night was very dark, I thought it prudent to return to the station. As soon as the other gentleman saw me, he came to me and replied, in a voice which this time I found very harmonious, to the question which I had asked him more than a quarter of an hour before: "ia, mein Heer, ia, Knesselaere."

At last! I sat down and waited. At the end of a second half-hour, the first man returned with horse and carriage and said to me: "ia, mein Heer, ia, Knesselaere, ia." I got in the carriage and we were off.

One can well imagine that the conversation along the way was not very animated; the horse was hardly more so. However, we ended by arriving. I got down at a hotel kept by the brother and the sister who, an astonishing thing, knew French.

I had them call, that very evening, Grave the notary, who had sent me the power of attorney of Ivon's father. It was agreed that he would come to pick me up the next day to take me to his home and to his children's house. Hardly had I supped when the hotel was invaded by a crowd of young people who, having learned of the arrival of Ivon Voet's friend, came to look at him and speak to him. Some of them understood French—more or less—and some others speaking a little English, conversation could begin. He was loved, poor Ivon, in his native place, and I spent the whole evening, until after midnight, in replying to the questions which they asked me on his account.

They did not withdraw until very late and never wanted me to pay my share of the drinks.

My interview next day with Ivon's father was sad—as one might well think. Three weeks before, he had lost another of his children, a daughter married in the village. Since the receipt of the letter which I had written them from Portland, in which I announced my visit to them, she had been impatiently awaiting my arrival; she died, the notary told me, holding my letter in her hand, and the last word she spoke was my name. All the members of the family gave me an excellent reception. Ida, Ivon's favorite sister, was married in Ghent; I went to see her on my return. This was a moving scene; when her husband had told her who I was, for she did not understand one word of French, she threw herself on my neck, embraced me effusively, then suddenly paled, collapsed on a chair and fainted. It took some time to bring her back to herself. Not knowing any more Flemish than she knew French, it was impossible for me to deliver the message to her with which Ivon had charged me; it was, as I said, a family secret which I was not to reveal except to her alone, and therefore I could not make use of an intermediary.

If necessary, I could have made myself understood by means of a French–Flemish dictionary, but it seems that this sort of work is unknown at Ghent, for I searched through the town for more than four hours without being able to encounter one; and again, did Ida know how to read? I wasn't sure; instruction, as one knows, even the most elementary, is a rare thing in Flanders.

The station of Alost being not far from the château of Moorsel, I got off there and went to pay a short visit to M. Van der Noot.[1] He appeared enchanted to see me; he welcomed me with great affability and that simplicity full of good nature which Flemish gentlemen add ordinarily to an exquisite urbanity. He took pleasure in recalling to me various incidents of our life on board ship and did not fail to inquire about the Señora.[2] I naively recounted to him my discomfiture; while laughing whole-heartedly, he expressed his condolences.

The château of Moorsel is a vast and solid construction, a true fortress of the Middle Ages. It dates from far back if it is true that a nephew of Saint Gudule, one of the ancestors of the present chatelain, had it, not built, but restored, which proves that it was old in those times.

1. Van der Noot had befriended Perlot on the trip from San Francisco to Nicaragua and New York in 1867. This appears to have been the only lasting friendship that grew out of the voyage.

2. Van der Noot was referring to Perlot's shipboard flirtations with Madame Cuvelier. See chap. 28 (p. 391).

M. Van der Noot showed me with pride the gallery of family portraits, a series which began in a very remote time, for I saw not a few old Sicambres. Saint Gudule figures there in the habit of a religious devotee, such as she was the day she took the veil. I have never understood how a country ruled by democratic institutions establishes or recognizes a hereditary nobility, but I understand and find legitimate the pride of one who counts a long list of ancestors; if I possessed, like the sire of Moorsel, the portraits of my ancestors, it seems to me that I would have, like him, some pleasure in seeing them and in showing them—supposing, all the same, that they were authentic.

On passing through Brussels, I also wished to go to see M. Sève, but he was absent and was not to return for three days; that is what his old mother told me, an excellent woman who received me literally with open arms, for she wished to embrace me. She knew me without ever having seen me, because her son had spoken to her of me. She insisted strongly that I await his return; but my time was limited. I left that same day and, the next day, I had returned to Herbeumont.

I found the village full of rumor; fourteen young men had resolved to expatriate themselves to go to tempt fortune beyond the seas and were preparing to accompany me to America. Fourteen young men of parts, that meant as many young girls condemned for a long time, perhaps forever, to celibacy: a veritable disaster in a locality of twelve hundred inhabitants—and I was the cause of it—the innocent cause, if one wishes; but none the less I feared having incurred the execration of the fairer half of the population.

During my absence two letters had arrived addressed to me, one of which was from my brother-in-law, Demouzon. It told me that my sister was in good health, she appeared calm, went about her ordinary occupations, but she remained somber, spoke little and never laughed. I showed this letter to my uncle; he read it, returned it to me without saying a word and began to weep. . . .

The other letter was from my elder brother; he expressed his regret at having seen me leave so suddenly and the hope of seeing me at Rennes on my return.

I wrote immediately to Demouzon to urge him to inquire of his wife if she would not prefer a stay in Herbeumont to that in Thonne-la-long, and in case of an affirmative answer, to come establish himself there with her, offering to compensate him if his interests would suffer from it. I asked a reply within three days; I received none.

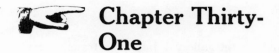 **Chapter Thirty-One**

Marriage to Victorine and Return to America

Some days after my return from Knesselaere, on a Sunday, I entered the home of Mme. Gaupin, my cousin.

I liked this house where I had received a welcome full of cordiality. Our two families, moreover, had at all times maintained the best of relations; no question of interest had divided them; but perhaps too, and without my quite realizing it, there was another liking which drew me to this sweet and peaceful hearth.

"Well, my cousin," Madame Gaupin said to me, "when at last will you do us the honor of dining with us?"—"It will be," I replied, "this very day, if you find it agreeable."

When I presented myself, at dinner time, I saw that there had been only three places set: we would dine then in a small party; I don't know why that gave me pleasure.

But this intimate feast, which on another account was remarkable in my life, lacked animation, and it was my fault, as one will see.

Victorine, by the delegation of her mother, did the honors of the table and acquitted herself to the general satisfaction—especially mine. I admired her good grace; her simple and natural manners charmed me, and I had discovered more serious qualities in her. I was telling myself that this young girl promised to be an accomplished wife and that the man who had the luck to spend his life at her side, would not have a bad lot. I went on dreaming for some time: I thought of the deserted hearth which was waiting for me back there, of the counsel of my uncle, of the eager adjurations of my sister; I remembered also the word of the wise king Solomon: *voe soli!*—and, finally, I resolved not to leave this house without having asked the hand of my young cousin.

I was forty-four years old; but it seemed equitable to me to deduct from that the years spent in California and in Oregon; the hard-working life, difficult, yes, but regular, in sum, which I had led back there, had preserved and conserved my youth rather than withered it; thus relieved of seventeen years, I was no more than twenty-seven and I became, it seemed to me, a suitable husband. I awaited no more than the opportunity to approach this delicate subject. She furnished it herself: seeing me absent-minded and taciturn, she spoke to me:

"So then, my cousin, you will leave us soon and besides that you will carry away from the village fourteen young men who are leaving with you?"

"And would there be in that number," I replied to her, "someone whose departure would afflict you, a claimant, a fiancé, perhaps?"

"Neither among those who leave nor among those who remain have I claimant or fiancé."

"So much the better; then, I will beg you to choose one before my departure."

"That's very short," she said, laughing; "but why before . . . ?"

"Because if your choice fell on me, Victorine, I would leave married and the happiest man on earth."

The declaration was unexpected, that is sure, for mother and daughter remained speechless—Victorine got up precipitately and went into the kitchen to see if the roast wasn't burning. I addressed myself to the mother, who promised me to make arrangements with her daughter, then went, in her turn, to look at the fire. When Victorine returned, somewhat recovered from her emotion, I pleaded my cause with all the eloquence of which I was capable—then I said in conclusion: "I will come tomorrow to learn my fate. Now, let us talk of other things and try to enliven this dinner. . . ."

We tried but we hardly succeeded; mother and daughter remained serious and preoccupied. A visitor arrived unexpectedly after dinner and I left.

When I returned the next day to learn "my fate," it had not been decided, it seemed, and I was put off until the following day. I was not disturbed about it otherwise: I knew the secret of Victorine's hesitations—she was willing, in order to follow a husband to distant lands, to leave her mother but not to abandon her. She had written to her sister, Madame Rogissart, of Muno, to make arrangements with her on this subject, and she was waiting for her arrival. I had let her know my intention of returning, after a few years, to settle in the country.

From the evening of that day, the news of my marriage with Mlle. Gaupin was already running through the village, and nevertheless I had not opened my mouth to anyone. On entering the hotel, I saw coming to me a notable inhabitant of the place, Father François: "Well," said he, "is it arranged, *the Victorine* is going away with you? Ah, you are right, she is the woman you need, an orderly woman, steady, a worker. With that, a heart of gold, but character too; ah, she will stand up to you, and you will not always be right with her! I, who know both of you, I am very happy about this marriage. I love Victorine, you see, *she is my goddaughter.* . . ."

At the word of *goddaughter,* I understood everything: they had consulted the godfather and I guessed without trouble what opinion he had given.

The next day, early, Rogissart and his wife arrived and when I presented myself, during the day, they told me that my proposal had been accepted. I was authorized to have the legal publications made, and the announcements from the pulpit. But then the difficulties began; the temporal power and the spiritual power, habitually in delicate relations, appeared for an instant in agreement to prevent our marriage.

M. le Bourgmestre refused outright to make the publications. I was no longer of

Herbeumont, I no longer figured on the registers of the commune, I was a stranger, he could not marry me without papers. "But, Cousin," I said to him, "if I am no longer of Herbeumont, I belong nowhere; I have no papers, for I come from a country where paper-work is unknown; I am therefore a vagabond, are you going to have me arrested?"

He protested that that was not his intention. After reflection, he consented to be guided by what the King's Procuror would decide, if I wished to send, at my expense, a messenger to Neufchâteau. The messenger—it was his son-in-law— took to that magistrate a letter which I had not seen, and brought back a reply which I did not see either; but M. le Bourgmestre assured me that it was negative. I telegraphed to the Minister of Foreign Affairs to ask if he would be able to go ahead with my marriage on the strength of a telegram coming from Oregon; the reply was: no, the telegraph not being infallible.

What to do? Write to Oregon and await the response? That was a delay of two months and I would have to be back in Portland for the month of March under pain of seriously compromising my interests! Defer our marriage until the year, and return from America to celebrate it? That still was a loss of time and money, but it was above all to create a delicate and almost ridiculous situation for my fiancée. So I proposed this: to be affianced before the two united families—the true marriage, after all—to leave together, cross the Atlantic and, on arrival in the United States, be married according to the formula. A demoiselle Lamkin who was going to rejoin her brother established in Kentucky, made a part of our expedition; she would chaperone my fiancée as far as New York, where the marriage was to take place. All the relatives whose opinions counted, including my uncle and M. Vasseur, the hotel-keeper, Victorine's uncle, were of the opinion that it was the only means of solving the difficulty. The approbation of the relatives having removed her scruples, Victorine said yes—and it was a settled thing.

I wished at least to have our banns published at the church. M. le curé faced me with the same refusal as had M. le Bourgmestre. Did they obey the same instigator? I had no doubt in that regard. M. le curé consented, however, on my insistence, to refer it to Monseigneur, the Bishop of Namur.

Every day letters arrived for my uncle, for the curé, for M. Vasseur, for Victorine herself; all advised against her departure: "she could not leave, there could not be any question of it, it was inexplicable." It happened that an express was sent from Bertrix to make her change her decision: she remained immovable. Some people said then that the *American* had thrown a spell over her.

The time of departure, which I had had to delay by eight days, was approaching. All those who were getting ready to follow me, good Catholics, and leaving for . . . the other world, went to confession and communion. Victorine wished to go as the others, went to confession and returned much dismayed—they had refused her absolution! That had had its effect: she was willing to be married, but to be damned! M. le curé had told her: it was a matter of her salvation.

Happily, I was soon able to comfort her again. I was on good terms with the postman, I knew where he entered the village and I did not fail to encounter him each day on my morning promenades; when the distribution was done, I went into the houses where I knew a letter had just arrived. So it was that I made a visit to M. le curé to ask if he had received the reply of the bishopric. "Yes," he said. — "Would you show me the letter?" He drew it from a piece of furniture and read it to me. I held out my hand as if to read it in my turn, he gave it to me. "M. le curé," I said to him, "I wish to keep this letter." "That's understood." He saw very well, no doubt, that it would have been useless to try to take it back from me. I went immediately to read it to Victorine; it said, in substance, that the best for the future spouses, taking into consideration the circumstances and the time, which pressed, was to go to be married in America, where the bishops had special privileges which permitted them to grant at need all the necessary dispensations.

Having the approbation of the Bishop, Victorine was consoled for not having had the absolution of the curé.

All was then working out for the best when Doctor Gaupin arrived, the blood brother of Victorine, whom she had invited to the engagement dinner. He had, unfortunately, passed through Jamoigne, where he had dined with the curé Mangin, and you can imagine all that that one had put in his head. Informed and prepared by that excellent man, he was not up to date on the situation and almost spoiled everything. His sister could not leave like that, we would have to find another expedient; such was the theme which he developed to me when we found each other again that evening at Vasseur's—for I had let mother, brother and sisters converse freely and had not attended their conference. I showed him again that all the expedients had been tried or examined and that the one on which we had settled had been recognized as the only one possible. "But," he said, "my sisters and their mother are of my opinion." Victorine, in agreement with all her people, gave up going! I could not give any other interpretation to what her brother had just said to me. I was filled with consternation, not in the least expecting this reverse.

My departure had been irrevocably fixed for the day after next: I was resolved to avoid an interview which would have been painful and to write a letter of farewell to Victorine—saving the continuation, from Portland, of this correspondence— unless our marriage had been definitely broken.

The doctor, in the course of our conversation, had said to me that the Curé Mangin had shown him a scarf forgotten by me at his house and that he had not wanted to give it to him to bring to me, desiring, he said, to keep it as a souvenir. It was the scarf which the Señora Cuvelier had given me. I didn't want in the least to leave this souvenir in the hands of the Curé Mangin and, the next morning, I sent an agent to reclaim it.[1]

---

1. Madame Cuvelier had given Perlot a green scarf as a token of thanks for his gallantry on board ship and for assisting her in her return to Paris. There is a remarkable irony in the fact that Perlot, who was determined to appear a solid and respectable character to the clergy, should have left the symbol of his dalliance with Madame Cuvelier, a married woman, at the house of Curé Mangin!

But before leaving for Jamoigne, the same agent came, on the part of Mme. Gaupin and Victorine, to invite me to breakfast with them; they insisted that I accept, they would wait for me. After having had this message repeated, I decided to go in response to their invitation, and I was astonished and ravished to find my fiancée still firm in her resolution; the brother had not understood or had not expressed himself well. But he had made me pass a really bad night!

The engagement dinner took place; all the relatives had been invited and all were present except M. le Bourgmestre Henrotte; he, no doubt, had not obtained the authorization. . . . As this engagement dinner was, at the same time, a farewell dinner, gaiety, without being excluded, was discreet. We separated fairly late. The doctor, who seemed no longer to remember what he had said the night before, wished luck and happiness to the future bride and groom, and left.

Toward evening, the agent I had sent to Jamoigne brought back to me, with my scarf, the malicious gossip of the Curé Mangin. The good apostle had informed him, with a joy that he did not seek to dissimulate, of the very latest news, which he had from a sure source, very sure: Mademoiselle Gaupin would not leave.

How did he know it! and how was he so sure as that? he had not told the messenger, but it was easy to see that the good Curé Mangin counted on the effect of the letters he had written or dictated, the advice he had given, the refusal of absolution, the objections of the brother, finally on all of the apparent or hidden maneuvers which he had employed and in which he was a past master. He thought himself sure in advance of success, in advance he announced it, and gave himself the pleasure of letting me know where the blow came from; it must have been a bitter disappointment for him to learn that, this time, the blow did not go home.

On the 23rd of January, at five o'clock in the morning, the drum was beating the call to arms in the village, in order, said the crier, that everybody might be up to witness the departure of those who were going off to the other end of the world and to shake them by the hand for the last time; he was followed by a group of young men singing at the top of their lungs the *Song of Departure* (*Chant du Départ*), and all this noise awoke with a start the small number of emigrants who had been able to sleep during the last night spent under the paternal roof. The day came slowly, the snow which had fallen all night in big flakes ceased little by little to darken the air, carriages and wagons were prepared, and at seven o'clock the caravan started to move.

The main route to the slate quarries crosses the Semois on a bridge situated a kilometer from Herbeumont; it is there usually that the farewells are made to those who, tired of toiling in the quarries, the sole industry in the place, for a hardly remunerative salary, go away to seek a better destiny. That day, the numerous cortège of relatives and friends expanded over the whole length of the road. But the newspaper, the *Voice of Luxembourg* (*Voix du L.*), in a contribution which it published the next day, took the trouble to sketch the spectacle presented by this exodus. Here it is: it is a traveler passing through Herbeumont who speaks.

"I light a cigar and I listen; I hear talk of the United States, of a gentleman with a big moustache, bearing the name of Jean-Nicolas Perlot, originally of Herbeumont, who, having left some twenty years ago for America, had returned temporarily after having made a fortune and who proposed soon to return there, accompanied by a female relation of his, who was said to be very nice and pretty enough, and whom he planned to marry immediately after his return to the promised land, and by a dozen young men who had let themselves be overcome by the coarse attractions of easy money. I understand, after that, the tears which I have seen flowing. I quite naturally attributed those of the mothers to the departure of a well-beloved son and those of the young girls to the loss of a brother or even more to the cruel ingratitude of an adored being! Like Peter with Caïaphas, I succumbed to the temptation of wanting to listen to the end; I learned that the young emigrants belonged almost all to honest families and enjoyed suitable comfort, but that purely local motives had determined them to take the extreme resolution of tearing themselves from the tenderness of their relatives and from all the charms of the native soil to go to seek beyond the seas the guarantee of probity, contentment, pure joy, and the share of fortune which they would have promised themselves in vain in the country which saw their birth. The scantness of the land suitable to cultivation, the lack of money . . . the continual dangers involved in the extraction of slate-rock, the low price of manpower and the difficulty for the workman to obtain a pension big enough to sustain him, when, enervated by a long and painful exercise, his arm obstinately refuses to work; in short, all these motives were discussed one after another and admitted unanimously. I could only approve them in my turn and internally address my warmest felicitations to the young intelligences which had known how to comprehend them. My curiosity was satisfied; I left, while accompanying with my best wishes the interesting caravan in its transatlantic peregrinations. Farewell then, I said to them, future children of the new world! May the Lord follow you to those distant shores, to watch day and night in guard of that probity of which you say you are so jealous, to smooth for you the path of fortune and to guide you as by the hand to the realization of all your dreams.

"Rich with the precious fruits of the land of Columbia, may you return one day to the paternal roof there to rejoice by the sweet effects of your gratitude the old relatives whom your departure has left inconsolable, and to show all your childhood friends as well as your former companions at work, what can be done by intelligence, decision, work, perseverance, order, and economy."

I left last from the village with my fiancée; I encountered on my way the relatives of the emigrants, returning from the escort; I gave to each a word of consolation, for I had the hope, with the help of my friends back there, of housing all soon after their arrival; while waiting I was responsible for them.

We arrived at Paris the next day at six o'clock in the morning. We were to leave it three days afterward to go to embark at Liverpool on board the *City of Paris*. In the interval, I recruited a fifteenth emigrant in the person of a native of Herbeumont, named Willaime, who, unhappily married in Paris and having unsuccessfully tried to get a divorce—that was too expensive—wanted to profit by this occasion to escape his wife by taking refuge in Oregon—the part of America farthest from Europe. I thought I should, in humanity, favor his evasion of the conjugal prison; he secretly took a ticket for the crossing and—secretly—left with us.

I could not think of passing through Rennes again, as I had promised; I wrote to my brother to bring him up to date on the situation and to make my excuses. I counted on finding or receiving in Paris a letter from my sister, whom I had not been able to see again and to whom I had written before my departure, asking for a reply; I had not received it and that inspired disquietude which was only too well founded.

The fourth day we left for Dieppe, where we embarked for England; from there, crossing London, we reached Liverpool and went on board the steamer *City of Paris*.

I had obtained cabin tickets for Victorine and for me: our companions slept between the decks (*dans l'entrepont*).

Each cabin was seven feet long, six wide, nine high, and contained three beds; I occupied one with two other passengers; Victorine shared hers with two English-women who did not understand a word of French. At the end of some days, seeing that she was sad, I questioned her: she informed me that her two companions, with whom, moreover, she could not converse, received frequent visits and had rather low manners. I spoke of it to the captain, who asked me how that could interest me.

I told him about our situation and asked his advice. "It's very simple," he said, "get married on board, I have the necessary powers, and then Miss Gaupin, become Madame Perlot, will be under your protection."

"I informed Victorine of this proposition, which she rejected at first; this marriage on the open sea without the ceremonial used in Belgium and without papers, did not seem regular to her. She ended, however, by deciding on it. She had joined forces on board with a lady who, having heard her reply to me in French, had approached her, happy to find someone with whom to talk: she was a Bretonne, Madame Monjoie, whose husband, who had taken part in the Exposition of 1867 and had been a member of the jury of awards, was returning from it to New Orleans. In Paris he had made the acquaintance of this young Bretonne, had asked for and obtained her hand; but like me, he had no *papers*, and—like me—had not been able to marry—without waiting. The two fiancés had found nothing better than to leave together and to be married—in passing—at London. The two ladies had exchanged confidences—Victorine asked me if this marriage, without papers, was good. "Perfectly," I told her, "and they won't marry us any other way in Portland; don't you want to finish with it and get married here?"—"No, no," she said, "it is better to wait till we are at home, back there."

But soon she declared to me that she had had enough of the society of her two companions and that she would sleep no more in the same cabin. I had an interview with an American whom the steamer's steward pointed out to me, and who occupied all by himself a half-cabin with two beds: he had paid for both places in order to have nobody in with him: he gave up his cabin to me and replaced me in mine. I installed Victorine in this cabin, where she found herself alone and at ease. As for me, finding myself without domicile, I spent the night, in spite of the rules and by means of a tip to the watchman, on one of the sofas in the salon. "But if they chase you away?" Victorine asked me. — "I'll still have the deck; moreover we'll soon be in New York."—"In eight or ten days, perhaps; it's too long, you won't be able to stand it."—"If I were your husband, I could enter your cabin at any time and we could occupy it turn by turn, you at night, me in the morning."—"If your marriage is celebrated here, what will they say in Herbeumont?"—"What they want. Nothing will prevent us, besides, from marrying again at Portland, even if it's only before the curé, the only marriage, I think, which would be valid in the eyes of your mother and my uncle."

With pity helping, and also the advice and example of the Monjoie couple, Victorine let herself be persuaded. M. Manjoie made me a marriage instrument modeled on his, a copy of which was left in the hands of the captain. He served as witness with the steamer's mate. The next day, at three o'clock in the afternoon, I was in possession of our marriage instrument in due form; I entertained as magnificently as possible my witnesses and their wives, who, the first to do so, saluted Miss Gaupin with the title of Mrs. Perlot.

This happened on the sixth of February, 1868; the eleventh in the evening we were tying up at New York. In spite of the advanced hour, they landed us immediately and took the steerage passengers, fairly numerous to the station of Castle Garden, where the Government lodges, feeds—and guards—the immigrants while waiting till they know where to go. I kept, however, Mlle. Lamkin and a man named Toussaint, whom I sent the day after next to their respective uncles living in Louisville (Kentucky), giving each of them, with their ticket, a basket of provisions and written instructions to permit them to manage the matter by themselves.

The day after our arrival, early in the morning, I went to the Belgian consul, M. Mali; he informed me immediately that he had written to the newspapers to learn the fate of Joseph Chénot and that he hoped to receive from them, before long, some news by means of the officers who had served in the same regiment.

I next spoke to him of my business, showed him my marriage instrument and asked him what there was left for me to do. After having read this piece, he said to me: "You are married as they marry in England, it is the same formula here, I don't see what use it would serve to marry again; in any case, it is better either to be remarried in your County, where you ought to go to get your license, or to have your instrument registered there; it's the same thing and it doesn't cost any more."

I thanked M. Mali and resolved to follow his counsel.

I went to deliver the guests of Castle Garden but there I had some difficulty. The government agents imagined that I had gone to Europe to recruit workmen and that I had made them take an engagement—a thing that was illegal and null in the United States. But after explanation, my men were able to follow me to the city, and lodged in a French restaurant while awaiting our departure, which took place two days later on a steamer leaving for Aspinwall (Colombia).[2] When we left New York, the cold was sharp, the streets were covered with six inches of snow.

By degrees as we advanced, heading south, the cold decreased; after four days, we enjoyed a summer temperature; the weather was superb and everybody appeared on deck; I say *appeared,* for considering the number of passengers (1200), it was impossible to promenade there, it was necessary to remain there, without budging, seated or standing. We passed between the islands of Cuba and Haiti and the eighth day the steamer was tied up at the wharf of Aspinwall.

We debarked toward noon and all went together to dine at the restaurant. Menu: omelette, fish, chicken, oranges, bananas, etc.; cost: 15 francs per head. Seeing the big eyes my companions made: "Consider, Gentlemen," I told them, "that here we are far from the banks of the Semois."

Aspinwall, alias Colón, is or at least was at that time a place composed of a hundred houses of brick, iron, wood, canvas, and even of woven reeds (*roseaux à claire voie*), forming, on the two sides of the railway which ties it to Panama, a street a hundred feet wide. It is inhabited by a population of mulattoes mixed with some blacks and with a very small number of whites.

At two o'clock we took the train for Panamá, a town situated on the Pacific, fifteen leagues from Aspinwall. It took four hours to cover this distance. For a part of its length, the road is on piles, the rails are eighteen inches above the water, salt, I think, and covered with marine weeds which give the illusion of a prairie. This prairie begins to narrow, and one ends by perceiving that he is going up the Chagres, a river which the tracks follow as far as the station of Gorgona. During the stop, which is a quarter of an hour, some negresses and mulattoes came to offer refreshments: eggs, bananas, oranges, limes, pineapples, etc.; beside and in the interior of the houses, built of rushes, latticed to daylight, one sees chickens, geese, pigs, dogs, monkeys, and children sporting, frolicking, and eating together, all absolutely naked, the ones as much as the others; the animals did not have hair, and the children weren't dressed; the vendors who offered us their fruits, were not any more so. Victorine, little used to seeing women and girls so completely décolletées, was quite scandalized at it and turned away her head.

After leaving this station, the railroad is built on an almost flat terrain, a sort of immense plain covered here and there with small hills (*taupinières*—mole-hills) one or two hundred feet high, between which it caracoles with curves of a hundred and fifty meters in radius. This terrain is covered with bushy but not very tall trees.

The train stopped on a wharf where they put us down on a flat boat which took us out a league to sea, where the steamer for San Francisco was found at anchor.

Panamá is built on a promontory, a sort of bare rock slightly elevated above the

2. Aspinwall was founded in 1850 as the Caribbean terminus of the Panama railway that after 1855 took passengers across the isthmus. Although the town was first named to honor William H. Aspinwall, one of the founders of the railway, it was eventually renamed Colón, and is known by that name today.

water. It seems to be a city of five to six thousand inhabitants; the houses, of stones and bricks with zinc roofs, have only one or two stories, so crowded one against another that there does not seem to be room for a garden; I did not observe, in fact, the least indication of vegetation.

The freight train which was to follow us at a distance of two hours, did not appear during the day; they feared a derailment, but the next evening it arrived, and we learned the cause of the delay. After our debarkation at Aspinwall, a revolt had broken out on board the ship which we had just left. There was a battle between-decks, the mutinied sailors took refuge at the bottom of the hold, lit fires under the boilers and closed all the cocks. The steamer would not have been slow to explode if the captain, the mate, and four policemen, revolver in hand, clearing themselves a path to the boilers, had not released the steam, which escaped with a strident noise. The mutineers left on the field of battle two dead and three wounded; the others, numbering eleven, had been put in the hands of the police.

This incident kept us two days in the roadstead of Panamá.

Between New York and the Isthmus, especially after having doubled the point of Cuba, when the heat had become overwhelming, ice had been allowed us at discretion, which had permitted us to arrive at the coast without being entirely melted. But once on the Pacific, if was no longer freely given us; it was sold at first for 12 sous a livre, then 40. Happily, we soon reached Manzanillo, where we put in; we profited from it to provide ourselves with fruits of all kinds, with which we filled our cabin, and we were able to arrive in San Francisco without having suffered too much from thirst.

Manzanillo, a small Mexican port in the state of Colima, is composed of forty to fifty houses scattered in a semi-circular valley surrounded by very high perpendicular mountains, which looks a lot like a half of a porringer which would be three leagues in diameter, the base being formed by the bay which serves as port. We saw there the pure-blooded Mexicans; they are not negroes, but very near it; they are small and spare, have long slender hands like thin women, for all clothing they have a very loose pair of pants and a strongly and heavily starched shirt, the whole of calico; they generally go barefoot or shod with *zapatos*, simple sandals held on the foot by straps. Their head is covered by a Panamá hat which touches only the top, with a horizontal brim of such dimensions that it is the center of a circle three feet in diameter.

One sees at Manzanillo neither highway, nor road, nor street, nothing but the grass and the bushes and shrubs between the houses; I think that transportation was done on the backs of animals.

Fourteen days after our departure from Panamá, we entered the bay of San Francisco. I learned that the steamer *Ajax* was leaving in two days for Portland; that left us just the time necessary to take a little rest. Nevertheless, I spent it in going to see the fairly numerous friends I had in this city, including M. Grisar, our consul, to inform them of my return and my marriage, which surprised nobody.

I had the time, in this short interval, to place two of my companions to advantage; the others, although I could have placed a good number just as well, preferred to follow me to the end.

The day came, we went on board the *Ajax*, all happy to accomplish the last stage in our long voyage. Numerous were the passengers on the deck of the steamer; I encountered, among them, several businessmen of Portland who had come to California to make their purchases for the season. They gave me the news of Portland: all was going well, the winter had been favorable in commerce, the city continued to grow. They did not fail to congratulate me on my happy return and especially on my marriage; neither did they fail to pay for the customary bottle of wine, which they drank to the health of my wife, who without understanding their compliments thanked them as best she could.

The *Ajax*, a solid steamer but slow sailing, and, moreover, heavily loaded, took four days to reach Portland.

We arrived on the 16th of March. As soon as we were debarked, I led my companions to a hotel kept by a Frenchman, perhaps a descendant of the Mérovingians, named Hildebrand; then I took my wife to my house; we supped with good appetite, one can well believe, while my brother and my sister-in-law overwhelmed us with questions on our relatives, on our friends, on what was happening at Herbeumont, etc.

Beginning the next day, I wrote to some of my friends scattered here and there in the country, to tell them of my return and of the workmen I had to place, asking them to let me know where men of good will could find work; at the same time, I gathered information in the city.

On the 18th, the Director of a sawmill at Oak Point wrote to me to send him six men, who would earn 75 francs a month, with board, room, and tools. Three days later, the rest of the expedition found places in the city under the same conditions. After that I had no more worries on the subject of my companions.

On the day after our arrival, I went to the Court (tribunal of the first instance), to get my license to be married. One takes an oath before a witness that one is not married, the judge gives you an instrument of this oath and this instrument constitutes the *license* by means of which one can proceed to the marriage. Strictly speaking, I could not swear to the oath in question, but I exhibited the instrument passed on board the *City of Paris*. According to the judge, this instrument sufficed, I was married; but as I insisted on satisfying everybody, I wanted anyway to be remarried in Portland. He therefore delivered to me a license which I placed under the eyes of Esquire Haufman, the justice of the peace, who was willing, after his hearing [audience], to come to marry us at home.[3]

But that was not all yet; I had to go find M. le curé Fierens, who married us also in his fashion, and it was not until after the accomplishment of this last ceremony

3. Undoubtedly "Squire Haufman" was J. J. Hoffman of the firm of Williams, Gibbs and Hoffman, attorneys-at-law in Portland. Hoffman was also a notary public and superintendent of schools. His office was on Front Street. See *Portland Directory, 1863*, p. 33.

that Victorine thought herself married at last. As for me, having been, in six weeks of time, married four times, including the family marriage at Herbeumont, I thought that that was enough and resolved to stop there for the moment.

There still remained a last formality to fulfill. I reported to the Court, took a copy of the pieces proving my marriage in Portland, and sent these documents to M. Grisar, Belgian consul in San Francisco, asking him to be so kind as to send them by administrative ways to M. Jacques Henrotte, *bourgmestre* of the community of Herbeumont, canton of Paliseul, arrondissement of Neufchâteau, province of Luxembourg (Belgium).

I wanted to take this way of sending these papers to my cousin the *bourgmestre*, so that he would not be able to say, later, that he had not received them.

XI

WAITING AT ARLON
1872–1900

"Mr. Perlot," he continued, "I see that you do not allow of mysteries, you judge everything through the eyes of human reason."
"Alas, Mr. Bell, I know no other; as for the word mystery, it is for me, synonymous with ignorance: everything is a mystery for the one who knows nothing."
Mr. Bell then asked me if, in what I called my religion there was a profession of faith, a credo?
"Yes," I said, "Mr. Bell, there is one."
"What is it?"
"Credo in unum Deum; that is all."
    Colloquy between Reverend
    Bell and Jean-Nicolas Perlot,
    Portland, Oregon, Summer, 1857

It was not without experiencing a lively emotion that I received the embraces of old and sincere friends and that I said goodbye to this land where during twenty-two years I had lived a life so intense, so free and, in sum, so happy.
    Jean-Nicolas Perlot
    San Francisco, April 21, 1872

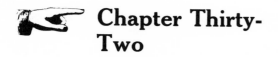

Chapter Thirty-Two

"The Smoke Which Rises . . ."

I went back to work with a new ardor. Circumstances, moreover, were propitious. Portland continued to prosper; during the year 1868 and the following ones, it had not stopped increasing in population, in size, and in beauty.

The city limits had just been extended and our gardens were included. The leveling of streets, within these limits, was decreed. These streets were rapidly being constructed and these lands were acquiring a great value from it. I profited from it as proprietor, but I lost as gardener. It had been permissible until then for me to enclose two neighboring blocks in a single holding, thus profiting by the space which separated them. Now this space became a public way which I must, as owner of the bordering property, level at my expense. And then I had too many neighbors around me, too many animals, chickens, pigs, cows, dogs—and too many marauders.

I had, after my return, increased my horticultural domain by various acquisitions and I found myself proprietor of five blocks. I had employed, in leveling and clearing them, those of my travel companions who were temporarily without occupation.

It seemed to me that the best thing I could do was to unload what I owned in town and establish myself in the outskirts. It was a good time to sell. The census of 1869 showed that Portland had more than 8000 inhabitants. It was lighted by gas, had a water system, and the greater part of the streets were paved, better than that, parqueted, for the pavement was of wood, an innovation justified here by reasons of economy, but which was later adopted elsewhere by reason of the special advantages it presented. They spoke of establishing a tramway, and a railroad under construction was going to put it in communication with the rest of Oregon, later with California.[1]

---

1. Perlot's interest in bringing a railroad to Portland was genuine, for in 1871 he subscribed $150 for a bonus "to help raise funds to bring the West Side Railroad (a Holladay project) to Portland." See "County Court House Meeting," *Oregonian*, January 5, 1871. I am indebted to Arthur C. Spence, III, of the Oregon Historical Society, Portland, for this information.

The result was that capital was flowing there. The value of the land had increased in unforeseen proportions. So I had acquired from Mr. Fierens for 500 dollars a block willed to the Church by poor Cambet; less than a year later, it could easily be resold for 2000 dollars. The dean, who very often, when walking, came to see us, claimed that I would never go to Paradise if I did not make restitution to him of three or four hundred dollars, which, he said, I had cheated him of by buying his block too cheaply. As he did not guarantee that I would enter there by means of this restitution, and considering above all that the Church itself had had this land for very little, I restored nothing.

I began to explore the environs in search of a property for sale where I could settle. While waiting to find one, I continued to cultivate what I had and to sell its produce, which I disposed of easily. I had among my principal clients the three brothers of whom I have spoken previously, who had established themselves in Portland, in a way, under my patronage, and whose business was prospering. Intelligent, hardworking, upright, they deserved to succeed. I was interested in them; I always reserved them my early crops and often sold them at a price lower than I was offered elsewhere.

Soon, I noticed that the one of the three who was in charge of purchases, received me coldly; he began to bargain with me; it even happened that he refused to take from me what he needed and bought it from another at the same price, without bargaining. When that had lasted fifteen days, I passed by their door and stopped selling to them.

This conduct of the three brothers astonished me at first and saddened me.[2] They had received from me services which they had hastened to accept—when they had not solicited them—and which I had been happy, moreover, to render them; I had shown them feelings of benevolence on every occasion, and I thought I had friends in them. Had they forgotten? No, there was at the bottom of their hearts a bad feeling; they had not forgotten, they remembered, on the contrary, and that memory, I saw very well, plagued them; now rich, or on the way to becoming so, they avoided the one who had known them when poor, and, which is worse, had obliged them: that is the explanation of their attitude in regard to me. I broke—which seemed neither to surprise nor to displease them—all relations with them; I who have always felt gratitude to anyone who has wished me well, I can have pity for those who let themselves be beaten down by adversity and dazzled by good fortune, but I have an insurmountable aversion for ingrates.

Since my return to Oregon, I had written several times to my sister and had received no response. My mother-in-law, in her letters, said little of her, for lack, according to what she said, of having news of her. This places us in an uncertainty easy to understand. She decided at last to inform us that as the illness from which my sister was suffering was increasing rather than improving, her husband had decided to take her back to the rest home, near Bar-le-Duc, where she had

2. Perlot was referring to the Cambet brothers, whom he described in chaps. 27 and 28.

previously been under treatment; if she had not spoken of it until now, it was because she hoped to be able to announce to us, from one moment to the next, her recovery. Vain hope! In the month of June 1869, my brother received from Herbeumont a letter telling him of her death. She had died without recovering her reason. She had died the victim of the machinations of a cheat, victim of one of those priestly hatreds which are not extinguished, which never relax!

And it was I, it was my unforeseen return which had finished troubling her reason and precipitated her end! I had killed her by embracing her!

To have the sister killed by the brother, vengeance was complete—for he had, no doubt, a vengeance to satisfy, this worthy priest—: how he must have savored it!

In the first moment, I wrote to my uncle a letter dictated by anger. On rereading it, I tore it up; I tore up twenty more of them. It took me a month to recover a little calmness. I could then write with a settled mind (à tête reposée); it seemed cruel to me to torment an unhappy old man who had only been an unconscious instrument in the hands of this Mangin, and whose soul was already goaded by remorse—he had let me see that clearly enough in the interview which I reported in its place.

I did not speak to him of my sister's revelations. I insisted only on one point: she had expressed the desire to be buried at Herbeumont, beside her people; I begged my uncle to watch over the execution of her last wishes and to remind her legatees of their duty, if they were capable of forgetting it. Could they leave her in a foreign land where those who had loved her would never come to give her a regret, a thought, a prayer? And he, her uncle, could he suffer it?

I awaited a response; it did not come.

The last wish of my sister was not granted: M. Henrotte and the others did not have her remains brought to Herbeumont; they were content with gathering her legacy.

Just a year after his niece, my uncle died. This coincidence struck me; it seemed to me that it was not due solely to chance. My uncle, I think, had no great fund of tenderness for me: I was not devout; on the other hand, he loved my sister very much; she was, like him, imbued with religious ideas; and, moreover, these weak spirits who abdicate their free will, do not keep for themselves even the choice of their affections. He knew of what she was dying, and remorse, I am still convinced, had hastened his own end. Whatever it was, I regretted him; I would have wished to find him living on my return, to tell him that I knew all, that I nursed no bitterness toward him, and to succeed in opening his eyes by showing him that heaven had not pursued me with its malediction, as they had tried to make him believe.

In the winter of 1870, while I was occupied in seeking a suitable location to which to move my business, the miners returning from the placers arrived in a crowd in Portland with a great deal of money, stopped there, settled there, and bought properties for which they paid cash. On the other hand, the railroad, completed and already in operation, gave an extraordinary activity to commerce.

The lots which I withheld represented, considering the high price reached by real estate, a certain capital. I followed events attentively in order to seize the most favorable moment to sell them; I kept myself informed of what was happening in San Francisco, metropolis of California, in Washington, where they were discussing the question of the establishment of a military port on the Pacific, at Portland, where the capitalists came from all directions to invest their funds.

The trade of dealer in lots becoming more lucrative and less fatiguing than that of dealer in vegetables, and not being able to follow these two trades at once, I recognized the impossibility of remaining a gardener any longer. It even seemed to me that the time of retirement had come for me. What was the good of struggling when the capital which I was going to have in hand should bring me more than my work would bring?

I let it be known to those whom I had brought with me from Herbeumont that I was going to stop my trade and my industry and that, if their hearts so moved them, they would find me disposed to abandon to them my installation and my clientele; in short, that I would abdicate in their favor.

Three of them came in a hurry, paid me for my tools and continued my business in my place (*en mon lieu et place, pour parler en style de notaire*).

I found myself thus with nothing more to do but to sell my lands, reserving the use of them for myself during two years, and also to give my successors the instructions they needed to make a success of the business. During the two years that they had been in the country, they had learned a little English, an essential thing in an Anglo-Saxon land; one of the three had worked with me almost all the time and could do without my explanations.

I had divided my blocks in lots, which I sold successively, without hurrying as long as the price of land continued to increase. I sold the last in April 1871; it included my house, which I was to occupy until the arrival of the purchaser, who was not in the country. In order not to find myself without refuge at the moment of giving up its possession, I bought, not far from there, a lot, with the intention of building there. While I was asking myself what sort of house I was going to build there, somebody came, three weeks after the purchase, to offer me 1500 dollars, which I accepted; it had cost me 1100. Some weeks after, I bought a half-block at 2500 dollars; but while I was leveling the land, to build, an admirer again presented himself, and I sold it to him for 4000 dollars.

I hadn't any luck, decidedly, and, this time, I gave up the idea of building, the more so as the purchaser of my house had let me know that he would not come to occupy it until the month of April of the following year.

It was soon necessary, moreover, to stop speculating on the purchase and sale of building lots. All the properties were, from then on, in the hands of holders who would no longer let go of them except at a good price, having themselves paid very high prices for them.

This stopped short the transactions and I found myself absolutely unoccupied. What to do then? I was forty-seven; I was no longer young enough to embrace a new career, nor old enough to remain lazy. From then on, my place was no longer in

America, where everybody works. And then my wife, who moreover was not yet well acclimated, thought often of her mother and sighed. The result was that, having held council, we decided, unanimously, to return to Belgium.

Before undertaking this long voyage, we had to be prepared. I didn't need preparation, that goes without saying; but it wasn't the same for my wife and our children, for we had two little girls, the last of whom was a few months old. Victorine, since her arrival, probably had not traveled a kilometer, except on Sunday to go to mass; and besides that, she had suddenly become rather stout; the children had never left the house. It was therefore prudent to prepare them for the trip by making them undergo some sort of training. Every day we went out, wandered through the town in all directions and returned very tired. That lasted a week.

Next it was necessary to become used to being cooped up in a wagon. I sent for a carriage; and with all four enclosed in this vehicle which I had chosen for its inconvenient design, we left for some point in the country surrounding the city, and so each day we covered two, four or five leagues.

Six weeks before our departure a compatriot, a man named De Conink, from Ghent, came to make our acquaintance.

His story is rather curious.

He had left Ghent, three years before, with three missionaries, with the intention of spending his life in evangelizing the savages. The bishop of Vancouver directed him with several missionaries to the northwest of the island. There, he had to do the chores, cut wood, clean the house, in case of need he did the cooking. In his moments of leisure and when—a rare thing—there were any savages within reach, he taught them the catechism, prayers, and tended them in their illnesses. It was fine, but he made the mistake of doing all this free. Hence, a complaint to the bishop against poor De Conink, *who was spoiling the Indians.*

Recalled to the bishopric, he was employed there as copyist, and also as drudge, agent, etc. Among other duties, he had to put in order, in fifteen days, more than four thousand cassocks, packed in the attics of the bishop's palace. They were the hand-me-downs of the priests who, believing the missionaries were clothed in rags, sent them their worn cassocks from Europe.

They did not know that the missionaries and the other ecclesiastics, in the United States, are, outside of their churches, dressed like everybody else. These cassocks were left in piles, moths ate them and, from time to time, they made an auto-da-fé to get rid of them.

In the meanwhile, the bishop fell ill; he wished to be cared for by nobody but his copyist, wished to eat and drink only what he prepared and presented to him with his own hands. One would have said, De Conink reported, that he was afraid that he would be poisoned.

The bishop died; they opened his will, written in English. De Conink, who did not know that language, heard only that his name was read; but, instead of receiving a legacy, he received some blows from fist and foot.

Monseigneur Blanchet called him to Portland to serve him as copyist. The priests of Victoria made him sign . . . he didn't know what, then sent him to Monseigneur, who employed him as copyist but did not pay him for it. He had to clean the church, light the candles, carry the holy water, ring the bells, etc. He was to have for salary the gifts made to the church on the occasion of first communions. But he left the bishopric before that period. The curés, of whom three were Belgian, wished to marry him to the cook, an Irishwoman who had bleary eyes and who drank. He refused, which raised a storm. He arrived one night at my house, his clothes in disorder and torn, his face bloody and one hand seriously cut; he came from the bishopric, firmly resolved not to return there any more, and he was going—he did not know where. He asked me to give him refuge until our departure; he was too unhappy, I could see, for me to able to refuse his request.

He looked for work in the city, but, known among the Catholics as a sort of vicar or *petit-frère*, he did not find it.

Some weeks later, he was called to the bishopric to receive a letter which had come from Europe addressed to him. It was impossible for me to persuade him to go there; I had to go myself to get the letter.

I received a kind reception from Monseigneur Blanchet, a very handsome and very gentle little old man. He asked me, on the subject of De Conink, a goodly number of questions which made me suppose that he considered him crazy; I saw nothing in him, myself, but a naive and good creature. The bishop thanked me warmly for having been willing to shelter a compatriot, and gave me the letter already opened.

This letter, in Flemish, was written to De Conink by his brother, vicar-dean (*curé-doyen*) somewhere in Flanders, and contained bitter reproaches on his *bad conduct!*

For three days, De Conink was occupied in writing out an interminable memoir of justification which he gave to me with the request that I myself take it to his brother the dean, and, if he questioned me, that I tell him everything without hiding a thing.

The poor devil followed us as far as San Francisco, where I presented him to M. Vénard, who employed him.

On the 13th of April 1872, we made our farewells and went on board the *Oriflamme*, leaving for San Francisco, where we arrived after four days of pleasant sailing. We stopped at a boarding house kept by a Belgian and I left my wife there to rest from the fatigues of these four first days of the trip, during which she had been indisposed the whole time.

By a singular chance, while at Portland I was making my preparations to return to Europe, Mr. Salomon, my former shipboard companion, in 1850, the same one who charmed away the tedium of the voyage with his recitations, was preparing, in San Francisco, to return also to the old continent.

As the settling of his affairs should keep him another few days in San Francisco, we planned to meet in New York, to cross together the Atlantic, which we had already crossed together in the opposite direction, twenty-two years before.

After eight days' rest, having paid a visit to my friends, including Huguet, ill in a middle class boarding house, a few leagues from San Francisco, we embarked on the *trans-continental railroad*. This time, instead of going around America by sea, we were going to cross it in all its length, from the west to the east. We had before us a ribbon of rails almost twelve hundred leagues long to cover at the rate of two hundred leagues a day.

It was not without experiencing a lively emotion that I received the embraces of old and sincere friends and that I said goodbye to this land where during twenty-two years I had lived a life so intense, so free and, in sum, so happy.

The train left, crossed the rich and populous plains of California, and by the evening of the second day was entering the gorges of the Sierra Nevada. On the plain it was summer, in the mountains it was winter; the locomotive, in the intervals of the *Showshades* [sic, i.e., showsheds]—sort of wooden tunnels with which the railroad cuts are covered—opened its way through a foot of snow.

At Reno, on the eastern side of the chain, a compatriot established in the country, Mr. Gillet, of Rossart, warned by a telegram I had sent him, climbed into our car and shared our trip as far as the Humboldt Mountains, where some mines were being worked in which he had interests.

Between the Sierra Nevada and the Rocky Mountains, we crossed arid plains, interwoven with forests and meadows inhabited especially by wild animals which scarcely seemed savage to me, hares, rabbits, prairie dogs, deer, gazelles, black bears. The stations consisted of a house near which is a well supplying the locomotives. The train follows the shore, on the north, of Salt Lake and we saw in passing the Latter Day Saints, alias the Mormons.

The crossing of the Rocky Mountains in a car is truly impressive. Often, on coming out of a long tunnel, one finds oneself on a bridge without railing, at a dizzy height above a torrent whose roaring can be heard; then the train is fastened to the flank, very precipitous, of the mountain. One of the rails is placed on the rock, the other is supported by stilts three to four feet high. If one looks down, one can believe himself suspended in the air; if one raises his eyes, it seems that he is in the gutter of a roof whose ridges cannot be seen, and one says to himself that, if the Sky rests on something, it must be on that.

Such was the impression which I received on staying for some time on the platform of the last car. Although not much subject to panic, I shuddered and soon reentered; instinctively, I came near to my children as if they were menaced by a danger against which I could have defended them.

After having reached Aspen, high point of the line (7540 feet) and which marks the point of separation of the two oceanic drainages [continental divide], the train heads for the pass at Cheyenne, then, turning to the south, descends toward Denver; the Rockies are crossed. It then traverses, from the west to the east, the limitless plains of Kansas. One sees hardly anything, along the line, but the skeletons of *Buffalos* [sic] killed by the hunters, who are content to take the skin, leaving the carcass to be eaten by vultures; sometimes too there are bands of antelope, frightened by the noise of the locomotive.

One station, in this desert, consists of two houses joined by a vast dining room; it is completely surrounded by a ditch twenty feet wide, by twelve in depth, whose scarp, extended by the extracted earth, forms a slope of twenty to twenty-five feet which rests against the houses. A drawbridge leads from the train to this sort of fortress. The purpose is to protect the station against the herds of *Buffalos*, which, when moving, are not to be deflected and upset everything they encounter. After the passage of a herd, which lasts from four to six hours, one usually finds in the ditch a dozen of these animals, which, pushed by those who follow them, have not been able to avoid falling in it.

The train passed not far from one of these herds, which, at a distance of about 1500 meters, had the appearance of a gathering of four thousand black cattle. Two of the buffaloes, withdrawn from the others, were traveling along the rail a few hundred meters away; the locomotive, furnished for this purpose with a special whistle, let a shrill noise be heard. They began to flee, but parallel to the progress of the train and in the same direction; it was amusing, when it approached them, to see their efforts to accelerate their course; soon overtaken, they stopped, watched it spinning away with all the marks of a profound astonishment, then making a half-turn began to run, in the opposite direction, with the same ardor.

The Buffalo hunters, mounted on small but light-running horses, carry behind them water and supplies for three days; then, a rifle on their shoulder, they range the plain; their supplies exhausted, they return—when they return—to the station with their spoils.

On approaching Kansas City, we at last encountered houses, stock, inhabitants. From there on, we entered the region of populous countryside and opulent cities; we found ourselves in the eastern part of the United States.

My wife, fatigued from the trip, was indisposed; we had to stop at St. Louis. All she needed was a little rest; at the end of three days she had recovered. But, under various pretexts, not wishing to tell her my real reason, I kept her there ten days in all: I had read in the papers that small-pox was raging in New York.

St. Louis is a large city, well built, which would be beautiful were it not for the immense and black cloud with which it is perpetually covered; the smoke vomited by the tall chimneys of its innumerable factories falls back on the city in a thick fog which fills the streets and whose emanations disagreeably affect the senses of smell and sight; if the fog clears a little, one sees through it the horribly blackened facades of the houses.

The Germans are numerous in this city, the Irish also; there are fewer Americans, very few French.[3]

To take the train to New York, one crosses the Mississippi on a ferry, which transported to the other side three hundred travelers, eighty cars and two-horse

---

3. Perlot was not in St. Louis long enough to learn that a number of its citizens were of French or French-Canadian origin, but through intermarriage with both Americans and Germans, the French names had begun to disappear.

wagons and all that the train was to carry. The river, at this place, is swift and flows with a yellowed, troubled, muddy water. Today one crosses it on a bridge, whose construction was already begun at that time, and which cost five millions.

We left, traveling across Illinois, Indiana, Ohio and Pennsylvania. What a beautiful day, what a beautiful country and what a beautiful trip! It repaid us very well for the boredom we had felt in the sad lands of Kansas. It is a garden, one would believe himself in Flanders, if it were not that the countryside is more agreeable and more varied. At certain points of the line, the railroad cuts are veritable coal-pits: one sees, twenty-five, forty or sixty feet above the track, a long chaplet of black holes out of which comes the coal, which, when one digs in the slope, rolls of itself onto the cars placed to receive it.

Nature has refused nothing to this happy land, which with the very riches she has so liberally dispensed, will succeed some day, no doubt, in ruining the old world, already threatened by the yellow peril. I am sorry for our great-nephews!

The next day, in the morning, we got off at New York. Three days afterward Mr. Salomon arrived, who spent two days with us, then left for Brest on the steamer the *Périere*, where I had not been able to find a place. The following day, we boarded the *Alexandria*, leaving for Glasgow. Peaceful crossing, except during the four days it took us to get out of the thick fog of the Newfoundland Banks; the light of the lanterns, powerless to pierce it, was replaced, on board, by the strident cries of the whistle, which from minute to minute tore our ear-drums, in concert—if concert can be said—with the formidable detonations of a cannon loaded to the muzzle. Impossible to sleep with that frightful racket, which was, unhappily, the sole means of avoiding a possible collision.

Fourteen days after our departure from New York, the *Alexandria* was going up the Clyde to Glasgow. The two banks, for a distance of five or six leagues, are occupied by yards covered with ships and iron boats, being built by numerous gangs of workmen. In a zigzag between the quais there slowly flow the black and muddy waters of the river, on which are fastened or circulating as many vessels as one sees carriages circulating on the most frequented streets of Paris.

The steamer *Grébé* was going to leave for Antwerp. We went aboard and descended the Clyde again, carried by the tide which had brought us. The weather was fair, but the following day, toward evening, it became overcast, and the wind suddenly rose; at midnight it was blowing a gale. When day came, only three passengers dared to get up and try to stay upright. It was a Sunday; on Saturday the captain had warned us that it was the night before the kermess of Antwerp and that the next day they would have a celebration on board.[4] But that day they did not even cook and, for that matter, no one thought of eating. Toward ten o'clock, I risked myself on the poop, where I found the captain, clothed in rubber from head

4. The captain referred to the celebrations in honor of the patron of the City of Antwerp and the founding of its church that were held in the Low Countries. The occasion was marked by a round of dances, feasts, and sporting events.

to foot and topped by a *Southwester* (sailor's hat), who was tied to the mizzen-mast: "Captain," I said to him, "it's the festival at Antwerp, but here is where the dancing is." Before he could reply to this pleasantry, a wave broke on the deck and buried me under a cubic meter of water. That was renewed three times; I had enough, and I hastened to return to our cabin.

My surprise was great to find there our little Florence, aged three, fallen from the bed to the floor, lost in the covers and blankets which had fallen with her; she had done herself no harm and was sleeping soundly. The mother, lying in the lower bunk and unable to sleep, had not observed the perilous leap the child had made; the creaking of the ship and its disordered movements, the howling of the tempest smothering all noises, and permitted her to see or hear nothing.

The day was passed this way: the tempest did not decrease. From moment to moment, without eating or sleeping, the captain remained fastened to the foot of the mast and ordered the maneuvers; three men, manning the wheel, made superhuman efforts to execute his orders, to resist the enormous waves which smothered the deck and to save, if possible, the ship with its passengers.

The sea was frighteningly beautiful to see. Five or six times again I risked myself on the deck to enjoy that grandiose and terrible spectacle: a tempest. Each time, alas! I returned soaked from head to foot.

My wife had not got up; she kept her children near her and passed her time in praying and in regretting her mother and all her family, who were going to be engulfed with her at the bottom of the sea; for it was ended, our last day had come, we were infallibly going to perish.

I did not know what to say to reassure her, but I refused to believe this tragic ending. How, after having traveled in my lifetime on seas that were from 10 to 11,000 leagues distant, and having escaped so many dangers, how could my destiny be to perish in the St. George Channel, from which one hears, in calm weather, cocks crowing in Ireland, in England and in France! It would have been too absurd, it was impossible.

It was I who was right: we were not drowned. Toward ten o'clock in the evening, the wind tired of blowing, and from hour to hour the sea became calmer. The next day, in the morning, everybody was up and we were sailing peacefully along the English coast; we had doubled the cape at Land's End, and we were in the Channel.

The following day, the eleventh of June, at seven o'clock in the evening, we debarked at Antwerp. It was the day of the legislative elections and it was raining. I had written from Glasgow to Herbeumont to announce our arrival, but nobody, on the wharf, was waiting for us.

The city, because of the elections, was much agitated, and I had some trouble, helped by the coachman who guided us, in finding a relatively peaceful hotel to spend the night in.

When my wife and my children were in bed, I wanted to go to a café to find out about the departure of trains; but the cafés and the streets were crowded with merry-making voters, singing, discussing, shouting at the tops of their voices: *Long live* or *down with . . .* I don't know whom; I had to return to the hotel and go to bed in my turn.

The next morning, as we were breakfasting quietly, we saw two ladies enter who came to embrace my wife; it was Madame Rogissart with her sister, Madame Malvaux; having come the evening before to Antwerp with my mother-in-law and the two little Rogissarts, they had walked the length of the quais a long time, awaiting our arrival; the rain had forced them to return to the hotel.

We left that very day, but we stopped at Brussels three weeks, long enough to be brought up to date on the European styles and to admire the splendors of the capital of the realm.

Finally, on the second of July we arrived at Herbeumont; it was again an election day, but for the community; there was less noise than in Antwerp.

My first care, as soon as I arrived, was to write to my friends Leborgne, in Paris, and Salomon, at Beaune, to tell them of my happy return. Salomon replied to me immediately: he too had had a happy crossing; he proposed to go soon to settle in Paris or its environs. I then wrote to him to get news of Leborgne, to whom I had written several times and who had not replied to me. He inquired and gave me the news I asked for; it was overwhelming.

Leborgne, whose property had been condemned by the city of Paris for the creation of the Boulevard St-Germain, was going to be, thanks to the indemnity he had obtained, added to the profits realized in his business, in a way to living tranquilly on his income. But, in the interval, the Franco-Prussian war broke out; there was no longer any question of continuing with the projects of beautification, and business was dead. The siege of Paris came to aggravate the situation further. Leborgne thought himself lost, ruined: he shot a revolver at his head, burned his eyes and made a large wound in his forehead. He was recovering from the wound but would not regain his sight. He was blind.

I spent the summer in fishing and the autumn in hunting. For fifteen years, that is, since the death of my poor Miraud, I had not touched a gun. I had to do my apprenticeship as a hunter all over again, very slowly, but I could not recover my former agility. What I had not lost, unfortunately, was a sort of tic contracted during my long sojourn in the middle of hostile Indians. When I was hunting, my gun on my shoulder, with the least noise produced by the fall of a branch, an acorn, a leaf, or by the step of a mouse, instantly and involuntarily I had my gun in hand, pointed at the suspected spot, and my finger on the trigger. It happened to me more than once when the noise came from a dog I didn't know was there, from livestock of some sort, or from a biped of my own kind, man or woman. It took me almost two years to succeed in getting rid of this habit, by making the firm resolution of never shooting without investigation. Without doubt, this way I missed many a good shot, but also I didn't kill anyone.

After the departure of my wife in 1868, my brother-in-law Rogissart had moved in with his family at Madame Gaupin's. The house was big, not enough so, however, to lodge three households. Respectful of the right of the first occupant, a very wise law, whatever Madame la Belette says of it, I thought that it was up to me to give up the place and go to house myself elsewhere. Where should I move my penates? I thought at first of Neufchâteau; but there wasn't a house there for me and there was no means of building one, for lack of stones; there are some houses, however, in that town but I do not know with what they were able to build them.

I pushed as far as Arlon; there, there were houses for rent or for sale, and materials in abundance to build them; I resolved to settle there. I found out first that the price of rentals had no relation to the value of the property: a house was rented for 1000 or 1100 francs which had cost only 15,000 francs to build and which one could buy for 10,000. I had not spent twenty-two years in America without having learned to count; instead of building or of putting myself in *quarters*, as they say in Arlon, I bought a house, the one I have occupied for twenty-five years with my wife and my four children. There is, behind it, a spacious garden; I cultivate it, not having been able to get the habit of being lazy. So I have remained a gardener, only I myself consume the vegetables I grow.

Until these last years, I relaxed from gardening by hunting; I have had to give it up, I am no longer active, "the years are the cause of it." From now on I am confined to my home and, like the hound of de La Fontaine, I dream; seated at my hearth or, in summer, at the bottom of my garden, I tranquilly smoke my pipe, while following with my eyes, with interest, the smoke which rises from it in bluish spirals soon to be dissipated. I see there the image of life, which passes so quickly and of which one enjoys so little. Death does not preoccupy me; I think little of it. I meditate on it even less. What's the use? It is enough that it will find me ready: I await it without impatience, certainly, but also without fear.

January 1898.

Index

447